The Lasting Significance of Etty Hillesum's Writings

Contributions by

Nancy JP Anderson
Fernando Arriero Peranton
Emilio Baccarini
Lotte Bergen
Ria van den Brandt
Pierre Bühler
John Cartner
Stephen Cherry
Marja Clement
Denise de Costa
Patricia Couto
Maria Essunger
Laura Fasani
Sara Gomel
Maribeth Kallemeyn
Marc P. Lalonde
Ulrich Lincoln
William C. McDonough
Barbara Morrill
Alexandra Nagel
Rosana Elena Navarro Sánchez
Maria Gabriella Nocita
William Augusto Peña Esquivel
Maria Luísa Ribeiro Ferreira
Bettine Siertsema
Klaas A.D. Smelik
Jurjen Wiersma
Patrick Woodhouse
Lucrezia Zanardi

In cooperation with

Julie Benschop-Plokker
Caroline Diepeveen
Ms. Michael Strange
Ron van Uum

The Lasting Significance of Etty Hillesum's Writings

Proceedings of the Third International Etty Hillesum Conference at Middelburg, September 2018

Edited by
Klaas A.D. Smelik

LONDON AND NEW YORK

This volume has been produced under supervision of the Etty Hillesum Research Centre, Middelburg.

First published in 2019 by Amsterdam University Press Ltd.

Published 2025 by Routledge
4 Park Square, Milton Park, Abingdon, Oxon OX14 4RN
605 Third Avenue, New York, NY 10158

Routledge is an imprint of the Taylor & Francis Group, an informa business

ISBN: 9789463722025 (hbk)
ISBN: 9781041188346 (pbk)
ISBN: 9781003706748 (ebk)
NUR 680

Cover illustration: Last page of the 11th diary (fragment)
Source: Collection Jewish Historical Museum Amsterdam

Cover design: Coördesign, Leiden

DOI: 10.5117/9789463722025

Table of Contents

List of Illustrations

We are grateful to the Jewish Historical Museum in Amsterdam for the permission to publish the illustrations 1, 4-6 in this volume, and to Uitgeverij Balans for the permission to publish illustration 7.

Preface

The diaries and letters of Etty Hillesum have a special place among the Jewish-Dutch testimonies of the Shoah (Holocaust). They contain not only a description of Camp Westerbork during the Nazi occupation of the Netherlands, but also a reflection of Hillesum's important, though unfortunately interrupted, existential search for spiritual, philosophical and literary fulfilment. Since her death in the extermination camp Auschwitz-Birkenau in 1943, the diaries have received worldwide attention and inspired hundreds of thousands of readers.

We have the honour to present in this volume the proceedings of the Third International Etty Hillesum Conference held in September 2018 meeting in Middelburg, Zeeland, the city where Etty Hillesum was born in 1914. The Etty Hillesum Research Centre in cooperation with University College Roosevelt invited scholars from around the world to exchange insights and to discuss problems that arise when studying Etty Hillesum's writings. Forty speakers presented papers and there was a wonderful performance of the theatre play *Blazing Harmonies* written by Stephen Cherry, Dean of King's College, Cambridge, and performed by him and the gifted English actress Rosie Hillal. In this volume, most of the papers presented at the conference have been included in revised and annotated versions.

Looking back at the conference with gratitude, we would like to thank the various people and organisations who made the meeting possible. First of all, we thank those who presented their papers and all others who accepted our invitation to attend the conference and through their enthusiasm and interest in Etty Hillesum's literary heritage made it an unforgettable experience. We especially thank Rosie Hillal for her most impressive performance, Bert van den Brink, Dean of University College Roosevelt Middelburg, for his cordial welcome, Han Polman, King's Commissioner in the province of Zeeland, for opening, and Harald Bergmann, Mayor of Middelburg, for closing the conference. Special thanks also to Ms. Michael Strange and Caroline Diepeveen, whose assistance in editing the texts has proven most helpful and whose dedication we appreciate very much.

A number of organisations and institutions provided us with indispensable aid, enabling us to carry out the conference in the beautiful surroundings of the ancient Town Hall of Middelburg. In alphabetic order, they are: the Etty Hillesum Foundation, Amsterdam, the Municipality of Middelburg, the Province of Zeeland and the University College Roosevelt. We express our sincerest thanks for their support.

We are grateful to Amsterdam University Press for recognizing the importance of the manuscript from the proceedings and for accepting it for publication. And we would like to thank Julie Benschop-Plokker for her continuous assistance in the process of producing this volume.

We end with a note to the reader: The quotations from Etty Hillesum's writings are taken from *Etty: The Letters and Diaries of Etty Hillesum 1941-1943*, translated by Arnold J. Pomerans (Grand Rapids: Eerdmans, 2002). This complete English edition of Etty Hillesum's literary heritage is indicated with the abbreviation E.T. In the footnotes, the reader will find the original Dutch (or German) text of the passages quoted from the diaries and letters. These quotations are cited from Etty Hillesum, *Het Werk* (Amsterdam: Balans, 2012). In this way, we hope to encourage our readers to become acquainted with Hillesum's original text.

15 April 2019
Klaas A.D. Smelik

Introduction

In autumn 1979, Klaas A.D. Smelik shared with the Dutch publisher, Jan Geurt Gaarlandt, a piece of Etty Hillesum's diaries transcribed by his half-sister Johanna Smelik, whom Hillesum called "Jopie" in her diaries. Unlike publishers in the 1950s, when his father Klaas Smelik Sr. had tried in vain to get Hillesum's diaries published, Gaarlandt immediately understood the value of the texts and moved to publish selections from them. An anthology appeared in 1981 under the Dutch title *Het verstoorde leven* [An Interrupted Life].[1] From the very beginning, the book was an overwhelming success. Many translations followed and Etty Hillesum became renowned internationally.[2] The remarkable global reception included some extreme reactions: hagiographic admiration, identification, lack of understanding and outright rejection. Every author claimed to know the truth about Etty Hillesum without any consideration of the research done by others.

The worldwide response to Hillesum's writings was, moreover, based on the selection of texts made by the publisher himself and taken from an unreliable transcription of the original manuscript.[3] An unabridged and scholarly edition of Hillesum's texts, both her diaries and letters, was required. The Etty Hillesum Foundation in Amsterdam asked Klaas A.D.

1 Later on, Gaarlandt published two other selection from Hillesum's writings: Etty Hillesum, *Het denkende hart van de barak: Brieven van Etty Hillesum*, with an introduction by J.G. Gaarlandt (Haarlem: De Haan, 1982), and Etty Hillesum, *In duizend zoete armen: Nieuwe dagboekaanteke-ningen van Etty Hillesum*, with an introduction by J.G. Gaarlandt (Haarlem: De Haan, 1984).

2 Meanwhile, the diaries have been translated in 18 languages: Czech, Danish, English, Finnish, French, German, Hungarian, Italian, Japanese, Modern Hebrew, Norwegian, Polish, Portuguese, Russian, Slovak, Slovenian, Spanish, and Swedish.

3 Jan Geurt Gaarlandt elucidates the criteria for his selection from the diaries in his contribution "Context, dilemmas, and misunderstandings during the composition and publication of *An Interrupted Life: Etty Hillesum's Diary, 1941-1943*," in: Klaas A.D. Smelik, Ria van den Brandt & Meins G.S. Coetsier (eds.), *Spirituality in the Writings of Etty Hillesum: Proceedings of the Etty Hillesum Conference at Ghent University, November 2008* (Supplements to The Journal of Jewish Thought and Philosophy, 11; Leiden/Boston, MA: Brill, 2010), 365-375.

Smelik, Klaas A.D. (ed.), *The Lasting Significance of Etty Hillesum's Writings: Proceedings of the Third International Etty Hillesum Conference at Middelburg, September 2018.*
Taylor & Francis Group 2019
DOI: 10.5117/9789463722025_INTRO

Smelik to address this need and, assisted by a group of young scholars, in 1986 he published a complete annotated edition of all then available texts of Etty Hillesum: *Etty: De nagelaten geschriften van Etty Hillesum, 1941-1943*.[4] The unabridged edition has been reprinted several times; the sixth edition appeared in 2012 with a different title: *Etty Hillesum, Het Werk*. In each new edition, annotations have been updated and revised where necessary, and newly discovered texts by Etty Hillesum added. In 2002, the complete edition appeared in English translation,[5] followed by a French version in 2008[6] and in 2012-2013 by an Italian translation in two volumes.[7] A German translation of the complete edition is in preparation.

In 1989, Jan Geurt Gaarlandt expressed his astonishment at the many reviews and essays on Etty Hillesum:

> It's shocking to read how many different aspects one can discover in her life and work. Literary, mystical, philosophical, historical, theological, psychological and therapeutic perspectives have generated material for many essays. She is compared and connected to people like Kafka, Meister Eckhart, Ruusbroec, Kierkegaard, Dostoevsky, Rilke, Jung, Seneca, Carry van Bruggen, Bonhoeffer, important representatives of literature, theology and philosophy. It has been said that her diary belongs to the most important documents of this century.[8]

The colourful but sometimes controversial reception of Hillesum's writings has continued long after 1989. Numerous books and essays have been written, conferences and seminars organized, classes given and artistic productions created. Each language, each cultural or religious domain seems to produce

4 *Etty: De nagelaten geschriften van Etty Hillesum, 1941-1943*. Edited by Klaas A.D. Smelik; text edition: Gideon Lodders & Rob Tempelaars (Amsterdam: Balans, 1986).

5 *Etty: The Letters and Diaries of Etty Hillesum, 1941-1943*. Edited by Klaas A.D. Smelik; translated by Arnold J. Pomerans (Ottawa, ON / Grand Rapids, MI: Novalis Saint Paul University / William B. Eerdmans Publishing, 2002).

6 *Hillesum: Les écrits d'Etty Hillesum: Journaux et lettres 1941-1943*. Edited by Klaas A.D. Smelik; translated by Philippe Noble & Isabelle Rosselin (Paris: Éditions du Seuil, 2008).

7 *Diario: Edizione integrale 1941-1942*. Edited by Klaas A.D. Smelik; translated by Chiara Passanti & Tina Montone (Milano: Adelphi Edizioni, 2012). *Lettere: Edizione integrale 1941-1943*. Edited by Klaas A.D. Smelik; translated by Chiara Passanti, Tina Montone & Ada Vigliani (Milano: Adelphi Edizioni, 2013).

8 Jan Geurt Gaarlandt, "Men zou een pleister op vele wonden willen zijn," in Jan Geurt Gaarlandt (ed.), *Men zou een pleister op vele wonden willen zijn: Reacties op de dagboeken en brieven van Etty Hillesum* (Amsterdam: Balans, 1989), ix-xi, especially p. x [translated from the Dutch].

a different image of her.[9] At the same time, the diverse readings from various countries show remarkable similarities and unexpected connections.[10] In this situation, an international exchange of ideas and perspectives became an imperative and in 2006 Klaas A.D. Smelik answered the call. The Etty Hillesum Research Centre was founded at Ghent University in that year with the express purpose of coordinating international Hillesum research.[11]

By 2008, the Etty Hillesum Research Centre had organized its first international conference in Ghent, focusing on two central themes in Hillesum's work: spirituality and writing. The papers were published in 2010 by Brill Boston in a volume in English, entitled *Spirituality in the Writings of Etty Hillesum*.[12]

In January 2014, one hundred years after Etty Hillesum's birth, a second international conference was organized by the Etty Hillesum Research Centre in Ghent.[13] Again, Hillesum scholars from all over the world presented papers and gathered in the beautiful university building 't Pand. The papers, revised and annotated, were (partly) published in 2017 by Brill Boston in English in a volume entitled *The Ethics and Religious Philosophy of Etty Hillesum*.[14]

And in September 2018, a third international conference on Etty Hillesum was organized by the Etty Hillesum Research Centre. Held in the ancient Town Hall of Middelburg, the centre of the University College Roosevelt, this conference was not only in the city of Etty Hillesum's birth, it began 75 years to the day when Etty Hillesum and her family arrived in Auschwitz-Birkenau, never to return again. The papers of the Hillesum scholars from this conference have been collected in this volume in revised and annotated

9 Cf. Ria van den Brandt & Klaas A.D. Smelik, "Etty Hillesum in facetten: Inleiding," in: Ria van den Brandt & Klaas A.D. Smelik (eds.), *Etty Hillesum in facetten* (Etty Hillesum Studies 1; Budel: Damon, 2003), 9-18.

10 See for instance Yukiko Yokohata, "Perceptions of Etty Hillesum in Japan," in: Klaas A.D. Smelik, Gerrit Van Oord & Jurjen Wiersma (eds.), *Reading Etty Hillesum in Context: Writings, Life, and Influences of a Visionary Author* (Amsterdam: Amsterdam University Press, 2018), 395-417.

11 In 2015, the Etty Hillesum Research Centre moved to Middelburg, the capital of the Dutch province of Zeeland, where Etty Hillesum was born on 15 January 1914.

12 Klaas A.D. Smelik, Ria van den Brandt & Meins G.S. Coetsier (eds.), *Spirituality in the Writings of Etty Hillesum: Proceedings of the Etty Hillesum Conference at Ghent University, November 2008* (Supplements to The Journal of Jewish Thought and Philosophy, 11; Leiden/Boston, MA: Brill, 2010).

13 Organized by the Etty Hillesum Research Centre, Ghent University, in cooperation with the Institutum Iudaicum, Interuniversity Centre for the Academic Study of Judaism in Belgium.

14 . Klaas A.D. Smelik, Meins G.S. Coetsier & Jurjen Wiersma (eds.), *The Ethics and Religious Philosophy of Etty Hillesum: Proceedings of the Etty Hillesum Conference at Ghent University, January 2014* (Supplements to The Journal of Jewish Thought and Philosophy, 28; Leiden/Boston, MA: Brill, 2017).

versions reflecting the different premises, approaches, and disciplinary tools of the conference participants. Each one is a unique contribution. Let us have a look at these papers.

In her contribution "Music as Metaphor in Etty Hillesum's Spirituality," the American researcher Nancy JP Anderson investigates the role of music in Hillesum's diaries and letters. She points to the fact that Hillesum's spirituality was not an awakening as much as a slow dawning composed over time. Hillesum used the metaphor of music to refer to the way she got in touch with her own spiritual melody. She learned to nurture the undertones that would sustain her through the difficulties she faced in occupied Holland.

In his essay "A 'staretz' in Camp Westerbork," the Spanish theologian Fernando Arriero Peranton investigates the connections between Slavic Orthodoxy and Etty Hillesum's spirituality. He maintains that it is possible to draw a parallel between her kind of spirituality and Russian Orthodox mysticism. He notes striking connections between the two: the need of muting the mind to reach the heart, the desire for a permanent state of prayer, non-violence, and the importance of being more than doing. Looked at in this way, Etty Hillesum could be seen as a "Russian spiritual father" – a *staretz* – in Camp Westerbork.

The Roman scholar Emilio Baccarini is very impressed with Etty Hillesum's writings. In his contribution "Etty Hillesum: Humanity as a Task," he says metaphorically that meeting Etty Hillesum through her diary and letters is like seeing a spark of light at the bottom of an abyss of evil. Hillesum's task on the road to humanity was to establish a balance between "inside" and "outside"; to find the centre of herself and fill every moment of life with meaning. The source from which this meaning originates, the author calls *ordo amoris* – a term dear to mystical theology and taken up by Max Scheler in his ontology.

In her contribution "Etty Hillesum & Albert Konrad Gemmeker: A Twofold Analysis of the Perpetration of the Westerbork Commander," EHOC scholar Lotte Bergen analyzes how Gemmeker, the commander of *Durchgangslager* Westerbork, became known as the "gentleman-commander". As well, the author deals with how Etty Hillesum did not follow along with this positive assessment of the key player in the *Entjudung* of the Netherlands – notwithstanding his polite and seemingly friendly behaviour towards the Jewish prisoners. During his trial after the war, Gemmeker, trying to minimize his role, declared – like many other Nazi perpetrators – that he did not know of the extermination of millions of innocent Jews in Eastern Europe. But Etty Hillesum – unlike Gemmeker's judges – was not blindsided by the commander's correct behaviour. In her letters, she described, criticized, and exposed the commander of Camp Westerbork as one of the most important executioners in the German system. Hillesum insisted that he had far more agency to act on his own responsibility than he would later admit during trial.

The Dutch scholar Ria van den Brandt has done extensive research into the friendship booklet *Levenskunst: Gedachten van week tot week* [Art of Living: Thoughts from Week to Week] that Etty Hillesum received from her friend Henny Tideman and in which she copied passages from authors she admired. In Van den Brandt's contribution, "'Now is the Time to Put into Practice: Love Your Enemies': Several Notes on Hillesum's 'Love for Enemies' in *Levenskunst*," she focuses on Hillesum's quotes related to love for one's enemy. She finds conspicuous the number of references to the Gospel of Matthew, particularly the Sermon on the Mount. Hillesum also often quoted Russian authors writing about the awareness of guilt and sin. Van den Brandt describes the literary-historical context of Hillesum's growing interest in the Gospel of Matthew and suggests a possible radicalization in Hillesum's later writings on the love for one's enemy.

Although Etty Hillesum briefly mentions the name of Kierkegaard in her diaries, we do not know if she read any of his work, or if she did, what exactly and how intensively. But when writing of her worries about the future, she regularly quoted chapter 6 of the Gospel of Matthew – a passage that Kierkegaard had commented upon extensively in his *Discourses*. Is it possible that Etty Hillesum knew these discourses? In his contribution "The Cares of the Pagans: The Reading of Matthew 6:25-34 by Søren Kierkegaard and Etty Hillesum," the Swiss scholar Pierre Bühler compares from several perspectives Kierkegaard's and Hillesum's reading of Matthew 6. He discovers in both authors what John D. Caputo has called *quotidianism*; for Søren Kierkegaard as well as Etty Hillesum, it was essential to devote all attention to living in the present.

In his essay, "Dialogizing Life amidst a Culture of Death: Etty Hillesum, Dostoevsky's *Grand Inquisitor* and Nazi Reductionism," the Australian scholar John Cartner stresses the difference between the discourse of the Nazis and that of Etty Hillesum. Her diaries and letters, in both their form and content, can be seen as a repudiation of the Nazis' monologically constituted, reductive discourse. Unlike her oppressors, Hillesum embraced the *Other* and allowed their voices to saturate her writings and inform her *Weltanschauung*. One such voice was that of the Russian novelist, Fyodor Dostoevsky. Through an examination of "The Grand Inquisitor" and Dostoevsky's novel *The Brothers Karamazov* of which it is a part, Cartner examines their influence on Hillesum's all-embracing worldview. In contrast to the diabolical markers of Nazi discourse, it is Cartner's seminal idea that Etty

Hillesum's dialogically constituted writings, which foreground a concern for the *Other*, actually reflected the discourse of the Deity.

The Cambridge scholar Stephen Cherry admits that it may seem an unlikely exercise to compare the fourteenth-century Christian visionary and anchorite, known as Julian of Norwich, with the twentieth-century Jewish author Etty Hillesum. Although Etty Hillesum longed for a convent cell at times, she committed herself to solidarity with her fellow Jews at a perilous time, while Julian opted for complete seclusion. Nevertheless, Cherry proves in his contribution, "Patience and Hope in the Writings of Julian of Norwich and Etty Hillesum" that such a comparison is fruitful. He shows that these two women can be seen as kindred spirits. He points out their openness to suffering, the way in which they related to others, and their determination to find beauty in the most unpromising of circumstances. For both of them, patience was hard but important work, and hope was a quality intrinsically connected to practical, intimate, mutual and vulnerable loving-kindness.

Most readers of Etty Hillesum's diaries are convinced that Julius Spier taught her to pray while kneeling, but the Dutch scholar Marja Clement does not share this opinion. In her essay "The Girl Who Could Not Kneel: Etty Hillesum and the Turn Inward," she examines the way Etty Hillesum described in her diaries her process of turning inward and finding the deepest and best in herself, which she called God. While admitting that Julius Spier played an important role in this process, Clement questions the general opinion that Hillesum discovered and developed the gesture of kneeling under his influence. She maintains that this gesture was encountered by Etty Hillesum herself and the process of discovery was well underway before Julius Spier suggested she pray in this rather Roman Catholic manner.

Both Etty Hillesum and Charlotte Salomon were creative and productive young women. They were of child-bearing age during the Second World War, but bore only cultural offspring. In her essay "Etty Hillesum and Charlotte Salomon: Pregnancy as a Theme in Their Lives and Works," the Dutch researcher Denise de Costa reflects on the lives and legacies of Charlotte Salomon and Etty Hillesum, emphasizing the connection between fertility in a biological and a cultural sense. The author of this chapter is influenced and inspired by the work of three women: Luce Irigaray and Hélène Cixous, both feminist theorists, and the late Dutch philosopher Rina Van der Haegen.

Etty Hillesum and Clarice Lispector were two brilliant authors who belonged to the same generation and were both victims of Nazi persecution. Most references to the two women consider them mystical writers who revealed an unconventional notion of God. For both, the use of language to represent reality meant being removed from full participation in the reality being described. For both, the search for the divine was connected to the failure of language. In her contribution "Wandering Beyond Words: Etty Hillesum and Clarice Lispector," the Dutch-Portuguese researcher Patricia Couto points to the fact that Hillesum's and Lispector's task was itself contradictory and impossible. After all, their medium was language and if it removed them from their own experience, how did they get beyond words? Hillesum and Lispector faced this paradox and did indeed meet finding ways to describe the world's turn towards darkness and to reveal their own journey through these events.

The suggestive testimonies of Etty Hillesum and Primo Levi urge the reader to reflect upon one of the most important questions of our time: What constitutes a human being? There are no answers given. But thanks to the poetical function in their narratives, and considering the vulnerable communication between author and reader, what emerges from Hillesum and Levi is a serious call to take responsibility, cooperate with the text, and let it affect you. In her essay "'Verbalize, Vocalize, Visualize': Creative Death and Performative Writing in the Testimonies of Hillesum and Levi," the Swedish scholar Maria Essunger argues that Hillesum's and Levi's writings affect us and change our perception of life as well as of our inner selves *if* we are willing to cooperate – critically and constructively – with their texts.

Although from different backgrounds and perspectives, Etty Hillesum and Simone Weil shared an attentive look at reality that made them able to understand contemporary events and to reject any kind of totalitarianism out of hand. As well, the two women believed in the need to re-found Europe upon a new humanism, and to create a new civilization based on a real sense of justice. In her contribution "A 'No' that Is an Affirmation: Etty Hillesum and Simone Weil Against the Laws of Force," the Italian researcher Laura Fasani focuses on the specifics of each woman's opposition to evil and shows that their choices led them both to say "no" to the outrages of history in the name of every human being.

Self-narration has often been perceived as a narcissistic display, a rupture with the outside world. Etty Hillesum's diary has not been spared this accusation. Italian researcher Sara Gomel, in her contribution, "From Enclosure to Disclosure: Images of the Self in Etty Hillesum's Diary," shows that the opposite process takes place in Hillesum's diaries, where narrative and ethics mingle and "dis-closure" of the Self is what enables the encounter with the other. Gomel analyzes this process of transformation from enclosure to disclosure by looking at the images Hillesum employed to portray the Self, images which were at first restricted, personal, and limited, but with time, evolved into wider, more open representations.

The diaries and letters of Etty Hillesum illuminate her path of individuation. In her contribution "A Story of Individuation in the Writings of Etty Hillesum: A Jungian Perspective," the American Jungian psychotherapist Maribeth Kallemeyn explores how Hillesum wrestled with individuation and shows the growing depth she attained, absorbing three key elements of individuation: a link with primal sources, genuine interpersonal encounter, and acknowledgment of pauses. In addition, the author discusses the risk of psychological projection when reading Etty Hillesum's writings.

The purpose of Marc P. Lalonde's essay "Mad Midrash in the Diaries of Etty Hillesum" is to examine Hillesum's wartime reflections on the divine-human interaction as a species of "mad midrash". According to the modern Jewish philosopher Emil Fackenheim, *mad midrash* is an inventive, theological narrative that responds to the inconceivable bond between the world, the divine and "the anti-world", i.e. Auschwitz. It is "mad" because the relationship strikes one as impossible, and yet it exists. In answer to such an aberration, mad midrash dares to voice, to protest against, and to partially mend an unthinkable history that is the Shoah. Hillesum's mad midrash, the author claims, involves a depiction of God without recourse and a human(e) existence that says "God lived, even in these times". To flesh out this idea, the author explores the act of diary writing as something that proliferates in times of historical turmoil, and finally, as a type of mad midrash.

In his contribution "The Mystery of Encounter: Poetry and Faith After Auschwitz in the Work of Paul Celan and Etty Hillesum," the German scholar Ulrich Lincoln constructs a dialogue between Etty Hillesum and the poet Paul Celan. Both writers try to come to terms, poetically and conceptually, with the Shoah. Both find their own language to search for the power of the human encounter in the face of existential nothingness and semantic levelling. Hillesum's work, just as Celan's poems, can be understood as a search for subtlety in language capable of expressing meaning in the face of meaninglessness.

The American scholar William C. McDonough's essay, "Can Religion Help Heal a World Broken by Trauma? Etty Hillesum as Our Ancestor in the *Qahal Goyim*," draws the reader's attention to the research on trauma. The author then goes on to state that Etty Hillesum is a religious model for responding to trauma. Tempted to withdraw from the horrors, Hillesum instead saw herself as part of a spiritual heritage and committed to acts of love for the other. The author concludes that Etty Hillesum can be seen as our contemporary Jacob, our ancestor in the assembly of peoples – a Hebrew idea going back to Genesis 35:11.

Etty Hillesum found an inner path to liberation, and in the face of the horror of her times, she discovered "union with the ground of her being". In her contribution "The Contours of These Times: Etty Hillesum as Chronicler of Love Transcending Hate in Her Times, for Our Time, for All Time," the American scholar Barbara Morrill explores aspects of Etty Hillesum's process of transcending the evil and hatred in her time, and posits that it can be seen as a model for opposing the seemingly ubiquitous rise of nationalism, neo-fascism and/or illiberalism throughout much of Europe and the United States in our time. In an even broader sense, the author cautions that the tension that exists between democratic and fascist principles, or open and closed systems is something that should concern us in all times.

Ever since the public read parts of Hillesum's diaries in *An Interrupted Life*, it has been obvious that Etty Hillesum's first encounter with Julius Spier was a major step in her personal development. In her essay "Etty Hillesum's Hand Analysis: The Prologue to Her Diaries," the Dutch researcher Alexandra H.M. Nagel finds powerful evidence to back up this assumption. The author argues that the report made during their first meeting on 3 February 1941, when Spier analyzed Etty Hillesum's hands, captured a pivotal moment. Several elements that Spier noted down about Hillesum when "reading" her hands, became themes in her diaries. Spier's report is thus a prologue to the diaries. This chapter contains the report in an amended, more easily readable version so that all Hillesum scholars may examine the content of this most unusual document.

The experience of pain and suffering accompanies the life of all human beings, in different ways, in the most diverse contexts throughout the history of humanity. The reality of the world we live in, is no exception; we are permanently "exposed". In her essay "Suffering, Silence, and Wisdom in the Life of Etty Hillesum," the Colombian scholar Rosana Elena Navarro Sánchez considers the evolution of the meaning of suffering in Etty Hillesum's writings. She wants to establish the relationship between the experience of suffering and the experience of silence. As well, she writes of the progressive emergence of wisdom in Hillesum's personal experience.

In her essay "Feeding the Soul: Etty Hillesum's Pedagogical and Spiritual Path," the Italian scholar Maria Gabriella Nocita reconstructs the path that Etty Hillesum followed during the years of the Shoah. On her way to the realization of the "self that one is", Hillesum understood that "body and soul are one", and that "the inner world is as real as the outer world" and that both need care. Taking care of one's soul is not as obvious as taking care of one's body; the soul's needs are commonly ignored or misunderstood. To decode the soul's needs, Hillesum developed a form of *philosophizing for life* that saw the human being as both subject and object of the enquiry and that humanized the individual who pursued this knowledge. The author concludes that through Etty Hillesum, we can learn to cultivate this knowledge of the soul.

In his contribution "Am I Really a Woman? A Question About Female Identity in Etty Hillesum," the Colombian researcher William Augusto Peña Esquivel sheds new light on the mystical itinerary of Etty Hillesum. He shows how her female identity is constituted in parallel to her inner search and her development as a mystic. Femininity and the realization of self as a woman, when taken from the particular perspective of Etty Hillesum's writings, emerges as a path to freedom.

Etty Hillesum and Dietrich Bonhoeffer lived in what Hannah Arendt called "Dark Times". Their lives and work show us that even in the worst places and situations, light is possible and hope can be maintained. Besides emphasizing how they both practised an ethics of care, the Portuguese scholar Maria Luísa Ribeiro Ferreira pays special attention in her essay "A Powerless God: Etty Hillesum and Dietrich Bonhoeffer" to their mutual concept of God – a powerless God who needs the help of human beings.

In her contribution "New Light on Etty Hillesum's Actions in Camp Westerbork," the Dutch scholar Bettine Siertsema draws our attention to a hitherto unknown testimony about Hillesum's activities in Camp Westerbork: a text written by Ies [later: Matthew] Spetter in the fall of 1945. Spetter was one of Etty Hillesum's colleagues on the Jewish Council in Camp Westerbork. Like Hillesum, he was opposed to the ways in which the Amsterdam Jewish Council responded to the Nazis' demands. In his post-war testimony, Spetter referred very briefly to cooperating with Etty Hillesum to smuggle children out of Camp Westerbork. Spetter managed to survive the Shoah, and his post-war activities show that to a great extent, he and Etty Hillesum shared the same views on life and humanity. This until now unknown testimony may well mandate a shift in how we interpret what has generally been viewed as Hillesum's total acceptance of her fate.

Etty Hillesum showed a special attachment to the desk in her room in Han Wegerif's house in Amsterdam. It was her favourite place to be even if other parts of her room were also very dear and had a special meaning for her. Nevertheless, she did not grieve when she had to leave because – as she explained – "In every place on earth, we *are* 'at home', when we carry everything within us." In his contribution "'My Beloved Desk, the Best Place on this Earth': Etty Hillesum Says Goodbye to Her Familiar Surroundings," Klaas A.D. Smelik analyzes Hillesum's remarks on the various parts of Wegerif's house and discusses the special meaning they had for her.

In his essay, "Etty Hillesum's Humanism," the Dutch scholar Jurjen Wiersma offers ethical, philosophical, and theological comments on Hillesum's diaries and letters. He stresses that excellent moral status provides leverage for the *humanum*, and elevates human persons to increased humanity. In Etty Hillesum's case, it inspired her to oppose hatred, anger, and barbarism. Hillesum wanted to be faithful to God, but also to all living co-creatures, to her own best moments, and to her creative talent. The author maintains that Hillesum displayed a specific Jewish identity when she, in spite of everything, committed herself to biblical humanism, to God and his creation.

In his essay "Etty Hillesum's Struggle to See Clearly: A Story of Two Worlds," the English scholar Patrick Woodhouse explores the question: How was it possible to continue to see the Nazis as human beings created in the image of God as Etty Hillesum did? The contribution begins with Etty Hillesum gazing at the brutal faces of the guards loading the train destined for the death camps, and explores her reaction to what she sees, noting that her reaction is a statement of what she has become. The essay traces how – in the midst of a world collapsing around her – Etty Hillesum learned to inhabit an inner world that shared characteristics common to the contemplative traditions of all the great faiths. This contribution is a reminder that her story is a story not of one, but of two worlds.

In "Present Traces of a Past Existence: Through the Lens of Photography" – the last contribution in this volume – the Italian artist and researcher Lucrezia Zanardi starts with the question: What happens to a space when it is inhabited by different people? Does the presence of its previous inhabitants persist? Is the space merely architectural or is it pervaded by the acts of the subjects and therefore bound in some way to the former occupants? The author, having photographed every space once inhabited by Etty Hillesum, presents a playful exploration of these questions. Photography is the perfect medium to work through these problems as it is able to suggest and maintain a trace of a presence alongside a look from the past. In addition, photography is a highly psychological medium that allows one, just like a diary, to review and rework a vision.

The 29 contributions in this volume reflect various new developments in the study of the literary heritage of Etty Hillesum. Since the first publication and translations of her diaries and letters in the 1980s, much creative work has been done and new approaches have been found. International research has shown how multifaceted her thought was and has stressed the viability of her views for our present situation. This Jewish woman, murdered 75 years ago by the Nazis, was convinced that humanity and human dignity could survive in a barbaric world. Etty Hillesum hoped for a better world after the war, but any daily newspaper today shows that we still have a long way to go. For our lives, her writings can serve as a guideline and they deserve our continued attention – which is the purpose of the Etty Hillesum Research Centre in Middelburg.

Music as Metaphor in Etty Hillesum's Spirituality

Nancy JP Anderson

Abstract

Etty Hillesum's spirituality was not a spiritual awakening as much as it was a slow dawning composed over time. One metaphor she used – music – is about getting in touch with her own spiritual melody. This undertone was one she learned to nurture, and which would sustain her through the many difficulties she faced. The use of metaphors can offer lasting significance to Hillesum's readers by providing various approaches to discovering one's inner life.

Keywords: music, spirituality, metaphors, "inner scale", Westerbork Camp, art, beauty

In this summary article,[1] I discuss the connection between music and spirituality in the span of Etty Hillesum's writings from 1941 to 1943. In her diaries and letters, Etty Hillesum frequently refers to music – both the external music she hears and the internal "music" she is experiencing as her own spirituality deepens. She refers to soul or spirit 266 times in her writings. Her references to music, melody, scale, tune, etc., and their derivatives are made 216 times. Her words "inner scale" first appear in Exercise Book Nine on Saturday, 6 June 1942, "I have my own inner scale".[2] This internal music is a metaphor for her spiritual self and the one on which I focus here. The framework for this article is music in Hillesum's life, music

1 This article is a summary of my graduate thesis, *The Undercurrent of Music in the Burgeoning Spirituality of Etty Hillesum,* fulfilling the requirements of a Master of Arts in Theology degree at St. Catherine University.

2 E.T., 397. *Het Werk*, 416; Saturday morning 6 June 1942: een eigen toon in me zit.

Smelik, Klaas A.D. (ed.), *The Lasting Significance of Etty Hillesum's Writings: Proceedings of the Third International Etty Hillesum Conference at Middelburg, September 2018.*
Taylor & Francis Group 2019
DOI: 10.5117/9789463722025_ANDERSON

and spirituality, and, finally, the metaphor of music used by Hillesum to describe her spirituality.

Music in the Life of Etty Hillesum

The references to music in the diaries and letters of Etty Hillesum commence with her first Exercise Book and end with her final postcard from the train. Hillesum takes us on a journey from "I too wanted to roll melodiously out of God's hand"[3] to "We left the camp singing".[4] References to music begin as a recognition of the music she hears around her in public spaces, as references found in her private reading, and in the musical soirees she attends with friends. As she continues journaling, there is a gradual awakening of her spiritual facet and the metaphor of music appears.

Hillesum's journals begin on Sunday, 9 March 1941. The first reference to music makes its appearance in the late evening of that same day when she recalls a line of poetry, "'Melodiously rolls the world from God's hand.' [...] I too wanted to roll melodiously out of God's hand."[5] A few days later, she journals about her experience as she registers her Jewish origin. On Wednesday, 19 March 1941, while standing in the "silent and depressed" line, Hillesum hears children singing in the next room and finds the singing "almost touching".[6] Later that same day, Hillesum recognizes a need for music in herself. She writes introspectively, noticing the way she has become more conscious of music in her life. "I surprised myself with a need for music. [...] And now, quite suddenly, music is beginning to press its claims."[7]

Hillesum moves from an external awareness of music to her personal inner tune. She attributes this to her deepening relationship with her God. The final specific reference we have to her inner music is in a diary entry on Saturday, 6 June 1942:

3 E.T., 7. *Het Werk*, 7; Sunday night 9 March 1941: Ik wilde dat ik zelf melodisch uit Gods hand rolde.

4 E.T., 577. *Het Werk*, 702; Letter 71, To Christine van Nooten, near Glimmen, Tuesday, 7 September 1943: We hebben zingende dit kamp verlaten [...].

5 E.T., 7, *Het Werk*, 7; Sunday night 9 March 1941: "Melodisch rolt de wereld uit Gods hand" [...]. Ik wilde dat ik zelf melodisch uit Gods hand rolde.

6 E.T., 31. *Het Werk*, 33; Wednesday morning 19 March 1941: bijna aandoenlijk.

7 E.T., 32-33. *Het Werk*, 35; Wednesday morning 19 March 1941: Ik betrap mezelf op een behoefte aan muziek. [...] en nu begint, in deze phase van m'n leven, de muziek z'n rechten op te eisen.

> I [...] have discovered that I have my own inner scale and that a melody is emerging, one to which I must give every chance and lots of space, and to which I must be true.[8]

In summary, Etty Hillesum appreciates listening to music and writes about music early on in her diaries. Her awareness of music around her is acute. The undercurrent of music as a metaphor for her spirituality is used only a few times, but with a growing awareness that this facet of herself is something she wants to share with others.

Music and Spirituality

Developing a strong, healthy spirituality initially requires as much attention as a strong, healthy emotional, physical, or social life. Tending to this part of being human starts with an *awakening* to this inner space; an awareness that there *is* a spiritual depth in each of us that desires nurturance. Some people find this through organized systems like religion or support groups. Others find their path through experiences like reading, listening to music, being in nature, or meditating. "Attending to the spiritual entails going within to the soul space, opening both the eye that looks into the Spirit and the eye that looks into the world."[9] In due course, one's spirituality will care for them if one is attentive to it, nurtures it, and allows it to sustain them.

Music has a way of gathering people together, creating community among us, and keeping communities unified. Richard Viladesau writes,

> Music seems to have a spiritual dimension which goes beyond mere sensible pleasure, and which somehow reflects a deeper reality. Anthropology makes it clear that primitive religion is inseparable from music and dance; and even for the most modern of cultures, music retains a mystical fascination.[10]

8 E.T., 397. *Het Werk*, 416; Zaterdagochtend [6 Juni 1942]: ... gehoord ondertussen hoe er toch een eigen toon in me zit en er zich een melodie ontwikkelt, die ik kans en de ruimte moet geven en aan welke ik trouw moet zijn.

9 John Shea, *Spirituality and Health Care: Reaching Toward a Holistic Future* (Chicago: Park Ridge Center, 2000), 106.

10 Richard Viladesau, "Music as an Approach to God: A Theology of Aesthetic Experience," *The Catholic World* (January/February 1989), 4-9, especially p. 5.

Kathleen Harmon states the power of music is more able to connect with the non-verbal portion of human thinking than words. She writes eloquently on music and spirituality when she states:

> Through music we can become present to that speechless realm within one another where the struggle with semantic overload is at rest and the peacefulness of our simple presence can communicate.[11]

Infants, long before they have the power of speech, respond to music and rhythm – even *in utero*. A baby is not born with a sense of individuation from the world surrounding it. Crying (singing) is one of the first vocalizations an infant uses to communicate with others. Music is as lifelong in our memory as the memory of aromas. Long after the initial experience with something musical has passed, music can conjure up long-distant memories in people, just as an aroma can bring memories of an event or person.

In the following quote, note the connection made between the arts and the survival of humanity when Karl Paulnack, Director of the Music Division at Boston Conservatory, addresses the 2014 freshman class:

> Given what we have since learned about life in the Nazi camps, why would anyone in his right mind waste time and energy writing or playing music? [...] And yet – even from the concentration camps, we have poetry, we have music, we have visual art; [...] many, many people created art. Why? Well, in a place where people are only focused on survival, on the bare necessities, the obvious conclusion is that art must be, somehow, essential for life. [...] Art is one of the ways in which we say, 'I am alive, and my life has meaning.' [...] You are here to become a sort of therapist for the human soul, a spiritual version of [...] someone who works with our insides to see if they get things to line up, to see if we can come into harmony with ourselves and be healthy and happy and well.[12]

Paulnack's references to music in the Nazi concentration and death camps are apparent in the texts of Hillesum, too. Etty Hillesum's eyewitness accounts of music at Camp Westerbork are incorporated into her letters to friends in Amsterdam, Deventer, and The Hague. One such letter, quoted

11 Kathleen Harmon, *The Mystery We Celebrate, the Song We Sing: A Theology of Liturgical Music* (Collegeville: Liturgical Press, 2008), 37 & 46.

12 Karl Paulnack, "Boston Conservatory Music Division," September 2014. www.bc.edu/content/dam/files/centers/boisi/pdf/s091/Welcome_address_to_freshman_at_Boston_Conservatory.pdf [Accessed February 2016].

here, was surreptitiously published with a pseudonym in 1943. While in Amsterdam in late December 1942, Hillesum writes to two sisters in The Hague about the experience of Camp Westerbork:

> The people from Rotterdam were in a class by themselves, hardened by the bombing raids. "We don't frighten easily anymore," you often heard them say. "If we survived all that, we'll survive this, too." And a few days later they marched singing to the train.[13]

When standing side-by-side with others and singing with them, we have joined a "collectivity of shared orientation and identity".[14]

In summary, music and spiritual practices, whether solitary or socially constructed, can work together to enliven the inner Presence. Music is innate in the human person. We respond to rhythm and tune at very early ages, before we can speak with each other. Music has an influence on an ailing humanity when facing times of darkness or uncertainty. Spiritual strength can exercise the same positive influence through the hope received through a private or public practice.

The Metaphor of Music

How did the undercurrent of Etty Hillesum's spirituality steady her through the remaining course of her life? Her journals and letters are stunningly written passages about dreadful events and actions. Her interior life is as much a topic in her journals as her exterior life at Camp Westerbork is in her letters. Hillesum is determined to nurture her inner melody (spiritual voice) and maintain it as a constant part of her life.

The phrase "basic tune" is used to describe the inner voice for which Etty Hillesum listens within herself. Hillesum first uses the metaphor "inner scale" or "melody" as a descriptor for her inner self on Monday, 4 August 1941. She is seeking a steady current inside her. "I still lack a basic tune; a steady undercurrent; the inner source that feeds me keeps drying up."[15]

13 E.T., 584-585. *Het Werk*, 622; Letter 23, To two sisters in The Hague, Amsterdam, end of December 1942: De Rotterdammers waren een klasse op zichzelf, gestaald door het bombardement in de oorlogsdagen. 'Wij zijn voor geen kleintje meer vervaard', hoorde men van velen, 'als we daar doorgekomen zijn, komen we hier ook wel door' en ze trokken enige dagen later zingende naar de trein.

14 Harmon, *The Mystery We Celebrate, the Song We Sing*, 39.

15 E.T., 72. *Het Werk*, 77; Monday, 4 August 1941: Ik heb nog geen grondmelodie. Er is nog niet één vaste onderstroom, de innerlijke bron waaruit ik gevoed word, slibt altijd weer dicht.

This metaphorical theme occurs three times over the next several months, between August 1941 and June 1942. Her desire to one day be a published writer assists her in developing various metaphors: a deep well, inner melody, thinking heart, etc. She continues the development of the inner melody metaphor on Monday, 20 October 1941:

> There is a strange little melody inside me that sometimes cries out for words. But through inhibition, lack of self-confidence, laziness, and goodness knows what else, that tune remains stifled, haunting me from within. [...] And then again it fills me with gentle, melancholy music.[16]

One month later, on Monday, 24 November 1941, Hillesum writes, "[...] let some music flow from me, let what is within me be given expression, it longs so desperately for that."[17] Her writing is her art form; her art gives voice to that inner tune. Through journaling, Hillesum can return to herself, her God and her inner tune whenever she finds it necessary to reconnect with that aspect of her life.

Etty Hillesum's conversations with her God illustrate to us, her readers, her confidence in the powerful, abiding Presence in her life and the lives of others. Her spirituality is her connection with/to others and is her strength to "lead them back to their own sources".[18] Her ministration to others prior to train departures from Westerbork is her way of being a calm presence in the dark chaos surrounding the deportees. She nods in the direction of her heritage when she writes:

> Your lessons are hard, oh God, let me be your good and patient pupil. [...] I feel that I am one of many heirs to a great spiritual heritage. I shall be its faithful guardian. I shall share it as best I can.[19]

Hillesum's desire to help people through difficult times is her way of expressing her spiritual life with and to others. She intends to give them

16 E.T., 131. *Het Werk*, 138; Monday, 20 October 1941: Er zit een eigen melodietje in me, dat er soms zo naar verlangt in eigen woorden te worden omgezet. Maar door geremdheid, gebrek aan zelfvertrouwen, luiheid en ik weet niet wat nog meer, blijft het nog steeds verstikt in me zitten en spookt in me rond. Soms holt het me helemaal uit en dan weer vervult het me met een hele zachte, weemoedige muziek.

17 E.T., 153. *Het Werk*, 161; Monday, 24 November 1941: laat U wat muziek uit me komen, laat dat wat er in me zit vorm vinden, het verlangt er zo naar.

18 E.T., 399. *Het Werk*, 418; Friday morning, 18 September 1942: terug te voeren naar de eigen bronnen.

19 E.T., 521. *Het Werk*, 551; Thursday night 17 September 1942: Uw lessen zijn moeilijk, God, laat mij Uw goede en geduldige leerling zijn. [...] Ik voel me een van de vele erfgenamen van een grote geestelijke erfenis.

Ik zal daarvan de trouwe behoedster zijn. Ik zal er van uitdelen, zoveel als ik bij machte zal zijn.

the strength they need by sharing her sense of purpose. Continuing in her determination to be an author, she is grateful for the opportunity to have lived her life and hopes that it will bear fruit someday in being published. Carol Lee Flinders describes Hillesum's journey in this way:

> When Etty first began writing the diary, she describes her desire for 'a tune': a thread, or medium, a calling that would make sense of her existence. By the end she has found it, and what she has found is so quiet it is almost intangible by ordinary standards.[20]

What Hillesum has discovered within herself is the steady undercurrent of spirituality in her life which flows to others without prejudice. In Letter 21, from Camp Westerbork written on Sunday, 29 November 1942, she confesses, "I should so much like to help provide some spiritual nourishment".[21] The desperate conditions of the camp do not destroy her. She knows she has the internal resources to bring a sense of "being human" to the lives of those continually being dehumanized within the barbed-wire confines of the camp.

In her article, *Etty Hillesum and Sophie Scholl: Sisters in Fate*, Marta Perrini writes cogently about the spiritual strength of these two non-violent resistors to Nazism.

> Several passages by Hillesum [...] focus on music. [...] The primary importance of music, like literature, was not [...] its dimensions of formal beauty and aesthetic pleasure, but its valuable support of spiritual activity.[22]

Hillesum's diaries abound with comments on her own written creations and the creations of other writers. Perrini continues,

> [...] especially Hillesum's, who saw diary writing as an exercise in style. Her need to 'find a new tone to go with this new attitude to life' was

20 Carol Lee Flinders, *Enduring Lives: Living Portraits of Women and Faith in Action* (Maryknoll, NY: Orbis Books, 2013), 66.

21 E.T., 577. *Het Werk*, 614; Letter 21, To Han Wegerif and others, Westerbork, Sunday, 29 November 1942: ik zou graag op dit gebied van geestelijk voedsel aan het werk willen gaan.

22 Marta Perrini, "Etty Hillesum and Sophie Scholl: Sisters in Fate", in: Klaas A.D. Smelik, Meins G.S. Coetsier & Jurjen Wiersma (eds.), *The Ethics and Religious Philosophy of Etty Hillesum: Proceedings of the Etty Hillesum Conference at Ghent University, January 2014* [Supplements to The Journal of Jewish Thought and Philosophy, 28] (Leiden/Boston, MA: Brill, 2017), 192-204; especially p. 192.

> deeply connected to her artistic and personal experiences, both internal and external.[23]

Richard Viladesau, whose expertise is theological aesthetics, resonates with Paulnack's speech with what is essential for surviving times of fear, horror, or personal darkness.

> [...] the fact that God is the 'horizon' of every experience of beauty explains why even the tragic emotions can be experienced in art as 'beautiful,' and why there is at the heart of every deep aesthetic experience – and perhaps particularly in music – an intense feeling of striving toward something beyond the moment itself.[24]

Beauty is essential for living towards something and not surrendering one's humanity to the current dark moment. The most transcendental aesthetic is music since human beings have an innate connection to this form.

In summary, music can be a solace in a wounded world. For Etty Hillesum, music is a metaphor for the undercurrent of her spirituality. Her inner tune is expressed in her desire to help others who were facing life-or-death possibilities on a day-in and day-out basis. She wants to bring a sense of humanness back to those for whom the dehumanization has taken hold. She uses metaphors to express what she hopes to do with her life: "let some music flow from me"[25] to "provide some spiritual nourishment".[26]

Conclusion

"We left the camp singing."[27] From a twenty-first century perspective, Etty Hillesum and her family boarding a transport train with a song on their lips is an amazing action. Surrounded by the cacophony of noises – screaming, howling, yelling, bargaining, crying, murmured praying – is the singing

23 Perrini, "Etty Hillesum and Sophie Scholl", 196.

24 Viladesau, "Music as an Approach to God", 8.

25 E.T. 153. *Het Werk*, 161; Monday late afternoon, 24 November 1941: En laat U wat muziek uit me komen.

26 E.T., 577. *Het Werk*, 614; Letter 21, To Han Wegerif and others, Westerbork, Sunday, 29 November 1942: op dit gebied van geestelijk voedsel aan het werk willen gaan.

27 E.T., 659. *Het Werk*, 702; Letter 71, To Christine van Nooten, near Glimmen, Tuesday, 7 September 1943: We hebben zingende dit kamp verlaten [...].

at the train an act of resistance? An act of acceptance? An act of spiritual confidence? A natural product of shared identity?

The metaphor of music in Hillesum's burgeoning spirituality is not about external music. It is about getting in touch with her own spiritual melody – a melody she could sustain, and which would sustain her. She found great hope, comfort, and safety in her God. Hillesum's conversations with her God were frequently written in her journals, sometimes spontaneously, other times trying to recall what had spilled out of her earlier. The inner tune or inner melody is one of the metaphors she uses to describe her spirituality.

Ultimately, she found in herself an unbreakable melody. Because of the strong melody within, she chooses to provide spiritual nourishment to those with whom she comes in contact. The unbreakable melody of Hillesum's spirituality transcends the sensory and "semantic overload" described by Harmon earlier in this work. Hillesum is then able to be the "peacefulness of [...] simple presence" in the lives of other prisoners at Camp Westerbork.[28] This undercurrent of Hillesum's spirituality is as strong and moving as any piece of music that touches something deep within each of us and, likewise, connects us to the greater Presence in all of us. This connection may be why, for decades now after her death, Etty Hillesum's life story continues to move us.

About the Author

Nancy JP Anderson (1957) earned a master's degree in theology with a focus on spirituality from St. Catherine University in St. Paul, Minnesota, USA. She is the sole owner of a wholesale distribution business for the graphics printing industry. She offers educational presentations about Etty Hillesum, incorporates Hillesum's writings into presentations about labyrinths as spiritual paths, and uses Hillesum's writings to keep her philanthropy, life, and business "human focused".

28 Harmon, *The Mystery We Celebrate, the Song We Sing*, 46.

A "staretz" in Camp Westerbork

The Connections Between Slavic Orthodoxy and the Spirituality of Etty Hillesum

Fernando Arriero Peranton

Abstract

It is possible to draw a parallel between the spirituality of Etty Hillesum and Russian Orthodox mysticism, since there are some striking connections: the need of muting the mind to reach the heart; the desire for a permanent state of prayer; non-violence; or the importance of being more than doing. In fact, Etty Hillesum could be seen as a "staretz" (Russian spiritual father) in Camp Westerbork. Moreover, this article shows that these connections are not casual.

Keywords: Russian orthodoxy, mysticism, *staretz*, Camp Westerbork, prayer, non-violence, kneeling, *hineinhorchen*

The aim of this article is to show that there are some interesting connections between the itinerary of Etty Hillesum and the spiritual path of Russian Orthodoxy. These links are not casual. Recall that Etty Hillesum inherited a love of Russia from her mother Rebecca, who was born in Pochep (Почеп), about 450 km from Moscow. Moreover, Etty Hillesum became deeply interested in Russian literature of the nineteenth century,[1] a literature steeped in the orthodox mysticism radiating out of Russian monasteries.

1 Etty Hillesum refers once to the geographer and philosopher P.A. Kropotkin and the short story master Anton Chekhov, and twice to the first modern Russian novelist, Nikolai Gogol. As for Alexander Pushkin, Etty Hillesum mentions two of his works: *Yevgeny Onegin* and *The Tale of Tsar Saltan*. On the other hand, she dedicated many hours to the translation of the works of Leo Tolstoy. Regarding Michail Lermontov, no textual citations are found, but the majority of the references appear in the first volume of the diary to express the inner battle between

Smelik, Klaas A.D. (ed.), *The Lasting Significance of Etty Hillesum's Writings: Proceedings of the Third International Etty Hillesum Conference at Middelburg, September 2018*.
Taylor & Francis Group 2019
DOI: 10.5117/9789463722025_PERANTON

In fact, there are some aspects in common held by both her spiritual development and Russian mysticism, which in her case could have been channeled through the literature. It is for this reason that Etty Hillesum could metaphorically be considered a *staretz*, a man of God dwelling in these monasteries. But Etty Hillesum's monastery was a Nazi transit camp called Westerbork.

The more relevant aspects are addressed below.

1.1 The Ascetic Battle

Orthodox religious practitioners take care of the corporal dimension of their spiritual advancement through physical and breathing exercises. They pay attention to the heart area, concrete bodily postures, and fasting, among other things.[2] Etty Hillesum, advised by Julius Spier, assumes similar practices, thus marking the beginning of her spiritual itinerary.[3] Moving forward on her spiritual path, however, soon demanded an attitude of deep listening or, as she called it, "hineinhorchen."[4]

Orthodox wisdom would say that Etty Hillesum was in the stage of the "common man," in which many thoughts or *pomysly* fill the mind when one is silent, and thus one avoids reaching the core of the self: the heart.[5] Thus, a necessary ascetic battle begins:

reading this author and getting carried away by the fantasies with respect to Julius Spier. Fyodor Dostoevsky is the second most cited author (35 times), even ahead of the Bible (33 times). Etty Hillesum approaches him in a direct way through his works, especially *The Idiot, The Brothers Karamazov*, and *Memories of the Dead House*. In addition, she immersed herself with great interest in the commentary prepared by the French author André Suarès. Hillesum fell in love with the main character of *The Idiot,* Prince Myshkin, whom she called my "new friend" (E.T., 214; *Het Werk*, 223; Friday, 2 January 1942: Er is een nieuwe vriend bijgekomen: Vorst Myschkin). In fact, she wanted to take these two volumes to Camp Westerbork, even if that meant sacrificing space for food. But the Austro-Hungarian poet Rainer Maria Rilke stands out among all her readings. The trips to Russia (1899 and 1900) left an indelible mark on the poet.

2 Saint Basil, bishop of Caesarea Mazaca in Cappadocia in the fourth century and a great defender of corporal prayer, invites us to consider "how the soul forces affect the body and how the feelings of the soul depends on the body" (Hom. In illud, Attende tibi ipsi 7 PG 31, 216b). Etty Hillesum mentions the practice of fasting on several days: 20 March 1941, 8 June 1941, 22 March 1942 and 11 June 1942. Indeed, to say monk in Slavic, the term *postnik* can be used, meaning "that who fasts."

3 Cf. E.T., 6. *Het Werk*, 6; Sunday, 9 March 1941.

4 Cf. E.T., 90. *Het Werk*, 96; Saturday, 23 August 1941.

5 This is, according to the Eastern Fathers, the main organ of psychic and spiritual life, the deepest sphere of being in which God manifests Himself to man (Cf. *Hom. Spirit.* XV), 20.

> It costs me a lot of pain and takes a great deal of strength, but if I can fight this fight to the end, I shall be stronger than ever before.[6]

To describe this descent into her inner core, Etty Hillesum uses various images: a well, a workshop, a laboratory, a granite block, a plain. Later, with a more mature practice, she adds two others. Etty Hillesum imagines an ocean crossed by a fleet of ships that transport treasures of incalculable value. Suddenly, a storm shakes the ships in such a way that one of them is shipwrecked. This ocean figures as the human being and the bottom of the ocean is where the valuable booty waits to be found. There lays the heart. To get to it, it becomes necessary to enter oneself.[7] Indeed, Etty Hillesum points out in her fourth notebook how this internal process is developing for her:

> The cosmos has moved from my head to my heart, or in my particular case, to my midriff – anyway from my head to another area. And once God had moved inside me to the space in which he still resides, well, I suddenly stopped having headaches and stomach aches![8]

Only after the battle was it possible to reach the most sacred source of her person and a state of stillness, the state which the Slavic mystics calls *hesykhia*. And only after the battle did Etty Hillesum make listening a permanent way of life. In fact, her deepest words about this attitude were written in September 1942 when she explained how a deep listening to herself, to others and to God could explain her life. That listening, from the depth of herself to the depth of the other, carried out a communion so intimate that it seemed to Etty Hillesum that God Himself listened to Himself in the wisdom of the other,

> Truly, my life is one long hearkening unto myself and unto others, unto God. And if I say that I hearken, it is really God who hearkens inside me.

6 E.T., 58. *Het Werk*, 62; Monday, 9 June 1941: Het doet een hoop pijn en kost veel kracht, maar wanneer ik deze strijd ten einde toe zal kunnen voeren, zal ik sterker staan in m'n leven dan ooit. The orthodox spiritual tradition compares ascetic practices with a combat against the enemies of the soul. Indeed, the monks were called "combatants" or *agonidzomenoi*. Cf. T. Spidlik, M. Tenace & R. Cemus, *El monacato en el Oriente* (Burgos: Monte Carmelo, 2004), 149-150.

7 Cf. E.T., 532. *Het Werk*, 563-564; Friday, 25 September 1942.

8 E.T., 555. *Het Werk*, 591; Letter 5, To Aimé van Santen; Amsterdam, Sunday 25 January 1942: De Kosmos is uit m'n hoofd verhuisd naar het hart, of voor mijnentwege naar het middenrif, in ieder geval uit m'n hoofd naar een ander regioon. En toen God eenmaal in me verhuisd was en de ruimte betrokken had, waar hij nu nog steeds woont, ja, toen had ik opeens geen hoofdpijn en geen maagpijn meer!

> The most essential and the deepest in me hearkening unto the most essential and deepest in the other. God to God.[9]

1.2 The Uninterrupted Dialogue with God

The radical transformation of Etty Hillesum is explained, among other things, by the discovery of God within. The God who initially bothered her became gradually her permanent interlocutor. In this way, Hillesum appears to have reached the aim of Orthodox spirituality: a permanent state of prayer.[10]

On 26 August 1941, Etty Hillesum discovers within herself, as if it were from a wellspring, God Himself.[11] The rock of her atheism and rationalism did not allow her quick or simple access,[12] but the mere awareness of being inhabited by the Presence supposed an irreversible dynamism.

Progressively, as she kneels physically and existentially, as she dares to pronounce the name of God, as she experiences the superabundance of peace, joy, strength, and love of God, she prepares to welcome Him inside her and to unearth Him in the hearts of others.

Additionally, Hillesum experiences for herself another of the spiritual keys of orthodoxy: the Holy Scriptures. These are the daily nourishment for any monk who wishes to reach *deification*.[13] Although Julius Spier is the person who encourages her to read the Bible, she takes a very personal approach. Thus on 28 November 1941, Etty Hillesum explains how she has

9 E.T., 519. *Het Werk*, 549; Thursday, 17 September 1942: Eigenlijk is mijn leven één voortdurend "hineinhorchen", in mijzelf, in anderen, in God. En als ik zeg: ìk "horch hinein", dan is het eigenlijk God in mij, die "hineinhorcht". Het wezenlijkste en diepste in mij dat luistert naar het wezenlijkste en diepste in de ander. God tot God.

10 The search for this continuous prayer marked the beginning of the itinerary of the Russian pilgrim; cf. Strannik (trad.), *El peregrino ruso* (Madrid: Espiritualidad, 2005), 14.

11 Perhaps Etty Hillesum took the image of a buried God from the imaginary of Rainer Maria Rilke. According to Rilke, God has retreated into the dark abyss of the incomprehensible, of nature and of inner faith, because He fears that poets will come to Him. In this way, God has been "self-buried"; cf. Fabián Soberón, "Dios y Rilke", in: pendientedemigracion.ucm.es/info/especulo/numero28/d_rilke.html [last query: 13-II-2017]. But the Austro-Hungarian poet warns that God will return to us from the bosom of the earth.

12 Cf. E.T., 102. *Het Werk*, 108; Wednesday, 24 September 1941.

13 The knowledge of the Holy Scriptures, having been inspired by the Spirit, "sows virtue, makes thought light, prevents us from being submerged by the unexpected vicissitudes of events, raises us above the darts of the devil, makes us stay very near the sky" (John Chrysostom, Hom. 5, *De studio praesentium1*, PG 63, 485) [translated into English by the author]. In this way, God, who is transcendent and inaccessible in his impartible essence, communicates Himself to finite man, making possible the real divinization of the believer (*theosis*).

chosen some passages and has given them a new, significant and experiential meaning. She chooses the commandment "love thy neighbor," the Pauline *Hymn of Charity*, and the creation of man in the image and likeness of God.[14]

Another suggestive connection between Etty Hillesum and orthodox spirituality is the relationship she finds between the physical body and the practice of prayer. The psychophysical dimension is acknowledged in how *Hesychasm* pays attention to bodily postures, breathing, or heartbeat. The most characteristic posture for Etty Hillesum is kneeling. She makes a point of describing herself as "*The girl who could not kneel*"[15] at the beginning of her diary, and as "*the girl who learned to pray*" at the end.[16] Far from a platonic vision, Etty Hillesum experiences the body as a home for God that must be preserved in good condition. By practicing corporal prayer in an ordinary context like her room, she sanctifies her own daily life.

In the Eastern tradition of the first centuries AD, kneeling prayer was, according to Origen,

> a symbol of that prostration and submission that Paul talks about when he writes: "I bow my knees before the Father" (Eph. 3,14). It is this spiritual kneeling, so called, that all creatures worship God in the name of Jesus and submit humbly to Him[...].[17]

Furthermore, it is interesting to point out that one of the times that Etty Hillesum wrote about kneeling is when quoting a letter from Rainer Maria Rilke. For the poet, this bodily gesture was connected to prayer and was the condition God needed to fill those who await him. From these verses, Etty Hillesum concludes that if God permeates and fills her, she herself will be the mediator of the Mystery, making sacred all that she experiences.[18]

1.3 Non-violence

Etty Hillesum shares with orthodox mystics an optimistic vision of the world related to the view of a kind and provident God Creator who protects His

14 A. Pleshoyano advocates that this truth was Etty Hillesum's *Leitmotiv*; cf. Alexandra Pleshoyano, "Etty Hillesum: For God and with God," in: *The Way* 44 (2005), 7-20, especially p. 11.

15 E.T., 145. *Het Werk*, 153; Friday, 21 November 1941, and E.T., 148. *Het Werk*, 156; Saturday, 22 November 1941: Het meisje, dat niet knielen kon.

16 E.T., 547. *Het Werk*, 580; Saturday, 10 October 1942: het meisje, dat leerde te bidden.

17 J. Daniélou, *Origène* (Paris: Éditions de la Table Ronde, 1948), 44.

18 Cf. E.T., 351. *Het Werk*, 262.

creatures. That is why Hillesum is also close to the Eastern understanding of evil; it has no substance, but is simply a corruption of good, an absence of good in the sense of realm or spiritual reality that was originally created in goodness. This approach led Hillesum to assume a posture of passive activity in the face of suffering.[19]

In the Eastern tradition, this attitude is known as *amerimnia*. It is a concept that may be misunderstood – as Etty Hillesum's attitude was by some of her friends – because it is close to apathy or lack of interest. But in monastic life, this term intends to describe a diametrically opposed attitude: "disregard for earthly things"[20] after struggling to "not having any desire for the things of this world any longer and to attend to God alone, assiduously and without distractions."[21]

The pacifist position of Etty Hillesum is also close to the view of Leo Tolstoy, who has drawn his inspiration from the Gospel according to Matthew. For the Russian author, revenge is not the way to build the Kingdom of God on earth. Love is the only force that will prevent humankind from distancing itself from its egocentric instincts in its actions. Hillesum, however, stands apart from a purely earthly Kingdom and finalizes her view on the foundation of evil by adopting the theological idea that human beings were created in the image and likeness of God (cf. Gen. 1:26-27).

The concept of being created in the image and likeness of God has been one of the theological truths studied by the greatest Fathers of the Church in the first centuries AD. In fact, Irenaeus, Origen, Basil, and Gregory of Nyssa distinguished between "image" and "likeness" to explain man's pull towards God; while "image" is a free gift from God, "likeness" refers to the free response of the human being, the effort made with the grace of God to assimilate and personalize the God within each person. Hillesum journeys along this orthodox path. As she recognizes God in her life, she knows herself better and recognizes others as images of God. Hence, in June 1942, when events accelerate and fear among the Jews intensifies, Hillesum tries not to express in her diary the separation between them (Nazis, executioners, evil) and us (Jews, victims, good). In fact, she refers to German soldiers as "our so-called enemies."[22]

19 Cf. E.T., 556. *Het Werk*, 591.

20 Pseudo-Efrem, *Ad renunciantes*, t. 3, 323F.

21 Dorotheus of Gaza, PG 88, 1109b. Cf. I. Hausherr, *Hésychasme et prière, Orientalia Christiana* (*Analecta*, 176) (Rome: Pontifical Institute of Oriental Studies, 1966), 216ff.

22 Etty Hillesum uses this expression on 23 September 1942 (cf. E.T., 529. *Het Werk*, 560); on 24 September 1942 (cf. E.T., 530. *Het Werk*, 561); and on 2 October 1942 (cf. E.T., 541. *Het Werk*, 573). See also B. Siertsema, "Etty Hillesum's Views on the Nazis and their Henchmen," in: K.A.D.

1.4 "Being more than doing"

Etty Hillesum, who welcomes with simplicity and confidence the superabundance given to her, decides to hand over everything she has learned and that has generated life in her.[23] This is how she breaks and shares herself like bread in the service of the inmates in Camp Westerbork, by sending the correspondence of the prisoners, helping to carry the suitcases of the deportees and visiting the sick. Moreover, Etty Hillesum discovers that "being [is] more than doing" and that her most worthy service consists in being herself – hopeful, full of vision, and present alongside others.

Thus, Etty Hillesum devotes more and more time to listening deeply (*hineinhorchen*) to those who approach her, reading their lives and understanding them as if they were houses with open doors that could be visited and where the God who inhabits them, could be found. Etty Hillesum, taking the witness of Julius Spier, her "midwife of the soul," becomes a mediator between divinity and humanity. Or, expressed with the analogy I am crafting here, she becomes a *staretz*, since the role assigned to *staretz* in the orthodox tradition is the same as what she has taken on.

> He is always directed to a human person with a unique destiny, a vocation and particular difficulties. Thanks to a special gift he sees each being as God sees them and looks for the right way to help them, opening the inner sense in a direct way without doing violence to their will, in such a way that they, liberated from his own hidden chains, can get to grace. To make this charismatic operation it is not enough to have a deep knowledge of human nature that is born from a long experience. It is necessary to have, each time, a vision of the person. A person cannot be known except through a revelation.[24]

The words offered by Etty Hillesum to the Westerbork prisoners are luminous and full of hope and compassion. The testimonies that have come from those who knew Etty Hillesum in these circumstances evoke the words of Macarius of Egypt,

Smelik, M.G.S. Coetsier & J. Wiersma (eds.), *The Ethics and Religious Philosophy of Etty Hillesum: Proceedings of the Etty Hillesum Conference at Ghent University, January 2014* [Supplements to the Journal of Jewish Thought and Philosophy, 28] (Leiden/Boston, MA: Brill, 2017), 270-281, especially p. 271.

23 Cf. E.T., 682. *Het Werk*, 640; Letter 60, To Henny Tideman; Westerbork, Wednesday, 18 August 1943.

24 John B. Dunlop, *Amvrosij di Optina* (Magnano: Qiqajon, 2002), 12-39.

> Those who carry within themselves the divine richness of the Spirit, when they talk with others about spiritual matters, transmit this wealth as if they extracted it from their own treasure [...]. Because, if we can say it that way, each of their words has returned to the place from where it had been taken.[25]

Ultimately, the most essential mission was not so much what was done, but what inner sense of being Etty Hillesum and others maintained. Indeed, a *staretz* could help a person not only with words and prayers, but simply with their presence, their being. Etty Hillesum expresses it in this way,

> And to be where one happens to be, to be there one hundred percent. My 'doing' will consist of 'being' there.[26]

1.5 Beauty and Patience

Contemplation of the beauty of creation aroused in Etty Hillesum inner peace and sharpened her sense of harmony and desire for a beautiful life. Amazement and admiration were transformed into interior attitudes such as adoration, praise and thanksgiving towards the Author of this beauty. In addition, Etty Hillesum enters into communion with the cosmos and understands that she is part of a whole in which each being has an incalculable value, in which everything is a comradeship and a gift. Everything is given to her and every gift is filled with the love of the Giver. Orthodox wisdom also speaks of this spiritual knowledge that allows one to understand the laws that govern the cosmos. In turn, this permits the spirit to sense a Presence that unifies all reality. This is what Saint Gregory of Sinai expresses when he says,

> Through the spirit and meditation of the heart, man sees clearly appear to the Word (Logos) of God from the 'logoi' of beings; see the personified wisdom of God Father appear from time leading into the 'logoi' of the models that print their strokes in beings.[27]

A similar approach, which goes beyond pure appearance, made it possible for Etty Hillesum to understand reality as a paradox; in spite of the horror, life

25 *Philocalia V,* 88, 55.

26 E.T., 536. *Het Werk,* 568; Wednesday 30 September 1942: En waar men is helemaal zijn, honderdprocentig zijn. Mijn 'doen' zal bestaan in er te 'zijn'.

27 *Philocalia X, Various sentences,* 134, p. 105.

is beautiful. Only one who has experienced Love as the last word standing stronger than death, can affirm that life is beautiful. Even the most inhuman terror can never wipe out the truth, the goodness, and the beauty of life. This was Etty Hillesum's *leitmotiv* and the core of her testimony to future generations.

1.6 Etty Hillesum: a "Staretz" in Camp Westerbork

A *staretz* possesses an "apostolic soul" of a very high order and is enabled to speak of God, to read hearts (*kardiognosis*), to prophesy the Kingdom, and to limit the power of demons.[28] In addition, a *staretz* has the gift of healing wounds of the soul by giving advice, sharing his presence, introducing silence, or offering prayers of intercession. These activities lead him to identify closely with his disciples in a way that makes their joys and sorrows his own, and he assumes the weight of their guilt or anxiety.[29]

A *staretz* is more than a priest because he is not appointed by a human authority in a hierarchy, but is chosen by the Spirit who offers him the gift of guiding others and healing them. Coming to his position in this way, he is a prophetic figure not tied to blind obedience.[30] Indeed, he knows well that each relationship of spiritual fatherhood is unique and does not follow a predetermined pattern. Rather, he knows that it grows under the influence of the Holy Spirit with each individual receiving the most appropriate word for their specific needs.

This figure from the oriental monastic evokes Julius Spier who had a role as mediator between Etty Hillesum and God, but the young Dutch woman also became a *staretz* while in Camp Westerbork. She guided dozens of people to whom she testified that life was beautiful in spite of everything. This commitment as a mediator was something Etty Hillesum assumed in front of the body of Julius Spier that 15 September 1942:

> You taught me to speak the name of God without embarrassment. You were the mediator between God and me, and now you, the mediator, have gone, and my path leads straight to God. It is right that it should be so. And I shall be the mediator for any other soul I can reach.[31]

28 Cf. O. Clement, *La Iglesia de los ortodoxos* (Madrid: Nerea, 2008), 20.

29 Cf. Kallistos Ware, *El Dios del misterio y la oración* (Madrid: Narcea, 1997), 146.

30 Cf. Spidlik, Tenace & Cemus, *El monacato en el Oriente*, 102.

31 E.T., 516. *Het Werk*, 545; Tuesday 13 October 1942: Jij hebt me onbevangen de naam van God leren uitspreken. Jij bent de bemiddelaar geweest tussen God en mij en nu ben jij, bemiddelaar

About the Author

Fernando Arriero Perantón (1979) holds a PhD in Theology from the Faculty of Northern Spain and a BA in Biblical Theology from the Pontifical University of Salamanca. He is the legal representative of the Etty Hillesum Foundation in Spain, which provides spaces for integral growth to the most vulnerable people. The author spends most of his time teaching Religion and Philosophy to Secondary and High School students, as well as listening to young people through spiritual accompaniment. He is Director of the Secretariat of Youth Ministry of the Diocese of La Rioja.

weggegaan en nu gaat mijn weg regelrecht tot God, het is goed zo, dat voel ik. En ik zal zelf weer de bemiddelaarster zijn voor al die anderen, die ik bereiken kan.

Etty Hillesum: Humanity as a Task

Emilio Baccarini

Abstract

Meeting Etty Hillesum through her diary and letters is like seeing a spark of light at the bottom of an abyss. Her achievement was to conquer and maintain a balance between "inside" and "outside." She was able to find the "centre" of the self, that point that allows one to fill every moment of life with meaning. To use a term dear to mystical theology and taken up by Max Scheler in his ontological value, *ordo amoris*; she found the centre where one encounters God.

Keywords: humanity, meaning of life, beauty of life, suffering, *ordo amoris*, Other, Max Scheler, inner self

Preliminary Remarks

Etty Hillesum died at Auschwitz-Birkenau 75 years ago. Some 40 years later when her work was published, it was immediately perceived as a vivid and direct testimony to the tragedy that took place in Europe during World War II. She considered her own writing as preparatory notes for a later narrative. But we are left without the follow-up. Her notebooks represent one of the most illuminating testimonies and concrete complaints coming out of the tragedy. Fortunately, with new scholarship focusing on the literature of memory, the analysis of the Shoah and its radical evil shows us that human beings are able to perform unconscionable acts. This lesson stands as a warning: We are again in a dangerous moment of narcissistic retreat leading many countries including Europe and the US, and even India and Brazil, to the exclusion of the other, to the rejection of the different and the needy. Dangerous forms of the exaltation of violence, of the ideology of death, and of the denial of humanity have returned to the scene. It is no longer so

Smelik, Klaas A.D. (ed.), *The Lasting Significance of Etty Hillesum's Writings: Proceedings of the Third International Etty Hillesum Conference at Middelburg, September 2018.*
Taylor & Francis Group 2019
DOI: 10.5117/9789463722025_BACCARINI

clear what we can assume by the word "humanity" or what the expressions "human" life or "human" existence imply. What does "human being" mean?

These are the questions that inspired my initial approach to the work of Etty Hillesum. My investigation developed along two complementary lines; the first sees Hillesum as a witness to the Shoah, and the second views her life and work from a philosophical-anthropological perspective examining how she manifested the sense of the human. Her answers to my questions – revealed to us in her writings – are a promising legacy applicable to the present and to our future. She embodied a real philosophical anthropology in practice.

A Spark of Light in the Abyss of Evil

Etty Hillesum's diaries are fully meaningful in the context of the time in which they were written, even if their origin was simply the desire of a young woman to solve the existential difficulties of life.[1] In this sense, they were first of all the "story of a soul" and we could say that they were a clear manifestation of what, after Plato and Augustine, we term *epimeleia tès psychès* [care of the soul]. The diaries, however, immediately display an awareness of the times. It was these times that Etty Hillesum wanted to chronicle[2] and she did it through her own osmosis between the exterior and its interior.

> Sometimes I long for a convent cell, with the sublime wisdom of centuries set out on bookshelves all along the wall and a view across the cornfields

1 Cf. E.T., 69-73. *Het Werk*, 72-77; Monday, 4 August 1941.

2 Cf. E.T., 86: I want to live to see the future, to become the chronicler of the things that are happening now (downstairs they are screaming blue murder, with Father yelling, "Go, then!" and slamming the door; that, too, must be absorbed, and now I am suddenly crying since I am not all that objective really and no one can breathe properly in this house; all right, make the best of it then); oh yes, a chronicler. I notice that, over and above all my subjective suffering, I have an irrepressible objective curiosity, a passionate interest in everything that touches this world and its people and my own motives. Sometimes I believe that I have a task. Everything that happens around me is to be clarified in my mind and later in my writing". *Het Werk*, 91; Wednesday afternoon, 13 August 1941: Ik wil de Kroniekschrijfster worden van veel dingen uit deze tijd (beneden moord en brand, vader brult: ga dan, en smijt met deuren; ook dat moet verwerkt worden en nou huil ik – brul opeens, zó objectief ben ik dus nog niet; eigenlijk kan je hier in huis niet leven, enfin, vooruit maar weer); o ja, Kroniekschrijfster, daar was ik gebleven. Ik neem bij mezelf waar dat naast al dat subjectieve lijden dat ik doe altijd weer een a.h.w. objectieve nieuwsgierigheid komt, een hartstochtelijke belangstelling voor alles wat deze wereld en z'n mensen en m'n eigen zieleroerselen betreft. Ik geloof soms dat ik een taak heb. Alles, wat er om me heen gebeurt moet in mijn hoofd tot klaarheid gedacht worden en later door mij beschreven worden.

> – there must be cornfields and they must wave in the breeze – and there I would immerse myself in the wisdom of the ages and in myself. Then I might perhaps find peace and clarity. But that would be no great feat. It is right here, in this very place, in the here and now, that I must find them. I must fling myself into reality, time and again, must come to terms with everything I meet on my path, feed the outer world with my inner world and vice versa. But it is all so terribly difficult, and I feel so heavyhearted.[3]

A passage from the diary clearly shows the "method" that Etty Hillesum intended to follow:

> I am sometimes so distracted by all the appalling happenings round me that it's far from easy to find the way back to myself. And yet that's what I must do. I mustn't let myself be ground down by the misery outside things around me out of some sense of guilt. Things must mature to clarity within you, you yourself must never succumb to things.[4]

One year later, on 20 and 21 July 1942, the path of existential maturation was advancing, as was her contact with suffering.

> They are merciless, totally without pity. And we must be all the more merciful ourselves. That's why I prayed early this morning: "Oh God, times are too hard for frail people like myself. I know that a new and kinder day will come. I would so much like to live on, if only to express all the love I carry within me; carry into that new age all the humanity that survives in me, despite everything I go through every day. And there is only one way of preparing for the new age, by living it even now in our

3 Cf. E.T., 71. *Het Werk*, 75-76; Monday, 4 August 1941: Soms verlang ik naar een kloostercel, met de gesublimeerde wijsheid van eeuwen op boekenplanken langs de muur en met het uitzicht op korenvelden – dat moeten nu eenmaal korenvelden zijn en ze moeten golven ook – en daar zou ik me dan willen verdiepen in de eeuwen en in mezelf en op den duur zou er dan wel rust en klaarheid komen. Maar dat is geen kunst. Hier, op deze plek, in deze wereld en nú, moet ik tot klaarheid en rust en evenwicht komen. Ik moet mezelf iedere keer weer gooien in de realiteit, moet me auseinandersetzen met alles, wat ik op m'n weg tegenkom, de buitenwereld moet voedsel ontvangen van mijn innerlijke wereld en omgekeerd, maar het is zo verschrikkelijk moeilijk en waarom heb ik toch zo een beklemd gevoel van binnen.

4 E.T., 86. *Het Werk*, 92; Wednesday afternoon, 13 August 1941: Je wordt soms zo afgeleid door de schokkende gebeurtenissen om je heen, dat je je later maar moeizaam de weg tot jezelf terug kunt banen. En toch moet dat. Je mag niet ten onder gaan in de dingen om je heen, uit een soort schuldgevoel. De dingen moeten in jóu tot klaarheid komen, je mag niet zelf in de dingen ondergaan.

> hearts. Somewhere in me I feel so light, without the least bitterness and so full of strength and love. I would so much like to help prepare for the new age and to carry that which is indestructible within me intact into the new age, which is bound to come, for I can feel it growing inside me, every day."[5]
>
> [...] I feel as if I were the guardian of a precious slice of life, with all the responsibility that entails. I feel responsible for that great and beautiful feeling for life I carry within me, and I must try to shepherd it safe and sound through these times, towards better ones. That is all that really matters, and I am always conscious of it. There are moments when I feel like giving up or giving in, but I soon rally again and do my duty as I see it: to keep the spark of life inside me ablaze.[6]

There was a continuity with what had been her reaction to the news of the suicide of her professor in March 1941.[7] This is the task that Etty Hillesum

5 E.T., 497. *Het Werk*, 526; Monday evening, 20 July 1942: Onbarmhartig, onbarmhartig! Maar des te barmhartiger moeten wij innerlijk zijn, dat is toch het enige. Waar mijn gebed vanochtend in de vroegte op neer kwam: Mijn God, dit tijdperk is te hard voor broze mensen als ik ben. Ik weet ook, dat er hierna weer een ander tijdperk komen zal, dat humanistisch zijn zal. Ik wil zo graag blijven leven om al de menselijkheid, die ik in me bewaar, ondanks alles, wat ik dagelijks meemaak, over te dragen in dat nieuwe tijdperk. Dat is ook het enige, waardoor wij de nieuwe tijd kunnen voorbereiden, door haar nu al in ons voor te bereiden. En ergens ben ik zó licht vanbinnen, zo zonder enige verbittering en heb zoveel kracht en liefde in me. Ik wil zo graag blijven leven om de nieuwe tijd te helpen voorbereiden en om dat onverwoestbare in mij behouden over te dragen naar de nieuwe tijd, die zeker zal komen, ze groeit immers al in mij, iedere dag, ik voel het toch?

6 E.T., 498. *Het Werk*, 527; Tuesday evening, 21 July 1942: Ik voel me als de bewaarplaats van een stuk kostbaar leven, met alle verantwoordelijkheid daarvoor. Ik voel me verantwoordelijk voor het mooie en grote gevoel voor dit leven dat ik in me heb en dat moet ik onbeschadigd door deze tijd heen trachten te loodsen, naar een betere tijd toe. Dat is het enige waar het om gaat. Daar ben ik me voortdurend bewust van. En er zijn momenten, waarop ik denk te zullen moeten resigneren of te bezwijken, maar steeds komt er weer dat verantwoordelijkheidsgevoel om dat leven, dat in mij is, ook werkelijk levend te houden.

7 E.T., 53: Nevertheless, we who are left behind are just a little bit destitute, though inwardly I still feel so rich that the destitution is not fully brought home to me. However, one must keep in touch with the real world and know one's place in it; it is wrong to live only with the eternal truths, for then one is apt to end up behaving like an ostrich. To live fully, outwardly and inwardly, not to ignore external reality for the sake of the inner life, or the reverse – that's quite a task. *Het Werk*, 56; Tuesday, 25 March 1941: Maar de wereld zal verder gaan en ik ga voorlopig nog mee, vol goede moed en goede wil. Maar we blijven toch een beetje berooid achter, maar ik voel me vanbinnen nog zo rijk, dat de berooidheid nog niet volledig tot me doordringt. Toch moet men goed contact houden met de tegenwoordige werkelijke wereld en daarin zijn plaats trachten te bepalen, men mag niet alleen leven met de eeuwigheidswaarden, dat zou ook kunnen ontaarden

set for herself and to which she tried to remain faithful. To find and preserve the harmony between "inside" and "outside" meant finding the "centre" of her being, that point that would allow her to fill every moment of life with meaning. Max Scheler in his ontological valence, takes up this term dear to mystical theology: *ordo amoris*. On 17 September 1942, Hillesum wrote,

> My love of life is so great and so strong and calm and makes me so grateful that I shall refrain from putting it into words again. There is such perfect and complete happiness in me, oh God. What he called "reposing in oneself." And that probably best expresses my own love of life: I repose in myself. And that part of myself; that deepest and richest part in which I repose, is what I call "God."[8]

At this time, Etty Hillesum was dealing with health problems, but this was not her obstacle. Rather it was her need to acquire the capacity to have a deeper look, and to listen "inside" (here she uses the German *hineinhorchen*). She writes,

> It is all to the good that my body has called a 'halt', oh God. For I must rest a while if I am to do what I have to do. Or perhaps that is just another conventional idea. Even if one's body aches, the spirit can continue to do its work, can it not? It can love and *hineinhorchen* – "hearken unto" – itself and unto others and unto what binds us to life. *Hineinhorchen* – I so wish I could find a Dutch equivalent for that German word. Truly, my life is one long hearkening unto myself and unto others, unto God. And if I say that I hearken, it is really God who hearkens inside me. The most essential and the deepest in me hearkening unto the most essential and deepest in the other. God to God.[9]

in struisvogelpolitiek. Volledig leven, naar buiten en naar binnen, niets van de uiterlijke realiteit opofferen terwille v.h. innerlijk en ook niet andersom, ziehier een schone taak.

8 E.T., 519. *Het Werk*, 549; Thursday morning, 17 September 1942: Het levensgevoel is zo groot en sterk en rustig en dankbaar in me, dat ik maar helemaal niet meer proberen zal het in één woord uit te drukken. Er is zo een volmaakt en volkomen geluk in me, mijn God. Het is toch weer het beste uitgedrukt met zijn woorden: "ruhen in sich". En hiermee is misschien het meest volkomen uitgedrukt mijn levensgevoel: ik rust in mijzelve. En dat mijzelve, dat allerdiepste en allerrijkste in mij, waarin ik rust, dat noem ik "God".

9 E.T., 519. *Het Werk*, 549, Thursday morning, 17 September 1942: Het is zeker goed, dat je mijn lichaam "halt" hebt laten roepen, mijn God. Ik moet helemaal gezond worden om te kunnen doen, wat ik allemaal zal moeten doen. Of misschien is dat ook een conventionele voorstelling. Zelfs als men een kwaal in z'n lichaam heeft kan de geest toch doorwerken en vruchtbaar zijn? En liefhebben en "hineinhorchen" in zichzelf en in anderen en in de samenhangen van dit leven en

This inner listening allowed her to become the "thinking heart" of Camp Westerbork. The question of God appeared many times in her diaries. An annotation of 26 August 1941 is particularly significant for the Chassidic – as well as Augustinian – resonances that one finds there:

> There is a really deep well inside me. And in it dwells God. Sometimes I am there, too. But more often stones and grit block the well, and God is buried beneath. Then He must be dug out again. I imagine that there are people who pray with their eyes turned heavenward. They seek God outside themselves. And there are those who bow their head and bury it in their hands. I think that these seek God inside.[10]

On 14 December of the same year, the young woman who did not know how to kneel, wrote,

> Last night, shortly before going to bed, I suddenly went down on my knees in the middle of this large room, between the steel chairs and the matting. Almost automatically. Forced to the ground by something stronger than myself. Some time ago I said to myself, "I am a kneeler in training." I was still embarrassed by this act, as intimate as gestures of love that cannot be put into words either, except by a poet.[11]

The slow work she did on herself transformed her life into one that manifests the elusive "meaning of life." The human being does not simply *be*. Rather one "builds himself on what he is," to use an expression of Edith Stein whom Etty Hillesum met in Camp Westerbork ("the two nuns with the yellow star"). Existence is not only a datum, statically defined and immutable,

in jou. "Hineinhorchen", ik wilde dat ik daar een goede hollandse uitdrukking voor kon vinden. Eigenlijk is mijn leven één voortdurend "hineinhorchen", in mijzelf, in anderen, in God. En als ik zeg: ìk "horch hinein", dan is het eigenlijk God in mij, die "hineinhorcht". Het wezenlijkste en diepste in mij dat luistert naar het wezenlijkste en diepste in de ander. God tot God.

10 E.T., 91-92. *Het Werk*, 97; Tuesday evening, 26 August 1941: Binnen in me zit een heel diepe put. En daarin zit God. Soms kan ik erbij. Maar vaker liggen er stenen en gruis voor die put, dan is God begraven. Dan moet hij weer opgegraven worden. Ik stel me voor, dat er mensen zijn, die bidden met hun ogen naar de hemel geheven. Die zoeken God buiten zich. Er zijn ook mensen, die het hoofd diep buigen en in de handen verbergen, ik denk, dat die God binnen in zich zoeken.

11 E.T., 181. *Het Werk*, 190; Sunday, 14 December 1941: Gisterenavond, vlak voor het naar bed gaan, lag ik opeens geknield midden in deze grote kamer, tussen de stalen stoelen en op het lichte matting. Zó maar vanzelf. Naar de grond gedwongen door iets, dat sterker was dan ik zelf. Een tijd geleden zei ik tegen mezelf: ik oefen me in het knielen. Ik geneerde me nog te veel voor dat gebaar, dat even intiem is als de gebaren der liefde, waarover men ook niet spreken kan, als men geen dichter is.

but an event in continuous transformation. With its plastic nature, it takes on the form that we are called to give it. The process of formation and transformation constitutes the very exercise of existence. Etty Hillesum found the internal light by digging mercilessly within herself and thus giving us all a valid paradigm path. Evil is born from the heart of man and only when we have the courage to dig into our own interiority ("listen to ourselves inside") can we find both the source of evil and the spark of love capable of transforming the world.

> Ultimately, we have just one moral duty: to reclaim large areas of peace in ourselves, more and more peace, and to reflect it toward others. And the more peace there is in us, the more peace there will also be in our troubled world.[12]

Today, just as 75 years ago, hatred and violence are never only political or social, though that may be a convenient thought. Their origin is elsewhere. On 24 July 1942, Hillesum wrote a message from which we can learn today:

> I am terribly tired. I can bear these times. I can even understand them a little. If I should survive and keep saying, "Life is beautiful and meaningful," then they will have to believe me. If all this suffering does not help us to broaden our horizon, to attain a greater humanity by shedding all trifling and irrelevant issues, then it will all have been for nothing.[13]

If suffering is cancelled out, the very meaning of life is cancelled out.

Humanity as a Task

The adjective "human" with which we determine the specific existence of a type of being compared to other creatures, is not a simple qualification. It

12 E.T., 535-536. *Het Werk*, 567; Tuesday, 29 September 1942: Dit is eigenlijk onze enige morele taak: in zichzelf grote vlaktes van rust ontginnen, steeds meer rust, zodat men deze rust weer uitstralen kan naar anderen. En hoe meer rust er ìn de mensen is, des te rustiger zal het ook in deze opgewonden wereld zijn.

13 E.T., 502. *Het Werk*, 531; Friday morning, 24 July 1942: Ik ben erg moe. Ik kan deze tijd dragen, ik begrijp haar zelfs een beetje. Als ik deze tijd overleef en als ik dan zal zeggen: het leven is mooi en zinrijk, dan zal men mij toch moeten geloven. Als al dit lijden niet tot een horizonverruiming leidt, tot een grotere menselijkheid, daartoe dat alle kleinheden en bijzaken van dit leven van je afvallen, dan is het voor niets geweest.

is not only an adjective. It has an ontological value: humanity is a mode of being. I think that Etty Hillesum perceived and experienced this in depth. Her diaries were the deposit of this reality in its continuous variations. In the course of her writing, her life happened, and she realized its meaning. Her biography became a phenomenology of the event of being human. She was able to manifest an awareness of her day-to-day existence, and to give meaning to the course of her life.

From this perspective, Hillesum's writings were her description of a metamorphosis in which she reached the ontological source of existence, which gave rise to her sense of humanity. For her, existence did not simply happen; it flowed in a current of meaning, and as a result, her life became meaningful. A note of 15 June 1941 is particularly enlightening. We find it at the conclusion of the first notebook:

> We are but hollow vessels, washed through by history. Everything is chance, or nothing is chance. If I believed the first, I would be unable to live on, but I am not yet fully convinced of the second.[14]

And further on she adds,

> For a moment yesterday, I thought I couldn't go on living, that I needed help. Life and suffering had lost their meaning for me; I felt I was about to collapse under a tremendous weight. But once again I put up a fight and now I can face it all, stronger than before. I have tried to look that "suffering" of mankind fairly and squarely in the face. I have fought it out, or rather something inside me has fought it out, and suddenly there were answers to many desperate questions, and the sense of emptiness made way for the feeling that there was order and meaning after all, and I could get on with my life. All was smooth going again after a short but violent battle from which I emerged just a fraction more mature.
> I said that I confronted the "Suffering of Mankind" (I still shudder when it comes to big words), but that was not really what it was. Rather I feel like a small battlefield, in which the problems, or some of the problems, of our time are being fought out. All one can hope to do is to keep oneself humbly available, to allow oneself to be a battlefield. After all, the problems must be accommodated, have somewhere to struggle and come to rest, and

14 E.T., 62. *Het Werk*, 66; Sunday, 15 June 1941: We zijn maar holle vaten, waar de wereldgeschiedenis doorheen spoelt. Alles is toeval of niets is toeval. Wanneer ik het eerste geloofde, zou ik niet kunnen leven, maar van het laatste ben ik nog niet overtuigd.

> we, poor little humans, must put our inner space at their service and not run away. In that respect, I am probably very hospitable; mine is often an exceedingly bloody battlefield, and dreadful fatigue and splitting headaches are the toll I have to pay. Still, now I am myself once again, Etty Hillesum, an industrious student in a friendly room with books and a vase full of oxeye daisies.[15]

Listening inside becomes clearer in this passage; we see that though it is not the most "natural" thing to do, we can become better at existing humanly when we know our own internal resources. On 19 and 20 February 1942, Etty Hillesum wrote,

> I said, "Human beings, you say, but remember that you're one yourself." And strangely enough he seemed to acquiesce, grumpy, gruff old Jan. "The rottenness of others is in us, too," I continued to preach at him. "I see no other solution, I really see no other solution than to turn inward and to root out all the rottenness there. I no longer believe that we can change anything in the world until we have first changed ourselves. And that seems to me the only lesson to be learned from this war. That we must look into ourselves and nowhere else."[16]

15 E.T., 63. *Het Werk*, 66-67; Sunday, 15 June 1941: Gisteren heb ik één moment gedacht, dat ik niet verder kon leven, dat ik hulp nodig had. Ik was de zin van het leven en de zin van het lijden kwijt, ik had het gevoel onder een geweldig gewicht "zusammen zu brechen", maar ook hier heb ik iets doorgevochten, waardoor ik opeens weer verder kon, sterker dan vroeger. Ik heb het "Lijden" der mensheid vlak en eerlijk in de ogen proberen te kijken, ik heb me ermee uiteengezet, of liever: iets in mij heeft zich er mee uiteengezet, op veel wanhopige vragen zijn antwoorden gekomen, de grote zinneloosheid heeft weer plaats gemaakt voor iets meer orde en samenhang en ik kan weer verder. Het was weer even een korte, maar hevige slag, waar ik een ondeelbaar beetje rijper uit tevoorschijn ben gekomen. Ik zeg, dat ik me uiteengezet heb met "Het Lijden der Mensheid" (ik griezel nog steeds van die grote woorden). Maar dat is het toch eigenlijk niet. Ik voel me veeleer een klein slagveld, waar de vragen of een enkele vraag van deze tijd uitgevochten wordt. Het enige wat je kunt doen, is je deemoedig ter beschikking te stellen en jezelf tot slagveld te laten maken. Die vragen moeten toch een onderdak hebben, moeten toch een plek vinden, waar ze kunnen strijden en tot rust komen en wij, arme kleine mensen, moeten onze innerlijke ruimte voor ze openstellen en niet weglopen. Ik ben misschien, wat dat betreft, wel heel gastvrij, het is daar soms een allerbloedigst slagveld bij mij en af en toe een overgrote vermoeidheid en zware hoofdpijn zijn de tol hiervoor. Maar nu ben ik alweer alleen nog maar mezelf, Etty Hillesum, een vlijtig studente in een vriendelijke kamer met boeken en een vaas margrieten.

16 E.T., 245. *Het Werk*, 254; Thursday & Friday, 19 & 20 February 1942: Ik zeg: De mensen, ja de mensen, maar bedenk, dat je daar zelf ook onder valt. En dat wilde hij onverwachts zo maar toegeven, de bokkige, norse Jan. En die rottigheid van de anderen zit in ons ook, preekte ik door. En ik zie geen andere oplossing, ik zie werkelijk geen andere oplossing dan in je eigen

> [...] It is a great deal merely to realize that one comprises part of a great growing process, indeed simply to be aware of such a process. I believe that for far too many people life still consists of rather disconnected, accidental moments. [...] You can only help others if you yourself live according to what you want to explain, and I feel that I am increasingly in a position to lend others a bit of a helping hand simply by making it clear to them that no one else can really help them and that they should accept that, not as something that makes one unhappy, but as something that may make one aware of one's own strength and inner voice, to which one should listen patiently until one accrues certainties from within – but one must be patient.[17]

That the origin of evil is in one's interior was a basic belief that Etty Hillesum constantly reaffirmed. From this reality arises the need for self-education if one is to become capable of responding to evil with the authentic human retort: "life is beautiful." On 28 March 1942, this expression was repeated several times, accompanied by the awareness of pain and by the realization that we must take on the pain of others.

> And finally: ought we not, from time to time, open ourselves up to cosmic sadness? One day I shall surely be able to say to Ilse Blumenthal, "Yes, life is beautiful, and I value it anew at the end of every day, even though I know that the sons of mothers, and you are one such mother, are being murdered in concentration camps. And you must be able to bear your sorrow; even if it seems to crush you, you will be able to stand up again, for human beings are so strong, and your sorrow must become an integral part of yourself; part of your body and your soul, you mustn't run away

centrum in te keren en daar uit te roeien al die rotheid. Ik geloof er niet meer aan, dat we in de buitenwereld iets verbeteren kunnen, wat we niet eerst in ons zelf moeten verbeteren. En dat lijkt me de enige les van deze oorlog, dat we geleerd hebben, dat we het alléén in onszelf moeten zoeken en nergens anders.

17 E.T., 246 & 247. *Het Werk*, 256 & 257; Friday morning, 20 February 1942: Het is al zoveel, wanneer men weet, dat men deel uitmaakt van één groot groeiproces, dat men bewust is van zo'n proces. Ik geloof, dat nog voor veel te velen het leven uit toevallige momenten bestaat zonder al te veel samenhang [...]. Men kan alleen helpen, wanneer men zelf lééft, wat men anderen wil duidelijk maken en ik voel steeds meer kracht in me groeien om anderen een kleine helpende hand te bieden, alleen al door ze duidelijk te maken, dat een ander ze eigenlijk niet helpen kàn en dat ze dat moeten accepteren, maar niet als iets, dat je ongelukkig moet maken, maar als iets dat je bewust doet worden van de eigen krachten en van het eigen innerlijk, dat men met geduld beluisteren moet, totdat je zekerheden toevallen uit je eigen innerlijk, maar men moet geduldig zijn.

> from it, but bear it like an adult. Do not relieve your feelings through hatred, do not seek to be avenged on all German mothers, for they, too, sorrow at this very moment for their slain and murdered sons. Give your sorrow all the space and shelter in yourself that is its due, for if everyone bears his grief honestly and courageously, the sorrow that now fills the world will abate. But if you do not clear a decent shelter for your sorrow, and instead reserve most of the space inside you for hatred and thoughts of revenge – from which new sorrows will be born for others – then sorrow will never cease in this world and will multiply. And if you have given sorrow the space its gentle origins demand, then you may truly say: life is beautiful and so rich. So beautiful and so rich that it makes you want to believe in God.[18]

In the profound depths of oneself, we "listen" and discover our own destination – not destiny – but precisely the *ordo amoris* where the sense of being human is manifested. We find God, but we also meet the other. In returning to the interior, we do not close in on ourselves. We are returned to the other, to each other. This was what allowed for Etty Hillesum's capacity to go beyond reason and approach poetry... to take on the pain of the other.

> To carry the other with one, always and everywhere, privately within oneself, and to live with him there. And not just with one, but with many. To draw the other into one's inner space and to let him go on flourishing there, to assign him a place where he can grow and unfold. To live

18 E.T., 308-309. *Het Werk*, 321; Saturday morning, 28 March 1942: Und schließlich: muß man der Weltentraurigkeit nicht dann und wann eine kleine Unterkunft verleihen? En tegen Ilse Blumenthal zal ik op een goede dag misschien zeggen: Ja, het leven is mooi, aan het eind van iedere dag prijs ik het, terwijl ik toch wéét, dat Zonen van Moeders, zoals U ook een Moeder bent, in concentratiekampen vermoord worden. En het verdriet daarover moet je dragen, je kunt er je onder laten verpletteren, je zult ook wel weer opstaan, een mens is zo iets sterks en het verdriet daarover moet a.h.w. een bestanddeel van jezelf worden, een stuk van je lichaam en van je ziel, je hoeft er niet voor weg te lopen, draag het, maar als een volwassen mens, reageer je gevoelens niet af in een haat, die zich wreken wil op alle duitse moeders, die toch nu, op dit ogenblik, hetzelfde verdriet te dragen hebben als jij om hun gesneuvelde en vermoorde zonen. Dit verdriet moet je in jezelf alle ruimte en onderdak verschaffen, die het toekomt en op die manier zal het verdriet in de wereld misschien verminderen, als iedereen draagt, eerlijk en loyaal en volwassen draagt, wat hem wordt opgelegd. Maar als je het verdriet niet het eerlijke onderdak verleent, maar de meeste ruimte openstelt voor haat en wraakgedachten, waaruit weer nieuw verdriet voor anderen geboren zal worden, ja dan neemt het verdriet nooit een einde in deze wereld en zal zich steeds vermeerderen. En als je het verdriet de plaats en de ruimte gegeven hebt, die het krachtens zijn nobele geboorte toekomt, ja, dan mag je toch zeggen: het leven is zo schoon en zo rijk. Het is zo, dat je in God zou kunnen geloven.

> genuinely with another, to live with him even if you should not see him for years and allow him to go on living within you – that is the fundamental thing. And that way you can be with someone sheltered from the external vicissitudes of life. It makes for great responsibility.[19]

Work on oneself, responsibility for oneself also becomes responsibility for the other.

> Because this, too, is a new truth for me: one must not just "work" on one's own inner life but also on the lives of all those one has taken into one's heart. We actually reserve a place within us for our friends, a place where they can flourish, we try to define them more clearly within ourselves, and that is bound to help them in the long run, even if we tell them nothing about it. Including in oneself all the gestures and looks and words and problems of others and allowing their lives to unfold in oneself and throwing fresh light on them that is our inner task.[20]

Etty Hillesum had reached what we call the kenotic dimension of existence: Through the emptying of self we make room for the other, we become responsible for them. Decades later, again in the context of Jewish thought, Emmanuel Levinas developed similar beliefs using the expression *l'autre dans le meme* to indicate a new definition of subjectivity as the *for-other*. The fundamental category of this anthropology is proximity. It is an anthropology that has not yet found the way to realization but whose ultimate aim is the fulfilment of an authentically human existence.

19 E.T., 281. *Het Werk*, 292; Friday morning, 13 March 1942: De ander met zich meedragen, altijd en overal, besloten in zich zelf, en daar met hem leven. En niet zo met een, maar met velen. De ander opnemen in de innerlijke ruimte en hem daar verder laten gedijen, een plaats geven, waar hij uitgroeien en zich ontplooien kan. Werkelijk mèt de anderen leven, ook al ziet men iemand soms jaren niet, hem tòch in je laten doorleven en mèt hem leven, dat is het wezenlijke. En zo kan men met iemand samen voortleven, beschut tegen de uiterlijke wisselvalligheden van dit leven. Het schept een grote verantwoordelijkheid.

20 E.T., 287. *Het Werk*, 298; Monday morning, 16 March 1942: Want ook dit is een nieuw opgekomen waarheid voor mij: men moet niet alleen aan z'n eigen innerlijke leven "werken", maar ook aan het leven van diegenen, die men in z'n innerlijk besloten heeft. Men geeft eigenlijk z'n vrienden een ruimte in zichzelf, waar ze kunnen gedijen en men probeert ze in zichzelf tot klaarheid te brengen en dat moet de anderen op den duur toch helpen, zelfs al zou men ze daar nooit iets van vertellen. De gebaren en blikken en woorden en problematiek en het leven van anderen in zich opnemen en dat leven van die anderen ìn zich zelf verder laten leven en tot klaarheid brengen. Hier ligt een innerlijke taak.

On 23 September 1942, Etty Hillesum talked to her friend Klaas Smelik Sr., who would become the keeper of her diaries:

> We shan't get anywhere with hatred, Klaas. Appearances are so often deceptive. Take one of my colleagues. I see him often in my thoughts. The most striking thing about him is his inflexible, rigid neck. He hates our persecutors with an undying hatred, presumably with good reason [...]. Klaas, all I really wanted to say is this: we have so much work to do on ourselves that we shouldn't even be thinking of hating our so-called enemies. We are hurtful enough to one another as it is. And I don't really know what I mean when I say that there are bullies and bad characters among our own people, for no one is really "bad" deep down. [...] And I repeat with the same old passion, although I am gradually beginning to think that I am being tiresome, It is the only thing we can do, Klaas, I see no alternative: each of us must turn inward and destroy in himself all that he thinks he ought to destroy in others. And remember that every atom of hate we add to this world makes it still more inhospitable.
>
> And you, Klaas, dogged old class fighter that you have always been, dismayed and astonished at the same time, say, "But that – that is nothing but Christianity!"
>
> And I, amused by your confusion, retort quite coolly, "Yes, Christianity, and why ever not?[21]

21 E.T., 528 & 529. *Het Werk*, 559 & 560-561; Wednesday, 23 September 1942: En we komen er tòch niet met die haat, Klaas, de dingen liggen in de realiteit toch heel anders, dan wij ze in onze gekunstelde schema's willen zien. Er is bij ons b.v. een medewerker. Ik zie hem in gedeelten dikwijls voor me. Het opvallendste aan hem is die onbuigzame, rechte nek. Hij haat onze vervolgers met een haat, waarvan ik aanneem, dat hij er gegronde redenen voor heeft. [...] Klaas, ik wilde je eigenlijk alleen dit zeggen: we hebben nog zoveel met ons zelf te doen, dat we aan haat tegenover onze zogenaamde vijanden nog niet eens toe zouden moeten komen. We zijn elkaar onderling nog vijand genoeg. En ik ben er ook niet mee klaar, wanneer ik zeg, dat er onder onze eigen mensen ook beulen en slechte elementen zijn. Ik geloof eigenlijk helemaal niet in wat men noemt "slechte mensen". [...] En ik herhaalde met dezelfde hartstochtelijkheid van altijd, hoewel ik mezelf langzamerhand vervelend begon voor te komen, omdat ik altijd weer op hetzelfde uitkwam: het is het enige en het enige, Klaas, ik zie geen andere weg, dat ieder van ons inkeert in zichzelf en in zichzelf uitroeit en vernietigt al datgene, waarvoor hij meent anderen te moeten vernietigen. En laten we ervan doordrongen zijn, dat ieder atoompje haat, dat wij aan deze wereld toevoegen, haar onherbergzamer maakt dan ze al is. En Klaas, oude en verbeten klassestrijder, zei ontsteld en verwonderd tegelijkertijd: Ja maar dat – maar dat zou immers weer Christendom zijn! En ik, geamuseerd over zoveel plotselinge verwarring, zei heel koelbloedig: Ja, waarom eigenlijk ook niet – Christendom?

God becomes one of the most interesting "interlocutors" in the final pages of Hillesum's diaries. Was hers a mystical "drift" or was it the simple recognition that at the end of the tunnel where darkness seemed absolute, the original is hidden, urging us to accept the assignment to responsibility?

We conclude these reflections with a prayer – as Hillesum herself called it – of Sunday, 12 July 1942. It was a passage of great philosophical, theological, and most importantly, anthropological value.

> Dear God, these are anxious times. Tonight for the first time I lay in the dark with burning eyes as scene after scene of human suffering passed before me. I shall promise You one thing, God, just one very small thing: I shall never burden my today with cares about my tomorrow, although that takes some practice. Each day is sufficient unto itself. I shall try to help You, God, to stop my strength ebbing away, though I cannot vouch for it in advance. But one thing is becoming increasingly clear to me: that You cannot help us, that we must help You to help ourselves. And that is all we can manage these days and also all that really matters: that we safeguard that little piece of You, God, in ourselves. And perhaps in others as well. Alas, there doesn't seem to be much You Yourself can do about our circumstances, about our lives. Neither do I hold You responsible. You cannot help us, but we must help You and defend Your dwelling place inside us to the last.[22]

In this testimony of inner torment, there is also the gift of another sense of existence. The diaries not only hold Hillesum's biography. They introduce ways in which humanity is constituted, and they reveal how we can construct the sense of a human. Etty Hillesum had somehow anticipated a path: life is continually given to us, but it's up to us to realize its meaning as human life.

22 E.T., 488-489. *Het Werk*, 516; Sunday morning prayer, 12 July 1942: Het zijn bange tijden, mijn God. Vannacht was het voor het eerst, dat ik met brandende ogen slapeloos in het donker lag en er vele beelden van menselijk lijden langs me trokken. Ik zal je een ding beloven, God, een kleinigheidje maar: ik zal mijn zorgen om de toekomst niet als evenzovele zware gewichten aan de dag van heden hangen, maar dat kost een zekere oefening. Iedere dag heeft nu aan zichzelf genoeg. Ik zal je helpen God, dat je het niet in mij begeeft, maar ik kan van te voren nergens voor in staan. Maar dit éne wordt me steeds duidelijker: dat jij ons niet kunt helpen, maar dat wij jou moeten helpen en door dat laatste helpen wij onszelf. En dit is het enige, wat we in deze tijd kunnen redden en ook het enige, waar het op aankomt: een stukje van jou in onszelf, God.

About the Author

Emilio Baccarini (1948) graduated in Philosophy from the University of Rome "La Sapienza." He teaches Philosophical Anthropology and Philosophy of Religion at the University of Rome "Tor Vergata." He has dedicated himself to the study of Husserl (Phenomenology: Philosophy as vocation, Studium, Rome 1981) and contemporary Jewish thought (Levinas: Subjectivity and infinity, Studium, Rome 1985), on which he has written many essays. In recent times, he has dealt with an anthropology of difference and otherness (*Il pensiero nomade: For a Planetary Anthropology*, Assisi: Cittadella, 1994); *The Person and His Faces: Ethics and Anthropology*, Rome: Anicia, 1996; *La soggettività dialogica*, Rome: Aracne, 2002); translation and introduction by E. Levinas, *Entre nous: Essai sur le penser-à-l'autre*, Milan: Jaca Book, 1998). He founded and directs the online philosophy magazine *Dialegesthai*.

Etty Hillesum & Albert Konrad Gemmeker

A Twofold Analysis of the Perpetration of the Westerbork Commander

Lotte Bergen

Abstract

Albert Konrad Gemmeker, Commander of *Durchgangslager* Westerbork, became to be known as the "gentleman-commander," because of his polite and friendly behaviour. After the war, he declared, during his trial, like many perpetrators, that he didn't know of the massive extermination of millions of innocents. Etty Hillesum, unlike Gemmeker's judges, was not blindsided by his behaviour and in her letters she described and criticized the commander, exposing him as one of the most important executors of the extermination system, the key player in the *Entjudung* of the Netherlands.

Keywords: Albert Konrad Gemmeker, Westerbork Camp, deportation of Jews, Nazism, prosecution of Nazi war crimes, "gentleman-commander", Westerbork letters of Etty Hillesum

"My God, are the doors really being shut now?"[1] Hillesum asks herself on 24 August 1943. Through the small openings at the top of the train, she catches a glimpse of the passengers. She sees only heads and hands. Hands that will wave to the ones who will be left behind, when the train leaves. This time, the transport consists of more than a thousand innocent men, women,

1 E.T., 654. *Het Werk*, 697; Letter 64, To Han Wegerif and others, Westerbork, Tuesday, 24 August 1943: Mijn hemel, gaan die deuren werkelijk allemaal dicht?

Smelik, Klaas A.D. (ed.), *The Lasting Significance of Etty Hillesum's Writings: Proceedings of the Third International Etty Hillesum Conference at Middelburg, September 2018.*
Taylor & Francis Group 2019
DOI: 10.5117/9789463722025_BERGEN

and children destined for Auschwitz-Birkenau where the train will arrive in three days. Between July 1942 and September 1944, 93 of such transports departed from Camp Westerbork for the camps in Eastern Europe.[2]

Camp Westerbork was established by the Dutch government on 9 October 1939 as the Central Refugee Camp Westerbork. The place was to provide a safe haven for Jews who had fled Germany and Austria. But on 1 July 1942, the Germans took over control of the camp and Camp Westerbork fell under the *Befehlshaber der Sicherheitspolizei und des SD*. Camp Westerbork continued under the official name *Polizeiliches Durchgangslager Westerbork*.

The organization of the camp that had already been introduced and put into motion by Jacques Schol,[3] the first Westerbork commander, was taken over by the Germans. Security in the camp was tightened. The military police present in the camp together with the *Ordedienst* (OD; Jewish camp police) took care of surveillance of the interior. An SS unit was responsible for surveillance outside.[4] Barbed wire and watchtowers gave the camp a different appearance. With the German takeover, the former refugee camp was transformed into a transit port for Jews being sent to their deaths.

Albert Konrad Gemmeker, an *SS-Obersturmführer* from Düsseldorf, was the commander of Camp Westerbork. His main concerns were prisoner quota, i.e. numbers to be transported out, and the time schedule for the deportation trains. Under his command, between October 1942 and April 1945, more than 80,000 Jews and 245 Roma and Sinti[5] were efficiently and almost silently sent out of the Netherlands to the camps in the East.

Gemmeker, who became known as the "gentleman-commander," declared during his trial after the war, like many perpetrators of the Shoah, that he didn't know of the massive extermination of millions of innocents. In addition to his "*nicht gewusst*," Gemmeker also appealed to the well-known excuse: "*Befehl ist Befehl*." The *Entjudung* was *kriegsnotwendig* and he, as commander of a Jewish Camp, carried out the political and military orders from Berlin.[6]

2 The first transport from Camp Westerbork left on 15 July 1942 with 1137 persons to Auschwitz-Birkenau. On 13 September 1944 the last transport with 279 people went to Bergen-Belsen.

3 The first commander of Camp Westerbork during the German occupation was Jacques Schol, reserve captain of the Dutch army. He was appointed commander in June 1940. He remained as commander alongside Gemmeker, but was only allowed to engage in internal camp matters. Because of Gemmeker, he left in January 1943.

4 Frank van Riet, *De bewakers van Westerbork* (Amsterdam: Boom, 2016), 65.

5 On 19 May 1944, the transport with Roma and Sinti departed from Camp Westerbork. Only 30 of the 245 Sinti and Roma survived the war.

6 Lotte Bergen, *Albert Konrad Gemmeker: Commandant van Westerbork* (Soesterberg: Aspekt, 2013), 95.

In various sources, diaries, letters, memoirs, and interviews, Gemmeker generally appeared "proper" and because of this behaviour he was not judged negatively by many. Even after the war, during his trial, his judges were swayed by his appearance. However, not everyone in the transit camp allowed themselves to be fooled by Gemmeker's behaviour. Klaas A.D. Smelik indicates that Hillesum was not at all blindsided by the appearance of the commander and she made a severe judgement.[7]

Historian Eva Moraal, in her comprehensive study based on diaries, camp letters, and memoirs, chronicled daily life in Camp Westerbork.[8] She recognized Hillesum and the Jewish journalist, Philip Mechanicus,[9] as two of the most important interpreters of life in the camp. According to Moraal, neither was a typical camp resident. Instead, in their texts and camp letters, they provided penetrating observations of life behind barbed wire on the piece of heath in Drenthe.

Etty Hillesum mentions the commander for the first time in her letter written to two sisters in The Hague at the end of December 1942. In that letter, she gives a detailed description of life in Camp Westerbork. She writes that there is a Dutch commander and a German one and that the German is said to be a music lover and a "gentleman."[10]

In her letter from 24 August 1943, Hillesum gives a searing account of a transport and depicts the anxiety and worry that preceded it the night before. She describes the commander issuing orders just before the train is about to leave. By doing so, she exposes him as one of the most important executioners in the extermination system, and a key player in the *Entjudung* of the Netherlands.

In this article, I will focus on Gemmeker's behaviour and Hillesum's description of him as outlined in her letters. I will go on to her ideas about the Nazi system and the role the individual played within that system. I will also dwell on the commander's view of his own role in the persecution of the Jews, views which came to light during his interrogation after the war and in later interviews.

7 Klaas A.D. Smelik, "Ik geloof eigenlijk helemaal niet in wat men noemt "slechte mensen": Etty Hillesums visie op het kwaad in de mens", in: Klaas A.D. Smelik, *et alii* (eds.), *Etty Hillesum 1914-2014* [Etty Hillesum Studies, 6] (Antwerpen & Apeldoorn: Garant, 2014), 24-47.

8 Eva Moraal, *Als ik morgen niet op transport ga...: Kamp Westerbork in beleving en herinnering* (Amsterdam: De Bezige Bij, 2014), 20.

9 Philip Mechanicus was a Jewish journalist who ended up in Camp Westerbork via Camp Amersfoort on 7 November 1942 as a criminal case. He met Etty Hillesum and her family in the camp. In his diary, published after the war under the title *In Depôt*, Mechanicus mentioned the Hillesum family. He was deported to Auschwitz where he was shot on 12 October 1944.

10 E.T., 582. *Het Werk*, 620; Letter 23, To two sisters in The Hague, Amsterdam, end of December 1942.

Albert Konrad Gemmeker

Albert Konrad Gemmeker was born in Düsseldorf on 27 September 1907. He grew up in a Roman Catholic family and visited the *Volksschule*. At eighteen, he started working for an insurance company, but this was not the best career choice and he soon quit the job. After being unemployed for a while, he enrolled in a police administration training course for a year at the Police Academy in Bonn. Then Gemmeker worked at the municipal police department in Duisburg until 1933. He was, however, more interested in obtaining an administrative position and with the help of a friend he managed to secure a post as an administrative police officer in his hometown.[11] Two years later, in 1935, he was hired as *Büroassistent-Anwärter* at the *Gestapo* [Secret State Police]. On 1 May 1937, he officially joined the NSDAP and in May 1940 he became a member of the SS. In August 1940, Gemmeker left Düsseldorf and moved to The Hague to fulfil the function of *Personalreferent* at BdS, the *Befehlshaber der Sicherheitspolizei und Sicherheitsdienstes*.

For a short time in June 1942, Gemmeker was appointed as commander of hostage Camp Beekvliet in Gestel near the city of Den Bosch.[12] One of the hostages, Hendrik Algra, described Gemmeker in a letter to his dearly beloved E. and the children as follows:

> The commander is quite approachable. He is even very flexible. We hardly ever see him. But he wishes to assist the people as much as possible, as far as business visits are concerned and also for furlough in case of serious illnesses.[13]

Another hostage, Robert Peereboom, wrote about Gemmeker's transfer to Camp Westerbork:

> For such a camp, the man is undoubtedly a weak figure: he cannot even bark and sneeze, like the ordinary representatives of the German regime, and we can hardly imagine that he will take the initiative for physical abuse. So we have hope that the poor Jews in the *Durchgangslager* might be better off with him than with his predecessor. We know that it is

11 Van Riet, *De bewakers van Westerbork*, 84.

12 Bergen, *Albert Konrad Gemmeker*, 55-56.

13 Hendrik Algra, *In den aap gelogeerd: Brieven van Hendrik Algra, Geschreven vanuit gijzelaarskamp Beekvliet Sint Michielsgestel 1942-1943* (Leeuwarden: Utjouwerij Frysk en Frij, 2002), 107: De commandant is nogal geschikt. Hij is zelfs zeer soepel. Wij zien hem practisch nooit. Maar hij is de menschen zoveel mogelijk ter wille, wat zakenbezoek betreft en ook het verlof bij ernstige ziekten.

> worse in the concentration camps compared to our situation. We are only threatened with death.[14]

Nevertheless, in October 1942, Gemmeker was appointed as Commander of transit camp Westerbork. On 9 October 1942, *Polizei-Inspektor* Bohrmann replaced the last commander Josef Hugo Dischner for the duration of three days. Gemmeker would have been present at the camp already. With Bohrmann as a temporary observer, he had a few days to get acquainted with the transit camp.[15] His predecessors, Erich Deppner and Josef Hugo Dischner had both proven to be unsuitable for the function of camp commander. They cursed and behaved aggressively towards the camp residents, and Dischner was also an alcoholic.[16] Gemmeker, however, had already proven in Beekvliet that he had the right leadership skills. After all, the Nazis favoured a silent *Entjudung* of the Netherlands and Gemmeker, with his generally correct behaviour, would be able to satisfy his superiors in Berlin. Because the Jewish camp organization functioned well, Gemmeker needed little effort to properly carry out his duties as commander.[17] Under his leadership, Westerbork was a "model camp," and Gemmeker ordered the Jewish filmmaker and photographer, Rudolf Werner Breslauer, to capture that apparent reality on film. Breslauer obliged him with a movie about camp life.[18]

For more than two years, Gemmeker ensured that the trains to the East left on time with the right quota of people loaded into them. Because of his excellent merits, he received an award on 1 September 1944: the *Kriegsverdienstkreuz mit Schwertern*.[19] He remained Commander until shortly before the

14 Robert Peereboom, *Gijzelaar in Gestel* (Zwolle: De Erven Tijl, 1945), 88.: Voor zo'n kamp is de man ongetwijfeld een slappe figuur: Hij kan niet eens keffen en snauzen, zoals de gewone vertegenwoordigers van het Duitsche regime en wij kunnen ons moeilijk voorstellen, dat hij het initiatief tot lichamelijke mishandeling zal nemen. Dus hebben wij hoop, dat de arme joden in het *Durchgangslager* wellicht iets beter met hem af zullen zijn dan met zijn voorganger. Wij weten dat het in de concentratiekampen erger is dan bij ons. Wij worden alleen maar met de dood bedreigd.

15 Van Riet, *Bewakers van Westerbork*, 83.

16 Bergen, *Albert Konrad Gemmeker*, 30-31.

17 *Ibidem*, 33.

18 In 1938, Breslauer and his family fled the Nazi terror in Germany. They settled in the Netherlands. In February 1942, the family was deported to Camp Westerbork. Gemmeker ordered Breslauer to take photos of camp residents and aspects of life in the camp. In 1944, he was ordered to make a film. Together with photographer and camp resident Willem Loeb, Breslauer made a 70-minute 16 mm film. Breslauer and his family were deported to Theresienstadt on 4 September 1944 and from there they were sent to Auschwitz-Birkenau. Only his daughter Ursula survived the Nazi horrors.

19 Bergen, *Albert Konrad Gemmeker*, 56.

liberation of the camp by the Allies on 12 April 1945. He left Camp Westerbork with his married secretary and mistress Elisabeth Helena Hassel-Mullender, also known as *Frau* Hassel. Gemmeker went to Amsterdam, where he was arrested on 5 May 1945. He was later transferred to Assen for interrogation. While awaiting trial, he himself was imprisoned in his own camp. The trial against the former commander began on 9 December 1948. A little over a month later, on 20 January 1949, he was sentenced to 10 years in prison with the three and a half years deducted for time already served. Because of good behaviour and a pardon granted by queen Juliana, Gemmeker was released in 1951, after only six years of imprisonment.[20]

Supposed Correct Behaviour of the "Gentleman-commander"

The sole purpose of *Durchgangslager* Westerbork was to eradicate Judaism from the Netherlands. The Jewish camp inmates had to be made to disappear quietly from Dutch soil. Circumstances in Camp Westerbork, compared to the other camps, were relatively favourable notwithstanding the poor hygiene conditions, the lack of privacy, and the terror associated with deportation and the unknown. Camp Westerbork did not give the impression that it was the last stop before destruction in the East. An illusion was created that it was not so bad after all, and life behind barbed wire was only temporary.[21] Gemmeker, with his air of "correct" commander, contributed to this façade in Camp Westerbork. What did this correct behaviour look like?

First of all, Gemmeker did not tolerate violence in the camp. The camp residents, in general, were not abused, beaten, or kicked. The Dutch SS man Van Dam was transferred out of the camp by Gemmeker, because he beat the Jews, and *Dienstleiter* Todtmann was relieved of his duties because he barked at the female camp inmates and at his subordinates.[22] Gemmeker's disapproval of violence can also be seen in his reaction to an incoming transport of heavily abused Jews from the labour camp in Ellekom.[23] The group arrived in Camp Westerbork on 27 November 1942. According to an

20 *Ibidem.*

21 Jurjen Wiersma, "Men zou de kroniek moeten schrijven van Westerbork", in: Klaas A.D. Smelik, *et alii* (eds.), *Etty Hillesum weer thuis in Middelburg* [Etty Hillesum Studies, 7] (Antwerpen-Apeldoorn: Garant, 2015), 37-49.

22 Bergen, *Albert Konrad Gemmeker*, 34.

23 In Ellekom, an SS training institute was established. Approximately 175 people were employed in appalling conditions for the extension of the institute.

eyewitness report, the victims were in such a bad condition that they all had to be transferred to the camp hospital immediately. This eyewitness believed that the commander was very affected by the event and exempted the men from further transport at least until they could recover.[24] Etty Hillesum was very impressed by the drama that had taken place in Camp Ellekom. She wrote to Han Wegerif and her friends in Amsterdam describing how she sat at the bedside of the unfortunates in boundless astonishment. She wondered how it was possible that people were capable of inflicting such pain on one another and that some victims had survived to tell the tale.[25]

Gemmeker not only eschewed violence, he also acted kindly and politely towards the Jewish camp residents. Where other camp commanders, like his predecessors Dischner and Deppner, kicked the Jews into the train, Gemmeker was calm and friendly. An example of his behaviour is shown is his treatment of a woman who suddenly jumped out of the train at the last minute and begged the commander to allow her to go on a later transport so that she could leave together with her daughter. Gemmeker responded in a polite way to the desperate woman's request, "*Gnädige Frau, es tut mir außerordentlich Leid, aber der Zug fährt gleich ab. Bitte wollen Sie einsteigen.*"[26] In this regard, the well-known quotation from Hillesum's letter of 24 August 1943 is illustrative. She noted how she heard someone behind her, just before a transport departed, remarking, "Once upon a time we had a commandant who used to kick people off to Poland. This one sees them off with a smile."[27]

Gemmeker's Jewish housekeeper, Mrs Asch-Rosenthal, experienced the commander from close range and she remembered in an interview in 1997 that Gemmeker always behaved politely towards her and sometimes even complimented her, a Jewish woman, for her cooking skills.[28]

A third point illustrating Gemmeker's "correct" behaviour is his personal interest and involvement with the camp residents, especially the children in Camp Westerbork. He felt that the children in the camp shouldn't lack anything. For the youngest camp inmates, there was a crèche and a kindergarten. Education took place in a large barracks for children between

24 Bergen, *Albert Konrad Gemmeker*, 34.

25 E.T., 577. *Het Werk*, 614; Letter 21, To Han Wegerif and others, Westerbork, Sunday evening, 29 November 1942.

26 Bergen, *Albert Konrad Gemmeker*, 35.

27 E.T., 653. *Het Werk*, 696; Letter 64, To Han Wegerif and others, Westerbork, Tuesday, 24 August 1943.

28 Herinneringscentrum Kamp Westerbork, interview with B.E. Asch-Rosenthal by Q. Abuys (1997).

the ages of six and fourteen. The Dutch historian Jacob Presser wrote that school attendance was compulsory. There were even special inspectors who were appointed for the task to apprehend truant pupils.[29] Gemmeker also involved himself with the *Jugendbund* in Camp Westerbork. The *Jugendbund* was founded by Leo Blumensohn, one of the first inhabitants of the camp. He taught the children religion, culture, and Zionism. Gemmeker approved this group, but wanted the name *Jugendbund* to be changed. The activities of this youth club were to be included in the "regular" camp education, so the name was changed to *Schülerkreis*, "Students Circle." Gemmeker seemed to understand that the children needed a break once in a while and he allowed the *Schülerkreis* to organize occasional trips outside the camp. This was undertaken, of course, under surveillance because any escape attempt had to be prevented. Gemmeker also attended a children's toy exhibition and listened to the children sing Hebrew and German songs.[30]

The most striking example of Gemmeker's involvement with the children was his interest in the fate of baby Machieltje, who came from Camp Vught to Westerbork. The premature infant needed special care. Gemmeker arranged for the Jewish professor of paediatrics, Van Creveld, to come to Camp Westerbork and he also organized for an incubator to be brought from a hospital in Groningen. The commander ensured that the infant received a drop of brandy in his bottle to gain strength. He regularly visited the maternity ward to enquire about the health of the little boy. Machieltje's condition improved slowly and once he reached six pounds, he was found strong enough to be transported to the East.[31]

In addition to his interest in the children, Gemmeker also showed admiration for the Jewish artists in the camp. Under the name *Bühne Lager Westerbork* a revue company was founded, which included the best artists. Gemmeker was very proud that there were talented actors, musicians, and cabaret artists present in "his camp." Often on a Tuesday evening, after a transport had left the same morning, they staged a performance with music, dance, and cabaret. The camp inhabitants could attend the *Bunter Abend* by paying a small sum of money, allowing them to clear their minds for a while. The artists enjoyed a certain amount of freedom in composing their

29 Jacob Presser, *Ondergang: De vervolging en verdelging van het Nederlandse Jodendom 1940-1945*, deel 1 (Den Haag: Staatsuitgeverij/Martinus Nijhoff, 1965). The English edition used here: Jacob Presser, *Ashes in the wind: The destruction of Dutch Jewry*, translated by Arnold Pomerans (London: Souvenir Press, [1968] 2010), 446.

30 Bergen, *Albert Konrad Gemmeker*, 44-45.

31 Willy Lindwer, *Getuigen van Westerbork: Kamp van hoop en wanhoop 1939-1945* (Hilversum: Just Publishers, 2009), 190-191.

programmes, but Gemmeker wanted to be informed about the lyrics and the music beforehand. He would appear at the rehearsals, unannounced. During the performances, the commander sat in the front row with high Nazi officials, whom he had invited specially for that evening.[32] Etty Hillesum wrote about Gemmeker as "our artistic patron" and told how he visited the same show as many as three successive times and always laughed at the same jokes. Hillesum wonders, with cynicism, how Gemmeker invited artists to his house and personally escorted an actress home and shook hands with her to say goodbye.[33] But artists enjoyed certain privileges. For example, they were exempted from transport because Gemmeker wanted to enjoy their talents for as long as possible. On 3 August 1944, this privilege dried up. The war no longer allowed for such entertainments and Gemmeker abolished the cabaret and music company. Most artists ended up in the "privileged" Jewish prisoners city Theresienstadt.[34]

Besides cabaret and music, there was also the opportunity to engage in all kinds of sports: football, handball, korfball, and there were chess tournaments, athletics, and boxing matches. Commander Gemmeker was willing to accommodate all these activities. The Dutch boxing champion Benny Bril got permission from Gemmeker to organize a competition which the commander attended together with German officers he had invited. Hans Schlomo, who worked as a gardener in the camp, remembered how Gemmeker came to see him one morning. The commander wanted to congratulate him personally for winning a sports competition.[35] Gemmeker came to see the Jews themselves and willingly joined in, mingling with the camp population on his own accord.

Sometimes the Commander Steps out of his Role

In general, the commander behaved correctly. He did not condone violence and showed interest in the camp residents. But there are a number of events that show Gemmeker stepping out of his role of "gentleman." Maintaining order and discipline was for the commander almost as important as the quota and the timetable of the trains. Those who did not adhere to the rules and regulations in Camp Westerbork, were in serious trouble.

32 Bergen, *Albert Konrad Gemmeker*, 46-47.

33 E.T., 652. *Het Werk*, 696; Letter 64, To Han Wegerif and others, Westerbork, Tuesday, 24 August 1943.

34 Bergen, *Albert Konrad Gemmeker*, 47.

35 *Ibidem*, 48-49.

Several regulations had already been laid down under Commander Jacques Schol but Gemmeker also issued various orders and instituted many rules. These were made known to the camp residents by means of a notice board with *Lagerbefehlen* and by the barrack leaders, so that everyone was aware of his duties and "rights." The members of the OD ensured that the camp laws and rules were carried out. In some cases, the commander himself determined what punishment a violator should receive and signed the criminal order to ensure it happened. Punishments could be such things as extra-hard labour in the camp or detention in the penal block.[36]

In his study on Westerbork guards, historian Frank van Riet extensively discusses a number of cases in which Gemmeker imposed severe penalties for serious offenses such as theft and maltreatment. For example, in winter, a number of camp residents were made to stand outdoors facing the camp fence throughout the day. For some, this punishment took place over several days.[37] Moreover, one of the witnesses who had to undergo such a punishment thought that the sanction was not too bad and despite the fact that people also had to stand at the fence under bad circumstances, he still judged the commander positively. Furthermore, this witness had been in German and Dutch camps. Then there is also the example of a Jewish camp resident who had to undergo a punishment because of theft. Before his deportation, the unfortunate man had to walk around, for three days after work, with a sign bearing the text: "I am a thief, because I have robbed my fellow prisoners."[38]

In addition to strict enforcement of the rules and devising severe punishments, there were a few incidents in which the commander himself acted brutally and violently. During a walk in the company of his mistress, Frau Hassel, the commander came across a camp prisoner who was walking around with a briefcase under his arm and wearing a hat, in the "forbidden zone," being too close to the camp fence. Then – as Gemmeker explained later during his interrogation – after being warned several times, the Jewish man still did not listen and continued to ignore him, so the commander shot him with his hunting rifle. Gemmeker explained that he had aimed low intentionally, because he did not want to injure the man seriously. The fact that the "courteous" commander walked around with a hunting rifle allegedly had to do with the wild rabbits scurrying around the camp farm,

36 Van Riet, *Bewakers van Westerbork*, 106.
37 *Ibidem*, 107.
38 *Ibidem*.

causing damage. Frau Hassel was shocked and she asked her beloved to warn her first, if there were a next time.[39]

Another camp prisoner testified that Gemmeker had behaved brutally towards a woman while a train was being prepared for deportation. It was Mrs Becker who had to go on transport and she begged the commander to let her stay in Camp Westerbork. According to the witness, Gemmeker grabbed the woman's handbag roughly from her hands, took something from the bag and then threw it back at her and pushed her towards the train.[40] Despite these harsh punishments and the sometimes brutal behaviour of the commander, these were exceptions in the impeccable appearance of the "gentleman-commander."

Hillesum's Description of the "Gentleman-commander"

> This morning he is putting fifty extra Jews on transport because a boy in blue pyjamas hid away in a tent.[41]

Etty Hillesum was aware of the image that had arisen around the commander. She writes about how legends were fabricated around Gemmeker, the commander with all his charm and well-disposed behaviour towards the Jewish camp residents.[42] Hillesum finds it all the more remarkable that his love of children apparently couldn't prevent so many children from dying in the camp.[43] The deportation of the sick, infants, and the elderly also raises doubts about the good intentions of the commander. In her letter from December 1942 to two sisters in The Hague, she writes about this remarkable phenomenon that virtually everyone – with the exception of those on the list of the commander, such as the artists – was sent to the labour camps as a working force in the

39 National Archives, Official Record No. 414, dated 4 June 1948, drawn up by J. Schoenmaker.
40 *Ibidem.*
41 E.T., 653. *Het Werk*, 696; Letter 64, To Han Wegerif and others, Westerbork, Tuesday, 24 August 1943: Hij stuurt vanochtend vijftig Joden meer mee op transport, omdat een jongen in een blauwe pyama zich verstopte in een tent.
42 E.T., 652. *Het Werk*, 695; Letter 64, To Han Wegerif and others, Westerbork, Tuesday, 24 August 1943.
43 In her study about Westerbork, Eva Moraal indicates that child mortality in Westerbork was relatively low. She refers to an overview of the ages among the deaths in the period from 15 July 1942 to 31 December 1943. The absolute mortality of infants under one year of age during this period was not very high. On average, it involved three to four deaths per month. In May 1943, the number was higher when six boys and girls one year of age and four infants under one died. In the age category 2-2.5 years the maximum number of deaths in a month was three boys and five girls.

East. One morning in the summer, Hillesum met a fellow camp prisoner who expressed his bewilderment about a transport that had just arrived and consisted of masses of old people who were later deployed for the *Arbeitseinsatz*.[44]

The sick who were actually not *transportfähig* went along with the train anyway. Hillesum's father also marvelled at this. On 2 September 1943 – five days before the Hillesum family was deported – he asked a male nurse from the last transport in amazement:

> How can people who are near death in the hospital be forced to go? Surely that's against all medical ethics. And the nurse answered solemnly, "The hospital gives up the corpses in order to hang on to the living."[45]

In August 1943, Hillesum gives a description of the commander during his performance just before a transport:

> He appears at the end of the asphalt path, like a famous star making his entrance during a grand finale.[46] [...] He walks along the train, his gray, immaculately brushed hair just showing beneath his flat, light green cap. That gray hair, which makes such a romantic contrast with his fairly young face, sends many of the silly young girls here into raptures – although they dare not, of course, express their feelings openly. On this cruel morning his face is almost iron-gray. It is a face that I am quite unable to read. Sometimes it seems to me to be like a long, thin scar in which grimness mingles with joylessness and hypocrisy. And there is something else about him, halfway between a dapper hairdresser's assistant and a stagedoor Johnny. But the grimness and the rigidly forced bearing predominate. With military step he walks along the line of freight cars, bulging now with people.[47]

44 E.T., 587. *Het Werk*, 625; Letter 23, To two sisters in The Hague, Amsterdam, end of December 1942.

45 E.T., 657. *Het Werk*, 700; Letter 68, To Maria Tuinzing, Westerbork, Thursday, 2 September 1943: Hoe kan dat nou, dat men uit het ziekenhuis mensen laat gaan, die ongeveer dood zijn, dat is toch tegen de medische ethica? 'De broeder antwoordde: Het ziekenhuis levert een lijk, om een levende hier te houden'.

46 E.T., 652. *Het Werk*, 695; Letter 64, To Han Wegerif and others, Westerbork, Tuesday, 24 August 1943: Hij verschijnt aan het begin van de asfaltweg, zoals de beroemde ster, die pas opkomt in de grote finale van een revue.

47 E.T., 653. *Het Werk*, 696; Letter 64, To Han Wegerif and others, Westerbork, Tuesday, 24 August 1943: Hij loopt langs de trein, zijn grijze, keurig geborstelde haren komen van achteren onder zijn platte lichtgroene pet te voorschijn. Met dat grijze haar, dat zo romantisch afsteekt tegen een nog betrekkelijk jong gezicht, dwepen vele onnozele bakvissen hier, al durven ze daar niet

Hillesum describes how the commander walked along the transport train to inspect "his troops: the sick, infants, young mothers, and shaved men" before departure. Gemmeker made an impatient gesture, while a number of patients on stretchers were being brought to the train. This morning, the courteous commander was somewhat displeased. A Jewish boy in blue pyjamas had escaped from the camp hospital and had hidden in a tent. After a manhunt, he was found and as a retaliatory measure fifty more Jews were added to the transport.[48] Because of the ill-considered action of the boy, he made fifty additional victims, or rather, Hillesum notes: "he didn't drag them away – our commandant did, someone of whom it is sometimes said that he is a gentleman."[49] It was the unrelenting judgment of Gemmeker, Hillesum writes, noting that this system functions by collective punishment.

In February 1943, the *Obersturmführer* issued the notorious *Lagerbefehl* No. 5 to prevent escape attempts. This order stipulated that on penalty of a successful escape attempt, ten additional Jewish camp residents would be added to the next transport, as a so-called *S-Falle* (a criminal case)[50]. In anticipation of the departure, these unfortunates stayed in the so-called penal barracks, the transit camp's prison.[51] In addition to these extra passengers, Hillesum writes how 20 more passengers were added to the transport, in case of death on the way because many sick people, without nursing, were deported this time.[52] Since the numbers needed to be correct, the commander decided to play it safe. The fate of the Jews was in the hands of the commander. He was lord and master over the life and death of the Jewish camp population.

Hillesum then examines the various "Jewish headpieces of camp life", who gathered around Gemmeker before the train left. The commander was

zo openlijk voor uit te komen. Zijn gezicht is op deze boze ochtend bijna ijzerkleurig. Het is een gezicht, dat ik nog lang niet ontcijferen kan, het komt me soms voor te zijn als een smal litteken, waarin verbetenheid, vreugdeloosheid en onoprechtheid met elkaar vergroeid zijn. En dan heeft hij iets in zijn type, dat het midden houdt tussen een verzorgde kappersbediende en de stamgast van een artistenkroeg. Maar de verbetenheid en de geforceerde stramheid. overwegen. In militaire pas loopt hij naar de goederenwagens, die uitpuilen van de mensen.

48 E.T., 652. *Het Werk*, 695; Letter 64, To Han Wegerif and others, Westerbork, Tuesday, 24 August 1943.

49 E.T., 645. *Het Werk*, 687; Letter 64, To Han Wegerif and others, Westerbork, Tuesday, 24 August 1943: [...] hij maakte ze niet, onze commandant, van wie men dikwijls zegt, dat hij een gentleman is, maakte ze.

50 After the war, Gemmeker claimed that this reprisal was only carried out once. Van Riet indicates that this statement is incorrect, as different sources and the information from the police report show otherwise.

51 Bergen, *Albert Konrad Gemmeker*, 38.

52 E.T., 654. *Het Werk*, 697; Letter 64, To Han Wegerif and others, Westerbork, Tuesday, 24 August 1943.

in company of his smartly dressed Jewish secretary and they were suddenly joined by a brown gun dog. This scene reminded Hillesum of something from a picture in an English society paper. The Dutch Jewish *Oberdienstleiter*, head of the Camp Service Corps, Kurt Schlesinger, joined the company and next to him the commander looked slight and insignificant. The three of them – the light green commandant with his military bearing, the fawn, impassive secretary, and the black bully-boy figure of the *Oberdienstleiter* – paraded past the overcrowded train before the doors were closed.[53] The train left and the commander had once again satisfied his superiors in Berlin.

Hillesum's younger brother Mischa, who arrived in Camp Westerbork with his parents on 21 June 1943, was, like his sister, not at all impressed by the commander and he did not fall into his apparent correctness.

In July 1943, Hillesum wrote to her friend Milli Ortmann that she had to keep an eye on her brother at the moment. After the "favoured camp" Barneveld was rejected for Mischa, his parents were now also eligible for transport. Mischa was allowed to stay in Camp Westerbork, but he didn't want to stay there without his parents. He was very upset about this and Hillesum could hardly keep her brother quiet. Mischa wanted to tell Gemmeker the truth: "I'm going to go and tell the commandant he is a murderer."[54]

Hillesum was aware of the game that was being played with the Jewish camp population, a game from which she and her family would not escape. When all stamps[55] expired at the beginning of July 1943 and the transport lists had to be made again, Hillesum wrote: "They are playing a game with us, but we allow them to do so, and that will be our shame for generations to come."[56]

The Functioning of the System and the Role of the Commander

> The terrifying thing is that systems grow too big for men and hold them in a satanic grip [...].[57]

53 E.T., 653-654. *Het Werk*, 696-697; Letter 64, To Han Wegerif and others, Westerbork, Tuesday, 24 August 1943.

54 E.T., 627. *Het Werk*, 668; Letter 51, To Milli Ortmann, Westerbork, Friday, 9 July 1943: Ik loop naar de commandant en zeg, dat hij een moordenaar is.

55 In the course of 1942, a system was introduced. Jews received a so-called stamp in their identity card. With this stamp exemption from deportation, "*Bis auf Weiteres*" was granted.

56 E.T., 620. *Het Werk*, 661-662; Letter 47, To Han Wegerif and others, Westerbork, Thursday afternoon, 8 July 1943: Men speelt een aardig spelletje met ons, maar wij láten dit spelletje ook met ons spelen en dit is onze onuitwisbare schande voor alle nageslachten.

57 E.T., 259. *Het Werk*, 269; Friday morning, 27 February 1942: Het angstaanjagende is, dat systemen boven mensen uitgroeien en mensen in een satanische greep houden [...].

Several months before Hillesum went voluntarily to Camp Westerbork, she wrote about the functioning of the Nazi system and the role of the individual within that system, at the end of February 1942, after visiting the Gestapo where she had to face the screaming and barking of an "unfortunate Gestapo boy," as Hillesum described him. Hillesum, instead of being intimidated by the aggressive behaviour of the Gestapo boy, thought that he, above all, was actually a pitiful figure and he interested her psychologically. Smelik states that Hillesum did not surrender to the intimidation techniques of the Gestapo. She did not go along with the opposition of friend or foe, which was related to her ideas about human hatred. It's about human beings and therefore, according to Hillesum, hate and fear are unnecessary.[58]

Hillesum was convinced that hatred only brings more hatred into the world. She felt that her own feelings of hatred had to be fought first, which was an active process. In no way should the Nazi barbarism get a grip on one's mind, for this might evoke the same kind of barbarism, which might work according to the same mechanisms.[59] This did not mean that Hillesum saw only the good in men, or in this case "the unfortunate Gestapo boy." Hillesum's ideas about the role that the individual plays in the functioning of the system is important. All the gruesome things that are happening, are part of human nature and this makes it familiar and less frightening, according to Hillesum.

She continued to write in her diary, however, that the terrifying thing is that systems grow too big for men and when that happens, both the builders of the system and its victims become entangled in what they have erected. Hillesum compared this process with buildings and towers, saying that first, they are built by men's hands and they rise above men. Then they collapse and bury men.[60] For Hillesum, the system's architects are the most pitiable, certainly as long as they can do no harm. But as soon as they are let loose on mankind, they become dangerous.[61] Hillesum understood that culprits such as the "unfortunate Gestapo boy" can become dangerous and turn into murderers. "But all the blame must be put on the system that uses these men."[62]

Smelik argues that Hillesum's way of thinking about the enemy, the German occupier, is paradoxical. The abandonment of hatred against the

58 Smelik, "Ik geloof eigenlijk helemaal niet in wat men noemt 'slechte mensen'", 32.

59 E.T., 21. *Het Werk*, 22; Saturday morning, 15 March 1941.

60 E.T., 259. *Het Werk*, 269; Friday morning, 27 February 1942.

61 *Ibidem.*

62 *Ibidem.*: Maar misdadig is alleen het systeem, dat deze kerels gebruikt.

enemy as an individual did not mean, according to Hillesum, that evil should not be eradicated. This had to be done and with all possible means. The Nazi system had to be eliminated, but not the individual person. Smelik points out that Hillesum's view was hard to realize in practice. The National Socialist system could only be destroyed if the allies killed German soldiers en masse. However, Hillesum did not write about the practical implementation.[63]

When in Camp Westerbork Hillesum was confronted with one of the main executors of the system, she noted that the word "gentleman" was actually a rather peculiar term for a commander of a Jewish camp. But it was precisely this "gentlemanly" attitude which made Gemmeker the perfect executor of the Nazi system.

Gemmeker was released on mankind, on the Westerbork camp population. Hillesum wrote that it is not the individual who is the criminal, but the system that uses these men. However, as Gemmeker himself pointed out, he was not just a dangerous executor of the system, he also had a certain room for manoeuvre and was able to make decisions on his own. He had been maintaining the system.

The Agency of the Commander Within the System

Every week, Gemmeker received from *Hauptsturmführer* Willy Zöpf the deportation order by telephone or telex connection with the required number of Jews. This number was determined by the *Reichssicherheitshauptamt* (RSHA), the head office of the German Security Service in Berlin, and then communicated to *Referat IVB4* in The Hague. *Referat IVB4* was a subdivision of the RSHA, which was in charge of the deportation policy and fell under the command of Zöpf. For Gemmeker, the quota was crucial, seeing he as commander was responsible for the execution of the deportations. Everything revolved around the trains, not only for Gemmeker, but also for those on the other side of the system, the victims.

As soon as the deportation order arrived, Gemmeker called in on the Jewish *Dienstleiter* who were involved in the execution of the transports. The deportation list was drawn up on the basis of cartel cards from the administrative centre of Camp Westerbork, the so-called *Zentralkartei*. The night before the departure, the barrack leaders read the names of the unfortunates who had to be transported. The commander demanded that during the reading of the deportation list it was always mentioned that the

63 Smelik, "Ik geloof eigenlijk helemaal niet in wat men noemt 'slechte mensen'", 35-36.

order was commissioned by his superiors. The barrack leader announced first: "*In Auftrag vom*" or "*In Anlassung vom*" followed by the name of one of Gemmeker's superiors and that was usually *Hauptsturmführer* Zöpf.[64]

For Gemmeker, the execution of orders from his superiors meant that he had to ensure that the trains, with the prescribed quota of people, left for the East on time.

Gemmeker stated after the war that he was just following orders. But a number of events show that the commander was able to make some decisions on his own. As an example, he determined that his beloved artists should stay in the camp for as long as possible, and he had his own list of Jews whom he considered to be important for different kinds of work. Camp prisoners were therefore not randomly sent out on transport.[65]

Gemmeker also allowed baby Machieltje and the wounded from Ellecom to first recover in the camp hospital before having them deported. Another example of Gemmeker's independent action is a remarkable transport of the sick on Tuesday, 8 February 1944. This transport was not ordered by his superiors, but departed on the initiative of Gemmeker himself. It is this transport that the historian Loe de Jong cited after the war as possible proof that the commander must have been aware of the Jewish fate. On 4 February 1944, Gemmeker sent a telex message to Zöpf, in which he requested to organize the transport of the sick. At that time, there were about 6500 Jews in the camp, including 900 sick persons. To relieve the camp hospital, the commander therefore considered it to be necessary to deport 400 to 500 sick persons. Without taking into account the condition of the sick and the possible risk of infection, this transport left for Auschwitz-Birkenau on 8 February 1944.

In addition, Gemmeker, together with Ferdinand aus der Fünten, who was in charge of the *Zentralstelle für jüdische Auswanderung* in Amsterdam, was involved in the evacuation of the Jewish psychiatric asylum, *het Apeldoornsche Bosch* on 21 January 1943. Fifty employees and 1200 patients went into trucks to Apeldoorn Station, from where they would continue their journey by train in freight wagons. This transport arrived in Auschwitz-Birkenau on 24 January 1943.[66]

Also the notorious *Lagerbefehl* No. 5 is an example of Gemmeker's own decision-making power. After all, it was an order issued by Gemmeker himself. No one was allowed to attempt a flight in his "model camp." From the above, it can be concluded that Gemmeker, while part of the system, still

64 Bergen, *Albert Konrad Gemmeker*, 39-40.

65 *Ibidem*.

66 *Ibidem*.

had a certain degree of agency. He sometimes acted according to his own judgment when it came to deportations; he determined that some "chosen ones" were given stay of execution while sending others on transport without deportation order from The Hague.

Gemmeker about his Role in the Shoah

How Gemmeker perceived his own role in the genocide became clear during his trial and in interviews he gave after the war. The commander declared that he did not know anything about the mass extermination of the Jews. According to him, he heard about this immense tragedy only after the war from the officers who interrogated him.[67]

For Gemmeker, the Jews had been put to work in the East. The commander admitted that this work was very heavy, and benefited the German war industry. The deportations as such, in his view, were *kriegsnotwendig* – a necessity of war.[68]

He also stated that Germany had the right to take such measures. After all, the Jews were extremely ill-disposed towards Germany and could have hindered and done damage to the war effort. Internment and deportation were therefore necessary.[69] With the exception of some details, for example the manner in which people were transported, Gemmeker did not find his task morally reprehensible:

> So personally I have had no moral objections to the internment and deportation of the Jews, but I do have some difficulty with some details of their execution, such as the unworthy way in which the deportees were packed together in the train carriages. However, I have not been able to do anything about it, although I made efforts to do so.[70]

But even the so-called attempts by Gemmeker to mitigate the misery of the transports were actually limited to placing paper mattresses in the wagons

67 National Archives, Official Record No. 414, dated 4 June 1948, drawn up by J. Schoenmaker.
68 *Ibidem*.
69 National Archives, Central Archive Special Jurisdiction, from the public hearing, 9 December 1948, inv. 454 II, doss. B.G. Assen 4/49.
70 *Ibidem*: Ik heb dus persoonlijk geen morele bezwaren gehad tegen internering en deportatie der Joden, maar wel tegen sommige details van de tenuitvoerlegging daarvan, zoals het op mensonwaardige wijze op elkaar pakken der gedeporteerden in de treinwagons. Ik heb daartegen echter niets kunnen doen, hoewel ik daartoe wel pogingen heb aangewend.

for the benefit of the sick.[71] Gemmeker explained that the deportation of the sick, the children, and the oldest camp residents was necessary to preserve family ties among the Jews, adding that he thought the people were well taken care of in Auschwitz: "There were large homes in Auschwitz. Modern furnished children's homes and well-equipped hospitals."[72] This statement is an outright repudiation of what Hillesum knew to be true about the fate of the Jews after Camp Westerbork. She wrote, "We are being hunted to death all through Europe [...]."[73]

In addition to his attempts to ease the inhumane transports, Gemmeker explained that he himself had tried to make a labour camp out of Westerbork, a so-called *Arbeitslager.* This idea was, however, rejected by his superiors and the transports continued.[74]

Gemmeker was interviewed in 1959 for a documentary by the Norddeutsche Rundfunk.[75] In the film, he acknowledged that, in retrospect, the "Jewish danger" had been exaggerated. He even stated, once again correctly, that anti-Semitism was based on prejudice and that this had become clear to him through his experiences in Camp Westerbork. He described his involvement with the Jewish residents he deported weekly to the extermination camps as follows:

> In those two and a half years, I have had many contact with the Jews. I have seen, heard, and experienced so much about and with these people that I cannot understand when someone is being anti-Semitic. It is particularly necessary to maintain relationships with Jews, to get to know them, and to conclude that all the prejudices against the Jews are not justified.[76]

71 E.T., 650. *Het Werk*, 693; Letter 64, To Han Wegerif and others, Westerbork, Tuesday, 24 August 1943.

72 National Archives, Official Record No. 414, dated 4 June 1948, drawn up by J. Schoenmaker.

73 E.T., 650. *Het Werk*, 693; Letter 64, To Han Wegerif and others, Westerbork, Tuesday, 24 August 1943: Wij worden doodgejaagd, dwars door Europa heen.

74 National Archives, Central Archive Special Jurisdiction, from the public hearing, 9 December 1948, inv. 454 II, doss. B.G. Assen 4/49.

75 The documentary from 1959 was broadcast in 2010 in the Dutch television series *Andere Tijden* produced by NTR and VPRO. The transcript of the interview can be found on: www.anderetijden.nl/programma/1/Andere-Tijden/aflevering/664/Albert-Gemmeker-commandant-van-Westerbork.

76 *Ibidem*: Ik heb in die tweeënhalf jaar, waarin ik zeer veel omgang had met de Joden, zoveel van die mensen gezien, gehoord en meegemaakt, dat ik niet kan begrijpen, als nu iemand met antisemitische zaken aankomt. Het is juist noodzakelijk om zich met Joden te onderhouden, om hen te leren kennen. En op deze wijze te kunnen concluderen dat alle vooroordelen tegen de Joden niet terecht zijn.

Gemmeker was also asked whether he really did not know what happened to the Jews in Poland. Gemmeker explained that he had tried to learn more about the rumours circulating in the camp. He went to his superior to obtain information. However, he was told that these rumours were terrible war propaganda.[77] Finding this information unsatisfactory, Gemmeker told the interviewer that he would still consult a transport supervisor who was regularly in Auschwitz:

> Of course I did not ask the man directly, I wanted to know in an indirect way what was happening. He told me that the transport at a station before Camp Auschwitz was taken over by the camp staff, an officer and his staff, and he had never seen the camp himself.[78]

In addition to "not knowing," Gemmeker appealed to "*Befehl ist Befehl*" after the war. He could not refuse his appointment as commander of Camp Westerbork. He had accepted his position without protest. There was no point in asking to be relieved of his new task. According to Gemmeker, this would have been without result, because his superiors had appointed him as the most suitable person for the job.

In Germany, attempts were made to put Gemmeker on trial again. In 1960, a preliminary investigation had been started in response to a lawsuit against a number of communists. One of the defendants had exclaimed, during interrogation, that it was the fascists and not the anti-fascists who had to be dealt with. One of those fascists, Albert Konrad Gemmeker, had been walking around in Düsseldorf, according to this witness. Because of this statement, the court had to restart an investigation into Gemmeker. This preliminary investigation yielded too little new information which could serve as evidence, and therefore the commander went free.[79]

In 1967, former commander Gemmeker was interviewed by a journalist from the *Haagsche Post*. He had at that time been living for thirteen years

77 "Albert Gemmeker, commandant van Westerbork", in: *Andere Tijden* (2010).

78 *Ibidem*: Ik heb natuurlijk niet op de man afgevraagd; ik wilde indirect te weten zien te komen wat er gebeurde. Die heeft me gezegd dat het transport op een station vóór het kamp Auschwitz door de kampbezetting, een officier en zijn personeel, werd overgenomen en hij nog nooit het kamp zelf had gezien. Johannes Houwink ten Cate (NIOD researcher and professor of Holocaust and Genocide studies) indicates that this is not true. For practical reasons, the attendants went along to the Auschwitz-Birkenau platform, where the selections for the gas chambers took place. It is, therefore, very unlikely that the transport supervisors would never have heard about what was happening in the extermination camp.

79 Van Riet, *Bewakers van Westerbork*, 315.

in his hometown together with his wife, whom he had married in 1953.[80] She was twenty-one years his junior. At that point, the District Attorney of Düsseldorf had begun a new investigation, and had been collecting evidence for a year in order to start a new trial against the former camp commander.[81] The journalist asked how Gemmeker felt about the German judiciary which was still actively tracking down war criminals twenty years after the fact. Gemmeker answered,

> I cannot make judgments about it, because there are great prejudices against me and my comrades. People will never judge my words objectively. No matter how much effort I put into achieving self-reflection.[82]

In this interview, Gemmeker also emphasized how he had been stuck in a system and had had to obey his superiors. In Düsseldorf, he was living a free life as a tobacconist and worked no less than ten hours a day. But he still thought that this was better than being a government official. He had sworn never to become a civil servant again. He did not want to be used again in a capacity such as had happened in Camp Westerbork. He never received a pension, but in any case, he was a free man able to make his own choices.[83]

Conclusion

Etty Hillesum and Albert Konrad Gemmeker were on two sides of the same system. Hillesum as victim and chronicler, Gemmeker as perpetrator. The commander – he claimed after the war – had no idea that he was the key figure in a murderous system. He knew nothing of the fate that awaited the people he deported. All he was doing, by his own account, was carry out the orders from Berlin and making sure that everything in the camp functioned well and deportation orders were executed *pünktlich*. In contrast to his claims, however, are examples that show the agency of the commander within the system. Gemmeker was able to influence the formation of the transports and he requested transports on his own initiative, for example a transport of the sick to relieve the overcrowded camp hospital.

80 *Ibidem.*

81 Once again, Justice could not prove Gemmeker's "gewusst".

82 NIOD (Institute for War, Holocaust and Genocide Studies), collection of newspaper articles, KBI7744, Haagsche Post, 25 February 1967.

83 *Ibidem.*

In the fall of 1943, journalist David de Koning published Hillesum's Westerbork letters in a clandestine edition entitled *Drie brieven van den kunstschilder Johannes Baptiste van der Pluym (1843-1912)* [Three Letters by the Painter Johannes Baptiste van der Pluym (1843-1912)]. A hundred copies of this illegal booklet were printed, the proceeds benefitting those in hiding.[84] In these letters, Hillesum showed her clear insight into how Camp Westerbork and the commander played a criminal role in the Nazi system of persecution and destruction. Hillesum had her doubts about Gemmeker and commented on the appearance of the commander and his remarkable behaviour – remarking on the Jewish actress who was escorted home and was even helped by Gemmeker, relaying Gemmeker's deep involvement with baby Machieltje, telling how Gemmeker facilitated and allowed amusement in the transit camp and how every week the "gentleman-commander" sent "his troops" eastwardsto the East. As the tragedy played out, Hillesum revealed in her letters the game the commander was playing to maintain the façade of Camp Westerbork. Judges at his trial did not know the part that Gemmeker, the commander who "laughed the Jews to Poland," had played in the system and were misled by his appearance. Similarly, many eyewitnesses did not judge Gemmeker harshly. The minor sentence that was imposed on him bore no relationship to the actual crimes he had committed. If Gemmeker's judges had read the Westerbork letters written by Etty Hillesum, they might have come to a different conclusion about the role the "gentleman-commander" played in the extermination of the Jews.

About the Author

Lotte Bergen (1978) studied History at Leiden University (the Netherlands) with a specialization in Political Culture and National Identities. In 2013, she wrote a book about the commander of Transit Camp Westerbork entitled *Albert Konrad Gemmeker: Commandant van Westerbork* (Soesterberg: Aspekt 2013). She is a PhD candidate at the faculty of Humanities, Utrecht University. Her thesis will focus on Hillesum's philosophical way of life and her agency.

84 E.T., VII, *Het Werk*, IX.

"Now is the Time to Put into Practice: Love Your Enemies"

Several Notes on Hillesum's "Love for Enemies" in *Levenskunst*[1]

Ria van den Brandt

Abstract

This contribution focuses on Etty Hillesum's quotes of love for one's enemy and related thoughts in her friendship booklet *Levenskunst: Gedachten van week tot week* [Art of Living: Thoughts from Week to Week]. Conspicuous is the number of fragments referring to the Gospel of Matthew, in particular to the Sermon on the Mount, combined with quotes about extreme guilt and sin awareness by Russian authors. The author shows the literary-historical context of Hillesum's growing interest in the Gospel of Matthew and suggests a possible radicalization of Hillesum's later thoughts on love for one's enemy. The author's research is based on her recently published research project *Veel mooie woorden: Etty Hillesum en haar boekje Levenskunst* [Many Beautiful Words: Etty Hillesum and her Booklet "Art of Living"]. Her contribution may be considered as an appetizer to further research into the "late" ideas from Etty Hillesum about love for your enemies and related themes.

Keywords: *Levenskunst* booklet, Matthew Gospel, Sermon on the Mount, Russian literature, love for enemies, forgiveness, Dostoevsky, meekness

1 This contribution is a sligthtly revised version of my Dutch article "'Dit is een tijd om in toepassing te brengen: hebt Uwen vijanden lief': Enkele notities bij Hillesums vijandsliefde in Levenskunst," in: Klaas A.D. Smelik, *et al.* (eds.), *Etty Hillesum en de contouren van haar tijd* [Etty Hillesum Studies, 10] (Oud-Turnhout: Gompel & Scavina, 2018), 53-67. Translator: Michelle Mellion-Doorewaard.

Smelik, Klaas A.D. (ed.), *The Lasting Significance of Etty Hillesum's Writings: Proceedings of the Third International Etty Hillesum Conference at Middelburg, September 2018.*
Taylor & Francis Group 2019
DOI: 10.5117/9789463722025_BRANDT

What is the appropriate stance to take when facing one's enemies, and particularly when the enemies are the Nazis? Etty Hillesum gave much thought to this question when writing in her diary during the Second World War. What stands out are her notes concerning how to display forgiveness towards one's enemy, a topic which has been questioned before and slightly modified by various researchers.[2] Most of this research uses the legacy left behind in Hillesum's complete and critical literary edition as a point of departure.[3] Recently, this textual base has been extended to include, up until now, relatively unknown texts in Hillesum's later work: quotations which were copied down after her initial experiences in Camp Westerbork and also presumably for the most part after finishing her eleventh diary notebook in October 1942. Therefore, our recent study, *Veel mooie woorden: Etty Hillesum en haar boekje Levenskunst* [Many Beautiful Words: Etty Hillesum and her Booklet "Art of Living"], which edits these copied quotations, provides a noteworthy enlargement for studying Hillesum's thoughts on interacting with the enemy.[4]

2 Cf. Klaas A.D. Smelik, "De houding van Etty Hillesum tegenover de vervolging van haar volk," in: Klaas A.D. Smelik, *et al.* (eds.), *Etty Hillesum in relatie* [Etty Hillesum Studies, 5] (Gent: Academia Press, 2013), 17-42; Hannah Wunderlich, "'Und damit muss ich nun versuchen, fertig zu werden...': Eine psychologische Studie zu Etty Hillesums Bewältigung der nationalsozialistischen Verfolgung," in: Smelik, *Etty Hillesum in relatie*, 43-83; Klaas A.D. Smelik, "'Ik geloof eigenlijk helemaal niet in wat men noemt 'slechte mensen'": Etty Hillesums visie op het kwaad in de mens," in: Klaas A.D. Smelik, *et al.* (eds.), *Etty Hillesum 1914-2014* [Etty Hillesum Studies, 6] (Antwerpen: Garant, 2014) 27-47; Bettine Siertsema, "'Wij mogen die haat niet aankweken in ons': Etty Hillesums visie op de nazi's," in: Smelik, *Etty Hillesum 1914-2014*, 49-58; L. Bergen, "Handelingsvrijheid binnen nazibegrenzing: Etty Hillesum en haar invulling van het 'Massenschicksal,'" in Klaas A.D. Smelik, *et al.* (eds.), *Etty Hillesum weer thuis in Middelburg* [Etty Hillesum Studies, 7] (Antwerpen: Garant, 2015) 51-83. Most of these essays by Smelik, Siertsema and Bergen have been translated. Cf. Klaas A.D. Smelik's essay "Etty Hillesum's Reaction to the Persecution of Her People," and Bettine Siertsema's essay "Etty Hillesum's Views on the Nazis and Their Henchmen," in: Klaas A.D. Smelik, Meins G.S. Coetsier & Jurjen Wiersma (eds.), *The Ethics and Religious Philosophy of Etty Hillesum: Proceedings of the Etty Hillesum Conference at Ghent University, January 2014* [Supplements to the Journal of Jewish Thought and Philosophy, 28] (Leiden/Boston, MA: Brill, 2017), 235-269, 270-281. Cf. also Lotte Bergen, "Agency within Nazi Constraints: Etty Hillesum and Her Interpretation of the Jewish Fate," in: Klaas A.D. Smelik, Gerrit Van Oord & Jurjen Wiersma (eds.), *Reading Etty Hillesum in Context: Writings, Life, and Influences of a Visionary Author* (Amsterdam: Amsterdam University Press, 2018), 103-141.

3 Cf. *Het Werk* and the English translation of this complete and unabridged edition *Etty*: E.T.

4 This study consists of a facsimile, transcription (with footnotes) of Etty Hillesum's and Henny Tideman's 95 copied quotations in the pre-printed friendship booklet *Levenskunst* [Art of Living]. For more information about this text edition, see the first part of *Veel mooie woorden*: "De citaten van Etty Hillesum en Henny Tideman in *Levenskunst*: Facsimile, transcriptie en notenapparaat," [The Quotations of Etty Hillesum and Henny Tideman in "Art of Living": Facsimile, transcription and annotation], prepared by Ria van den Brandt & Alexandra Nagel,

It was while preparing the text edition of *Veel mooie woorden* that it occurred to us that quite a few of the quotations found in Hillesum's *Levenskunst: Gedachten van Week tot Week* [Art of Living: Thoughts from Week to Week][5] deal with the tendency to show forgiveness towards the enemy. Some of these fragments and their authors have never been cited in Hillesum's diary. In the fragments that Hillesum copied down and decided to include in her booklet *Levenskunst* the "enemy" is depicted as an executioner, a criminal, a villain, and a persecutor. Quite a few quotes evoke one's own sense of forgiveness towards one's enemies and one's own responsibility in cases of enmity. The quotes are consistent in their plea to show tenacity in maintaining meekness during times of conflict. Moreover, the references to the Gospel of Matthew – particularly regarding the Sermon on the Mount (Matthew 5-7) – play a striking role.[6] The appeal to show meekness is emphasized by an explicit condemnation of violence. Just as she had done in her diary, Hillesum also copied a fragment in *Levenskunst* from a text written by Walther Rathenau, which stated that each individual should bear a bit of the world's suffering, and that this should definitely not be done in a violent way, because each act of violence has a perpetual effect: "All violent deeds in this world, like all acts, live on."[7]

It is not without significance that approximately a quarter of Hillesum's 43 quotes in *Levenskunst* deal with possessing a forgiving demeanour towards one's enemy and that Hillesum drew inspiration from both the

11-117 [from now on: Hillesum, "De citaten"]. The second part of the book consists of 22 chapters pertaining to the backgrounds and sources of inspiration derived from the quotations and the context of the booklet. The study was published by Verloren (Hilversum, 2017) and appeared under the editorship of Ria van den Brandt and Peter Nissen. Cf. Ria van den Brandt, "Lopend onderzoek: De citaten van Etty Hillesum in Levenskunst," in: Smelik, *Etty Hillesum weer thuis in Middelburg*, 171-188; Ria van den Brandt, "Newly Discovered Sources of Etty Hillesum," in: Smelik, Coetsier & Wiersma, *The Ethics and Religious Philosophy of Etty Hillesum*, 299-313.

5 Written on the 52 blank pages in the friendship and quotation booklet *Levenskunst: Gedachten van week tot week* (edited by A.J.C. van Seeters and published by Ten Have [1942]). For more information about the booklet: Ria van den Brandt, "Etty Hillesum en haar boekjes *Levenskunst*: Een document voor onderzoek," see: Van den Brandt, *Veel mooie woorden*, 121-133. For more information about the anthologist, see: Bettine Siertsema, "De spiritualiteit van A.J.C. van Seters," in: Van den Brandt & Nissen, *Veel mooie woorden*, 135-145.

6 Cf. Van den Brandt, "Etty Hillesum en haar boekje *Levenskunst*," 133, note 49.

7 "Jede Gewalt in der Welt wirkt fort, wie jede Tat." Hillesum, "De citaten," 34-35. Cf. Hans Ester, "'Jede Gewalt in der Welt wirkt fort...': Etty Hillesum en Walther Rathenau," in: Van den Brandt & Nissen, *Veel mooie woorden*, 237-244. Cf. E.T., 132. *Het Werk*, 139; Monday, 20 October 1941. Cf. Jurjen Wiersma, "'... merken, dat het leven werkelijk eenvoudig is': Etty Hillesum en Walther Rathenau," in: Smelik, *Etty Hillesum 1914-2014*, 141-149.

Sermon on the Mount and texts concerning the Sermon, as well as from the texts written by Russian authors (for whom the Sermon on the Mount never seems to be far from mind).[8] In *Levenskunst*, we come across Hillesum's very own patchwork or *bricolage*[9] relating to love for one's enemy; a plea for the "soft powers." This essay intends to serve as an overture for those researchers who would like to research Hillesum's notes concerning love for one's enemy further and who would like to refer to the sources of inspiration contained in *Levenskunst*. The Gospel of Matthew, and particularly the Sermon on the Mount, appear to play a central role in this. Before we examine the quotations pertaining to Hillesum's love for one's enemy in *Levenskunst*, we outline the context of this theme in Hillesum's diary. Moreover, we show how Hillesum's reading of the Gospel of Matthew has been prompted by two people who were close to her in those years of her life: her teacher Julius Spier (1887-1942)[10] and her female friend Henny Tideman (1907-1989), from whom she received the booklet *Levenskunst* as a gift.[11]

A Therapeutic Process

As is well known, many reflections found in Hillesum's diary belong to a therapeutic process of self-realization, a kind of "working on one's self", in which Hillesum had embarked and a process in which the German-Jewish psycho-chirologist Julius Spier played an important role.[12] Therefore, the language she employs in her diary is also a language of introspection and

8 Other authors mentioned in *Levenskunst*, who she does not mention in her diary, are Ebba Pauli, Kees Schuurman, Charles Alexander Eastman and Frederik van Eeden. For more information about these authors, see: Van den Brandt, "Newly Discovered Sources of Etty Hillesum." Cf. also Van den Brandt & Nissen, *Veel mooie woorden*.

9 Cf. Ria van den Brandt, "'... comme dans mille éclats d'un miroir': Le bricolage d'Etty Hillesum," in: F. Nault & M. Viau (eds.), *Reconstruction et bricolage dans la réflexion théologique contemporain* [special issue], *Religiologiques* 26 (2003) 1, 163-174; Ria van den Brandt, *Steeds een ander uitzicht: Een inleiding in het denken en leven van Etty Hillesum* (Heeswijk: Berne media, 2015), 43-49.

10 Alexandra Nagel, "Julius Spier zocht en vond houvast in de Bijbel – Etty Hillesum volgde hem," in: Ria van den Brandt & Klaas A.D Smelik (eds), *Etty Hillesum in discours* [Etty Hillesum Studies, 3] (Gent: Academia Press, 2011), 77-91.

11 For more information about the relationship shared among these three people, see: Ria van den Brandt, "Vriendschap op het tweede gezicht: Aantekeningen bij de vriendschap van Etty Hillesum en Henny Tideman," in: Ria van den Brandt & Klaas A.D Smelik (eds), *Etty Hillesum in context* [Etty Hillesum Studies, 2] (Assen: Van Gorcum, 2007), 4-15.

12 Cf. Alexandra Nagel, "'*Wie was de S. van Etty Hillesum?' Op zoek naar de psychochiroloog Julius Spier*" [PhD Thesis, Leiden University, 2019, forthcoming].

confrontation with herself. She wanted to "work on herself" in an honest way and, in so doing, to understand the different emotions which arose within her. The fact that this process occurred during the Second World War and that she felt threatened as a Jewish woman, caused Hillesum increasingly to pose questions about how one should interact with the enemy and what had led to the war. As Klaas Smelik has emphasized, Hillesum made a distinction between "the system" and "the people" in her reflections concerning the Nazis. Hillesum believed more in "bad systems" than she did in "bad people."[13] It are the systems that "grow too big for men and hold them in a satanic grip."[14] It is exactly this distinction between "system" and "people" which, according to Bettine Siertsema, reveals that Etty Hillesum "was aware of how human behaviour, no matter how negative, was still always human, and that in principle, it could also be found hiding in herself, and therefore, it should first be combatted in herself."[15] What is more, according to Lotte Bergen, Hillesum also kept "combatting the hatred she encountered in herself" in Camp Westerbork.[16]

Such reflections are related to the basic thought behind Hillesum's philosophy: if you want to fight evil in the world, then start with yourself. Apart from the role of satanic systems, Hillesum makes an appeal to one's own sense of responsibility. This appeal to one's own sense of responsibility can also be recognized in a large number of quotations found in *Levenskunst*. In her diary, Hillesum writes that each individual should try not to nurture feelings of hatred in him or herself. She believes this is only possible when each individual learns to forgive him or herself.[17] This thought seems to have only become stronger after her first stay in Camp Westerbork. On 22 September 1942, she wrote in her diary that "to forgive one's own mistakes and lapses" is perhaps "the hardest thing" for a person to learn. However, according to Hillesum, it is necessary that people "come to recognize all the good and bad qualities of mankind." It is only when people teach themselves to forgive their own "bad qualities" that they can forgive others.[18] Three weeks after having written down this thought, Etty Hillesum stopped keeping a diary

13 Cf. E.T., 529. *Het Werk*, 560; Wednesday, 23 September 1942. Cf. Smelik, "'Ik geloof eigenlijk helemaal niet in wat men noemt 'slechte mensen'," 32-33.

14 Cf. E.T., 259, *Het Werk*, 269; Friday, 27 February 1942.

15 Siertsema, "'Wij mogen die haat niet aankweken in ons'," 52.

16 Bergen, "Handelingsvrijheid binnen nazibegrenzing," 62.

17 E.T., 526. *Het Werk*, 557; Tuesday, 22 September 1942.

18 *Ibidem.*

for a while. It was around that time, perhaps a bit later, that she started to jot down quotations in *Levenskunst*.[19]

"Working on one's self," a process on which her diary had an important impact, was for Hillesum also related to "improving human relations." One's inner space was "the only place where one can start." She saw no other way than to start "with oneself, in oneself."[20] Not to create a larger ego, but to help let go of the "small me" and to achieve a reality that is free of egocentricity ["Ich-haftigkeit"],[21] and to create a space in which the divine can be experienced. In her diary, we can read how the path Hillesum pursued coincides with a growing faith in God. Hillesum views it as a human task to "take one's own seriousness seriously," to "work on one's self" and according to her, that it is "not a morbid form of individualism."[22] It is much more than that; it is a prerequisite for true peace, for only then can "true peace" come into being,

> when each individual finds peace within himself; when we have all vanquished our hatred for our fellow human beings whatever their race may be – transforming it even into love one day.[23]

In order to carry out the task to love, Hillesum "gropes" increasingly for inspiration that she finds in biblical texts, particularly I Corinthians 13.[24] Even though this biblical reference can also be found in *Levenskunst*, it appears that during the last year of her life, Hillesum referred more and more often to Matthew's verses, in particular to his Sermon on the Mount. As mentioned before, this had to do with her teacher Julius Spier and her friend Henny Tideman, with whom she copied the quotations down into the booklet *Levenskunst*.

"Love Your Enemies" as an Appeal

During the first year that Hillesum kept her diary, she hardly quoted from the Gospel of Matthew. It was Spier himself who, inspired by Henny Tideman, read

19 For the date of the copied quotations, see: Alexandra Nagel, "Wanneer schreven Henny Tideman en Etty Hillesum in *Levenskunst*?" in: Van den Brandt & Nissen, *Veel mooie woorden*, 147-158.

20 E.T., 285. *Het Werk*, 296; Monday morning, 16 March 1942.

21 Cf. E.T., 416. *Het Werk*, 437; Monday morning, 15 June 1942.

22 E.T., 434. *Het Werk*, 458; Saturday night, 20 June 1942.

23 *Ibidem*.

24 E.T., 256. *Het Werk*, 266; Friday morning, 27 February 1942.

this Gospel and it was Spier who passed on his growing love for this Book of the Bible to Hillesum, particularly for the Sermon on the Mount.[25] In the spring of 1942, she mentions that she would like to read Matthew "systematically".[26] It seemed to serve as a new source of inspiration for her, because she wrote soon afterwards "my dear Matthew."[27] Again, a few months later, just before her departure to Camp Westerbork, she noted down a passage from Spier in her diary, which was related to the Sermon on the Mount (Matthew 5:44).

> He [Spier] says, now is the time to put into practice: love your enemies. And if *we* [Jews] do say that, surely we must also believe that it can be done?[28]

To Hillesum, "love your enemies" seemed to function as an ethical appeal directed at "us Jews." Following her initial experiences in Camp Westerbork and Spier's death on 15 September 1942, it appears that her love for Matthew's verses had grown enormously. During this time, she was not able to deal with everything and express herself in words, but the time she spent in Camp Westerbork was one of "the most intensive and enriching" periods of her life as it provided "a confirmation" of "the final and highest values."[29] Matthew's "love your enemies" was included among these highest values. More than ever before, she seemed convinced that "every atom of hatred added to the world makes it an even more inhospitable place."[30] In the last diary notebook known to us – which she began writing on the day that Spier died and which ends on 13 October 1942 – she quotes Matthew's verses several times again, including Matthew 5:23-24.

> So if you are offering your gift at the altar and there remember that your brother has something against you, leave your gift there before the altar and go. First be reconciled to your brother, and then come and offer your gift.[31]

25 Nagel, "Julius Spier zocht en vond houvast in de Bijbel."

26 E.T., 323. *Het Werk*, 337; Saturday, 4 April 1942. Cf. also Door Brouns-Wewerinke, "'Zijt niet bezorgd om Uw leven…': Etty Hillesum, Matteüs, en 'de jood Paulus'," in: Van den Brandt & Nissen, *Veel mooie woorden*, 255-267, especially p. 259.

27 E.T., 331 [revised]. *Het Werk*, 346; Wednesday morning, 15 April 1942.

28 E.T., 503 [revised]. *Het Werk*, 532; Saturday morning, 25 July 1942: Hij [Spier] zegt: Dit is een tijd om in toepassing te brengen: hebt Uwen vijanden lief. En als wíj [Joden] dat zeggen, dan moet men toch geloven, dat zoiets mogelijk is?

29 E.T., 520. *Het Werk*, 550-551; Thursday, 17 September 1942.

30 E.T., 590. *Het Werk*, 560; Wednesday, 23 September 1942.

31 E.T., 532 [revised]. The English Standard Version is used here. *Het Werk*, 563; Friday, 25 September 1942: Zo gij dan uwe gave zult op het altaar offeren, en aldaar gedachtig wordt, dat uw

At the same time, she underlines the passages “and there remember that your brother has something against you” and “First be reconciled to your brother.” It is exactly this same quote that we find once again in *Levenskunst,* the friendship booklet in which texts from Etty Hillesum and her pious, Bible-reading friend, Henny Tideman, can be found.

Moreover, it is not inconceivable that Hillesum, who at first had trouble getting along with Tideman and who was even sometimes jealous of her,[32] considered the biblical task of reconciliation as a task that both she and her “sister” Tideman should carry out. From Hillesum’s perspective, she and Tideman became much closer friends *after* Spier’s death. It was during that same period that they probably had begun copying down the quotations into the booklet *Levenskunst.*[33] The fact that Etty Hillesum, within the context of *Levenskunst,* had chosen several texts from the Sermon on the Mount, either directly or indirectly, might also possibly have stemmed from her desire to address Tideman as her “sister.” During that time, Tideman was a member of the Oxford Group, a group which had been much inspired by the Sermon on the Mount. Moreover, it was due to Tideman that Spier had started reading in the Bible.[34] Hillesum’s choice to copy Matthew’s “love for enemies” and other texts from the Sermon on the Mount may have been determined by her desire to reconcile with her “sister.” Perhaps she chose to honour Spier after his death by using the texts that she had read together with him and Tideman, more than she had done in the past.[35] Honouring Spier seems to play a role in the quotations she decided to choose, and this was especially true for Tideman. Nevertheless, the way in which Henny Tideman preferred to jot down Julius Spier’s words of wisdom in *Levenskunst* is quite conspicuous.[36]

broeder iets tegen u heeft, laat daar uw gave vóór het altaar, en ga henen, verzoen u eerst met uwe broeder, en kom dan en offer uwe gave. This quotation (Hillesum, “De citaten,” 30-31) has been taken from the “Statenvertaling” (first Authorized Version of the Bible in Dutch).

32 Cf. Van den Brandt, “Vriendschap op het tweede gezicht,” 7-9.

33 Cf. Nagel, “Wanneer schreven Henny Tideman en Etty Hillesum in Levenskunst?”; Cf. Van den Brandt, “Vriendschap op het tweede gezicht.”

34 Cf. also Siertsema, “De spiritualiteit van A.J.C. van Seters,” 143-144.

35 In Hillesum’s diary, for example, she never chose a text from Spier’s favourite author Thomas a Kempis, but in *Levenskunst* she did exactly that in Week 6 for the theme ‘Life’s truths’ (Hillesum, “De citaten,” 24-25). Cf. also Peter Nissen, “‘... onverdeeld van hart en innerlijk eenvoudig...’,” in: Van den Brandt & Nissen, *Veel mooie woorden,* 289-292.

36 In Tideman’s quotations, Julius Spier’s words of wisdom are prevalent. Cf. Alexandra Nagel, “Henny Tideman en de wijsheden van Julius Spier en anderen,” in: Van den Brandt & Nissen, *Veel mooie woorden,* 159-167.

Hillesum's "Love for Enemies" in *Levenskunst*

Apart from *Levenskunst*'s specific context, Hillesum clearly continued to ponder about the enemy after finishing her eleventh diary notebook on 13 October 1942. The appeal to "Love your enemies" seems to be the guiding principle. Her notes in *Levenskunst* show that her thoughts continue to include a radical form of forgiving demeanour, just as the same thoughts can be found in the Sermon on the Mount. As pointed out earlier, we find the task of reconciling with one's brother (Matthew 5:23-24) in the third quotation under the theme of "Love" in Week 9 of *Levenskunst*. After the well-known first lines found in 1 Corinthians 13,[37] Hillesum subsequently notes a fragment concerning forgiveness from *The Idiot* by Fyodor Dostoevsky. This quotation also reflects an extremely forgiving demeanour.

> You will forgive those who have hurt you, and also those who have not hurt you. And this is much more difficult, precisely because they have not hurt you and your emotion lacks justification.[38]

This phrase comes from "Prince Myshkin," who according to Van den Bercken had a "permanent place" in the diary and who had "embodied the absolute demeanour of forgiveness and unselfish neighbourly love."[39] One should also be aware that *after* this text Hillesum also cites Matthew again in verse 5:23-24:

> So if you are offering your gift at the altar and there remember that your brother has something against you, leave your gift there before the altar and go. First be reconciled to your brother, and then come and offer your gift.[40]

37 Hillesum, "De citaten," 30-31. Hillesum used the "Statenvertaling": "Al ware het, dat ik de talen der mensen en der engelen sprak, en de liefde niet had, zo ware ik een klinkend metaal, of luidende schel geworden." Tideman jotted down "1 Kor. 13." for the theme "Love" in week 35.
38 This quotation in *Levenskunst* (Hillesum, "De citaten," 30-31) has been taken from: F.M. Dostojewski, *Der Idiot: Roman in zwei Bänden* [Sämtliche Werke, II] (München: R. Piper & Co. Verlag, 1920) 1057. Original German: "Sie werden denen verzeihen, die Sie gekränkt haben, und auch denen, die Sie nicht gekränkt haben – das ist ja doch noch viel schwerer, gerade weil sie Sie nicht gekränkt haben und Ihr Gefühl folglich unbegründet ist." For the background and context of this quotation see: Wil van den Bercken, "'Denn wenn ich selbst gerecht wäre…': Etty Hillesum en Fjodor Dostojevski," in: Van den Brandt & Nissen, *Veel mooie woorden*, 195-212.
39 Van den Bercken, "'Denn wenn ich selbst gerecht wäre…'," 196-197, 200. See: E.T., 214. *Het Werk*, 223; Friday, 2 January 1942.
40 Matthew 5:23-24 (English Standard Version). Original: "Zo gij dan uwe gave zult op het altaar offeren, en aldaar gedachtig wordt, dat uw broeder iets tegen u heeft, laat daar uw gave

By combining these texts, Hillesum twice evokes that true love is related to unselfish neighbourly love, in the form of extreme forgiveness and reconciliation: love your enemies! The quotations concerning the theme of "Love" in Week 9 are exemplary. The combination of the selected biblical and Russian (literary) fragments on one and the same page shows Hillesum's preference for a radical way of thinking. Therefore, in her *bricolage,* regarding the love of one's enemies, we can distinguish between the two groups of quotations previously mentioned: quotations taken directly or indirectly from the Sermon on the Mount, and quotations derived from Russian writers. In the latter case, Hillesum chose quotations which evoked an enormous sense of sin – or a sense of guilt. The combination of using different quotations suggests that Hillesum's "later" texts were not only a continuation of her thoughts from her diary in *Levenskunst,* but that they also possibly indicate a further radicalisation of her thoughts.[41] It seems that she is making a great appeal to one's sense of responsibility in her *Levenskunst* texts. By making use of our extensive research project concerning *Levenskunst,* I have placed the quotations in a sequential order and in doing so, I hope to have furthered subsequent research in the field.

1 Quotations with References to the Sermon on the Mount

The theologian Brouns-Wewerinke has spent much time studying Hillesum's biblical quotations in *Levenskunst.*[42] She has shown that there are a striking number of direct and indirect references to Matthew. In addition to the quotations from the Sermon on the Mount – which were previously mentioned as appearing in Matthew 5:23-24, but also Matthew 6:25 and 6:34 (see Week 50, the theme "Dedication to Live"), Etty Hillesum also copied Matthew 16:25-26 (see Week 8, the theme "To Serve"). Moreover, there is an explicit reference to the Sermon on the Mount (Matthew 5:5) in a quotation taken from Giovanni Papini's writing as well as an implicit reference to Matthew 5:38-39 in a (double) quotation of Eli Stanley Jones.[43]

vóór het altaar, en ga henen, verzoen u eerst met uwe broeder, en kom dan en offer uwe gave." This quotation in *Levenskunst* (Hillesum, "De citaten," 30-31) has again been taken from the *Statenvertaling.* For more information see: Brouns-Wewerinke, "'Zijt niet bezorgd om Uw leven…'," 256-257.

41 The 'later' Hillesum refers to the texts that Hillesum wrote during the last year of her life in the Netherlands.

42 Cf. Brouns-Wewerinke, "'Zijt niet bezorgd om Uw leven…'," 255-267.

43 Etty Hillesum jotted down the verses of Matthew 6:25, 34 and Matthew 16:25-26 from the "Statenvertaling" (Hillesum, "De citaten," 112-113, 28-29). Cf. also Brouns-Wewerinke, "'Zijt niet

Brouns-Wewerinke distinguishes between three themes with reference to the quotations related to Matthew: 1) trust and letting go, 2) love for the enemy and conquering evil in oneself, and 3) letting go of one's own ego.[44] The connection of "love for the enemy" and "conquering evil in oneself" in the second theme is an important consideration in Hillesum's quotations concerning love for the enemy; in order to love the enemy, control of "the evil in oneself" should have first taken place. This is directly related to Hillesum's idea of "working on oneself." Ideally, one should practice controlling "the evil in oneself" to achieve an attitude of meekness. Although Hillesum believed that anger could sometimes be well justified,[45] she also saw it as one's task to work on acquiring a gentle attitude towards life. Therefore, Hillesum wrote "Selig sind die Sanftmütigen" ["Blessed are the meek"] (Matthew 5:5) in Week 41 of *Levenskunst,* whose theme is "Life as a Task." The third beatitude can be found in the first sentence of the quote that Hillesum copied from *Lebensgeschichte Christi* [Life of Christ] written by the Italian philosopher Giovanni Papini (1881-1956). This concerns the German translation of Papini's *Storia di Cristo* that was published in 1921.

> "Blessed are the meek: for they shall inherit the earth."
> The soldier who fights for the earthly earth needs to be fierce ["zorngrimmig"]; but he who fights within himself ["seines eigenen Ich"] for the conquest of the new Earth and the new Heaven must not abandon himself to anger, the counsellor of evil, nor to cruelty, the negation of love.
> The meek are those who endure close contact with evil men and with themselves – often harder to bear – who do not break out into brutish rage when things go badly, but conquer their inner enemies with that quiet perseverance which more than sudden sterile furies shows the force of the soul.[46]

bezorgd om Uw leven...'," 256-259.

44 Brouns-Wewerinke, "'Zijt niet bezorgd om Uw leven...'," 259-263.

45 We find in Hillesum's diary (E.T., 397-398. *Het Werk*, 417; Monday, 8 June 1942) a quotation copied from Eli Stanley Jones concerning "legitimate and illegitimate anger" ["gewettigde en ongewettigde toorn"]: "If our anger is rooted in moral indignation, in moral pain and not in personal resentment, then that anger is good and valuable and healthy." Before this, she had written: "The soul rises up and, with deep indignation, resists evil. Nietzsche was probably right when he said, 'Virtue is of little importance if it cannot be whipped up into rage'."

46 Freely translated from Italian by Dorothy Canfield Fischer. See: Giovanni Papini, *Life of Christ* (New York: Harcourt, Brace & Company, 1923), 88-89. The original quotation in *Levenskunst* (Hillesum, "De citaten," 94-95) has been copied from: Giovanni Papini, *Lebensgeschichte Christi* (München: Allgemeine Verlagsanstalt, 1923), 112. This work has been translated from Italian by Max Schwarz. Zie ook: Annette van Dijk, "'Selig sind die Sanftmütigen...': Etty Hillesum

After writing down "Blessed are the meek, for they shall inherit the earth," Hillesum skips a few lines from Papini's translated text and immediately starts with "the soldier" who – in situations where he fights for "earthly goods" – must be "fierce" ["zorngrimmig"], but when he fights an internal battle to conquer "the new Earth" and "the new Heaven," he should not submit to rage or anger, for rage is a bad counsellor. He should also not submit to cruelty, because cruelty is a denial of love. After these banning orders, Papini explains who he believes "the meek" are, and Hillesum copies this down. "The meek" tolerate the existence of evil as well as their own existence, which for many is more difficult to bear and endure than the alien (evil). The meek do not fight evil, but instead they conquer it through patience. They do not act like an animal enraged, but rather conquer the animal in themselves with "that alert state of endurance" ["mit jener heiteren Ausdauer"], which costs more strength than a sudden and disturbing outburst of anger. Conquering evil in oneself and assuming a continual state of meekness requires particular power and effort. Hillesum seemed to believe in such a victory of the "soft power," which is supported for example by a short quotation that she copied down in Week 20 ("Life's Truths") and that she had taken from Frederik van Eeden's diary: "He who feels great power is gentle. All roughness or sharpness is weakness."[47]

That Etty Hillesum had a special interest in maintaining a meek attitude towards life as it was preached in the Sermon on the Mount, is also evidenced in the text that she had copied down and included in Week 47. The theme is "Attitude towards Life." Here as well, the Sermon on the Mount is referred to (Matthew 5:38-39), even though Matthew is not mentioned in the quotation. It concerns two fragments which Etty Hillesum copied from various works

en Giovanni Papini," in: Van den Brandt & Nissen, *Veel mooie woorden*, 269-272. The original quotation in German: "Selig sind die Sanftmütigen, denn sie werden das Land erben." Der Soldat, der sich schlägt um Erdengüter, muß zorngrimmig sein; wer hingegen innerhalb seines eigenen Ich kämpft um das neue Land, den neuen Himmel, der darf sich nicht dem Rasen überlassen, das zu jeder Untat rät, nicht der Grausamkeit, die die Liebe verleugnet.
Die Sanftmütigen, die das Mitsein der Bösen ertragen, und auch das eigene Sein, das manchem noch schwerer zu ertragen ist als das Fremde: die lehnen sich nicht auf gegen die Bösen, sondern überwinden sie mit Geduld; sie werden nicht zum Tier beim erstbesten Widerstand, sondern besiegen das Tier in der eigenen Brust, mit jener heiteren Ausdauer, die mehr Kraft erfordert als die plötzlichen, nur zerstörenden Ausbrüche.

47 This quotation was taken by Hillesum ("De citaten," 52-53) from: Frederik van Eeden, *Mijn dagboek, Eerste deel* (Amsterdam: N.V. Van Munster's Uitgevers-maatschappij, s.d. [1931]), 172. Cf. Annette van Dijk, "'Wie grote kracht voelt is zacht': Etty Hillesum en Frederik van Eeden," in: Van den Brandt & Nissen, *Veel mooie woorden*, 191-193.

completed by the American Methodist minister and missionary Eli Stanley Jones (1884-1973) and from which she composed one text:

> Wie terugslaat als hij geslagen wordt, wekt in zijn tegenstander de vechtinstincten. Wie wegvlucht als hij geslagen wordt, wekt de jachtinstincten van zijn vervolgers, maar wie de andere wang toekeert, wekt de diepste, de tederste instincten op.
>
> De moeilijkheid zit niet in het toekeren van de andere wang, de moeilijkheid zit in het opgeven van het eigen ik. Doe dat, en het toekeren van de andere wang is een noodzakelijke en vanzelfsprekende consequentie.[48]
>
> Whoever strikes back when being beaten, arouses the fighting instincts in his opponent. Anyone who flees when he is beaten, awakens the hunting instincts of his persecutors. Whoever turns the other cheek, however, arouses the deepest, most tender instincts.
>
> The rub [difficulty] is not at the place of turning the other cheek; the rub [difficulty] is at the place of letting go the essential self. Do that, and turning the other cheek is a necessary and natural outcome.[49]

Hillesum's choice of quotations and how she has edited them – she is the one who took the two fragments from the various works written by Eli Stanley Jones and combined them – clearly shows that she considered that "letting go" one's own ego was a precondition for having a meek and forgiving demeanour. Once freed from one's "own ego" ("Ich-haftigkeit"), "turning the other cheek" would be a self-evident act. Etty Hillesum unites both texts in a clever way. She appears to be quite at home with Stanley Jones's writing; moreover, she was friends with Johanna Kuiper who translated his work into Dutch. In his day and time, Stanley Jones was a well-known preacher of Mahatma Gandhi's teachings and had even given lectures in Amsterdam on this topic.[50] It is generally

48 Hillesum has copied these two quotations ("De citaten," 106-107) from two Dutch translations of Eli Stanley Jones's work, namely: *Christus en het menselijk lijden*, Amsterdam: H.J. Paris, 1934, 78 and *Christus op den Berg*, Amsterdam: H.J. Paris, 1935, 53. Both books have been translated by Johanna E. Kuiper. See also: Ria van den Brandt, "'... wie de andere wang toekeert...': Etty Hillesum en Eli Stanley Jones," in: Van den Brandt & Nissen, *Veel mooie woorden*, 273-281.

49 Original English texts of Eli Stanley Jones in: Eli Stanley Jones, *Christ and Human Suffering* (London, Hodder & Stoughton, 1933), 80, and *The Christ of the Mount: A Working Philosophy of Life* (New York: Abingdon, 1931), 76.

50 Van den Brandt, '"... wie de andere wang toekeert...'," 274-275.

known that this icon of non-violence had been inspired by the Sermon on the Mount and Tolstoy. This combination of biblical and Russian sources will have undoubtedly appealed to Hillesum. It is practically for certain that she will have had an affinity for Gandhi's call to the Jews to resist in a non-violent way.[51]

2 Russian Quotations on Becoming Aware of One's Guilt and Sin

There are two Russian authors who play a crucial role here: the previously mentioned and very well-known Dostoevsky and the forgotten Julia de Beausobre (1893-1977). Let us start with Dostoevsky. In Week 9, we saw how the combination of biblical and Russian (literature) fragments evoked a radical form of love for one's enemies. In this radical approach, the words of Dostoevsky's character Prince Myshkin – the symbol of "absolute forgiveness and unselfish neighbourly love" – among others, played an important role. In *Levenskunst,* three of the four quotations by Dostoevsky contribute to Hillesum's views on love for one's enemies. It is particularly the monk Zosima, a character from Dostoevsky's *The Brothers Karamazov*, who receives attention. Whereas a figure such as Myshkin was already known in Hillesum's diary, the monk Zosima was not.[52] According to Van den Bercken, both characters can be considered as ambivalent figures. The monk Zosima stands out due to his exaggerated propensity to show forgiveness and his special outlook on love. Etty Hillesum copies the first quotation regarding the character of Zosima down under the theme "Life's Truths" in Week 6; and the second quotation under the theme "Love" in Week 23:

> (1) Denn wenn ich selbst gerecht wäre, gäbe es vielleicht auch den Missetäter nicht, der vor mir steht.[53]

> (1) For if I was righteous myself, then the criminal standing in front of me would not be here either.

> (2) Brüder, die Liebe ist eine Lehrmeisterin, doch muss man verstehen, sie sich anzueignen, denn nur schwer lernt man sie und sie wird teuer

51 Hillesum must have read Gandhi's call in her daily newspaper *Algemeen Handelsblad* on 6 December 1938. Nine months later (5 September 1939), the same newspaper mentioned Gandhi's letter to Hitler, written on 23 July 1939.

52 Van den Bercken, "'Denn wenn ich selbst gerecht wäre…'," 196.

53 This quotation in *Levenskunst* (Hillesum, "De citaten," 24-25) has been copied from: F.M. Dostojewskij, *Die Brüder Karamasow*, I (Berlijn: Axel Juncker Verlag, 1930), 514. See also: Van den Bercken, "'Denn wenn ich selbst gerecht wäre… '."

> erkauft durch lange Arbeit und erst nach langer Zeit, denn man soll ja nicht für einen zufälligen Augenblick lieben, sondern für alle Zeiten. Zufällig kann ein jeder lieben, auch der Bösewicht.[54]
>
> (2) Brothers, love is a teacher, but one has to understand to acquire it, for love is difficult to learn and costs much by lasting and hard work. For one should not love incidentally, but forever. Everyone can love incidentally, also the villain.[55]

From the point of view of having a forgiving demeanour, the first quotation is worth noting: when you are righteous, then perhaps even the criminal – who is standing before you – will cease being a criminal. According to the monk Zosima – and Etty Hillesum seems to agree with him – the great evil in the world is connected to the small evil, which can be found in each individual.[56] Insight into one's own guilt and sinfulness can therefore offer something to humanity. In the Dostoevskyian approach to self-confrontation, the Russian soul seeks a confrontation with its own dark sides, endures suffering and then reaches self-rectification. According to Van den Bercken, Hillesum has been "contaminated" by this romantic notion concerning the Russian soul.[57] He thereby points out that Dostoevsky has an exceptional view of humanity: "On the one hand, he is optimistic regarding the possible self-rectification of the criminal, on the other hand, he is an evangelist in regard to becoming aware of one's own sinfulness while referring to the Sermon on the Mount: 'Judge not lest you be judged'."[58]

The ethos from the Sermon on the Mount seems to resound in this quotation as well, just as it does in Zosima's second quotation.

In the second quotation concerning love as a teacher, Van den Bercken explains how Zosima's text is immersed in a paragraph where he connects "real and actual" love to forgiveness and meekness. According to Van den Bercken, this "real" love, unselfish neighbourly love, is a key concept in Zosima's spirituality and it is the opposite of "illusory" and "abstract" love. It is about love that is just as encompassing as forgiveness and that is not based on reciprocity but on meekness. Moreover, it is this meek love that

54 This quotation in *Levenskunst* (Hillesum, "De citaten," 58-59) has been copied from: Dostojewskij, *Die Brüder Karamasow*, 512. See also: Van den Bercken, "'Denn wenn ich selbst gerecht wäre...'."

55 Free translation.

56 Van den Bercken, "'Denn wenn ich selbst gerecht wäre...'," 201.

57 *Ibidem*, 199.

58 *Ibidem*, 198.

is a precondition for achieving actual forgiveness and love for the enemy, who – being depicted as a "villain" – is not capable of this type of love. Van den Bercken points out that immediately after this fragment in *The Brothers Karamazov,* the character Zosima believes that we should even ask the birds for forgiveness:

> Then you would pray to the birds, driven by an all-encompassing love, as if in ecstasy, praying that you will be forgiven for your sins.[59]

Etty Hillesum's copied quotation for the theme "Sin" in Week 42 captures the same overpowering sense of sin that can be found in Dostoevsky's quotations. This particular quotation concerns a fragment from *The Women Who Could Not Die* (1938), a testimony written in poor English by Julia de Beausobre, a Russian Orthodox-Christian author.[60] The theme of the quotation chosen by Hillesum fits almost perfectly with Dostoevsky's quotation in Week 6 ("For if I was righteous myself, then the criminal standing in front of me would not be here either"), in the sense that one's own guilt and sinfulness can be part of the criminality of the other. Even when cast in the role of victim, a person can be a part of the evil and suffering inflicted. That is what we read in the quotation that Etty Hillesum copied from *The Women Who Could Not Die*:

> It is unperdonable [sic] that anyone should be tortured, even you – if you merely leave it at that. But, surely, when you overcome the pain inflicted on you by them, you make their criminal records less villainous. But when, through weakness, cowardice, lack of balance, lack of serenity, you augment your pain, their crime becomes so much the darker and is darkened by you.[61]

The fragment has been formulated in a rather complex way. Aside from that, this fragment evokes an overpowering sense of sin. In fact, the fragment reads as if it were a lesson concerning the appropriate stance that a victim should take when being tortured. Even the victim can be guilty of the seriousness of the executioner's crime. The "sin" (the guilt) of the victim

59 *Ibidem*, 200, 201-202.

60 Ria van den Brandt, "'... when you overcome the pain...': Etty Hillesum en Julia de Beausobre," in: Van den Brandt & Nissen, *Veel mooie woorden*, 213-221.

61 This quotation (Hillesum, "De citaten," 96-97) has been copied from: Iulia De Beausobre, *The Woman Who Could Not Die* (London: Chatto & Windus, 1938), 86. See also: Van den Brandt, "'... when you overcome the pain...'."

is the reinforcement of the suffering that has been inflicted on him or her by "weakness, cowardice, lack of balance, lack of serenity." In so doing, the victim enhances the criminality of the perpetrator even more and contributes to the dark side of the executioner's crime. From the fragment that has been copied over, it appears once again that Hillesum holds a fascination for the talent that (according to her) Russians possess in being able to look into their own souls and to confront suffering and evil. Dostoevsky and those who interpret his work, such as Walter Schubart, play an important role in this fascination. It is not a mere coincidence that Hillesum quotes Schubart in *Levenskunst*: "Physical well-being is not as important as the loss of ethical freedom."[62] According to Schubart, love and not justice should be the highest principle in Russian ethics. We can also find this stream of thought in Hillesum's diary.[63] This love – in Dostoevsky's and De Beausobre's worldview – is capable of seeing the sinfulness of one's own self and to forgive the sins of the greatest criminal (who would not exist if you yourself were free from sin) and to love him as your neighbour.

Conclusion

The combination of references that Hillesum makes regarding the Sermon on the Mount and her references to the overpowering "Russian" sense of sin and guilt – together with Rathenau, Schubart, and Van Eeden's quotations – have led us to suspect that Hillesum, when copying her quotations down into the booklet *Levenskunst*, maintained the same train of thought that she had developed earlier regarding love for one's enemies. During that period, she may also have borne witness to a number of new sources by searching for texts which could articulate this love for one's enemy in greater detail. In that sense, her quotations in *Levenskunst* seem to be an exploration of Spier's words: "Now is the time to put into practice: Love your enemies."

62 This quotation (Hillesum, "De citaten," 72-73) has been copied from: Walter Schubart, *Dostojewski en Nietzsche: De symboliek van hun leven* (Haarlem: Uitgeverij De Librije [1939]), 75. For more information: Hans Ester, "'Verschrikkelijker dan het godsgericht…': Etty Hillesum en Walter Schubart," in: Van den Brandt & Nissen, *Veel mooie woorden*, 205-212.

63 E.T., 501. *Het werk*, 531. Zie verder: Ester, "'Verschrikkelijker dan het godsgericht…'," 206-207, 212; Van den Bercken, "'Denn wenn ich selbst gerecht wäre…'," 199. Van den Bercken points here to Dostoevsky's "slavophile ideology" and his view of the Russian soul as "a philosophical and spiritual opposite to the rationalistic and legalistic West." According to Van den Bercken, such ideological views held by Hillesum can be traced back to Schubart.

About the Author

Ria van den Brandt (1960) is philosopher and researcher at the Faculty of Philosophy, Theology and Religious Sciences of the Radboud University in Nijmegen (the Netherlands). Her fields of research are Jewish testimonies of World War Two, spiritual studies, thanatology, and "art of living". She is an internationally known Etty Hillesum scholar, lecturer, and adviser. With Klaas A.D. Smelik, she was the initiator and editor (until 2012) of the *Etty Hillesum Studies*. Among her many publications are: *Etty Hillesum: Amicizia, ammirazione, mistica* (2010), *Etty Hillesum: An Introduction to Her Thought* (2014), and (with Peter Nissen) *Veel mooie woorden: Etty Hillesum en haar boekje Levenskunst* (2017).

The Cares of the Pagans

The Reading of Matthew 6:25-34 by Søren Kierkegaard and Etty Hillesum

Pierre Bühler

Abstract

We do not know if Etty Hillesum has read anything of Kierkegaard's work, and if so, what exactly and how intensively. But speaking of her worries about future, she quotes several times Chapter 6 of the Gospel of Matthew, a passage that Kierkegaard has commented upon several times, especially in his edifying discourses of 1848 entitled *Cares of Pagans*. Could it be that Etty Hillesum knew these discourses? This article compares from several perspectives Kierkegaard's and Hillesum's reading of Matthew 6. It concludes by discovering in both authors what John D. Caputo has called "quotidianism": for both, it is essential to devote all attention to living today.

Keywords: Matthew Gospel, Søren Kierkegaard, Care of the Pagans, quotidianism, worry about future, concentrating on present

My latest treasure: the birds of the heavens and the lilies of the fields[1]
– *Etty Hillesum*

Introduction

My article is inscribed in a kind of a triangle: a possible connection between Etty Hillesum, the Danish philosopher Søren Kierkegaard (1813-1855), and the

1 E.T., 530. *Het Werk*, 562; Thursday, 24 September 1942: Mijn verrijking van de laatste dagen: de vogelen des hemels en de leliën des velds.

Smelik, Klaas A.D. (ed.), *The Lasting Significance of Etty Hillesum's Writings: Proceedings of the Third International Etty Hillesum Conference at Middelburg, September 2018.*
Taylor & Francis Group 2019
DOI: 10.5117/9789463722025_BÜHLER

Gospel of Matthew, specifically 6:25-34 where Jesus speaks of the birds of the heavens and the lilies of the fields. This passage must have touched Etty Hillesum as she was attuned to nature as God's creation, and especially to flowers. Reflecting, for example, on her roses that went on quietly blossoming in Amsterdam while she was in Camp Westerbork, she wrote, "Many say, 'How can you still think of flowers!'"[2]

But how was Etty Hillesum's attention drawn to Matthew's parable? Could it be that she found "the birds of the heavens and the lilies of the fields" in Kierkegaard's edifying discourses on Matthew 6? This is the basic query that I shall try to answer.

In fact, we do not know if Etty Hillesum had read *anything* of Kierkegaard's work. If she had, we do not know which passages nor how intensively she may have focused on them. There are only four occurrences where she even mentioned Kierkegaard in *Het Werk*, and these references to the Danish philosopher were quite unspecific, often inside of a list of several authors.

> I don't want you to think of anything today, not of Freud, not of Jung, not of Kierkegaard, not of Dostoevsky and not of Stendhal.[3]

> S. arrived from Friesland so fresh and rested, bubbling over with 'life after death' and Kierkegaard and new ideas. And I was too tired to draw breath.[4]

> And Kierkegaard. And the boundary between psychology and literature. And du Perron and Jung.[5]

> And there is the bookcase, within reach of my bed. I have only to stretch out my hand to touch Dostoevsky or Shakespeare or Kierkegaard. But I do not stretch out my hand. I feel so dizzy.[6]

2 E.T., 499. *Het Werk*, 529; Thursday evening, 23 July 1942: Velen zeggen: hoe kun je nu nog aan bloemen denken.

3 E.T., 119. *Het Werk*, 126; Sunday morning, 5 October 1941: Ik wil niet, dat je vandaag aan iets denkt, niet aan Freud, niet aan Jung, niet aan Kierkegaard, niet aan Dostojewski en niet aan Stendhal.

4 E.T., 139. *Het Werk*, 146; Tuesday morning, 28 October 1941: S. kwam zo fris en uitgerust uit Friesland, tjokvol met 'het leven na de dood' en Kierkegaard en nieuwe ideeën. En ik was te moe om adem te halen.

5 E.T., 149. *Het Werk*, 156; Saturday evening, 22 November 1941: En Kierkegaard. En de grens tussen psychologie en literatuur. En Du Perron en Jung.

6 E.T., 515. *Het Werk*, 544; Tuesday afternoon, 15 September 1942: En zijn boekenkast staat er, op een meter afstand van mijn bed. Ik hoef mijn linkerarm maar uit te strekken en dan heb ik Dostojewski in mijn handen of Shakespeare of Kierkegaard. Maar ik strek m'n hand niet uit. Ik ben zo duizelig.

This last quotation is most interesting for this investigation because it stands closest in time to the pages of the diaries where Etty Hillesum referred repeatedly to Matthew (July and September 1942, in exercise books 10 and 11). In those months when she wrote of her worries about the future, Etty Hillesum referred several times to "the birds of the heavens and the lilies of the fields." What inspired her to take this particular passage as a kind of a shelter for her fears? Could it be that she did indeed stretch out her hand on occasion to take one of Kierkegaard's books from Julius Spier's library?

Matthew 6:25-34 – an Important Passage for Etty Hillesum

Matthew's text belongs to a longer discourse referred to as the Sermon on the Mount (Matthew 5-7). Jesus was speaking in public to instruct his disciples about living faith and love in daily life. In Chapter 6, Jesus underlines how unnecessary and senseless it is to worry instead of trusting in God, because God knows what every one of his creatures needs. The passage culminates in the recommendation not to worry about tomorrow, because "each day has enough trouble of its own."

> Therefore I tell you, do not worry about your life, what you will eat or drink; or about your body, what you will wear. Is not life more important than food, and the body more important than clothes? Look at the birds of the air; they do not sow or reap or store away in barns, and yet your heavenly Father feeds them. Are you not much more valuable than they? Who of you by worrying can add a single hour to his life? And why do you worry about clothes? See how the lilies of the field grow. They do not labour or spin. Yet I tell you that not even Solomon in all his splendour was dressed like one of these. If that is how God clothes the grass of the field, which is here today and tomorrow is thrown into the fire, will he not much more clothe you, O you of little faith? So do not worry, saying, 'What shall we eat?' or 'What shall we drink?' or 'What shall we wear?' For the pagans run after all these things, and your heavenly Father knows that you need them. But seek first his kingdom and his righteousness, and all these things will be given to you as well. Therefore do not worry about tomorrow, for tomorrow will worry about itself. Each day has enough trouble of its own.[7]

7 Quoted according to: *The Holy Bible: New International Version* (London/Sydney/Auckland: Hodder & Stoughton, 1999), 983.

Julius Spier recommended Etty Hillesum to read the Bible.[8] Among her biblical readings, she developed a special relationship to Paul's hymn of love in Chapter 13 of the First Epistle to the Corinthians, and to the Gospel of Matthew. In April 1942, she decided to read Matthew's Gospel regularly, "After breakfast started on Matthew, every morning now, systematically."[9] And some days later, she spoke of reading her "good Matthew," instead of noting down a thousand things.[10] On 13 April 1942, she noted a quotation from Matthew 10:18-19, which is an instruction to the disciples not to worry about what they would say if they were brought before a governor or a king.[11] This passage is interesting, because in her comment on it, Etty Hillesum started to think about her own attitude, attributing the fact that she didn't worry in those difficult times, to a kind of incapacity to face reality.[12] This first, slightly negative reaction to worrying and not worrying was soon revised when she encountered the text of Matthew 6.

The importance of the Gospel of Matthew for Etty Hillesum is made clear by the many quotations in her diaries as well as those found in the little meditation book *Levenskunst* that she was preparing together with Henny Tideman in the last months of her life.[13] Beside the quotation of Matthew 10, there is Matthew 5:23-24, about the spirit of forgiveness,[14] and Matthew 16:25-26, on losing or saving one's life.[15] In *Levenskunst*, there are also two indirect quotations from Matthew: Matthew 5:5, from the beatitudes ("Blessed are the meek"), quoted in a passage of Giovanni Papini, in week

8 Cf. Alexandra Nagel, "Julius Spier zocht en vond houvast in de Bijbel – Etty Hillesum volgde hem," in: Ria van den Brandt & Klaas Smelik (eds.), *Etty Hillesum in discours* [Etty Hillesum Studies 3] (Gent: Academia Press, 2011), 77-91.

9 E.T., 323. *Het Werk*, 337; Saturday morning 4 April 1942, 9 o'clock: Na het ontbijt begonnen met Mattheüs, nu iedere ochtend, systematisch.

10 E.T., 331 (instead of "good Matthew", the English text has "Saint Matthew"). *Het Werk*, 346; Wednesday morning 15 April 1942, 8.30: Nog duizend dingen te schrijven, maar ik lees nog even mijn goede Mattheüs [...].

11 E.T., 329. *Het Werk*, 344. Monday morning 13 april 1942, 8.30: en gij zult ook voor Stadhouders en Koningen geleid worden.

12 E.T., 329. *Het Werk*, 344; Monday morning, 13 April 1942, 8.30: Dat ikzelf geen angst en bezorgdheid ken in deze tijd komt misschien ook wel daardoor, dat ik de realiteit nog steeds niet goed zie, dat ik in een andere realiteit leef; maar daarom moet men toch ook wel rekening houden met déze.

13 Cf. Ria van den Brandt & Peter Nissen (eds.), *Veel mooie woorden: Etty Hillesum en haar boekje* Levenskunst (Hilversum: Verloren, 2017).

14 *Levenskunst*, 30-31 (in week 9); E.T., 532. *Het Werk*, 563.

15 *Ibidem*, 28-29 (in week 8).

41, and Matthew 5:38-39 ("If someone strikes you on the right cheek, turn to him the other also"), in a quotation from Stanley Jones, in week 47.[16]

But the most often quoted passage of the gospel is the text under study, Matthew 6:25-34. In *Levenskunst*, verses 25 and 34 (the first and the last verse of the passage) are quoted in week 50.[17] As we will see below, there are several quotations of Matthew 6 and allusions to the lilies of the fields and the birds of the heavens in the diaries, mainly in July and September 1942. And in July 1943, Matthew 6:34 is mentioned again in a letter to Christine van Nooten. All these references show how important this passage had become for Etty Hillesum in this increasingly difficult period of her life.[18]

But was her adoption of this text influenced by Kierkegaard?

Kierkegaard's *Christian Discourses* (1848)

Besides his philosophical works, Kierkegaard has published several series of so-called "upbuilding discourses," a type of written sermons. They consisted of comments on a biblical text addressed to the readers for their spiritual edification, their upbuilding. The readers were invited by the author to emulate the biblical text in their own existence. On three different occasions, Kierkegaard devoted upbuilding discourses to Matthew 6. In a collection called *Upbuilding Discourses in Various Spirits* published in 1847,[19] he developed three discourses on what we can learn from the lilies of the fields and the birds of the heavens. Two years later, Kierkegaard published a small series of three short discourses on the same topic. But his most famous series on Matthew 6 is to be found in the *Christian Discourses* of 1848.[20] This book is known to have had an early German translation and therefore it is possible that it was in Julius Spier's bookcase, close to Etty Hillesum's bed, within easy reach. If she once opened the book, she would

16 *Ibidem*, 94-95; 106-107.

17 *Ibidem*, 112-113.

18 For an extensive description of Etty Hillesum's relationship to the Gospel of Matthew, cf. Door Brouns-Wewerinke, "'Zijt niet bezorgd om Uw leven...'. Etty Hillesum, Matteüs en 'de jood Paulus'," in: Van den Brandt & Nissen, *Veel mooie woorden*, 255-267.

19 Søren Kierkegaard, *Upbuilding Discourses in Various Spirits*, in: *Kierkegaard's Writings*, ed. and translated by Howard V. Hong & Edna H. Hong (Princeton, NJ: Princeton University Press, vol. 15, 1993).

20 Søren Kierkegaard, *Christian Discourses*, in: *Kierkegaard's Writings*, ed. and translated by Howard V. Hong & Edna H. Hong (Princeton, NJ: Princeton University Press, vol. 17, 1997).

have found at its very beginning the quotation of Matthew 6:25-34, followed by Kierkegaard's meditation on it.

The *Christian Discourses* are organized in four sections of seven discourses each. The discourses of sections 2-4 comment on different biblical texts, under the following titles: "States of Mind in the Strife of Suffering," "Thoughts that Wound from Behind – for Upbuilding" and "Discourses at the Communion on Fridays." The first section, entitled "The Cares of the Pagans," devotes all 7 discourses to a single text: Matthew 6. "The Cares of the Pagans" defines cares that are typical to a pagan way of life ("the pagans run after all these things"). Kierkegaard writes that the birds of the heavens and the lilies of the fields can teach humans to free themselves from the "cares of the pagans." Humans can learn to trust in the love of the heavenly Father instead of counting on human effort.

Kierkegaard's first two discourses, "The Care of Poverty" and "The Care of Abundance" deal with the human relationship to material things, properties, home, food, clothes. He points out that some people worry about their poverty and try to get rich, while others guard their wealth and fear losing it. The next two discourses, "The Care of Lowliness" and "The Care of Loftiness," concern the human feeling of being small and insignificant or, conversely, big and important. And again, some people fear losing their importance, while others suffer from their insignificance and try to gain importance. The 5th and 6th discourses, "The Care of Presumptuousness" and "The Care of Self-Torment," are devoted to the tension created by the effort to have everything under control and mastery over life, and the worry and constant self-torment that comes from knowing life has no guarantees. The last discourse, "The Care of Indecisiveness, Vacillation, and Disconsolateness," deals with the consequences of self-torment: there is no constancy, no confidence, and therefore no comfort. For this reason, indecisiveness and vacillation abound.

Cares of the Pagans in Etty Hillesum

Although we do not know if Etty Hillesum has read these discourses, there are striking parallels between Kierkegaard's meditations and Etty Hillesum's diaries. Without pretending to be exhaustive, I will give a few examples of Hillesum's passages that are like echoes of Kierkegaard. It may just be fortuitous that she hit upon such similar opinions and wording, but it is nothing if not striking.

a) Care of Poverty and Abundance

In Etty Hillesum's diaries, there are many passages about attachments to property that she noticed in herself and others; for example, to property and the comforts of home. As well, Hillesum cautioned that one's task was to learn *detachment*. What makes us rich or poor? Being too attached to our possessions can make us poor, and thus Etty Hillesum saw the "cares of pagans" all around her. She wrote,

> There are, it is true, some who, even at this late stage, are putting their vacuum cleaners and silver forks and spoons in safekeeping instead of guarding You, dear God.[21]

In contrast to this attitude, Etty Hillesum herself struggled to achieve detachment, for example with respect to the house in which she lived, her room, and her desk.

> This house, I feel, is slowly losing its hold on me. It's a good thing to be able to cut all ties with it. Very carefully, with great sorrow, but also in the certainty that it is all for the best and that there can be no other way, I let go, day by day.[22]

Earlier on the same day, she made a connection with Matthew 6:

> I would love to be like the lilies of the field. Someone who managed to read this age correctly would surely have learned just this: to be like a lily of the field.[23]

But later, considering what things she would put in her rucksack for an "unknown destination," she made a list. She realized she wanted to take a

21 E.T., 489. *Het Werk*, 517; Sunday morning prayer, 12 July 1942: Er zijn mensen, het is heus waar, die nog op het laatste ogenblik stofzuigers in veiligheid brengen en zilveren vorken en lepels, inplaats van jou, mijn God.

22 E.T., 527. *Het Werk*, 558; Tuesday, 22 September 1942: Dit huis hier, ik voel het, begint langzaam van m'n schouders te glijden. Het is goed, dat het zo is, de losmaking ervan gaat zich nu geheel voltrekken. Heel voorzichtig, met grote weemoed, maar ook met de zekerheid, dat het goed is zo en niet anders kan zijn, laat ik het glijden, dag voor dag.

23 E.T., 526. *Het Werk*, 557; Tuesday, 22 September 1942: Ik wil wel graag zo leven als de leliën des velds. Als men deze tijd goed begreep, zou men het van haar kunnen leren: te leven als een lelie des velds.

shirt, a small Bible, her Russian dictionaries, Tolstoy's folk tales, a volume of Rilke's letters and a lambswool sweater, and then, with self-irony she wrote, "what a lot of possessions I have, my God, and someone like me wants to be a lily of the field!"[24]

b) Care of Disconsolateness

In July-September 1942, Etty Hillesum often expressed her sadness, distress, and despair. "Care of disconsolateness," Kierkegaard would call it. So, for example, at the beginning of her often-quoted Sunday morning prayer of 12 July 1942, in a direct connection with Matthew 6:34, she wrote,

> Dear God, these are anxious times. Tonight for the first time, I lay in the dark with burning eyes as scene after scene of human suffering passed before me. I shall promise You one thing, God, just one very small thing: I shall never burden my today with cares about my tomorrow, although that takes some practice. Each day is sufficient unto itself.[25]

The despair she felt in herself was caused by the distress that with her characteristic empathy she observed in mankind. She worried if her small heart would have enough strength to support this burden,

> With a sharp pang, all of suffering mankind's nocturnal distress and loneliness passes now through my small heart. What shall I be taking upon myself this winter?[26]

Again and again, however, Etty Hillesum placed her gratitude in opposition to her disconsolateness. She expressed thanks for the beautiful life her Creator had given her and for her confidence that made her sure she would be sheltered in His arms, come what may,

24 E.T., 527. *Het Werk*, 558; Tuesday, 22 September 1942: – wat heb ik nog veel bezittingen, mijn God en zo iemand wil een lelie des velds zijn?

25 E.T., 488. *Het Werk*, 516; Sunday morning prayer, 12 July 1942: Het zijn bange tijden, mijn God. Vannacht was het voor het eerst, dat ik met brandende ogen slapeloos in het donker lag en er vele beelden van menselijk lijden langs me trokken. Ik zal je een ding beloven, God, een kleinigheidje maar: ik zal mijn zorgen om de toekomst niet als evenzovele zware gewichten aan de dag van heden hangen, maar dat kost een zekere oefening. Iedere dag heeft nu aan zichzelf genoeg.

26 E.T., 531. *Het Werk*, 562; Thursday, 24 September 1942: Alle nachtelijke nooden en eenzaamheden van een lijdende mensheid trekken nu plotseling met een weeë pijn door dat éne kleine hart van mij. Wat ben ik toch van plan deze winter op me te nemen?

> In Tide's diary I often read, 'Take him gently into Your arms, Father.' And that is how I feel, always and without cease: 'As if I were lying in Your arms, oh God, so protected and sheltered and so steeped in eternity.'[27]

But this confidence is always confronted by doubt. God is, after all, a God of mysteries, leaving humans without answers, allowing them to carry His mysteries. In the passage where she spoke about Julius Spier's bookcase, with the books of Dostoevsky, Shakespeare, and Kierkegaard, Etty Hillesum underlined this idea.

> I feel so dizzy. 'You have placed me before Your ultimate mystery, oh God, I am grateful to You for that, I even have the strength to accept it and to know there is no answer. That we must be able to bear Your mysteries.'[28]

c) Care of Vacillation

In many passages, Etty Hillesum spoke of her spirit being disturbed by thousands of things. The number "thousands" comes up often in her diaries: thousands of things to write;[29] thousands of concerns of every day;[30] thousands of fears and oppressions and despondencies,[31] etc. All of these perturbations caused vacillation. In connection with Matthew 6, Etty Hillesum spoke of thousands of small worries that divert the spirit from the essential thing, its confidence in God, and its only moral duty – working for peace.

> We have to fight them daily, like fleas, those many small worries about the morrow, for they sap our energies. We make mental provisions for the days to come, and everything turns out differently, quite differently. Sufficient unto the day. The things that have to be done must be done, and for the rest we must not allow ourselves to become infested with

27 E.T., 519. *Het Werk*, 549; Thursday morning, 17 September 1942: In Tide's dagboek ben ik vaak tegen gekomen: Neem hem zachtjes in Uw armen, Vader. En zo voel ik me, altijd en ononderbroken: of ik in jouw armen lig, mijn God, zo beschut en zo geborgen en zo van eeuwigheidsgevoel doortrokken.

28 E.T., 515. *Het Werk*, 544; Tuesday afternoon, 15 September 1942: Ik ben zo duizelig. Je stelt me voor je laatste raadselen, mijn God, ik ben dankbaar, dat je me ervoor stelt, ik heb ook de kracht ervoor gesteld te staan en te weten dat er geen antwoord is. Men moet jouw raadselen kunnen dragen.

29 See above, footnote 10.

30 E.T., 474. *Het Werk*, 500; Sunday evening, 5 July 1942.

31 E.T., 507. *Het Werk*, 537; Monday evening, 27 July 1942: om God als een banier uit te tillen boven de duizend angsten en beklemmingen en moedeloosheid van de aldag.

> thousands of petty fears and worries, so many motions of no confidence in God. [...] Ultimately, we have just one moral duty: to reclaim large areas of peace in ourselves, more and more peace, and to reflect it toward others. And the more peace there is in us, the more peace there will also be in our troubled world.[32]

d) Care of Self-torment about Tomorrow

The centrepiece in Etty Hillesum's reading of Matthew 6 is directly akin to what Kierkegaard called "the care of self-torment," the worry about tomorrow. She explicitly quoted verse 34 when introducing the passage about "becom(ing) infested with thousands of petty fears and worries".

> Let me just note down one more thing for myself: Matthew 6:34: Take therefore no thought for the morrow; for the morrow shall take thought of the things of itself. Sufficient unto the day is the evil thereof.[33]

As early as July 1942, she already realized the contradiction between believing in God and worrying about tomorrow,

> This afternoon on my long walk home, when worries assailed me wildly and refused to go away, I suddenly said to myself, if you really believe in God, then you must surrender yourself completely and live in faith. Then you must take no thought for the morrow.[34]

32 E.T., 535. *Het Werk*, 567; Tuesday, 29 September 1942: Men moet ze dagelijks bestrijden als flooien, de vele kleine zorgen om komende dagen, die de beste scheppende krachten in de mens aanvreten. Men tracht in gedachten regelingen te treffen voor komende dagen – en het komt alles anders, heel anders. Elke dag heeft genoeg aan zijn eigen kwaad. De dingen, die gedaan moeten worden moet men doen en dan voor de rest zich niet laten infecteren door de vele kleine angstjes en zorgjes, even zovele moties van wantrouwen tegenover God. [...] Dit is eigenlijk onze enige morele taak: in zichzelf grote vlaktes van rust ontginnen, steeds meer rust, zodat men deze rust weer uitstralen kan naar anderen. En hoe meer rust er in de mensen is, des te rustiger zal het ook in deze opgewonden wereld zijn.

33 E.T., 535. *Het Werk*, 567; Tuesday, 29 September 1942: Laat ik het nog maar weer eens voor mezelf opschrijven, 6 Mattheüs 34: Zijt dan niet bezorgd tegen den morgen, want de morgen zal voor het zijne zorgen; elke dag heeft genoeg aan zijn eigen kwaad.

34 E.T., 498. *Het Werk*, 526-527; Tuesday evening, 21 July 1942: Vanmiddag op mijn lange wandeling naar huis, toen de zorgen me plotseling weer wilden bespringen en geen einde schenen te zullen nemen, zei ik me plotseling: Als je dan al beweert aan God te geloven, dan moet je ook consequent zijn, dan moet je je helemaal overgeven en vertrouwen. Dan mag je je ook geen zorgen maken voor de dag van morgen.

And one year later, in a letter to Christine van Nooten, she again explicitly quoted Matthew 6:34 (wrongly cited as Matthew 24) as "the great lesson from Matthew," taught to her by her "unforgettable friend" Julius Spier.

> This is the only attitude that allows you to carry on at Westerbork. And so every night, with sure peace of mind, I lay down my many earthly cares at the feet of God Himself.[35]

e) Seeking First God's Kingdom and Justice

To free oneself from disturbing cares and finding peace of mind, it is necessary to have a main orientation and know what counts as primary in life. In this sense, Etty Hillesum quoted Matthew 6:33 to give an ethical accent to her discovery of the birds and lilies.

> My latest treasure: the birds of the heavens and the lilies of the fields in Matthew 6:33: But seek ye first the kingdom of God, and his righteousness, and all these things shall be added unto you.[36]

When writing in the note of 29 September 1942, "The things that have to be done must be done", Hillesum was referring to, for example, working actively for love, peace, and justice. Being free from care did not mean for her being indifferent and passive. She inveighed against any such suggestion. "Many accuse me of indifference and passivity when I refuse to go into hiding. They say that I have given up."[37] She insisted that acceptance was not being out of touch with reality; it included moral indignation and a fight against evil in the world. As for the "things that must be done...", she helped victims, acted as a balm for all wounds, and had both feet firmly planted in reality:

> I shall always be able to stand on my own two feet even when they are planted on the hardest soil of the harshest reality. And my acceptance is

35 E.T., 631. *Het Werk*, 672; Letter 55, To Christine van Nooten [communicated by Maria Tunzing in a letter to Christine van Nooten dated 31 July 1943], Wageningen, 31 July 1943: Dit is de eenige instelling, waaronder men het leven hier aan kan. Ik leg dan ook met een zekere gemoedsrust iedere avond m'n vele aardsche zorgen neer aan de voeten van God zelf.

36 E.T., 530. *Het Werk*, 562; Thursday, 24 September 1942: Mijn verrijking van de laatste dagen: de vogelen des hemels en de leliën des velds en Mattheüs 6,33: Maar zoekt eerst het Koninkrijk Gods en zijne gerechtigheid, en al deze dingen zullen u toegeworpen worden.

37 E.T., 487. *Het Werk*, 514; Saturday morning, 11 July 1942: Velen verwijten mij onverschilligheid en passiviteit en zeggen, dat ik me zo maar overgeef.

> not indifference or helplessness. I feel deep moral indignation at a regime that treats human beings in such a way.[38]

A simple sentence in a letter from Westerbork, "This morning, I read Meister 'Eckehardt,' the mystic, for a while and scrubbed W.C.'s,"[39] illustrates concretely Etty Hillesum's strong connection between spirituality and ethical activity.

Let us turn now to try – from another perspective – to deepen the analysis of the similarities between Kierkegaard's and Etty Hillesum's reading of Matthew 6:25-34.

Quotidianism

In 2006, the American philosopher and theologian John D. Caputo published a book with a title that could have come from Etty Hillesum: *The Weakness of God*.[40] It appears he is not acquainted with Hillesum however, and his book was more inspired by the last writings of Dietrich Bonhoeffer, the German theologian who also was murdered by the National Socialist regime.[41]

In Chapter 8 of his book, Caputo reflects on how the weakness of God influences the conception of time. It was the existential philosopher, Martin Heidegger, who stressed that the care of the future is a main preoccupation of humans, because they constantly project themselves into the future. Caputo engages in an intense dialogue with Heidegger and rereads Matthew 6 in light of Kierkegaard's discourses. He then defends a position he calls "quotidianism"

38 E.T., 487 [a very incomplete translation of this passage!]. *Het Werk*, 515; Saturday morning, 11 July 1942: Ik geef me rekenschap van alles tot in de kleinste details, ik geloof wel dat ik, in m'n innerlijke 'Auseinandersetzungen', met m'n twee voeten staan blijf op de hardste bodem van de hardste realiteit. En mijn aanvaarden is geen resignatie of willoosheid. Er is nog altijd plaats voor de elementaire zedelijke verontwaardiging over een regiem, dat zó met mensen omspringt.

39 Not included in E.T., *Het Werk*, 874; Letter D, Etty Hillesum to Hes Hijmans and other acquaintances in Amsterdam, Westerbork, Monday, 24 August 1942: Vanmorgen heb ik een poosje gelezen in de mysticus Meister Eckehardt en W.C.'s geschrobd. The English translation of this letter can be found in the bilingual edition Etty Hillesum: *The Complete Works 1941-1943: Bilingual, Annotated and Unabridged*, edited by Klaas A.D. Smelik & Meins G.S. Coetsier (Maastricht: Shaker Verlag, 2014), 2, 1114.

40 John D. Caputo, *The Weakness of God: A Theology of the Event* (Bloomington & Indianapolis, IN: Indiana University Press, 2006).

41 Cf. Jurjen Wiersma, "Etty Hillesum en Dietrich Bonhoeffer: Er zijn met en er zijn voor anderen," in: Klaas A.D. Smelik, Ria van den Brandt & Meins G.S. Coetsier (eds.), *Etty Hillesum in perspectief* [Etty Hillesum Studies, 4] (Gent: Academia Press, 2012), 5-14.

(Latin: *quotidianus, quotidie*, "quotidian," "daily")[42], which holds that the main task of human beings is not to worry about the future, but to devote all attention to the present day, to be aware of today, to be "really present to the present."

Caputo underlines first the apparent foolhardiness of this position,

> This all sounds a little mad, like a 'mad economics' without foresight, long-term investments, or long-range planning. It invests everything in today and makes no provisions for the future.[43]

But, as Caputo stresses, this foolishness is a paradox. We have to do both things, work for the future, not only our own future but the future of mankind and creation, and simultaneously surrender the future to God and not worry over it. Caputo expresses this paradoxical tension – which can also be found in Etty Hillesum's diaries – with constant references to Matthew 6,

> We are enjoined both to work for our bread and to trust God to give us our bread, to plan for the future and to realize that the future is in God's hands. Both together, not one without the other. But God *first*. We trust God *first*. Seek *first* the kingdom of God and then these daily supplements will be added to you. Get up and go to work in the morning, but thank God for the gift of the day.[44]

Therefore, worrying about the future has its place in quotidianism, but with an inner distance; allowed to be free from worry about the future, paradoxically, humans are free to worry without worry.

> Life is a risky business, and we worry constantly about the future, about what is coming, for ourselves and for others – and so we must, but we should worry without worry, and do so in the name of Elohim, who said that everything he made is good. Tomorrow it may be better or *perhaps* it will be worse, but that is another day. Today is the day to say yes. Life is a beautiful risk, and the lilies are the beautiful part."[45]

Couldn't these sentences have been written by Etty Hillesum?

42 Cf. chapter 8: "Quotidianism: Every Day, or Keeping Time Holy", in: Caputo, *The Weakness of God*, 157-181.

43 *Ibidem*, 165.

44 *Ibidem*, 173.

45 *Ibidem*, 181.

Conclusion: Quotidianism in Søren Kierkegaard and Etty Hillesum

What John D. Caputo defines as quotidianism, resonates in Søren Kierkegaard's writings as well as in Etty Hillesum's diaries. If we use quotidianism as an overarching framework to understand the connection between Hillesum and Kierkegaard, this approach suggests a strong tie between them, even with no concrete proof that Etty Hillesum ever read Kierkegaard. To illustrate their commonality, let us consider two quotations. Both express metaphorically a dedication to the *present* day by turning one's back to the *future* and by relaxing one's grip on the *past.*

Kierkegaard:

> The one who rows a boat turns his back to the goal toward which he is working. So it is with the next day. When, with the help of the eternal, a person lives absorbed in today, he turns his back to the next day. [...] When he turns around, the eternal becomes confused before his eyes and becomes the next day. But when, in order to work toward the goal properly, he turns his back, he does not see the next day at all, whereas with the help of the eternal he sees today and its tasks with perfect clarity.[46]

Hillesum:

> Relaxing one's rigid grip on the day. I think many people keep hanging on to a portion of the day with their greedy, grasping claws even at night. There must be an act of surrender and release every evening: a letting go of the day, and of everything that has happened in it. [...]. One must, so to speak, enter the night with empty, open hands from which one has deliberately allowed the day to slip. For only then can one have a good rest. And into one's rested and empty hands, which are no longer trying to cling on to anything and from which all desire has gone, one receives a new day upon awakening.[47]

46 *Kierkegaard's Writings* (cf. above, footnote 20), vol. 17, 73 (in the discourse about the care of self-torment).

47 E.T., 421. *Het Werk*, 443; Wednesday morning, 17 June 1943: De krampachtige greep om de dag ontspannen. Ik denk, dat velen in /gretige/begerige/ klauwen nog een stuk dag omklemd houden, ook in hun nachten? Dat zou iedere avond weer een gebaar van overgave en ontspanning moeten zijn: de dag loslaten, met alles wat er in was. [...] Men moet a.h.w. met lege, open handen in de nacht liggen, handen, waaruit men de dag vrijwillig heeft laten wegglijden. En dan pas kan men werkelijk uitrusten. En in z'n uitgeruste en leege handen, die niets hebben willen vasthouden en waarin geen enkele begeerte meer was, ontvangt men bij het wakkerworden een nieuwe dag.

About the Author

Pierre Bühler (1950) is a retired professor for Protestant Theology of the Universities of Neuchâtel and Zurich (Switzerland). Born in the Swiss Jura region, he studied Protestant Theology and Philosophy in Lausanne and Zurich. He was ordained as minister of the Reformed Church of Zurich. After having been assistant of Professor Gerhard Ebeling in Zurich (1974-1982), he was Professor of Systematic Theology in Neuchâtel (1982-1997) and in Zurich (1997-2015), and director of the institutes for Hermeneutics in Neuchâtel and Zurich.

Dialogizing Life amidst a Culture of Death

Etty Hillesum, Dostoevsky's *Grand Inquisitor* and Nazi Reductionism

John Cartner

Abstract

Etty Hillesum's diaries and letters, in both their form and content, stand as a repudiation of the Nazis' monologically constituted reductive discourse. Unlike her oppressors, Hillesum embraced the *Other* with its voices saturating her writings and informing her *Weltanschauung*. One such voice is that of Russian novelist, Fyodor Dostoevsky. Through an examination of his fable of "The Grand Inquisitor" and *The Brothers Karamazov* of which it is a part, their likely influences on Hillesum's all-embracing worldview are examined. In contrast to the diabolical markers of the Nazis' discourse, it is the seminal proposition of this paper that Hillesum's dialogically constituted writings, which foreground a concern for the Other, reflect the discourse of the deity.

Keywords: Other, diabolical speech, "Grand Inquisitor" legend, Fyodor Dostoevsky, suffering of innocents, dialogical writings, Shoah, Nazi rhetoric

According to Rowan Williams, "It is characteristic of diabolical speech to move toward silence, not a listening silence but that of incommunicable, self-enclosedness, death. To speak as if the other's responses were already known and could be dealt with or circumvented in advance."[1] Such a

1 Rowan Williams, *Dostoevsky: Language, Faith and Fiction*. (London: Bloomsbury, 2008), 109.

Smelik, Klaas A.D. (ed.), *The Lasting Significance of Etty Hillesum's Writings: Proceedings of the Third International Etty Hillesum Conference at Middelburg, September 2018*.
Taylor & Francis Group 2019
DOI: 10.5117/9789463722025_CARTNER

characterization can be attributed to the rhetoric of Hitler and his Nazis. The disconnect between language and life that marked their representations of the Jews revealed a narrative void of any of the signifiers of encounter so frequently found in Hillesum's writing; whether it be Hitler's proclamation of genocidal vengeance upon the Jews who laughed at his prophecies,[2] or the recycled fables of the dark-haired Jew preying on the virginal Aryan girl,[3] Hitler's references to Jews belong firmly in the realm of the abstract – divorced, not only from the reality of their existence, but from reality according to every possible measure. This wilful deafness to the Other promotes rigid representations with no relation to time and space; the Other is removed from his/her embodied reality and transposed into a fictional chronotope, where they become a plaything for the oppressor. The fantastical and, ultimately, ghastly consequence of such discourse is related by Melita Maschmann, a member of the girls' division of the Hitler youth and daughter to prosperous and educated parents, in her confessional memoir to a lost childhood Jewish friend:

> In preaching that all the misery of the nations was due to the Jews or that the Jewish spirit was seditious and Jewish blood was corrupting, I was not compelled to think of you or old Herr Lewy or Rosel Cohen: I thought only of the bogeyman, "the Jew." And when I heard that Jews were being driven from their professions and homes and imprisoned in ghettos, the points switched automatically in my mind to steer me round the thought that such a fate could also overtake you or old Lewy. It was only *the* Jew who was being persecuted and made "harmless."[4]

Maschmann's testimony exhibits the dangerous consequences of the divorce of language from life: the sacrifice of reality upon the altar of ideology by the Nazis and the broader German population produced a Holocaust of diabolical proportions. Given the apocalyptic consequences of the Nazis' one-sided rhetoric, one could justify its characterization, in eschatological terms, as the discourse of the Devil. According to Williams, "the Devil's priority is [...] to freeze human agency in the timelessness of a 'rational'

2 Andreas Musolff, *Metaphor, Nation and the Holocaust: The Concept of the Body Politic.* (New York: Routledge, 2010), 51.

3 Adolf Hitler, *Mein Kampf: The Official 1939 Edition.* (Warwickshire: Coda Books LTD., 2011), 206.

4 Daniel Jonah Goldhagen, *Hitler's Willing Executioners: Ordinary Germans of the Holocaust.* (New York: Vintage, 1997), 88.

order in which love or reconciliation is impossible."[5] Echoing synonymous intent in an eschatologically framed oration, Hitler fatefully declared:

> [...] we are animated with an inexorable resolve to seize the Evil [the Jews] by the roots and to exterminate [*auszurotten*] it root and branch. To attain our aim we should stop at nothing, even if we must join forces with the Devil.[6]

Pronounced to an audience of 1200 in 1920, Hitler's declaration utilizes the same reductive characterizations of the Jews as found in *Mein Kampf* and elsewhere.[7] Deaf to the target of its derision, both the uncompromising tone and genocidal intent of the statement lead to demonic silence – silence that militates against communication and leads to destruction and death. Such ends are intrinsically situated in the formalistic markers of diabolical speech acts: the rejection of genuine otherness, a fundamental characteristic of Hitler's statements pertaining to the Jews, serves as a linguistic signifier which enacts in speech that which it foreshadows. As Williams notes,

> someone who has lost the capacity to hear and speak, to engage humanly with others and to change in response, is already potentially a murderer. The crime comes out of the inner dialogue that is practically never interrupted by a real other."[8]

As the disseminator of discourse, which has no true Other, Hitler acts as the demonic narrator, as do all who take up his narrative.

If the demonic narrative leads to incommunicable silence, the Deity's narrative leads to dialogue. Whilst the former ends in nihilism and death, the latter enacts an interminable recognition and openness to the Other, which assures the continued growth of its participants. Herein lies one of the fundamental, indeed, defining characteristics of Hillesum's writings. Through openness to the voices of her Other, an attitude demonstrated and nurtured through her voracious reading of literature and the book of life – within the pages of which she encountered and dialogized with the Other clothed in flesh and blood – Hillesum guaranteed her growth as subject while simultaneously defining the nature of her resistance and

5 Williams, *Dostoevsky*, 108.
6 Goldhagen, *Hitler's Willing Executioners*, 134.
7 *Ibidem*.
8 Williams, *Dostoevsky*, 116.

discovering the meaning of her existence. What then were the possible lessons taken by Etty Hillesum from the writings of Dostoevsky?

While Hillesum's stated aspiration to write the next *Brothers Karamazov*[9] suggests Dostoevsky's novel made a profound impression on her, beyond a tantalizing promise to further develop a fleeting reflection on the lessons of the legend of "The Grand Inquisitor" for her generation,[10] Hillesum leaves only a few other clues as to her thoughts regarding the work.[11] While these clues do suggest Dostoevsky played a formative role in Hillesum's outlook, their relative scarcity, in comparison to her musings on a writer such as Rilke, will necessitate an inductive approach be taken to our task.

The legend of "The Grand Inquisitor" is relayed by Ivan, during the course of a conversation he has with his younger brother, Alyosha, regarding "the eternal questions."[12] As a poem of Ivan's conception, it reflects his beliefs or, rather, disbelief pertaining to the world created by God, which Ivan admits cannot be grasped by his own Euclidean mind.[13] The essence of Ivan's dilemma is his incapacity to make sense of the suffering of innocents, especially the suffering of children; furthermore, the idea that all this suffering, all the humiliating absurdity of human contradictions will vanish like a pitiful mirage[14] amidst some eschatological love-fest (Heaven) is intolerable. "To Ivan, reconciliation without recompense – a recompense

9 E.T., 94. When I do a simple translation, the whole of Russia spreads out before my mind's eye and I feel I must write another *Brothers Karamazov*. *Het Werk*, 100; Friday morning, 5 September 1941: Als ik een eenvoudige Russische vertaling maak, staat daar op de achtergrond in m'n geest het hele Rusland en vind ik ook, dat ik minstens zo een boek als de gebroeders Karamazow moet schrijven.

10 E.T., 21: With Communism in Russia, immediately after 1917, the problem, I think, was different. A new world had to be cobbled together from scratch, and there was no time for deeper thought, for taking an objective view. But yes, basically, it was still the same contempt for the masses, who must not be left to their own devices, who must not be allowed to choose between good and evil for themselves. This puts me in the mind of Dostoevsky's "Grand Inquisitor", but I shall work that out later. *Het Werk*, 22; Saturday, 15 March 1941: In het Communisme, vlak na 1917 in Rusland, lag het probleem geloof ik iets anders. Er moest een nieuwe wereld uit de grond gestampt worden en de aandacht mocht niet afgeleid worden door de diepere dingen, door het relativeren der dingen. Maar ja, im Grunde is het toch dezelfde minachting voor de massa, die men niet aan zichzelf durft over te laten, die zelf niet mag kiezen tussen goed en kwaad. Ik moet hierbij denken aan de 'Groot-Inquisiteur' van Dostojewski, maar dat werk ik later nog wel eens uit.

11 Due to her premature death at Auschwitz, Hillesum was denied the opportunity to pursue her literary ambitions; neither did she complete her promised reflections on *The Grand Inquisitor*.

12 Fyodor Dostoevsky, *The Karamazov Brothers* (Hertfordshire: Wordsworth Editions Limited, 2010), 255.

13 *Ibidem*, 257.

14 *Ibidem*.

that is immediate and visible – equates to a harmony that is bought too dearly and beyond our means to pay so much to enter on it."[15]

While there is no reason to doubt the genuineness of Ivan's distress and his concern for the suffering of innocent children, it appears largely a result of cognitive dissonance rather than being experientially induced. This is borne out in the litany of miseries he relays to his brother, Alyosha, as he seeks to justify his rejection of God's world. From his account of a peasant lashing the eyes of his overloaded and exhausted horse,[16] to the story of "[a] well-educated, cultured gentleman and his wife beat[ing] their own child with a birch rod,"[17] to the disturbing tale of a serf-boy being torn apart by a general's hounds as punishment for an accident brought about from his innocent play[18] – Ivan's stories are collected from historical accounts; thus, whilst horrific, and historically grounded, they are nevertheless second-hand and, therefore, removed from Ivan's experience. Though of a different order to Hitler's fabrications regarding the Jews, their recollection reflects an individual similarly disconnected from the present time and space and thus, disengaged from authentic human relations. The results of such exercises in abstraction are often catastrophic, a fact of which Dostoevsky was all too aware. Rejecting the reductive impact upon the human story brought about by such cognitive dissonance, he insisted on subjecting all ideologies to narrative embodiment, where their real impact could be fully played out; herein lies the defining trait of his artistic endeavours.

Sharing Dostoevsky's distrust of abstractionism, Hillesum, as one who lived and died amidst the diabolical event that was the Holocaust, refused to submit to the nihilistic narrative it enacted. Unlike Ivan, Hillesum witnessed and experienced the suffering of innocents and looked searchingly into the faces of its perpetrators for traces of humanity. In an extensive and moving letter written to Han Wegerif, a mere fortnight prior to her own deportation, she recounted the impact of watching the loading of a transport at the hands of the *Ordnungspolizei*,[19] otherwise known as the *Grüne Polizei*:

> When I think of the faces of that squad of armed, green-uniformed guards – my God, those faces! I looked at them, each in turn, from behind the safety of a window, and I have never been so frightened of anything in

15 *Ibidem*, 268.

16 *Ibidem*, 263.

17 *Ibidem*.

18 *Ibidem*, 265.

19 The Ordnungspolizei played a significant role in loading the transports during the Holocaust. Due to their uniforms, they were often referred to as the Green Police.

> my life. I sank to my knees with the words that preside over human life: And God made man after his likeness.[20] That passage spent a difficult morning with me.[21]

Watching the Nazis' extermination process unfold before her eyes at the hands of those whom, based on Hillesum's reaction, betrayed little humanity as they turned the cogs of the Nazis' genocidal machine, it is little wonder that the scripture so seminal to Judeo-Christian anthropology proved difficult to comprehend; more surprising is the fact she sought to reconcile the absurdity surrounding her.

Like Ivan, the suffering of children proved the most incomprehensible; unlike Ivan, Hillesum's recollections were not drawn from the pages of history but the pages of her life:

> [...] those tiny piercing screams of the babies, dragged from their cots in the middle of the night to be carried off to a distant land. I have to put it all down quickly, in a muddle, because if I leave it until later I probably won't be able to go on believing that it really happened. It is like a vision, and drifts further and further away. The babies were easily the worst.[22]

Hillesum recounts a throng of Dantesque images as they unfolded around her: a young girl wondering aloud at the meaninglessness of her short life; a woman with a sick child in distress at the lack of provisions allowed on the transport; the preparation of small bottles of milk for the infants being conveyed to their deaths; the gentle chiding of a mother telling her crying child that unless it behaves she won't allow it to accompany her on

20 Hillesum is referencing Genesis 1:27: "So God created humankind in his image, in the image of God he created them; male and female he created them."

21 E.T., 644: From a passage further on in this letter, it appears that Etty Hillesum had sneaked into the barracks that was situated opposite the leaving train. This was strictly forbidden: on the morning of the transport everyone not involved had to stay in his/her barracks. *Het Werk*, 686; Letter 64, To Han Wegerif and others, Westerbork, Tuesday, 24 August 1943: Als ik denk aan die gezichten van het groengeüniformeerde, gewapende begeleidingspeloton, mijn God, die gezichten! Ik heb ze stuk voor stuk bekeken, verdekt opgesteld achter een venster, ik ben nog nooit van iets zo geschrokken als van deze gezichten. Ik ben in de knoei geraakt met het woord, dat het leidmotief van mijn leven is: En God schiep de mens naar Zijn Evenbeeld. Dat woord beleefde een moeilijke ochtend met mij..

22 E.T., 644-645. *Het Werk*, 687; Letter 64, To Han Wegerif and others, Westerbork, Tuesday, 24 August 1943: [...] die kleine doordringende kreten der babies, die midden in de nacht uit hun kribben gehaald werden om vervoerd te worden naar een ver land. Ik moet het gauw alles door elkaar neerschrijven, later zal ik het niet meer kunnen, omdat ik geloven zal, dat het niet echt waar is geweest, het is nu al als een visioen, dat steeds verder van me wegdrijft. Die babies waren wel het ergste.

the transport; another mother hysterically pleading with Hillesum to hide her child; one of her colleagues feeding poison to a dying woman, who also happened to be her mother; another mother who recently witnessed her husband being dragged away and, having just seen her own child die, remarked at the crying babies around her, "I'll have good work to do on the train, I still have lots of milk"; a woman in her ninth month of pregnancy being readied for the transport; a dying man, reciting the Shema to himself as he is carried away, and the loading of the elderly, frail, sick, disabled, infants, children, mothers and fathers onto the train for their final journey, it is little wonder Hillesum exclaimed, "So that's what Hell is like," before asking, "God Almighty, what are you doing to us?"[23]

Though immersed in desolation on an apocalyptic scale and understandably confounded by the absurdity of the needless suffering of her fellow Jews, Hillesum refused to return her ticket by seeking, to her final moments, meaning amidst the meaningless:

> I have told you often enough that no words and images are adequate to describe nights like these. But still I must try to convey something of it to you. One always has the feeling here of being the ears and eyes of a piece of Jewish history, but there is also the need sometimes to be a still, small voice.[24]

Unlike Ivan, for whom the concept of intolerable suffering was sufficient to see him make the decision to close the book on the narrative of his own existence, Hillesum, living amidst a cataclysmic event that would claim her life, continued to add to the pages of her narrative, one which today stands in perpetuity as testimony to humanity's capacity for goodness amidst the most desperate of circumstances.

As one who lived prior to the Shoah, Dostoevsky set his challenge to faith amidst the flames of the Spanish Inquisition. Set in 16th-century Seville, at a time "when fires were lighted every day to the glory of God, and 'in the splendid *auto da fe* the wicked heretics were burnt,'"[25] the legend of

23 E.T., 646 and 647. *Het Werk*, 689 and 690; Letter 64, To Han Wegerif and others, Westerbork, Tuesday, 24 August 1943: Zo, nu ben ik dus in de hel. [...] Allemachtig, wat hebben we hier, wat bent U van plan?

24 E.T., 644. *Het Werk*, 687; Letter 64, To Han Wegerif and others, Westerbork, Tuesday, 24 August 1943: Dat woorden en beelden niet toereikend zijn voor nachten als deze, heb ik jullie al vaak genoeg verteld. Toch moet ik proberen iets voor jullie neer te schrijven, men voelt zich steeds oren en ogen van een stuk joodse geschiedenis, men heeft soms ook de behoefte een kleine stem te zijn.

25 Dostoevsky, *The Karamazov Brothers*, 271.

"The Grand Inquisitor" has Christ make his promised return during an age dominated by the fear of official seriousness; a time when humanity sacrificed its Other on the altar of ideology. Arriving the day after the burning of a hundred heretics at the hands of the Grand Inquisitor, "He came softly, unobserved, and yet, strange to say, everyone recognised Him."[26]

> The people are irresistibly drawn to him, they surround Him, they flock about Him. He moves silently in their midst with a gentle smile of infinite compassion. The sun of love burns in His heart, light and power shine from His eyes, and their radiance, shed on the people, stirs their hearts with responsive love. He holds out His hands to them, blesses them, and a healing virtue comes from contact with Him, even with His garments.[27]

Through Ivan, Dostoevsky here paints a picture reminiscent of the Gospels, though, perhaps even more than the evangelists' accounts, there is an emphasis on the unspoken, visible power of Christ which, though transmitted in silence, is immediately recognizable to all. Christ utters only two words during Ivan's tale: "maiden arise,"[28] a command with the power to resurrect a child from her coffin, which sees the grim figure of the Grand Inquisitor enter the scene. Unlike Christ, who commands the crowd's affection with active love, the Grand Inquisitor sees them cower in fearful obedience. Whilst, at this stage of the tale, neither relies on words to enact their commands, Christ's actions elicit responsive excitement and life, while the Grand Inquisitor's every gesture invokes deathlike silence. It is a silence reminiscent of the demonic, incommunicable silence, of which Williams speaks; a silence that leads to death.

The juxtaposition of the Grand Inquisitor with Christ reflects the opposition between the official and unofficial seriousness of the Middle Ages, a conflict revisited in the twentieth century in the contrast between the discourse of Hitler and that of Hillesum. In all of these instances, the discourse of the former is monologic, authoritarian, given and oppressive, while the latter is dialogic, anti-authoritarian, posited and liberating; in the former, truth takes the form of a closed system of inflexible propositions, in the latter, truth is discovered in dialogue and embodiment; the former is deaf to the voice of the Other, while, in the case of the latter, the Other is its indispensable, constitutive centre. The former represents satanic

26 *Ibidem*, 272.
27 *Ibidem*.
28 *Ibidem*.

discourse – which is divorced from love of self or the Other – clashing with the latter, which is reminiscent of the Deity's narrative.

"Bound within the gloomy vaulted prison in the ancient palace of the Holy Inquisition,"[29] Christ is met by the Grand Inquisitor who had ordered his arrest. With light in hand, the old cardinal rhetorically enquires as to his "guest's" identity. Though greeted by silence, it is immediately evident he has no interest in anything Christ may say, and he demands his continued silence: "What canst thou say indeed, indeed? I know too well what Thou wouldst say. And Thou hast no right to add anything to what Thou hadst said of old."[30] He then proceeds, during the course of an extensive monologue, to take umbrage with the burden of freedom Christ placed on humanity and, referencing Christ's rejection of Satan's offerings in the desert, he praises the greater understanding of man's needs, expressed through the three temptations posed by "the wise and mighty spirit in the wilderness,"[31] while conducting a defence of the way the Church has corrected Christ's work.[32]

As Ivan's creation and mouthpiece, in his condemnation of Christ's work, the Grand Inquisitor aligns himself with the diabolical, underpinned as it is by an impoverished vision of humanity. Like Ivan, the ageing cardinal's vision is limited to observing humanity's weaknesses and, in a Foucauldian will to power, he steps into the breach, to remove the burden of freedom from the shoulders of feeble humanity. Replacing Christ's freedom with happiness, the Inquisitor enslaves humanity by giving them the very things Christ had rejected: miracle, mystery and authority.[33] Though cognizant of the appropriateness of Christ's rejection of Satan's offerings, the Inquisitor nevertheless ridicules the decision as one that places too heavy a responsibility on humanity's capacity for goodness; a humanity he assesses as weak and vile.[34]

29 *Ibidem*, 273.
30 *Ibidem*.
31 *Ibidem*, 276.
32 *Ibidem*, 279.
33 *Ibidem*.
34 *Ibidem*, 280: Thou wouldst not enslave man by a miracle, and didst crave faith given freely, not based on miracle. Thou didst crave for free love and not the base raptures of the slave before the might that has overawed him forever. But thou didst think too highly of men therein, for they are slaves, of course, though rebellious by nature. Look round and judge; fifteen centuries have passed, look upon them. Whom hast Thou raised up to Thyself? I swear, man is weaker and baser by nature than Thou hast believed him! Can he, can he do what Thou didst? By showing him so much respect, Thou didst, as it were, cease to feel for him, for Thou didst ask far too much from him – Thou who hast loved him more than Thyself! Respecting him less, Thou wouldst have asked less of him. That would have been more like love, for his burden would have been lighter. He is weak and vile.

The Inquisitor's lack of faith in humanity's capacity for goodness is matched only by his lack of belief in his Deity's benevolence. Ignoring the divine promise of grace, he replaces freedom with another totalitarian system, within which truth, discovered in embodiment and dialogue, is exchanged for adherence to abstract ideology. As far as the Inquisitor is concerned, "no one really wants liberty, yet people want the semblance of it; they want to fantasize that they are free."[35] It is thus the illusion of freedom, without real responsibility, that the cardinal provides by demanding assent to his religious power. Thus, by presiding over and reinforcing the precepts of the paternal state, the Inquisitor propagates the totalitarian project, which, according to Gorman Beauchamp,

> seeks to keep its subjects in a state of perpetual childishness, insecure, seeking approval from authority, dependent upon the surrogate parent to make decisions for them. It does not, that is, find man slavish, servile, childish by nature, but attempts to make him so.[36]

In language that starkly concurs with Beauchamp's assessment, the Grand Inquisitor confesses to Christ:

> [...] in their leisure hours we shall make their life like a child's game, with children's songs and innocent dance. Oh, we shall allow them even sin, they are weak and helpless, and they will love us like children because we allow them to sin.[37]

All too aware of the mechanizations of the totalitarian state, Hillesum observed, in the political systems surrounding her, a similar disdain for freedom and truth. Reflecting on the Third Reich's propaganda chiefs' determination to "incite people with theories they don't believe in themselves",[38] Hillesum writes:

> It is essentially a boundless contempt for the masses. Keeping the truth to oneself in the supposition that the masses can't take it. For strategic reasons, of course, the masses cannot be told the truth, because that

35 Williams, *Dostoevsky*, 28.

36 Gorman Beauchamp, "'The Legend of the Grand Inquisitor': The Utopian as Sadist," *Humanitas* 20 (2007) 1-2, 146.

37 Dostoevsky, *The Karamazov Brothers*, 284.

38 Hillesum's assessment reflects her generosity as there is much evidence to suggest that the majority of Germans supported the Nazis' anti-Semitic measures.

would weaken their resolve. But that means something is being imposed and foisted upon them [...]. This puts me in the mind of Dostoevsky's 'Grand Inquisitor'.[39]

Illuminating the Deity

According to Williams, "if we are to avoid the politics of the Devil [...] we have to develop a political imagination that resists abstraction and generality."[40] It is interesting then, that in formulating his response to the diabolical narrative of the Grand Inquisitor, Dostoevsky avoids the path of rationalism adopted by Ivan, instead choosing, through his characterization of Zosima and his protégé, Alyosha, to paint an image of active love. In the opening of book 6, "The Russian Monk," the portrayal of Zosima – Alyosha's master and mentor – prompts the recollection of Christ's characterization in Ivan's tale of "The Grand Inquisitor." Like Jesus, Zosima is a force of attraction. While anticipating his death, it is as the embodiment of joyful Christian love that people are drawn to him. Though weak, Zosima is "engaged in a quiet and joyful conversation,"[41] with his focus, even in his dying hours, on the welfare of others: Upon noticing Alyosha standing at the doorway of his room, he joyfully implores him to enter; comforting Alyosha in his sorrow, he enquires as to whether his offering of sixty kopecks had reached the "good woman from Vishegorye, with her little Lizaveta in her arms;"[42] assured that it had, Zosima then asks Alyosha about his brother, Dmitri, in whose face he had observed a future of trails.[43]

Juxtaposed as Ivan's antithesis, Zosima is one in whom love is visible. While Ivan, the embodiment of Dostoevsky's belief that "those who love men in general, hate men in particular,"[44] expresses scepticism regarding love for humanity beyond its conceptual possibility, Zosima, demonstrates love through encounter with one's Other in their embodied, individual

39 E.T., 21. *Het Werk*, 22; Saturday, 15 March 1941: Het is in de grond een grenzenloze minachting voor de massa. De waarheid voor zichzelf houden en menen, dat de massa die niet verdragen kan. Nee, vanuit hun doelstellingen kan de massa de waarheid natuurlijk niet verdragen, omdat die verslapt in de strijd. Maar het gaat hier om een geforceerde, opgedrongen strijd. [...] Ik moet hierbij denken aan de 'Groot-Inquisiteur' van Dostojewski [...].

40 Williams, *Dostoevsky*, 82.

41 Dostoevsky. *The Karamazov Brothers*, 310.

42 *Ibidem*, 311.

43 *Ibidem*, 312.

44 Ellis Sandoz, *Political Apocalypse: A Study of Dostoevsky's Grand Inquisitor* (Baton Rouge LA: Louisiana State University Press, 1971), 125.

form. Importantly, in the aforementioned cases, encounter is followed by action. Having observed in Dmitri's eyes present distress and future suffering and, due to his own proximity to death unable to check on him directly, he sends his brother, Alyosha, to secure his welfare. Similarly, having encountered the woman from Vishegorye and her child, he sends after them an offering with the instruction it be given anonymously, "from an unknown benefactress."[45] It is in this same spirit that Zosima, having reminded Alyosha of the carnivalesque scriptural injunction that, "Except a grain of wheat fall into the ground and die, it abideth alone; but if it die, it bringeth forth much fruit,"[46] commands his protégé to go beyond the walls of the monastery in order to "live like a monk in the world."[47] Zosima's actions reflect a *Humanism of the Other*[48] of the sort advocated by Jewish philosopher, Emmanuel Levinas, which also resonates in the words and actions of Hillesum.

"Am I my brother's keeper?" Etty Hillesum's Response

Across the pages of Etty Hillesum's diaries and letters, a significant personal and spiritual transformation can be traced. Commencing on 8 March 1941, the therapeutic origins of her writing reveal an individual looking to discover herself and her place in the world. By 7 September 1943, when, as one of 987 Jews being transported to Auschwitz-Birkenau, she scrawled her final words on a postcard and threw it from the train of human misery, Hillesum had discovered that her meaning lay securely in her Other.[49] Arguably the most radical demonstration of this was Hillesum's refusal to go into hiding.[50] This choice, to stand in solidarity with her fellow Jews, signifies her retreat from self-concern and her entrance into the time of the Other. No longer is her life lived for the fulfilment of her own existential possibilities, rather, her existential possibilities are directed towards, and realized through, the service of her Other into perpetuity – this is

45 *Ibidem*, 312.

46 Dostoevsky, *The Karamazov Brothers*, 312.

47 *Ibidem*.

48 Emmanuel Levinas, *Humanism of the Other* (Urbana: University of Illinois Press, 2003).

49 Meins Coetsier, *The Existential Philosophy of Etty Hillesum: An Analysis of her Diaries and Letters* [Supplements to The Journal of Jewish Thought and Philosophy, 22] (Leiden/Boston, MA: Brill, 2014), 69: Included in the transport of 7 September 1943 were 170 children. Only eight of the 987 prisoners who accompanied Hillesum, survived Auschwitz-Birkenau.

50 Coetsier, *The Existential Philosophy of Etty Hillesum*, 62.

guaranteed by the preservation of her writings. Though she had not forsaken the desire to live a long life, the quality of her existence – measured by the service she could provide those who came after her – took precedence.[51] As such, by working for a time beyond the span of her life, by setting her sights beyond the horizon of her own time, Hillesum embodies the Levinasian notion of ethical transcendence, "which is irreducible to the immanence of the self's interest (essence) structured by time and death."[52] She simultaneously stands as an embodied rejection of the Grand Inquisitor's damning anthropology.

"Surrounded by [her] writers and poets"[53] and informed by their vision, Hillesum rejects the Nazis' demonic narrative by entering into and embracing the ambivalent and enigmatic nature of existence; through her descent into Otherness, Hillesum transcends the fearful circumstances of her life, and discovers both meaning and joy. Her diaries and letters testify to a life in which the embrace of the carnivalesque death-life dialectic at the heart of the scriptural injunction that "unless a grain of wheat falls into the earth and dies, it remains just a single grain; but if it dies, it bears much fruit" (John 12:24), was played out in full.

About the Author

John Cartner (1973) teaches in the English Literature programme at The University of Notre Dame Australia (Fremantle Campus). He has acted as course coordinator for a range of units including World Literatures, The Western Literary Tradition, The Novel in English, Children's Literature and Australian Literature. The author's MA focused on refugee representations and self-representations in Australia between 2001 and 2007, while his PhD examined carnival laughter in the writings of Etty Hillesum. The author continues to conduct research in the areas of Postcolonial literatures, Etty Hillesum studies and Holocaust literatures.

51 E.T., 462: And that is why I must try to live a good and faithful life to my last breath: so that those who come after me do not have to start all over again, need not face the same difficulties. Isn't that doing something good for future generations? *Het Werk*, 487; Friday evening, 3 July 1942: [...] en daarom moet ik het zo goed en zo volledig en zo overtuigd mogelijk leven tot de laatste ademtocht, zodat diegene, die na mij komt niet helemaal opnieuw hoeft te beginnen en het niet meer zo moeilijk heeft. Is dat ook niet iets doen voor het nageslacht?

52 Glenn Morrison, *A Theology of Alterity: Levinas, von Balthasar and Trinitarian Praxis* (Pittsburgh PA: Duquense University Press, 2013), 20.

53 E.T., 527. *Het Werk*, 557; Tuesday, 22 September 1942: Tussen m'n schrijvers en dichters [...].

Patience and Hope in the Writings of Julian of Norwich and Etty Hillesum

Stephen Cherry

Abstract
It may seem unlikely that comparing a fourteenth-century Christian visionary and anchorite with Etty Hillesum might be a fruitful exercise. After all, although Etty Hillesum sometimes longed for a convent cell, she committed herself to solidarity with her fellow Jews at a perilous time. However, these two women can be seen as kindred spirits in their openness to suffering, the way in which they relate to others, and their determined attention to the possibility of beauty in the most unpromising of circumstances. For both of them, patience is hard but important work, and hope is a quality that is intrinsically connected with practical, intimate, mutual and vulnerable loving-kindness.

Keywords: Julian of Norwich, love, anchorites, visions, patience, hope, *agape*

Introducing Julian of Norwich

One of the surprising and encouraging turns in English-language theology of recent years is the amount of attention and respect given to the short fourteenth-century book, *Revelations of Divine Love*, by Julian of Norwich.[1] It is often said that *Revelations* was the first book-length text we have written by a woman in English. It is, in fact, two books, consisting of a relatively

1 References to *Revelations of Divine Love* (*Revelations*) are all to the Long Text, except where indicated as Short Text (ST). The number given (e.g. #51) is the chapter in that text. There are 86 short chapters. The translation quoted is that of Barry Windeatt in the Oxford Word Classic's Series, 2015.

Smelik, Klaas A.D. (ed.), *The Lasting Significance of Etty Hillesum's Writings: Proceedings of the Third International Etty Hillesum Conference at Middelburg, September 2018.*
Taylor & Francis Group 2019
DOI: 10.5117/9789463722025_CHERRY

"short text" written when Julian was in her early thirties and the so-called "long text" written twenty years later. Her writing was occasioned by a short period of acute illness when she was thirty years old in which she, and those around her, were convinced that she was going to die.[2] It was in this state that she experienced a series of what she called "shewings" which are often thought of as visions because some of them are so visually vivid, but the better word is "revelations" because not all of what is "shown" to Julian is visual. Indeed, one feature of her writing style is that she often uses the word "see" to mean "understand." So to a considerable extent, it is possible to say that when we describe Julian as a *visionary* or *mystic*, we mean that she was a *thinker*; and when we talk about her "revelations," we are talking about her "reflections."

In Julian's day, Norwich was the second largest city in England and while she was a child, it was half destroyed by the plague. The population of Norwich fell from thirteen thousand people to about six thousand over just a few years, and there is no doubt that the young Julian would have been exposed to the sights, sounds and smells of dying and death on a huge scale. Indeed, even without the plague a city of that size would have been most insanitary.

> Raw sewage and stinking garbage clogged the ditches on both sides of the roadways; blood and offal flowed out from the open doors of butcher houses and turned the streets red; servants threw the contents of chamber pots out of the windows; and the stench of tanneries, as well as of tallow and parchment makers, filled the air.[3]

Etty Hillesum famously and romantically wrote that she longed for a convent cell but she saw it as a temptation, a distraction from a more rigorous path. Julian, on the other hand, was walled up as an anchorite at St Julian's church, from which we now derive her name. While the ceremony involved reading the burial service over the still living anchoress, her subsequent life would not have been one of complete isolation. She would have had a younger woman to assist her in the tasks of living and many seekers after counsel or guidance would have found their way to the window through which she would have listened and dispensed advice.

2 She actually records the date "the year of our Lord 1373, on the eighth day of May," #2.

3 V.M. Rolfe, *Julian's Gospel: Illuminating the Life and Revelations of Julian of Norwich* (Maryknoll: Orbis Books, 2013), 32.

Julian, when compared with Hillesum, is very Christian and rather doctrinal, although she describes herself as illiterate or unlearned. Hillesum, when read against Julian, is a serious reader and scholar, and comes across as very Jewish and very exploratory. She is open to a wide variety of cultural influences – among them, psychoanalytic thought and practice of a certain kind, Russian literature, German poetry. She is a great-great-grandchild of the Enlightenment; something that Julian could never have imagined.

Julian's Theology

Julian's theology is thoroughly Trinitarian, writing that "where Jesus appears, the blessed Trinity is understood, as I see it" (#4) and her cast of mind is shaped by the mainstream Christian thinkers, especially Augustine. One interesting feature of Julian's style is her love of lists. These show a careful and detailed, almost forensic mind at its patient work. Nothing could be more different to Hillesum's passionate observations, her embracing of perplexity or her self-scolding than Julian's tidy lists.

Julian's visions are varied and include beautiful images of the natural world, ranging from a profound meditation on the vulnerability of all that is created through the medium of something round and of the size of a hazelnut (#5), to an almost psychedelic underwater scene (#10). But there is a focus in her first "shewing" on aspects of the passion of Christ, and in particular on the blood that flows from the wounds made by the impressed crown of thorns. She sees this blood as "hot and fresh, plentiful and life-like" and describes in detail its relentless flow (#4). It is sometimes difficult to get contemporary students beyond the "yuk-factor" when introducing them to Julian's writings, and yet they are not primarily about the horror of the crucifixion any more than Hillesum's diaries are about the horror of the occupation.

Julian's writing is infused with doctrine, driven by imagery and littered with lists, but most importantly it is theologically *creative,* revealing how someone thought about God using medieval categories in the aftermath of the plague. Hers is a genuine and lively theological text, written not only to share the pictures that popped up in her mind, but to inform the thinking and living of those she called, in the beautiful Middle English of her time and place, her "*evencristens*." Like Hillesum, she wrote in the hope that her writings might help others.

To the extent that she thought in words, Julian thought in Middle English. We have already come across "evencristen" and we shall inevitably come to the word "behovely" before we end. Another word is important too, and it lies at the heart of the way in which Julian understood incarnation. While modern translations say that Christ took our *nature* from the Virgin Mary, the Middle English word used by Julian is not "nature" but "kynde."[4] The meaning and associations of this word are far more domestic, intimate and personal than "nature." We might particularly think of "kin" (family relationship) and "kindness" (generosity and compassion). This frames Julian's understanding that God is present in Christ as one of us bodily beings. Julian's theology is one of solidarity with the flesh and in the flesh. Unlike many Christian theologians, she doesn't prioritize the mind, but affirms the whole of the human being. Equally, she doesn't step outside the temporal realm when she thinks about God, but sees the realm of time as theologically as well as humanly important. She is alert to the difficulties of life and yet her outlook is always warm and kind. This extends to her view of God who is not only Jesus and Trinity but also, perhaps surprisingly, our Mother (#59).

Just as Julian doesn't take a gloomy view of human nature, so she doesn't believe that God is (or can be) angry (#46) and she startlingly asserts that our sins are our glories (#38). According to Julian, we are saved by profound kinship; Christ is our sibling as well as our Mother. This explains the considerable extent of what one might call *horizontal* concern in Julian: genuine care for and identification with her human brothers and sisters, her *evencristens*. This is not a secondary matter; it is a primary concern and purpose, based not on any kind of turning away from God, or downplaying God's significance, but rooted in her understanding of the nature of God: God's *kynde*. God is perhaps in a formal way "Almighty" to Julian, but she doesn't celebrate the mightiness in God. In fact, what she values and esteems about God, is quite the opposite.

Patience

To understand what hope means to both Julian and Hillesum, we must also talk about patience. For Julian, patience is the virtue of enduring in faith,

4 J.M. Soskice, *The Kindness of God: Metaphor, Gender and Religious Language* (Oxford: Oxford University Press, 2008), especially chapter 7, "The Kindness of God: Trinity and the Image of God in Julian of Norwich and Augustine," (pp. 125-156). Soskice mentions in passing how very Augustinian Julian's basic theology is, and points out several sentences in the *Revelations*, which are paraphrases of Augustine's *Confessions*.

"serving God all the days of our life" whether that be a short time or over many years (#14). However, patience is threatened by "fear and perplexity" (#54). It is needed because we do not know when we will "be taken" (#64). But it is suffering that causes her to think about patience as much as uncertainty, though even sufferings can be of help if "patiently accepted" (#150). Julian associates patience with a cluster of virtues, such as "meekness, gentleness and pity" and connects it with "hatred of sin and wickedness" (#59). Her parabolic figure of "the servant" (whom she ultimately understands to be both Adam and Christ) is seen as a character of patience, obedience and humility (#51).

It is when Julian writes of the sufferings of Christ that the distinctiveness and strength of her views becomes most apparent. This comes in terms of her articulating a response to the spiritual sickness (or sin) of "sloth or impatience" (#73). The way in which she sees this as sin is worth comment. It's not the sin of a particular wrong action or of malevolent intention, but the sin of those who "love God and dispose themselves to do God's will" but, nonetheless, get things wrong through weakness and inclination which is not merely the pull of the flesh. As she puts it, "through our spiritual blindness and the burden of our bodies we are most inclined to these sins" (#73). The antidote to such sins is to be found in meditating on "the patience that he [Jesus] had in his cruel Passion and also the joy and the delight that he had in his cruel Passion because of love" (#73). This is a typically dense comment of Julian's, and it points to the intricate interconnectedness that she perceives between virtues and feelings, and between our lives and suffering and the life and suffering of Christ.

The word and quality of "patience" is as important for Hillesum as it was for Julian. In her earlier writings, patience is the quality that she knows she needs in order to allow her to persist with trying to write and develop as a writer. She learnt much from Rilke in this regard; and gets a sense of time and pace from his writing, even as she muses on how ill-fitted he would be to live through her experiences.[5]

5 What Rilke has to say about patience and the passage of time is so important that she quotes some of his words on no fewer than five occasions. For instance, on the evening of Monday 16 February 1942, she writes, "Trying to find the way back to myself once more with these words of Rainer Maria's:
'*Everything* is bearing and then giving birth. Allowing every impression and every germ of a feeling to reach perfection deep within us, in the dark, in the ineffable, the unconscious, in what is beyond the grasp of reason, and to await the hour of birth of a new clarity with deep humility and patience: only thus can you live artistically in understanding no less than in art. There is no measuring of time then, a year does not matter then and ten years are as nothing. Being an

Etty Hillesum also learnt about patience from Julius Spier. She copied these words of his from an early diary into one of her letters:

> Pessimistic depressions should be regarded as creative pauses during which one's strength is being restored. If one is aware of this, then the depressions will pass more quickly. One should never feel depressed about a depression.[6]

And she concluded her diaries with a second reference to his dictum, "One must acknowledge one's pauses." On the first occasion, she protested, "but I wilt during the pauses, or so it seems to me"[7] and on the second she put the quote in uppercase and following it with three exclamation marks.[8] The acknowledgement here, perhaps, is that although inner development is apparently "on hold" we should be confident that it will resume; or maybe she and Spier mean to imply that development occurs even during "pauses"; suggesting that we should not be particularly confident that we know what is going on within us; that our self-awareness is always limited.

This short saying about "pauses" is reflected in her more mature understanding, which connects patience with "acceptance" rather more than with

artist means not calculating and counting; coming to maturity like a tree which does not force its sap, which continues to stand confidently throughout the spring storms, never doubting that summer will come. It will. But it comes only to the patient, who behave as if eternity lay before them, so carefree, still and spacious are they. Every day I keep learning it, learning it painfully, for which I am grateful: *patience* is all!'" E.T., 243. *Het Werk*, 252; Monday evening, 16 February 1942: Weer bezig de weg naar mezelf terug te vinden door deze woorden heen van Rainer Maria: – *Alles* ist austragen und dann gebären. Jeden Eindruck und jeden Keim eines Gefühls ganz in sich, im Dunkel, im Unsagbaren, Unbewußten, dem eigenen Verstande Unerreichbaren sich vollenden lassen und mit tiefer Demut und Geduld die Stunde der Niederkunft einer neuen Klarheit abwarten: das allein heißt künstlerisch leben: im Verstehen wie im Schaffen. Da gibt es kein Messen mit der Zeit, da gilt kein Jahr, und zehn Jahre sind nichts. Künstler sein heißt: nicht rechnen und zählen; reifen wie der Baum, der seine Säfte nicht drängt und getrost in den Stürmen des Frühlings steht ohne die Angst, daß dahinter kein Sommer kommen könnte. Er kommt doch. Aber er kommt nur zu den Geduldigen, die da sind, als ob die Ewigkeit vor ihnen läge, so sorglos still und weit. Ich lerne es täglich, lerne es unter Schmerzen, denen ich dankbar bin: *Geduld* ist alles!

6 E.T., 556. *Het Werk*, 589; Letter 4, To Aimé van Santen, Amsterdam, Sunday, 25 January 1942: – Pessimistische Depressionen sind als schöpferische Pausen zu betrachten, in denen sich die Kräfte wieder herstellen. Wenn man sich hiervon bewußt ist, so werden die Depressionen schneller vorüber gehen. Man soll sich nie deprimiert fühlen über eine Depression.

7 E.T., 93. *Het Werk*, 99; Thursday night, 4 September 1941: Men moet z'n "Pausen wahr haben wollen". Maar ik zit wel heel erg midden in de "Pausen", lijkt me zo tenminste.

8 E.T., 550. *Het Werk*, 583; Tuesday, 13 October 1942: MAN MUSS SEINE PAUSEN WAHRHABEN WOLLEN!!!

development or improvement, which her psychotherapeutic adventures and self-educational efforts stressed and prioritized. This more mature "patience" seems to come not from the natural energy of her personality, but from the way in which she learns to see, in particular the way in which she came to see with the eyes of sympathy (the bullying Nazi shaped in his hate by his background and insecurity)[9] but also the way in which she sought the resilience necessary to avoid the snares of hatred.[10] Patience in the mature Hillesum is more a matter of attention, or attentiveness, than of purpose. It's not the determination to try harder or to have another go tomorrow. Rather, it's the conviction that it's important to bring to the process of perception a sense of ethical priorities, to focus on what matters most. Patience entails recognizing that suffering, cruelty and evil endure, while not being entirely preoccupied by them.

Something similar could be said about the significance of Julian's most famous phrase, "sin is behovely [necessary/inevitable] but all shall be well, and all shall be well and all manner of thing shall be well." The word "shall", which is stronger than "will", implies the belief that patient attention to that which endures is preferable to being distracted by suffering and sin. Such a belief could be considered to deflect attention from what matters to more abstract concerns. It is better perhaps to see it as a shift in attention from matters of power and politics to questions of meaning and grace, for it is these that abide.

The Quality of Hope

Although Hillesum does not think about hope against the same eschatological or eternal background as Julian, it is clear from her writings that the question of how to sustain hope is integral to her spiritual quest, and it seems that as time goes by she develops this *quality* of hope. This is not to say that she becomes optimistic about the way things will work out, or that she imagines any fulfilment of a particular purpose in the future (that would be the mindset

9 See E.T., 258-259. *Het Werk*, 268-269; Friday morning, 27 February 1942.

10 For instance: "But, Lord, help me not to waste a drop of my energy on fear and anxiety, but grant me all the resilience I need to bear this day." German soldiers were already drilling at the Skating Club. And so I also prayed, "God, do not let me dissipate my strength, not the least little bit of strength, on useless hatred against these soldiers. Let me save my strength for better things." E.T., 329. *Het Werk*, 344; Thursday morning, 9 April 1942: Maar God, geef me, dat ik geen atoompje kracht verspil aan angst of onrust, maar dat ik alle krachten ter beschikking houd om deze dag te dragen. Er oefenden al Duitse soldaten op het IJsclubterrein. En ik bad ook: God, laat me geen kracht, geen snippertje kracht verliezen aan haat, aan nutteloze haat tegen deze soldaten. Ik zal m'n kracht sparen voor andere dingen.—

and approach of project, power and politics), but that she has a perspective of calm acceptance, and a positive appreciation for all that is good, even in the context of manifest evil, cruelty and suffering. She is able to see, and to attest to, the beauty of life even in the transit camp. Most importantly, this doesn't seem to be a matter of striving or effort; she is not trying to look on the bright side. Rather, it is a sense of delight and joy that comes upon her unbidden and without a depressing downside or saddening shadow.[11]

After experiencing, reflecting on, and writing up her revelations, Julian tells her reader that she "often yearned to know what our Lord's meaning was." The answer came to her "spiritual understanding."

> Be well aware: love was his meaning. Who showed you this? Love. What did he show you? Love. Why did he show it? For love. Hold fast to this and you will know and understand more of the same; but you will never understand nor know anything else from this for all eternity.[12]

In their own ways, both Hillesum and Julian refer to hope in the context of faith and love. Hillesum does this when she refers to the 13th chapter of the letter that "the Jew Paul" wrote to the people of Corinth, and Julian by quoting the triplicate with which the chapter ends, "faith, hope and love" on several occasions. On 10 June 1942, she wrote this, which is not so much about love enduring as about love triumphing through some inner transformation.

> True peace will come only when every individual finds peace within himself; when we have all vanquished and transformed our hatred for our fellow human beings of whatever race – even into love one day, although perhaps that is asking too much. It is, however, the only solution.[13]

What becomes clear in the writings of Hillesum, in particular in her record of her spiritual searching and her prayers, is that it makes no sense to think of God acting with the kind of power that is disconnected from love. Love

11 One could imagine, for instance, glimpsing a golden sunset from a concentration camp and being more impressed by the contrast with the foreground than by the sheer transcending beauty of it.

12 All quotes in this paragraph are from #86.

13 E.T., 435. *Het Werk*, 458; Saturday night, 20 June 1942: En een vrede kan alleen een echte vrede worden later, wanneer eerst ieder individu in zìchzèlf vrede sticht en haat tegen medemensen, van wat voor ras of volk ook, uitroeit en overwint en verandert in iets, dat geen haat meer is, misschien op den duur wel liefde, of is dat misschien wat veel geëist? Toch is het de enige oplossing.

is not just benevolence but mutuality, and mutuality implies vulnerability on both sides.

Julian's way of making this point is by reference to the overflowing love shown in the passion of Christ, envisaged not in the acceptance of pain and isolation as punishment, but in the offering of the endless flow of life-giving blood that is her first revelation, and then by her creative insistence that we must not only see Jesus as our kin but as our mother – with all the aspects of motherly love: intimacy, bodyliness, temporality and co-vulnerability.

This returns us to the hymn to *agape* that was penned by the Jew Paul and which speaks of the gentleness and equality of love, and reminds us that it is above all else the way of being that involves giving life and then nurturing it to maturity – that it too may love. As Julian asserts, it is love that creates the context for everything else: "for of all the attributes of the blessed Trinity it is God's will that we find most certainty and delight in his love; for love makes power and wisdom very humble towards us [...]" (#73). Love for Julian and for Hillesum is always loving-kindness.

Conclusion

It is inevitably easy to find differences between a fourteenth-century English recluse and a modern young Jewish woman who died in the Holocaust. However, the very different writings of the two authors reveal some important similarities beyond the historical and doctrinal differences. Both are profoundly aware of suffering, but are spiritually and perceptually drawn away from it to the beautiful, the real and the good. Moreover, it cannot be said that hope was eclipsed for either writer, whether by the darkness of their days or by the way in which horrendous sights and sounds played on their imagination, but that hope was not a hope for a happy ending but was one of a peace that comes through transformative acceptance and wisely focused attention.

It is clear that for both Julian and Hillesum, love is of primary importance. In their own ways, they feel and share the horizontal dimension in this and move beyond the inherited and abstract categories of patriarchal and political theology. Hillesum's sense of *agape* is developed over a period of time and includes her thoroughgoing experiments with *eros*.[14] For Julian,

14 See the thorough analysis of *agape* and *eros* in Hillesum's writings by M.C.L. Bingemer, "The Journey of Etty Hillesum from Eros to Agape," in: Klaas A.D. Smelik, Meins G.S. Coetsier

the journey to a deep understanding of *agape* comes through the equally physical form of her deathbed visions of the bloody passion of Christ.

That "*agape* never ends," as Paul wrote, is their common faith. That it never ends temporally is the basis of patience and hope. That it never ends geographically and humanly is the challenge to each individual's sense of kin and practice of kindness: a challenge mediated to all who have a sense of a greater reality beyond the negativity of suffering and sin.

About the Author

Stephen Cherry (1958) is Dean of King's College, Cambridge, with responsibility for the life of the famous College Chapel. His published works include *Healing Agony: Reimagining Forgiveness* (2012) and *The Dark Side of the Soul: An Insider's Guide to the Web of Sin* (2016). He is an Anglican priest and worked in college chaplaincy, parish, diocesan and cathedral contexts before moving to his academic, administrative and ministerial role at King's in 2014.

& Jurjen Wiersma (eds.), *The Ethics and Religious Philosophy of Etty Hillesum: Proceedings of the Etty Hillesum Conference at Ghent University, January 2014* [Supplements to The Journal of Jewish Thought and Philosophy, 28] (Leiden/Boston, MA: Brill, 2014), 68-89.

The Girl Who Could Not Kneel

Etty Hillesum and the Turn Inward

Marja Clement

Abstract

Etty Hillesum wrote in her diaries about the process of turning inward and of finding the deepest and best in herself, which she called: her God. In this process, Julius Spier played an important role. But the question remains: did he also have an influence on her discovering and developing the gesture of kneeling which was so important in her expression of herself? That still awaits an answer.

Keywords: kneeling, prayer, Julius Spier, *hineinhorchen*, *hineinhören*, Henny Tideman, inner self

Introduction

In 1941 and 1942, Etty Hillesum filled notebooks with diary entries. In these diaries, the image appears of a young woman who was seeking and struggling in life, and who went through an important transformation. Julius Spier played an important role in that process; it was he who recommended that she start keeping a diary. As she wrote, Hillesum transformed from a person with many physical and psychological ailments to become a powerful, self-assured woman with a deep confidence in life.

A particular aspect of this transformation was that she gradually discovered that she could come into contact with her deepest self through the gesture of *kneeling*.[1] In October 1942, in the last section of the extant

1 Pierre Bühler describes how the kneeling has become a gesture embedded in her entire body. Cf. Pierre Bühler, "Het lichamelijke gebed bij Etty Hillesum," in: Klaas A.D. Smelik (red.), *Etty Hillesum weer thuis in Middelburg* [Etty Hillesum Studies, 7] (Antwerpen-Apeldoorn: Garant, 2015), 85-91.

Smelik, Klaas A.D. (ed.), *The Lasting Significance of Etty Hillesum's Writings: Proceedings of the Third International Etty Hillesum Conference at Middelburg, September 2018.*
Taylor & Francis Group 2019
DOI: 10.5117/9789463722025_CLEMENT

diaries, she wrote that she remembered with tremendous gratitude Julius Spier, who had died in September 1942. She described how she learned to kneel thanks to him.

> I think that I can bear everything this life and these times have in store for me. And when the turmoil becomes too great and I am completely at my wits' end, I still have my folded hands and bended knee. A gesture that is not handed down from generation to generation with us Jews. I have had to learn it the hard way. It is my most precious inheritance from the man whose name I have almost forgotten but whose best part lives on in me.[2]

The fact that Etty Hillesum herself remarked on the connection between Spier and kneeling fuels the assumption that it was Spier who taught her this gesture.[3] It was striking that she – a Jewish woman – learned to kneel, for it is

2 E.T., 547 [revised]. *Het Werk*, 580; Saturday evening, 10 October 1942: Ik geloof, ik kan alles van dit leven en van deze tijd dragen en verwerken. En wanneer de onstuimigheid te groot is, en wanneer ik er helemaal niet meer uit weet te komen, dan blijven me altijd nog twee gevouwen handen en een gebogen knie. Het is een gebaar, dat ons Joden niet van geslacht op geslacht is overgeleverd. Ik heb het moeizaam moeten leren. Het is mijn kostbaarste erfdeel van de man, wiens naam ik al bijna vergeten heb, maar wiens beste deel ik verder leef.

3 Klaas Smelik therefore concludes on the basis of this passage that Etty Hillesum learns to kneel under the influence of Julius Spier: "Onder Spiers invloed komt Etty Hillesum nog tot een andere activiteit in de badkamer: zij leert zichzelf knielend te bidden op de ruwe bruine kokosmat, die daar op de vloer ligt." Cf. Klaas A.D. Smelik, "'M'n lieve bureau, de beste plek op deze aarde': Etty Hillesum neemt afscheid van haar vertrouwde omgeving," in: Klaas A.D. Smelik (ed.), *Etty Hillesum en de contouren van haar tijd* [Etty Hillesum Studies, 10] (Oud-Turnhout/'s-Hertogenbosch: Gompel & Svacina, 2018), p. 242. See also the remark of Janny van der Molen and Klaas Smelik in their book about Etty Hillesum, that it is not a Jewish form of praying, but that she has nevertheless overcome her shyness, because Julius Spier stimulated her to kneel while praying: 'Het was niet de Joodse manier van bidden, zoals zij zelf ook opmerkt, eerder zoals in de rooms-katholieke kerk gebruikelijk is. Zij had niettemin haar schroom overwonnen op aanraden van haar leermeester Julius Spier. Die had haar overtuigd dat het belangrijk was om neer te knielen en dan tot God te bidden.' Cf. Janny van der Molen & Klaas A.D. Smelik, *Ik zou lang willen leven. Het verhaal van Etty Hillesum, 1941-1943* (Amsterdam: Uitgeverij Balans, 2014), 131. See also: "But why, then, did Etty Hillesum adopt from Spier a ritual that he borrowed from Christianity? Why kneel down to pray as if she were a Roman Catholic?" Cf. Klaas A.D. Smelik, "Etty Hillesum and her God," in: Klaas A.D. Smelik, Ria van den Brandt & Meins G.S. Coetsier (eds), *Spirituality in the Writings of Etty Hillesum: Proceedings of the Etty Hillesum Conference at Ghent University, November 2008* [Supplements to The Journal of Jewish Thought and Philosophy, 11] (Leiden/Boston, MA: Brill, 2010), 84. Meins Coetsier mentions that Etty Hillesum was influenced by Julius Spier and by reading Augustinus: "Naast de invloed die Julius Spier op haar heeft uitgeoefend, is het mogelijk dat Augustinus heeft bijgedragen aan het leren knielen en bidden – dat wil zeggen *Gott aus ganzem Herzen zu lieben*, in de vorm van een tweegesprek met God"; Coetsier sees the influence of Spier and Augustines: "Spier en Augustinus hebben ertoe

not a Jewish manner of prayer, but rather a Christian one.[4] It was Julius Spier who had introduced her to a Christian philosophy of life and who encouraged her to study it more closely. Under his influence, she also learned to look inwards and to connect with her "inner source,"[5] the divine presence within.

Etty Hillesum herself saw Spier's influence on her adopting the kneeling posture, and suggested that it was Spier who had taught her to do it. But was she exaggerating Spier's influence slightly? Did Etty Hillesum learn to kneel under the influence of Julius Spier? I would like to answer this by a close reading of the diaries. What can we conclude from Etty Hillesum's diaries about the process she went through while "learning to kneel"? And what do we learn about Spier's influence on this process?

A First Reference to "Kneeling"

It is notable that there are references to kneeling at the very beginning of the diary. On Sunday, 16 March 1941, a week after Etty Hillesum started writing her diary, she noticed something inside her had changed. She had a new sense of life and she felt a certain freedom and inner richness, all of which was new to her.[6] Surprised, she asked herself what it was exactly that Spier had done to her. For her, there was no doubt that Spier was behind the changes. That day, while sitting on a garbage can in the sun for half an hour, she had an intense sensory experience. She became acutely aware of the sunlight falling on the branches of the chestnut tree and the sound of chirping birds.

> As I sat there like that in the sun, I bowed my head unconsciously as if to take in even more of that new sense of life. Suddenly I knew how someone can impulsively sink to his knees and find peace there, his face hidden in his folded hands. —[7]

bijgedragen dat Etty Hillesum een vorm van communiceren en 'bidden' ontdekte, dat zij van thuis niet had meegekregen, maar waar zij zich wel geleidelijk aan goed bij voelde. 'Gevouwen handen en een gebogen knie' werden haar méér en méér vertrouwd." Cf. Meins Coetsier, "'Incipit exire, qui incipit amare': Augustinus en Etty Hillesum," in: Klaas A.D. Smelik (ed.), *Etty Hillesum 1914-2014* [Etty Hillesum Studies, 6] (Antwerpen & Apeldoorn: Garant, 2014), 124, 136.

4 Cf. Coetsier, "Incipit exire, qui incipit amare," 124. Pierre Bühler mentions that she presumably adopted the kneeling from her Christian environment: Cf. Bühler, "Het lichamelijke gebed bij Etty Hillesum", 86.

5 E.T., 72. *Het Werk*, 77; Monday afternoon, 4 August 1941: innerlijke bron.

6 E.T., 23-25. *Het Werk*, 25-26; Sunday afternoon, 16 March 1941.

7 E.T., 26 [revised]. *Het Werk*, 27; Sunday afternoon, 16 March 1941: [...] en toen ik daar zo zat in die zon had ik het hoofd, onbewust, gebogen, alsof ik daardoor nog meer onderging het nieuwe

So, just one week after she started her diary, she made a reference to the gesture of kneeling. She wrote, "I bowed my head unconsciously." And she felt drawn from within to the gesture of kneeling, an action that she would often describe in her diary.

The next day, she wrote that her "centre" was becoming more anchored by the day. The many impressions she absorbed from the outside world no longer made her restless and insecure. Rather, she discovered that she could guide everything toward her inner being.[8]

Listening

Several months passed without many diary entries. On 8 June, a Sunday morning, she suddenly made a decision. "I think I'll do it," she wrote, "in the morning before work, I'll 'turn inward' half an hour, listen to what's inside me."[9] Presumably, this was a recommendation from Spier since she used the German expression *sich versenken* when she talked about it.[10] It also seems as though she still had to get used to the idea, "You could also call it meditation. But I find that word a bit disturbing. But why not? A quiet half hour with your inner self."[11]

Under Spier's influence, she had learned to curb inner confusion and chaos through a little self-discipline; in the morning, she took a cold shower and did gymnastics in the bathroom, moving all her muscles. She explained to herself that, afterwards, it was good to be silent for half an hour and to look inward, to meditate. This created a solid foundation of calm and concentration from which she could get through the day. She emphasized that this was not an easy task and that it promised to be an intensive learning process.

> Not thinking, but listening to what is going on inside you. If you do that for a while every morning before you start work, you acquire a kind of

levensgevoel. En ik doorvoelde plotseling hoe een mens stormachtig op de knieën kan zinken en dan tot rust komen, het gezicht verborgen in de gevouwen handen.—

8 E.T., 29-30. *Het Werk*, 31-32; Monday evening, 17 March 1941.

9 E.T., 56 [revised]. *Het Werk*, 59; Sunday morning, 8 June 1941: Ik geloof, dat ik het maar zal doen: 's morgens voor het begin van het werk een half uurtje "naar binnen slaan", luisteren naar wat er binnen in me zit.

10 E.T., 56. *Het Werk*, 59; Sunday morning, 8 June 1941.

11 E.T., 56 [revised]. *Het Werk*, 59; Sunday morning, 8 June 1941: Je kunt het ook mediteren noemen. Maar van dat woord ben ik nog een beetje griezelig. Maar waarom eigenlijk niet? Een stil half uur in je zelf.

> calm that illuminates the whole day. You really ought to begin each day like that, until the last shreds of worry and all petty thoughts have been swept out of your head. Just as you sweep your room clean of dust and cobwebs in the morning, so you ought also to clean your inner self every morning. And only then should you start your work.[12]

She immersed herself in the work of Jung and copied in her diary passages from Jung in which he speaks of *die Tiefen des Selbst* [the depths of the Self].[13] This inspired her to experience her own depths, her inner landscape. She would sit hunched in her chair, her head bowed low. She discovered that her inner landscape was as wide as a Russian steppe, "My inner landscape consists of large, wide plains, infinitely wide, with hardly a horizon in sight – one plain merging into the next."[14] These experiences gave her a sense of well-being, of endlessness and tranquillity.

A few days later, however, her mood changed. The imminent and ominous reality of war, with "arrests, terror, concentration camps, the arbitrary removal of fathers, sisters and brothers,"[15] made her question the meaning of life. She felt an overwhelming sense of powerlessness and that everything was haphazard – reflections that made her deeply depressed. She wrote the next morning that these thoughts caused her to contemplate whether she could live any further. But she fought her way through that and emerged stronger than before.

A Second Reference to "Kneeling"

In the summer weeks that followed, she again did not often write in her diary. In the one entry on 4 July 1941, a theme emerged, and although this theme was only mentioned in a subordinate clause, it is of particular interest

12 E.T., 59 [revised]. *Het Werk*, 62; Tuesday morning, 10 June 1941: Niet denken, maar luisteren naar wat er binnen in je is. Wanneer je dat 's morgens, voor je aan het werk gaat, een poosje doet, dan geeft dat een rust, die de hele dag doorstraalt. Eigenlijk hoor je de dag zo te beginnen: tot alle flarden van gepieker en gedachtetjes eerst zijn weggevaagd uit je hoofd. Zoals je 's morgens stof en spinrag uit de kamer veegt, zo hoor je ook jezelf 's morgens innerlijk schoon te maken. En dan kun je pas beginnen met je werk.

13 E.T., 60. *Het Werk*, 63; Wednesday morning, 11 June 1941.

14 E.T., 60 [revised]. *Het Werk*, 64; Wednesday morning, 11 June 1941: Mijn innerlijke landschap bestaat uit grote, wijde vlaktes, oneindig wijd, er is nauwelijks een horizon, de ene vlakte gaat over in de andere.

15 E.T., 62 [revised]. *Het Werk*, 65; Saturday evening, 14 June 1941: Weer arrestaties, terreur, concentratiekampen, willekeurig weghalen van vaders, zussen, broers.

for the current project. She remembered a time when she was staying in Deventer and mentioned that she was so impressed by the wheat fields there that she almost fell to her knees.

> In Deventer the days were like great sunny plains, each one a long, uninterrupted whole; there was contact with God and with every person I met, possibly because I met so few. There were wheat fields I shall never forget, whose beauty nearly brought me to my knees; there were the banks of the IJssel with the colourful parasols and the thatched roofs and the patient horses. And the sun, which I drank in through all my pores.[16]

Hineinhorchen

She wrote in her diary again in August 1941. Her entry reveals that she longed for peace, clarity and balance, but instead she felt an inner oppression. And then she used the term *hineinhorchen* for the first time – a German word meaning "to listen carefully to your inner voice." She wrote that she must eat and sleep well, not think and worry too much, and that she must continue to listen carefully to herself, "*hineinhorchen*."[17]

> What I do is *hineinhorchen* (to hearken to) (I think this word is untranslatable). I listen to my inner self, to others, to the world. I listen very intently, with my whole being, and try to fathom the meaning of things. I am always very tense and attentive, I keep looking for something but don't know what. [...] I am working towards something, part of some greater framework, but it is all still undefined and yet it is going somewhere, striving towards a synthesis.[18]

16 E.T., 68 [revised]. *Het Werk*, 71; Friday 4 July 1941: In Deventer waren de dagen grote zonnige vlaktes, iedere dag van één groot, ongebroken geheel, er was contact met God en met alle mensen, waarschijnlijk omdat ik nauwelijks een mens zag. Er waren korenvelden, die ik nooit meer zal vergeten en waarbij ik bijna neergeknield was, er was die IJssel met de kleurige parasol en met het rieten dak en de geduldige paarden. En dan de zon, die ik door alle poriën liet binnenkomen.

17 E.T., 72. *Het Werk*, 77; Monday afternoon, 4 August 1941. For the meaning of the verb "hineinhorchen" see the article of Peter de Wind, "*Gelatenheid* volgens Meister Eckhart en Etty Hillesum", in: Klaas A.D. Smelik (ed.), *Etty Hillesum in weerwil van het Joodse vraagstuk* [Etty Hillesum Studies, 8] (Antwerpen/Apeldoorn: Garant, 2016), 121-138, especially p. 132-134.

18 E.T., 90-91 [revised]. *Het Werk*, 96; Saturday evening, 23 August 1941: Wat ik doe is "hineinhorchen" (dit lijkt me onvertaalbaar). "Hineinhorchen" in mezelf, in de anderen, in de wereld. Ik luister heel intensief met m'n hele wezen en tracht te luisteren tot op de bodem der dingen. Ik ben altijd strak gespannen en vol aandacht, ik zoek naar iets en weet nog niet naar wat. [...]

This is followed by a key passage in which Etty Hillesum expressed exactly how she looked inside herself and what she experienced when doing so. We readers after-the-fact know that she will discover kneeling and that this gesture will become important to her. In this passage, however, we can already read what happened when she knelt and why the motion of kneeling was bound to become essential to her.

> There is a really deep well inside me. And in it dwells God. Sometimes, I am there too. But more often stones and grit block the well, and God is buried beneath. Then He must be dug out again. I imagine that there are people who pray with their eyes turned heavenward. They seek God outside themselves. And there are those who bow their head and bury it in their hands. I think that these seek God inside.[19]

The fundamental difference between an outward prayer and searching within one's self by listening carefully tells us how purposefully Etty Hillesum was searching for "inner contentment."

Hineinhören

On 4 September 1941, Hillesum wrote that she was once again unhappy. She had broken down and did not know where to look. She could imagine that some people would turn to the bottle but she knew she had to get through the difficulty in a sober state with a clear head. Then she did something that turned out to be a remedy against those moments of deep despair.

> "Listen to my inner self." Yes, indeed. So I withdrew to the farthest corner of my little room, sat on the floor, squeezed myself in between two walls, my head bowed low. Yes. And sat there. Absolutely still, contemplating my navel so to speak, in the pious hope that new sources of inspiration would bubble up inside me. My heart was once again frozen and would

Ik werk ergens naar toe, ik werk in een groot kader, maar het is nog onbestemd, en tòch gaat het ergens naar toe, het streeft naar synthese.

19 E.T., 91-92 [revised]. *Het Werk*, 97; Tuesday afternoon, 26 August 1941: Binnen in me zit een heel diepe put. En daarin zit God. Soms kan ik erbij. Maar vaker liggen er stenen en gruis voor die put, dan is God begraven. Dan moet hij weer opgegraven worden. Ik stel me voor, dat er mensen zijn, die bidden met hun ogen naar de hemel geheven. Die zoeken God buiten zich. Er zijn ook mensen, die het hoofd diep buigen en in de handen verbergen, ik denk, dat die God binnen in zich zoeken.

> not melt; every outlet was blocked and my brain squeezed by a large vice. And what I am waiting for whenever I sit huddled up like that is for something to give, for something to start flowing inside me.[20]

Here she used a new term: *hineinhören*. She did this whenever she felt a sense of despair closing in. She was experiencing deep unhappiness, severe headaches, and intense sorrow. In the instance described, she crawled across the floor to a corner, bent her head toward her navel and listened to what came up inside her. If one looks for a sign of Spier's influence here, one will find no evidence to suggest that it was Spier who advised her to deal with her problems in this way. She had spent the evening alone and had not gone to see Spier, "It's a good job that rogue wasn't at home tonight. Otherwise I would have rushed to him again."[21] I believe that this method, this crawling into a corner and bowing her head, was a method she devised herself. She noted that this method of being passive and listening was hers. It created an openness, in which she came into contact with a calm, vast eternity.

> I have found my remedy. I just have to crouch, huddle up on the ground in a corner and listen to what is going on inside me.[22]

Apparently, this was the first time she had tried this, making herself small and huddling in a corner. Anyone who reads this part of the diary carefully, will not find any reference to conversations with Spier on this subject. While it is true that the use of the German *hineinhorchen* and *hineinhören* suggests that she had learned these terms from Spier,[23] nowhere does she mention that Spier suggested that huddling in a corner would be a remedy in

20 E.T., 92 [revised]. *Het Werk*, 98; Thursday evening, 4 September 1941: Ik wil hineinhören. Jawel. Nou, toen ben ik in de uiterste hoek van m'n kamertje op de grond gaan zitten, ingeklemd in een hoek tussen 2 muren, m'n kop heel diep naar beneden. Ja, en daar zat ik. Heel stil. A.h.w. starende op m'n navel, in vrome afwachting, of er nieuwe krachten in me wilden opborrelen. M'n hart zat weer in een klem, het wilde niet vervloeien van binnen, alle afvoerkanalen weer dichtgeslibd en de hersens in een zware schroef ingeklemd. En wanneer ik daar zo inelkaargedoken zit, wacht ik tot er iets wil smelten en iets wil gaan vloeien in me.

21 E.T., 92 [revised]. *Het Werk*, 98; Thursday evening, 4 September 1941: Het is goed, dat die schurk vanavond niet thuis was. Anders was ik er weer heen gerend.

22 E.T., 93 [revised]. *Het Werk*, 99-100; Friday morning, 5 September 1941: M'n remedie weet ik nu. Ik moet maar ineenhurken in een hoekje op de grond en zo in elkaar gedoken luisteren naar wat er binnen in me is.

23 Ria van den Brandt explains that the psychological vocabulary of Julius Spier and Carl Gustav Jung is taken over and is woven into the life program: "Het dieptepsychologisch vocabulaire van Julius Spier en Carl Gustav Jung wordt overgenomen en in het levensprogramma verweven." Cf. Ria van den Brandt, *Denken met Etty Hillesum* (Zoetermeer: Meinema, 2006), 37.

a crisis. She was the one who discovered this method and she experimented on her own to see if it worked. On 11 June 1941, she had already noted that, after reading the work of Jung, she searched for *die Tiefen des Selbst*, while sitting hunched on her chair with her head bowed low.[24] That was perhaps the first stage of her experiment.

Kneeling

On 24 September 1941, a few weeks after her use of the word *hineinhorchen*, she wrote that something suddenly happened in the bathroom – a room where she spent much time bathing in cold water, doing her gymnastics exercises, and savouring time alone.

> This afternoon I suddenly found myself kneeling on the brown coconut mat in the bathroom, my head hidden in my dressing gown, which was slung over the broken wicker chair. Kneeling doesn't really come easily to me, I feel embarrassed. Why? Probably because of the critical, rational, atheistic part of me. And yet every so often I have a great urge to kneel down with my face in my hands and to find some peace and to listen to that hidden source within me.[25]

That was the first time she wrote in her diary that she had knelt. On that Wednesday afternoon, she suddenly gave in to a great feeling that had been urging her on. She knelt in the bathroom, perhaps a strange choice of room, but a room that was already the only place in the house where she could be alone, undisturbed, and where she was accustomed to engaging in self-reflection.[26] She initially thought that she was not good at kneeling but she was actually feeling embarrassment. That was the voice of the atheist-still-present inside her. Nevertheless, on the spur of the moment, she sank to her knees.

24 E.T., 60. *Het Werk*, 63-64; Wednesday morning, 11 June 1941.
25 E.T., 103 [revised]. *Het Werk*, 109; Wednesday afternoon, 24 September 1941: Vanmiddag vond ik mezelf plotseling geknield op de bruine cocosmat in de badkamer, m'n hoofd verborgen in m'n badjas, die op die kapotte rieten stoel slingerde. Ik kan helemaal niet goed knielen, er is een soort gêne in me. Waarvoor? Waarschijnlijk voor het critische, rationele, atheïstische stuk, dat er ook in me zit. En toch is er af en toe een grote drang in me neer te knielen, met de handen voor m'n gezicht en op die manier een vrede te vinden en te luisteren naar een verborgen bron in me.
26 E.T., 7. *Het Werk*, 7; Sunday evening, 9 March 1941; E.T., 38. *Het Werk*, 41, Friday morning, 21 March 1941.

The following day, she wrote in her diary her memory of a conversation she had had with her friend, Henny Tideman, known as "Tide." The passage provides interesting information and contains a number of interesting clues.

> It was only a week ago that I had that talk with her, when she said, "In that, respect too, I am like a child. If I don't know what to do, I kneel down in the middle of my room and ask God." And when it was over and we were out on the doorstep, I gave her a kiss on the spur of the moment, and then she said that she wouldn't have dared to do that, and then she said, "Little Etty," and I, "Tide," and then I cycled off. But now I am gradually beginning to process that evening.[27]

A week before, on Thursday, 18 September, Tide had told Etty that she knelt when she no longer knew what to do.[28] What was the subject of the conversation Hillesum was recalling? Did Henny Tideman's remark ignite something in Etty Hillesum? Almost a week later, on 24 September, she noted for the first time in her diary that she knelt. It would appear that Tideman had kindled a change in Hillesum.

"The Girl Who Could Not Kneel"

In the months that followed, Hillesum wrote in her diary almost every day. Occasionally, she described how she crawled across the floor to a corner of her room to listen, to look inward, and to find peace in herself. This seemed to be her answer to being overstimulated by the outside world. On 21 November, she wrote,

27 E.T., 106 [revised]. *Het Werk*, 113; Thursday morning, 25 September 1941: Is het pas een week geleden, dat gesprek met haar, waarin ze zei: Ook daarin ben ik als een kind, als ik niet weet wat ik doen moet, kniel ik midden in m'n kamer en vraag het God. En toen na afloop buiten op de stoep, gaf ik haar spontaan een zoen en toen zei zij: dat durfde ik niet te doen en toen zei ze: Etteke en ik Tide en toen fietste ik weg. Maar nú begin ik pas langzamerhand die avond te verwerken.

28 Cf. F. Joke Vrijlandt-Postma, "Tide – Mijn Tante Henny: Persoonlijke herinneringen aan Henny Tideman," in: Klaas A.D. Smelik (ed.), *Etty Hillesum en het pad naar zelfverwerkelijking* [Etty Hillesum Studies, 9] (Antwerpen-Apeldoorn: Garant, 2017), 211-219; Ria van den Brandt, "Vriendschap op het tweede gezicht: Aantekeningen bij de vriendschap van Etty Hillesum en Henny Tideman," in: Ria van den Brandt & Klaas A.D. Smelik (eds.), *Etty Hillesum in context* [Etty Hillesum Studies, 2] (Assen: Van Gorcum, 2007), 4-15.

> It is odd that while I have been so full of creative impulses lately, and would like to write a novella – The girl who could not kneel, or something like that [...][29]

The next day, she wrote about the shame she felt in expressing her own truth.

> There is a sort of melancholy and tenderness as well as a little wisdom somewhere inside me that cry to be let out. Sometimes several different dialogues run through me at the same time, images and figures, moods, a sudden flash of something that must be my very own truth. Love for human beings that must be hard fought for. Not through politics or a party, but in myself. Still a lot of false shame to get rid of. And there is God. The girl who could not kneel but learned to do so on the rough coconut mat in an untidy bathroom. Such things are often more intimate even than sex. I would like to tell the story of this internal process I am experiencing, the story of the girl who gradually learned to kneel, in the fullest possible way. —[30]

She strived to describe and articulate the process she was going through, and again she repeated the title she would give the work, "The girl who could not kneel." The process that had taken place within her was very intimate, and it resulted in a kind of timidity to speak about it openly.

In the cold, dark days of December, she liked to sit in front of the small lamp at her desk in the early morning. There she sought the tranquillity of study and contemplation, calling this "the best hour of the day."[31] While sitting at her desk on a dark, quiet Sunday morning, 14 December 1941, she wrote that the night before, she suddenly fell to her knees in the middle of the room. It had just come to her naturally.

29 E.T., 145 [revised]. *Het Werk*, 153; Friday, 21 November 1941: Interessant is het, dat terwijl ik de laatste tijd vol scheppingsdrang zit en schrijven zou willen, een novelle: Het meisje, dat niet knielen kon of zo iets [...]

30 E.T., 148 [revised]. *Het Werk*, 156; Saturday morning, 22 November 1941: Er is ergens een weemoed en een tederheid en ook wat wijsheid in me, die daar een vorm zoekt. Soms lopen er hele dialogen door me heen. Beelden en figuren. Stemmingen. Het plotseling doorbreken naar iets wat m'n eigen waarheid zal moeten worden. Liefde voor de mensen, waarvoor gevochten moet worden. Maar niet in de politiek of in een partij, maar in jezelf. Maar nog valse schaamte om ervoor uit te komen. En dan God. "Het meisje dat niet knielen kon en het toch leerde op de ruwe cocosmat in een slordige badkamer." Maar deze dingen zijn haast nog intiemer, dan de sexuele. Dit proces in mij, van het meisje dat leerde knielen, zou ik willen uitbeelden in al z'n nuanceringen.

31 E.T., 174. *Het Werk*, 183; Friday morning, 12 December 1941.

> Last night, shortly before going to bed, I suddenly fell to my knees in the middle of this large room, between the steel chairs and the mat. Almost automatically. Forced to the ground by something stronger than myself. Some time ago I said to myself, "I am a kneeler in training." I was still embarrassed by this act, as intimate as gestures of love that cannot be put into words either, except by a poet.[32]

What is new here, is that she did not kneel in the bathroom where her privacy was protected, but in another room of the house where anyone could have entered at any moment. Here again, she talked about the intimacy of the gesture and about her timidity and embarrassment.

"Knien Sie auch?"

December days brought clarity, and reflection followed. As she wrote, reflecting upon the previous days, she mentioned conversations she had engaged in with Spier and noted that there was still so much she wanted to study and explore. She wanted to understand the interplay of all the relationships of life. Her words were: "steadfast, constant, patient."[33]

And then she suddenly described how she recently had asked Spier if he also knelt. She asked him in passing, casually, while she was busy doing something else.

> And while I was sewing on a button: "I must ask you something." And after a lot of urging on his part, I finally did ask the question, "Do you kneel as well?" I still can't write about it. Later.[34]

This is an important passage in our quest to find out the extent of Spier's influence. Apparently, she had been wondering whether Spier also knelt.

32 E.T., 181 [revised]. *Het Werk*, 190; Sunday morning, 14 December 1941: Gisterenavond, vlak voor het naar bed gaan, lag ik opeens geknield midden in deze grote kamer, tussen de stalen stoelen en op het lichte matting. Zó maar vanzelf. Naar de grond gedwongen door iets, dat sterker was dan ik zelf. Een tijd geleden zei ik tegen mezelf: ik oefen me in het knielen. Ik geneerde me nog te veel voor dat gebaar, dat even intiem is als de gebaren der liefde, waarover men ook niet spreken kan, als men geen dichter is.

33 E.T., 197. *Het Werk*, 206; Sunday morning, 21 December 1941: gestadig, bestendig, geduldig.

34 E.T., 197-198. *Het Werk*, 206; Sunday morning, 21 December 1941: En onder het aanzetten van een knoop: Ich muß Sie etwas fragen. En na heel lang aandringen van zijn kant, kwam mijn vraag eindelijk: Knien Sie auch? Ik kan dit nog helemaal niet opschrijven. Later.

After 24 September 1941, she went through a process in which she discovered kneeling. And now, in December, she wanted to know whether Spier also knelt.

We can ask ourselves: Had she never spoken to him about "The girl who could not kneel"? Was the act of kneeling so intimate for her, was it so delicate, was she so vulnerable, and was kneeling so new – that she had not even talked to Spier about it? In any case, after the months spent discovering kneeling, she wondered whether Spier also knelt. And when she asked him, it was not open and direct, not candid. It was asked shyly, timidly, casually, while she was sewing on a button.

First, she said that she had something to ask him. Suddenly, she dared not go through with it. He had to press her. Apparently, she did not find it easy to ask. And then finally, she asked: "Do you also kneel?" She had become a close friend of this man, whom she loved and desired, but she still addressed him with the formal *Sie*: "*Knien Sie auch*?" And she couldn't bring herself to write down his answer. This subject was still so fragile, so delicate. She could not find the right words.

This passage gives us a clear answer to our question whether or not Etty Hillesum learned to kneel under the influence of Julius Spier. The answer here seems loud and clear: No. It was only after she had gone through months of transformation on her own, in which she learned to kneel, and discovered what kneeling meant to her, that she finally asked Spier if he also knelt. Therefore, she could not have learned this act from him. It is doubtful that Spier ever spoke about kneeling for prayer. The fact that Etty Hillesum is unsure whether he kneels or not, suggests that they had never spoken about it before.

The following day, she mentioned more questions she wanted to ask Spier about kneeling because it appears that he said he did indeed kneel. She wanted to know exactly where and how he knelt and what he prayed for.

> I know the intimate gestures he uses with women, but I still want to know the gestures he uses with God. He prays every night. Does he kneel down in the middle of his small room? And does he bury his heavy head in his great, good hands? And what does he say? Does he kneel before he takes his dentures out or afterward? That time in Arnhem: "Let me show you how I look without my teeth. I look so old and so 'knowing'."
> "The girl who could not kneel." This morning, in the grey dawn, in a fit of nervous agitation, I suddenly found myself on the floor, between Han's stripped bed and his typewriter, huddled up, my head on the ground. As if I were trying to seize peace by force. And when Han came in and

seemed a bit taken aback by the spectacle, I told him I was looking for a button. But that was a lie. —[35]

The passage about Han Wegerif, who entered his bedroom while she was kneeling on the ground between his bed and the typewriter, is rather amusing. The lie she told the surprised Han, that she was looking for a button, indicates that she was still too shy to speak openly about kneeling.

A Natural Impulse

In the months that followed, Hillesum mentioned on a number of occasions that she found herself suddenly kneeling, and that she allowed herself to be guided by what was going on inside her.[36] She often knelt when she was overwhelmed by heaviness or restlessness, and almost always as a "sudden" impulse that emerged unexpectedly. It is also noticeable that she did not usually have a fixed place where she went calmly and quietly with a preconceived plan to kneel. Rather, she knelt wherever she happened to be in the house at the moment the impulse seized her.[37] She knelt in the middle of the room,[38] beside the stove in the living room,[39] near the white table,[40] in front of her bed,[41] in a corner,[42] in the living room, between the breadcrumbs on the carpet,[43] near the pearwood bookcase,[44] in Dicky's

35 E.T., 198. *Het Werk*, 207; Monday afternoon, 22 December 1941: Zijn intieme gebaren tegenover de vrouwen ken ik en nu zou ik nog willen kennen: de gebaren, waarmee hij met God omgaat. Hij bidt iedere avond. Knielt hij midden in die kleine kamer? En verbergt hij z'n zware kop achter die grote, goede handen? En wat zegt hij dan? En knielt hij vóórdat hij z'n gebit uit z'n mond heeft of daarna. Toen in Arnhem: Ich werde Ihnen mal zeigen wie ich aussehe ohne Zähne. Dann sehe ich so alt und so "wissend" aus. "Von dem Mädchen, das nicht knien konnte". Vanochtend, in de grauwe schemering, in een aanvechting van onvrede, vond ik mezelf opeens op de grond, geknield tussen Han's afgehaalde bed en m'n schrijfmachine, in elkaar gedoken, m'n hoofd op de grond. Een gebaar soms om vrede af te willen dwingen. En toen Han binnenkwam en wat verbaasd dat tafereel aanzag zei ik, dat ik een knoop zocht. Maar dit laatste is niet waar.—

36 E.T., 212. *Het Werk*, 221; Wednesday evening, 31 December 1941.

37 E.T., 301. *Het Werk*, 313; Friday morning, 27 March 1942.

38 E.T., 216. *Het Werk*, 225; Monday morning, 5 January 1942.

39 E.T., 250. *Het Werk*, 260; Saturday morning, 21 February 1942.

40 E.T., 256. *Het Werk*, 266; Friday morning, 27 February 1942.

41 E.T., 290. *Het Werk*, 302; Friday morning, 20 March 1942; E.T., 438. *Het Werk*, 462, Monday evening, 22 June 1942.

42 E.T., 296. *Het Werk*, 308; Sunday evening, 22 March 1942.

43 E.T., 329. *Het Werk*, 343; Thursday morning, 9 April 1942.

44 E.T., 418. *Het Werk*, 440; Monday morning, 15 June 1942.

room.[45] When she worked for the Jewish Council, she once suddenly had an urge to kneel in the middle of the stone floor among all the people.[46] The impulse to kneel came over her like a wave.[47] She wrote, "sometimes a natural impulse to kneel runs through my entire body."[48]

Even in Camp Westerbork, kneeling remained important to her. In the evening she conversed with her friend Joseph Vleeschhouwer, sitting on the moor under the stars. There she realized that one was at home under the sky: "We *are* 'at home.' Under the sky. In every place on earth, if only we carry everything within us."[49]

> It took me several nights before I could bring myself to speak of it to him, this most intimate of all intimate feelings. And I wanted to say it to him as much as I wanted to give him a gift. Yes, and you know, I ran out of the barracks that night. It was so beautiful. And then I, and then I – oh, it was so beautiful. And not until one night later could I put it into words: I knelt there then facing the great moor. It made him quite breathless and hushed and he looked at me and said, "How beautiful you are. —"[50]

Conclusion

Three months after Etty Hillesum had started to kneel, after she had already written about kneeling on several occasions (between September and December 1941) and had called herself "the girl who could not kneel," she wondered whether Spier also knelt when he prayed. She had to overcome a certain shyness to ask him this question. From this, it can be deduced that Spier had not been the one who taught her to kneel. Her relating to him on this subject came after the fact.

45 E.T., 496-497. *Het Werk*, 525; Sunday evening, 19 July 1942.

46 E.T., 500. *Het Werk*, 529; Thursday evening, 23 July 1942.

47 E.T., 328. *Het Werk*, 343; Wednesday evening, 8 April 1942.

48 E.T., 320 [revised]. *Het Werk*, 334; Friday morning, 3 April 1942: door mijn hele lichaam gaat soms een natuurlijke beweging van te willen knielen.

49 E.T., 524. *Het Werk*, 555; Sunday evening, 20 September 1942: Op iedere plek van deze aarde is men "thuis", wanneer men alles in zich draagt.

50 E.T., 524-525 [revised]. *Het Werk*, 555; Sunday evening, 20 September 1942: Ik heb er toen avonden lang over gedaan, voor ik het kon vertellen aan hem, het intiemste van het intiemste. En ik wilde het hem toch zo graag zeggen als om hem een geschenk te geven. Ja weet je, toen ben ik 's nachts m'n barak uitgelopen. Het was zo mooi weet je. En toen heb ik, toen heb ik, o, het was zo mooi. En een avond later pas kon ik het er uit brengen: toen heb ik geknield daar voor die grote hei. Hij was er helemaal ademloos en stil van en keek me aan en zei: Wat ben je toch mooi.—

But it appears that Spier himself did indeed kneel. A few passages in the diaries make clear that this gesture was also a way for him to express himself while praying.[51] Both Etty Hillesum and Julius Spier learned this, yet both were Jewish and this gesture is not a Jewish way to pray. Further research is necessary to understand how they both came to kneel. Perhaps Julius Spier learned from Augustine, whose work he studied. Etty Hillesum also studied Augustine, and other religious authors, and they might have influenced her too. And of course, the poet Rilke spoke about kneeling.[52] Given his importance to Hillesum, maybe he inspired her.

From the diaries, we know that Henny Tideman's remark that she often knelt, created a flash of recognition for Etty Hillesum. Tideman, a Christian, may have started Etty Hillesum's process of learning to kneel. At the same time, we must not overestimate Tideman's influence. Etty Hillesum had chosen independently to learn this gesture, a gesture that fascinated her. There are no indications that she talked with Tideman about her own learning process. Kneeling for Hillesum was the most intimate of all intimacies. In the diaries, there are only two persons mentioned with whom she talked about kneeling: Julius Spier and her friend Jopie Vleeschhouwer, with whom she had a deep friendship in Camp Westerbork.

There are a few other signals which indicate that Etty Hillesum followed an individual path. Her belief in God was authentic and not influenced by dogmas. The authenticity of her belief in God emerged from the fact that she sought God within, something that is not usual in Christianity. Also, Hillesum's speaking with God, using the informal form *je* instead of *u*, is not at all common in Christianity. Furthermore, it is not an almighty God, but a powerless God, with whom she speaks. Hillesum's kneeling was an authentic gesture, a way of expressing and shaping her own path. It was not the typical Roman Catholic gesture, where the body stays upright, the head bowed, and the hands folded. Etty Hillesum was kneeling, deeply bent, with her head to the ground, her face hidden in her hands. "Sometimes, in moments of deep gratitude, kneeling down becomes an overwhelming urge, head deeply bowed, hands before my face."[53] This gesture was akin to the gesture she used when she wanted to turn inward; huddling on the floor in a corner of the room, making herself very small.

51 E.T., 198. *Het Werk*, 207; Monday afternoon, 22 December 1941; E.T., 493. *Het Werk*, 521; Wednesday morning, 15 July 1942.

52 E.T., 351. *Het Werk*, 368; Monday morning, 27 April 1942.

53 E,.T., 320. *Het Werk*, 334; Friday morning, 3 April 1942: Soms, in momenten van grote dankbaarheid, is het me een onweerstaanbare behoefte neer te knielen, het hoofd diep gebogen, de handen voor het gezicht.

The diaries clearly show the overall influence of Julius Spier. He played an essential role in Etty Hillesum's spiritual development. She was very conscious about the fact that she owed a lot to Spier, and she was very thankful to him. He stimulated her search for God. He encouraged her to take time every day in the morning to turn inward. He created important conditions for the spontaneous emergence of her individual learning. But he also gave her the possibility of going her own way, of following her own path, independently. He may have stimulated her to pray, but the physical form, the gesture that she developed for praying, she learned on her own. He inspired her to listen to something inside, very deep, a hidden source. And she discovered the deepest and best inside herself: her God. But the movement that she used to go inside, the physical act of kneeling – that she discovered and developed by herself, independent of Spier. After his death, she realized how Spier had made it possible for her to discover kneeling, as we see in the quotation at the beginning of this article. Thus, indirectly, Spier had an influence. But the process by which she discovered kneeling was her own, and it proved to be invaluable to her. It was her "most precious inheritance."

About the Author

Marja Clement (1963) received her PhD from the University of Amsterdam with a linguistic thesis on the prose of the female Dutch writer Josepha Mendels. For ten years, she was Lecturer and Senior Assistant in Dutch Studies at the University of Zurich. At the moment, she is Lecturer at the Institute for Dutch Language Education of the University of Amsterdam.

Etty Hillesum and Charlotte Salomon

Pregnancy as a Theme in Their Lives and Works

Denise de Costa

Abstract
Both Etty Hillesum and Charlotte Salomon were extremely creative and productive young women. They were women of child-bearing age during the Second World War, but their offspring are cultural. In this text, De Costa reflects on the differences and similarities in the lives and legacies of Charlotte Salomon and Etty Hillesum, emphasizing the connection between fertility in a biological as well as cultural sense. Hereby, the author is influenced and inspired by the work of three women: the writer and philosopher Luce Irigaray, the fondly remembered Dutch philosopher Rina Van der Haegen, and the writer and philosopher Hélène Cixous.

Keywords: Charlotte Salomon, fertility, sociomaternal productivity, motherhood, pregnancy, abortion

Charlotte Salomon, a Jewish woman born in Berlin in 1917, left Nazi Germany in January 1939 and lived in exile with her maternal grandparents in the south of France on the famous Côte d'Azur. While there, she stayed on a large seaside estate owned by an American woman, Ottilie Moore. In Berlin, Charlotte had been a student at the art academy. Her passion was drawing. In the South of France from 1940 until her deportation in 1943, she created 1325 small gouaches, most of which form a rich series known as *Leben? oder Theater?*

Both Etty Hillesum and Charlotte Salomon were extremely creative and productive young women. They were women of child-bearing age during the Second World War, but due to circumstances, their offspring are solely cultural. Here, I will reflect on the differences and similarities in the lives

Smelik, Klaas A.D. (ed.), *The Lasting Significance of Etty Hillesum's Writings: Proceedings of the Third International Etty Hillesum Conference at Middelburg, September 2018.*
Taylor & Francis Group 2019
DOI: 10.5117/9789463722025_COSTA

and legacies of Charlotte Salomon and Etty Hillesum, emphasizing the connection between fertility in a biological sense and fertility in a cultural sense. I will focus on Etty Hillesum first and discuss the theme of pregnancy, and then address this same theme with Charlotte Salomon. In this investigation, I am influenced and inspired by the work of three women: the writer and philosopher Luce Irigaray, the fondly-remembered Dutch philosopher Rina Van der Haegen, and the writer and philosopher Hélène Cixous.

Etty Hillesum

Etty Hillesum was a freethinker in many ways, including in her approach to religion. Her image of God had a strong mother-child dynamic. She did not believe in a powerful God. She saw God as small and dependent, and she offered to protect him and to guide him safely through all hardship. It is as if she were pregnant with God: "living one's life with God and in God and God in me."[1] Surrounded by a system intent on the destruction of the Jewish people, she wanted to safeguard God from outside evil and continued to focus on the new life she felt within, writing in her diary,

> I would so much like to help prepare for the new age and to carry that which is indestructible within me intact into the new age, which is bound to come, for I can feel it growing inside me, every day.[2]

This symbolic pregnancy contrasted sharply to the unplanned and unwanted pregnancy she actually faced during this same period. The confirmation of this pregnancy led to the following outpouring of emotion.

> The mother instinct is something of which I am completely devoid. I explain it like this to myself: life is a vale of tears and all human beings are miserable creatures, so I cannot take the responsibility for bringing yet another unhappy creature into the world.[3]

1 E.T., 439 [revised]. *Het Werk*, 463; Monday night, 22 June 1942: [...] het is een leven met God en in God en God in mij [...].

2 E.T., 497. *Het Werk*, 526; Monday evening, 20 July 1942: Ik wil zo graag blijven leven om de nieuwe tijd te helpen voorbereiden en om dat onverwoestbare in mij behouden over te dragen naar de nieuwe tijd, die zeker zal komen, ze groeit immers al in mij, iedere dag, ik voel het toch?

3 E.T., 164. *Het Werk*, 173; Wednesday morning, 3 December 1941: Moederschapsinstinct ontbreekt geloof ik volledig bij me. Voor mezelf motiveer ik dat als volgt: In de grond vind ik het leven toch een grote lijdensweg en alle mensen maar ongelukkige wezens en ik kan voor

She decided to abort her pregnancy, fighting the unborn life first with quinine and cognac, and when that failed, with hot water and – in her own words – "bloodcurdling instruments."[4] Afterwards, she was convinced she had made the right decision, not only because of the war but more importantly, because of her fear of hereditary mental illness. Her mother had been admitted to a psychiatric hospital several times and both of her brothers were psychiatric patients as well. Very caringly, responsibly, and paradoxically full of love for the unborn child, she opted to end the pregnancy.

The fact that Etty Hillesum did not want to become a mother in the literal sense, did not detract from the pro/creative abilities that she put to use. In the last year of her life, her reasons for rejecting actual motherhood were the same as those for assuming symbolic motherhood.

My interpretation of the choices Etty Hillesum made is indebted to the philosophical reflections of Luce Irigaray, who wrote on the relationship between womanhood and motherhood. While Irigaray's illustrious predecessor Simone de Beauvoir advised women against motherhood because she felt that it stood in the way of their emancipation, Irigaray rejected this strategy because of its intrinsic danger of turning women into men, and advocated for a re-evaluation rather than a rejection of motherhood. She wrote,

> We [women] bring many things into the world apart from children. We give birth to many other things apart from children: love, desire, language, art, social things, political things, but this kind of creativity has been forbidden to us for centuries. We must take back this maternal creative dimension. That is our birthright as women.[5]

Irigaray's re-evaluation created room for women and their potential motherhood in the symbolic order, an order that was also radically changed by women taking their place in it.

Following in Irigaray's footsteps, the Dutch philosopher Rina Van der Haegen also pleaded for a place for women in the symbolic order where they could develop without having to deny who they were. In response to the traditionally restricted role of women as mothers, and inveighing against their exclusion from the symbolic order, Van der Haegen formulated the notion of "sociomaternal productivity,"

mezelf niet de verantwoording op me nemen de mensheid met nog een ongelukkig creatuur te vermeerderen.

4 E.T., 168. *Het Werk*, 177; Saturday morning, 6 December 1941: [...] griezelige instrumenten [...].

5 Cf. Luce Irigaray, *An Ethics of Sexual Difference* (Ithaca, NY: Cornell University Press, 1993), 18.

> Independent of actual motherhood, of reproduction in the strict sense of the word, I want to use the word conglomerate "sociomaternal productivity" to create an opening for a social actualization of her pro/creative powers.[6]

I think "sociomaternal productivity" is ultimately where Etty Hillesum was headed on her inward journey. In her diary, she tentatively wrote of her wish to help her fellow human beings. Her desire to be socially productive and treat others with love was stronger than a traditional motherly feeling. She went to Camp Westerbork to be a social worker, to take on the impossible task of ameliorating other people's suffering. Like a midwife assisting in childbirth, she brought God out of the hearts of others. She was not, or not only, a victim, but a strong woman with a great sense of responsibility who continually worked to give meaning to her own life and to the lives of others. At Camp Westerbork, but also in her diaries and letters, one recognizes a "sociomaternal productivity."

Hélène Cixous, another French writer and feminist thinker writing *écriture féminine*, states, "A woman is never far from 'mother.'"[7] Cixous points to "mother" outside her role functions; she means "mother" in a symbolic way. She writes, "There is always within her at least a little of that good mother's milk."[8] About Etty Hillesum she said, again speaking metaphorically about milk, "she wrote in white ink."[9] She means that Hillesum's writings belong in the genre of "nourishing books," books that map the path for living a spiritual life.[10]

Charlotte Salomon

Charlotte Salomon did not write in "white ink," but she painted in it. She painted to map paths to survival.

6 Cf. Rina van der Haegen, *In het spoor van seksuele differentie* (Nijmegen: SUN, 1989), 178-179: Los van het al dan niet feitelijk moeder zijn, van de voortplanting in strikte zin of anders gezegd van reproductiviteit ten koste van haarzelf, wil ik met het woordconglomeraat "maatschappelijke moederlijke productiviteit" een opening creëren voor een maatschappelijke realisering van haar scheppende vermogens.

7 Cf. Hélène Cixous, "The Laugh of the Medusa," in: Elaine Marks & Isabelle de Courtivron (eds.), *New French Feminisms: An Anthology* (Brighton: Harvester Press, 1981), 251.

8 *Ibidem.*

9 Cf. Denise de Costa, *Anne Frank and Etty Hillesum: Inscribing Spirituality and Sexuality* (New Brunswick, NJ & London: Rutgers University Press, 1999), 235.

10 *Ibidem*, 236.

For both Etty Hillesum and Charlotte Salomon, their mothers were their inspiration and their model – by negative example. Etty Hillesum wrote in her diary,

> Mother is a model of what I must never become. […]. I'm sure I always go in fear of becoming like my mother: one moment full of enthusiasm and life and interest in things, and the next moment worn out with fatigue and quite unable to cope. And by the time you are a fully alive human being again, you have lost faith in yourself and present a kind of façade to the outside world in which you yourself do not believe.[11]

The way her mother lived, chaotically, out of balance, inspired Etty Hillesum to work on herself, to analyze herself, to try to become the best version of who she really was.

Charlotte Salomon's situation was quite different. Her mother committed suicide when she was eight years old. Nobody told her that her mother had died in this manner, nor that several other members of her family, including her mother's sister, the aunt for whom she had been named, had also taken their own lives. For years, Salomon lived with the information that her mother had died from influenza. She learned about the suicide thirteen years after the fact, while living in France with her grandparents, as refugees from Nazi Germany. After Charlotte Salomon's grandmother finally succeeded in a suicide attempt in March 1940, her grandfather related the history of suicides in the family and became totally dependent on his granddaughter. Still, he treated her in a rejecting and contemptible way. He could not stand the way she was. Once he said to her, "Kill yourself too, so this yakking of yours can stop!"[12]

Months later, Charlotte Salomon formulated her response to the traumatic news about the maternal line of her family and came to a choice she felt she had to make, "She was faced with the question to take her own life or to do something very crazy."[13]

11 E.T., 141. *Het Werk*, 148-149; Thursday afternoon, 30 October 1941: Moeder is voor mij het voorbeeld, hoe ik niet worden moet. […] Ik geloof, dat ik altijd een angst heb zo te worden als mijn moeder: bij momenten vol enthousiasme en leven en belangstelling en voor de rest verterende in mezelf, me afplagende met moeheid en er niet uit kunnende komen. En op de momenten, dat je dan werkelijk weer eens een echt levend mens bent, geloof je daar zelf niet in en ben je maar een soort façade voor de buitenwereld, waar je zelf niet in gelooft.

12 Cf. Charlotte Salomon, *Leven? Of Theater?* (Amsterdam: Cossee, 2015), 787: Nun nimm dir doch schon endlich das Leben damit dies Geklöne endlich aufhört.

13 *Ibidem*, 790: […] Sie sah sich vor die Frage gestellt sich das Leben zu nehmen oder etwas ganz verrückt besonderes zu unternehmen.

In fact, what she did was to dedicate herself completely to painting and writing. She went deep into herself and her memories, and she painted the biography of her family. She tried to understand her mother. She did what her mother could not; Charlotte Salomon freed herself from her destined role in the bourgeoisie, which at that time would have meant that she had no role beyond the biological function of motherhood.

Charlotte Salomon lived the opposite of a bourgeois life. She left her grandfather and did the things she needed to do: create, live, follow her own dreams and passions. She expressed her madness in her art and in doing so, discovered that she did not need to do away with herself as her ancestors had. From the inner depths, she created her own world, her own context, her own roots, her own life.

From the more than 1300 gouaches she painted, she gathered nearly eight hundred into a work that she titled: *Life? Or Theatre? A play with music.* This series employs images and texts, along with musical and cinematic references. The narrative underlying the work, informed by Salomon's experiences as a talented, cultured and assimilated German Jew, depicts life lived in the shadow of Nazi persecution as well as the family history of suicide. It also reveals moments of intense happiness and hope. The major theme of *Life? Or Theatre?* is how the threat of self-destruction can lead to self-discovery, and how secrecy can lead to truth-seeking. Created on the eve of the Shoah, *Life? Or Theatre?* is a deeply moving meditation on life, art, and death. Charlotte Salomon gave birth to a very unique piece of art... and to herself. In her own words, she painted, as

> the war raged on and I sat by the sea and saw deep into the heart of humankind. I was my mother, my grandmother, indeed I was all the characters in my play. I learned to walk all paths and became myself.[14]

She finished her work in the summer of 1942. Her grandfather died six months later, and she and her unborn child were murdered in Auschwitz-Birkenau in October 1943.

While living on Ottilie Moore's estate, Charlotte Salomon began a relationship with another resident on the property, a German speaking Jewish refugee, Alexander Nagler. In a postscript to her work, she noted that, "The woman to whom this book is dedicated, had gone away in the meantime." The book was dedicated to Ottilie Moore, who had escaped to Spain with

14 *Ibidem*, 806: Der Krieg tobte weiter und ich sass da am Meer und sah tief hinein in die Herzen der Menschen. Ich war meine Mutter meine Grossmutter ja alle Personen die vorkommen in meinem Stück war ich selbst. Alle Wege lernte ich gehen und wurde ich selbst.

many children and from there had returned to the USA. When Moore left, Alexander Nagler remained on the estate. Salomon commented, "She left behind only one friend, and I had no idea how to deal with him."[15] We don't know what prompted Salomon's involvement with Nagler. Perhaps, in the midst of that chaotic time, Nagler gave her a certain sense of security. Perhaps, she fell in love with him because he valued the artist in her. Or perhaps their relationship had everything to do with the death of her grandparents and with finishing *Life? Or Theatre?* Once she had finished the work that was a creative therapy for her, and once it was no longer necessary to take care of her grandfather, maybe space cleared in front of her for new ties, for new life.

By the spring of 1943, Charlotte Salomon was pregnant and she and Alexander Nagler married on 17 June 1943. She was then twenty-six years old. The two behaved as any couple might on any June wedding day at the Nice Town Hall. But they were Jews surrounded by Nazis. What they did was daring; it was certainly dangerous.

If Charlotte Salomon had wanted to remain childless, this would not have been easy under a regime which didn't allow birth control. Moreover, the Nazis punished anyone involved in an abortion with a sentence of twenty years' hard labour. Perhaps, the rumour that the French did not deport pregnant women or the thought that the Italians who controlled the Côte d'Azur would respect her condition, influenced Salomon's decision to get pregnant.[16]

These questions are not answered by *Life? Or Theatre?* Charlotte Salomon had finished her autobiographical work ten months before the pregnancy. What we do know is that the young couple hid on the property of Ottilie Moore, but were betrayed and arrested at the end of September 1943. After a stay at the processing centre, Drancy, near Paris, Charlotte Salomon was deported to Auschwitz-Birkenau, where she was killed along with her unborn child.

Etty Hillesum and Charlotte Salomon

Etty Hillesum had one or more abortions; Charlotte was halfway through her pregnancy when she arrived in Auschwitz-Birkenau on 10 October

15 *Ibidem*, 806: Der das Buch gewidmet ist war inzwischen abgereist. Sie hinterliess nur einen Freund mit dem ich nicht viel anzufangen wusste.

16 Cf. Mary Lowenthal Felstiner, "Alysum (1942-1943)," in: *To Paint her Life: Charlotte Salomon in the Nazi Era* (Berkeley, Los Angeles, CA & London: University of California Press, 1997), 158-174, especially p. 173.

1943. Etty Hillesum had arrived in Auschwitz exactly one month earlier, on 10 September. It is likely Etty Hillesum was alive when Charlotte Salomon arrived and, had Salomon lived, they might have met. But Charlotte Salomon, obviously pregnant, was immediately sent to the gas chambers.

Though Etty Hillesum and Charlotte Salomon were of child-bearing age during the war, their offspring are not biological, they are cultural. Etty Hillesum the writer, and Charlotte Salomon the painter, are two extremely creative and productive human beings who gave birth to art and literature against all odds.

In the paintings of Charlotte Salomon and in the letters and diaries of Etty Hillesum we can recognize a "sociomaternal productivity." They dipped their pen and brush "in white ink." Both created so as to map out paths for survival. Even seventy-five years after their deaths, their work still nourishes us, feeds us, inspires us to live, to work. In spite of their tragic deaths as young fertile women, their drawings and words, created under such extreme and difficult conditions, inspire us to construct a free world where the possibility for developing oneself as a full human being exists. Their lives and work call on us to grow, to become who we are, to be original, unique, different.

About the Author

Denise de Costa (1958) wrote the first PhD dissertation on Etty Hillesum: *Anne Frank and Etty Hillesum: Inscribing Spirituality and Sexuality* (New Brunswick, NJ & London: Rutgers University Press, 1999; translation of the 1996 Dutch edition). She has written several books and articles on Etty Hillesum, Anne Frank and Charlotte Salomon, spirituality and women's lives.

Wandering Beyond Words

Etty Hillesum and Clarice Lispector

Patricia Couto

Abstract

Etty Hillesum and Clarice Lispector were two brilliant authors who belonged to the same generation and were victims of Jewish persecution. Most references to the two women consider them mystical writers who reveal an unconventional notion of God. For both, the search for the divine was connected to the failure of language. For both, the use of language to represent reality meant being removed from full participation in the reality being described. Their task was impossible and contradictory. When language failed, or removed them from their own experience, how did they get beyond words? After all, their medium was language. Hillesum and Lispector faced this paradox. It was their challenge to find ways to describe their world's turn toward darkness and to reveal their own journey through these events.

Keywords: Clarice Lispector, God, search for the divine, mysticism, language failure, new language

Silence.
If one day God comes to earth there will be great silence.
The silence is such that not even thought thinks.[1]

When surfing the internet or browsing through publications on Etty Hillesum, one occasionally notices her name linked to that of Brazilian

1 Clarice Lispector, *The Hour of the Star*, transl. B. Moser, intr. Colm Tóibín (New York: New Directions Paperbook, 2011), 111.

Smelik, Klaas A.D. (ed.), *The Lasting Significance of Etty Hillesum's Writings: Proceedings of the Third International Etty Hillesum Conference at Middelburg, September 2018*.
Taylor & Francis Group 2019
DOI: 10.5117/9789463722025_COUTO

writer Clarice Lispector (1920-1977). This has been especially true since Hélène Cixous wrote about both women.[2] Most references to the two women consider them mystical writers who reveal an unconventional notion of God. But between the two there are many more points of commonality. For both, the search for the divine was connected to the failure of language. For both, the use of language to represent reality meant being removed from full participation in the reality being described. Their task was impossible and contradictory. When language failed, or removed them from their own experience, how did they get beyond words? After all, their medium was language. Hillesum and Lispector faced this paradox. It was their challenge to find ways to describe their world's turn toward darkness and to reveal their own journey through these events.

In practical terms, Hillesum and Lispector came from quite similar backgrounds. They were both of Russian descent and Hillesum's mother as well as Lispector's family had been victims of pogroms. Both were rooted in Judaism, but neither practised their religion for the major part of their lives. In their works, it was clear that they were influenced by the New Testament and had a fascination with the Eucharist. Nevertheless, this did not prevent them from assuming their Jewish identity at critical moments; Lispector wished to be buried at the Jewish cemetery in Rio de Janeiro and Hillesum chose to stay at the transit camp Westerbork where she was certain to eventually share the destiny of her people. Both women were brilliant and attractive but they also suffered great inner turmoil and sought the help of psychoanalysis. They were familiar with mental illness in their families. Hillesum's brothers and Lispector's eldest son suffered from schizophrenia.

Readers of the works of Etty Hillesum may be unfamiliar with Clarice Lispector. It may be helpful to first review Lispector's life and writing so that we can then place their works beside one another. Knowing more about Lispector will help us to see how her world and writing style placed her in an author's universe quite similar to Etty Hillesum's.

Lispector was born in 1920, during her family's escape from Western Ukraine. What befell the Jews of the Ukraine was an unimaginable disaster.[3] It has been estimated that some 250,000 Jews were killed in pogroms, among them Lispector's grandfather. Her birth was considered a miracle because

2 Hélène Cixous, *Reading with Clarice Lispector*, edited, translated and introduced by Verena Andermatt Conley (Minneapolis: University of Minnesota Press, 1990). See also Hélène Cixous, *L'heure de Clarice Lispector, précédé de Vivre l'orange* (Paris: Éditions des Femmes, 1989).

3 Benjamin Moser, *Why this World: A Biography of Clarice Lispector* (Oxford: Oxford University Press, 2009), 11.

her mother had contracted syphilis after being gang-raped by Russian soldiers. There was a superstitious belief that giving birth might cure the disease; instead, Lispector's mother's health only deteriorated. By the time of their arrival in Brazil when Clarice was an infant, her mother's illness had left her paralyzed and mute, and she died when the girl was nine. After her father's death ten years later, Clarice abandoned Judaism, in part because she felt that religion had failed her.

Living in Rio de Janeiro in her teens, Lispector studied law and published works as a journalist. At the age of 23, her first novel, *Near the Wild Heart*, propelled her to fame with a style and language considered revolutionary in Brazil. At twenty-one, she had married a Roman Catholic diplomat and from 1944, she accompanied him to Italy, Switzerland, England and Washington D.C., living a glamorous life. Discontented with the diplomatic milieu and with living abroad, she divorced her husband in 1959, and returned to Brazil with her two sons.

Once back in Brazil she produced her most famous works, among them *The Hour of the Star* and *The Passion According to G.H.* Yet, during this period of her life, she had difficulty finding an editor willing to publish her works. Lispector's writing is replete with hermetic and introspective text, strange syntax, and lyrical, ambiguous formulations. She created a style with inconsistencies in punctuation and violations of traditional grammar. She wrote in a way that gave a sense of chaos and instability. In later years, she became withdrawn and suffered from depression. Clarice Lispector died of cancer in 1977.

Communion with the Divine

Lispector's *The Passion According to G.H.* is a monologue by a woman identified as G.H.[4] The title evokes Christ's passion but G.H. also stands for *género humano*, humankind, and unlike Christ's passion it is written in the first person. The novel is an account of G.H.'s violent and repulsive encounter with the divine.

G.H. is a pampered woman from Brazil's upper class, a dilettante sculptor, between lovers, childless and living in a penthouse. Her maid has resigned and she decides to clean the maid's room. Except for a cockroach, the room is completely empty and silent. G.H. accidently kills the insect

4 Clarice Lispector, *The Passion According to G.H.*, transl. Idra Novey, ed. B. Moser (New York: A New Direction Book, 2012).

and through this incident, she suffers a breakdown and enters a dimension beyond time, space and language. G.H. overcomes her repugnance and places the slime oozing out of the womb of the dead cockroach in her mouth and in an inverted ritual of the Eucharist, she becomes one with the insect/God.

Lispector chose a cockroach because it is one of the oldest continuously existing insects on earth; it existed before humanity and its presence evokes a time before civilization and language. In the novel, G.H. finds herself wandering through the barren Libyan Desert, a "hieroglyphic fragment of an empire," becoming more and more decivilized and dehumanized, going back in time to a prelinguistic period.[5]

Lispector's idea of God was influenced by reading Spinoza. In Spinoza, she found confirmation of her own rejection of a humanized and transcendental God. Spinoza equates God with Nature. Nature is amoral; good and evil are absent. For Lispector, what is real is the divine eminence present in Nature. Thus the divine is present in an unclean insect such as a cockroach, just as it is in G.H. herself. Time and again, Lispector's protagonist considers herself divine; she feels herself called to rename the world, and even takes on the idea that "on the seventh day, I would be free to rest."[6]

For G.H., the divine is "neutral," "indifferent," "empty," "inexpressive," "whatever is real," or "nothing." Benjamin Moser, citing Gershom Scholem, has explained that to many Jewish mystics, the notion that God equals Nothing (or Everything) means that Nothing is "beyond the reach of intellectual knowledge."[7] In Jewish tradition, the very name of God is one that cannot be written or spoken.[8] Or in Scholem's words: "Only when the soul has stripped itself of all limitation and, in mystical language, has descended into the depths of Nothing does it encounter the divine."[9] Lispector's novel describes the mystical experience of removing language to discover an ultimate nameless truth or "nothing that is the God – and has no taste."[10]

5 Lispector, *The Passion According to G.H.*, 27.

6 *Ibidem*, 37.

7 Moser, *Why this World*, 268; Gershom Scholem, *Major Trends in Jewish Mysticism* (New York: Schocken Books, [1941] 1995), 25.

8 Though Hillesum uses the word "God" abundantly, she admits that it is an improvised construction: "I find the word 'God' so primitive at times, it is only a metaphor after all, [...] I am sure that I don't even need the word 'God' which sometimes strikes me as a primitive primordial sound." E.T., 439. *Het Werk*, 463; Monday, 22 June 1942: Ik vind het woord God soms zo primitief, het is toch maar een gelijkenis, [...] ik geloof, dat ik het woord "God" niet eens nodig heb, het komt me soms voor als een primitieve oerklank.

9 Scholem, *Major Trends in Jewish Mysticism*, 25; Moser, *Why this World*, 226.

10 Moser, *Why this World*, 269; Lispector, *The Passion According to G.H.*, 118.

While Lispetor's frivolous protagonist finds God in the belly of a repulsive insect, Hillesum finds God in the mud and agonies of a concentration camp. In Hillesum's writings, we witness the transformation of an agnostic and egotistical girl into a mature woman. Hillesum's metaphor of wandering in the desert, similar to Lispector's, has her watching "blurred age-old visions" or deciphering hieroglyphs in order to become intelligible, "And how can I let others see the many inmates, who have to be deciphered like hieroglyphs, until they finally form one great readable and comprehensible whole?".[11] Etty Hillesum, too, becomes part of the divine, and using the Eucharistic metaphor, she compares her suffering with Christ's, "I have broken my body like bread and shared it out among men."[12]

Fragile God

In Lispector's *The Hour of the Star*, a highly self-reflective novella, the narrator, Rodrigo S.M., wants to write a tragic story of a poor Brazilian girl named Macabéa. Near the end of the novella, Rodrigo S.M. contemplates the need to finish his book,

> I'll go on to where the air runs out, I'll go to where the great gale leaps away howling, I'll go to where the void begins to curve, I'll go where my breath takes me. Does my breath deliver me to God? I am so pure that I know nothing. I only know one thing: I don't need to pity God. Or do I?[13]

For Rodrigo, writing is seen as another form of communion with the divine. The last two sentences of the narrator, however, suddenly add a nuance to Lispector's concept of God. It suggests that He must be pitied. In this view, humankind's fall has torn apart the perfect union between word and world and made humanity responsible for the imperfect world. It becomes the writer's task to forge a new language, to rename the world.

11 E.T., 650. *Het Werk*, 693; Letter 64, To Han Wegerif and others, Westerbork, Tuesday, 24 August 1943: vervagende, eeuwenoude visioenen; E.T., 527. *Het Werk*, 558; Tuesday, 22 September 1942: En hoe kan ik anderen laten meelezen in die vele mensen, die ontcijferd moeten worden als hiëroglyphen, [...] tot men tenslotte één groot leesbaar en begrijpelijk geheel voor zich ziet.

12 E.T., 549. *Het Werk*, 582; Tuesday, 13 October 1942: Ik heb mijn lichaam gebroken als brood en het uitgedeeld onder de mannen.

13 Lispector, *The Hour of the Star*, 108.

We see a shade of this same idea in Hillesum's diary when she, too, considers humankind responsible for this imperfect world: "Neither do I hold You responsible, although You may later hold us responsible."[14] As well, in Hillesum's sentence where she questions God's omnipotence, we see a comparable need to "pity" God. She writes, "And if God does not help me to go on, then I shall have to help God." This weighty suggestion comes after a reflective passage revealing for us what Hillesum sees as her most serious task – her role in chronicling the horrors of human imperfection.

> [...] my words will have to be so many hammer strokes with which to beat out the story of our fate and of a piece of history as it is and never was before. Not in this totalitarian, massively organized form, spanning the whole of Europe. Still, a few people must survive if only to be the chroniclers of this age.[15]

The Failure of Language

Though of a different nature than Hillesum's trauma, Lispector's main character in *The Passion According to G.H.* also goes through a harrowing experience for which there are no words, but which is one that nevertheless must be rendered.[16] For the authors to translate into words what they see, it seems necessary to be in a kind of trance. Lispector's novel begins with six dashes, and the first letter in lowercase. The narrator is stuttering, disoriented by her experience of the day before.[17] Even the coherence of her language has been smashed by what she has witnessed,

14 E.T., 488, *Het Werk*, 517; Sunday, 12 July 1942: Ik roep je er ook niet voor ter verantwoording, jij mag daar later ons voor ter verantwoording roepen.

15 E.T., 484. *Het Werk*, 512; Saturday, 11 July 1942: En als God mij niet verder helpt, dan zal ik God wel helpen; E.T., 484. *Het Werk*, 511; Friday, 10 July 1942: de woorden zouden even zovele mokerslagen moetenzijn, om te vertellen over een lot en over een stuk geschiedenis, zoals het er voor dien nog niet was. Niet in deze totalitaire en massaal georganiseerd een geheel Europa omspannende vorm. Er moeten toch een paar mensen overblijven om later de kroniekschrijvers te zijn van deze tijd.

16 G.H. confesses: "Because in myself I saw what hell is like," Lispector, *The Passion According to G.H.*, 139. Hillesum verifies: "So, now I am in hell," E.T., 646. *Het Werk*, 689; Letter 64, To Han Wegerif and others, Westerbork, Tuesday, 24 August 1943: Zo, nu ben ik dus in de hel.

17 In the English translation by Novrey, the dashes were replaced by a long line and the first word 'I' is always written in uppercase.

> —————— I saw. I know I saw because I didn't give my meaning to what I saw. I know I saw – because I don't understand. I know I saw – because there's no point to what I saw. Listen, I'm going to have to speak because I don't know what to do with having lived. Even worse: I don't want what I saw. What I saw smashes my daily life. Sorry for giving you this, I'd much rather have seen something better. Take what I saw, deliver me from my useless vision, and from my useless sin.[18]

G.H.'s bewilderment reminds us of Hillesum's hallucinatory depiction of her experience at Camp Westerbork, a passage that also describes a prior day and night. In an almost delusional state, Hillesum repeats the words "I see." Like Lispector, Hillesum goes back in time.

> I walk past scenes that loom up before my eyes in crystal-clear detail and at the same time seem like blurred age-old visions. I see a dying old man being carried away, reciting the Shema to himself. [...] I see an old man being carried away. [...] I see a father, ready to depart, blessing his wife and child and being himself blessed in turn by an old rabbi with a snow-white beard and the profile of a fiery prophet. I see... ah, I can't begin to describe it all....[19]

Both Hillesum and Lispector struggled with the fact that language cannot represent reality. Language can refer to reality but it stands in the way of participating in it. In Lispector's novel, G.H. refers to the destructive power of language, implying that it negates the actual concrete thing.

> How I entered whatever exists between the number one and the number two [...] A note exists between two notes of music, between two facts exists a fact, between two grains of sand no matter how close together there exists an interval of space, a sense that exists between senses. [...] The name is an accretion, and blocks contact with the thing. The name of the thing is an interval for the thing.[20]

18 Lispector, *The Passion According to G.H.*, 17-18.

19 E.T., 650. *Het Werk*, 693; Letter 64, To Han Wegerif and others, Westerbork, Tuesday, 24 August 1943: Ik ga door tafrelen, die voor mijn ogen opstaan in vele kleine kristalheldere details en die tegelijkertijd zijn als vervagende, eeuwenoude visioenen. Ik zie een doodzieke oude man wegdragen, sjeimes zeggende over zich zelf. [...] Ik zie een oude man wegdragen [...] Ik zie een vader, die voor het vertrek z'n vrouw en kind zegent en die zichzelf laat zegenen door een oude rabbijn met een sneeuwwitte baard en een vurig profetenprofiel. Ik zie... ach, ik kan het immers toch niet beschrijven...

20 Lispector, *The Passion According to G.H.*, 113-4.

In the novel, language cannot be trusted. G.H. writes that she "shall feel at the poverty of the spoken thing. As soon as it's out of my mouth, I'll have to add: that's not it, that's not it!"[21] Hillesum faces an identical problem. "I know that what I write will be only a feeble reflection of what is inside me."[22] Hillesum admits that, "We have to become as simple and as wordless as [...] the falling rain," and that,[23]

> I hate wordiness. The only words I want to write are those naturally woven into one great silence, not those that merely serve to drown out the silence and to pull it apart. [...] I would like to brush in a few words against a wordless background. To describe the silence and the stillness and to inspire them. What matters is the right relationship between words and wordlessness, the wordlessness in which much more happens than in all the words one can string together. And the wordless background of each short story [...] must have a distinct hue and a discrete content. [...] It is not some vague and incomprehensible silence, for silence too must have contours and form. All that words should do is to lend the silence form and contours.[24]

Thus, representation is best expressed by silence. In another example of Lispector's views, the narrator Rodrigo S.M., in Lispector's *The Hour of the Star*, says, "So that's why I'll try contrary to my normal habits to write a story with a beginning, middle and 'grand finale' followed by silence and falling rain."[25]

21 *Ibidem*, 21.

22 E.T., 112. *Het Werk*, 119; Monday, 29 September 1941: omdat ik weet, dat het maar een flauwe afschaduwing zal zijn van zoals het in me zit.

23 E.T., 483. *Het Werk*, 510; Thursday, 9 July 1942: En men moet weer zo eenvoudig en woordeloos worden als [...] de regen, die valt.

24 E.T., 394. *Het Werk*, 413; Friday, 5 June 1942: Ik haat veel woorden. Alleen woorden, die organisch ingevoegd zijn in een groot zwijgen, zou ik willen schrijven, niet woorden, die er alleen maar zijn om het zwijgen te overstemmen en uiteen te rukken. [...] dan zou ik enkele woorden willen penselen tegen een woordeloze achtergrond. En het zal moeilijker zijn die stilte en dat zwijgen aftebeelden en te bezielen, dan de woorden te vinden. Het zal dan gaan om de juiste verhouding van woorden en woordeloosheid, een woordeloosheid, waarin meer gebeurt, dan in alle woorden, die men bij elkaar vinden kan. En in iedere novelle [...] moet de woordeloze achtergrond weer anders getint zijn en een andere inhoud hebben, [...]. Het gaat niet om een vaag en onvatbaar zwijgen, ook dat zwijgen zal z'n eigen kantige contouren moeten hebben en z'n eigen vorm. En dus zouden de woorden alleen moeten dienen om het zwijgen z'n vorm en omtrekken te verlenen.

25 Lispector, *The Hour of the Star*, 20.

Forging a New Language

For both writers, the search for the divine is connected with the failure of language. But how does one go beyond words when one's medium is language? Hillesum has to strip down layers of language.

> I am sometimes afraid to call a spade a spade. Because nothing will then be left to the imagination? No, things ought to be called by their proper name. If they can't stand it, then they have no right to be. We try to save so much in life with a vague sort of mysticism. Mysticism must rest on crystal-clear honesty, can only come after things have been stripped down to their naked reality.[26]

This very same question – of names and naming – the process by which things are called into being, dominates Lispector's work.[27] In *The Hour of the Star*, she once again links religious and linguistic questions. Her opening sentence, "All the world began with a yes," reminds us of John 1:1: "In the beginning was the Word, and the Word was with God, and the Word was God."[28] According to Rodrigo S.M. in *The Hour of the Star*, creation began with a word and through that word all things were created. A word that creates the world, is God.

Rodrigo questions his writing and the ability of words to capture the truth about life. His task is to name. "But when I write – let things be known by their real names. Each thing is a word and when there is no word it is invented. This your God who commanded us to invent."[29]

Rodrigo S.M.'s aim is to write the tragic story of Macabéa, a nearly illiterate, naive girl who works as a typist. Unlike Rodrigo S.M., Macabéa – untroubled by the problem of the representation of reality through language – loves to type words even when she doesn't know their meaning and, in fact, to modify them, creating new, mysterious words – much to her employer's despair.[30]

26 E.T., 426. *Het Werk*, 448; Friday, 19 June 1942: Ik ben soms bang de dingen bij de naam te noemen. Omdat er dan misschien niets van over blijft? De dingen moeten kunnen velen, dat je ze precies bij de naam noemt. Kunnen ze daar niet tegen, dan hebben ze geen bestaansrecht. Men probeert veel in het leven te redden met een soort vage mystiek. Mystiek moet rusten op een kristalheldere eerlijkheid.

27 Moser, *Why this World*, 33.

28 Lispector, *The Hour of the Star*, 18.

29 *Ibidem*, 26.

30 *Ibidem*, 54.

For Hillesum, writing is a desperate struggle "like a bloody battlefield of words fighting and struggling with one another."[31] Though bloody, the struggle is also *zaligmakend* [sanctifying]. This Dutch word has a strong religious connotation. It means "redemption from sin, salvation by God." Hillesum considers writing as a way of salvation, a mystical experience,

> I shall become the chronicler of our adventures. I shall forge them into a new language and store them inside me should I have no chance to write things down [...] one day I may perhaps discover a peaceful space round me that is mine alone, and then I shall sit there for as long as it takes [...] until life begins to bubble up in me again and I find the words that bear witness where witness needs to be borne. —[32]

In Lispector's case, in *The Passion According to G.H.*, the new language is ambiguous, consists of oxymora and deconstructs any certainty about the linguistic sign,

> My destiny is to search and my destiny is to return empty-handed. But – I return with the unsayable. The unsayable can only be given to me through the failure of my language.[33]

The unsayable is G.H.'s brief encounter with the divine, an experience beyond intellectual knowledge and thus beyond words. In the end though, G.H. does not forsake language even if she does not understand it,

> I am not understanding whatever it is I'm saying, never! never again shall I understand anything I say. Since how could I speak without the word lying for me? how could I speak except timidly like this: life just is for me. Life just is for me, and I don't understand what I'm saying. And so I adore it. ——————————————.[34]

31 E.T., 523. *Het Werk*, 553; Sunday, 20 September 1942: als een bloedig slagveld van strijdende en elkaar bevechtende woorden.

32 E.T., 510. *Het Werk*, 540; Tuesday, 28 July 1942: Ik zal de latere kroniekschrijfster worden van onze lotgevallen. Ik zal me in mijzelf een nieuwe taal tezamen smeden en ik zal haar in mij bewaren, als ik niet de gelegenheid zal hebben iets neer te schrijven. [...] misschien krijg ik dan heel veel later nog eens een rustige ruimte om me heen, die voor mij alleen is en dan zal ik er zo lang blijven zitten [...] tot het leven weer in me gaat borrelen en tot de woorden tot me zullen komen, die zullen getuigen van datgene, waarvoor getuigd zal moeten worden.—

33 Lispector, *The Passion According to G.H.*, 205.

34 *Ibidem*, 210.

The hope expressed in Lispector's *Passion* reminds us of Hillesum's conviction that life is meaningful, a conviction that goes beyond words,

> It is the only way one can live nowadays, with unreserved love for one's tortured fellow creature, no matter of what nation, race or creed. And when that struck me during a completely disconsolate moment, I knew that I could go on living, not merely a surrogate life in a Jewish transit camp during the Second World War, as most people here do, but genuinely, with a good deal of zest and joy and conviction and an inkling of all the connections there are and that ultimately still make life a meaningful whole – but this is something about which one cannot really write for lack of the right words.[35]

Hillesum's last letter, in which she describes the appalling hours preceding deportation, belongs among the most sublime testimonies of the Holocaust. The increasing numbers of readers and scholars interested in Hillesum's writings, and those who have translated her diary into 18 languages, can say with confidence that Hillesum did indeed find the right words.[36]

About the Author

Patricia Couto (1950) was born in the Netherlands, studied Germanic Philology in Coimbra (FLUC 1975) and holds an MA in Comparative Literature (FLUL 1996) and a PhD in Translation Studies (FLUL 2012). She has taught Dutch Language and Culture at the University of Lisbon and is an integrated member of the Centro de Estudos Compatatistas (FLUL). With Ana Leonor Duarte, she has translated Etty Hillesum's letters into Portuguese.

35 E.T., 629. *Het Werk*, 671; Letter 54, To Maria Tuinzing, Fragment, Westerbork, Undated; end of July 1943: Het is de enige manier waarop men het leven tegenwoordig leven kan, uit de voorkeurloze liefde tot de gekwelde medecreatuur, van wat voor natie, ras of gezindheid hij ook is. En toen dat in een volkomen troosteloos moment weer over me kwam, kon ik weer verder leven, niet zo maar een surrogaatleven in een joods doorstuurkamp in de tweede wereldoorlog, zoals de meesten hier doen, maar echt, met een hoop élan en vreugde en overtuiging en een vaag vermoeden van samenhangen, die er zijn en die in de diepte het leven toch tot een zinrijk geheel maken – maar daarover kan men eigenlijk nog lang niet schrijven, omdat men de woorden niet weet.

36 E.T., 644-654. *Het Werk*, 686-698; Letter 64, To Han Wegerif and others, Westerbork, Tuesday, 24 August 1943.

"Verbalize, Vocalize, Visualize"

Creative Death and Performative Writing in the Testimonies of Hillesum and Levi

Maria Essunger

Abstract
The suggestive testimonies of Etty Hillesum and Primo Levi challenge us to reflect upon one of the most important questions of our time: What constitutes a human being? Thanks to the poetical function in their narratives, and taking into account the vulnerable communication between the authors and their readers, there are no answers given in their texts, only a serious call to take responsibility, cooperate with the text, and let it affect you. The author argues that their writing affects us and changes our perception of life as well as of our inner selves *if* we cooperate – critically and constructively – with the texts in question.

Keywords: Primo Levi, essence of human beings, poetical language, communication, conception of God, Other, death

All philosophical knowledge has its unique expression in language.
– *Walter Benjamin*

Stories are much bigger than ideologies. In that is our hope.
– *Donna Haraway*

Theoretical Reflections

Neither Etty Hillesum nor Primo Levi could be labeled a novelist or poet. Both Jewish thinkers and writers have, however, through their very different

Smelik, Klaas A.D. (ed.), *The Lasting Significance of Etty Hillesum's Writings: Proceedings of the Third International Etty Hillesum Conference at Middelburg, September 2018.*
Taylor & Francis Group 2019
DOI: 10.5117/9789463722025_ESSUNGER

narratives, helped us understand the systematic cruelty and surprising complexity of the Shoah. Their texts are far from fiction and have no reference to "*l'art pour l'art*", art for its own sake, nor to the more exact expression: *an aesthetic conception of art as independent in relation to motives and morals*. Nevertheless, the texts of the concentration camp victim, Hillesum, and the survivor, Levi, are definitely driven by an effective *poetical function*. Is this a contradiction? No. There is no contradiction if we think along lines laid out by Roman Jakobson (1896-1982), a Russian-born linguist and philosopher active in the inter-war period and still highly topical today.

Jakobson wrote about *the poetical function*, which he said was found not only in what we normally call "poetry" such as lyrics and poems, but also in other genres. At the same time, he insisted upon the fact that poetry cannot be reduced to its poetical function only. He pointed out that the poetical does not reside in a specific theme or a choice of motive. Indeed, what is defined as poetry is not found in a set of poetic artefacts; the history of art testifies to the inconsistency of artifacts over time. For example, the most banal jokes can be built up from the same style elements as brittle poetry. Lived life and written poetry interact dynamically with one another; art is not simply a mechanical reproduction of reality. The *poetical function* in a text offers "resistance towards established formulas and schedules and thereby counteracts a conventional and automated perception of reality. This special function in the text assures our formulas of love and hate, revolt and reconciliation, faith and resistance, against automation and rust formation."[1]

Another Russian thinker, linguist and writer, Viktor Sklovskij (1893-1984) coined a concept that vigorously described the poetical function in a single word: *defamiliarization* or *estrangement* (from Russian: остранение, ostranenie). The point is that with estrangement, what is written upsets one's conventional perception of reality. Let me give an example: *The earth is blue like an orange*. Saying this makes one's brain confused. The earth looks blue from a great distance and a certain perspective, and its spherical shape becomes obvious. But even if it is round, round oranges are not blue. When you bump into an expression like this in a text you probably need an extra moment to think: What does this mean? How does it interact with the context and co-text of the other words and

1 The reasoning and the quotation are taken from a text by Bengt Landgren, "Vad är en litterär text?" in: Staffan Bergsten (ed.), *Litteraturvetenskap- en inledning* (Lund: Studentlitteratur, 1998), 27-28, based on e.g. Roman Jakobson's text *Linguistics and Poetics* (1960).

phrases in the same text? And what consequence does this special *form* of expression have on the content? *The point* is that the text upsets your conventional perception of reality. *The question* then becomes: What does one do about it?

This question is an important starting point for my reasoning in this article, as it is in all my research. I am convinced that poetic language and stories have a special ability to lay bare different and even conflicting perspectives and meanings. Language and stories can do this because they are often characterized by intriguing paradoxes, suggestive symbols, provocative lacunas and other stylistic figures, all of which only work *if* the reader cooperates in a hermeneutical interaction with the text.[2] My conviction is based on having faith in the vulnerable communication between the addressee and the addressed, which is always broken in one way or another, *and* on the insight that all communication – and knowledge – is perspectival.[3] We always stand somewhere in a certain context or a certain mood when we communicate, read or interpret, and that matters. As Nancy Tuana puts it:

> [...] we always have to ask whose interests are served by the knowledge that mainstream science believes it is important to develop, and whose interests are served by the knowledge projects that are overlooked or ignored.[4]

Thanks to their manifold rhetorical figures, one can say that poetical language and narratives comprise *creative silence*. They encourage the reader to interact independently and sensitively with the messages and meanings in the text. Nevertheless, this is a risky business. How can one know if the reader interacts with the text in a constructive way? There is no guaranty that they will, and thus we talk about communication as *vulnerable*. In this vulnerability, however, also resides the hope of an engaged and responsible reader or interpreter who, through meeting the text, sheds new light not only on the text, but on herself as well.

2 Hermeneutical does not necessarily mean harmonic; it is often critical, but never detached or uninterested.

3 I share this conviction with, for example, Paul Ricœur, e.g. *Qu'est-ce qu'un texte?* 1986, Jacques Derrida, e.g. *Limited Inc*, 1990, Hélène Cixous, e.g. *Rootprints*, 1997, and Donna Haraway, e.g. *The Companion Species Manifesto*, 2004.

4 Nancy Tuana, "Gendering Climate Knowledge for Justice: Catalyzing a New Research Agenda," in: Margaret Alston & Kerri Whittenburg (eds.), *Research, Action and Policy: Addressing the Gendered Impact on Climate Change* (London: Springer, 2013), 18.

Etty Hillesum – the Passionate Testifier of Potentiality

Between 1941 and 1943, a Jewish woman from the Netherlands, Etty Hillesum, kept a diary and wrote letters under the infernal gaze of the Nazi regime.[5] Through her passionate and personal writings, she exposed her inner self while depicting her everyday life at the same time. The outside world, mean and colored by despair, was not her focus. Either she was naively unaware of this world, or, more likely, she transmitted a kind of hope through her passive approach to the world outside. I see her diaries as a self-portrait, both multilayered and mysterious, even mystical. She described the world through her microcosm – herself and her reality – rather than through the macrocosm that surrounded her. Nevertheless, it is through this very microcosm that we get *a special entry* into the larger context that she is part of, the extreme reality that she faces.

Her writings have, as I see it, two great sources of inspiration, and both are of equal importance. On the one hand, she puts her trust in literature, from poets and novelists such as Rainer Maria Rilke and Fyodor Dostoevsky, through the stories of the Bible and mystical writers as Meister Eckhart, to psychoanalytical theory, especially C.G. Jung. *She uses literature to understand the world and to be part of the world.* Literature for her has nothing to do with reading for amusement or distraction. She oscillates between seeing her own literature – her diaries – as both important and serious, and frivolous and silly. In the end they become necessary. In time, she scrapes away the superfluous in her personal belongings as well as in her words. Only the important and serious are left, only that which can help. On the other hand, but in the same way, *she uses her relation to God to understand the world and to be part of it.* This again has nothing to do with amusement or a simple search for well-being. No specific religious formulas or artefacts are indefeasible or absolute for Hillesum. Only important and serious considerations are left to help what is great but weak, to help the Other – whoever that is: yourself, your neighbour, or your God.

Hillesum's two sources of inspiration make her writing acts of both introversion and extroversion. She simultaneously listens inwards for herself, and writes outwards for her fellow human beings. The extrovert act is most obviously materialized in her decision to volunteer to work in a Nazi transit camp, and to share the destiny of all Jews. She does this out of the conviction that she can "attain a sense of inner harmony and peace

5 For further reading on (different aspects of) Hillesum, see e.g. various publications of Klaas A.D. Smelik, Denise de Costa, Meins G.S. Coetsier and Maria Luísa Ribeiro Ferreira.

amid the distressing outer turmoil" and so transform that turmoil, at least to some small degree. She summarizes this as being "true to myself." What is at stake, is a life in God. Here, the heart of Hillesum's conception of God unfolds; *the god within is only active if the human being interacts with it.*[6] But she does not stop here. In the interaction with God she also claims that one needs to take *responsibility for God*, so that life in God is still an option in a future setting. She expresses this in terms of helping God, "And if God does not help me to go on, then I shall have to help God."[7] What remained the only feasible obligation at the time was to save the remains of God that existed in herself and, she hoped, in others. For Hillesum, the nest of God in the human being needed to be defended, because God was unable to act on his own. Hélène Cixous's wordings on God and the need for the *word* God in our world can be seen as a kind of mirror image, reinforcing the recognition of *the place* of God in the world, without providing God with any determinate description.

> [...] God is of my making. [...] But god, I say, is the phantom of writing, it is her pretext and her promise. God is the name of all that has not yet been said. Without the word *Dieu* to shelter the infinite multiplicity of all that could be said the world would be reduced to its shell and I to my skin.[8]

Etty Hillesum had a special meaning as a human being. She was composed of flaws – as are the rest of us. She was passionate and incomplete. To me she was, above all, *human*, not a Saint, nor a Mother of God.[9] She is corporal and sensual, and still reflective, all of which become obvious on reading her sentence on how to kiss a man,

> Perhaps that is the only way of kissing a man. Not just out of sensuality but also from a desire to breathe for one moment through a single mouth. So that a single breath passes through both. And it was with S. that I had

6 Cf. my reasoning in Maria Essunger, "The Phantom of God in the (Auto-) Biographical Writings of Hélène Cixous and Etty Hillesum," in: Klaas A.D. Smelik, Meins G.S. Coetsier & Jurjen Wiersma (eds.), *The Ethics and Religious Philosophy of Etty Hillesum: Proceedings of the Etty Hillesum Conference at Ghent University, January 2014* [Supplements to the Journal of Jewish Thought and Philosophy, 28] (Leiden/Boston, MA: Brill, 2017), 205-220.

7 E.T., 484. *Het Werk*, 512; Saturday morning, 11 July 1942: En als God míj niet verder helpt, dan zal ik God wel helpen.

8 Hélène Cixous, *Stigmata: Escaping texts* (London/New York: Routledge, 1988), 150.

9 This said without neglecting the importance of seeing Hillesum as the Mother of God *in other contexts*, cf. e.g. the interesting reasoning of Denise de Costa in this volume.

> this experience for the first time. Ever since, my kisses for Han have been platonic. But yes, bodies have their own laws.[10]

In the same way that both literature and God inspired Hillesum, the sexual and the spiritual life dueled within her, a recognizable dilemma – or chance – for many human beings. This may be most relevant for those in the Judeo-Christian tradition where sin, sacredness, and sexuality are at stake when discussing the human-god relation and the human godlikeness.[11] Or as Hillesum put it straightforwardly, "It is difficult to be on equally good terms with God and your body."[12] Nevertheless, she was, in body and spirit, *materializing* a living relation between a (non-flawless but devoted) human being and a (responsive but weak) God. One example of this can be seen in the following expression that is a distinct example of Sklovskij's *defamiliarization* or *estrangement*, and shows the poetical function in action.

> There is no hidden poet in me, just a little piece of God that might grow into poetry. And a camp needs a poet, one who experiences life there, even there, as a bard and is able to sing about it.[13]

Here we have to stop and reflect. Our perception of reality oscillates; why should the horrible death camps have a poet? How could the victims of the Shoah be inspirational to a bard? And if a poet or a bard were to witness the life of the destructive camps, why sing about it? This expression makes the reader think on her own and meditate about the obvious contradiction that it lays bare. But if we bear in mind the passive approach to the outer world that characterized Hillesum's worldview, it makes a lot of sense. Only a poet can bring out the stories of the detainees in a way that does not violate the muted voices of the death camps but *re-presents* them so clearly that we can understand the camp and the voices in our own way. And the singing can be interpreted as hopeful

10 E.H., 333. *Het Werk,* 348; Thursday morning, 16 April 1942: Misschien is dit de enige juiste manier om een man te kussen. Niet alleen uit zinnelijkheid, maar uit een verlangen een ogenblik te ademen door één en dezelfde mond. Dat er één adem door beiden gaat. En bij S. is het voor het eerst, dat ik het zo beleef en Han kus ik sindsdien alleen nog maar Platonisch. Maar ja, lichamen, die hebben hun eigen wetmatigheden.

11 Cf. the reasoning in e.g. Kari Elisabeth Børresen (ed.), *Image of God and Gender Models in Judeo-Christian Tradition* (Oslo: Solum Forlag, 1991).

12 E.H., 70. *Het Werk,* 74; Monday, 4 August 1941: Het is moeilijk om met God en met je onderlichaam op gelijkelijk goeie voet te staan.

13 E.H., 542. *Het Werk,* 575; Saturday morning, 3 October 1942: Er is geen dichter in mij, er is wel een stukje van God in mij, dat tot dichter zou kunnen aangroeien. In zo een kamp moet toch een dichter zijn, die het leven daar, ook daar, beleeft als dichter en die er van zal kunnen zingen.

resistance to the fact that often we cannot change the reality that we are part of. We can only *relate* to it in different ways. One should notice that the very last testimony from Hillesum was written on a postcard blown in the wind from the boxcar when she is on her way with her family to meet death. Here she wrote – whether being a poet or not – "We left the camp singing."[14]

Primo Levi – the Dedicated Testifier of Deeds

In 1946, the Italian-Jewish chemist, Primo Levi, wrote a book entitled *Se questo è un uomo* [*If This is a Man*].[15] Primo Levi's challenging depiction of hell on earth, i.e. daily life in a concentration camp during the Second World War, starts with a poem. This poem sets in motion the hard work of reflecting philosophically on the complex question of *what constitutes a human being*, especially in the inhumane setting of the Shoah. It is a poem that invites the reader to hear the story of what Levi calls in his narrative, "sub-human lives" and to keep on telling that story over and over again. By the end of the poem, the wording – in its form as well as in its content – alludes to the Jewish prayer (*w'ahavta*) that commands believers to remember and carry on the teaching and traditions of their faith. The poem also mirrors Levi's mission to pass on the story of sub-human lives – not to allow them to fall into oblivion – but to narrate the experiences of the Jew, the Roma, the homosexual, the disabled person, and other Others, of which he is himself a representative. But, as a survivor, he is not what he calls a "real witness" to the Holocaust because real witnesses, the ones who faced their final end, no longer have voices, they do not narrate anything, and they do not share stories.[16] This statement highlights the well-known problem of representation. *How to (respectfully) give voice to another creature, human or non-human?* This is not the place for an exhaustive examination of philosophical reflections on this problem. I would, however, like to highlight a common core of these discussions, namely the need for a nuanced sensibility and acknowledgement of imperfection in all our attempts to represent or "speak for" someone, or to re-present, i.e. "to present anew" reality or the Other whoever it may be; another fellow being, an animal, or God.[17]

14 E.H., 659. *Het Werk*, 702; Tuesday, 7 September 1943: We hebben zingende dit kamp verlaten.

15 Primo Levi, *Se questo è un uomo* (Turin: Einaudi, 1978 [1946/1947], 8th ed.), E.T., *If This is a Man/The Truce*, trans. Stuart Woolf (London: Abacus, 1988/2003).

16 Primo Levi, *The Drowned and the Saved*, trans. Raymond Rosenthal (New York: Vintage International, 1989). Originally published as *I sommersi e i salvati*, 1986.

17 What could be called the problem of representation, has been discussed by many thinkers. For further reading, see e.g. the reasoning of Sölle, Focault and Deleuze, interestingly elaborated

Levi's introductory poem, *If This is a Man,* not only embodies the fundamental question of who and what we are, but also asks *how we ought to* relate to each other in our shared, shattered world. The poem starts by contrasting the reader's secure life with the extreme situation of the detainees of the concentration camp. It asks the reader to reflect upon whether the dehumanized lives in the camp are human at all,

You who live safe
In your warm houses [...]
Consider if this is a man
Who works in the mud [...]
Who fights for a scrap of bread
Who dies because of a yes or a no [...].

Levi's piece of art, of testimony, of politics, of philosophy, and of ethics presents the vulnerability of human dignity. It asks rather firmly, for human responsibility, encouraging the reader to be accountable for the continued actualization of the victims of the Shoah,

Meditate that this came about:
I commend these words to you.
Carve them into your hearts [...]
Or may your house fall apart [...]
May your children turn their faces from you.

It depicts inhuman and inhumane conditions where human dignity is not only questioned but denied. In the middle of this explicitly anthropocentric poem there is a simile highlighting a frog in winter,

Consider if this is a woman
Without hair and without name [...]
Her eyes empty and her womb cold
Like a frog in winter.

by Petra Carlsson in *Theology beyond Representation: Foucault, Deleuze and the Phantasms of Theological Thinking* (Uppsala: Acta Universitatis Upsaliensis, 2012), or the immense reflections in the wake of Gayatri Chakravorty Spivak's fundamental question: can the subaltern speak? in Rosalind C. Morris (ed.), *Reflections on the History of an Idea: Can the Subaltern Speak?* (New York: Columbia University Press, 2010).

This is a double alienation – a vivid example of Sklovskij's *defamiliarization* or *estrangement* – that awakens the reader. Why this frog? Why a frog in winter?

Levi's book *If This is a Man* is not characterized by poetical language. It is an unsentimental, nude, and yet astonishingly illuminating text that registers and presents raw life. Perhaps the unsentimental stylistic figuration is the only possible way to speak about this inconceivable sub-life. Yet, the text opens with a poem that contains what, at first, seems like a rather non-decisive simile. A woman with no hair or name, with empty eyes, a weak mind, and a cold womb is compared to a frog in winter. At first glance, one might only associate the woman with the creature because neither is where they should be; the woman is far from home and warmth, and the frog is frozen in wintertime. But if one reflects upon what kind of animal the frog is, and remembers that the reader is explicitly asked to *meditate* upon what is stated, there is far more information than imagined available within this simile.[18]

The frog does not have an external ear so the eardrum is attached directly to the skin. Nevertheless, the frog has good hearing and, in amplitude, it resembles the hearing capacity of a human being. The frog has a vocal cord, is good at communicating, and uses several warning calls and a range of noises. When frogs emerge from the egg, they have gills. As they grow, they develop lungs that they use in adulthood. There is real *metamorphosis* in a frog's life, starting from a tadpole that swims smoothly in water, and transforming into a four-legged animal bumping around on the ground. Frogs eat insects and, at the same time, are prey for other insects as well as bigger animals. Moreover, amphibians' way of life and fertility are adapted to a high mortality rate. During the annual spawning season, a female field frog produces an egg mass of about 1500 eggs. Of these, between five and ten eggs survive until adulthood when they themselves can participate in reproduction. The rest of the female reproductive effort that year contributes to the ecosystem in the form of nutrition and food for other creatures.

When connecting the cold woman deprived of liberty in the concentration camp to a frog in winter, Levi is giving a concentrated depiction of the sub-human lives that the Jews – and other Others – are leading in Auschwitz. With no possibility to speak for themselves, or for their friends, they seem mute, but – like a frog – they hear and they communicate well with one another. For the Nazi's, their whispering, wording and singing seem like

18 Cf. the strophe from the poem "Meditate that this came about" and especially note its location; it is placed directly *after* the simile and *before* the severe exhortation.

incomprehensible noises, but among the prisoners, there are many distinct voices to be heard.[19] Every prisoner experiences some kind of metamorphosis during their stay in the camp. One may enter as a healthy and flourishing person and die as a stripped skeleton. Or, one may develop what could be called useful skills in the camp, such as the ability to bargain, to win, to steal, to invent, to lie, to survive, which, simultaneously, could be seen as destructive and terrible proficiencies. One may, more likely, change from human to sub-human in this dehumanizing milieu. Symbolically speaking, one will even eat another. The mortality rate is sky-high in the camps, and the ones who perish, or their few belongings, will be recycled among the detainees.

One well-chosen simile, between a half-dead woman and a frozen frog evokes the unsafe and unlivable lives of the detainees in Auschwitz. Levi continues elaborating on this rich and vivid image, but as readers, we are already meditating upon the existential question that permeates the narrative from the opening poem to the bitter end: What constitutes a human being? If the poem succeeds in awakening the reader's imagination and engagement, it has managed to combine a feeling of being close and yet very far from what is evoked. Meditating on the simile, one realizes that if there are so many unexpected similarities between humans and frogs, there are many, many more similarities between one human and another, even if some are *defined* as *Other.* It becomes striking in this context how extremely construed is the borderline between the Norm and the Other. In a way, I am always your Other. Levi's simile manages to materialize the vulnerability of human dignity in extreme situations as well as to open our ears so that we may hear the unheard voices of the real witnesses, the Others that could be you or me.

Levi's need to tell us, and to let us take part in his lived reality, was so immediate and demanding – both before and after liberation – that it competed with his other basic needs. In the foreword, he states that the book was written to appease that need. But his text is also asking for action, from himself and from all of us, to rethink – and try to imagine – what

19 Cf. the reasoning of Aristotle who claims that it is *the speech* of the human being (*logos*) that distinguishes us from the animal that (only) makes sounds or noises (*phone*). If a human being is not capable of using comprehensible speech, but only makes sounds and noises, she will be condemned to be without morality as well, and, consequently, she will lose her status as a complete social being (excluded from the public society/*polis* as well as the private home/*oikos*). Helen Andersson discusses this thoroughly in relation to Frans Kafka's writings in: Elena Namli *et al.* (eds.), *Etiska undersökningar: Om samhällsmoral, etisk teori och teologi* (Uppsala: Acta Universitatis Upsaliensis, 2010), 87-105.

really happened some seventy years ago, and to continue to reflect upon this ongoing history. To the reader, his text might actualize a willingness to hear what seems to be the mute screaming of the real human witnesses in the concentration camps.

Conclusion

To conclude, I would like to actualize the title of this article: *"Verbalize, Vocalize, Visualize": Creative Death and Performative Writing in the Testimonies of Etty Hillesum and Primo Levi.* I start with the suggestive alliteration of Hillesum. On Sunday night, 20 September 1942, she stated in her diary, "Many people are still hieroglyphs to me, but gradually I am learning to decipher them. It is the best I can do: to read life from people."[20] Primo Levi stated in the preface to his testimony *If This is a Man* that his text was not written to bring forth new accusations towards the concentration camps or the masters of this dehumanizing machinery, but rather to serve as a quiet study of the human soul. Both writers wanted to transmit words, sounds, and images – to verbalize, vocalize, and visualize in the wordings of Hillesum.[21] In my opinion, they succeeded. Their suggestive testimonies challenge us to reflect upon one of the most important questions of our time: What constitutes a human being? Thanks to the poetical function in their narratives, and taking into account the *vulnerable communication* between the authors and their readers, there are no answers given in their texts, only a serious call to take responsibility, cooperate with the text, and let it affect you. In that way, the writings of Hillesum and Levi are not just performative for them, in the sense that their writing affects only them, changing their perception of life and their inner selves. Their writing is also performative in relation to the reader. Their writing affects us and changes our perception of life as well as of our inner selves if we cooperate – critically and constructively – with the texts in question.[22]

20 E.H., 522. *Het Werk,* 552; Sunday evening, 20 September 1942: Veel mensen zijn nog hiëroglyphen voor me, maar heel langzaam leer ik ze dan ontcijferen.

21 E.H., 522. *Het Werk,* 552; Sunday evening, 20 September 1942: Verwoorden, verklanken, verbeelden.

22 I use "performative" in its most simple signification seeing performativity as denoting the action aspects of linguistic observations, focusing the effects and impression of words and writing rather than their meaning. Cf. e.g. John Langshaw Austin, and his reflections on performativity in his lecture *How To Do Things With Words* by the end of the 1950s, publishes in 1962 (Oxford: Oxford University Press, 1962/1976) and their development by thinkers as Jacques Derrida and Judith Butler.

Finally, I tried to use an unexpected combination of words as a manifest example of Sklovskij's *defamiliarization* or *estrangement.* I combined "creative" and "death." These words connote different spheres of meaning, a good and constructive one, and a bad and destructive one. When you try to interpret this combination of words, you will have to stop, reflect, and meditate. What could they possibly mean especially when placed together? The words make perfect sense in relation to the story that I have told of the testimonies of Hillesum and Levi and their importance for us today. Living – or writing – in front of death could definitely be creative. To live in the vicinity of death affects human beings in many ways. Life might become clearer and even more fully or truthfully described when death is the undesired partner in the dialogue.

About the Author

Maria Essunger (1972) is Assistant Professor of Systematic Theology and Studies in Worldviews, Uppsala University, Sweden. Her research is in the field of cultural theology focusing on the relation between worldviews and literature. She is currently working in a research project entitled "The Politics of Writing: Membership, Testimony and Representation" with a special interest in the philosophical and poetical texts of Hélène Cixous, Walter Benjamin and Birgitta Trotzig.

A "No" that Is an Affirmation

Etty Hillesum and Simone Weil Against the Laws of Force

Laura Fasani

Abstract
Although from different perspectives and backgrounds, Etty Hillesum and Simone Weil shared an attentive look on reality that made them able to understand contemporary historical events and to reject any kind of totalitarianism from its roots. The two women also believed in the need of re-founding Europe upon intertwining values for a new humanism and a new civilization based on a real sense of justice. This contribution focuses on their specific but somewhat similar opposition against evil: a choice that led them to say "no" to the outrages of history in the name of every human being.

Keywords: justice, force, totalitarianism, resistance

> Pour moi, la résistance consiste à dire non.
> Mais, dire non est une affirmation.
> C'est positif. C'est dire non à l'assassinat, au crime.
> Il n'y a rien de plus créateur que de dire non
> à l'assassinat, à la cruauté, à la peine de mort
> – *Germaine Tillion*

In the midst of Western civilization's 20th century crisis, a generation of female writers and extraordinary thinkers was able to read into contemporary historic events and take a stand against the blind laws of force. They did this with an exceptional clear-headedness. Though they never met, the fates of two of them, the passionate and yet very different personalities of

Smelik, Klaas A.D. (ed.), *The Lasting Significance of Etty Hillesum's Writings: Proceedings of the Third International Etty Hillesum Conference at Middelburg, September 2018.*
Taylor & Francis Group 2019
DOI: 10.5117/9789463722025_FASANI

Simone Weil and Etty Hillesum, crossed in the struggle to defend humanity against the cult of history of their time.

Born within five years of each other in two different countries, both faced death at an early age. Their existences show only a few points of convergence. While Hillesum didn't feel herself cut out to be "a social worker or a political reformer," on the contrary Simone Weil's life and philosophical adventure was shaped by militancy in the French revolutionary trade union movement and by her work as a laborer in a factory. While Etty Hillesum was fresh and ironic and readers of her work come away with a feeling of intimacy and an understanding of her life as a model of self-actualization, Simone Weil was both a political activist and a mystic, a combination so rare she was nicknamed "the Martian" as a student at Lycée Henri IV by her teacher, the philosopher Alain. Both women were Jewish. Etty Hillesum accepted persecution to share her people's fate; Simone Weil rejected any recognition of her Jewish origin, preferring instead exile and the French resistance.

Their main points of departure though, are related to their analytic and conceptual tools. While the approach to historical events in Etty Hillesum's diaries is deeply intertwined with taking an inner path – the key subject of her diaries, for Weil, the same inner path represents a temptation to be avoided. Weil was always driven by a rigorous need for thinking and writing in an impersonal spirit of truth. Etty Hillesum, on the other hand, wrote about her desire to become an artist, and she was able to make sense out of the meaningless thanks to her singular poetic expression.

Despite their different temperaments, important analogies emerge when comparing the two women's take on reality. They were able to name things for what they were at a time when words and their meaning were systematically divorced from one another. For this reason and others, they came to similar conclusions about the nature of evil, and they shared views on resistance against barbarism. Moreover, belief in the need to act personally without thought of the possible consequences was an imperative of the conscience for both of them in spite of being well aware of the demands their choices might entail.

A similar look on reality

When, during the summer of 1932, Simone Weil went to Berlin to observe first-hand the German political situation, she witnessed the long, dramatic crisis that led to Hitler's ascent. Over the next several months, she continued to follow the news, worried about how events were evolving. She turned out to be a sharp observer at the age of 23, and in her treatise, *L'Allemagne en attente*, she showed how the political and economic crisis had broken every habit, tradition, and social class and had shattered security. Her view was that in the face of this unprecedented collapse, the great force of Nazism sprung from propaganda based upon the German sense of failure and oppression. The force of the Hitlerian movement "bursting everywhere" – she wrote in another essay about the situation in Germany – "in parades, in attacks, in airplanes engaged for the propaganda; and all those weak people just being drawn like flies to a flame."[1] A new form of power was emerging before the young philosopher's eyes. In addition to violence, Weil understood that Nazi power was making use of speeches and spectacle to affect the collective imagination. From this initial shrewd analysis, Simone Weil drew the conclusion that National Socialism could only mean "organized massacre, the suppression of every freedom and culture."[2]

Moreover, the crisis of the political forces in Germany, alongside the Soviet Union's authoritarian development, meant to Weil the rise of a new form of oppression operating "in the name of function." At the top of this unheard-of power was the bureaucratic and technocratic caste of the centralized state. According to Weil, this power had no flags. In fact, its main feature was to appear in a number of guises both in European dictatorial systems as well as in Roosevelt's liberal America. In her long article entitled *Prospectives*, which provoked Trotsky's personal attack, the young philosopher pointed out how the features of a new kind of regime were basically founded on the systematic oppression of the population.

It is not surprising to find these poignant words in an article Simone Weil wrote a few years later, reflecting on the double threat of fascism and communism,

> One has only to examine the present-day meaning of the two words to discover two almost identical political and social conceptions. In each of them, the State seizes control of almost every department of individual and social life; in each, there is the same frenzied militarization, and the same artificial unanimity, obtained by coercion, in favour of a single party [...]; there is the same serfdom imposed upon the working masses

1 "La force éclate partout, dans les défilés en uniforme, dans les attentats, dans les avions employés pour la propagande; et tous ces faibles vont vers cette force comme des mouches vers la flame". Simone Weil, *La situation en Allemagne*, in: *idem*, *Œuvres complètes: Écrits historiques et politiques*, II/2 (Paris: Gallimard, 1991), 155.

2 *Ibidem*, 141.

> in place of the ordinary wage system. No two nations are more similar in structure than Germany and Russia.[3]

For Weil, however, to understand 20th-century totalitarianism, one needed a wider historical lens. For the young activist what was happening on the continent at war in the 1930s only proved a historical law that had been devastating the world for thousands of years. She summed this up in *The Need for Roots*, "There is no other force on this earth except force."[4] Thus, in her view, Nazism was not merely an incidental phenomenon, but rather a long-practiced cult of force implemented to extreme consequences. For Simone Weil, it was urgent to search out the origin of the evil that was the scourge of Europe. She found it in the concept of power as an exercise of force, which she saw as having taken root in the Western world during the Roman Empire and further developed into the modern nation during the reign of Richelieu and Louis XIV. In her essay *Quelques réflexions sur les origines de l'hitlerisme*, she claimed that it was easy to believe that after two thousand years, Hitler had simply been able to copy the Romans.

In addition to being a recurring part of human history, this strange analogy had a strong negative impact on everyday life. The social idolatry at its peak within totalitarianism and the moral fracture of the population led the French philosopher to think that,

> [...] today, it is only belonging unconditionally to some brown, red or other totalitarian system which is able to give, as it were, a solid illusion of an inward unity. Which is why it constitutes such a strong temptation for so many distraught minds.[5]

A few years later, Etty Hillesum would write in her diaries of the experience of an interior resistance to the very same oppression. One may imagine Weil's thoughts as a bird's eye view of the whole of Europe, while Hillesum's diary and letters focus on smaller episodes of her everyday life. Nevertheless,

3 "Car si on examine le sens qu'ont aujourd'hui ces deux termes, on trouve deux conceptions politiques et sociales presque identiques. De parte et d'autre, c'est la même mainmise de l'État sur presque toutes les formes de vie individuelle et sociale: la même militarisation forcenée; la même unanimité artificielle, obtenue par la contrainte au profit d'un parti unique [...]; le même régime de servage imposé par l'État aux masses laborieuses à la place du salariat classique. Il n'y a pas deux nations dont la structure soit plus semblable que l'Allemagne et la Russie." *Ibidem*, 261.

4 Simone Weil, *The Need for Roots* (London: Taylor & Francis, 2005), 215.

5 *Ibidem*, 241.

Hillesum's considerations show an understanding equal to Simone Weil's of the deep mechanisms underlying Nazism. While Weil is driven by the need to take inventory of her degraded civilization, Hillesum pushes with "an almost demonic urge"[6] to personally read her time and the human soul.

> I notice that, over and above all my subjective suffering, I have an irrepressible objective curiosity, a passionate interest in everything that touches this world and its people and my own motives. Sometimes I believe that I have a task. Everything that happens around me has to be clarified in my mind and later in my writing.[7]

As a matter of fact, in her diaries, restrictions against the Jews are gradually recorded and scrupulously integrated into Etty Hillesum's interior. She believed that "humiliation always involves two. The one who does the humiliating, and the one who allows himself to be humiliated."[8] One day, after biking in one of the last streets Jews were permitted to use, she noted, "They can't do anything to us, they really can't. They can harass us [...], but we ourselves forfeit our greatest assets by our misguided compliance."[9] The harsher the bans and prohibitions became, the clearer it was to the young Dutch woman that the only thing that really mattered was the inner attitude, not the exterior facts. Hillesum believed that it was possible to face the evil of her time if she were able to bear the deprivations and not be overwhelmed by them. In her opinion, most people lived with the wrong approach, "without dignity" and lacking "a historical sense."[10] She thought they were overly worried about their bodies, not focused enough on their souls nor on their personal attitude toward events.

6 E.T., 511. *Het Werk*, 541; Tuesday morning, 28 July 1942: een bijna demonisch gadeslaan van alles.

7 E.T., 86. *Het Werk*, 91; Wednesday afternoon, 13 August 1941: Ik neem bij mezelf waar dat naast al dat subjectieve lijden dat ik doe altijd weer een a.h.w. objectieve nieuwsgierigheid komt, een hartstochtelijke belangstelling voor alles wat deze wereld en z'n mensen en m'n eigen zieleroerselen betreft. Ik geloof soms dat ik een taak heb. Alles, wat er om me heen gebeurt moet in mijn hoofd tot klaarheid gedacht worden en later door mij beschreven worden.

8 E.T., 434. *Het Werk*, 457; Saturday night, 20 June 1942: Om te vernederen [...] er twee nodig [zijn]. Diegene, die vernedert en diegene, die men wil vernederen en vooral: die zich láát vernederen.

9 E.T., 434. *Het Werk*, 457-458; Saturday night, 20 June 1942: Men kan ons niets doen, men kan ons werkelijk niets doen. Men kan het ons een beetje lastig maken [...] wij roven ons onze beste krachten door onze verkeerde instelling.

10 E.T., 492. *Het Werk*, 520; Tuesday evening, 14 July 1942: Men heeft te weinig historisch besef. Men gaat te ver in zijn angsten voor dat ongelukkige lichaam. En de geest, die vergeten geest, verschrompelt ergens in een hoekje.

As a reader of Dostoevsky, Saint Augustin and Rilke, Hillesum felt she could bear living through the history of her times because she had learnt to accept sorrow and death as part of life. In this regard, the following lines are emblematic:

> One moment it is Hitler; the next it is Ivan the Terrible, one moment it is the Inquisition and the next war, pestilence, earthquake, or famine. Ultimately what matters most is to bear the pain, to cope with it, and to keep a small corner of one's soul unsullied, come what may.[11]

She always managed to be faithful to this aim even when she became a member of the Jewish Council. It was a choice that she judged as an absurd and shameful attempt to stay afloat while everything else was drowning. Being conscious of the role the Council played, Etty Hillesum succeeded in preserving an interior space where many things still took place – from human relations to readings, from illegal musical soirées to flowers, all just as real as the misery lived in a day.

These quick references are enough to show the differences between Etty Hillesum and Simone Weil's approaches to totalitarianism. Nevertheless, in their examination of external forces, what emerges is a similar intuition about evil. Beyond political concepts and ideologies, the two women understood that every person was able to think and do evil, since both Weil and Hillesum considered evil as innate to human beings. And it is precisely from this understanding that their opposition to Nazism began.

According to Weil, human beings were always ready to subjugate one another in their relentless drive for power. She realized that as long as we think in the first person, everyone tends to make use of others as if they were inert things. Therefore, barbarity should be considered "as a permanent and universal feature of human nature, whose development is greater or smaller depending on the circumstances."[12] Clearly in this view, barbarity was not a peculiarity of Nazism. The same conviction appears in Hillesum's diaries and letters. For her, whether a population happens to be oppressed instead of oppressing depended on mere contingencies. Turn the tables and the play of forces easily trades places,

11 E.T., 483. *Het Werk*, 510; Friday morning, 10 July 1942: De ene keer is het een Hitler en de andere keer voor mijn part Iwan de Verschrikkelijke, en de ene eeuw is het de inquisitie en een andere keer oorlogen, of de pest en aardbevingen en hongersnood. Het gaat er in laatste instantie om, hoe men het lijden, dat toch essentieel aan dit leven is draagt en verdraagt en verwerkt en dat men een stukje van z'n ziel ongeschonden bewaren kan door alles heen.

12 S. Pétrement, *La vie de Simone Weil*, I (Paris: Fayard, 1973), 370.

> Nazi barbarism evokes the same kind of barbarism in ourselves, one that would involve the same methods if we could do as we wanted right here and now.[13]

In her diaries, Hillesum frequently repeated that she didn't believe in wicked people. This didn't mean she was indulgent. On the contrary, she thought it was necessary to "make a stand, wax indignant at times," but also to acknowledge that "indiscriminate hatred is the worst thing there is. It is a sickness of the soul."[14]

In 1936, despite her pacifism, Simone Weil joined the Anarchist column of Buenaventura Durruti in the Spanish Civil War. During the short period she spent with the Republican fighters, she had the chance to see how hatred and force were able to contaminate everyone, the good as well as the bad. In her famous letter of 1938 to Georges Bernanos, the young philosopher wrote in regard to the anarchists:

> When they knew it was possible to kill without risking neither punishment nor responsibility, they killed; or, at least, they smiled at those who were killing. If by chance one felt a bit of disgust, they silenced it and soon ignored it for the fear of showing lack of virility, because of a sort of entertainment impossible to resist to.[15]

Simone Weil understood that the one who makes use of violence ends up becoming inebriated by it and losing control of their own actions regardless of what they're fighting for. What she had foreseen at that time would actually take place again in Europe in 1943, when supposedly normal people proved ready to commit endless atrocities.

Etty Hillesum and Simone Weil both noticed how evil acts were frequently the result of mental distress or interior emptiness. During a visit to the Gestapo headquarters, Hillesum happened to see an SS officer walking

13 E.T., 21. *Het Werk*, 22; Saturday, 15 March 1941: [...] het nazibarbarisme roept in ons eenzelfde barbarisme wakker, dat met dezelfde methoden zou werken, wanneer we mochten doen wat we wilden vandaag aan den dag.

14 E.T., 18. *Het Werk*, 19; Saturday, 15 March 1941: [...] op gezette tijden verontwaardigd [is] over bepaalde dingen [...] die ongedifferentieerde haat [...] het ergste [is] wat er is. Het is een ziekte van de eigen ziel.

15 Cf. Simone Weil, *Lettre à Georges Bernanos*, in: *idem*, *Écrits historiques et politiques*, 223. In the original French: [Q]uand on sait qu'il est possible de tuer sans risquer ni châtiment ni blâme, on tue; ou du moins on entoure de sourires encourageants ceux qui tuent. Si par hasard on éprouve d'abord en peu de dégoût, on le tait et bientôt on l'étouffe de peur de paraître manquer de virilité [because a sort of] entraînement, une ivresse à laquelle il est impossible de résister.

among the Jews looking for a pretext to yell at them. Later in her diary, she described the person she had seen as a glum and anguished boy. She remembered not being afraid, but instead having felt the desire to ask him, "Did you have a very unhappy childhood, has your girlfriend let you down?"[16] The idea of human evil as a projection of the evil inside people also can be found in Weil's *Cahiers*, in her *Intuitions préchretiennes*, and in *Venise sauvée*. Weil conceived of evil as a "transfer" of emptiness or suffering that everyone carries within oneself and which they try to get rid of by shifting it on to someone else; the one who is hurt wants to suppress evil by "abolish[ing] it from his own existence and for this reason he casts it outside."[17]

Totalitarianism set aside an entire array of moral values on which civil society had been based. It also demolished the basic capacity for judgment that allows one to distinguish the fair from the unfair and the good from the bad. In this regard, Etty Hillesum could see in Camp Westerbork how deep the moral rupture had become. She noted with astonishment that in the space of half a kilometer squared, the camp held "every class, ism, conflict, and current of society."[18] Describing a meeting with a girl who was wearing worn-out shoes but was proud to live in what was considered a prestigious barrack, Hillesum wrote that "one suddenly realizes that it is not enough to be an able politician or a talented artist. In most extreme distress, life demands quite other things."[19] While all the efforts to conceal terror and/or evil under social status or prestige were in vain in Westerbork, only a few inmates realized they were being given the ultimate test of discerning human values.

Indeed, Etty Hillesum's and Simone Weil's opposition to evil comes from an awareness that "the rottenness of others is in us, too"[20] Therefore for them, there was no solution other than to start with oneself and take the responsibility daily to get rid of negative instincts towards the other. In the *Prélude à une declaration des devoirs envers l'etre humain*, Weil seems to echo Hillesum's words when she writes,

16 E.T., 259. *Het Werk*, 269; Friday morning, 27 February 1942: [...] heb je zo een ongelukkige jeugd gehad of heeft je meisje je bedrogen?

17 Translated from the Italian edition: Simone Weil, *Quaderni*, vol. IV, edited by G. Gaeta (Milano: Adelphi, 1993), 194.

18 E.T., 588. *Het Werk*, 626; Letter 23, to two sisters in The Hague, Amsterdam, end of December 1942: er alle aspecten, klassen, ismen, tegenstellingen en stromingen van de hedendaagse maatschappij [...] (En de oppervlakte blijft nog steeds één halve vierkante kilometer).

19 E.T., 590. *Het Werk*, 627; Letter 23, to two sisters in The Hague, Amsterdam, end of December 1942: dat het in het leven niet voldoende is alleen maar een bekwaam politicus of een begaafd kunstenaar te zijn, in de grootste nood vraagt het leven om heel andere dingen.

20 E.T., 245. *Het Werk*, 254; Thursday, 19 February 1942: die rottigheid van de anderen zit in ons ook.

> It is chimerical and due to the blindness induced by national hatred to imagine that one could exclude Hitler from the title to greatness without a total transformation, among the men of today, of the idea and significance of greatness. And in order to be able to contribute towards such transformation, one must have accomplished it in oneself.[21]

Against the totalitarianism arising inside, and driven by the need to act and answer their times, the two women opposed extreme choices even if it meant paying with their own lives. It is in this light that Etty Hillesum's decision to share the *Massenschicksal* and Weil's projects with the French resistance should be considered. For the latter, especially the *Plan for an Organization of Front-Line Nurses* comes to mind. That project aimed to establish a unit of first-aid nurses, chosen because of their willingness to die in order to save the soldiers. Weil attended a first-aid course in New York to get ready to join these nurses, but when she sent a proposal for the project to De Gaulle in London, he judged it completely foolish and rejected it. The project was never carried out.

The apparent contradictions and the choices made by the two women are sometimes hard for admirers to accept; their ideas and actions raise legitimate doubts among those who read their works. These doubts risk diverting from real questions of the depth of their thought and actions. Simone Weil was so aware of this that she wrote about it in a letter just before she died, and no one took the time to ask, "Is she telling the truth?"[22]

In my opinion, *The Need for Roots*, Weil's last important work, and Hillesum's letters can be considered as two founding texts of a new idea for Europe, a document that is still a mere draft today. With their new tone, the two thinkers laid the foundations for a new civilization. The resistance found in Hillesum's letters are a first step. As already pointed out by Tzvetan Todorov,[23] Etty Hillesum's path demonstrates that individual moral acts are the real base of collective political life. It is not possible to build a community, whether small or big, local or international, where only the basest human emotions rule: private hates, mutual distrust, blatant egotism, ignorance, and spiritual and cultural poverty. Hillesum needed to be a "viable generation" even in the prison camp, able to transform the hard facts of the times "into impulses through which we can grow and from which we

21 Simone Weil, *The Need for Roots* (London: Taylor & Francis, 2005), 222.

22 Simone Weil, *Lettres à ses parents*, in: *idem*, *Écrits de Londres et dernières lettres* (Paris: Gallimard, 1957), 234.

23 Cf. Tzvetan Todorov, *Resistenti*, translated by Emanuele Lana (Milan: Garzanti, 2016), 30-31.

can draw meaning."[24] She responded with a sense of responsibility towards future generations, so that they wouldn't have to start all over again from the beginning.

Simone Weil for her part, understood and passionately asserted in her work that every human being has physical and moral needs, and that such needs are obligations to be respected. She emphasized that any instance of uprooting mutilates a person and that the destruction of a city is one of the worst crimes that can be committed. She understood that science was not something beyond good and evil, and that technology should serve people and not the other way around. She affirmed that work has dignity and that artists and writers must draw inspiration from good and beauty without getting lost in meaningless trends. Finally, she was clear that real politics doesn't belong to parties that are totalitarian in nature, but must be founded on mutual consent based on justice; politics must be inspired by love of the homeland, the people's history, the beauty of the world itself, for individuals and the oppressed. In essence, organization of the body politic must spring from the holy part in the human being, the personal and impersonal parts that equate everyone and relentlessly long for the good.

In the end, Etty Hillesum and Simone Weil were resisters in the sense meant by Germaine Tillion and Albert Camus: they were able to say no as an affirmation. They were able to say no that was a yes to life and to human beings against the miseries and outrages of history, and its law of force.

About the Author

Laura Fasani (1993) graduated in Italian Philology and Literature at Ca' Foscari University, Venice (Italy) in 2018, with a thesis on Simone Weil. Her main studies focus on 20th-century writers and philosophers such as Albert Camus and Cristina Campo. Currently, she is a contributor for *Giornale di Brescia*, the Italian most read local newspaper, writing about technology, innovation, culture and for the news section.

24 E.T., 586. *Het Werk*, 624; Letter 23, to two sisters in The Hague, Amsterdam, end of December 1942: En wanneer wij de harde feiten, waarvoor wij onherroepelijk gesteld staan, aan hun lot overlaten, wanneer we ze geen onderdak verlenen in onze hoofden en in onze harten, om ze daar te laten bezinken en te veranderen in feiten, waaraan wij zouden kunnen groeien en waarop wij een zin zouden weten te winnen, dan zijn wij geen levensvatbare generatie.

From Enclosure to Disclosure

Images of the Self in Etty Hillesum's Diary

Sara Gomel

Abstract

Self-narration has often been perceived as a narcissistic display of the self, a rupture from the outside world. Etty Hillesum's diary has not been spared the accusation, though being the setting of an opposite process, where narrative and ethics mingle: the "dis-closure" of the Self, which enables the encounter with the other. This process of transformation from enclosure to disclosure will be analyzed in this article through the images Hillesum employs to portray the Self, images which are at first restricted, personal, and limited, and will, with time, evolve into wider, more open ones.

Keywords: Self, literary images, process, disclosure, Carl Gustav Jung, coincidence of opposites, God, otherness

There are still many ongoing discussions to determine whether Etty Hillesum was mainly a writer, a spiritual figure, a philosopher, a poet, or a social worker. Be that as it may, it is certain that the rhythm of her writing was highly poetical. It depends not only on her rich figurative language,[1] but also on the abundance of images that she employs. Hillesum worked closely with images, as a means to explore and enlighten her experiences and conceptions. Thus, if we want to outline her "philosophy," we cannot avoid studying and analyzing her imagery. And if we think of her cherished authors, those who inspired her, even when they were universally recognized as authorities

1 For an in-depth study on this topic, see Marja Clement's essay, *"Hineinhorchen* and Writing: The Language Use of Etty Hillesum," in: Klaas Smelik, Gerrit Van Oord, and Jurjen Wiersma (eds.), *Reading Etty Hillesum in Context: Writings, Life, and Influences of a Visionary Author* (Amsterdam: Amsterdam University Press, 2018), 51-77.

Smelik, Klaas A.D. (ed.), *The Lasting Significance of Etty Hillesum's Writings: Proceedings of the Third International Etty Hillesum Conference at Middelburg, September 2018.*
Taylor & Francis Group 2019
DOI: 10.5117/9789463722025_GOMEL

in their disciplines (Jung as a psychologist, Rilke as a writer, St Augustine as a theologian), they had, at times, been considered "unconventional" because of their fascination with the power of images.

In this article, I will focus on the conception of the Self in Etty Hillesum through the images she uses in her diary. Hillesum never makes the Self her concept, even if she seems to make reference to such an entity when she speaks of being in "contact" with herself. I adopt this terminology from Carl Gustav Jung, who capitalizes Self as a proper noun, which helps me stress that, despite the diversity of images, Hillesum implicitly refers to the same concept. I have chosen to use "Self," rather than "ego," "consciousness," or "psyche," because it immediately gives the idea of a totality: it represents the experience that we have of ourselves as a whole.

I have identified two main tendencies in the poetical imagery of Hillesum, when she makes reference to the Self. One is the development from small, restricted images to vast, limitless ones – a process that I have called "disclosure," as the blossoming of a flower. This progress is also mirrored in Hillesum's existential choices, when she decides to leave her little circle and "open up" to the world, renouncing certainties and devoting herself to others and to the unknown.

On the other hand, Hillesum, to represent the Self, often uses opposite images simultaneously, which makes it difficult to determine any chronology in her conception. One image does not replace the other, but they will resist together. In this perspective, enclosure and disclosure are not two opposite tendencies: they can coexist and one is produced by the other. Poetry allows Hillesum to reveal that it is in the inner retreat, through introversion, that an *ouverture* can be found. The Self that at first seems a restricted, limited reality, is discovered to have the characteristic of vastness. Only poets can embrace this contradiction, and in this sense Hillesum's conception of the Self is not different from Rilke's *Weltinnenraum* [the outer space within], which finds outwardness enfolded in inwardness.

The Self as a Workshop and a Craftsman

What Julius Spier asks Etty Hillesum to do at the beginning of the psychoanalytic therapy, giving her the task to write a journal, is to register her thoughts day after day so as to constantly keep in touch with herself: a form of inner listening that Hillesum will later call *hineinhorchen*.

As readers, we have the impression that Hillesum immerses herself in the process naturally, but a closer look reveals that her first attempts at a diary were extremely difficult. But why exactly? What did Etty Hillesum find while searching inside, listening to what was alive within?

At first, major chaos. Listening to herself turns out to be a difficult exercise: it reveals the inside struggles of the psyche. She portrays her inner life as the reign of an uninterrupted and uncontrolled flow of emotions and sensations, in which the Self appears to be a laboratory where thoughts and feelings are constantly shaped. Her early images are of confusion and turbulence, of movement, of continuous oscillations between extremes. In some passages, Hillesum describes her inner life as a solid, heavy block of granite, weighing on her, senseless and purposeless. A pure, conflictual matter with a certain tendency to resist her, and that the therapy asks her to confront and control. Her battle becomes, then, the titanic battle of the sculptor, who uses all his forces to mould materials and give them shape:

> but inside me, inside my brain, there is an enormous workshop where fashioning, forging, labouring, suffering and sweating all go on. But what the end product may be I do not know. [...] Something is demanding to be given shape.[2]

> Yet I must start slowly on that great block of uncut granite I carry within me if I am to model my small figures, or else I am bound to get crushed one day. If I don't seek and discover my form, I will end up in night and in chaos [...].[3]

The Self, therefore, appears not only as a chaotic laboratory, but also as the craftsman who tries to take control over it. His effort lies in avoiding to be carried over by the ever-continuing flow of matter, and to give it a precise direction, yet without compressing or denying such movement. It is a continuous effort which cannot be put to rest by a single act: beauty, peace, and order – or, we could ultimately say, "form" – are the result of a lengthy work, and can be reached only through discipline over time. Hillesum was very much aware of this, and we can see it not only in her constant

2 E.T., 149. *Het Werk,* 157; Saturday evening, 22 November 1941: Maar in mij, in m'n brein is een geweldige werkplaats en daar wordt gewerkt en gesmeed en gezwoegd en geleden en gezweet. Maar wat het werkstuk zal zijn weet ik niet [...]. Er wil iets uitgekristalliseerd worden.

3 E.T., 73. *Het Werk,* 78; Tuesday noon, 5 August 1941: Toch moet je langzamerhand beginnen in het grote blok onbehouwen graniet, dat je in je draagt, de kleine figuren te gaan modelleren, anders zul je op den duur verpletterd worden. Wanneer je niet je vorm zoekt en vindt, zul je in nacht en chaos te gronde gaan [...].

reminders to order her life more consistently,[4] but also in the small tasks that Spier used to give her: to wake up early, to wash with cold water, to do some physical exercise in the morning. This is only the beginning, or the preparatory phase, to the process that Carl Gustav Jung, and his disciple Julius Spier with him, called *individuation*, a process through which an individual becomes an integrated human being, aware of his unconscious battles, and developed to his/her own full potential.

Ultimately, it is the process through which we become who we really are. Therefore, it is a process of differentiation, which allows us to reveal ourselves in our distinctiveness: we humans may all share common "matter," but it is the "form" we give to our own lives, the unique way we assemble the material we own, that really determines who we are. This was clear to Spier, who wrote, with the same images of Hillesum, that a "mould"[5] was necessary for the development of the individual. Only through shaping and moulding, the piece of granite will become that unique, inimitable statue that it was meant to be, with its own, defined, and peculiar characteristics.

No surprise then that with the deepening of the therapy the image of the artisan gains more and more importance in Hillesum's language, becoming, in her words, "a powerful central authority of the soul." Without this authority which gives order it is impossible to find peace in the inner life. Only its ruling power will enable her to feel grounded and in harmony with herself and with others:

> God, I thank You for having given me so much strength: the inner centre regulating my life is becoming stronger and more pivotal all the time. [...] after a day like yesterday I feel entitled to say with some conviction:

4 E.T., 72. Monday afternoon, 4 August 1941: I must stop and listen to myself, sound my own depths, eat well, and sleep properly if I am to keep my balance, or it will turn into something altogether too Dostoevskian. *Het Werk*, 77: Ik moet maar blijven luisteren naar mezelf, "hineinhorchen" in mezelf en goed eten en slapen voor het evenwicht, anders wordt het zo Dostojewski-achtig, maar in onze tijd ligt het accent weer ergens anders.

5 E.T., 420. Tuesday evening, 16 June 1942: Creative energy has to be forced into a mould if the creative element is to be kept alive. Conversely, one might say that only the right mould can give expression to man's creative energy and help him to reach out to others. *Without a mould that energy is but narcissistic hedonism, intoxication with one's own feelings and passions.* The mould alone impels man's energies to act and hence to fertilize as a reaction. *Het Werk*, 441-442: Schaffende Kraft muß in eine Form gegossen werden, so, daß doch immer das Schöpferische lebendig bleibt. Im Gegenteil kann man sagen, daß die richtige Formung erst das Schöpferische im Menschen zum Ausdruck bringen kann, der auch andere in seiner Umgebung erreicht. *Ohne Formung ist es eine Art narzistisches Genießertum; man berauscht sich an seinem eigenen Gefühl, Leidenschaft.* Aber erst die Formung dringt alle diese Kräfte zur Weiterwirkung, und dadurch wieder in der Rückwirkung zu neuer Befruchtung.

> peace reigns in my inner domain because a powerful central authority is in control there.[6]

This powerful image reminds us of the structure of the soul in Plato's *Phaedrus*, where the head represents the central power governing the entire psyche. Plato uses the allegory of the chariot to represent the different parts of the soul and their structure: the charioteer governing the two horses (one representing the moral impulses, the other the appetites, the irrational passions) is the intellect, the rational guiding part, whose task is to take control over all restless inclinations. For Hillesum, however, the inner centre is not identified with reason, and impulses, pleasures and desires are never denied as such. On the opposite: to find our own centre, for Hillesum, we need to explore our desires, to be aware of our personal inclinations, and to embrace movement and change as the essence of life. The horses cannot be stopped and locked up in their stables if we want the chariot – symbolizing the soul as a *living* being – to pursue its run: for the soul to be alive, horses are needed as movement is. If authority becomes a prohibition on living fully, then its power becomes dangerous and unfruitful. This means that, in order to find balance, the effort of the patient must be the integration of the two opposite tensions we have evoked: movement (the hegemony of matter) and stillness (the hegemony of form). Or, in Hillesum's figurative language, "the workshop" and "the craftsman." Not differently than Jung, who conceives the Self as a whole, composed of both the "ego," consciousness, and the undercurrent of unconsciousness, Hillesum imagines it as coincidence of opposites: *coincidentia oppositorum*, the attribute that Nicholas of Cusa referred to God in his *De Docta Ignorantia* (1440), and that Jung recalled as the attribute of the Self in his work on alchemy and psychology, *Mysterium Coniuctionis* (1955). When it comes to Hillesum, a well-defined centre where everything flows unceasingly.

The Self as a Source

One of the most frequent images in Hillesum' diary, which perfectly represents the unity of opposites, is the one of the source. By listening to the

6 E.T., 223. *Het Werk*, 232; Friday morning, 9 January 1942: God, ik dank je voor zoveel kracht, die je me geeft: Het innerlijk centrum, waaruit m'n leven geregeerd wordt, wordt steeds krachtiger en middelpuntiger. [...] En na een dag als gisteren durf ik met een zekere overtuiging zeggen: in mijn innerlijke rijk heerst vrede doordat er een krachtig centraal gezag is.

inside, Hillesum suggests, one gets to a source, a centre that keeps balance between the streams of time. While the source can be located in a precise place in space, a stream flows out from it freely at the rhythm of *panta rei*, each instant running into the next one. To stay still and yet to flow like a stream: this is the paradox that the spring embodies and the ideal type that Hillesum tries to attain.

Initially, however, because of her natural inclination to dispersion, Hillesum strongly expresses the need to re-centre, and the image of the source perfectly represents this process of conversion into the inside. Indeed, geographically, the spring is a point in space, usually well-protected by its surroundings and enclosed between rocks, often hard to find. Psychologically, it is an excellent representation of enclosure and inwardness, intimately related to words like "corner" and "shelter," and for Hillesum, the deepest and most essential voice of the Self, so remote that it can only be reached through a profound retreat in self-listening, only when one is able to make silence around. Some of the most common expressions found in her diary, in this respect, are:

> [...] to listen to that hidden source within me.[7]

> Because there is now so palpable, so vital, so moving and deep a source within me [...].[8]

But the source, with its fresh, regenerating water, also corresponds more generally to vital energy, and in this sense, it represents something that transcends the purely personal voice of the individual. Therefore, as restricted as it initially appears, this image reveals that at the very core of the soul there is an opening, a starting point for a process of dis-closure. It is not by chance that Etty Hillesum uses "source" and "God" as synonyms: God is to be found through a strenuous personal training, at the heart of each human being, but God also represents an impersonal energy that belongs to each of us independently of our contingent traits. What is unique in Hillesum, then, differently from the classical theological paradigm, is that the impersonal is to be found at the core of the personal, which is why the experience of God – a word that

7 E.T., 103. *Het Werk,* 109; Wednesday, 24 September 1941: [...] te luisteren naar een verborgen bron in me.

8 E.T., 229. *Het* Werk, 239; Wednesday, 14 January 1942: Doordat er nu zo een voelbare, levende, steeds in beweging zijnde bron diep in je is [...].

Hillesum points out as "primitive"[9] and that we use repeatedly without questioning it to signify the unintelligible – does not require abstraction, the unrobing of the Self of its individual characteristics, but a personal, daily, existential practice.

However, this tension towards an "opening," inherent in the image of the spring itself, is also portrayed by a concrete evolution in the language of Hillesum. With time, the image of the spring will be often associated with – and sometimes even replaced by – the image of a "flowing river," giving way to a new texture in Hillesum's portrayal of the internal processes of the psyche.

She makes use of it since the beginning of the diary, when she affirms that the most precious miracle that has been produced by the encounter with Julius Spier is a new sense of freedom that she had never experienced before:

> Suddenly I was living differently, more freely, more *flowingly* [...].[10]

Or:

> I am flowing again in my own narrow riverbed [...].[11]
>
> So this is my attitude to life at the moment: it flows through me as a great, rich, mighty river, fed by an infinite number of small tributaries – etc.[12]

To portray herself as a "rich, mighty" river, means to have discovered vastness and openness at the core of what had appeared to be a small, personal, and restricted reality, and to such an extent that it brings *con-fusion* between the individual existence and life in general, so that it seems impossible to know whether it is life that is flowing through us, or we who are flowing through life.

9 E.T., 439. Monday night, 22 June 1942: I find the word "God" so primitive at times, it is only a metaphor after all, an approach to our greatest and most continuous inner adventure; I'm sure that I don't even need the word "God," which sometimes strikes me as a primitive, primordial sound. A makeshift construction. *Het Werk*, 463: ik vind het woord God soms zo primitief, het is toch maar een gelijkenis, een benadering van ons grootste en ononderbrokenste innerlijke avontuur, ik geloof, dat ik het woord "God" niet eens nodig heb, het komt me soms voor als een primitieve oer-klank. Een hulpconstructie.

10 E.T., 6. *Het Werk*, 6; Sunday, 9 March 1941: En ik leefde opeens anders, bevrijder, "fließender" [...].

11 E.T., 63. *Het Werk*, 67; Sunday, noon, 15 June 1941: Ik loop weer in m'n eigen smalle bedding [...].

12 E.T., 301. *Het Werk*, 313-314; Friday morning, 27 March 1942: En zo is mijn levensgevoel tegenwoordig: mijn leven gaat als een grote, rijke, machtige stroom door me heen, gevoed door oneindig vele kleine bijriviertjes – enz.

Furthermore, a flowing river is an image of expansion, movement, and growth, and therefore of progression towards otherness. For the Self, learning to flow like a river means not having to contain the vital energy being discovered within, but to be able to partly let it go and nourish others with the same lively water.

In this perspective, stagnation – an equivalent to death – must be avoided, just as much as dispersion. The solution to both dangers is represented by the image of a river that, while flowing, always remains in its own riverbed. Hillesum borrows this image from a letter of Rainer Maria Rilke written to his beloved Lou-Andreas Salomé:

> I keep on dividing and flowing apart – and I would so like to grow great coursing along a single bed. For that is how it should be, Lou, shouldn't it – we should be like a river, not diverted into canals carrying water to the meadows. We should hold ourselves together and rush ahead, shouldn't we? Perhaps when we are very old we may just once at the very end give way, spread out and flow into a delta…[13]

The Self as God

> I regained contact with myself, with the deepest and best in me, which I call God.[14]

Once you discover your inner voice, the source of the soul, Hillesum writes, there you find God. If we compare one of her most fundamental intuitions to the common reception of Western theology, the contrast seems immeasurable. To say that God lives within us is for any monotheistic religion an absurdity, even a blasphemy: if God is the most unreachable, distant entity from humankind, the almighty creator of the universe and the most perfect reality, how could he be found within material and imperfect beings as humans are?

13 E.T., 324. *Het Werk,* 338; Saturday morning, 4 April 1942: und ich teile mich immer wieder und fließe auseinander, – und möchte doch so gerne in *einem* Bette gehn und groß werden. Denn, nicht wahr, Lou, es soll so sein: wir sollen wie ein Strom sein und nicht in Kanäle treten und Wasser zu den Weiden führen? Nicht wahr, wir sollen uns zusammenhalten und rauschen? Vielleicht dürfen wir, wenn wir sehr alt werden, einmal, ganz zum Schluß, nachgeben, uns ausbreiten und in einem Delta münden… Rilke's letter of the 8 August 1903 is published in *Briefe 1902-1906,* edited by Ruth Sieber-Rilke and Carl Sieber (Leipzig: Insel Verlag, 1929), 115-17.

14 E.T., 83. *Het Werk,* 88; Sunday morning, 10 August 1941: Ich bekam wieder Kontakt mit mir selber, mit dem Tiefsten und Besten was in mir ist und was ich Gott nenne.

But unfrightened of irreverence, this is exactly what Hillesum discovers and argues: a "divinity" of the Self. When she meets herself, indeed, Hillesum speaks of God; when she loses herself, God is absent, and one must seek him over again in each instance, like a hidden spring from which one craves to drink.

In the absence of the Self and of God, which for Hillesum are the same thing, the act of praying reveals the longing for the encounter. Prayer makes possible an intimate connection with God; it is a search, by means of the word, for a presence we do not find. What is characteristic of Etty Hillesum's discourse, however, is that this quest does not imply an address to the outside, but a retreat in the inside. She discovers that by withdrawing into herself, her hands upon her chest, her forehead touching the ground, God's presence will be revealed to her. This is why it is necessary for Hillesum, in order to pray, to kneel. The very posture of her body in prayer is significant; it is connected to her representation of God, as she states in one of her most quoted passages:

> I imagine that there are people who pray with their eyes turned heavenward. They seek God outside themselves. And there are those who bow their head and bury it in their hands. I think that these seek God inside.[15]

The posture of the body, here, is a posture of enclosure, and it reveals that God is to be found in the inside. It is a reversal of the ecstatic posture: ecstasy[16] represents the act of exiting from oneself with the aim of joining the divine. At the roots of mysticism lays the same idea: God is outside, and in order to reach him it is necessary to distance oneself from one's own material reality, including one's body, perceptions, and thoughts.

In her diary, however, Hillesum speaks of an opposite movement: a turn inward, which is the beginning of a process of *conversion*, which, after all, etymologically means nothing more than to change direction. This representation of God as the core of the Self can also be found, in a sort of spiritual fraternity, in one of the fathers of Christianity, Augustine of Hippo. For Augustine, God is *interior intimo meo*: more intimate for me than my own intimacy. That is why, as Augustine suggests in his

15 E.T., 92. *Het Werk,* 97; Tuesday evening, 26 August 1941: Ik stel me voor, dat er mensen zijn, die bidden met hun ogen naar de hemel geheven. Die zoeken God buiten zich. Er zijn ook mensen, die het hoofd diep buigen en in de handen verbergen, ik denk, dat die God binnen in zich zoeken.

16 The word comes from Ancient Greek *ekstasis*, formed of *ek* ("out") and *histemi* ("to stand"), meaning "to stand outside."

Confessions when he remembers his unfruitful juvenile attempts to reach for God, we will always be unable to discover his presence in the outside world:

> Belatedly I loved thee, O Beauty so ancient and so new, belatedly I loved thee. For see, thou wast within and I was without, and I sought thee out there. Unlovely, I rushed heedlessly among the lovely things thou hast made. Thou wast with me, but I was not with thee.[17]

Ab exterioribus ad intima: the process that Augustine recalls is the passage from a continuous projection out to the world, into a retreat within the inner space of the divine. In his conception, therefore, God represents the most familiar entity we can confront. The same intuition can be found in Hillesum, who addresses God with such a simple and direct voice, and with such a real, palpable tenderness, that it is nearly impossible to know whether she is talking to herself or to someone else. But if in the beginning it is necessary to protect one's intimacy – the sanctuary of God – with walls and fortresses, with time the presence of God becomes so immediate and evident that no further research is needed, and the role of personal will becomes marginal.

What becomes essential instead, is to learn to "welcome" God, to open ourselves to the point that he can pass through us, exactly as happens with the breath: the air entering our bodies is intimately ours because during inhalation it only belongs to us, but as soon as we exhale, the same air flows beyond our body, spreading throughout the world. Even if Hillesum didn't specifically make use of this image, the biblical motifs resonating here seem in tune with her evolution towards dis-closure: in the Old Testament, God is referred to at times as *Ruach ha-Qodesh*, the Holy Spirit, where the word *ruach* means, in the first place, "wind," and "breath." If breath intimately belongs to the individual, it also belongs to any other human being, and to the space existing between them. If we embrace the metaphor, it means that every man can reach for God, and can also meet the other "through" God. In this respect, revelation is not only given in moments of solitude, but in moments of communion and connection as well, as if in those instants God "happened" between people, precisely like the breath.

This conception of reality suffused by the divine breath is to be called pantheism, the immanence of God into the world. The aim of this article

17 Augustine of Hippo, *Confessions*, Book X, 27.38, translated by Albert C. Outler.

is not to venture into the hypothesis of a pantheistic reading of Etty Hillesum,[18] but it is undoubted that the images of her diary evolve towards the idea of a pervasiveness of God into the world, which also explains Hillesum's fascination for the natural world, as the eternal testimony of his existence.

The Self as Home

A plaque hangs on the wall of the house where Hillesum was born in Middleburg, in remembrance:

> Op iedere plek van deze aarde is men "thuis", wanneer men alles in zich draagt.
>
> We *are* "at home" in every place on earth, if only we carry everything within us.[19]

Words taken from the diary where Etty Hillesum recalls a conversation with her friend Jopie under a starry sky in Camp Westerbork. How could she feel at home in a place that was for so many a place of devastation? Yet,

18 There is something of the *Deus Sive Natura* of Spinoza resonating in Hillesum's experience of God, but also something of the conception of God as *anima mundi* (peculiar to Renaissance Neoplatonist philosophers such as Ficino, Bruno and Campanella), where God represents the pattern of an invariably animated world. However, if we want to give justice to Hillesum's thought, we must mention that, alongside the image of God as a personal, interior voice and of God as the pattern of the world, there is also – and maybe even with a greater importance – the image of a transcendent God, the God *persona* of the Jewish-Christian tradition, which she addresses in the prayer. How to explain, otherwise, the act of kneeling and praying without any reference to faith or to the belief in the presence of an external divine entity? As Klaas A.D. Smelik has justly stressed in his essay "Ulrich Beck and Etty Hillesum" (in: Klaas Smelik, Gerrit Van Oord & Jurjen Wiersma (eds.), *Reading Etty Hillesum in Context: Writings, Life, and Influences of a Visionary Author* [Amsterdam: Amsterdam University Press, 2018], 456), what is peculiar to Hillesum, and makes her writing even more fascinating, is that "interdependently opposing visions exist alongside each other without replacing one another," and that the different statements about God "are comparable to the layers of an onion: one idea is enfolded in another, and the notion of the transcendent God functions as the inner core." For reasons of space, I cannot comment any further, but I have largely discussed the topic in my MA Thesis *Il racconto di sé come apertura etica: Un'analisi filosofica del diario di Etty Hillesum* (Roma 2018), in the chapter on Hillesum's conception of God, showing how essential to her growth is the relation to Otherness, and in particular to God as the Other. For an in-depth study, see Klaas A.D. Smelik's book *Il concetto di Dio in Etty Hillesum* (Sant'Oreste [Roma]: Apeiron editori, 2014).

19 E.T., 524. *Het Werk*, 555; Sunday night, 20 September 1942.

no nostalgia for home. "We *are* at home. Under the sky. In every place on earth [...]."[20] Even in Camp Westerbork, one can be like a snail who always carries around its little house.

It is no accident that to remember Etty Hillesum's short and intense life, one of the most frequent images of her writing was chosen: home as the space of intimacy. Home is the first space we experience, the place from which we come and where we return, but also a place where we are sheltered from the world and its hardships. It represents a nest, a protected space on which Etty Hillesum wrote extensively, making it one of her most enchanting motifs.

First, speaking about home, she refers to the small space in the apartment where she lived in Amsterdam on Gabriël Metsustraat. Later she narrows her notion of home to her room, the desk full of books and the window overlooking the Rijksmuseum. And then, the space she needs to feel at home shrinks to a tiny corner where she can kneel and hide. Lastly, something new happens. Hillesum discovers while praying that an airy space has opened within herself, a place where she can settle down. Now these loved spaces can be carried around: if the Self is made our home, then we are no longer alone since our home is always with us. Thus, anywhere in the world we are not alone, for we can plant roots wherever we wish if we are rooted in ourselves.

It is astonishing that in the years of major devastation, when millions of Jews were forcibly taken away from their homes and deported to places forgotten by mankind, Etty Hillesum wrote about roots. Her age was, as Martin Buber would have suggested, a "homeless" age, where one does not even own "four pegs to mount a tent,"[21] and is forced in the face of loneliness to confront the question of the Self. Etty Hillesum, who lived in one of those times, sought in herself the home that a hideous history had taken away from her. And again, in the images she chose we find the same progression: at first, home is a confined internal space, similar to a monastery, a place of silence, separated from the outside world through high, thick walls:

> I draw prayer round me like a dark protective wall, withdraw inside it as one might into a convent cell [...]. Withdrawing into the closed cell of prayer is becoming an ever-greater reality for me as well as a necessity.

20 *Ibidem*: Men is "thuis". Onder de hemel is men thuis. Op iedere plek van deze aarde is men "thuis",

21 Martin Buber, "What is man?", in: *idem, Between Man and Man* (London and New York: Routledge Classics, 2002), 150. The English edition of the text was firstly published in 1947. In the same year, the text was published in German as "Das Problem des Menschen", in the volume: *idem, Dialogisches Leben: Gesammelte philosophische und pädagogische Schriften* (Zürich: Müller, 1947).

> That inner concentration erects high walls around me within which I can find my way back to myself, gather myself together into one whole, away from all distractions.[22]

And later, once she feels grounded in herself, owning her home to the extent that she is able to bring the "quiet room" she has discovered through prayer always with herself, the images change. Having found her own solid shape and contour, she can open the doors of her "house" and let the world cross it with its lights and shadows. The Self will then be portrayed as an immense, open, limitless landscape, which looks in Hillesum's words like the vast plains of Russia she was longing for:

> My inner landscape consists of great, wide plains, infinitely wide, with hardly a horizon in sight – one plain merging into the next.[23]

> Last night I felt suddenly that my inner landscape was like a vast ripening cornfield.[24]

With this last image, we see clearly that the concept of the Self in Etty Hillesum is an entity in which opposites are reunited. It may sound as a contradiction, but it is precisely through the act of enclosing that vastness – and Otherness – will be discovered. And this is why Hillesum can imagine the Self, progressively and simultaneously, as chaos and discipline, as a source and a river, as a familiar and personal God and the energy governing life, as a convent cell and an infinite prairie.

About the Author

Sara Gomel (1993) received her master's degree in Philosophy at the University of Rome la Sapienza, with a thesis on self-narration and ethics in

22 E.T., 364. *Het Werk,* 380; Monday, 18 May 1942: Ik trek het gebed om me heen als een donkere beschuttende muur, in het gebed trek ik me terug als in een kloostercel [...]. Zich terugtrekken binnen de gesloten cel van het gebed, dit wordt voor mij een steeds grotere realiteit en ook noodzakelijkheid. Die innerlijke geconcentreerdheid richt hoge muren om mij heen op, waarin ik mezelf weer terugvind, me uit alle verstrooiingen weer bijeenraap tot één geheel.
23 E.T., 60. *Het Werk,* 64; Wednesday morning, 11 June 1941: Mijn innerlijke landschap bestaat uit grote, wijde vlaktes, oneindig wijd, er is nauwelijks een horizon, de ene vlakte gaat over in de andere.
24 E.T., 246. *Het Werk,* 255; Friday morning, 20 February 1942: Ik had opeens het gevoel vannacht, dat m'n innerlijke landschap er uitzag als wijde graanvelden, die te rijpen stonden.

Etty Hillesum's diaries. For her thesis, she has had the opportunity to make research at the EHOC in Middelburg. She received her bachelor degree in Philosophy at the University of Paris 1 – Panthéon La Sorbonne in 2015. Since the beginning of her studies, she has been working on educational and social projects for children and more specifically on projects of philosophy for children in schools and museums.

A Story of Individuation in the Writings of Etty Hillesum

A Jungian Perspective

Maribeth Kallemeyn

Abstract

The diaries and letters of Etty Hillesum illuminate her path of individuation. This contribution explores how Hillesum wrestled with and deepened into three key elements of individuation: linking with primal sources, genuine interpersonal encounter, and acknowledging pauses. A discussion of the risks of psychological projection in relationship to Etty Hillesum is included.

Keywords: individuation, Carl Gustav Jung, Julius Spier, acknowledgement of pauses, interpersonal encounters, linking to primal sources, projection

Beginnings

The diaries and letters of Etty Hillesum offer a compelling and concentrated account of her path of individuation. Carl Gustav Jung coined the term "individuation," and he described it as the process of "the coming-to-be of the self."[1] It was Jung's belief and discovery that human development does not stop with young adulthood, but continues for a lifetime.

"Become what thou art" was the chosen maxim of Julius Spier, who had been influenced deeply by Jung, and who became Etty Hillesum's chirologist,

1 Carl Gustav Jung, "On the Nature of the Psyche", in: *idem, The Structure and Dynamics of the Psyche* [Collected Works, vol. 8, edited by H. Read, M. Fordham & G. Adler, translated by R.F.C. Hull] (Princeton, NJ: Princeton University Press, 1960), para. 432.

Smelik, Klaas A.D. (ed.), *The Lasting Significance of Etty Hillesum's Writings: Proceedings of the Third International Etty Hillesum Conference at Middelburg, September 2018.*
Taylor & Francis Group 2019
DOI: 10.5117/9789463722025_KALLEMEYN

depth psychotherapist, mentor, lover, and friend.[2] Etty Hillesum was drawn to the process of becoming her own, full person. She wrote:

> this is the beginning, the first beginning of all:
>
> To take yourself seriously and to be convinced that it makes sense to find your own shape and form.[3]

The path of individuation is far from easy, as Etty Hillesum and Jung knew from personal experience. Jung wrote:

> Everything good is costly, and the development of personality is one of the most costly of all things. It is a matter of saying yea to oneself, of taking oneself as the most serious of tasks [...]. Truly a task that taxes us to the utmost.[4]

To engage in the process of becoming one's own full self requires a capacity and willingness to face unknown territory, descend into one's depths, and confront that which is "other." It requires saying "Yes" to large encounters, both inner and outer. It is not a "safe" path. It is this path to which Etty Hillesum repeatedly assented.

Why give attention to one's inner being, to finding one's own "shape and form"? Why take the risk of large encounters in unknown territory? Jung discovered, out of his own arduous, rich encounter with his depths, that the seeds of new growth, aliveness, and relationship are found there. Etty Hillesum quoted Jung in this regard:

> Nowhere are we closer to the sublime secret of all origination than in the recognition of our own selves, whom we always think we know already. Yet we know the immensities of space better than we know our own depths.[5]

2 Julius Spier, *The Hands of Children: An Introduction to Psycho-Chirology* (New Delhi: Sagar, 1944), 1.

3 E.T., 398. *Het Werk*, 418; Monday night, 8 June 1942: [O ja, maar dat wilde ik zeggen:] hier is het begin, het allereerste begin: het ernstig nemen van zich zelf en er van overtuigd zijn, dat het zin heeft z'n eigen vorm te vinden.

4 Carl Gustav Jung, "Commentary on 'The Secret of the Golden Flower'", in: *idem*, *Alchemical Studies* [Collected Works, vol. 13, edited by H. Read, M. Fordham & G. Adler, translated by R.F.C. Hull] (Princeton, NJ: Princeton University Press, 1967), para. 24.

5 E.T., 60. *Het Werk*, 116; Wednesday morning, 11 June 1941: Nirgends stehen wir näher dem vornehmsten Geheimnis aller Ursprünge als in der Erkenntnis des eigenen Selbst, das wir immer schon zu kennen wähnen. Aber die Tiefen des Weltraumes sind uns bekannter als die Tiefen

Etty Hillesum's beginning path toward finding her own shape and form is evidenced in her first two entries in her first exercise book, begun on 8 March 1941. She began with an interpersonal communication, a letter she wrote to Julius Spier.[6] The next day she wrote her first regular diary entry, embarking on a new relationship with her inner world.[7] Writing each of these entries required courage of her. Throughout the next two and a half years, until her deportation from Camp Westerbork on 7 September 1943, Etty Hillesum experienced and chronicled a profound deepening in both her intrapsychic and interpersonal relationships.[8] She lived into five key elements of individuation, in her own words and her own way.[9] Three of these five elements are discussed below: linking with primal sources; genuine interpersonal encounter; and acknowledging pauses.

Linking with Primal Sources

> If after a long and arduous process, day in, day out, you manage to reach your primal sources, which I will call God now, and if you make certain that your path to God is unblocked – which you can do by 'working on yourself' then you can keep renewing yourself at these sources and need never again be afraid of wasting your strength.[10]

des Selbst. Citing Carl Gustav Jung, "Analytical Psychology and *Weltanschauung*", in: *idem*, *The Structure and Dynamics of the Psyche* [Collected Works, vol. 8, edited by H. Read, M. Fordham & G. Adler, translated by R.F.C. Hull] (Princeton, NJ: Princeton University Press, 1960), para. 737.

6 E.T., 3. *Het Werk*, 3; Saturday 8 March 1941.

7 E.T., 4. *Het Werk*, 4; Sunday 9 March 1941.

8 Jung identified the intrapsychic and interpersonal aspects of individuation: "Individuation has two principal aspects: in the first place it is an internal and subjective process of integration, and in the second it is an equally indispensable process of objective relationship. Neither can exist without the other." See Carl Gustav Jung, "Specific Problems of Psychotherapy", in: *idem*, *The Practice of Psychotherapy* [Collected Works, vol. 16, edited by H. Read, M. Fordham & G. Adler, translated by R.F.C. Hull] (Princeton, NJ: Princeton University Press, 1954), para. 448.

9 Maribeth Kallemeyn, *A Story of Individuation in the Diaries and Letters of Etty Hillesum: A Jungian Perspective* [Unpublished manuscript, 2018], 32-83.

10 E.T., 535. *Het Werk*, 566; Monday, 28 September 1942: Wanneer men, na een lang en moeizaam proces, dat dagelijks verder gaat, is doorgebroken tot die oerbronnen in zichzelf, die ik nu maar God wens te noemen, en wanneer men er voor zorgt, dat die weg tot God vrij en onverbarricadeerd blijft – en dat geschiedt door "werken aan zichzelf" – dan vernieuwt men zich steeds weer aan die bron en dan hoeft men ook niet angstig te zijn, dat men te veel krachten geeft.

A key aspect of Etty Hillesum's "long and arduous process" was letting go of familiar reliance on her intellect as a primary way of approaching the world. She articulated her struggle and diagnosed herself:

> That is your disease: you want to capture life in formulas of your own. You want to embrace all aspects of life with your intellect instead of allowing yourself to be embraced by life.[11]

> I still lack a basic tune... The inner source that feeds me keeps drying up and, worse still, I think much too much.[12]

Jung had a similar struggle near the beginning of his inner journey:

> I am still a victim of my thinking. When can I order my thinking to be quiet, so that thoughts, those unruly hounds, will crawl to my feet? How can I ever hope to hear your voice louder, to see your face clearer, when all my thoughts howl?[13]

These two confessions, alive with language written out of direct experience, draw us into a feeling-proximity with the struggle to let go of privileging thinking and the intellect, in order to link to a deeper realm and hear a deeper voice.

Etty Hillesum discovered the act of inner listening, or hearkening, in her process of making contact with and trusting her primal sources: "I listen in to myself; allow myself to be led, not by anything on the outside, but by what wells up from deep within."[14] From a Jungian perspective, Hillesum's ego was becoming relativized as she nudged her intellect and outer authorities off to the side. She turned inward, and she said "Yes" to what she found.

Later that same evening (31 December 1941), Etty Hillesum wrote that she "hope[d] to make some progress with Jung this evening." Still later in the evening, she quoted Jung at length, including this:

11 E.T., 119. *Het Werk*, 126; Saturday night, 5 October 1941: Dat is je ziekte: je wilt het leven vangen in eigen formules. Je wilt alle verschijnselen van dit leven omvatten met je geest inplaats van je zelf te laten omvatten door het leven.

12 E.T., 72. *Het Werk*, 77; Monday, 4 August 1941: Ik heb nog geen grondmelodie... de innerlijke bron waaruit ik gevoed word, slibt altijd weer dicht en bovendien denk ik te veel.

13 Carl Gustav Jung, *The Red Book: Liber Novus, A Reader's Edition*, edited by Sonu Shamdasani, translated by Mark Kyburz, John Peck & Sonu Shamdasani (New York/London: Norton, 2009), 148.

14 E.T., 212. *Het Werk*, 221; Wednesday, 31 December 1941: Het je laten leiden, niet meer door dat wat er van buiten op je afkomt, maar wat er van binnen in je opstijgt.

> From Jung: 11 o'clock
> "A high regard for the unconscious psyche as a source of knowledge is not nearly such an illusion as our Western rationalism likes to suppose. We are inclined to assume that in the last resort all knowledge comes from without. Yet today we know for certain that the unconscious has contents which would bring an immeasurable increase of knowledge if they could only be made conscious."[15]

The words Hillesum wrote early in the evening are synchronous with this passage from Jung which later that same evening she read and copied into her diary. These are two expressions of the validity and value of the inner depths. Etty Hillesum speaks with immediacy and in vivid detail about her way of linking to an inner source of knowledge. Jung's expression is more abstract, drawn from his own direct experience of contact with primal sources.

Approximately one year after beginning her diary, Etty Hillesum summarized her perspective on the movements that had taken place within her that year, in a letter to her friend, Aimé van Santen:

> What I have gone through this year is really quite simple, but I believe of incisive bearing on my further life. The cosmos has moved from my head to my heart, or in my particular case, to my midriff – anyway from my head to another area.[16]

The "cosmos" within Etty Hillesum had moved downward, out of head and intellect. In the same letter, she continued with a quote from Jung:

> And now I shall again quote someone else's words, this time C.G. Jung's:

15 E.T., 213. *Het Werk,* 222; Wednesday, 31 December 1941: Die Wertschätzung der unbewußten Psyche als Erkenntnisquelle ist keineswegs so illusionär, wie unser westlicher Rationalismus es haben möchte. Unsere Neigung ist es, anzunehmen, daß alle Erkenntnis in letzter Linie immer von außen stamme. Wir wissen aber heute bestimmt, daß das Unbewußte über Inhalte verfügt, die, wenn sie bewußt gemacht werden könnten, einen unabsehbaren Erkenntniszuwachs bedeuten würden. Citing Carl Gustav Jung, "The Basic Postulates of Analytical Psychology", in: *idem, Modern Man in Search of a Soul,* translated by W.S. Dell & Cary F. Baynes (New York/ London: Harcourt Brace Jovanovich, 1933), 185.

16 E.T., 557. *Het Werk,* 591; Letter 4, To Aimé van Santen, Amsterdam, Sunday morning, 25 January 1942: Het proces, dat ik dit laatste jaar heb doorgemaakt, is eigenlijk zo eenvoudig, maar ik geloof dat het doorslaggevend is voor het hele verdere leven. De Kosmos is uit m'n hoofd verhuisd naar het hart, of voor mijnentwege naar het middenrif, in ieder geval uit m'n hoofd naar een ander regioon.

> "… So experienced, 'god' too is a theory in the most literal sense, a way of looking at the world, an image which the limited human mind creates in order to express an unfathomable and ineffable experience. The experience alone is real, not to be disputed; but the image can be soiled or broken to pieces…"[17]

Here, Jung discriminates between image and "unfathomable experience." This discrimination is essential, for it creates a separation which makes room for a human being to participate directly with primal sources. Without the separation, the ego (the ordinary, familiar human self) either reduces the unfathomable to the comprehensible or gets swallowed up in a state of identification and inflation. With a separation, the potential for a free relationship with primal sources is possible. Etty Hillesum lived into this kind of relationship. It was a relationship marked by encounter, dialogue, Eros, and exquisite care.[18]

17 E.T., 557. *Het* Werk, 591; Letter 4, To Aimé van Santen, Amsterdam, Sunday morning, 25 January 1942: '… Auch "Gott" in diesem Sinne ist eine Theorie, eine Anschauung, ein Bild, das der menschliche Geist in seiner Beschränktheit sich erschafft, um ein unausdenkbares, unaussprechbares Erlebnis auszudrücken. Das Erlebnis ist das einzig Wirkliche, das nicht Wegzudisputierende. Bilder aber können beschmutzt und zerrissen werden' citing Carl Gustav Jung, "Meaning of Psychology" [Collected Works, vol. 10, edited by H. Read, M. Fordham & G. Adler, translated by R.F.C. Hull] (Princeton, NJ: Princeton University Press, 1970), para. 330.

18 See e.g. E.T., 488: […] all that really matters: that we safeguard that little piece of You, God, in ourselves. *Het Werk*, 516; Sunday morning, 12 July 1942: En dit is het enige, wat we in deze tijd kunnen redden en ook het enige, waar het op aankomt: een stukje van jou in onszelf, God.; E.T., 489: I look after You, I bring you not only my tears and my forebodings on this stormy, gray Sunday morning, I even bring you scented jasmine. And I shall bring You all the flowers I shall meet on my way. *Het Werk,* 517; Sunday morning, 12 July 1942: Je ziet, ik zorg goed voor je. Ik breng je niet alleen mijn tranen en bange vermoedens, ik breng je op deze stormachtige, grauwe Zondagochtend zelfs geurende jasmijn. En ik zal je alle bloemen brengen, die ik op mijn wegen tegenkom.; E.T., 494: I hold a silly, naïve, or deadly serious dialogue with what is deepest inside me, which for the sake of convenience I call God. *Het Werk,* 523; Wednesday evening, 15 July 1942: […] ik houd een dolzinnige of kinderlijke of doodernstige dialoog met dat allerdiepste in me, dat ik gemakshalve maar God noem.; E.T., 519: The most essential and the deepest in me hearkening unto the most essential and deepest in the other. God to God. *Het Werk,* 549; Thursday morning, 17 September 1942: Het wezenlijkste en diepste in mij dat luistert naar het wezenlijkste en diepste in de ander. God tot God.; E.T., 640: My life has become an uninterrupted dialogue with You, oh God, one great dialogue. *Het Werk,*682; Wednesday, 18 Augustus 1943: Mijn leven is geworden tot één ononderbroken samenspraak met jou, mijn God, één grote samenspraak.; E.T., 657: And if we just care enough, God is in safe hands with us despite everything. *Het Werk,* 701; Thursday, 2 September 1943: En als wij er maar zorg voor dragen, dat ondanks alles, toch God bij ons in veilige handen is […].

A Meeting of Two Personalities

Genuine interpersonal encounter is a second key element of individuation. Jung wrote: "The meeting of two personalities is like the contact of two chemical substances: if there is any reaction, both are transformed."[19]

When a genuine meeting happens, two-way change is catalyzed. The contact between Etty Hillesum and Julius Spier was such an encounter. Their meeting impacted both. We have in-depth access to how this unfolded in Etty Hillesum through her diary, which she used to express and reflect on her experience with Spier. While we have less direct access to Spier's inner world, there are indications that he was willing to be marked by their encounter as well.

Spier was significantly influenced by Jung because he underwent training analysis with him in the late 1920s.[20] Later, in his book *The Hands of Children,* Spier wrote: "Whenever I make reference to analysis I mean Professor C.G. Jung's system of analytic psychology, which I know, theoretically as well as empirically."[21] Spier also wrote a description of analysis:

> an analysis, if properly conducted, transfers things from the intellectual sphere to the sphere of emotional and spiritual experience [...]. Analysis is not merely a method that can be grasped and fathomed by the intellect but an inner experience which affects the personality as a whole and leaves a deep and indelible mark on the person's innermost being.[22]

Spier had an "empirical" knowledge of analysis, born out of personal experience, rather than a knowing by intellect only. From his words here, it is safe to assume that he had an analytic experience with Jung that left a "deep and indelible mark" on his "innermost being." This is important contextual background to the encounter between Spier and Hillesum.

19 Carl Gustav Jung, "Problems of Modern Psychotherapy", in: *idem, The Practice of Psychotherapy* [Collected Works, vol. 16, edited by H. Read, M. Fordham & G. Adler, translated by R.F.C. Hull] (Princeton, NJ: Princeton University Press, 1954), para. 163.

20 Klaas A.D. Smelik, "A short biography of Etty Hillesum (1914-1943)", in: Klaas A.D. Smelik, Ria van den Brandt & Meins G.S. Coetsier (eds.), *Spirituality in the Writings of Etty Hillesum: Proceedings of the Etty Hillesum Conference at Ghent University, November 2008* [Supplements to The Journal of Jewish Thought and Philosophy, 11] (Leiden/Boston, MA: Brill, 2010), 21-28, especially p. 24.

21 Spier, *The Hands of Children*, 102, footnote.

22 *Ibidem*, 103-104.

Etty Hillesum wrote about an early therapy session with Spier, which took place prior to her first letter to him. One of Spier's maxims was: "Body and soul are one":

> But to go back. 'Body and soul are one.' That was no doubt why he began to test my physical strength in a sort of wrestling match. It was apparently more than adequate, for, remarkably enough, I floored the man, big though he was. All my inner tensions, the bottled-up forces, broke free, and there he lay, physically and also mentally, as he told me later, thrown. No one had ever been able to do that to him before, and he could not conceive how I had managed it. His lip was bleeding. I was allowed to dab it clean [...]. An embarrassingly intimate thing to do. But then he was so 'free', so guileless, so open, so unaffected in his movements, even as we tumbled about together on the ground. And even when I, held tightly in his arms and finally tamed, lay under him, he remained 'objective', pure, while I surrendered to the physical spell he emanated. It all seemed so innocent, this wrestling, new and unexpected, and so liberating. It was not until later that it took hold of my fantasies.[23]

This account is a problem for any thoughtful, contemporary therapist, raising large ethical questions. It would seem a given that Spier's breach of professional boundaries would inflict damage. And yet a deeper look at Hillesum's account suggests that something potentially transformative happened in this forbidden territory.

In Hillesum's account we get clues that she and Spier were both willing to be subject to something outside of and larger than their egos, that is, something along the lines of an interpersonal "chemical reaction." Hillesum threw her full weight into the encounter and so did Spier. Neither hid. Spier was thrown by her physically and psychically. "No one had ever been able to do that to him before," and Spier let Hillesum know it. He gave her access

23 E.T., 6-7. *Het Werk*, 6-7; Sunday, 9 March 1941: Aber jetzt. "Körper und Seele sind eins." Op grond daarvan begon hij zeker m'n lichamelijke krachten te meten in een worstelpartij. Die krachten van mij bleken nogal erg groot te zijn. En toen gebeurde het merkwaardige, dat ik deze grote kerel tegen de vlakte smeet. Al mijn innerlijke gespannenheid, samengebalde kracht brak los en daar lag hij, lichamelijk en ook psychisch, zoals hij me later vertelde, tegen de grond gesmeten. Dat had nog nooit iemand bij hem gepresteerd. Hij begreep niet hoe ik het had klaargespeeld. Z'n lip bloedde. Die mocht ik schoonwassen met eau-de-cologne. Een unheimisch, vertrouwelijk werkje. Maar hij was zo "vrij", zo argeloos, open, ongekunsteld in z'n bewegingen, ook toen we samen over de grond rolden, en ook toen ik stijf in z'n armen gekneld, eindelijk getemd, onder hem lag, bleef hij "zakelijk", zuiver, hoewel ik me even overgaf aan de lichamelijke bekoring, die er van hem voor mij uitging. Maar het was alles nog goed, zuiver, voor mij iets nieuws en onverwachts en ook iets bevrijdends, dat worstelen, hoewel het later te sterk op m'n phantasie werkte.

to that. She was embarrassed. Both of their egos had moved off to the side, a necessary surrender for any real encounter to happen.

As their relationship unfolded, Etty Hillesum and Spier became a creative problem for one another. Both were individually required to grapple with and suffer things through their relationship, and both acknowledged it.

Hillesum wrote repeatedly of Spier's impact on her and of the value of the relationship to her: "he has dug up God in me and brought Him to life [...] Jul [= Julius Spier] [...] my most precious and most radical experience."[24] On the occasion of his death, Hillesum, as perceptive witness, gives an intimate window into Spier's being:

> All the bad and all the good that can be found in a man were in you – all the demons, all the passions, all the goodness, all the love – great discerner, God-seeker, and God-finder that you were. You sought God in every human heart that opened up before you – and how many there were! – and found a little bit of him in each one. You never gave up, you could be so impatient about small things, but about the important things you were so patient, so infinitely patient.[25]

Here Etty Hillesum's voice rings with clarity and potency. She has travelled many miles from the beginnings of her encounter with Spier to this penetrating eulogy upon his death. Her words bear witness to the quality of their encounter, to her own capacity to see deeply into another, and to her strong link to her own inner authority. She had been marked by the encounter with Spier, and she was also free.

Acknowledging Pauses

"One must acknowledge one's pauses!!!"[26] With this declaration, Etty Hillesum ended Exercise Book 11 and the diaries to which we have access.

24 E.T., 567. *Het Werk,* 602; Friday, 11 September 1942: hij heeft God in mij opgegraven [...] Jul [...] mijn kostbaarste en ingrijpendste belevenis.

25 E.T., 517. *Het Werk,* 547; Tuesday night, 15 September 1942: Al het slechte en al het goede, wat er in een mens kan zijn, was er in jou. Alle demonen, alle hartstochten, alle goedheid, alle mensenliefde, jij, grote begrijper, godzoeker en godvinder. Overal heb je God gezocht, in ieder mensenhart, dat zich voor je opende – en wat zijn dat er vele geweest – en overal vond je een stukje God. Je gaf het nooit op, in kleinigheden kon je zo ongeduldig zijn, maar in het grote was je zo geduldig, zo oneindig geduldig.

26 E.T., 550. *Het Werk,* 583; early morning Tuesday, 13 October 1942: MAN MUSS SEINE PAUSEN WAHRHABEN WOLLEN!!!

She first came into contact with this notion through Spier.[27] She was drawn to the idea and over time she made it her own. It took on unique meaning for her. Klaas Smelik noted: "This concept [...] bec[a]me one of Etty's leading thoughts."[28]

"Pauses" for Etty Hillesum were difficult inner emotional experiences. In several diary entries, she wrote her way through these painful experiences and worked to acknowledge the pause rather than fight it or flee into dissociation.[29] She was working with an important aspect of individuation: Coming into relationship with the weak, inferior, struggling aspect of being human, in the shadow territory of life.

Hillesum's stance toward "pauses" was related to her stance toward suffering. Both Jung and Hillesum discriminated between genuine suffering and false, or neurotic, suffering. Neurotic suffering is actually a refusal to suffer, where an authentic touching of a wound is avoided. Jung wrote: "Neurosis is always a substitute for legitimate suffering."[30] Hillesum wrote: "most of us in the West do not understand the art of suffering and

27 Etty Hillesum copied these quotations from Spier into her diary: E.T., 28: "Pessimistic depressions should be regarded as creative pauses during which one's strength is being restored [...]. *One should never feel depressed about a depression." Het Werk,* 30; Monday, 17 March 1941: Pessimistische Depressionen sind als schöpferische Pausen zu betrachten, in denen sich die Kräfte wieder herstellen; E.T., 29: "One must have the courage to pause and to feel tired. If one goes beyond one's powers, then one will also refuse to *acknowledge* one's relapses." *Het Werk,* 31; Monday, 17 March 1941: Man muß den Muth haben zum Pausenmachen und zum Müdesein. Wenn man sich übersteigert, so will man die Rückfälle *nicht wahr haben.*

28 E.T., 692, note 93. *Het Werk,* 734, note 99.

29 See e.g. E.T., 92-93: On days like this I am sure that no one suffers as much as I do. Imagine somebody in pain all over his body, unable to bear anyone touching him even with the tip of a finger that's the feeling in my soul [...]. Sometimes I don't feel like carrying on [...]. One "must acknowledge one's pauses", but I wilt during the 'pauses', or so it seems to me. *Het Werk,* 98-99; Thursday night, 4 September 1941: Ik verbeeld me op zo een dag als vandaag dat er niemand zo erg lijdt als ik. Wanneer een mens pijn heeft over z'n hele lichaam en niet kan velen dat een ander hem ook maar met één vinger aanraakt, zo is het dan met mijn ziel [...]. Ik heb er soms niets geen zin meer in. [...] Men moet z'n "Pausen wahr haben wollen". Maar ik zit wel heel erg midden in de "Pausen", lijkt me zo tenminste.; E.T., 378: I [...] must have the courage to be alone with my weakness, to be that small bundle of exhausted and not very inspired humanity I happen to be at the moment and nothing more. *Het Werk,* 396; Tuesday night, 26 May 1942: Ik moet me nu dwingen om [...] met m'n krachteloosheid alleen te durven zijn en net dàt hoopje vermoeide en niet zeer bezielde mens te zijn, dàt ik op het ogenblik ben en niet meer.

30 Carl Gustav Jung, "Psychology and Religion", in: *idem,* Psychology and Religion: West and East [Collected Works, vol. 11, edited by H. Read, M. Fordham & G. Adler, translated by R.F.C. Hull] (Princeton, NJ: Princeton University Press, 1958), para. 129.

experience a thousand fears instead. We cease to be alive."[31] She also wrote: "We suffer most by playing hide and seek with suffering and calling curses down upon it."[32]

In the last two diary entries to which we have access, Etty Hillesum wrote a detailed account of her work with a pause. She was in Amsterdam, hoping to return to Camp Westerbork, but she was quite ill, grounded by her body's limitation. Spier had died a few weeks prior. She was not able to "do" anything, only to be in bed, with insomnia making matters worse:

> And then again there are moments in which life is dauntingly difficult. Then I am agitated and restless and tired all at once [...]. All I can do is to lie motionless under my blankets and be patient until I shed my dejection and the feeling that I'm cracking up being scattered to the four winds. When I felt like that in the past, I used to do silly things: go out drinking with friends, contemplate suicide, or read right through the night, dozens of books at random [...]. One must have the courage to call a halt, to feel empty and discouraged – Goodnight, dear gorse —[33]

As in earlier entries, here again Etty Hillesum worked to acknowledge the pause. She bore witness to the experience as she gave it expression on paper, articulating the paradoxically active stance of simply being with the felt sense of limitation. She recognized the courage it took to stay present with the pain. Out of this solitary, difficult inner work, something potent emerged: care. She used a term of endearment, "dear gorse," as she bid herself good night. In that moment, she was not at internal odds. She was not neurotic. She was not caught in destructive self-criticism. She did not cast blame. She was linked with herself.

Etty Hillesum's acceptance of her anguish and the care she offered herself in the midst of it was a significant psychic act. This acceptance and care

31 E.T., 459. *Het Werk,* 484; Thursday morning, 2 July 1942: de meeste Westerlingen verstaan de kunst van het lijden niet en ze krijgen er duizend angsten voor in de plaats. Dit is geen leven meer,

32 E.T., 183. *Het Werk,* 192; Monday morning, 15 December 1941: Men lijdt het meest door verstoppertje te spelen met het lijden en er tegen te vloeken.

33 E.T., 549. *Het Werk,* 582; Monday evening, 12 October 1942: En dan komen er weer van die ogenblikken, waarop het leven zo ontmoedigend moeilijk is [...]. En nu heb ik niets anders te doen dan dit: roerloos onder m'n dekens gaan liggen en geduldig zijn tot die moedeloosheid en verstovenheid naar vele kanten weer van me afvalt. Vroeger ging ik in zo een toestand gekke dingen doen: drinken met vrienden of over zelfmoord nadenken of nachten lang lezen in honderd boeken door elkaar [...]. Men moet eens leeg en moedeloos durven zijn – Goeienacht lieve duindoorn –

for the struggling, limited aspect of being human is an essential task of individuation. Jung wrote of its importance and difficulty:

> simple things are the most difficult. In actual life it requires the greatest discipline to be simple, and the acceptance of oneself is the essence of the moral problem and the epitome of a whole outlook upon life.[34]

Early the next morning, 13 October 1942, Etty Hillesum wrote her final diary entry to which we have access. She ended this entry in a striking way: "ONE MUST ACKNOWLEDGE ONE'S PAUSES!!!"[35] As is visually apparent on a photograph of this page, she drew a messy, horizontal line near the bottom of the page, under everything she had written thus far (see Figure 1). She then wrote her final sentence in darker lettering, ending it with three exclamation points.

Given Etty Hillesum's emphasis on this final sentence, it is of note that it has been ignored by multiple Hillesum scholars. The problem begins with *An Interrupted Life*, a selection of Etty Hillesum's writings compiled and edited by Jan Geurt Gaarlandt. Hillesum's final sentence is not included in that selection.[36] But what is more, in his introduction, Gaarlandt explicitly and incorrectly claims that the diary ends with the sentence just above the horizontal line, and he gives that sentence great weight.[37] Several scholars after Gaarlandt do the same.[38]

In addition to the erasure of Etty Hillesum's last sentence, there is an additional problem for those reading the English translation. Arnold Pomerans, the translator of Etty Hillesum's works into English, translated the sentence

34 Carl Gustav Jung, "Psychotherapists or the Clergy", in: *idem*, *Modern Man in Search of a Soul*, translated by W.S. Dell & Cary F. Baynes (New York/London: Harcourt Brace Jovanovich, 1933), 235.

35 E.T., 550. *Het Werk*, 583; Tuesday, 13 October 1942, early morning: man muss seine pausen wahrhaben wollen!!!

36 Etty Hillesum, *An Interrupted Life: The Diaries of Etty Hillesum, 1941-1943*, edited by J.G. Gaarlandt, translated by Arnold J. Pomerans (New York: Washington Square Press, 1985), 243.

37 Jan Geurt Gaarlandt, "Introduction", in: *An Interrupted Life: The Diaries of Etty Hillesum, 1941-1943* (New York: Washington Square Press, 1985), x.

38 Frans Maas, *Spirituality as Insight: Mystical Texts and Theological Reflection* (Leuven: Peeters, 2004), 142; Meins G.S. Coetsier, *Etty Hillesum and the Flow of Presence: A Voegelinian Analysis* (Columbia, MO: University of Missouri Press, 2008), 16-17; Patrick Woodhouse, *Etty Hillesum: A Life Transformed* (London & New York: Continuum, 2009), 153; Maria Clara Lucchetti Bingemer, "The Journey of Etty Hillesum from Eros to Agape", in: Klaas A.D. Smelik, Meins G.S. Coetsier & Jurgen Wiersma (eds.), *Ethics and Religious Philosophy of Etty Hillesum: Proceedings of the Etty Hillesum Conference at Ghent University, January 2014* [Supplements to The Journal of Jewish Thought and Philosophy, 28] (Leiden/Boston, MA: Brill, 2017), 67-89, especially pp. 80-81.

Figure 1 Last page of the 11th diary

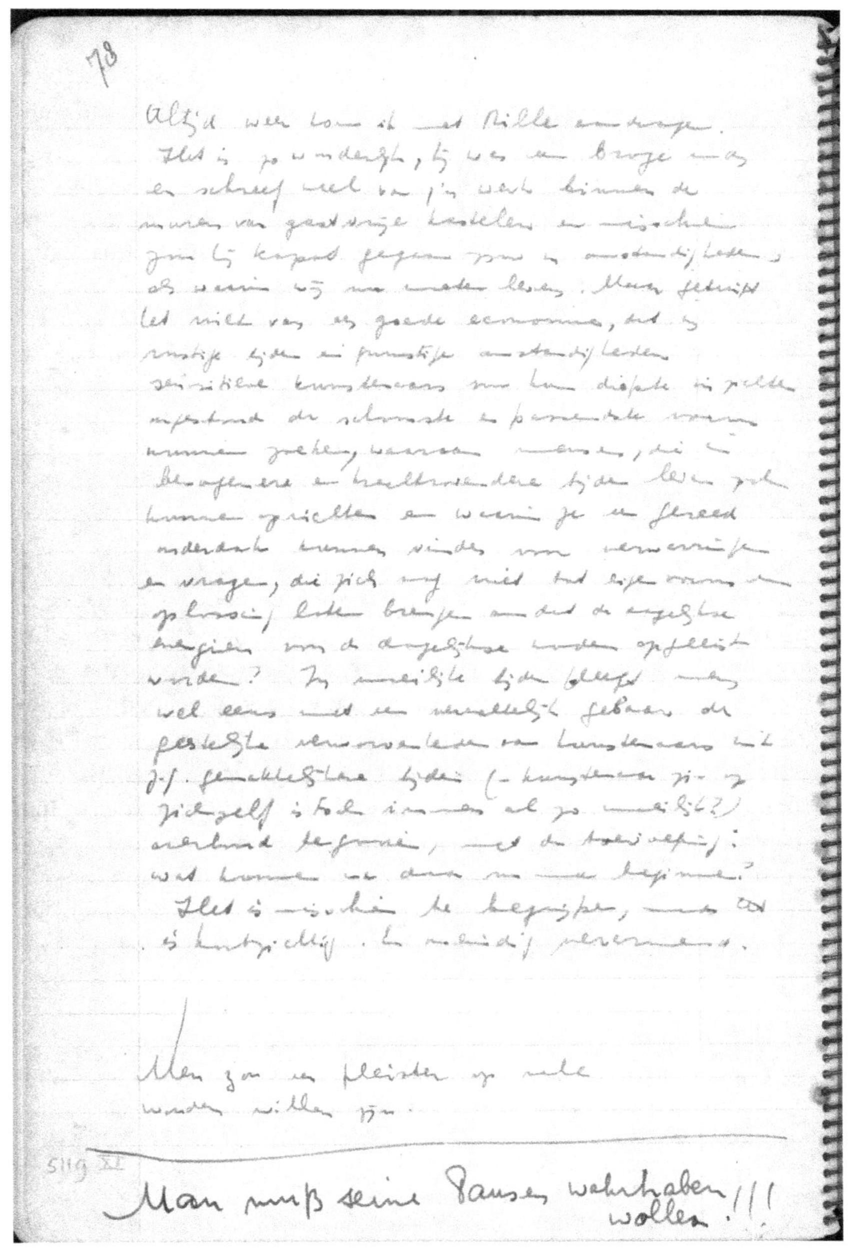

78

Altijd weer kom ik met Rilke aandragen. Het is zo wonderlijk, hij was een broze man en schreef veel van zijn werk binnen de muren van gastvrije kastelen en misschien zou hij kapot gegaan zijn in omstandigheden als waarin wij nu moeten leven. Maar getuigt het niet van een goede economie, dat in rustige tijden en gunstige omstandigheden sensitieve kunstenaars van hun diepste en zuiverste inzichten de schoonste en passendste vormen kunnen zoeken, waarin mensen, die in bewogener en krachtmetender tijden leven zich kunnen oprichten en waarin ze een gereed onderdak kunnen vinden voor verwarringen en vragen, die zich nog niet tot eigen vormen en oplossing laten brengen omdat de dagelijkse energieën voor de dagelijkse nooden opgebruikt worden? In moeilijke tijden pleegt men wel eens met een minachtend gebaar de geestelijke verworvenheden van kunstenaars uit z.g. gemakkelijke tijden (– kunstenaar zijn is zelf is toch immers al zo moeilijk?) overboord te gooien, met de toevoeging: wat kunnen we daar nu mee beginnen?
Het is misschien te begrijpen, maar het is kortzichtig. En onzinnig verarmend.

Men zou een pleister op vele wonden willen zijn.

5119 XI

Man muß seine Pausen wahrhaben wollen!!!

Collection Jewish Historical Museum, Amsterdam

just above the horizontal line as: “We should be willing to act as a balm for all wounds.”[39] A more accurate translation is: “One would like to be a balm on many wounds.”[40]

Pomerans used the words “We should” rather than “One would like.” And he used “all” rather than “many.” This is a marked discrepancy in word choice and the resulting difference in meaning is clear.[41]

What does it mean that Etty Hillesum ended Exercise Book 11 as she did? Of what import did the act of drawing the line have for her? We get a clue from an earlier diary entry in which she did not actually draw a line on the page, but she spoke of drawing a line, metaphorically:

> Yes, I am still at the same desk, but it seems to me that I am going to have to draw a line under everything and continue in a different tone. I must admit a new insight into my life and find a place for it: what is at stake is our impending destruction and annihilation, we can have no more illusions about that.[42]

In this passage, Hillesum wrote of drawing a line under everything she had written thus far, as a way to emphasize her felt need to “continue in a different tone.” It appears that the “different tone” here included seeing clearly, free of illusion, the stark reality of the Nazi intent to destroy.

In her final entry, Etty Hillesum did actually draw a line, and I suggest that she did so for a similar reason: to emphasize, on this occasion with an actual physical action, her wish to “continue in a different tone.” The “different tone” with which she continued is suggested by the darker lettering, the three exclamation points, and the statement itself.

To summarize: Etty Hillesum expressed a wish to be a balm for many wounds. But she did not end there. She drew a line. And then she made her final forceful statement: “ONE MUST ACKNOWLEDGE ONE’S PAUSES!!!” This

39 E.T., 550. *Het Werk,* 583; Tuesday morning, 13 October 1942: Men zou een pleister op vele wonden willen zijn.

40 See also Ria van den Brandt, *Etty Hillesum: An Introduction to Her Thought* (Munster: LIT Verlag, 2014), 19.

41 For a critique of Pomerans’s Dutch-to-English translation, see Harry Monkel, “Translator’s Forward”, in: Van den Brandt, *Etty Hillesum*, 9-10.

42 E.T., 461 [emphasis added]. *Het Werk,* 486; Friday evening, 3 July 1942: Het is waar, ik zit nog aan het zelfde bureau, maar het is me, of ik een streep onder al het vorige zetten moet en op een nieuwe toon verder gaan. Men moet een nieuwe zekerheid in zijn leven een onderdak geven, men moet er even een plaats voor vinden: het gaat om onze ondergang en onze vernietiging, daarover hoeft men zich geen enkele illusie meer te maken.

is not a sentence to ignore or erase. It is one of Etty Hillesum's hard-won, leading thoughts.

The errors of omission and translation suggest that projection may at times get in the way of seeing Etty Hillesum clearly. She is a likely target for projection for multiple reasons. She died an untimely, unjust death, murdered by the Nazis, which is a recipe for idealization. She was an introspective, articulate woman, uninterested in conventional living or thinking. Finally, she gave intimate access to her inner being through her writings. This profound access naturally brings up hopes, longings, and fears in those who encounter her, and when these are activated, the temptation to project, to reduce, or to redefine who she was is great [D. Carpenter, personal communication, 2018]. But Etty Hillesum asked herself, and she asks us, for more than that. She asks us to stay open, even as she worked to stay open to the complexity, ambiguity, and paradoxes of life and of her own personhood. She asks us to meet her on her individuating path in the same way she herself did, for, in her words, "Life cannot be forced into a system. Nor can people."[43]

About the Author

Maribeth Kallemeyn (1955) lives in Salem, Oregon, USA, where she has maintained a psychology practice since 2001. She received her PhD in clinical psychology from Fuller Graduate School of Psychology in Pasadena, California in 1995. She received certification as a Jungian analyst in 2018, having completed her analytic training through the C.G. Jung Institute Pacific Northwest. Her thesis was entitled *A Story of Individuation in the Diaries and Letters of Etty Hillesum: A Jungian Perspective.* She is a member of the Pacific Northwest Society of Jungian Analysts and the International Association for Analytic Psychology.

43 E.T., 180. *Het Werk,* 189; Sunday morning, 14 December 1941: Het leven is niet in een systeem te vangen. Ook niet een mens.

Mad Midrash in the Diaries of Etty Hillesum

Marc P. Lalonde

Abstract

The purpose of this essay is to examine Etty Hillesum's wartime reflections on the divine-human relation as a species of "mad midrash." According to the modern Jewish philosopher Emil Fackenheim, mad midrash entails an inventive, theological narrative that responds to the inconceivable bond that joins the world, the divine and "the anti-world" that is Auschwitz. It is "mad" because the relation strikes as impossible, yet relation there is. In answer to such aberration, mad midrash as mad dares to voice, protest against and partially mend an unthinkable history that is the Holocaust. Hillesum's mad midrash, the author claims, involves a depiction of God without recourse and a human(e) existence that bears witness "that God lived, even in these times." These creative theological stories express, protest and restore, in some measure, the unimaginable history that is the Holocaust. To flesh this out, the author explores the character of the diary as such; as that which proliferates in times of historical turmoil, including the Holocaust; and finally, as a type of mad midrash.

Keywords: "mad midrash", Auschwitz, Shoah, God, wartime diary writing, Emil Fackenheim, trauma

The purpose of this essay is to examine Etty Hillesum's wartime reflections on the divine-human relation as a species of "mad midrash." According to the modern Jewish philosopher Emil Fackenheim, mad midrash entails an inventive, theological narrative that responds to the inconceivable bond that

Smelik, Klaas A.D. (ed.), *The Lasting Significance of Etty Hillesum's Writings: Proceedings of the Third International Etty Hillesum Conference at Middelburg, September 2018.*
Taylor & Francis Group 2019
DOI: 10.5117/9789463722025_LALONDE

joins the world, the divine and "the anti-world"[1] that is Auschwitz. It is "mad" because the relation strikes as impossible, yet relation there is. In answer to such aberration, mad midrash as mad dares to voice, protest against and partially mend an unthinkable history that is the Holocaust. Such is its spirited yet precarious aim. Hillesum's mad midrash, I claim, involves a depiction of God without recourse and a human(e) existence that bears witness "that God lived, even in these times."[2] These creative theological stories express, protest, and restore, in some measure, the unimaginable history that is the Holocaust. To flesh this out, I explore the character of the diary as such; as that which proliferates in times of historical turmoil, including the Holocaust; and finally, as a type of mad midrash.

In "The courage to write: Biography and religion in Etty Hillesum and Søren Kierkegaard," Ulrich Lincoln asks a question that bears repeating: "We know Etty Hillesum mainly as a writer of a diary. But what does that mean [...]?"[3] Indeed, Hillesum begins her journals with some apprehension: "This is a painful and well-nigh insuperable step for me: yielding up so much that has been supressed to a blank sheet of lined paper."[4] As Bunkers and Huff confirm, the choice to keep a diary emerges from the need to "give shape and meaning to life with words."[5] What, then, is the shape and meaning provided by Hillesum's words? What do her diaries, as diaries, involve?

It should be underlined that the character of the diary "as such" is wide ranging.[6] Scholars who have studied the genre stress there is no ideal type.[7] This amorphous feature is especially the case for the modern diary which focuses on the writer's interior life and transitory experience.[8] As

1 Cf. Emil L. Fackenheim, "Midrashic existence after the Holocaust," in: Michael L. Morgan (ed.), *The Jewish Thought of Emil Fackenheim: A Reader* (Detroit, MI: Wayne State U.P., 1987), 332.

2 E.T., 506. *Het Werk*, 536; Monday, 27 July 1942: [...] dat God ook in deze tijd nog geleefd heeft.

3 Cf. Ulrich Lincoln, "The courage to write: Biography and religion in Etty Hillesum and Søren Kierkegaard," in: Klaas A.D. Smelik, Meins G.S. Coetsier & Jurjen Wiersma (eds.), *The Ethics and Religious Philosophy of Etty Hillesum: Proceedings of the Etty Hillesum Conference at Ghent University, January 2014* [Supplements to The Journal of Jewish Thought and Philosophy, 28] (Leiden/Boston, MA: Brill, 2017), 158-169, especially p. 158.

4 E.T., 4. *Het Werk*, 4; Sunday, 9 March 1941: Dit wordt een pijnlijk en haast onoverkomelijk moment voor mij: het geremde gemoed prijs geven aan een onnozel stuk lijntjespapier.

5 Cf. Suzanne L. Bunkers & Cynthia A. Huff, "Issues in studying women's diaries: A theoretical and critical introduction," in: Suzanne L. Bunkers & Cynthia A. Huff (eds.), *Inscribing the daily: Critical essays on women's diaries* (Amherst, MA: University of Massachusetts Press, 1996), 12.

6 Cf. Amos Goldberg, *Trauma in the first person: Diary writing during the Holocaust* (Bloomington, IN: Indiana U.P., 2017), 10.

7 Cf. Alexandra Garbarini, *Numbered days: Diaries and the Holocaust* (New Haven, CT: Yale U.P., 2006), 17.

8 Cf. Goldberg, *Trauma in the first person*, 12.

echoed in the diaries of Hillesum, "This writing is a sort of rough draft; I try things out, discard this and that and hope all the pieces will fit together in the end."[9] Thus, modern diaries represent a disjointed chain of responses to the writer's current set of circumstances.[10] Two opposing effects follow from this disjunctive focus on the lived life.

First, the erratic character of the modern diary is matched by an "underground poetic," to borrow Dostoevsky's phrase.[11] Namely, it entails an account marked by fragmentation, paradox and an absence of an overarching narrative.[12] The diary's "plot" hurdles from event to event, from idea to idea, and from image to image without forging a coherent connection between them. Second, the modern diary still constitutes a "tale." The accent on the diarist's personal history obtains an autobiographical shape where a life story is carved out as a first-person narrative.[13] According to Amos Goldberg, the modern diary entails "all the identity-creating characteristics of the life story and autobiography [...] [but] in a far more fragmentary fashion."[14] Indeed, narrative, life story, autobiography, etc. are key to the ways a diary creatively transforms human experience into literature.[15] The modern diary may thus be said to establish a hybrid text: shapeless, yet not without a rough outline; and flexible, yet not without an approximate goal.[16] Such an amalgam seems key.

Beyond this characterization of the modern diary, there is an additional facet that bears upon a more complete understanding of Hillesum's work; one that classifies the diary as a type that proliferates during periods of historical upheaval. When one's yesterday can no longer explain one's today, then keeping a daily log may help to conserve a modicum of continuity. In such a disturbing context, writes Goldberg, the diary provides a measure of coherence as it "weaves a fine narrative thread between the fragments of the protagonist's disintegrating world."[17] It comes as no surprise, then, to learn

9 E.T., 70. *Het Werk*, 74; Monday, 4 August 1941: Dit is een soort kladschrift, ik zal af en toe maar eens iets proberen, er iets uitgooien, misschien worden alle stukjes nog eens een geheel [...].

10 Cf. Garbarini, *Numbered days*, 17.

11 *Ibidem*, 6.

12 Cf. Goldberg, *Trauma in the first person*, 10.

13 *Ibidem*, 6.

14 *Ibidem*, 36.

15 Cf. James Olney, "Autobiography and the cultural moment: A thematic, historical, and biographic introduction" in: James Olney (ed.), *Autobiography: Essays theoretical and critical* (Princeton, NJ: Princeton U.P., 1980), 10.

16 Cf. Bunkers and Huff, "Issues in studying women's diaries," 1.

17 Cf. Goldberg, *Trauma in the first person*, 36.

that diary writing flourished during the Second World War.[18] In regard to the Jewish community, the same holds true. Goldberg contends that most Jews "who began to write diaries did so under the Nazi occupation."[19] The reason? To bear witness, but also to partially escape the iron grip of a totalitarian regime by turning inward. There some degree of self-determination holds sway.[20] So Hillesum writes: "I'll 'turn inward' for half an hour each morning before work, and listen to my inner voice."[21] Thus, the diary obtains a therapeutic function that deals with the stress of a historical moment that imperils the diarist's very framework of meaning.[22]

This feature of the modern diary leads to a consideration of the Holocaust diary. Holocaust diaries, says Garbarini, represent desperate responses to life "in the shadow of annihilation."[23] Indeed, it is precisely the confrontation with such destruction that instigates the initial compulsion to write.[24] As Hillesum expresses this in relation to the devastation of Dutch Jewry, "And I shall wield this slender fountain pen as if it were a hammer, and my words will have to be so many hammer strokes with which to beat out the story of our fate and of a piece of history as it is and never was before."[25] While the Holocaust diarist is trying to make sense of the genocidal events unfolding around them, it is still unwise to reduce the Holocaust diary to one specific type. Rather, it is prudent to recognize the diversity of forms. There is no single type of Holocaust diary. Garbarini clarifies how Holocaust diaries reflect the "heterogeneity of the victims, [...] of their war-time perceptions and [their different] coping strategies."[26] What we encounter is a diversity of witness with "multiple layers of testimony."[27] These layers are shaped by various concerns: the diarists' theological beliefs, historical sensitivities, personal relationships, etc. Thus, Jews wrote diaries during the Holocaust for a whole host of reasons.

18 *Ibidem*, 10.

19 *Ibidem*, 8.

20 Cf. Garbarini, *Numbered days*, 2.

21 E.T., 56. *Het Werk*, 59; Sunday morning, 8 June 1941: 's morgens voor het begin van het werk een half uurtje "naar binnen slaan", luisteren naar wat er binnen in me zit.

22 Cf. Goldberg, *Trauma in the first person*, 7, 43.

23 Cf. Garbarini, *Numbered days*, 1.

24 Cf. Goldberg, *Trauma in the first person*, 90, and Garbarini, *Numbered days*, 4.

25 E.T., 484. *Het Werk*, 511; Friday morning, 10 July 1942: En met deze slanke vulpen zou ik nu moeten zwaaien als was het een hamer en de woorden zouden even zovele mokerslagen moeten zijn, om te vertellen over een lot en over een stuk geschiedenis, zoals het er voor dien nog niet was.

26 Cf. Garbarini, *Numbered days*, 3.

27 Cf. Zoe Vania Waxman, *Writing the Holocaust: Identity, testimony, representation* (Oxford: Oxford U.P., 2006), 1.

Nevertheless, typical of many Holocaust diaries is the battle between the diary as life story and as confrontation with extreme trauma. Holocaust diaries constitute "texts of struggle"[28] that document the determination to uphold a sense of self and purpose even as both modes of import dissolve. "It is my contention," states Goldberg, "that in the case of radical and immense traumatic events like the Holocaust [...] the narratives recounted by the victims [...] help to create a framework for traumatic experience that protects them from breaking down [...]."[29] Life story, then, helps to resist life destruction.

How does this characterization of the Holocaust diary apply to Hillesum?

Undoubtedly, there are times when Hillesum's diaries appear to be more "texts of crises" than "texts of struggle." Following Goldberg's analysis, a text in crisis mode suggests a work where personal problems are resolved by the unbeatable human spirit. It thus entails some sense of historical continuity while simultaneously conveying the potential for new life.[30] In keeping with this, Hillesum asserts that "I seem to be achieving a state of complete equilibrium. [...] I now listen all day long to what is within me, and even when I am with others I [...] am able to draw strength from the most deeply hidden sources in myself."[31] Hillesum appears to be dealing with existential challenges rather than moments of distress. In the process, she imparts the sense that things are unfolding as planned.

Still, I think it is equally evident that Hillesum is struggling with a sense of trauma. For example, she is painfully aware of the "Nazi barbarism;"[32] mindful how "The threat grows greater, and terror increases from day to day."[33] She mentions the ongoing arrests of Dutch citizens;[34] the disturbing suicides of former professors;[35] and the onslaught of anti-Jewish measures. On 1 July 1942, Hillesum observes: "This morning around seven o'clock, I was cast into a hell of alarm and despondency brought on by the new regulations."[36] Then we abruptly read:

28 Cf. Garbarini, *Numbered days*, 9; Goldberg, *Trauma in the first person*, 67-68.

29 Cf. Goldberg, *Trauma in the first person*, 89.

30 *Ibidem*, 56.

31 E.T., 234. *Het Werk*, 244; Monday morning, 19 January 1942: Er schijnt een volledig evenwicht in me tot stand te zijn gekomen. [...] ik luister de hele dag naar wat er binnen me is, ook wanneer ik tussen anderen ben, [...] put (ik) geregeld krachten uit de verborgenste en diepste bronnen in mezelf.

32 E.T., 21. *Het Werk*, 22; Saturday, 15 March 1941: nazi-barbarisme.

33 E.T., 364. *Het Werk*, 380; Monday, 18 May 1942: De bedreigingen van buiten steeds groter, de terreur stijgt met de dag.

34 E.T., 62. *Het Werk*, 65; Saturday, 14 June.

35 E.T., 53. *Het Werk*, 55; Tuesday, 25 March 1941.

36 E.T., 458 [revised]. *Het Werk*, 483; Wednesday morning, 1 July 1942: Vanochtend om een uur of 7 had ik even de hel van onrust en gejaagdheid in me over al die nieuwe verordeningen en

Mortal fear in every fiber.
Complete collapse.
Lack of self-confidence. Aversion. Panic.[37]

While I have alluded to these passages in an earlier essay as instances of personal crisis,[38] I now think they represent moments of personal trauma. For Hillesum seems drained; "lapsing into her own 'Dark Ages'"[39], nearly destroyed.

How does Hillesum respond to this ordeal? How does her narrative "create a framework for traumatic experience that protects [her] from breaking down"[40]? I would like to suggest that it does so by adopting a version of "mad midrash" that constitutes a creative theological narrative addressing the impossible bond between the world, God, and the "anti-world" that is the Holocaust. In Hillesum's case, her surprising revision of the divine-human relationship marks her peculiar aggadic-midrash as mad in its own way. But first some thoughts on aggadic-midrash.

Aggadah, says Joseph Heinemann, derives from the verb *le-haggid,* meaning "to say" or "to tell;"[41] while "midrash," notes S.M. Lehrman, stems from *darash,* meaning to "search in order to explain."[42] It constitutes an inventive scriptural exegesis in response to historical disruption. Here the unsettling event at play is the destruction of the Second Temple. This incident served to generate new forms of exegesis that yield "new understandings of Scripture for a time of crisis and [...] conflict [...]."[43] The goal? To demonstrate that living in step with the Torah is still on despite the historical upheaval. While Hillesum writes at one point that "I have recently been picking odd sentences from the Bible and endowing them with what for me is a new, meaningful, and experiential significance,"[44] her concern for the Torah is

dat is goed, ik kan daardoor iets van de angst van de anderen navoelen.

37 E.T., 141. *Het Werk*, 148; Thursday, 30 October 1941: Levensangst over de hele linie. Volledige inzinking. Gebrek aan zelfvertrouwen. Afkeer. Angst.

38 Cf. Marc P. Lalonde, "The religious meaning and significance of the Holocaust today: The diary of Etty Hillesum," *Journal of Jewish Identities* 9/1 (2016): 61-65.

39 E.T., 141. *Het Werk*, 148, Thursday afternoon, 30 October 1941: ... terugvallen in m'n eigen "zwartste middeleeuwen".

40 Cf. Goldberg, *Trauma in the first person,* 89.

41 Cf. Joseph Heinemann, "The nature of Aggadah," in: Geoffrey H. Hartman & Sanford Budick (eds.), *Midrash as Literature* (New Haven, CT: Yale U.P., 1986), 41.

42 Cf. S.M. Lehrman, *The world of midrash* (London: Thomas Yoseloff, 1961), 11.

43 Cf. Heinemann, "The nature of Aggadah," 42.

44 E.T., 157. *Het Werk*, 165, Friday morning, 28 November 1941: Ik heb het de laatste tijd dat af en toe een enkele zin uit de Bijbel voor me oplicht in een duidelijke, nieuwe, inhoudsrijke en

nominal. However, like aggadic-midrash, her diaries constitute a creative-literary response to historical change involving "new understandings of" the divine-human relationship for a time of disaster and "conflict." In the process, new values are fashioned in response to exacting historical circumstances. So the following passage from Heinemann on aggadic-midrash would seem to hold true of Hillesum's diaries as well. Namely, they represent a "poetic creation which has a vitality [...] which elevates and inspires the soul. Aggadic[-midrashic] creativity partakes of the power of the productive imagination; it embodies not only religious and moral values, but also artistic and aesthetic values of beauty and symmetry."[45]

In many respects, this approach to Hillesum's diaries is already shaped by a contemporary reading of aggadic-midrash as literature.[46] This interpretation stresses the overlap with postmodern literary theory and the parallel appreciation of "deep spontaneity;"[47] a "variety of 'open' modes of interpretation;"[48] a "waywardness" and "ability to function without apparent boundaries;"[49] and the "enduring power of the provisional"[50] that understands itself as provisional. More emphatically, the contemporary fascination with aggadic-midrash stems from the discovery of a "mode of creativity" which represents "more than just historical knowledge [...]."[51] The result? A popular form of contemporary Jewish spirituality[52] that is felt in Hillesum's diaries *avant la lettre*. As she notes, "All that matters now is the 'deep inner serenity for the sake of creation.' [...] I do believe that it is possible to create [...] by simply 'molding' one's inner life."[53]

Another voice concerning the significance of aggadic-midrash today has been that of Emil Fackenheim. This religious thinker has always considered

doorleefde betekenis.

45 Cf. Heinemann, "The nature of Aggadah," 52.

46 Cf. Geoffrey Hartman & Sandford Budick, "Introduction," in: Geoffrey H. Hartman & Sanford Budick (eds.), *Midrash as Literature* (New Haven, CT: Yale U.P., 1986); David Stern, *Midrash and theory: Ancient Jewish exegesis and contemporary literary studies* (Evanston, IL: Northwestern U.P., 1996): Barry W. Holtz, 1992. "Midrash and modernity: Can Midrash serve a contemporary religious discourse?" in: Jack Wertheimer (ed.), *The uses of tradition: Jewish continuity in the modern era* (New York: The Jewish Theological Seminary of America, 1992).

47 Cf. Hartman & Budick, "Introduction," ix-x.

48 *Ibidem*, xi.

49 *Ibidem*, xiii.

50 Cf. Hartman & Budick, "Introduction," xiii.

51 Cf. Stern, *Midrash and theory*, 10.

52 *Ibidem*, 2.

53 E.T., 318. *Het Werk*, 323; Wednesday, 1 April 1942: Het gaat alleen nog maar om het 'tiefes Gesammelt sein um des Bildens willen' [...]. Maar ik geloof, dat men ook zonder ooit één woord te schrijven of één schilderij te schilderen "bilden" kan, al is het het eigen innerlijke leven.

classical rabbinic aggadic-midrash as an indispensable way to explore the enigmatic religious situation of humankind;[54] namely, that which emerges from "the living relation between the infinite God and finite man [...]."[55] To be sure, this relation is not seamless. Says Fackenheim, the "bond between God and the world is always problematical."[56] The result? Paradox and ambiguity. However, "[t]he most authentic Word expressing this bond," writes Fackenheim, "is midrash."[57] Why? Because "[t]he midrashic Word is story. It remains story because it both points to and articulates a life *lived with* problems and paradox – the problems and paradox of a divine-human relation."[58] In effect, aggadic-midrashic thought is aware of such paradox yet does not aim to rationally resolve it.[59] Rather, it lets the paradox stand as story, as narrative and reaffirms the existence of the divine-human relation as such.

However, does the aggadic-midrashic bond hold if the finite world includes the anti-world, that is, Auschwitz? While Fackenheim's argument vacillates, he intimates that dissolution is the outcome. "Midrash is meant for every kind of imperfect world," he writes, but "[i]t is not meant for Planet Auschwitz, the anti-world."[60] This is because the anti-world entails far more than paradox: it occasions caesura.[61] How, then, does the Jewish thinker bridge such an abyss? The answer is not obvious. However, one thing is clear: after Auschwitz, the traditional aggadic-midrash is subject to revision if not rejection. Morgan states the matter unequivocally: "no attempt to understand Auschwitz within the framework of traditional midrashic thinking is satisfactory; if there can be midrashic thinking [...] it must have to chart a new direction."[62] And what is that new direction? "Mad midrash."

Thinking of the post-Holocaust literary corpus of Elie Wiesel, Fackenheim suggests that mad midrash is a narrative that simultaneously gives voice to, protests against, and partially mends the impossible bond that joins the

54 Cf. Michael Morgan, *Fackenheim's Jewish philosophy: An introduction* (Toronto: University of Toronto Press, 2013), 220.

55 Cf. Morgan, *Fackenheim's Jewish philosophy*, 226.

56 Cf. Fackenheim, "Midrashic existence after the Holocaust," 331.

57 *Ibidem*, 331.

58 *Ibidem*, 331.

59 Cf. Emil L. Fackenheim, *God's presence in history: Jewish affirmations and philosophical reflections* (New York: Harpertorchbooks, 1970), 20-25.

60 Cf. Fackenheim, "Midrashic existence after the Holocaust," 331.

61 Cf. Arthur A. Cohen, *The tremendum: A theological interpretation of the Holocaust* (New York: Crossroad, 1981).

62 Cf. Morgan, *Fackenheim's Jewish philosophy*, 237.

world, the divine, and the anti-world that is the Holocaust. This complex adumbrates a madness that cannot be eluded in a post-Holocaust context.[63] Consider, for example, the distressing episode of the sad-eyed angel in Wiesel's novel *Night*. After witnessing the brutal hanging of a young boy, a nameless inmate asks: "'Where is God? Where is He? [...] Where is God now?'"[64] The narrator responds to himself: "'Where is He? Here He is – He is hanging here on this gallows [...].'"[65] Is God, indeed, hanging on the gallows? Did God die in Auschwitz? Perhaps. Or is God imagined on the side of the victim? A form of desolate solidarity? Perhaps. The episode of the sad-eyed angel expresses, disputes, and partially restores an unbearable relation between the world, the divine, and the anti-world.

Is something like mad midrash at play in Hillesum's diaries? Do her reflections on the divine-human relationship during an age of trauma simultaneously voice, protest, and partially restore the difficult bond between the world, the divine, and the anti-world?

I want to begin with Hillesum's jarring claim that "God lived, even in these times."[66] Jarring because "in these times," people are being arrested and imprisoned en masse. Jarring because "in these times," "The latest news is that all Jews will be transported out of Holland through the province of Drenthe and then on to Poland."[67] Jarring because "in these times," God may be dead. May be. And yet for Hillesum, it is clear: "God lived, *even* in these times."

But what kind of God is she referring to? Surely not the traditional Jewish or Christian deity who directly intervenes in history in order to save. Indeed, the term "God," for Hillesum, is a metaphor for "our greatest and most continuous inner adventure [...]. [W]hen I [...] speak to God," she notes, "[...] it is [...] as if I were addressing something in myself, trying to plead with a part of myself."[68] Hillesum intends an indwelling "God" who wants an interior relationship. At the start of 1942, Hillesum writes, "God, I thank You [...] for wanting to dwell within me."[69] And in June of the same

63 Cf. Fackenheim, "Midrashic existence after the Holocaust," 333.

64 Cf. Elie Wiesel, *Night* (New York: Bantam Books, 1960), 61-62.

65 *Ibidem*, 62.

66 E.T., 506. *Het Werk*, 536; Monday, 27 July 1942: dat God ook in deze tijd nog geleefd heeft.

67 E.T. 455. *Het Werk*, 480 Monday morning, 29 June 1942: Het laatste bericht is, dat alle Joden uit Holland weggetransporteerd zullen worden, via Drenthe naar Polen.

68 E.T., 440. *Het Werk*, 463; Monday night, 22 June 1942: dan is het toch nèt of ik iets toespreek dat er in mijzelf is, of ik een stuk van mezelf te bezweren probeer.

69 E.T., 231. *Het Werk*, 240; Thursday, 15 January 1942: God, ik dank je [...] dat je in me wonen wilt.

year, "It means [...] living one's life with God and in God and God in me."[70] A number of consequences follow.

To start, this "God," as indwelling, means an involved, exposed, and vulnerable God ("'Where is [God]? Here He is – He is hanging here on this gallows [...].'") This "God" is not wholly transcendent but subject to the horrible things human beings inflict upon one other "in these times." Hillesum concludes: "[O]ne thing is becoming increasingly clear [...] that You [God] cannot help us [...]."[71] God appears helpless; ineffective; without saving power ("'Where is [God]?'"). A sense of abandonment ensues. Hillesum writes: "I must admit a new insight into my life [...]: what is at stake is our impending destruction and annihilation, we can have no more illusions about that."[72] However, rather than collapsing in the face of such abandonment, Hillesum sounds a note of resistance and protest: for "if God does not help me to go on," she declares, "then I shall have to help God."[73] God, too, must be safeguarded, fortified, and defended. "And that is all we can manage these days," writes Hillesum, "and also all that really matters: that we safeguard that little piece of You, God, in ourselves."[74] Herein lies a partial mending of the world. A moral task is advanced, spiritual aspirations are sounded, hope springs forth, however fragmentary. "You cannot help us, but we must help You and defend Your dwelling place inside us to the last."[75]

To conclude, Hillesum's reflections on the divine-human relation during the age of trauma advances an inventive way to articulate, dispute, and partly repair the difficult bond between the world, the divine, and the anti-world. "At difficult moments like these, I often wonder what You intend with me, oh God, and therefore what I intend with You."[76] The response? Mad midrash.

70 E.T., 439. *Het Werk*, 463; Monday night, 22 June 1942: ... het is een leven met God en in God en God in mij.

71 E.T., 488. *Het Werk*, 516; Sunday morning prayer, 12 July 1942: Maar dit éne wordt me steeds duidelijker: dat jij ons niet kunt helpen [...].

72 E.T., 461. *Het Werk*, 486; Friday evening, 3 July 1942: Men moet een nieuwe zekerheid in zijn leven een onderdak geven [...]: het gaat om onze ondergang en onze vernietiging, daarover hoeft men zich geen enkele illusie meer te maken.

73 E.T., 484. *Het Werk*, 512; Saturday morning 11 July 1942: En als God mij niet verder helpt, dan zal ik God wel helpen.

74 E.T., 488. *Het Werk*, 516; Sunday morning prayer, 12 July 1942: En dit is het enige, wat we in deze tijd kunnen redden en ook het enige, waar het op aankomt: een stukje van jou in onszelf, God.

75 E.T., 488-489. *Het Werk*, 517; Sunday morning prayer, 12 July 1942: [...] jij ons niet kunt helpen, maar dat wij jou moeten helpen en dat we de woning in ons, waar jij huist, tot het laatste toe moeten verdedigen.

76 E.T., 531. *Het Werk*, 562; Wednesday, 23 September 1942: Ik vraag me, op een moeilijk moment als vanavond, wel eens af, wat je bedoelingen met me zijn, jij God. En misschien zal het dáárvan

About the Author

Marc P. Lalonde (1961) is a Senior Lecturer in the Department of Religions and Cultures, Concordia University, Montreal, Canada. He is the author of "The Religious Meaning and Significance of the Holocaust Today: The Diary of Etty Hillesum", and "Moral Authenticity in a Turbulent Age: Charles Taylor and the Diaries of Etty Hillesum" [forthcoming].

afhangen, welke mijn bedoelingen met jou zijn?

The Mystery of Encounter

Poetry and Faith After Auschwitz in the Work of Paul Celan and Etty Hillesum

Ulrich Lincoln

Abstract
The article constructs a dialogue between Etty Hillesum and the poet Paul Celan. Both writers try to come to terms, poetically and conceptually, with the event of the Shoah. Both find their own respective language to search for the power of the human encounter in the face of existential nothingness and semantic levelling. Thereby Hillesum's work, just as Celan's poems, can be understood as a search for subtle languages that are truly capable of expressing meaning in the face of meaninglessness.

Keywords: Paul Celan, poetry, poetic language, language after Auschwitz, silence, dialogical writing

1 After Auschwitz: What is left of Language?

In 1949, Theodor Adorno famously remarked: "After Auschwitz, writing poetry is barbaric."[1] Adorno argued that culture was ineradicably affected by the experience of the Shoah. Auschwitz represents an ultimate historical divide. Adorno claims that not only poetry but all realms of society and culture are affected by this rift. And no part of human culture is able to reclaim a status out of it, as if there was an innocence untouched by the inherent barbarism of human culture as revealed in the events of the Shoah. The political and social circumstances that made Auschwitz possible, leave

1 Theodor W. Adorno, "Kulturkritik und Gesellschaft", in: *idem*, *Prismen: Kulturkritik und Gesellschaft* (Munich: Deutscher Taschenbuch Verlag, 1963), 26.

Smelik, Klaas A.D. (ed.), *The Lasting Significance of Etty Hillesum's Writings: Proceedings of the Third International Etty Hillesum Conference at Middelburg, September 2018.*
Taylor & Francis Group 2019
DOI: 10.5117/9789463722025_LINCOLN

no part of human culture untouched. If Adorno is right, this applies also to language, especially to the German language. It is this language which was polluted by the Nazis. This language in all its performative power was used to express and organize "the depth of scapegoating anger and hatred that the human soul can fall prey to," as Charles Taylor puts it. And even more, this language was used again to give cover for this crime in the years after the war:

> Not only in its terrible deviancy, but in its blindness to this deviancy, the pollution was contagious, threatening to spread through the whole system.[2]

Therefore, after Auschwitz the question arises: What is left of human language? Can language ever be used again to express meaning?

Etty Hillesum did not live to see the other side of the Auschwitz divide, the time after Auschwitz. She died *in* Auschwitz. However, she was keenly aware of the deep epochal change that her time was going through. From a certain time on, she writes her diary with the clear knowledge of her task: to write for the people who come after her:

> I shall become the chronicler of our adventures. I shall forge them into a new language and store them inside me should I have no chance to write things down.[3]

Etty Hillesum wants to be a chronicler and a witness for a new age. Beyond her own personal role, Hillesum also has a vision of this new age towards which she writes already now:

> I feel a new period is beginning in our lives, more serious and more intense, one in which we shall concentrate on the essentials.[4]

It seems that Etty Hillesum did have trust in the fate of humankind. She senses new life after Auschwitz. But what does that mean with regard to language? She writes of a new language. How would a new language be

2 Charles Taylor, *Celan and the Recovery of Language*, in: *idem*, *Dilemmas and Connections: Selected Essays* (Cambridge, MA: Belknap Press, 2011), 64.

3 E.T., 510. *Het Werk*, 540; Tuesday, 28 July 1942: Ik zal de latere kroniekschrijfster worden van onze lotgevallen. Ik zal me in mijzelf een nieuwe taal tezamensmeden en ik zal haar in mij bewaren, als ik niet de gelegenheid zal hebben iets neer te schrijven.

4 E.T., 464. *Het Werk*, 489; Friday, 3 July 1942: Het lijkt me of er nu een nieuw tijdperk in ons leven begint. Nòg ernstiger en ook nòg intensiever en een nog meer zich concentreren op het allernoodzakelijkste.

possible in the face of terror and genocide? Can we find resources in her work that hint towards a healing of polluted languages?

In what follows, I will try to sharpen the search for these hints by also looking at the work of another author who was trying to come up with an answer to Adorno's question: Paul Celan. It is as if both give an answer to Adorno, although their answers come from different sides of the divide called Auschwitz.

2 Meaning out of Nothing: Paul Celan's attempt to save language

Paul Antschel aka Paul Celan was born in 1920 to German-speaking Jewish parents in Czernowitz, then a part of Romania. During the war, Celan was deported; he survived and could return, only to learn that his parents were murdered by the Nazis. After the war, Celan continued writing in German, and his poems quickly established him as one of the foremost voices in post-war German literature. In 1970, Celan took his own life.

Celan writes in German, the language which is contaminated by the very crimes that destroyed his own family. Celan tries to find words and language in the face of this historic fate. He searches for truth and meaning within the very language that has been corrupted and contaminated to serve the Shoah. He says:

> In this language I have sought, during those years and the years since then, to write poems: so as to speak, to orient myself, to find out where I was and where I was meant to go, to sketch out reality for myself.[5]

Within the fearsome fragility of being and language, Celan tries to find a path for meaningful speech. But for that, he needs to step deep down into the abyss of pain and trauma, and begin his search at this low point where loss and brokenness take away someone's voice, even someone's breath, and make him gasp at this point of "breath turn" [Atemwende]:

> Poetry – that can mean an *Atemwende*, a breath turn. Who knows, perhaps poetry follows this route – also the route of art – for the sake of such a breath turn?[6]

Language sends the poet towards this point of gasping. And the poet follows language on its journey.

5 Paul Celan, *Collected Prose*, translated by Rosemarie Waldrop (New York: Routledge, 2003), 34.

6 *Ibidem*, 47.

> Only one thing remained reachable, close and secure amid all losses: language. Yes, language. In spite of everything, it remained secure against loss. But it had to go through its own lack of answers, through terrifying silence, through the thousand darknesses of murderous speech. It went through. It gave me no words for what was happening, but went through it. Went through and could resurface, "enriched" by it all.[7]

Language and art need to go through the experience of silence and nothingness. Therefore, it are these notions of nothing and nothingness, of nobody and nowhere, that Celan circles around in ever new figures and images. As in the poem titled "Psalm":

> No one kneads us again out of earth and clay,
> no one incants our dust.
> No one.
>
> Blessèd art thou, No One.
> In thy sight would
> we bloom.
> In thy
> spite.
>
> A Nothing
> we were, are now, and ever
> shall be, blooming:
> the Nothing-, the
> No-One's-Rose.
>
> With
> our pistil soul-bright,
> our stamen heaven-waste,
> our corona red
> from the purpleword we sang
> over, O over
> the thorn.[8]

7 *Ibidem*, 34.

8 Paul Celan, *Selected Poems and Prose, translated by John Felstiner* (New York: W.W. Norton & Company, Inc., 2001), 156 -157.

This poem reflects Celan's struggle with his Jewish heritage and with biblical faith. It is a prayer, and there is a "thou" spoken to, at least in the beginning. But at the same time, this addressee really is but a No one. The god of Jewish faith is still present but only as someone who is unknown. The God of Exodus, the God of Abraham, Isaak and Jacob, has lost his name: "Blessed are thou, No One". That God has a name, is one of the most important features of biblical, and indeed ancient, faith. It is the name that carries the aura of power, interaction and speech. In Celan's psalm there is no name left, only a trace, a distant memory. And accordingly, the collective We also is only a Nothing, a Nobody – but at the same time it is a living Nobody, a blossoming creature, homeless and bereft of any belonging: a No-One's-Rose.

That is how Celan climbs down into the underworld of language, religion and culture, into its storage, in order to search for fragments, shards and splinters, that make it possible to speak meaningfully and truthfully. By deconstructing the German language and the heritage of German poetics, of Hölderlin, Rilke and Stefan George, Celan attempts to give an answer to Adorno's verdict. He agrees with Adorno that any kind of aestheticization or poetic transfiguration of the Shoah in works of art is impossible. But this danger should not be allowed to render real poetry impossible.

3 Etty Hillesum and the Search for Subtle Languages

Hillesum's poet was Rilke. It is Rilke, who seems to be the natural partner for any attempt to understand Hillesum's ideas about language, about poetry, and about her own writing. However, we have already noticed that sometimes Hillesum's texts seem to jump forwards, beyond her own time, and look into a future after war and genocide. In that future, she found her calling as a writer. And what I would like to propose is that in that future there is another poet waiting for her, without ever getting to know her work or her story. Paul Celan is like a distant cousin, with a different life story, and yet in a sense sharing a similar destiny. His work as a poet is very different from all she ever produced; and yet, he is engaged in a very similar project: namely in the midst of destruction to find meaning and healing through the power of writing. Charles Taylor calls this the search for "subtle languages," a search that is characteristic for modern poetry and that can be found, among others, in Celan's work. Subtle languages are resonating languages in a world void of guaranteed or established meanings.[9] I believe that Hillesum should be recognized as being engaged in that very same endeavour.

Etty Hillesum did not write poetry. However, she wrote about the particular kind of language that was able to resonate, a language capable of gathering dimensions of reality that are deeper and wider than the blunt reality in front of our eyes:

> The landscape man carries within him he also seeks without. Perhaps that is why I have always had that strange longing for the wide Russian steppes. My inner landscape consists of great, wide plains, infinitely wide, with hardly a horizon in sight – one plain merging into the next. As I sit huddled up in this chair, my head bowed low, I roam across those bare plains, and when I have been sitting like that for a while, a feeling of well-being, of infinity and peace, comes over me. The inner world is as real as the outer world. One ought to be conscious of that. It, too, has its landscapes, contours, possibilities, its boundless regions. And man himself must be a small centre in which the inner and outer worlds meet.[10]

I believe what Hillesum here describes as the language of inner landscapes is exactly what Taylor has in mind when he talks about the subtle language of resonance. It is a particular way of thinking about reality: a deepening and listening kind of thought. A soundboard for reality. It is the same kind of resonating thought that a hundred years earlier Søren Kierkegaard had called the inwardness of human existence, by which he had meant: the absolute passion by which a person lives her life and takes responsibility for it. The same kind of a resonating inwardness, a deepening of life through language, we find in Hillesum's diaries and letters. And it is this approach to the power of language that makes her a relative also of Celan.

Hillesum did not write poems. But she did write a kind of poetics. Her reflection on the inner landscape is a first step towards that poetics. But

9 *Celan and the Recovery of Language*, 60; cf. Charles Taylor, *Sources of the Self: The Making of the Modern Identity* (Cambridge, MA: Harvard University Press, 1989), 456-493.

10 E.T., 60. *Het Werk*, 64; Wednesday morning, 11 June 1941: Het landschap, dat de mens in zich draagt, zoekt hij ook buiten. Misschien heb ik daarom altijd dat merkwaardige verlangen gehad naar de wijde Russische steppen. Mijn innerlijke landschap bestaat uit grote, wijde vlaktes, oneindig wijd, er is nauwelijks een horizon, de ene vlakte gaat over in de andere. En wanneer ik zo in elkaar gedoken zit op deze stoel, het hoofd heel diep gebogen, dan zwerf ik over die blanke vlaktes en wanneer ik een tijdje zo blijf zitten komt er een weldadig gevoel van eindeloosheid en rust over me. De binnenwereld is even reëel als de buitenwereld. Men moet dit bewust weten. Zij heeft ook haar landschappen, haar contouren, haar mogelijkheden, haar onbegrensde gebieden. En zelf is men het kleine centrum, waar binnen- en buitenwereld elkaar ontmoeten.

there is more, especially with regard to the process of writing and to the performance of language. In June 1942 she writes:

> The few great things that matter in life can be said in a few words. I hate the accumulation of words. If I should ever write – but what? – I would like to brush in a few words against a wordless background. To describe the silence and the stillness and to inspire them. What matters is the right relationship between words and wordlessness, the wordlessness in which much more happens than in all the words one can string together. And the wordless background of each short story – or whatever it may be – must have a distinct hue and a discrete content, just like those Japanese prints. It is not some vague and incomprehensible silence, for silence too must have contours and form. All that words should do is to lend the silence form and contours. Each word is like a small milestone's – a slight rise in the ground beside a flat, endless road across sweeping plains.[11]

This short notice is Hillesum's very poetical theory of poetic writing. Writing a text is a process of grasping, comprehending and of symbolizing, of putting into words what has been grasped. But this grasping and symbolizing begins in the space between the words and the wordlessness. This space-between is silence. Silence is the background from which words, stories, images step forward. And to shape and form this silence is the actual performance of writing. Writing is born out of the silence of language. Silence is an essential part of every language.

I find this is an astonishing text. It might be inspired by Hillesum's reading of Rilke. But it also brings to mind the poetics of Paul Celan: because for Celan as well silence is essential for language and for poetry, although perhaps for different reasons. We already have heard about Celan's notion of

11 E.T., 394. *Het Werk*, 413-414; Friday evening 5 June 1942: Ik haat een opeenhoping van woorden. Men kan eigenlijk met zo weinig woorden zeggen de paar grote dingen, waar het om gaat in het leven. Als ik ooit zal schrijven – wat eigenlijk? – dan zou ik enkele woorden willen penselen tegen een woordeloze achtergrond. En het zal moeilijker zijn die stilte en dat zwijgen af te beelden en te bezielen, dan de woorden te vinden. Het zal dan gaan om de juiste verhouding van woorden en woordeloosheid, een woordeloosheid, waarin meer gebeurt, dan in alle woorden, die men bij elkaar vinden kan. En in iedere novelle – of wat het ook zijn mag – moet de woordeloze achtergrond weer anders getint zijn en een andere inhoud hebben, zoals dat ook bij die Japanse prenten het geval is. Het gaat niet om een vaag en onvatbaar zwijgen, ook dat zwijgen zal z'n eigen kantige contouren moeten hebben en z'n eigen vorm. En dus zouden de woorden alleen moeten dienen om het zwijgen z'n vorm en omtrekken te verlenen. En is ieder woord als een kleine mijlpaal of als een kleine verheffing langs eindeloos vlakke en uitgestrekte wegen en wijde vlaktes.

"breath turn," the experience which makes somebody gasp. The breath turn is the moment of silence, and as such it is the origin of poetic language: "Poetry is perhaps this: an *Atemwende.*"[12] But we also noticed that the possibility of falling silent for Celan is not only something productive but also a terrifying danger constantly looming in the background of the historical experience of the 20th century. In his speech titled "The Meridian", Celan says:

> It is true, the poem, the poem today, shows – and this has only indirectly to do with the difficulties of vocabulary, the faster flow of syntax or a more awakened sense of ellipsis, none of which we should underrate – the poem clearly shows a strong tendency towards silence.[13]

Notice that this tendency emphatically is claimed only for the modern poem, that is the poem after Auschwitz. Silence is the absolute challenge for poetry, and it cannot be avoided or made undone. But then he continues:

> The poem holds its ground on its own margin. In order to endure, it constantly calls and pulls itself back from an "already-no-more" into a "still-there".[14]

Against the silencing of time and mortality stands the promise of staying in the present. But it is a dim promise. It is as if Celan's notion of silence was a dark reflection of Hillesum's emphatic understanding of the silence of language. Or do her words about the wordlessness perhaps also, consciously or unconsciously, reflect the looming danger of actually becoming nothing, of physical and mental nihilation, that very danger which surrounded her life every day? Or to put the question differently: How did Hillesum understand her work as a writer from that moment on when she was aware of her own fatal destiny? What did the silence around the words that she sensed in her writing have to do with the numbness and wordlessness that the world was thrown into during the war?

4 Celan and Hillesum: From Silence to Encounter

Our question was: Given the collective experience of the Shoah, what can we learn from Celan and Hillesum about the possibility of meaningful

12 Celan, *Collected Prose*, 47.

13 *Ibidem*, 48f.

14 *Ibidem*, 48f.

language resonating with truth and humanity? And we saw that Celan felt urged to face this experience in his work and to wrest the language of poetry from that very negativity. Etty Hillesum – in the midst of the ultimate danger of her own annihilation – found her own special way into that sacred inner space where meaning and love resonated. Sometimes, she would call that sacred space "God", and slowly and surprisingly she became fluent in a religious language that had not been with her before. In this, she obviously is very different from Celan who had abandoned the belief in God. And yet, there is more: Celan's work is very much shaped by a strong element of dialogue and encounter even at the edge of speechlessness and silence. For him, a Thou is still there. This Thou is not a god. But it does have the spark of a transcendent reality. Once, he describes the dialogical character of poetry as the way of a "Flaschenpost" [bottle message], and then he continues:

> Poems are *en route*. They are headed toward. Toward what? Toward something open, inhabitable, an approachable you, perhaps, an approachable reality. Such realities are, I think, at stake in a poem.[15]

For all its necessary loneliness, poetry is dialogical to its core. Celan wants us to see poetry as the very act of setting free, of opening up towards someone or something else in a way that no other action or experience could do. Poetry always orbits around silence, but at the same time it is always headed towards someone else.

> The poem intends another, needs an opposite. It goes towards it, bespeaks it. For the poem, everything and everybody is a figure of this other towards which it is heading.[16]

It seems that these sentences still harbour some remains of biblical faith. The strong notion of the other, in many figures, invokes the image of the God of covenant and Exodus, and the God of creation. And yet, the mystery of encounter is not a happy occasion. Celan calls it a "desperate conversation."[17] Mortality and loss are necessary ingredients of poetry. The poem has an inherent drive towards someone else, but it has no name to give or to address. No one's Rose.

15 *Ibidem*, 35.
16 *Ibidem*.
17 *Ibidem*, 50.

When Celan talks of the mystery of encounter, he has a strong sense of what encounter actually means. Encounter is nearness, free exchange, acknowledgement, concession, even vulnerability. These are qualities of humanity which are highly endangered in the time of Totalitarianism. Actually, the free and open encounter with the other, the acknowledgement of her face, freedom, and difference, these characteristics are the very things that the Nazis were most afraid of. Against the demons of that time, the mystery of true encounter has to be found and set free with the help of poetry.

It is exactly this performative quality of encounter which we also meet in Hillesum's texts. Her writing is dialogical through and through. Once she writes:

> *Hineinhorchen* – [...] Truly, my life is one long hearkening unto myself and unto others, unto God. And if I say that I hearken, it is really God who hearkens inside me. The most essential and the deepest in me hearkening unto the most essential and deepest in the other. God to God.[18]

Hillesum's diaries are one big conversation with her own life based on the encounter with God. And at the same time, many other voices and interlocutors are woven into this conversation. And so are the readers of today.

> Exactly that is the mystery of Hillesum's diary style: The Reader is not only listening, but is drawn into Etty Hillesum's self-conversation as another narrator [...]. These unpretentious sentences, that flow of self and God-talk allows the reader to immerse into the horizon of the other own life.[19]

However, the truly dialogical quality of this author becomes clear only once she climbs down into the depths of herself – and when she takes the reader along down that road. She writes:

> I have grown very humble. I no longer want to be this century's most famous writer. All I want is to find a few little words now and then to accommodate my gathering feelings. Just for myself. And I want always

18 E.T., 519. *Het Werk*, 549; Thursday morning, 17 September 1942: "Hineinhorchen" [...] Eigenlijk is mijn leven één voortdurend "hineinhorchen", in mijzelf, in anderen, in God. En als ik zeg: ìk "horch hinein", dan is het eigenlijk God in mij, die "hineinhorcht". Het wezenlijkste en diepste in mij dat luistert naar het wezenlijkste en diepste in de ander. God tot God.

19 Ulrich Beck, *Der eigene Gott: Friedensfähigkeit und Gewaltpotential der Religionen* (Frankfurt a.M.: Verlag der Weltreligionen, 2008), 22.

> to keep in touch with those depths from which the words well up, lest I feel like a ship that has lost its bearings. I know that I have a mooring. I don't lose my bearings all that often these days. And I always return, that is something I now know for certain. And when I do feel homesick now, I also know what for. I no longer look outside myself, but within – that, too, is something I have learned this year.[20]

She only wants to write for herself, but in that she wants to travel far out on the ocean of expression and language. This journey far out certainly includes encounters and new horizons. And a homecoming. Once again we are reminded of the way Paul Celan talks about the journey of the poem:

> The paths on which language becomes voice. They are encounters, paths from a voice to listening You, natural paths, outlines for existence perhaps, for projecting ourselves into the search for ourselves... A kind of homecoming.[21]

Encounter begins within the silent horizon of words, but it carries far beyond it. At the same time, it also carries a sense of home, of homesickness. Etty Hillesum walks this very path of searching for speech within the mystery of encounter, but she discovers that she can do that only as a religious path, as a journey to God, and with God. For her, God is just this very mystery, this transcendence on the ground of the self, which carries the self beyond itself.

Adorno later said about Paul Celan: "Celan's poems want to speak of the most extreme horror through silence."[22] And so does Etty Hillesum. In the end, she falls silent. Her diaries break off. Her last words to the world after her diaries are written on a postcard from the train to Auschwitz. But her testimony remains.

20 E.T., 237-238. *Het Werk*, 247-248; Friday afternoon, 23 January 1942: Ik ben heel bescheiden geworden. Ik wil niet meer de beroemdste schrijfster van deze eeuw worden. Ik wil af en toe maar een paar kleine woorden vinden, die de zwellende gevoelens herbergen. Alleen maar voor mezelf. En met die diepte, waaruit die woorden opwellen, wil ik steeds voeling houden, anders voel ik me als een losgeslagen schip. Ik weet, dat ik een ankerplaats heb. Ik sla niet vaak meer los. En ik keer toch altijd weer terug, dat weet ik nu heel zeker. En als ik tegenwoordig wel eens Heimweh heb, dan weet ik ook, waarnáár ik het heb. De gebieden, waarnaar ik Heimweh heb, moet ik niet meer buiten me zoeken, maar binnen me, ook dàt heb ik geleerd dit jaar.

21 Celan, *Collected Prose*, 53.

22 Theodor W. Adorno, *Aesthetic Theory* (London: Bloomsbury, 1998), 322.

About the Author

Ulrich Lincoln (1963) is a Lutheran pastor and area dean in Wolfsburg, Germany. He earned his theological doctorate at Goethe University in Frankfurt, Germany. He has published books and articles on Kierkegaard, Bonhoeffer, Hillesum and theological aesthetics (*Die Theologie und das Hören*, 2014).

Can Religion Help Heal a World Broken by Trauma?

Etty Hillesum as Our Ancestor in the *Qahal Goyim*

William McDonough

Abstract

Etty Hillesum is a religious model for responding to trauma. Tempted to withdraw by "splitting [herself] up" (4 June 1942), she instead saw herself as "heir to a great spiritual heritage" (18 September 1942), committing to "love everyone […] made in God's image" (18 August 1943). She is our contemporary Jacob, our ancestor in the *qahal goyim* (Genesis 35:11).

Keywords: recovery from trauma, survivors, religious responses to trauma, hands, Jacob, *qahal goyim*

Introduction: We are survivors seeking a life that is not "counterfeit"

American psychiatrist Robert Jay Lifton has focused much of his life's work on the psychic lives of Holocaust survivors and perpetrators. Yet he claims that all human beings living in the nuclear age are survivors:

> A survivor is one who has encountered, been exposed to, or witnessed death and has himself or herself remained alive. On that basis (and without in any way equating ordinary life to the experience of holocaust), we all have in us something of the survivor.[1]

1 Robert Jay Lifton, "Concept of the Survivor," in *The Future of Immortality and Other Essays for a Nuclear Age* (New York: Basic Books, 1987), 235, 231. For Lifton's writings on the holocausts of the Second World War, see his *Death in Life: Survivors of Hiroshima* (New York: Random House,

Smelik, Klaas A.D. (ed.), *The Lasting Significance of Etty Hillesum's Writings: Proceedings of the Third International Etty Hillesum Conference at Middelburg, September 2018.*
Taylor & Francis Group 2019
DOI: 10.5117/9789463722025_MCDONOUGH

Survivors, Lifton adds, often settle for "counterfeit nurturance [...] divesting the survivor experience of some of its psychological horror." To settle in this way is to trap ourselves in "patterns of distrust in human relationships and the sense that much of the world, even life itself, is counterfeit."[2] And religion, continues Lifton, is too often an accomplice to counterfeit survival: "We find little solace in the idea of a 'divine spirit' continuing on after the annihilation of humankind [...]. We need to experience the nurturing affirmations of everyday human life."[3]

Struggling myself with a tendency toward counterfeit religious survival, I search here for a more authentic religious response to survivorship. In this study, I am led by contemporary American writer Carol Flinders's contention that Dutch Jewish diarist and Holocaust victim Etty Hillesum (1914-1943) is a model for a more authentic religious life. Flinders reflects on what she calls Hillesum's terror of "splitting off" common in victims of trauma. Her trajectory argues that there is no situation within which it is impossible to have a spiritual practice, to come to life, to wake up.[4]

I wish here to understand something of how Hillesum "came to life," asking whether and how she can aid our own "waking up." Like Lifton, I do not mean to equate my suffering with hers. Yet I do want to develop the undoubtedly paradoxical claim that Hillesum – though murdered at Auschwitz – is a religious model for what we might call an imaginative return to everyday life.

This essay comprises three main sections and a conclusion. First, I survey the scientific research on trauma and its healing in the fifty years since Lifton first worked with survivors. Part two focuses briefly on what adequate religious-spiritual responses to trauma might look like. This leads to Hillesum as religious model in part three. To conclude. I claim her as a successor to the biblical patriarch Jacob. She is ancestor to all seeking wholeness in the *qahal goyim*, the religious assembly of all peoples.

1968) and *The Nazi Doctors: Medical Killing and the Psychology of Genocide* (New York: Basic Book, 1986).

2 Lifton, "Concept of the Survivor," 241-242.

3 *Ibidem*, 274.

4 Carol Flinders, *Enduring Lives: Portraits of Women and Faith in Action* (New York: Tarcher/ Penguin, 2006), 91-2, 95-6.

Part one: Insights into non-counterfeit survival from fifty years of psychology, neurology and neurobiology

After his work with Holocaust survivors, Lifton worked with US soldiers returning from Vietnam.[5] Together they convinced the American Psychiatric Association to recognize a new diagnosis; posttraumatic stress disorder (PTSD) appears for the first time in the third edition of APA's *Diagnostic and Statistical Manual* (1980). A researcher summarizes:

> PTSD described a cluster of symptoms that was common, to a greater or lesser extent, to all veterans, giving a name to the suffering of people overwhelmed by horror and helplessness [...]. This led to an explosion of research and attempts at finding effective treatments.[6]

Here, I survey that "explosion of research," outlining three developments in the scientific literature on trauma over the last fifty years.

a Feminist psychiatry on the everyday pervasiveness of trauma

Probably the most important broadened understanding has come in research into the trauma caused by childhood sexual abuse and spousal violence. Harvard psychiatrist Judith Herman's 1992 book *Trauma and Recovery* radically expanded the number and circumstances of those to be counted as direct victims of trauma.[7]

Herman cites Lifton repeatedly while subtly shifting his idea that survivors often settle for counterfeit nurturance. The pressure to settle comes from the survivor's environment, not from within. Her work with girls and women led Herman to outline a threefold process of recovery, beginning first when a survivor finds a basic sense of safety.[8]

In a second stage, Herman claims a survivor must take distance from her familiar environment.[9] Recovery's third stage is "reconnection": by

5 See Robert Jay Lifton, *Home from the War: Learning from Vietnam Veterans* (New York: Simon and Schuster, 1973).

6 Bessel van der Kolk, *The Body Keeps the Score: Brain, Mind and Body in the Healing of Trauma* (New York: Penguin Books, 2014), 19.

7 Judith Lewis Herman, *Trauma and Recovery: The aftermath of violence-from domestic abuse to political terror* (New York: Harper Collins, 1992).

8 *Ibidem*, 133.

9 *Ibidem*, 178, 196.

participating in groups, survivors rediscover that they are more than victims – finding a public role and renewed belonging to ordinary, everyday life.[10]

b Neuroscience on the embodied damage of trauma

Just as Herman published her research, new technology made for what fellow psychiatrist Bessel van der Kolk calls a "neuroscience revolution" in our understanding of trauma:

> Novel brain-imaging techniques [...] showed that when traumatized people are presented with images, sounds, or thoughts related to their traumatic experience the amygdala [the brain's "mammalian part"] reacts with alarm, even years after the event. Monitors record this physiological state of frantic arousal even when people never lose track of resting quietly in a scanner.[11]

Trauma damages persons more deeply than they can know in their "rational" brains:

> The bodies of traumatized people experience terror, rage, and helplessness, but these feelings are almost impossible to articulate [...]. This doesn't mean people can't talk about a tragedy [...]. These stories, however, rarely capture the inner truth of the experience.[12]

Thus, our usual methods of treating the traumatized through talk therapy are of little help.

c Interpersonal neurobiology on the social exacerbations of trauma

Another discovery revealed the social nature of trauma. In 1994, a group of psychologists discovered so-called "mirror neurons" and so pioneered the field of "interpersonal neurobiology." Van der Kolk writes: "Our mirror neurons make us vulnerable to others' negativity, so we respond to their anger with fury or are dragged down by their depression."[13]

10 *Ibidem*, 236.

11 Van der Kolk, *The Body Keeps the Score*, 39, 42.

12 *Ibidem*, 43.

13 *Ibidem*, 59.

Mirror neurons mean that, years after suffering trauma, the sufferer can be re-traumatized by anyone or anything reminiscent of the trauma. And so we must all be co-involved in trauma's healing. Van der Kolk writes: "*We* have to overcome our natural reluctance to confront the reality of trauma and cultivate the courage to listen to the testimonies of survivors."[14]

But who precisely is the *we* who "must cultivate the courage to listen"? Who is this *we* in relation to "survivors"? Lifton claimed "*we* all have in us something of the survivor," but did not ask whether *we* (all of us) live and relate in ways that are more like or unlike those of the directly traumatized. With its heightened awareness of how deeply we affect one another, interpersonal neurobiology forces the question of how fundamentally alike human beings are. Yet to this question, Van der Kolk gives a disturbing if unclear response: "Each patient demands that *we* suspend *our* sense of what is normal and accept that *we* are dealing with a dual reality: the reality of a relatively secure and predictable present that lives side by side with a ruinous, ever-present past."[15] He often seems to split human experience into two types: "normal" and traumatized. Interpersonal neurobiology appears unable to answer its own question of how alike we are.

By contrast, let us briefly hear from Canadian physician Gabor Maté, who works with street addicts in Vancouver. He knows interpersonal neurobiology but is straightforward in claiming that whatever differences exist among us, the similarities are greater:

> Trauma in the strict sense is not required for a young human being to suffer the loss of essence, the sense of oneness with all that is. Infants soon begin to shut down parts of themselves that their environment is unable to recognize or accept with love. As a consequence [...] one or more essential qualities such as love, joy, strength, or courage may be suppressed.[16]

We have all lost "essence" and "courage," and so *we* all develop addictive behaviours. Maté counts us all among the addicted, adding that his own addictions are simply more socially acceptable than those of the street addicts with whom he works. His understanding of our brokenness has roots in his

14 *Ibidem*, 196-197; emphasis added [WMcD].

15 *Ibidem*, 197; emphasis added [WMcD].

16 Gabor Maté, *In the Realm of Hungry Ghosts: Close Encounters with Addiction* (Berkeley, CA: North Atlantic Books, 2010), 418-419.

personal history. Born of Jewish parents in the ghetto in Budapest, Hungary in 1944, Maté saw his father taken away to a forced labour camp before his mother smuggled him to relatives living outside the ghetto. He writes:

> My relatives were caring people, but the small child's natural response to overwhelming emotional loss is a defensive shutdown. I've had a lifetime of resistance to receiving love, to accepting love vulnerably on a visceral, emotional level.[17]

We are all spiritually hurt, and Maté's words show us where we need to go next:

> Misplaced attachment to what cannot satiate the soul is the common condition of mankind. It is this ubiquitous mind-state that calls prophets, spiritual masters, and great teachers into *our* midst.[18]

Part two: The search for authentic survival as search for spiritual-religious wholeness

On the question of dual realities or a shared condition, the spiritual masters universally agree that we have all lost essence. Religion exists for our mutual healing. Yet, if it is really to help heal trauma, religion must support communal, participative processes of healing – much more so than it has done until now.

Australian biblical scholar Mark Brett provides one model for how religion might help. Though Christian, Brett makes his entire case for a religious communal life adequate to trauma without adverting to uniquely Christian texts. He focuses on what he calls "an inner-biblical conversation" within the pages of the Hebrew Bible – where he sees three competing religious self-understandings, each formed in response to trauma.[19]

The first came about in response to Assyria's invasion of Israel in the eight century BCE: "The social vision of the 'Deuteronomistic' history reflects a classic model of nation-building, a violent territorial claim, assertions of sovereignty, and exhortations of national unity."[20]

17 *Ibidem*, 242.

18 *Ibidem*, 414; emphasis added [WMcD].

19 Mark G. Brett, *Political trauma and healing: Biblical ethics for a postcolonial world* (Grand Rapids, MI: Eerdmans, 2016), 6 and *passim*.

20 *Ibidem*, 77-78.

This worldview was left behind in the sixth-century BCE Babylonian invasion of Judah and subsequent exile of the Judahite people. The exile occasioned another intra-communal argument about the nature of the Hebrew community (*qahal*). Two competing self-understandings were at stake in that argument and remain inscribed in the Bible. The first was a model of withdrawal:

> [It called] for a separation from foreign impurities even in cases where Israelites had intermarried with the so called 'peoples of the lands.' Where Deuteronomy's law called for slaughter of Canaanites, Ezra-Nehemiah called for divorce, but nevertheless, the clear boundaries of a holy nation were to be maintained.[21]

A second model offered a broader self-understanding:

> The Priestly tradition constitutes a remarkable case of healing following the traumatic loss of political sovereignty. Displacing the national imaginary, it exchanges political hegemony for divinely-given identity that is free to engage with strangers in the same social space.[22]

Brett sees evidence for this self-understanding in the textual revisions the Priestly editor made in the Book of Genesis. Genesis chapter one announces "a radically inclusive covenant that encompasses also the unity of humanity, both male and female, made in the 'image of Elohim.'" And while Genesis chapter twelve calls Abraham the father of a great nation, Genesis chapter seventeen calls him instead the father of "many nations."[23]

Brett gives further evidence from the Jacob narrative in Genesis that I will save until the end of this study. He sums up by saying the Priestly editor has inserted into the Hebrew Bible "a universalizing scheme, an 'inclusive monotheism' [...]. Israel responded to her own political traumas by reconnecting with creation and by reframing the particularities of her identity within much larger contexts of accountability."

This is the model for contemporary religious communities if they want to help heal trauma, claims Brett: "Actually engaging with the other means our original standards of judgment may be transformed [...] proceeding

21 *Ibidem*, 99.
22 *Ibidem*, 109.
23 *Ibidem*, 94.

from the concreteness of actual friendship and love, context by context."[24] Inclusive monotheism sides with Maté on both our shared "essence" and our loss of it: the experience of trauma is not evidence of two realities but of our one, very incomplete reality struggling to wake up.

Part three: Hillesum as survivor seeking wholeness

We now return to Flinders's claim that Hillesum's having woken up should help us wake from whatever our traumas are. In asking *how* Hillesum can mentor us, we do well to notice a second contention from Flinders – namely, that splitting off parts of ourselves is already the beginning of "othering" those around us in hatred, the one simply a less serious "maladaptation" than the other:

> My ability to 'other' someone else to the degree that I can kill him may be directly related to my ability to alienate myself from myself as well. Both states are surely maladies, but they may also be understood as *maladaptations*.[25]

What might Hillesum teach us about adapting and maladapting to trauma? Here, I examine five realities about trauma that we have learned from our scientists and religionists, asking what Hillesum might teach us about each.

a Learning from Hillesum about the everyday origins of trauma

Early in her diaries, Hillesum often writes about her fear of "splitting off" and "collapsing" in response to her difficulties. Interestingly, she uses the same language to describe her responses to both world threatening and ordinary events. Three kinds of events seem to trigger the same terrified response in her: the murder, arrest or suicide of her teachers after the 1940 Nazi occupation; an impending or just finished visit from her mother; and a quarrel with psychoanalyst Julius Spier, her mentor, colleague, lover and friend.

We encounter Hillesum's fear at the beginning of her journals. For example, on 25 and 26 March 1941, after news of the death of her teacher and of "professors who have been thrown into concentration camps," Hillesum

24 *Ibidem*, 14, 100, 33.
25 Flinders, *Enduring Lives*, 91.

writes that "a whole world of learning has collapsed (*in elkaar gezakt*) [...] a whole world has fallen apart (*in elkaar gezakt*) [...] [Her dead professor] has become part of a collapsed world (*in elkaar gezakt*)." These events leave her in a "state of numbness" (*verdoofde toestand*).[26] After hearing of the arrest of more than 300 Jews she writes: "I felt I was about to collapse (*zusammen zu brechen*) under a tremendous weight."[27]

Hillesum uses the same language to describe her response to encounters with her mother. For example, on 8 August 1941, she writes that she feels overwhelmed after such an encounter with her mother and writes: "I always used to go to pieces (*altijd kapot*) in this madhouse."[28] Two months later, she writes that her mother's visit has left her "feeling just as if a big building had collapsed (*ingestort*) on top of me."[29]

She uses the same language in regard to Spier. After Spier made casual remarks about whether she would marry, Hillesum writes: "Breakdowns (*instortingen*) and relapses can occur at any moment."[30] After another disagreement with Spier, she writes: "I have the feeling that I am splitting myself up (*versplinter*) and [...] feel torn into pieces (*zerrissen*)."[31]

Before reporting to Camp Westerbork, she uses the same language even while beginning to notice something changing in her response: "Had all of this happened to me only a year ago, I should certainly have collapsed (*in elkaar gezakt*)."[32]

With respect to trauma's sources, then, world-shaping and personal hurts are equally at work in Hillesum's life, and she feels as if she is collapsing under both. Before looking at how she adapts to trauma, let us allow Hillesum to instruct us in the ways of maladapting.

26 E.T., 50, 53. *Het Werk*, 52, 56; Tuesday evening, 25 March 1941: Er zitten professoren in concentratiekampen [...]. Er is een wereld van wetenschap zomaar, plotseling, geruisloos in elkaar gezakt. [...] Een wereld van kennis en wetenschap is ingezakt [...] een soort verdoofde toestand.

27 E.T., 63. *Het Werk*, 66-67; Sunday, 15 June 1941: ik had het gevoel onder een geweldig gewicht "zusammen zu brechen".

28 E.T., 79. *Het Werk*, 84; Friday morning, 8 August 1941: Vroeger ging ik altijd kapot in dit gekkenhuis.

29 E.T., 141. *Het Werk*, 148; Thursday afternoon, 30 October 1941: Het is weer of er een zwaar huis boven op me is ingestort.

30 E.T., 382. *Het Werk*, 400; Friday morning, 29 May 1942: En instortingen en vallen is daar ieder ogenblik mogelijk.

31 E.T., 392. *Het Werk*, 411; Thursday night, 4 June 1942: [...] heb ik een gevoel, dat ik me zo versplinter, dan voel ik me zo "zerrissen".

32 E.T., 501. *Het Werk*, 530; Thursday evening, 23 July 1942: Als een jaar geleden me gebeurd was datgene, wat er nu allemaal is, dan was ik zeker na 3 dagen in elkaar gezakt.

b Learning from Hillesum about maladapting through intellectualist flight

From the opening of her diaries, Hillesum knew trauma was at work in her: "[...] at times I am nothing more or less than a miserable, frightened creature, despite the clarity with which I can express myself."[33]

She was also quite aware of her tendency, in response, to "split off" into fantasy. Let us see just two texts in this regard, the first from her second journal entry, in which she acknowledges her escape into fantasy in a "wrestling" session with Spier: "There was an immediate and mighty collision of my extravagant fantasy life (*phantasieleven*) with the sober reality."[34] A short time later she writes: "[...] you're so full of vanities and fantasies (*phantasieēn*) you have not made much progress in the art of forgetting yourself."[35]

Though she has real insight, Hillesum is often caught in her intellectual tricks. She sees that her intelligence is not much help in this regard: "I keep encouraging myself to put the hand of my intellect, so to speak, first on this and then on that sore spot of my psyche, but the basic pain remains."[36]

So much for maladaptation. My next task is to describe what she teaches us about adapting and seeking wholeness, beginning with the communal support she needed for healing.

c Learning from Hillesum about embodied, participative communities as external supports for healing trauma

In part one of the study, we learned that, in order to heal, we need two things from those around us: first, an embodied experience (beyond ideas) of being held in safe hands; second, an experience of being part of a community that also needs our hands. I pursue these insights by collating texts in which Hillesum speaks both of being held in safe hands and of her hands being needed by others.

33 E.T., 4; *Het Werk*, 4; Sunday, 9 March 1941: [...] ik ben af en toe toch maar een angstige stakkerd, ondanks het heldere denken.

34 E.T., 8. *Het Werk*, 8; Monday morning, 10 March 1941: Het was opeens een geweldige botsing tussen mijn ausschweifend phantasieleven en de ontnuchterende werkelijkheid.

35 E.T., 57. *Het Werk*, 61; Sunday morning, 8 June 1941: [...] maar zolang je nog zo vol met die ijdelheid en phantasieën zit, heb je het nog niet zo ver gebracht in het vergeten van jezelf.

36 E.T., 124-145. *Het Werk*, 132; Tuesday morning, 7 October 1941: Ik probeer ook van alles en spreek mezelf toe en leg a.h.w. de hand v.h. intellect nu eens op deze en dan weer op die wonde plek van m'n psyche, maar de grondpijn blijft [...].

We begin with Spier, for it was in his hands that she first felt safe. Hillesum experienced something of both the safety of being held and the strength of being respected there. Let us take these texts about hands in two different groups – each arranged chronologically and each suggesting what communities of healing must be like.

So, first, Hillesum writes on at least ten occasions of being held in Spier's hands. Here are the first and the final instances: "He took me metaphorically by the hand [...] for all my apparent self-reliance, if someone came along, took me by the hand [...] I would deliver myself up to his care"[37]; "Did he not lead me to God, after first paving the way with his imperfect human hand?"[38] She also writes of the safety of others' hands.[39] So, Hillesum, too, needed the physical, embodied safety provided by others.

There is another set of "hands texts" getting at a further quality that communities must have in order to support healing. Hillesum needed to experience her own agency within the safe community. So, she also writes of holding others in her hands. Here, again, I report just two such texts – first: "Something you can do for your fellow men [...] take them by the hand and lead them back to their own sources."[40] Second, in the end, the people she holds in her hands include Spier – whom she comforts as he dies: "For the last time you took my hand and led it to your lips."[41] In the end, we need participative communities that are both safe and mutual.

37 E.T., 6. *Het Werk*, 6; Sunday, 9 March 1941: Hij nam me a.h.w. aan het handje [...]. M'n leven lang heb ik het gevoel gehad: kwam er maar iemand, die me bij de hand nam en die zich met me bemoeide, ik lijk flink en doe alles alleen, maar ik zou me zo verschrikkelijk graag uitleveren.

38 E.T., 540. *Het Werk*, 572; Friday, 2 October 1942: [...] heeft hij de weg voor me vrijgemaakt regelrecht tot God, na eerst die weg, met zijn onvolmaakte mensenhanden, gebaand te hebben. Other references to Hillesum's safety in Spier's hands include: E.T., 85. *Het Werk*, 90; Wednesday, 13 August 1941; E.T., 207. *Het Werk*, 216; Monday, 29 December 1941; E.T., 240. *Het Werk*, 250; Saturday, 24 January 1942; E.T., 340. *Het Werk*, 356; Wednesday, 22 April 1942; E.T., 350. *Het Werk*, 367; Sunday, 26 April 1942; E.T., 361. *Het Werk*, 378-379; Thursday, 30 April 1942; E.T., 442. *Het Werk*, 466; Tuesday, 23 June 1942.

39 For example, Etty Hillesum writes about Henny Tideman laying her hand on Hillesum (E.T., 139. *Het Werk*, 146-147; Tuesday, 28 October 1941).

40 E.T., 398-399; *Het Werk*, 418; Monday night, 8 June 1942: [...] dat men aan medemensen verrichten kan [...] ze dan aan de hand te nemen en terug te voeren naar de eigen bronnen.

41 E.T., 516; *Het Werk*, 546; Tuesday night 15 September 1942: [...] je hebt nog eens een keer mijn hand genomen en naar je lippen gebracht. Other similar texts appear at: E.T., 250. *Het Werk*, 259-260; Friday morning, 20 February 1942, and E.T., 548. *Het Werk*, 581; Sunday, 11 October 1942.

d Learning from Hillesum about courage as the internal source of healing

Communities of support are necessary external resources. But the sources for healing trauma are internal to the human being. Here, I suggest that the primary internal source that enabled Hillesum to adapt to trauma was the courage we saw Maté write about above. A month after Spier's death and in her own exhaustion, Hillesum writes: "We must have courage (*de moed*) to call a halt, to feel empty and discouraged (*moedeloos*)."[42]

This courage to stop is the internal source of the search for wholeness. And there are several texts in which Hillesum describes what she discovered when she "called a halt." I will again report just two here: "I'll 'turn inward' for half an hour each morning before work and listen to my inner voice"[43] and "I shall go early to bed, be patient and listen inwardly for what I have to do."[44]

42 E.T., 549. *Het Werk*, 582; Monday, 12 October 1942: Men moet de moed hebben tot een pauze. Men moet eens leeg en moedeloos durven zijn.

43 E.T., 56. *Het Werk*, 59; Sunday morning, 8 June 1941: [...] 's morgens voor het begin van het werk een half uurtje "naar binnen slaan", luisteren naar wat er binnen in me zit.

44 E.T., 238. *Het Werk*, 248; Friday afternoon, 23 January 1942, 5 o'clock: vroeg naar bed gaan en geduldig zijn en naar binnen luisteren wat ik doen moet. See also E.T., 62: I have become just a little stronger again. I can fight things out within myself. Your first impulse is always to get help from others, to think you can't make it, but then suddenly you notice that you've fought your way through and that you've pulled it off all by yourself, and that makes you stronger. *Het Werk*, 66; Sunday, 15 June 1941: Ik ben weer een klein beetje sterker geworden. Ik kan de dingen binnen mezelf uitvechten. Eerst is er wel de neiging om hulp te halen bij anderen, om te denken, ik kom er niet door, maar opeens merk je, dat je weer iets hebt doorgevochten en dat je dat alleen klaar hebt gespeeld en dat maakt je weer sterker; E.T., 72: I must stop and listen to myself, sound my own depths [...]. But alas the emphasis these days is on speed, not on rest. *Het Werk*, 77; Monday, 4 August 1941: Ik moet maar blijven luisteren naar mezelf, [...] maar in onze tijd ligt het accent weer ergens anders.; E.T., 97: I seem to be calmer and more at peace than I have been for years. *Het Werk*, 103; Friday, 5 September 1941: Ik ben zo vredig en rustig als ik, naar het me lijkt, in jaren niet geweest ben.; E.T., 100: No chance of doing any work now, all I can do is write down last night's dream as carefully as I can. I must not ignore anything that can add the least little light. *Het Werk*, 107; Tuesday, 9 September 1941: Van werken komt nu niets meer, ik zal nog maar eens nauwgezet die droom van vannacht opschrijven, alles wat wat helderheid kan brengen, moet ik er maar bij slepen.; E.T., 119: Now and then I must shut my ears more to the outside world and listen to the voice within. *Het Werk*, 125; Saturday, 4 October 1941: Ik moet af en toe weer véél dover zijn naar buiten en luisteren naar binnen.; E.T., 120: [...] all that matters is finding a little piece of eternity in myself [...] Redirect your ears and your 1 senses to your inner centre once more and try to find peace in yourself again. *Het Werk*, 127; Sunday, 5 October 1941: Maar waar het om gaat bij mij is om de verovering van een stukje eeuwigheid in mezelf. [...] Verleg je oren en je zintuigen weer eens helemaal naar binnen en probeer weer te rusten in je zelf.

Hillesum's courage to stop and listen uncovered an internal strength that allowed her to support others in listening. We have already seen that her experience of being held led to her holding others. But we must notice that the source of courage is always internal, only the supports are external. Recall Hillesum's text above about leading other human beings "back to their own sources."

Trauma is everywhere, and Hillesum shows that our most important response is to find the courage to stop running so something internal to us can lead us back toward wholeness. As Maté knows, the real reason communities must learn to listen is because precisely the same fear is at work in all of us, but so is a deeper source. This leads to the fifth and final way that we learn about healing from Hillesum.

e Learning from Hillesum about larger hands in healing trauma

I return to Hillesum's use of the metaphor of hands to see her understanding of the ultimate source of courage. We notice three chronological steps, one beginning before she went to Camp Westerbork and two taking place there.

The first further set of "hands texts" expresses Hillesum's sense of finding herself more and more "in God's hands." I report the first and last of these texts, one earlier and the other just after Spier's death: "God, take me by Your hand, I shall follow You [...]. I shall follow wherever Your hand leads me"[45] and "I accept everything from Your hands, oh God, as it comes."[46]

Not all of Hillesum's final "hands texts" express full confidence in God, as we see in a second set of references – this time in letters from and about Camp Westerbork. I gather three of these five negative hands texts here before commenting further:

45 E.T., 154. *Het Werk*, 162; Tuesday, 25 November 1941: God, neem me aan Uw hand [...]. Ik zal overal meegaan aan Uw hand.

46 E.T., 515. *Het Werk*, 545; Tuesday afternoon, 15 September 1942: [...] ik aanvaard alles uit jouw handen, mijn God, zoals het komt. See three other texts on God's hands: E.T., 197: Feeling safe and secure in Your hands, oh God. I am no longer cut off quite so often from that deep undercurrent within me. *Het Werk*, 206; Sunday, 21 December 1941: Een zich geborgen voelen in jouw hand, mijn God. Ik sta niet meer zo dikwijls afgesneden van die diepe onderstroom in me.; E.T., 494: Well, I am in God's hands. My body with all its aches and pains as well. *Het Werk*, 523; Wednesday, 15 July 1942: Enfin, ik ben toch in Gods hand. M'n lichaam met al z'n kwaaltjes ook.; E.T., 509: There are moments when I feel like a little bird, tucked away in a great protective hand. *Het Werk*, 538; Tuesday, 28 July 1942: Ik heb momenten, waarop ik me voel als een klein vogeltje, verborgen in een grote, beschuttende hand.

> At night the barracks [...] like a plaything that had slipped from God's preoccupied hand.[47]
>
> When the first transport passed through our hands, there was a moment when I thought I would never again laugh and be happy.[48]
>
> Through small openings at the top [of the transport wagons] we can see heads and hands, hands that will wave to us later when the train leaves.[49]

The horror leads one to wonder whether there are two realities side by side to each other – a terrifying "real life" one and a comforting one of religious fantasy. Yet before we settle for such a view, we must notice a final set of three references to hands. The first two are Hillesum's last "hands texts."

First, one paragraph into her final letter to Henny Tideman, Hillesum breaks off into direct address to God: "You have made me so rich, oh God, please let me share out Your beauty with open hands."[50] And she writes in a final letter to Maria Tuinzig: "[...] if we just care enough, God is in safe hands with us despite everything, Maria."[51]

47 E.T., 529. *Het Werk*, 561; Wednesday, 23 September 1942: Zoals die barak daar soms 's nachts lag [...] als een stukje speelgoed, ontgleden aan God's verstrooide hand.

48 E.T., 584. *Het Werk*, 621-622; Letter 23, To two sisters in The Hague, Amsterdam, end December 1942: Toen het eerste transport door onze handen ging, kwam er één moment, waarop men meende, dat men nu nooit meer zou kunnen lachen en vrolijk zijn.

49 E.T., 654. *Het Werk*, 697; Letter 64, To Han Wegerif and others; Westerbork, Tuesday, 24 August 1943: Door de smalle openingen aan de bovenkant ziet men hoofden en handen, die later wuiven, wanneer de trein vertrekt. The other two texts are: E.T., 628: I would like to pack their cases with the best things I can lay my hands on, but I know perfectly well that they will be stripped of everything; about that we have been left in no doubt. So why bother? *Het Werk*, 670; Letter 52, To Maria Tuinzing; Westerbork, Saturday, 10 July 1943: Ik zou zo goed mogelijk hun bagage willen verzorgen, maar tegelijkertijd weet ik: het zal hun toch worden afgenomen (dat weten we hier steeds zekerder), dus waarom nog al dat gesleep. and E.T., 645: Whenever misfortune strikes, people have a natural instinct to lend a helping hand and to save what can be saved. Tonight I shall be helping to dress babies and to calm mothers – and that is all I can hope to do. I could almost curse myself for that. *Het Werk*, 688; Letter 64, To Han Wegerif and others; Westerbork, Tuesday, 24 August 1943: Wanneer er ergens een ongeluk gebeurt, dan is het een natuurlijk instinct in de mens, dat hij te hulp loopt en redt wat er te redden valt. Maar ik ga vannacht alle babies aankleden en moeders kalmerend toespreken en dat noem ik dan "helpen", ik zou me hier bijna om kunnen vervloeken [...].

50 E.T., 640. *Het Werk*, 682; Letter 60, To Henny Tideman; Westerbork, Wednesday, 18 August 1943: Je hebt me zo rijk gemaakt, mijn God, laat me ook met volle handen uit mogen delen.

51 E.T., 657. *Het Werk*, 701; Letter 68, To Maria Tuinzing, Westerbork, Thursday, 2 September 1943: En als wij er maar zorg voor dragen, dat ondanks alles, toch God bij ons in veilige handen is, Maria.

The very last hands text, chronologically speaking, is from Hillesum's friend Jopie Vleeschhouwer's description of his final encounter with her before she was deported to Auschwitz: "[...] a friendship like hers can never be lost; it is, and it endures. That is what I wrote on the slip of paper I pressed into her hand at the last moment."[52]

It seems fitting that this final reference to hands describes an act of everyday kindness done to Hillesum by a member of her community. In writing this, I do not mean to hide from the terror; rather, I mean to side with Maté rather than Van der Kolk: what our spiritual teachers give and receive with their hands suggests we all share an "essence" to which we struggle to reconnect.

Conclusion: Jacob, Hillesum, the *qahal goyim* and us

I promised to come back to the patriarch Jacob, specifically to something about him that Brett claims the Priestly editor of Genesis inserted into the Bible. After reporting on Abraham as the father of "many nations," Brett continues:

> Instead of fathering 'many' nations, [in Genesis 35.11] Jacob is to be the ancestor of an 'assembly' of nations, a *qahal goyim* – using the term *qahal* which is normally associated with the cultic congregation [....]. The descendants of Jacob were themselves something of a mixed multitude.[53]

Jacob's descendants were a mixed multitude most immediately because he adopted the two sons his son Joseph had fathered by an Egyptian woman; Jacob took outsiders as sons (Genesis 48:5).[54]

But Jacob's descendants (all of us) are a mixed multitude in a much wider sense. We are a multitude, each having our own traumas and needing our own communities in which to be healed and help others heal. This multitude is being mixed or called together into an ever-larger *qahal* by the God of all peoples for healing the cosmos. Our efforts in this will always be incomplete; as Brett writes, "the final task of mending the world belongs

52 E.T., 668. *Het Werk*, 712; Letter 78, Jopie Vleeschhouwer to Han Wegerif and others, Westerbork, Monday, 6 September/Tuesday, 7 September 1943: Dat schreef ik ook nog op een klein stukje papier, dat ik haar op 't laatst in haar hand drukte.

53 Brett, *Political trauma and healing*, 101, 104.

54 See Avivah Zornberg, *The Beginning of Desire: Reflections on Genesis* (New York: Doubleday, 1996), 369.

to God."[55] But we always have tasks, and our hands testify to whether we are attending to them.

Etty Hillesum is our Jacob, our contemporary ancestor in the *qahal goyim*. I admire her courage in moving out of fantasy and into shared everyday human life. And I must let hers be an insistent voice waking me and calling me to courage, which means opening myself to healing hands and extending my own hands to others in my community and to all whom God sends into my path.

About the Author

William McDonough (1956) is Professor of Theology at St. Catherine University in St. Paul, MN, USA, where he teaches courses in theological ethics and spirituality.

55 Brett, *Political trauma and healing*, 126.

The Contours of These Times

Etty Hillesum as Chronicler of Love Transcending Hate in Her Times, for Our Time, for All Time

Barbara Morrill

Abstract
Etty Hillesum, a young Dutch Jewish woman of twenty-seven, found an inner path to liberation, and "union with the ground of her being" in the face of the horror of her times, the Nazi genocide sweeping across Europe, which ultimately engulfed Etty Hillesum and her family in late 1943. This paper explores aspects of Etty Hillesum's process of transcending the evil and hatred in her time, which may be seen as a model for engaging the seemingly ubiquitous rise of nationalism, neo-fascism, and/or illiberalism throughout much of Europe and the United States in our time, and in a broader sense, the tension that exists between democratic and fascist principles, or open and closed systems in all times.

Keywords: transcendence of evil, rejection of hatred, contemporary nationalism, illiberalism, Carl Gustav Jung, Other

> And then, it suddenly happened: I was able to feel the contours of these times with my fingertips. How is it that this stretch of heathland surrounded by barbed wire, through which so much human misery has flooded nevertheless remains inscribed in my memory as something almost lovely? How is it that my spirit, far from being oppressed seems lighter and brighter there? It is because I read the signs of the times and they did not seem meaningless to me...
>
> – *Etty Hillesum*[1]

1 E.T., 526. *Het Werk*, 557; Tuesday 22 September 1942: Het is me daar werkelijk geweest, alsof ik met gevoelige vingertoppen getast heb langs de contouren van deze tijd en van het leven. Hoe komt het toch, dat dat met prikkeldraad omrasterde stukje heidegrond, waar zoveel mensenlot

Smelik, Klaas A.D. (ed.), *The Lasting Significance of Etty Hillesum's Writings: Proceedings of the Third International Etty Hillesum Conference at Middelburg, September 2018.*
Taylor & Francis Group 2019
DOI: 10.5117/9789463722025_MORRILL

Etty Hillesum, a young Dutch Jewish woman of twenty-seven, found an inner path to liberation, and "union with the ground of her being" in the face of the horror of her times, the Nazi genocide sweeping across Europe, which ultimately engulfed Etty Hillesum and her family in late 1943. The life of Etty Hillesum moved from chaotic family dysfunction, to the healing of her own inner distress, depression, mood swings and somatic complaints, toward a vast inner life of spaciousness and presence, even with the awareness of the Nazi evil that awaited European Jewry. Her mode of resistance was journal writing, and contributing to others, and as Denise de Costa says, "It was with her pen, rather than with her sword that she battled to save humanity."[2]

This paper explores aspects of Etty Hillesum's process of transcending the evil and hate in her time, which may be seen as a model for engaging the seemingly ubiquitous rise of neo-fascism or illiberalism throughout much of Europe and the United States in our time, and in a broader sense, the tension that exists between democratic and fascist principles, or open and closed systems in all times.

Her Times: Her Response; Love Transcends Hate

Hitler's final solution was formally articulated and put into place by a small group of Nazi elite in January 1942. Etty Hillesum was murdered at Auschwitz-Birkenau eighteen months later, a victim of the Nazi attempt to "protect" Aryan Europe from the infection of Jewish contamination, a sentiment held toward the Jews since the first century. Given the context of the German takeover of Amsterdam, the months after the occupation in 1940 were relatively calm. For Etty Hillesum and others such as the Frank family, it was a slow, steady process of becoming fully aware of the destructive intention of the Nazis. We can see the evolution of her inner response to these unfolding events in her words. She writes in February of 1941:

> Last night I wondered again if I was so "unworldly" simply because the German measures affect me so little personally. But I don't fool myself for one single moment about the gravity of it all. Yet sometimes I can take

en -lijden áán- en dóórspoelde, als bijna liefelijk in m'n herinnering is achtergebleven? Hoe komt het, dat m'n geest daar niet verduisterd, maar veeleer verlicht en verhelderd is? Ik heb er iets gelezen van deze tijd, die me niet zinneloos lijkt.

2 Denise de Costa, *Anne Frank and Etty Hillesum: Inscribing Spirituality and Sexuality* (New Brunswick, NJ & London: Rutgers University Press, 1998), 141.

> the broad historical view of the measures; each new regulation takes its little place in our century, and I try then to look at it from the viewpoint of a later age. And the suffering, the ocean of human suffering, and the hatred and all the fighting?[3]

And, as she goes to bed early one night in May 1942, she tells us:

> And it was once more as if life with all of its mysteries was close to me, as if I could touch it. I had the feeling that I was resting against the naked breast of life, and could feel her gentle and regular heartbeat. I felt safe and protected.[4]

Yet, rather than remain within herself, "safe and protected," she was acutely aware of the suffering around her, developing the inner strength to move beyond her personal safety in order to fully touch the events of her time:

> I know the persecution and oppression and despotism and the impotent fury and the terrible sadism. I know it all and continue to confront every shred of reality that thrusts itself upon me.[5]

Shortly after her commitment to confront even the most uncomfortable elements of her reality, she engages a more profound quest, to take on her time; in doing so, she becomes both a very human, loving presence, and at the same time a transcendent figure, a conduit of knowledge and inspiration to future generations:

> Ours is now a common destiny, and that is something we must not forget [...]. And that part of our common destiny that I must shoulder myself; I strap it

3 E.T., 358. *Het Werk*, 375; Thursday evening, 30 April 1942: Ik heb me gisteren weer afgevraagd of ik toch echt "weltfremd" ben, omdat al die maatregelen me persoonlijk zo weinig raken, terwijl ik toch werkelijk geen moment mezelf in het duister laat omtrent de ernst van dit alles. Maar soms kan ik zo een maatregel plotseling ondergaan als iets indrukwekkends vanwege de historische merkwaardigheid, iedere nieuwe verordening krijgt a.h.w. direct z'n plaatsje toebedeeld in de eeuwen en dan bezie ik haar, vanuit een verdere eeuw. En het lijden, het vele menselijke leed, en de haat en de strijdbaarheid?

4 E.T., 386. *Het Werk*, 404; Saturday morning, 30 May 1942, 7.30: En het was weer net of het Leven, met al z'n geheimen, vlàk bij me was, of ik er aan raken kon. Ik had een gevoel of ik rustte tegen de naakte borst van het leven en haar zachte en regelmatige harteklop hoorde. Ik lag in de naakte armen van het Leven en het was er zo veilig en beschut.

5 E.T., 386. *Het Werk*, 404-405; Saturday morning, 30 May 1942, 7.30: ik weet van de vervolging en onderdrukking en willekeur en machteloze haat en veel sadisme. Ik weet het allemaal en blijf steeds oog in oog met ieder stukje werkelijkheid, dat zich aan me opdringt.

> tightly and firmly to my back, it becomes part of me as I walk through the streets even now. And I shall wield this slender fountain pen as if it were a hammer, and my words will have to be so many hammer strokes with which to beat out the story of our fate and of a piece of history as it is and never was before [...] Still, a few people must survive if only to be the chroniclers of this age. I would very much like to become one of their number.[6]

Etty Hillesum's response to her times, simply put, is to work on herself, to "repose in herself," and to find the beauty in life, even in the very darkest of times. Through this fiercely vulnerable Self, as Jung would call it, Etty Hillesum will become a chronicler of her age, and her chronicle will transcend the darkness of her time, to become a model for living in our own hate-filled times.

Through her mentor, Julius Spier, Etty Hillesum becomes introduced to, and infused by, Jung's worldview and psychology. "I keep being drawn towards Jung," she writes in 1941.[7] It is as if Jung is speaking when Etty Hillesum quotes Spier:

> What you expect from others, that is, from the outside, you carry unconsciously in you. Instead of expecting it from the outside, you ought to develop it yourself, by making it conscious [...] that is, develop yourselves.[8]

Her realization of her inner demons and those found in the external world was particularly acute. In a movement that seems to channel the Jungian notion of the "shadow," Etty Hillesum recognizes that the eradication of evil must begin internally:

> The rottenness of others is in us, too [...]. I [...] see no other solution than to turn inward and to root out all rottenness there. [...] And that seems

6 E.T., 484. *Het Werk*, 511; Friday morning, 10 July 1942: Het is nu een "Massenschicksal" geworden en dat moet men weten.[...] En datgene van dat "Massenschicksal" dat ik kan dragen dat gesp ik als een bundeltje steeds steviger en vaster op m'n rug en ik vergroei er mee en ga er nu al mee door de straten. En met deze slanke vulpen zou ik nu moeten zwaaien als was het een hamer en de woorden zouden even zovele mokerslagen moeten zijn, om te vertellen over een lot en over een stuk geschiedenis, zoals het er voor dien nog niet was. [...] Er moeten toch een paar mensen overblijven om later de kroniekschrijvers te zijn van deze tijd. Ik wil graag zo een klein kroniekschrijfstertje zijn later.

7 E.T., 56. *Het Werk*, 59; Friday, 8 May 1941: Ik word alweer naar Jung getrokken.

8 E.T., 17. *Het Werk*, 18; Thursday, 13 March 1941: Das, was man vom andern, also von aussen erwartet, hat man unbewußt in sich. Statt es von aussen zu erwarten, soll man es in sich entwickeln, indem man es in sich bewußt macht. [...] d.h. sich entwickeln.

> to me the only lesson to be learned from this war. That we must look into ourselves and nowhere else.[9]

Etty Hillesum was often filled with hatred against the occupiers, yet she recounted a moment when a liberating thought emerged in her:

> If there were only one decent German, then he should be cherished despite that whole barbaric gang, and because of that one decent German, it is wrong to pour hatred over an entire people.[10]

Etty Hillesum knew the way to achieve this freedom was to "work on oneself" and she understood that "hatred was a sickness of the soul."[11] She believed that strength would come from seeing the good in people, and that a profound form of resistance would emerge; in facing horror, one did not have to become horrible.

As her story unfolds and deepens, she realizes that hatred actually "does not lie in [her] nature."[12] She understood human vulnerability, and believed that hatred and evil could not be allowed to triumph. For Etty Hillesum, love was everything; for family and friends, the other, as well as the "love that you can apply to small everyday things,"[13] things one does that come from experience. She sums up this wish for active loving, "let everyone spring from a greater central core of devotion and love."[14] In short, the core principle of Etty Hillesum's response to fully living through her times, until her murder by the Nazi machine, is this:

> My love of life is so great and so strong and calm and makes me so grateful that I shall refrain from putting it into words again. There is such perfect and complete happiness in me, oh God. What he [Spier] called "reposing

9 E.T., 245. *Het Werk*, 254; Thursday, 19 February 1942: En die rottigheid van de anderen zit in ons ook, [...] En ik zie geen andere oplossing, ik zie werkelijk geen andere oplossing dan in je eigen centrum in te keren en daar uit te roeien al die rotheid.

10 E.T., 18. *Het Werk*, 19; Saturday, 15 March 1941, 9.30: En al zou er nog maar één fatsoenlijke Duitser bestaan, dan zou die het waard zijn in bescherming genomen te worden tegen de hele barbaarse bende en om die éne fatsoenlijke Duitser zou men dan niet zijn haat mogen uitgieten over een geheel volk.

11 E.T., 18. *Het Werk*, 19; Saturday morning, 15 March 1941: Het is een ziekte van de eigen ziel.

12 *Ibidem*: Haat ligt niet in mijn karakter.

13 E.T., 57. *Het Werk*, 60; Sunday morning, 8 June 1942: maar liefde, waar je iets mee kunt doen in de kleine dagelijkse practijk.

14 E.T., 165. *Het Werk*, 173; Wednesday morning, 3 December 1941: laat iedere kleine handeling komen uit één groot, centraal gevoel van bereidheid en liefde.

in oneself." And that probably best expresses my own love of life: I repose in myself. And that part of myself; that deepest and richest part in which I repose, is what I call "God."[15]

In July of 1942, Etty Hillesum volunteered, through the Jewish Council, to go to Westerbork, a Dutch transit camp in the province of Drenthe. She wanted to be a social worker and help others, initially young women and girls, as well as her parents and brother who eventually arrived at the camp. It is here that Etty Hillesum both struggled and flourished, ultimately finding the purpose of her life in the most difficult of times, amidst the ubiquitous dust, mud, and winding barbed wire of the camp, working with the sick and persecuted, living in fear of the continual transports east, to "work" in Poland.

For Etty Hillesum, Camp Westerbork was "now a focus of Jewish suffering," with its "great waves of human beings [...] from all the nooks and crannies" of the Netherlands, waiting anxiously "to meet their unknown destiny."[16] Yet, it was at Camp Westerbork that Etty Hillesum found life in herself. She writes: "And there among the barracks, full of hunted and persecuted people, I found confirmation of my love of life."[17] Her love of the other tapped into her internal, "elementary life force, springing straight from my heart," giving her the will to resist "[a]gainst every new outrage and every fresh horror, we shall put up one more piece of love and goodness, drawing strength from within ourselves. We may suffer, but we must not succumb [...]."[18]

Etty Hillesum's decision to go to Camp Westerbork and not to go into hiding has been considered controversial; however, this decision was the cornerstone of her resistance and transformation. For Etty Hillesum, freedom

15 E.T., 519. *Het Werk*, 549; Thursday morning, 17 September 1942: Het levensgevoel is zo groot en sterk en rustig en dankbaar in me, dat ik maar helemaal niet meer proberen zal het in één woord uit te drukken. Er is zo een volmaakt en volkomen geluk in me, mijn God. Het is toch weer het beste uitgedrukt met zijn woorden: "ruhen in sich". En hiermee is misschien het meest volkomen uitgedrukt mijn levensgevoel: ik rust in mijzelve. En dat mijzelve, dat allerdiepste en allerrijkste in mij, waarin ik rust, dat noem ik "God".

16 E.T., 583. *Het Werk*, 619 en 621; Letter 23, To two sisters in The Hague, Amsterdam, December 1942: nu een brandpunt van Joods lijden [...] mensenmassa's er binnenspoelen [...] uit alle hoeken en gaten van Nederland [...] hun onbekende bestemming tegemoet.

17 E.T., 527. *Het Werk*, 557; Tuesday, 22 September 1942: En daar tussen de barakken, vol opgejaagde en vervolgde mensen, heb ik de bevestiging gevonden van mijn liefde voor dit leven.

18 E.T., 616. *Het Werk*, 657; Letter 46, To Johanna en Klaas Smelik and others, Westerbork, 3 July 1943: en tegen iedere wandaad te meer en gruwelijkheid te meer hebben wij een stukje liefde en goedheid te meer tegenover te stellen, dat we in onszelf veroveren moeten. We mogen wel lijden, maar we mogen er niet onder bezwijken.

was found through her engagement with the suffering of others, not in her individual survival:

> They say that everyone who can, must try to stay out of their clutches, it's our bounden duty to try. But that argument is specious. For while everyone tries to save himself, vast numbers are disappearing. [...] I certainly do not want to go out of some form of masochism, [...] but, I don't think I would feel happy if I were exempted from what many others have to suffer.[19]

Etty Hillesum's response to the common fate of the Jews was her particular form of resistance, as well as a deep confirmation of solidarity with her Jewish roots. She rejected Nazi dehumanization, choosing instead to lean into the terror and panic that confronted her. Her openness and presence in the face of the surrounding horror actually allowed her to become free "from their clutches" at an inner level. This internal freedom, her resistance through engagement with the fear, pain, anxiety, and suffering of others was her calling, her destiny:

> At night as I lay in the camp on my plank bed surrounded by women and girls, gently snoring, dreaming aloud, quietly sobbing, tossing and turning, women and girls who often told me during the day, 'We don't want to think, we don't want to feel, otherwise, we are sure to go out of our minds', I was sometimes filled with an infinite tenderness, and lay awake for hours [...] and I prayed, 'Let me be the thinking heart of these barracks.'[20]

A search for a deeper truth in the midst of chaos becomes a central part of Etty Hillesum's message to us today, one that is equally meaningful in our time, as we attempt to make sense of the uncertainty that is unfolding throughout the Western world.

19 E.T., 487. *Het Werk*, 514-515; Saturday morning, 11 July 1942: En zeggen: ieder, die uit hun klauwen kan blijven, moet dat proberen en is dat verplicht. En ik moet iets dóen voor mezelf. Dit is een sommetje, dat niet op gaat. Iederéén is op het ogenblik n.l. bezig iets voor zichzelf te doen om er onder uit te komen en er moet immers toch een aantal, een zeer groot aantal zelfs, gaan? [...] Ik wil niet uit een soort masochisme beslist mee gaan [...] maar ik weet nog niet eens of ik me prettig zou voelen, als ik verschoond bleef van datgene, wat zovelen moeten ondergaan.

20 E.T., 543. *Het Werk*, 575; Saturday morning, 3 October 1942: 's Nachts, als ik daar zo lag op m'n brits, temidden van zachtjes snurkende, hardop dromende, stilletjes huilende en woelende vrouwen en meisjes, die overdag zo dikwijls zeiden: 'we willen niet denken', 'we willen niet voelen, anders worden we gek', dan was ik soms van een eindeloze vertedering en lag wakker [...] en dacht: 'laat mij dan het denkende hart van deze barak mogen zijn.'

Our Time

What are the contours of our time? It appears, at least currently, that some Western democracies, once modelled on Enlightenment principles, have discarded the basic fabric underlying democracy itself in favour of authoritarianism, exclusion, fear mongering, and hatred. After centuries of colonialism, wars of conquest, and slavery, we embarked on a painfully slow, and inherently flawed trajectory towards more freedom, more empathy, more inclusion, and greater understanding of the differences that exist in our societies, yet now find ourselves again, even more blatantly, building walls, cataloguing our "enemies," rejecting the vulnerable and helpless, and literally closing our eyes to suffering. Under the guise of populism, nativism, "freedom" parties, or "making America great again," the very soul of democratic institutions around the world is being replaced by misguided versions of neo-fascism, or at least the nascent forms of authoritarian regimes.

Scholars point to a number of specific events as the harbingers of this phenomenon: The rise of the Austrian Freedom Party, the Brexit vote in the UK, the successes of Geert Wilders in the Netherlands, the National Front in France, and most recently, and for many, most shockingly, the election of Donald Trump in the USA in 2016.

These political events share common underlying themes, always beginning with a fear of the "other," blamed for the ills of contemporary society. Regardless of how the "other" is articulated in a specific context, the message is the same: we are now engaged in an existential struggle, a zero-sum game, if you will, in which one segment of the population, often "white," or "Christian," sees itself in opposition to the "hordes of immigrants" and usurpers, taking what is "ours," or destroying traditional culture and values from within. Trump's worldview substantively overlaps with his neo-authoritarian cohorts in Europe, who promise a return to an idealized past; safe, secure, and free of the unwanted other. Trump's refusal to consider facts that are contrary to his "truth," along with his inability to admit error or shame, stand in direct opposition of Etty Hillesum's openness and willingness to love the other, and reflects the personality type that personifies evil, according to Scott Peck. In his book, *The People of the Lie*, Peck notes, "the imposition of one's will upon others by overt or covert coercion is done in order to avoid spiritual growth." In other words, evil turns outward and attacks others instead of the far more difficult process of turning inward to engage one's own shadow material, and over time, transform it.[21]

21 Cf. Scott Peck, *People of the Lie: The Hope For Healing Human Evil* (New York: Simon & Schuster, 1985), 74.

Jungian psychology is very much concerned with shadow work, of both the individual, which Etty Hillesum was drawn to, but also of the group psyche. Thomas Singer, a Jewish-American Jungian analyst and psychiatrist, along with Samuel Kimbles, an African American Jungian analyst and psychologist, have developed a working model of the theory of cultural complexes. This theory is helpful in understanding the psychological elements of Trumpism and today's changing societal norms. Since the 2016 election, we have had to come to terms with the ways in which Trump reflects our materially oriented, achievement-focused, white privileged, narcissistic culture. He both mirrors it and greatly amplifies it, says Singer. Trump seems to have tapped into the severely wounded unconscious of a portion of the American voter, who, feeling left behind by the technical revolution propelling both coasts forward, the recent structural changes in our social mores, including, but not limited to affirmative action and the legalization of same-sex marriage, have been able to openly articulate their pent-up frustration and anger under the cover of a Trump presidency that discourages neither racism nor homophobia. According to Singer, Trump's attacks on "political correctness" have acted as a switch to unleash a torrent of decades-old, unresolved shadow energies.[22]

Mirroring Hitler's promise of a return to a mythical German past, Trump harkens to an antebellum America, when the brutality of slavery, and the destruction of Native American culture were sublimated in favour of a more heroic American self-image. Trump's charged rhetoric glorifying this collective past creates a space for the public airing of racist, homophobic, and misogynist rhetoric, creating, what Robert J. Lifton referred to as "malignant normality," in his study of the German medical profession's role in the Final Solution. Lifton notes that normality is fluid, and "can be much affected by the political and military currents of a particular era."[23]

All Time

This exploration has offered a historical, contemporary, psychological, and transcendent perspective of Etty Hillesum's radical evolution of

22 Cf. Thomas Singer, "Trump and the American Collective Psyche," in: Lee B. Bandy (ed.), *The Dangerous Case of Donald Trump: 27 Psychiatrists and Mental Health Experts Assess a President* (New York: Thomas Dunne Books, 2017), 292-293.

23 Robert J. Lifton, "Our Witness to Malignant Normality," in: Lee (ed.), *The Dangerous Case of Donald Trump*, xvi.

consciousness that we glimpse in a "moment" of her time, that is relevant to our time, and is, indeed, timeless. As we look through the lens of her "sacred resistance," a model of resistance that is meaningful today, we see those essential aspects of life and spirit that Etty Hillesum not only discusses in her journal, but was able to fully live in the moment and also carry a larger perspective of history. She helps us understand the hatred and fears and reactions of her times as well as the losses, fears, and threats to existence, perceived and real in all times. Both her lived and written guidance has shown us the essential aspects of potential that dwell within us in all time: courage, beauty, love of the other, truth, the union of opposites, and presence.

Courage

Above all, Etty Hillesum personifies the values of bravery and courage, which we have held as ideals since Socrates, who taught us that courage is more than conquering the other, and that an unexamined life is not worth living. Courage seems more about the ability to conquer not others but oneself, the courage to be open and just, the courage to cultivate your soul. Etty Hillesum knew this profoundly, and lived this kind of courage. Her choice to volunteer at Camp Westerbork, live the suffering of her people, and resist the dehumanization of the Nazis by finding beauty and meaning in life are pure articulations of the Socratic notion of courage.

The Face of the Other

While it is clear that Etty Hillesum was on a psychological and spiritual journey in order to "repose in" and "hearken unto herself" to a place she called God, her primary motivation was for the "Other." Emmanuel Levinas, the French-Jewish philosopher, who languished in a German POW camp while Etty Hillesum was struggling at Camp Westerbork, was "convinced that only our responsibility for the 'Other' will free us from our awful anonymity and nakedness."[24] Levinas's work helps us to discover the ethics behind her

24 Meins G.S. Coetsier, *The Existential Philosophy of Etty Hillesum: An Analysis of Her Diaries and Letters* [Supplements to the Journal of Jewish Thought and Philosophy, 22] (Leiden/Boston, MA: Brill, 2014), 338.

open, face-to face encounters (*le visage de l'autre*) between Etty Hillesum and those she met at Camp Westerbork.

We are facing the same urgency today, as in all times, to discover our own fear and distrust of the other. This remains the core of sacred teachings of all religions in all times, to love one another and to look out for the poor and traumatized. It remains the deepest work of our human condition for all time.

Beauty

Etty Hillesum's connection to the "beauty of life" is expressed throughout her writing; her narrative "poetry" is laced with symbols reflective of nature. Her references to the "sky," "purple lupins," and "fingertips," all bring a sense of immediacy to the page, for example,

> the sky is full of birds, the purple lupins stand up so regally and peacefully, two little old women have sat down on the box for a chat, the sun is shining on my face – and right before our eyes, mass murder. The whole thing is simply beyond comprehension.[25]

Etty Hillesum's love of beauty begins with existence itself, and her developing experience of being at one with her own existence.

The Union of Opposites

Etty Hillesum's narrative reveals an emerging truth arising from her ongoing struggle between the opposing forces of light and dark. As Jung would say, "waxing and waning make one curve," and that wholeness is the result. What is remarkable about Hillesum is that she approached both the human and the divine aspects of human existence in the same way, with a sense of moving toward wholeness. She did not reduce experience to one or the other. She was simultaneously a transcendent figure as well as a grounded, open, vulnerable woman with a strong will and open heart.

25 E.T., 602. *Het Werk*, 642; Letter 37, Probably to Han Wegerif, Westerbork, Tuesday, 8 June 1943: De lucht is vol vogels, de paarse lupinen staan daar zo vorstelijk en vredig, op die kist zijn twee oude, keuvelende vrouwtjes gaan zitten, de zon schijnt op m'n gezicht en vlak voor onze ogen geschiedt een massamoord, het is zo onbegrijpelijk alles.

Presence

Etty Hillesum channelled presence. It was through integrating her flaws and vulnerability that she was able to "kneel," surrender, accept, and touch presence. Reality became radiant to itself within her, in the language of metaphysics, and she became at one with existence itself.

From a Buddhist perspective, the "present" moment contains everything, not only a person's immediate perception and emotional experience, but all experience in all times. This gives an ineffable depth to what we conventionally call the "present" moment, which includes life, and also death. It includes joy, and it includes suffering. Etty Hillesum's focus in her life, in keeping with Zen precepts, was to be present in the fuller sense of what every moment includes. To be fully present, it seems, we have to go considerably beyond ourselves. As we see with Etty Hillesum, as well as ourselves, it requires a powerful identity shift, a different way of "being" within experience.

May we, in our times of societal devolution, or closed systems, know this presence and resistance that Hillesum knew so deeply in her times, that gives us courage and guidance in our time and that we, too, can live into these essential elements of the soul's journey in all time.

About the Author

Barbara Morrill (1950) is core faculty of the Integral Counseling Psychology Program at the California Institute of Integral Studies in San Francisco, CA. She is a clinical psychologist licensed in CA, and has been in private practice for 25 years. The author has spent much of her life exploring women's social, psychological, and spiritual development, with an emphasis on intergenerational trauma. Etty Hillesum has been a focus of her study since 2006 and she presented *Unfolding Toward Being: Etty Hillesum and the Evolution of Consciousness* in January 2014 at the Second International Conference of the Etty Hillesum Research Centre at Ghent University in Belgium.

Etty Hillesum's Hand Analysis

The Prologue to Her Diaries

Alexandra H.M. Nagel

Abstract

Ever since the publication of *An Interrupted Life*, it has been obvious that Etty Hillesum's first encounter with Julius Spier was a major stepping stone in her personal development. In this paper, it is argued that the notes made during their first meeting, i.e. the report of Spier's hand analysis dated 3 February 1941, are powerful evidence to back up this assumption. Several elements that Spier noticed about Hillesum through "reading" her hands, became themes in Hillesum's diaries. Consequently, the report can be viewed as the prologue to these diaries. However, to understand this particular text, first the content is examined and an amended, more easily readable version is presented.

Keywords: Julius Spier, hand analysis, protocol of Etty Hillesum's hand analysis, personal development, balance between feelings and thinking, Dicky de Jonge, Adri Holm

On 3 February 1942, Etty Hillesum, Julius Spier, and Adri Holm celebrated Hillesum's "spiritual birthday."[1] Precisely one year prior, Hillesum had had

1 E.T., 558-559. *Het Werk*, 592-593; Letter 5, Etty Hillesum to Gera Bongers; Amsterdam, Friday morning, 6 February 1942. To celebrate the event, Hillesum prepared a long letter, now lost, that she called her "annual confession," cf. Alexandra Nagel & Denise de Costa, "'With You, I Have My Anchorage,' Fifteen Letters From Etty Hillesum to Julius Spier,' in: Klaas Smelik, Gerrit Van Oord & Jurjen Wiersma (eds.), *Reading Etty Hillesum in Context: Writings, Life, and Influences of a Visionary Author* (Amsterdam: Amsterdam University Press, 2018), 285-301, 291-292 (letter VIII).

Smelik, Klaas A.D. (ed.), *The Lasting Significance of Etty Hillesum's Writings: Proceedings of the Third International Etty Hillesum Conference at Middelburg, September 2018.*
Taylor & Francis Group 2019
DOI: 10.5117/9789463722025_NAGEL

her hands analyzed by Spier and a few of his students, including Dicky de Jonge. The report on Hillesum's hand analysis made by Holm in that session in 1941, was among the papers that De Jonge carefully safeguarded from her time as a student of Spier.

In this article, I will argue that Holm's report should be considered the prologue to Hillesum's diaries. To understand the importance of Spier's analysis, I will first examine the content of Holm's report on Hillesum's hands and then go on to present an amended, more easily readable version of this initial report.

Hillesum's protocol consists of a series of eighty-five statements

When a person attended Spier's course as the subject of study with the aim of having his/her hands analyzed by Spier and his students, one of the students present made a handprint of the "subject" for each student present at the meeting. Usually, the student making these handprints was the one who had invited the person to serve as a subject of study. Additionally, one of the students took notes during the session. At the time Hillesum attended, this was often Adri Holm, but Dicky de Jonge was also willing to do this task. Afterwards, the note taker typed up copies of the notes for every student in attendance. In this way, all who had been present would get a copy to keep.

Julius Spier called the subject of study *Objekt* [Object, as if it was a name]. The final copy of the report from the notes of the hand analysis was called the *Protokoll* [protocol]. Each protocol combined with the appropriate handprint became a file in what was to become a reference book of sorts for Spier's students.[2]

Most files in De Jonge's extant collection are anonymous. In principle, the subjects were described only by their sex (male/female), age, and marital status (married/unmarried). Sometimes, the date of the session was included on the report, on the handprint, or both. Hillesum's file is marked as *Mädchen 27 J[ahr]* (see Figure 2).

Several sentences in the three-page report, typed on thin paper by Adri Holm, give a clue that the unmarried girl, aged twenty-seven, was Etty Hillesum. On the corresponding handprint, De Jonge had scribbled a few notes (see Figure 3).

After making the handprints, Spier, the subject, and the other students sat together around a table. They then observed the hands of the subject

2 Information of Dicky van de Heuvel-de Jonge to the author, 20 November 2017.

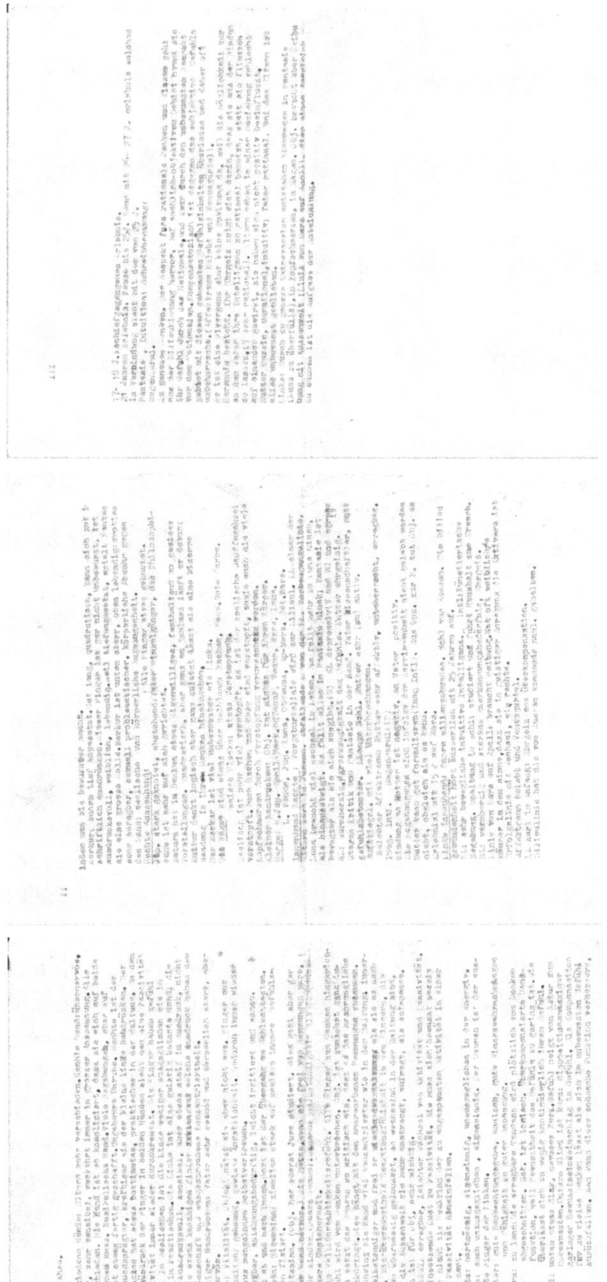

Figure 2 **Report of the hand analysis of Etty Hillesum, 3 February 1941**

Archive Dicky van de Heuvel-de Jonge

Figure 3 The handprints of Etty Hillesum, 3 February 1941

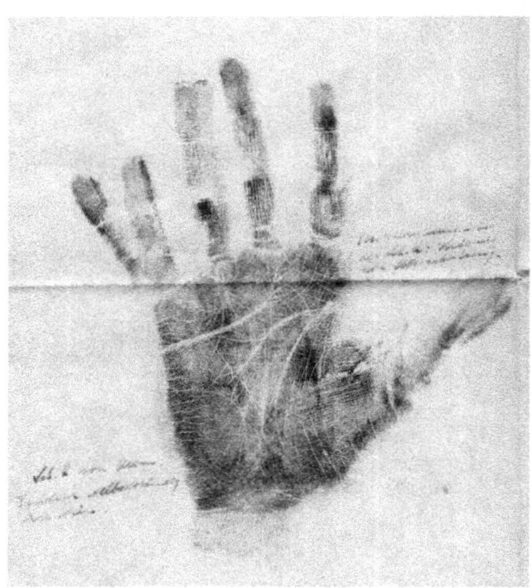
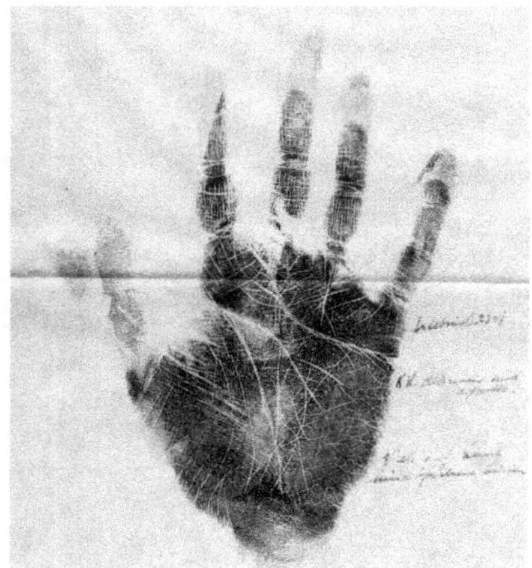

Archive Dicky van de Heuvel-de Jonge

from three different positions. First, Object put his/her elbows firmly on the table, hands held up, and fingers pointing somewhat loosely toward the ceiling. The palm was held toward Object while Spier and his students viewed the backside of the pair of hands. The second posture had the subject put his/her hands flat on the table, the palms downwards. For the third posture, Object was asked to turn the hands 180 degrees, so the palms were visible to everyone. Between the first and the second postures, Spier gripped one of Object's hands to determine the "consistency." He did this with a particular grasp that allowed him to feel the structure of the hand, so he could conclude whether it was hard, weak or something in between.

Each of the three hand postures was designed to show particular aspects of the hands, for example, the whole hand, the individual fingers, the thumbs, the nails, the color of the skin, how the fingers connected to the lower part of the hand, how particular fingers "related" to other fingers, the lines and mounts in the palm, and differences between the left and the right hand. Step by step, all these features were observed and interpreted. Sometimes, when Spier wasn't sure how to interpret a particular feature, he would ask Object a question in order to gain a better, more defined understanding.

This three-phased procedure shows up in almost every protocol kept in De Jonge's private collection. Each report consists of the same type of chronologically ordered observations and interpretations beginning with observations of the hands held up, and ending with notes on the palms-up position. In Hillesum's case, eighty statements can be identified in her protocol. In addition, De Jonge jotted down five statements on the sheet with Hillesum's handprints.

The content of these statements varies from clear information written in German to obscure psychochirological vocabulary. For instance, the comment on Hillesum's "stiff thumb" on her left hand, mentioned that her thumb demonstrated "obstinacy; pretty much fixed on certain inner feelings" [*Starrer Daumen: Eigensinn; ziemlich stark auf gewisse innere Gefühlsvorstellungen fixiert*]. The remarks on her fingers say that she had a feel for rhythm [*Die Finger haben Gefühl für Rhythmus*] and a tendency to think [*Alle Finger zum Denken hingerichtet*]. Yet the way in which Hillesum held some fingers tightly together was interpreted as illustrating that she was inhibited and somewhat timid [*Finger eng zusammen gehalten: gehemmt, gewisse Ängstlichkeit*]. With regard to psychochirological vocabulary, one would have to know that Mercury was a hand-reader's name for the pinky. Knowing this, one could understand the cryptic statement, "Mercury: excitable, in need of support, slightly irritated and shy" [*Merkur: anregbar, anlehnungsbedürftig, leicht irritiert und scheu*]. Basically, the shape and expression of Hillesum's little finger informed Spier that Hillesum was "excitable" in nature, and "in need of support."

Why or how the whole hand, its individual fingers, nails, lines, and mounts related to its owner's health, character, or even his or her upbringing, is a mystery. Spier couldn't explain these connections; he simply believed that there was a correlation between a pair of hands and a person's nervous system.

Many statements in Hillesum's protocol combine a description of a hand feature, and Spier's interpretation of that particular feature. Often, the meaning was enclosed in the description itself. For example, the remark "pre-natal line" meant, according to Spier, that Etty Hillesum, while a fetus in her mother's womb, was affected by an intense experience by her mother during the pregnancy.[3] Similarly, Spier's mention of a "line of prevention" was meant to indicate that he believed Hillesum to have a weak constitution, along with the tendency, unconsciously, to undertake counteractions as soon as she sensed an illness overtaking her.[4]

3 Julius Spier, *The Hands of Children: An introduction to psycho-chirology*, foreword by Carl G. Jung; translated by Victor Grove (London: Kegan Paul, Trench, Trubner & Co, 1944), 79: "I have very often come across this line [the *Pre-natal Line*] in the many years of my practice, and as my observations have taught me that the mothers of children who possess this line have had a decisive and palpable experience during the period of pregnancy which definitely influenced the psychical development of the child."

4 Spier, *The Hands of Children*, 73: "[The *Line of Prevention*] very often appears in the hands of people of a more or less weak constitution who unconsciously try to counteract this by preventive

The report of Hillesum's hand analysis is replete with abbreviations and idiosyncratic hand-reading terminology. It also contains various rather arbitrary statements. The text ultimately boils down, however, to a Jungian psychological report based on the inspection of Hillesum's hands. I have tried here to create an easier, more readable report. All the psychochirological jargon is eliminated, the repetitive fragments are cut to the essentials, and the remaining sentences are reorganized and rewritten. The result is the following report, still in sync with the original version, but written for the modern ear and eye.

The protocol: A psychological portrait of Etty Hillesum[5]

The subject of 3 February 1941 is a young, unmarried woman, twenty-seven years of age. She studies, and in order to earn an income, she helps in someone's household.

Object is extremely restless, very peckish, very sensitive, easily irritated and in a constant state of stress. She is stubborn and ambitious. At the same time she is shy and in need of recognition. She is artistic, can write well [*Schreibbegabung*!], has a lively, intuitive intelligence, possesses a sense of justice, a talent to observe; she has well-functioning senses, can adapt well to circumstances [*Fähigkeit zu guter Anpassung*], and is emotionally generous and warm-hearted. Despite her many talents, Object has in no area achieved anything of consequence. Her thinking is sometimes quirky, sometimes tenacious with regard to holding certain inner ideas and feelings. Her energy is not balanced.

Object has a weak constitution. She suffers from a stuffy nose, stomach aches; she has problems with her throat, and many headaches. However, out of an unconscious impulse, she tries to take preventive measures.

Regarding sexuality, Object gets easily aroused [*erotisch sehr anregbar*]. This is so strong that it is probably problematic. She has had various relationships, and is receptive to effeminate men in the sense that she, mentally, is the more active one.

The cause of Object's problems is roughly twofold. There is a predisposition on the one hand (biological cause), and there is the environment of her upbringing on the other (psychological cause). Born with a strong capacity

measures."

5 Ria van den Brandt convinced me to do a proper text analysis of Hillesum's protocol. Thanks to her, I have been able to rewrite the hand-analysis report of *Mädchen, 27 J.*

to think, Object is focused on the mind. However, she is little aware of her feelings. Her feelings naturally tend to the unconsciousness. Object inherited these tendencies from her parents. Her parents are very different. The father is healthy and physically strong, but also very nervous and a "loner." He is an academic and very rational. The mother, Russian, is an emotional person. She is very affective, quickly stimulated, (too) active, ambitious, and out of control. She has a predisposition to gastrointestinal problems. The mother is also intuitive and can formulate well. However, in her thinking, toward the end of her thought process, she undergoes a bizarre turn [*Mutter denkt logisch aber ganz zuletzt läszt sie eine bizarre Wendung in ihr Denken hineingehen*]. In their mutual relationship, the parents have not positively influenced each other. They have remained rather unaware.

While in the womb, Object was psychologically burdened by traumatic experiences of her mother. This burden has continued during Object's lifetime. Furthermore, the connection between Object and her mother is negative; between Object and her father the connection is positive. The philosophical nature of Object, and the respect she has for thinking, is reinforced by the positive bond with her father. Object naturally is impulsive, extroverted, and, like her mother, she can formulate well. She does not do so, however, to demonstrate her opposition to her mother. As a result of her unconscious, strong respect for thinking (the positive father bond), Object too often inhibits her feelings in daily life. When authentic feelings emerge, her thinking moves toward the critical and serves to reduce these feelings. Object's feelings are always interrupted by her thinking and lead, unconsciously, to an overload of feelings. Unaware of this process, more feelings fall down into the "unconscious" than rise up out of it. As a result, Object can no longer find relaxation in the outside world. Her feelings become overstimulated, and abruptly and uncontrollably switch from activity to passivity. To compensate for her many thoughts, Object lets herself fall back into unconscious feelings.

At the level of the soul, this has caused much clogging. This is the cause of the nasal and throat problems, the stomach complaints, the headaches. Also, Object neglects her body.

From the disunity between the parents and a lack of self-confidence, Object hasn't developed her talents. Still, she is much more independent within herself than she outwardly shows.

It is important to note that Object possesses a "tendency for development" [*Neigung zur Entwicklung*]. The key here is for her to become aware of her (unconscious) feelings. Therefore, Object must learn to regularly make herself passive, and not to let introversion take place only in response to overwhelming activities. Through awareness, she can learn to let her intelligence flow (instead of using it purely rationally), and she can learn to become aware of her weak emotional life (her feelings). The possibility for harmony exists.

Object needs friction with the outside world. The task inherent in her personal development is to find a balance between her feelings and her thinking. When Object is relieved of inhibitions, she has a great sense for children.

Past experiences ([often meaning relationships, AN]) that have left a mark in the palms of her hands, took place when Object was aged seventeen-eighteen, twenty-one, twenty-five, and between twenty-six and twenty-seven. Around her thirtieth year, an important event or experience will occur. (This last is a prediction, noted on the sheet with the handprints.)

In her diaries Hillesum refers to the hand analysis more than once

Several elements in Etty Hillesum's hand analysis seem remarkable. It is generally accepted that Spier knew nothing about Hillesum on Monday, 3 February 1941. In the session, Spier "saw" that Object had a weak constitution, acted more insecure outwardly than she felt inwardly, and that she had not been able to properly develop her many talents. Spier perceived that the main cause of Object's problems was the underdeveloped sense of awareness of her feelings. He ascertained, upon meeting her, that her "biologically" inclined tendency to think more than to feel had grown due to her positive father's bond posed against the negative bonding with her mother. This mattered mainly because – according to Spier – Hillesum's father was a very rational person, whereas her mother was emotional and intuitive. This was seen as the root cause of why Hillesum constantly overruled her feelings in favor of her thoughts. Spier, however, appreciated that Hillesum had a capacity for personal development; he thought she would be able to overcome her problems. We can surmise that Spier's advice had been to start a diary in order to help Hillesum become aware of her inner life, her feelings. At the same time, writing a diary would activate her talent for writing.

On Friday, 7 March 1941, the day before Hillesum wrote Spier the letter that would become the opening page of her diaries, she held a private session with Spier. It is not certain if this was her first or second private meeting with the man who would eventually become her lover. It was during this 7 March session that Spier assured Hillesum that she was "not mad," but simply needed "to do a lot of work" on herself.[6] In other words, Spier repeated what he had said a month earlier, namely that she had the "tendency for development," and that the "possibility for harmony within herself" was genuine. Within days Hillesum began to write a diary.

Right from the beginning, there are direct, and sometimes indirect, references to the protocol from the hand analysis encounter. For instance, the third sentence of her notes on 9 March 1941 reads, "The thoughts in my head are sometimes so clear and so sharp and my feelings so deep, but writing about them comes hard."[7] This is Hillesum expressing in her own words what Spier had told her, namely that her thinking overruled her rather unconscious feelings. She felt the difficulty associated with writing about her feelings. It is easy to imagine his words ringing in her ears.

Ten days later, on 19 March 1941, Hillesum notes in her diary, "I catch myself with a need for music. I don't seem to be unmusical."[8] According to the protocol, Hillesum had a "musical hand" [*Musikalische Hand*], and her fingers showed a feeling for rhythm [*Die Finger haben Gefühl für Rhythmus*]. Then on 24 March, she writes about wrestling with Spier, an experience that had aroused erotic feelings in her. "Well, my friend," she writes, "you ought to know just how 'excitable' I am, because you told me so yourself."[9] This links to the statement in the protocol: "Mercury [the little finger] is rigid below, alive above: erotically very 'excitable'" [*Merkur ist unten starr, oben lebendig: erotisch sehr anregbar*]. In the beginning of August 1941, Hillesum again refers to Spier having told her that she had a talent for writing. "He also once said: 'Well, you are a born writer'."[10] On 22 October 1941, Hillesum herself adopts psychochirological lingo in writing, "Luckily, my Jupiter is not my biggest mount, Apollo-Mercury is even bigger."[11] And a month later

6 E.T., 3. *Het Werk*, 3; Saturday, 8 March 1941: Und als ich von Ihnen nach Hause fuhr, hätte ich gern überfahren werden wollen von einem Auto und dachte: Ach ja, ich werde auch wohl verrückt sein sowie meine ganze Familie, ein Gedanke, den ik immer bekomme, wenn ich mich irgendwo verzweifelt fühle. Aber jetzt weiß ich schon wieder, daß ich das nicht bin, nur daß ich noch sehr viel an mir selber arbeiten muß um ein erwachsener und hunderprozentiger Mensch zu werden.

7 E.T., 4. *Het Werk*, 4; Sunday, 9 March 1941: De gedachten zijn soms zo klaar en helder in het hoofd en de gevoelens zo diep, maar opschrijven, dat wil nog niet.

8 E.T., 33. *Het Werk*, 34; Wednesday, 19 March 1941: Ik betrap mezelf op een behoefte aan muziek. Ik schijn niet onmuzikaal te zijn [...].

9 E.T., 44. *Het Werk*, 47; Monday morning, 24 March 1941: Ik dacht toen wel zoiets van: Ja ventje, jij moet toch drommels goed weten, hoe erotisch "anregbar" ik ben, dat heb je me zelf verteld [...].

10 E.T., 74. *Het Werk*, 78; Tuesday, 5 August 1941: Hij zei ook een keer: Sie sind ja die geborene Schriftstellerin.

11 E.T., 137. *Het Werk*, 47; Wednesday afternoon, 22 October 1941: Jupiter is bij mij gelukkig toch niet het grootste, Apol. Merkur is de nog grotere berg.

she takes up Spier's views on her relationship with her mother. "I have an unresolved antipathy for my mother, and that is precisely why I do the things that I abhor in her."[12]

Hillesum's diary writing also reveals that she followed up on issues regarding her physical well-being:

> I used to think that headaches, stomach aches, rheumatism and similar disagreeable conditions were nothing but physical, but now I can see in myself that their main causes are psychological. Body and soul are very much one in my case. The moment something goes wrong with my psyche something goes wrong with my body as well. That is why mental hygiene is so terribly important for me. The great gain of these past six months is that I have become aware of that and that I shall no longer put me blame on my body.[13]

> True, I've got a headache and a stomach ache right now, but I am no longer in their thrall as I used to be [...].[14]

As these two passages show, Hillesum noted progress in her efforts to become healthier and more balanced. Another clear reference to Spier's initial "diagnosis" concerns the progress she felt she was making with regard to her strong need to fall back into solitude so that her unconscious feelings could take flight if she felt herself overstrained herself by the outside world. On 22 April 1942 she shared in a letter to Henny Tideman (copied in her diary), "At certain fixed times – though less and less often now – I have a tremendous need to cut myself off; to be quite alone for a while."[15]

12 E.T., 44. *Het Werk*, 154; Friday, 21 November 1941: [...] ik heb een oppositie tegen m'n moeder, die is nog steeds niet in elkaar gezakt, en daarom doe ik die dingen, die ik in haar verafschuw, precies zo.

13 E.T., 121; *Het Werk*, 128; Sunday afternoon, 5 October 1941: Vroeger heb ik gemeend, dat die lichamelijke onprettige toestanden, zoals hoofdpijn, maagpijn, rheumatische verschijnselen, ook alleen maar lichamelijk waren, maar ik kan nu aan mezelf constateren dat ze in hoofdzaak psychisch bedingt zijn. Lichaam en ziel zijn heel sterk één bij mij. Zodra er iets stokt in de ziel, zit het ook in het lichaam. Daarom is hygiëne v.d. ziel zo verschrikkelijk belangrijk voor me. Het is de winst van het laatste halve jaar, dat ik dat heel bewust weet en ik zal de schuld ook nooit meer aan m'n lichaam kunnen geven.

14 E.T., 253; *Het Werk*, 263, Sunday evening, 22 February 1942: Ja, het is waar, ik heb nu hoofpijn en maagpijn, maar ik word daar niet meer door beheerst, zoals vroeger.

15 E.T., 336. *Het Werk*, 351; Wednesday morning, 22 April 1942: Op gezette tijden – maar met steeds grote tussenpozen, komt dat bij me terug: een verschrikkelijk sterke behoefte me af te zonderen en tijdenlang helemaal alleen te zijn.

Conclusion

In short, ever since the publication of *An Interrupted Life*, a selection of Hillesum's diary, it has been obvious that Hillesum's first encounter with Julius Spier was a major stepping stone in her personal development. The notes of the hand analysis made during the February 1941 meeting are now powerful evidence to back up that assumption. What is more, the fact that several passages in Hillesum's diaries can be traced back to the protocol from that first meeting indicates that the original hand analysis was a kind of reference point for Hillesum. The report was indeed a prologue to Hillesum's diaries.

About the Author

Alexandra H.M. Nagel (1961) has an MA in History of Western Esotericism at the Faculty of Religious Studies, University of Amsterdam. She hopes to defend in 2019 her PhD thesis about Julius Spier. Currently, she is still enrolled as a PhD candidate at the Institute for Philosophy, Leiden University, the Netherlands.

Suffering, Silence, and Wisdom in the Life of Etty Hillesum

Rosana E. Navarro Sánchez

Abstract

The experience of pain and suffering accompanies the life of all human beings, in different ways and in the most diverse contexts, throughout the history of humanity. The reality of the world we live in is no exception; we are permanently "exposed." The author will consider the evolution of the meaning of suffering in Etty Hillesum's writings. She wants to establish the relationship between the experience of suffering and the experience of silence, as well as the progressive emergence of wisdom in Hillesum's personal experience.

Keywords: suffering, silence, wisdom, Raimon Panikkar, search for inner self

All human beings throughout the history of humanity, in different ways and in the most diverse contexts, have experienced the pain and suffering that accompany life. Our own reality is no different; we are permanently "exposed." Understanding and approaching this reality, however, is different for different people.

In this reflection, I will consider the evolution of the meaning of suffering in Etty Hillesum's writings. Her personal experience and her relationship to silence and wisdom are written in the diaries, and every word contributes to our understanding of the meaning of life today where we find ourselves in the midst of multiple crises and human conflicts.

Much has been written on Etty Hillesum. Nevertheless, it is my intention to deepen our understanding of the experience of suffering, an experience woven silently and yet tightly into Hillesum's life by the circumstances of her times. Etty Hillesum was an eyewitness to the rupture of society

Smelik, Klaas A.D. (ed.), *The Lasting Significance of Etty Hillesum's Writings: Proceedings of the Third International Etty Hillesum Conference at Middelburg, September 2018.*
Taylor & Francis Group 2019
DOI: 10.5117/9789463722025_SÁNCHEZ

and the collapse of all that seemed consolidated in the Western world, and especially in Europe. Hillesum wrote of physical pain in her body, of the pain of impotence when observing the pain of others, and she wrote of the exponential growth of suffering amid the meaninglessness of war. These same realities endure today and even increase. We consider pain and suffering as mutually implied and we note that pain is also caused by the negative, by what is *not* present... by indifference, abandonment, loss, or the lack of love.

Fernando Bárcena has written that in pain there is *"an excess of existence,"*[1] and surely this is so. The stories of the many who suffer attest to this. One of them was Etty Hillesum. While our whole existence is weighted with suffering, in body, mind, and spirit, the question is, what do we do with it? How do we live with suffering? Do suffering and human life give meaning to one another?

We can use our own existence to approach and reflect upon human suffering. Not just abstract nor purely discursive, suffering confronts us, challenges us, and questions our sense of humanity and our aspirations for ourselves. Suffering appears before us in illness and death. It grows from life's vulnerabilities, the soul's relationships, and the consequences we bring on ourselves by what Gabriel Marcel[2] calls "the denial of being."

Suffering in Etty Hillesum's Life

Etty Hillesum's life was full of oscillations and changes, of acute crises and elevated moments. Nevertheless, life went on for her amidst these oscillations. She sought to comprehend and reach the bottom of the falls and the summit of the peaks. That is why such a myriad of influences was intertwined in her story: her personal experiences, her sources of inspiration,

1 Fernando Bárcena, "La Prosa del dolor: El aprendizaje de un instante preciso y violento de soledad," in: F. Bárcena, and others, *La autoridad del sufrimiento / The authority of suffering* (Barcelona: Anthropos, 2004), 65. Fernando Bárcena, a doctorate in Philosophy and Education Sciences and professor of philosophy of education at the Universidad Complutense de Madrid. He has participated in recent years in the research project Philosophy after the Holocaust, at the Institute of Philosophy of the National Research Council (Madrid).

2 French existentialist philosopher (1889-1973), described man's place in the world in terms of such fundamental human experiences as relationships, love, fidelity, hope, and faith. His trend of existentialism was said to be largely unknown in the English-speaking world, where it was mistakenly associated with that of Jean-Paul Sartre. Marcel's view of the human condition was that "beings" are beset by tension, contradiction and ambiguity. He was also interested in life's religious dimension.

her affective relationships, her family. And of course, she was inextricably linked to the situation in society at large; for example, the fate of the Jews, the advance of the war. For her, there was an awareness that pain arises from different directions and expresses itself in different forms. Without a doubt, Hillesum suffered the pain caused by the war, but initially her suffering was associated with her physical ailments and the complexity of her affective relationships.

In the physical realm, Hillesum's body was an almost constant source of pain manifesting in headaches and stomach aches. Facing the threatening events of a war that occupied a central place of fear for the entire population, Etty Hillesum was torn between fear and calm, between her thoughts that sought to comprehend, and her body that felt itself disintegrating.[3]

In line with this, Hillesum's fundamental resource was her own experience. Her reflections always remained closely related to reality, her only existential security. In the course of her story, she described how she learned to live with pain. Indeed, suffering played an important role for her. It was the subject of many of her annotations, not as an intellectual diversion, but as something which gave meaning to the reality of her pain. Hillesum's home life gave rise to substantial pain. Rebecca, her Russian-Jewish mother, had witnessed pogroms in her native land and during Etty's life, she endured a turbulent marriage to Hillesum's father, a reserved man strongly under his wife's influence.[4]

In addition to the complex family dynamic, the war also constituted a source of reflection for Etty Hillesum. When praying, she felt the suffering of herself and all humanity, and this led to new levels of understanding of the meaning of "with," the "other," and "you." As well, she began to experience the importance of union with others to strengthen shared hope before the imminence of death. Hillesum's emerging understanding of the "you" was accompanied and animated by her readings, particularly her engagement with the works of the poet Rainer Maria Rilke.

Sometimes, Etty Hillesum seemed confused when talking about suffering. In everyday life, what she called suffering was closely tied to her affective-sexual desire. Initially her descriptions of "suffering" depended upon feelings she was going through such as attachment, jealousy, or rejection. An example

3 E.T., 456. *Het Werk*, 481; Wednesday morning, 1 July 1942: Het is uiteengevallen in duizend stukken en ieder stukje heeft een andere pijn.

4 Cf. "Mischa announced that Father would be arriving on Saturday evening [...]." E.T., 157. *Het Werk*, 165; Friday morning, 28 November 1941: Mischa kondigde mij zijn komst aan voor Zaterdagavond.

of this is her diary entry where she states, "and perhaps a night may yet come when I shall pray for you, without any petty reservations or jealousy."[5]

The evolution in the meaning of suffering in Hillesum's writings goes hand in hand with advances in her spiritual growth. The incessant questions that moved her interior dialogue were a combination of the intensifying restrictions on Jews, together with her vital experiences of affection and sexuality. Her affective life and temperament gathered and integrated her lived experiences into a mature understanding of suffering. For Hillesum, passion was a powerful appetite. She felt a deep yearning in her relationships with Han Wegerif and Julius Spier. But with any human connection there is also vulnerability, and inevitably – suffering. Etty Hillesum represents a way in which the "I," when open to the other, suffers and, occasionally, renounces and collapses.

Hillesum's woman's consciousness, her curiosity and intellectual lucidity, cannot be separated from her spiritual development and real suffering. She discovered the impossibility of dividing her personal experience into compartments – one for painful events, another for reflection and spiritual growth.[6] Suffering for Hillesum acquired its own traits, drawn from her own experiences. In her narrative, there are striking phrases resonating from the works of the authors she had read. But at the beginning, she was simply overwhelmed and unable to, as yet, understand the complexity of suffering.

Gradually, as her understanding grew, she saw suffering as an inescapable reality, and her challenge became accepting the inevitable; she turned to face vulnerabilities and sorrows instead of evading them. Her perspective began to reveal an interesting lucidity. If suffering is a part of life, there is no point in not facing it; still, one should not seek it out either. Moreover, authentic suffering leads the human being to what she called – echoing Spier's annotations – an "active passiveness" that "consists in accepting and enduring something irrevocable, and that is how new forces are released."[7] In this recapitulation of Spier, Hillesum maintains that suffering strengthens.

5 E.T., 443. *Het Werk*, 467; Tuesday morning, 23 June 1942: [...] en misschien zal er toch nog eens een avond zijn dat ik voor je zal bidden, bevrijd van iedere kleine achtergedachte en jaloezie.

6 Cf. E.T., 24: And so I wanted to own him [...]. *Het Werk*, 26; Sunday morning 16 March 1941: Ik wilde hem dus op de een of andere manier bezitten.

7 Cf. [...] The passive activity of genuine suffering involves bearing and accepting what is inalterable and this releases new powers. E.T., 27. *Het Werk*, 29; Monday evening, 17 March 1941 Die passive Aktivität beim richtigen Leiden besteht darin, daß etwas unabänderliches ertragen und akzeptiert wird und gerade dadurch neue Kräfte frei werden.

The awareness of suffering as a part of progressive maturity was becoming entrenched in Etty Hillesum.[8] The point at which this awareness became fully mature, was when she integrated into her own life the real suffering of others, and especially when she acknowledged the pain of others from a position of strength built on her own trust in God. Her spiritual pursuit bore fruit, but it was a painful path – challenging, disciplined, and dotted with multiple colours. The emotions and experiences of her daily life and in her relationships gave her a particular way of seeing and approaching reality.[9]

In that progressive existential lucidity, Etty Hillesum discovered that suffering could give her a humanizing potential. Suffering could be lived in dignity, and human beings could even face death with no loss of self. For this, all that was necessary was to live beyond the stigmas that humans place on things because of their fear. And again, for Hillesum, suffering was viewed as a source of strength and life, for both oneself and for others.

Etty Hillesum gave her view of the hidden secret of the meaning of pain, which – she implied – one could access when they were prepared internally.[10] This secret consisted in the strength that emerges when suffering is assumed and integrated. She wrote, "If all this suffering does not help us to broaden our horizon, to attain a greater humanity by shedding all trifling and irrelevant issues, then it will all have been for nothing."[11]

In brief, Etty Hillesum experienced suffering in close correspondence with the many elements of her life – the complex world of her family, her affective relationships, her personal contradictions, and the real threat of imminent war. In all this, she witnessed the pain of others as well as of herself. And it was in this scenario that her inner search – her desire to know everything, her tireless task of observing what was happening around her, her

8 Cf. E.T., 370: I know already that in years to come I shall be grateful for everything that has been churned up inside me by what I have had to suffer through him [...]. *Het Werk*, 387; Saturday night, 23 May 1942: Ik weet nu al, dat ik na vele jaren dankbaar zal zijn voor alles wat er in mij omgeploegd is door alles wat ik door hem heb moeten lijden [...].

9 Cf. E.T., 433: [...] I also have great faith in God, and a spirit of sacrifice and love of mankind. [...] I experience people, and I also experience the suffering of people [...]. *Het Werk*, 456; Friday evening, 19 June 1942: daarnaast ken ik ook het grootste godsvertrouwen en offervaardigheid en mensenliefde. [...] Ik beleef de mensen en ik beleef ook het lijden der mensen.

10 Cf. E.T., 494: The greatest cause of suffering in so many of our people is their utter lack of inner preparation [...]. *Het Werk*, 523; Tuesday evening, 16 July 1942: En dit is het grootste lijden voor de velen: de volkomen innerlijke onvoorbereidheid [...].

11 E.T., 502. *Het Werk*, 531; Friday morning, 24 July 1942: Als al dit lijden niet tot een horizonverruiming leidt, tot een grotere menselijkheid, daartoe dat alle kleinheden en bijzaken van dit leven van je afvallen, dan is het voor niets geweest.

relationships, her grievances, her struggles, and her longings – allowed her to patiently weave her own understanding and attitude towards suffering. Ultimately, she saw suffering as a matter intimately linked to life, and as necessary if one was going to learn to live life fully.

All of her experience was succinctly noted in this one central discovery, "Ultimately what matters most is to bear the pain, to cope with it, and to keep a small corner of one's soul unsullied, come what may."[12]

The Experience of Silence in Etty Hillesum's Life

In the richness of Etty Hillesum's existence, what place did silence occupy? And in what way were silence and suffering connected?

Hillesum's encounter with silence was not sudden. It happened gradually, in the midst of personal confusion over mixed feelings, and with full awareness of her inner chaos. In this process, she felt led by the midwife of her soul, under the force of a physical attraction that spilled over her boundaries.[13] Hillesum's experience of war – its reality of exclusion, hatred, deep suffering, and death, also played a central role in her discovery of silence.

As Etty Hillesum consolidated the daily discipline of writing in her diary, she began with the desire to "listen to herself." There were many voices resonating, but she sensed a particular one that she longed to listen to. Curiously, everything started with an exercise "on the floor," tilting her head in a way that, at the beginning, was not very productive.[14] Nevertheless, through the effort of this daily practice, Hillesum found the attractive force of silence, and discovered its risks, its dangers, and its emptiness.

> Sometimes I feel that every word spoken and every gesture made merely serve to exacerbate misunderstandings. Then what I would really like is to escape into a great silence and impose that silence on everyone

12 E.T., 483. *Het Werk*, 510; Friday morning, 10 July 1942: Het gaat er in laatste instantie om, hoe men het lijden, dat toch essentieel aan dit leven is draagt en verdraagt en verwerkt en dat men een stukje van z'n ziel ongeschonden bewaren kan door alles heen.

13 Along with the desire of a stable partner, although she questions herself about it.

14 Cf. E.T., 92: [...] Yes. And sat there. Absolutely still, contemplating my navel so to speak, in the pious hope that new sources of inspiration would bubble up inside me [...]. *Het Werk*, 98; Thursday night, 4 September 1941: Ja, en daar zat ik. Heel stil. A.h.w. starende op m'n navel, in vrome afwachting, of er nieuwe krachten in me wilden opborrelen.

> else. Yes, every word can aggravate the misunderstanding on this too crowded world.[15]

Hillesum's inner struggle led her to short moments of "stillness." Yet, she reproached herself for not allowing "stillness to develop in all its extension," and for not allowing stillness to become her natural state. She recognized that the stillness, the silence she sought, came through interior restlessness, struggle, and discomfort. Ultimately, silence and/or stillness for her would be born of her suffering.[16]

The need for stillness accompanied her. And she discovered that silence was not only found when she retired in solitude; it simply *was* within the hustle, the company, the study, and the questions. Silence inhabited her very being. It consisted in the art of finding the source from which each moment of life was nourished.[17]

Strongly influenced by Rainer Maria Rilke, Etty Hillesum knew she needed to encounter herself, to discover herself in the ongoing monitoring of the experience of herself. She became more and more aware that her silent, secret inner space must remain even in the midst of the vast hustle of life.[18] Thus, she wrote of her desire to fill her diary with only those words "naturally woven into one great silence, not those that merely serve to drown out the silence and to pull it apart. They should simply emphasize the silence."[19]

In relation to words, what Etty Hillesum desired was closely related to what the Catalan philosopher and theologian, Raimon Panikkar endorsed

15 E.T., 131. *Het Werk*, 138-139; Monday morning, 20 October 1941: Soms heb ik het gevoel of ieder woord, dat er gesproken wordt en ieder gebaar dat er gemaakt wordt, het grote misverstand vergroot. Dan zou ik willen ondergaan in een groot zwijgen en ook ieder ander het zwijgen willen opleggen. Ja, ieder woord maakt soms het misverstand op deze veel te drukke aarde, groter.

16 Cf. E.T., 245: [...] but being satisfied with those far too brief moments of peace and introspection which are increasingly being woven into my everyday life [...]. *Het Werk*, 255; Friday morning, 20 February 1942: [...] maar al tevreden zijn met de korte momenten van rust en zelfinkeer, die weliswaar steeds meer door m'n dagelijkse leven heengeweven raken.

17 Cf. E.T., 310: [...] one must always carry a great silence within one, [...] even in the midst of all the hustle and bustle and in the midst of the most animated conversations [...]. *Het Werk*, 323; Sunday evening, 29 March 1942: altijd een grote stilte met zich meedragen [...] ook tenmidden van het grootste gewoel en midden in het intensiefste gesprek.

18 Cf. E.T., 336: [...] We must carry our experience within us, place it at the centre of a quiet space within us [...]. To be alone. Stillness [...]. *Het Werk*, 351; Friday morning, 17 April 1942: [...] men moet zijn "Erleben" in zich meedragen, het in zich midden in een ruimte van stilte plaatsen [...]. Alleen zijn. Stilte.

19 E.T., 394. *Het Werk*, 413; Friday evening, 5 June 1942: die organisch ingevoegd zijn in een groot zwijgen, zou ik willen schrijven, niet woorden, die er alleen maar zijn om het zwijgen te overstemmen en uiteen te rukken. De woorden moeten eigenlijk het zwijgen accentueren.

when he wrote, "Silence is one. Words are many."[20] Ultimately, it was the search for what Panikkar calls, "the spirit in the word," or the primacy of myth over logos, or the innocence of the one who has nothing to say because everything has been said.

> And everything is silent. However, in the vast silence there is
> A new beginning, a signal and a change.[21]

For Etty Hillesum, learning about suffering and silence was a daily task that blended hurry, anguish, hope, restlessness, joy, words, absence, rejection, and even the embrace. Suffering and silence were intertwined for her. Suffering became the path to silence. Silence was nourished by awareness and acceptance of that which tears at us and touches us from the inside. Thus, for Hillesum, the inevitable pain and violence caused by hatred were transformed. She emerged as the artist who could describe and colour with hope that which human senses lack. With the brush and pen of an artist, she made silence become eloquent and lucid; she no longer allowed suffering to intimidate her. In place of suffering, the joyful certainty of a Greater Love was patiently carved in her heart, mind, and body.

Wisdom or "catching the flavour of things"

Wisdom is not understood in the same way by everyone. In today's world, so saturated by examples of technical complexity, luxury, wealth, comfort, academic rigour, and power, conceptions of wisdom are very diverse. Some believe that wisdom consists of doing things well or having the knowledge to solve life's problems and human coexistence. Others think that having a mature and integrated personality is the equivalent of wisdom – at least some schools of psychology believe this. Then there are those with a philosophical perspective who consider that wisdom consists of deep knowledge of reality. And of course, there is the theological perspective that holds that wisdom is the knowledge of God.

20 Raimond Panikkar, *Obras Completas/Complete Works*, Book 1, Volume 2. (Barcelona: Herder, 2015), 275.

21 Rainer María Rilke, *Sonnets to Orpheus*. Rilke (1875-1926) is considered the greatest lyric poet of modern Germany. His work is marked by a mystical sense of God and death. He was a great inspiration for Etty Hillesum.

"And there I stood nought knowing, all science transcending"[22]

These words of John of the Cross provide the framework for the final phase of our reflection. Etty Hillesum's path, crowded by experiences, questions, pain, books, embraces, confusion, and desire, is a path "in wisdom," if by wisdom we understand:

> [...] a basic attitude that depends on our own transparency, on the authenticity of our life. Wisdom is personal harmony with reality, unity with Being, Dao, Heaven, God, nothingness [...].[23]

In our reflection on suffering and silence in Etty Hillesum, we have established that suffering – the awareness of an absence, the feeling that something is missing, the deep need for relief[24] – represents an evolution in her consciousness. In Hillesum's case, this was achieved by integrating spiritual growth, affective maturity, and a sense of otherness. The experience of suffering led her to silence, which, from a spiritual perspective, means availability, purity of heart, and the essence of detachment.[25]

> From the first pages of her diary, Etty is aware of the need to "forget about herself," and of the inner struggle that this implies; therefore, she states: "Everything must be more natural and simple: I myself must completely disappear." [...] [O]blivion of herself became, from the beginning, a firm purpose and desire. At the end of her diary, she even sees the need to forget those words that have vitiated her meaning. That is the purpose of "forgetting oneself," a return to the origins, to the easy and simple, in order to recover our authentic being.[26]

When Etty Hillesum began her journey, she referred to wisdom as knowledge-to-be-conquered, that "sublime wisdom of centuries" that rested in books.

22 Expression of John of the Cross in one of his mystic poems. He lived from 1542 to 1591 and was a major figure of the Counter-Reformation, a Spanish mystic, Carmelite friar and priest. John of the Cross is considered as one of the foremost poets in the Spanish language.

23 Panikkar, *Obras Completas/Complete Works*, 477.

24 As soon as it was made into conscious experience that accepts "that which is missing."

25 For Eckhart, detachment is the maximum virtue that a human being has to cultivate, as complete abandonment of himself so that the void gives place to the encounter with the Divine. Cf. Eckhart, *On Detachment*, 237-244.

26 Rosana Navarro, *Etty Hillesum: Mística y humanidad / Mysticism and Humanity* (Bogotá: PUJ, 2017), 85.

She wrote about the desire to immerse herself in the "wisdom of the ages," sure that it would lead her to the depths of herself.[27] Motivated by her own interests and readings, and accompanied by Julius Spier's mentoring, Etty Hillesum discovered the intention of power behind her search for knowledge and asked God for wisdom.[28]

Conclusion

As the ensuing war uncovered desolation and anguish, the darkest forces of human beings came to the fore. And just when the feeling of desolation and hopelessness grew, and suffering thrust men and women down into meaninglessness, in Etty Hillesum's heart, suffering was transformed with silence, and she vowed to maintain trust in humanity at all costs.

Both the inner and outer worlds with all their movement and noise gave rise to the existential queries Etty Hillesum asked during her life. Her answer was not to flee, nor to victimize herself. She took the option of continuous learning with no evading of events, even the most painful and difficult ones. How did this happen? Her path was to patiently learn silence, where, she felt, transformation took place. It was a *metanoia*, in which her daily life and her inexorable future became her treasure. Thus, her conscious experience of suffering, along with her progressive comprehension of the depths of silence, made it possible for her to open to wisdom's harmony. *Not knowing* filled her interior and invited her to come out of herself, to "unearth God from hearts," to "help God," and to "be a balm on so many wounds" of the people she met straining to live in those disastrous times.

About the Author

Rosana Navarro Sánchez (1963) holds a PhD in Theology and M.Ed. (Master of Education) at the Pontifical Xavierian University, Bogotá, Colombia. She

27 Cf. E.T., 71: [...] and there I would immerse myself in the wisdom of the ages and in myself. Then I might perhaps find peace and clarity. *Het Werk*, 75-76; Monday, 4 August 1941: en daar zou ik me dan willen verdiepen in de eeuwen en in mezelf en op den duur zou er dan wel rust en klaarheid komen.

28 Cf. E.T., 94: Knowledge is power, and that's probably why I accumulate knowledge [...]. But Lord, give me wisdom, not knowledge [...]. *Het Werk*, 100; Friday morning, 5 September 1941: Kennis is macht, dat weet ik en misschien verzamel ik ook daarom kennis [...]. Maar Heer, geef me liever wijsheid inplaats van kennis.

is Associate Professor, Faculty of Theology, Pontifical Xavierian University (since January 1991), Professor of Practical Theology (since January 1996), Professor in History and Education Researches (since January 2004), and Professor in Spiritual Theology, Carmelite Institute of Spirituality (since January 2016), and Director of the Etty Hillesum Foundation in Colombia.

Feeding the Soul

Etty Hillesum's Pedagogical and Spiritual Path

Maria Gabriella Nocita

Abstract

During the years of the Shoah, Etty Hillesum engages a particular path intended to promote a process of human edification. Along the way to the realization of the "self that one is," she understands that "body and soul are one," and that "the inner world is as real as the outer world." Both elements need to be cared for. While taking care of one's body comes quite naturally, deciding to take care of one's soul is not such an obvious choice. The soul has its own particular needs, which are very commonly ignored or misunderstood. It is necessary to decode the soul's needs. To follow this path, she develops a form of *philosophizing for life* that sees man as both subject and object of the enquiry and that humanizes the individual who pursues it. Together with Etty Hillesum, we learn how to cultivate this knowledge of the soul.

Keywords: unity of body and soul, caring/nourishing of soul, decoding needs of soul, philosophizing for life, pedagogical path

The thoughts I would like to share in this article, range from the philosophical to the pedagogical. All are based on considerations that arose in the aftermath of the Shoah. The turn towards mass extermination became possible when the general trend of events shifted to "making man no longer human."[1] So our question becomes: is it possible to experience the opposite

1 Cf. Maria Gabriella Nocita, "Etty Hillesum and Primo Levi among the *Drowned* and the *Saved* Experiences of Inner Freedom," in: Klaas A.D. Smelik, Meins G.S. Coetsier & Jurjen Wiersma (eds.), *The Ethics and Religious Philosophy of Etty Hillesum: Proceedings of the Etty Hillesum*

Smelik, Klaas A.D. (ed.), *The Lasting Significance of Etty Hillesum's Writings: Proceedings of the Third International Etty Hillesum Conference at Middelburg, September 2018.*
Taylor & Francis Group 2019
DOI: 10.5117/9789463722025_NOCITA

– a "path *towards* humanization?" How can we embark on a journey towards the full realization of our human nature?

During the years of the Shoah, Etty Hillesum set forth on just such a journey. She created and engaged a pedagogical and spiritual path intended to remove the causes of dehumanization and promote a process of human edification. As a young woman of twenty-seven in Holland in the nineteen-forties, she realized it was her existential priority to work on herself and discover what it would take to attain completeness as a human being. She began on 8 March 1941, when she wrote on the first page of her diary, "but I know again now that [...] I simply need to do a lot of work on myself before I develop into an adult and a complete human being."[2] While she wrote, she noticed "a small slice of chaos was suddenly staring at me from deep down inside my soul."[3] Yet from such *inquietude*, she was able to muster the strength to confront herself and ask who she wanted to be. Believing that "life poses a different riddle for every person," she set out to solve "the riddle of life" – or better: *the riddle of her own life*; "the riddle that has been set for her."[4]

For Etty Hillesum, delving into such a mystery meant trying to contact the realities that made up one's being; to have "the courage to be oneself."[5] Not to do so meant to her to have no right to exist. In her discovery of how to do this, Julius Spier loomed large. He came to represent the person to whom Hillesum's soul and all that mattered most could be entrusted. For her, Spier seemed attuned to the inner tension whereby the most original part of one's being was able to make the transition from potentiality to action. He was the person "[who] would bring order to [her] inner chaos, harness the force now at loggerheads within [her]."[6] On his tombstone it reads: "He taught and lived: 'Become the one you are'."[7] Hillesum felt exactly the same

Conference at Ghent University, January 2014 [Supplements to The Journal of Jewish Thought and Philosophy, 28] (Leiden-Boston, MA: Brill, 2017), 170-191, especially p. 174.

2 E.T., 3. *Het Werk*, 3; Saturday, 8 March 1941: Aber jetzt weiß ich schon wieder, daß ich das nicht bin, nur daß ich noch sehr viel an mir selber arbeiten muß um ein erwachsener und hundertprozentiger Mensch zu werden.

3 *Ibidem*: [...] ein kleines Stückchen Chaos schaute mich mit einemmale tief unten aus der Seele an.

4 Cf. E.T., 151. *Het Werk*, 158; Sunday morning, 23 November 1941: Het leven geeft ieder een ander raadsel op, al naar de aard en gesteldheid van de mens. Ik wil hèt raadsel van het leven oplossen. Maar moet eigenlijk zeggen: míjn raadsel of liever: het raadsel dat mij gesteld wordt.

5 Cf. E.T., 158. *Het Werk*, 167; Sunday morning, 30 November 1941: De moed hebben tot zich zelf.

6 E.T., 6. *Het Werk*, 6; Sunday, 9 March 1941: En hij zou orde brengen in de innerlijke chaos, zich aan 't hoofd stellen van de innerlijke tegenstrijdige krachten, die er in me werken.

7 E.T., 744 note 516. *Het Werk*, 777 note 546: Julius Philipp Spier / Frankfurt 25 April 1887 / Amsterdam 15 September 1942 / Er lehrte und lebte: / ‚Werde der du bist'. / Nun bleibet Glaube / Hoffnung Liebe / diese drei aber / die grösseste unter / ihnen ist die Liebe.

thing: that Spier could set an example for everyone near him because "he himself lives precisely as he teaches."[8] She immediately fell under his spell which she characterized as an "inner freedom that seemed to emanate from him."[9] She had no doubt she would follow him.

"Become what you are" are the opening words of Julius Spier's book *The Hands of Children*. Published posthumously, Spier had written the book with the explicit intent "to point out the road of development which leads towards perfection."[10]

Ortega Y Gasset, in *Man and People* (1957) wrote,

> To such an extent, unlike all the other beings in the universe, is man never surely *man*; on the contrary, being *man* signifies precisely being always on the point of not being man, being a living problem, an absolute and hazardous adventure, or, as I am wont to say: being, in essence, drama! [...] While the tiger cannot stop being a tiger, cannot be de-tigered, man lives in perpetual danger of being dehumanized. [...] but at times what happens to man is nothing less than *ceasing to be man*. [...] The majority of men perpetually betray this *self* which is waiting to be; and to tell the whole truth, our personal individuality is a personage which is never completely realized, a stimulating Utopia, a secret legend, which each of us guards in the depths of his heart. It is thoroughly comprehensible that Pindar summarized his heroic ethics in the well-known imperative: "Become what you are".[11]

Along the way to the realization of the "self that one is," Etty Hillesum began to understand that "body and soul are one,"[12] and that both elements of the self need to be cared for. She could also see, however, that while taking care of one's

8 E.T., 59. *Het Werk*, 63; Tuesday morning, 10 June 1941: [...] hij zelf alles leeft, wat hij leert. It was Spier himself who taught her the importance of all this and Etty Hillesum reported his teaching on a page of the month of March in German: "One cannot teach what one has not mastered oneself." E.T., 29. *Het Werk*, Monday, 17 March 1941: Was man nicht beherrscht, kann man auch nicht lehren.

9 E.T., 5. *Het Werk*, 5; Sunday, 9 March 1941: Toen onder de indruk gekomen van een soort innerlijke bevrijdheid [...].

10 Julius Spier, *The Hands of Children: An Introduction to Psycho-Chirology*, edited by Herta R. Levi, foreword by Carl G. Jung, foreword; translated by Victor Grove (London: Kegan Paul, Trench, Trubner & Co, 1944; 1955, revised edition; 1973, reprinted by New Delhi, Sagar Publications, 1973, and London: Routledge, 1999), 1.

11 José Ortega Y Gasset, *Man and People*, translated by Willard R. Trask (New York: Norton, 1963), 25.

12 E.T., 6. *Het Werk*, 6; Sunday, 9 March 1941: "Körper und Seele sind eins."

body comes quite naturally, deciding to take care of one's soul is not such an obvious choice. In order to develop the soul, it is first essential to understand its own particular needs, which are very commonly ignored or misunderstood.

So how is one to decode the soul's needs? In Plato's *Protagoras*, when Hippocrates asks, "But what is it that nourishes a soul?"[13] Socrates answers that the soul takes its nourishment from "*matemata*," teachings. Etty Hillesum received her initial teachings concerning the soul from Spier. She duly records in her diary, on 13 March 1941, what she has heard from Spier and describes her struggle to make his teachings *flesh and blood*.

Spier had noted first of all that "development must not bother with time" and that "what you expect from others, that is, from the outside, you carry unconsciously in you." Nonetheless, he observed the necessity "to develop it in yourself, by making it conscious," adding that the development of one's self consists of immersing oneself within the soul in order to then "raise it into consciousness."[14] Referencing 2 Corinthians 5:5, where it is written that God has given unto Man the *pledge of the Spirit,* Spier remarked that it is Man who is in charge of administering his own soul and he should do it well – "live on his spiritual strength, be inspired."[15]

As essayist and philosopher, María Zambrano phrased it, Spier's teachings had awakened in Hillesum the need for a *Knowledge of the Soul* that would put her inner life in order. Moreover, a diary entry from 4 August 1941 informs us that Etty Hillesum regarded herself a *devourer* of books from an early age[16] with interests ranging from literature to poetry and art, and under Spier's influence, to psychology, theology, and philosophy. Indeed, we know that several authors sustained Hillesum along her journey and nourished her with their teachings. The most frequently cited were Rilke, Dostoevsky, Jung, and St Augustine, authors she loved and who became part of her daily life, were addressed with words of affection, and referred to as though they had become life companions.[17]

13 Plato, *Protagoras and Meno*, translated by W.K.C. Guthrie (Harmondsworth, Middlesex: Penguin Books, 1956), *Protagoras* 313 C.

14 E.T., 16-17. *Het Werk*, 17-18; Thursday, 13 March 1941: Entwicklung darf nicht mit Zeiten rechnen. [...] J. –Das, was man vom andern, also von aussen erwartet, hat man unbewußt in sich. Statt es von aussen zu erwarten, soll man es in sich entwickeln, indem man es in sich bewußt macht. Die Seele ist nicht zeitgebunden, sie ist ewig. Man soll sich in sie vertiefen, sie ins Bewußtsein heben, d.h. sich entwickeln. These concepts are reaffirmed by Etty Hillesum also in other pages: cf. E.T., 65. *Het Werk*, 69; Wednesday morning 18 June 1941; and E.T., 556. *Het Werk*, 590; Letter 4, To Aimé van Santen; Amsterdam, 25 January 1942.

15 Cf. E.T., 17. *Het Werk*, 18; Thursday, 13 March 1941: –Der Mensch kriegt seine Seele in Verwaltung (zie ook 2 Corinthiërs, 5:5) und soll sie gut verwalten; aus seinen Seelenkräften leben, beseelt sein.

16 Cf. E.T., 70-71. *Het Werk*, 75; Monday, 4 August 1941.

17 Cf. E.T., 383. *Het Werk*, 401; Friday morning, 29 May 1942.

To what extent the manner in which she chose to nourish her soul would prove fitting to the fate that awaited her, is something we shall evaluate shortly.

Etty Hillesum was not born a philosopher, and did not regard herself as such. The elaboration of an unshakable system of thought meant little to her, and indeed would have felt like a prison for her mind. She had, rather, a fundamental interest in the form of human understanding that was comparable to what Socrates termed "antropine sofia" [human wisdom][18] – a form of human reflection that sees the human being as both subject and object of the enquiry and which (and here lies its chief merit) *humanizes* the individual who pursues it. Hers, then, was a form of *philosophizing for life* – in which reflection could guide life's experience and vice versa.

At the end of March 1941, Etty Hillesum wrote an entry relating to a task she had set herself, namely "to live fully, outwardly and inwardly, not to ignore external reality for the sake of the inner life, or the reverse."[19] Just over a month later, she sensed, among other things, that her life had become "so clear [...] and so intense" that she felt she had come into contact "with the outer and inner worlds" and that this progress was life-enriching, and involved a broadening of her personality.[20]

On 11 June 1941, she wrote about these recent experiences,

> The inner world is as real as the outer world. One ought to be conscious of that. It, too, has its landscapes, contours, possibilities, its boundless regions. And man himself must be a small centre in which the inner and outer worlds meet.[21]

Etty Hillesum was certain that these two worlds "are fed by each other" and that "[to] neglect one at the expense of the other" is not possible. As well, it should not be possible "[to] deem one more important than the other" because "[o]therwise you impoverish your own personality."[22]

18 Plato, *The last days of Socrates*, translated by Hugh Tredennick (Harmondsworth, Middlesex: Penguin Books, 1954), *The Apology* 20 d 6.

19 E.T., 53. *Het Werk*, 56; Tuesday, 25 March 1941: Volledig leven, naar buiten en naar binnen, niets van de uiterlijke realiteit opofferen terwille v.h. innerlijk en ook niet andersom [...].

20 Cf. E.T., 54. *Het Werk*, 57; Friday afternoon, 8 May 1941.

21 E.T., 60. *Het Werk*, 64; Wednesday morning, 11 June 1941: De binnenwereld is even reëel als de buitenwereld. Men moet dit bewust weten. Zij heeft ook haar landschappen, haar contouren, haar mogelijkheden, haar onbegrensde gebieden. En zelf is men het kleine centrum, waar binnen- en buitenwereld elkaar ontmoeten.

22 *Ibidem*: De beide werelden worden door elkaar gevoed, men mag de ene niet verwaarlozen ten koste van de andere, de ene niet belangrijker vinden dan de andere. Anders verarmt men de eigen persoonlijkheid. She reaffirmed this concept on the 4th of August writing. Cf. E.T., 71. *Het*

For Hillesum the idea began to form that in time, her own journey toward self-awareness might open the way for others. She felt strongly that the inner world of the people she met was "fallow, uncultivated ground which does not seem worth tilling" because those people did not acknowledge it as a real place and treated it in fact as "terra incognita." In the face of such a situation she could "[feel] the urge to start the work of reclamation, to create order and to bring it into consciousness." She wondered if in the long run, opening up consciousness for others might be her life's work.[23]

During the month of August 1941, Etty Hillesum wrote about her own development along lines of the metaphor of *tilling* piece by piece, an unsown plot of land that is the field of the spirit.[24] At that time, she nourished constantly herself with *the highest and most precious goods of the spiri*t, but she was also aware of the danger of becoming alienated from "the masses, who must content themselves with far coarser food."[25] Still, she had come to terms with what seemed to her an indisputable fact: the presence of "a dogged spirit in me that wants to wrest as many secrets from life as possible."[26]

One of her favourite practices became "[j]ust to crouch huddled up on the ground in a corner and listen to what is going on inside me" – a practice that enabled her to "make [her]self passive" and so "reestablish contact with a slice of eternity."[27]

Werk, 76; Monday, 4 August 1941: Ik moet mezelf iedere keer weer gooien in de realiteit, moet me auseinandersetzen met alles, wat ik op m'n weg tegenkom, de buitenwereld moet voedsel ontvangen van mijn innerlijke wereld en omgekeerd, maar het is zo verschrikkelijk moeilijk en waarom heb ik toch zo een beklemd gevoel vanbinnen.–

23 Cf. E.T., 61. *Het Werk*, 64; Wednesday morning, 11 June 1941: Die binnenwereld is bij hun een braakliggend, onontgonnen terrein, waar ze zich niet de moeite voor nemen om aan te werken. Het is geen erkend reëel gebied. En ik voel dan een soort neiging in me opkomen aan het ontginnen te gaan en orde te scheppen en bewust te maken. [...]?

24 Cf. E.T., 76. *Het Werk*, 81; Thursday, 7 August 1941: Werk maar rustig door, bewerk maar de akker van de geest en leef ook een beetje en laat het met elkaar in harmonie zijn.

25 E.T., 77. *Het Werk*, 81; *ibidem*: Maar door me voortdurend te voeden met de hoogste en kostbaarste geestelijke goederen ben ik misschien bang te ver verwijderd te raken van de grote massa, die zich met veel grover voedsel voedt.

26 *Ibidem*: Dan zou ik zo eenvoudig willen zijn dat het leven als iets vanzelfsprekends in me was, waar ik verder niet over hoefde te denken. Er is eigenlijk heel diep in me een verlangen naar het heel eenvoudige, het rustige en gelijkmatige. Of verbeeld ik me dat en is het toch weer iets anders? Maar er zit nu eenmaal een ploeterende geest in me, die het leven zoveel mogelijk geheimen ontrukken wil, er is niets aan te doen, je weg zal waarschijnlijk nog moeilijk genoeg zijn.

27 Cf. E.T., 93-94. *Het Werk*, 99-100; Friday morning, 5 September 1941: Ik moet maar ineenhurken in een hoekje op de grond en zo in elkaar gedoken luisteren naar wat er binnen in me is. Met denken kom ik er toch nooit uit. Denken is een mooie en trotse bezigheid in je studie maar uit moeilijke gemoedsgesteldheden kun je je nooit "heraus" denken. Dan moet er iets anders

That "slice of eternity" Etty Hillesum discovered, she believed is an inalienable part of each human being – something each one holds within themselves.[28] But she cautioned, so as not to smother the impulse toward eternity that lies within, humans have a duty to "reestablish contact" with that slice. Later on, as she advanced in her experience of inner discovery, Hillesum wrote that, ultimately, her life was "one long hearkening unto myself and unto others, unto God. And if I say that I hearken, it is really God who hearkens inside me. The most essential and the deepest in me hearkening unto the most essential and deepest in the other. God to God."[29]

Etty Hillesum experienced in her own "slice of eternity," a form of presence that was transcendent and immanent at the same time.[30] Initially, the insight into this inner reality came in the guise of minor intuitions, but as the months passed Hillesum's increasing awareness fell in line with that disclosed to her by Rilke, her favourite poet, and by Spier, the mentor of her soul. What she understood and described as an "outer space within,"[31] or an *interior universe*[32] that contacts and *partakes of* a reality common to all, was for Rilke "our ancestral experience whereby beings recognize one another," the *Weltinnenraum*.[33]

As she progressed in her search for the "heaven [which] lives in her,"[34] Hillesum refined the technique of *active contemplation*. She learned the process through which one "become[s] lost in oneself" in order to recompose

gebeuren. Dan moet je je passief maken en luisteren. Weer contact vinden met een klein stukje eeuwigheid.

28 Cf. E.T., 435. *Het Werk*, 458; Saturday night, 20 June 1942.

29 E.T., 519. *Het Werk*, 549; Thursday morning, 17 September 1942: Eigenlijk is mijn leven één voortdurend "hineinhorchen", in mijzelf, in anderen, in God. En als ik zeg: ìk "horch hinein", dan is het eigenlijk God in mij, die "hineinhorcht". Het wezenlijkste en diepste in mij dat luistert naar het wezenlijkste en diepste in de ander. God tot God.

30 Cf. Klaas A.D. Smelik, *Etty Hillesum and her God,* in: Klaas A.D. Smelik, Ria van den Brandt & Meins G.S. Coetsier (eds.), *Spirituality in the Writings of Etty Hillesum: Proceedings of the Etty Hillesum Conference at Ghent University, November 2008* [Supplements to The Journal of Jewish Thought and Philosophy, 11] (Leiden/Boston, MA: Brill, 2010, 75-102, especially pp. 85-86.

31 E.T., 515. *Het Werk*, 545; Tuesday, 15 September 1942: Weltinnenraum.

32 Cf. Maria Gabriella Nocita, "Feeling Life: Etty Hillesum *Becomes* Word", in: Smelik, Van den Brandt & Coetsier (eds.), *Spirituality in the Writings of Etty Hillesum*, 279-295, especially pp. 282-284.

33 Cf. Rainer Maria Rilke, "Es winkt zu Fühlung fast aus allen Dingen", in: *idem*, *Gedichte 1906-1926* (Sämtliche Werke, II), 92: [...] Wer rechnet unseren Ertrag? Wer trennt / uns von den alten, den vergangnen Jahren? / Was haben wir seit Anbeginn erfahren, / Als daß sich eins im anderen erkennt? [...] Durch alle Wesen reicht der *eine* Raum: / Weltinnenraum. Die Vögel fliegen still / durch uns hindurch. O, der ich wachsen will, / ich seh hinaus, und *in* mir wächst der Baum.

34 E.T., 515. *Het Werk*, 545; Tuesday, 15 September 1942: [...] de hemel leeft in mij.

the fragments of the soul.[35] When she found herself on the route to rediscovering herself, she saw it as an act of inner *re-unification*.[36]

Within the abode of her inner space, Etty Hillesum also learned to give sorrow the space its gentle origins demanded.[37] She understood that if she failed to reconcile sorrow in her own life, it would be hard "to keep a small corner of one's soul unsullied."[38]

All of these conquests from her interior journey eventually enabled her to describe herself as "mature enough to take your destiny upon yourself" and stop "living an accidental life."[39] She could finally take upon herself the task of keeping her soul perfumed.[40] For, in her eyes, the spirit "withers" and "shrivels up in some corner"[41] if it goes unheeded and is not nourished.

As early as July 1942, once she had embarked on her soul's journey, Etty Hillesum realized that "unless we provide an alternative, a dazzling and dynamic alternative with which to start afresh somewhere else, then we are lost, lost permanently and for all time."[42] The alternative she devised began in her inner world with the *transformation* of self and then turned outward spreading in a kind of positive *contagion*.

Months later, in September 1942, while on leave in Amsterdam, she expanded her caretaking of the soul to others. She recalled how during the previous summer she had walked through the Westerbork transit camp with members of the Jewish Council, and reflected on their character and behaviour. She expressed in her diary, "if only I could enter a small piece of their soul."[43] This desire sprang from her wanting to be "the receptacle of

35 E.T., 59. *Het Werk*, 62; Monday morning, 9 June 1941.

36 Cf. E.T., 144. *Het Werk*, 152; Friday, 31 October 1941.

37 Cf. E.T., 308-309. *Het Werk*, 322; Saturday morning, 28 March 1942.

38 Cf. E.T., 483. *Het Werk*, 510; Friday morning, 10 July 1942.

39 E.T., 359. *Het Werk*, 376; Thursday, 30 April 1942: Maar ik vind ze opeens terug en ze maken me weer een beetje trots en heel ernstig. Inplaats van voor een toevallig leven voel je je, zo in alle stilte, gerijpt voor een "Schicksal".

40 Cf. E.T., 448. *Het Werk*, 473; Saturday morning, 27 June 1942: Met meerderen in één benauwde cel. En is het dan niet onze taak temidden der bedorven uitwasemingen onzer lichamen onze ziel geurig te houden?

41 E.T., 491. *Het Werk*, 520; Tuesday, 14 July 1942: En de geest, die vergeten geest, verschrompelt ergens in een hoekje.

42 E.T., 505. *Het Werk*, 534; Monday morning, 27 July 1942: En tegelijk wist ik ook: wanneer we hier niet iets tegenover stellen, iets stralends en krachtigs, dat ergens op een heel andere plek weer helemaal opnieuw begint, dan zijn we verloren, voor goed en voor altijd verloren.

43 E.T., 518. *Het Werk*, 547; Wednesday morning, 16 September 1942: [...] ach, laat mij maar een stukje ziel van jullie zijn.

their better nature, which is sure to be present in all of them."[44] She wanted to feel that she was their *guardian*, or better... the *guardian of the soul.*

Etty Hillesum gave guidelines for a profound meditation on the events unfolding around her. They were of such a nature that "in the past the our reason would not have been judged possible," and surmised that, possibly, human beings "have faculties other than reason in [them], faculties that in the past they didn't know [they] had but that possess the ability to grapple with the incomprehensible."[45] Hillesum was convinced that for every event, "man has a faculty that helps him deal with it."[46] This formidable intuition became manifest for her: "[what] matters is not whether we preserve our lives at any cost, but how we preserve them."[47] That was the point at which Hillesum declared, "yet if we have nothing to offer a desolate post-war world but our bodies saved at any cost, if we fail to draw new meaning from the deep wells of our distress and despair, then it will not be enough."[48] Several months later, in a letter of 3 July 1943, she added that only when "we should survive unhurt in body and soul, but above all in soul, without bitterness and without hatred, then we shall have a right to a say after the war."[49]

Metaphorically, the course she believed everyone should seek was likened to a spider spinning its web. She asked, "[when] a spider spins its web, does it not cast the main threads ahead of itself; and then follow along them from behind?" In the same way, she felt, that "the main path of [her] life stretches like a long journey before [her] and already reaches into another world."[50]

44 *Ibidem*: Laat ik maar de opvangbarak zijn van het betere in jullie, dat er toch zeker in ieder van jullie is.

45 Cf. E.T., 586. *Het Werk*, 624; Letter 23, To two sisters in The Hague, Amsterdam, end December 1942.

46 *Ibidem*: Ik geloof, dat er voor ieder gebeuren in de mens een orgaan is, waardoor hij dat gebeuren ook kan verwerken.

47 *Ibidem*: Het gaat er toch immers niet om, dàt men ten koste van alles dit leven behoudt, maar hóe men het behoudt.

48 *Ibidem*: [...] maar toch, wanneer wij een na-oorlogse, berooide wereld niet méér te bieden hebben dan onze ten koste van alles geredde lichamen en niet een nieuwe zin, die komt uit de diepste putten van onze nood en onze vertwijfeling, dan zal dat te weinig zijn.

49 E.T., 616. *Het Werk*, 657; Letter 46, To Johanna and Klaas Smelik and others; Westerbork, Saturday, 3 July 1943: En als we deze tijd ongeschonden overleven, naar lichaam en naar ziel, maar vooral naar ziel, zonder verbittering, zonder haat, dan hebben we ook het recht om een woord mee te spreken na de oorlog.

50 *Ibidem*: Ik zal eens proberen jullie te beschrijven, hoe ik me voel, ik weet niet, of het beeld juist is. Wanneer een spin haar web weeft, werpt ze dan al niet de hoofddraden vooruit en klimt ze er dan niet zelf achteraan? De hoofdweg van m'n leven strekt zich al een heel eind voor me uit en reikt al in een andere wereld.

This young woman experienced a journey of the soul that, in turn, prepared her for the fate destiny had in store for her. Could her path not also be a valid route for the scores of malnourished souls who live in our own times? I'm inclined to think it could. Etty Hillesum helped open a pedagogical and spiritual passageway for everyone and every epoch, offering us what she was looking for: "a dazzling and dynamic alternative with which to start afresh."[51]

About the Author

Maria Gabriella Nocita (1977) is Adjunct Professor of History of Philosophy and Intersubjective Pedagogy at the Angelicum University of Rome. She wrote her PhD dissertation on Etty Hillesum: *Dalle tenebre della Shoah una paideia per umanarsi* (2012). Her studies focus on the Philosophy of Education but she is also involved in Special Educational Needs. She wrote "Etty Hillesum and Primo Levi among the *Drowned* and the *Saved*" (2017); "Quale Dio? Un modello del Dio personale di Ulrich Beck?" (2012), and "Feeling Life: Etty Hillesum *Becomes* Word" (2010).

51 E.T., 505. *Het Werk*, 534; Monday morning, 27 July 1942: Ik zal de weg naar dat stralende en nieuwe wel weer vinden [...].

Am I Really a Woman?

A Question About Female Identity in Etty Hillesum

William Augusto Peña Esquivel

Abstract

The configuration of human identity is not an isolated process of mystical experience. That is why, in the mystical itinerary of Etty Hillesum, her female being is intimately linked with an identity that is being constituted in parallel to her inner searches. Femininity, as a path of freedom and realization of being a woman, has a particular perspective from Etty Hillesum.

Keywords: identity, femininity, female identity, mysticism, liberation, love, Simone de Beauvoir, emancipation

The question, *who am I?* with all its possible answers, serves as an existential engine in the inner life processes of many human beings who consider themselves, or are considered, mystical. In the vital itinerary narrated in her diaries, Etty Hillesum embarked on a path of self-discovery independent of any particular religious belief. It is important to bear in mind that the mystical experience is often conceived of as the affirmation of an identity that revolves around the doctrinal assumptions of a particular religion. For Hillesum, however, the mystical experience was a path of self-affirmation on a simple human scale. Therefore, in Hillesum we find an identity that broke with all sorts of stereotypes of her time and that was marked by the concept of personal liberation. Considering these things, *Le deuxième sexe*, by Simone de Beauvoir is relevant.[1] The French philosopher exposes the

1 Simone de Beauvoir was a French philosopher and writer. Her work *Le deuxième sexe* was published in 1949, and is considered one of the most important publications on feminism. I think the book is close to Etty Hillesum's context insofar as it describes the problems of women

Smelik, Klaas A.D. (ed.), *The Lasting Significance of Etty Hillesum's Writings: Proceedings of the Third International Etty Hillesum Conference at Middelburg, September 2018.*
Taylor & Francis Group 2019
DOI: 10.5117/9789463722025_ESQUIVEL

subject of feminine identity that is germane to Etty Hillesum as it relates to the same cultural context.

First, I will establish that the fundamental presupposition of the subjective constitution in Hillesum's writings is the existence of the *other* or otherness. Starting by looking at the first description that Etty Hillesum wrote of herself, I will address the process of emancipation that led Hillesum to an experience of inner liberation. Finally, I will lay out Hillesum's mystical experience as a process of inner liberation and affirmation of her womanhood.

1 The Role of the Other in the Configuration of Etty Hillesum's Identity

The foundation of authenticity for determining what is human is the *relationship*.[2] To think of ourselves as existing, requires conceiving of ourselves as not being the other.[3] The constitution of identity has as its starting point the *relationship* with the other: I am not me without you. In the mystical experience, the subjectivity of the mystic manifests itself as openness and availability towards the other. In Hillesum's case, the first clue was her relationship with Julius Spier, in which she felt moved by the emotions that Spier aroused. Such emotions did not present themselves passively; they induced change in her. For Hillesum, her relationship with Spier led her to try to answer essential questions about herself.

Along this line of thinking, we must consider that the constitution of identity, which includes intersubjectivity, is not a path that is given by antonomasia. Etty Hillesum struggled to preserve the clarity of her emotions and confirm her identity; it was never an absolute or finished experience for her. Hers was a conquered identity. The identity discovered along Hillesum's path sprang from a particular unseen experience that had as its source the usual: A relationship with another human being that was not exempt from desire or human passions.

Hillesum's passions were a battlefield on which she was open and exposed to everything surrounding her. There was no place for her to evade events. Etty Hillesum's availability to the world also included a social and cultural understanding that she was a woman.

in the first part of the 20th century and addresses women's stigmas and their possible paths of liberation.

2 Cf. Anna Bissi, *El color del trigo* (Bogotá: Paulinas, 2006), 39.

3 Cf. Gabriel Marcel, *Être et avoir* (Paris: Editions Universitaires, 1991), 97.

2 And Deep Inside Me Something is Still Locked Away

On the first page of her diaries, Etty Hillesum provided a description of herself,

> I am blessed enough intellectually to be able to fathom most subjects, to express myself clearly on most things; I seem to be a match for most of life's problems, and yet deep down something like a tightly wound ball of twine binds me relentlessly, and at times I am nothing more or less than a miserable, frightened creature, despite the clarity with which I can express myself.[4]

The sensation that Hillesum described, of intuiting herself as something more than she thought she was, was an intuition linked to the constitution of identity. At the core of what she stated was a question about her being: Who am I? From the leading French, Christian existentialist, Gabriel Marcel's perspective, this question only acquires real meaning when the subject can distinguish between life and *being.*[5] Because Hillesum's "I" was not that of life, it had the possibility of judging it, and taking a position before it.

Etty Hillesum perceived about herself that Julius Spier could be the engine that caused her to release what she sensed was a blockage within herself. Spier not only led her to this discovery, he also ignited her identity process through the relationship that was established between them.

Sexuality was one of the first internal movements that unties the Julius-Etty relationship. Erotic experiences find human beings in the midst of their most ambiguous condition; as flesh, and as spirit. For women, this conflict is even more dramatic, considering that a woman's sexual life depends entirely on her social and economic situation.[6] Etty Hillesum's diaries had a lot to say about the role human sexuality played in the essential constitution of her womanhood. She integrated her sexuality in the search for her identity. She spared nothing of her being in the search for what was veiled in her interiority. Narrating and unravelling her emotions and passions were fundamental steps taken to consolidate an internal

4 E.T., 4. *Het Werk*, 4; Sunday, 9 March 1941: Intellectueel ben ik zo geoefend dat ik alles kan peilen, alles kan aanroeren met heldere formules, ik lijk zeer überlegen in vele problemen des levens, maar toch, daar heel diep zit een samengebalde kluwen, er houdt me iets vast in de greep en ik ben af en toe toch maar een angstige stakkerd, ondanks het heldere denken.

5 Cf. Marcel, *Être et avoir*, 101.

6 Cf. Simone de Beauvoir, *Le deuxième sexe Vol. II* (Paris: Gallimard, 1990), 133.

unity, even if it meant she had to talk about her personal process of sexual liberation.

Hillesum thought there was no place for the social prejudices of her times, especially because she wanted to clarify her sensuality as a woman. If she wanted to undergo an authentic identity process, she – as a mystical human being – could not bring recrimination down upon her human condition. To annul or ignore the passionate side of her human self would have resulted in creating an identity that would not have been able to enjoy complete freedom. Specifically, Etty Hillesum undertook the task of placing her sensuality at the service of love. Gradually, in her eagerness to constitute her real being, she identified in her passions the vital challenge of liberation. She was determined not to exclude the sensual from her being, but rather, to detach herself from the possessiveness that sometimes accompanies the sensual.[7] In Hillesum's internal task, one can sense an itinerary of feminine emancipation. To fully face being a woman in her epoch was an inner struggle.

3 Etty Hillesum's Adulthood and Female Emancipation

Ridding herself of the desire to possess everything was the first task Etty Hillesum set for herself in order to achieve emancipation. Possessiveness was identified by Hillesum as a form of immaturity, of pettiness,

> Whenever I saw a beautiful flower, what I longed to do with it was press it to my heart, or eat it all up. It was more difficult with a piece of beautiful scenery, but the feeling was the same. I was too sensual, I might almost write too greedy. I yearned physically for all I thought was beautiful, wanted to own it.[8]

This meant that she struggled to get rid of the stereotypes that, to a certain extent, prevented her from feeling free,

> I am an ordinary twenty-seven-year-old girl, and I too am filled with love for all mankind, but for all I know I shall always continue to be in

7 Cf. Richard Gaillardetz, "Sexual vulnerability and a spirituality of suffering: Explorations in the writing of Etty Hillesum", *Pacífica* 22 (2009), no. 1, 85.

8 E.T., 22-23. *Het Werk*, 25; Sunday morning, 16 March 1941: Wanneer ik een bloem mooi vond, dan had ik die het liefst aan het hart gedrukt of opgegeten. Met een heel stuk natuurschoon ging dat moeilijker, maar het gevoel was hetzelfde. Ik was te zinnelijk, ik zou haast zeggen "hebberig" ingesteld. Naar wat ik mooi vond, verlangde ik veel te sterk lichamelijk, ik wilde het hebben.

> search of my one man. And I wonder to what extent that is a handicap, a woman's handicap. Whether it is an ancient tradition from which she must liberate herself, or whether it is so much part of her very essence that she would be doing violence to herself if she bestowed her love on all mankind instead of on a single man. (I can't yet see how the two can be combined.) Perhaps that's why there are so few famous women scientists and artists: a woman always looks for the one man on whom she can bestow all her wisdom, warmth, love and creative powers. She longs for a man, not for mankind.[9]

Etty Hillesum's reflections were in consonance with the descriptions that Simone de Beauvoir makes about the situation and the character of women. For the French philosopher, women have been culturally destined to immanence. To achieve transcendence, they must escape through men, who can make them a wife or a mother. The fact that women have been excluded from the transcendent, prevents them from accessing the highest human attributes such as science and art.[10] For Hillesum, going against the condition of women as expressed by de Beauvoir represented an essential struggle. In Hillesum's diaries, she described that she sometimes observed a woman in the street, and longed to understand her beauty in the same way that men did. Perhaps she did this because Hillesum also wanted to be a sought-after woman desired by men enthralled by all the feminine stereotypes prized in the culture.

Along these lines, Etty Hillesum was configuring her identity so she could assume a feminist character. To reach the fullness of her being meant to engage in the struggle as a free woman. De Beauvoir affirms that the only path for women is to fight for their liberation.[11] And this was exactly Etty Hillesum's choice:

> Perhaps the true, the essential emancipation of women still has to come. We are not yet full human beings; we are the "weaker sex." We are still

9 E.T., 69. *Het Werk*, 73; Monday, 4 August 1941: Ik ben een kleine vrouw van 27 jaar en draag ook heel sterk in me de liefde tot de hele mensheid, maar ik vraag me af of ik toch niet altijd zoeken zal naar één man. En ik vraag me af inhoeverre dat een beperking, een begrenzing is van de vrouw. In hoeverre dat een eeuwenoude traditie is, waar ze zich uit zou moeten losmaken of misschien hoort het zózeer bij het wezen van de vrouw dat ze zich zelf zou verkrachten als ze haar liefde gaf aan de hele mensheid inplaats van aan één man.

10 Cf. de Beauvoir, *Le deuxième sexe*, 366.

11 *Ibidem*, 369.

> tied down and enmeshed in centuries-old traditions. We still have to be born as human beings; that is the great task that lies before us.[12]

It is important to take into account, however, that Etty Hillesum did not think of the female struggle as an individual fight. She struggled as a way to help other women:

> There is nothing else for it, I shall have to solve my own problems. I always get the feeling that when I solve them for myself I shall have also solved them for a thousand other women. For that very reason I must come to grips with myself.[13]

The process of the liberation of women for Simone de Beauvoir, cannot be an individualistic process. To her, a solitary way to salvation for women is absurd; an individual path is nothing more than an attempt to justify the existence of women in their own immanence. Thus, de Beauvoir identifies three common roles women adopt as they move toward emancipation: the narcissist, the lover and the mystic.[14]

The lover, according to de Beauvoir, is the one who dreams through the eyes of a man. It is in his eyes she believes she finds herself. She who is in love is tyrannized in the name of her lover. For her, the only option is to be owned and own at the same time.[15] Etty Hillesum debated with herself all the time on this question, moving between the one in love, and the free woman – an inner movement that directly reflected her relationship with Julius Spier.

In Hillesum's diaries, we find questions about whether or not to lead an exclusive life with only one man:

> Yes, we women, we foolish, idiotic, illogical women, we all seek paradise and the Absolute. [...] We women want to perpetuate ourselves in a man. Yes, I want him to say, "Darling, you are the only one, and I shall love you

12 E.T., 69. *Het Werk*, 73; Monday, 4 August 1941: Misschien moet de ware, de innerlijke vrouwenemancipatie nog beginnen. We zijn nog geen echte mensen, we zijn wijfjes. We zitten nog vastgebonden en omstrikt door tradities van eeuwen, we moeten nog geboren worden als mens, er ligt hier nog een grote taak voor de vrouw.

13 E.T., 70. *Het Werk*, 74-75; Monday, 4 August 1941: Er is niets aan te doen, ik zal m'n problemen moeten oplossen en ik heb altijd het gevoel, dat, wanneer ik ze voor mij oplos, ze ook voor duizend andere vrouwen oplos. En daarom moet ik me "auseinandersetzen" met alles.

14 Cf. de Beauvoir, *Le deuxième sexe*, 369.

15 *Ibidem*, 386-390.

> for evermore." I know, of course, that there is no such thing as eternal love, but unless he declares it for me, nothing has any meaning. And the stupid thing is that I don't really want him, don't want him forever or as the only one in my life, and yet I demand it of him [...].[16]

Her narration of this struggle turned the diaries into a feminine testimony for achieving complete inner freedom. At times, we see Etty Hillesum expressing herself as if having already won the fight. At other times, she falters again. And yet, between victories and defeats she discovered that being a woman was not limited to the characterization of the lover described by de Beauvoir. On the contrary, Hillesum achieved the independence that she so desired.

How do we define the lover's liberation process? Simone de Beauvoir's description outlines the state that Etty Hillesum managed to achieve. Authentic love, according to the French philosopher, is based on the reciprocal recognition of two freedoms. Neither de Beauvoir nor Hillesum would forego the ability to transcend simply to gain love. De Beauvoir affirms that women must learn to love from a position of strength, not weakness. Love should never be a reason for a woman to dismiss herself as a human being. Love should be a source of affirmation.[17] This is what happened to Etty Hillesum.

> Life itself must be our fountainhead, never something or someone else. Many people, especially women, draw their strength from others, instead of directly from life. A man is their source, instead of life. That attitude is as distorted and unnatural as it possibly can be.[18]

Little by little, Etty Hillesum reached this state of freedom through changes in her relationship with Julius Spier. She came to understand that the centre of her being was life itself and not a man. Hillesum began to intuit love in a different way. The process of independence of her identity allowed her to strongly reaffirm the self of her inner experience. That is why she could

16 E.T., 105. *Het Werk*, 111; Thursday morning, 25 September 1941: Ja wij vrouwen, wij dwaze, idiote, onlogische vrouwen, wij zoeken het Paradijs en het Absolute. [...] Wij vrouwen willen ons vereeuwigen in de man. Het is zo: ik wil dat hij tegen me zegt: Liefste, jij bent de enige en ik zal je eeuwig lief hebben. Dat is een fictie. En zolang hij dat niet zegt, heeft al het andere geen zin, zie ik het andere over het hoofd. En dat is het gekke: Ik wil hem toch helemaal niet, ik zou hèm niet als enige en eeuwige willen en ik eis het wel van de ander.

17 Cf. de Beauvoir, *Le deuxième sexe*, 409.

18 E.T., 66. *Het Werk*, 70; Wednesday morning, 18 June 1941: Het leven zelf moet steeds de oerbron blijven, nooit een ander mens. Veel mensen, vrouwen vooral, putten uit hem hun kracht, inplaats van regelrecht uit het leven, hij is hun bron en niet het leven. Dat is zo verdraaid en onnatuurlijk als het maar kan.

question whether she really was a woman. Hillesum sensed that she had left behind stereotypes of the feminine and that she had opened up to a different way of being a woman.

4 Etty Hillesum, the Mystical Woman

Independence strongly marked Etty Hillesum's female identity. According to her, to accept one's own strengths and limitations increased the life force. In this way, Hillesum defined independence as an act of self-affirmation of life. From the woman in love, Hillesum became the mystical woman. Simone de Beauvoir criticizes the conception of the mystical woman when it is simply a state where a woman transfers from belonging to a man, to belonging to the divinity. When women do this, human love and divine love are confused. The woman in love, to try to save her contingent existence, must join a Whole which is incarnated in a Sovereign person.[19] For the French philosopher, a mystical woman who does not merely transfer from man to the divine, is a woman of action. She can use her spiritual experience to give objectivity to her certainties and trace her own authentic paths to identity.[20]

This is where we can place Etty Hillesum. Her path to emancipation allowed her to direct her inner experience to an objective end: engagement with the world of human beings. Hillesum's testimony was never solipsistic. Even as she clarified that people imitate an imaginary obligation or a false idea of what a human being should be, she was geared up to help others achieve clarity in their own processes and to constitute their own identity built on an inner attitude of facing life itself.

According to Hillesum, the only secure way to know how to live and what should be done, was to bring it up from the depths of one's *being*. Hillesum's path to emancipation was a self-affirmation of her own life. She believed that one had to teach people to eliminate the fear of their reality, which is only possible if they have the courage to recognize their feelings and emotions. Achieving unity of identity requires including opposite elements and irrational moments. If a path of nullification or rigidity is chosen, the very flow of life that connects us to our innermost being, is violated.

19 Cf. de Beauvoir, *Le deuxième sexe*, 419-422.

20 Simone de Beauvoir highlights the courage of Teresa de Avila, Joan of Arc and Catherine of Siena. She conceives her mystical experience as an exception to the image of the mystical woman who annuls herself in a sovereign deity. Cf. de Beauvoir, *Le deuxième sexe*, 426.

Conclusions

For Etty Hillesum, the path of her emancipation and the constitution of her identity cannot be separated from the mystical experience. We can find in her diaries a close relationship between the affirmation of her identity and the defining moment of her encounter with God. The being's full identity and the experience of God in Etty Hillesum were essentially linked,

> And that probably best expresses my own love of life: I repose in myself. And that part of myself; that deepest and richest part in which I repose, is what I call "God."[21]

Subjectivity, the core of the mystical experience, guarantees that such an experience is human. The freedom that springs from the individuality of the mystical human being, is the experience of love in its fullness. In Hillesum's case, having constituted herself as a free woman, she was, in turn, able to experience divine love. The internal process of liberation from the stereotype of the feminine was what made her fully a mystical woman.

Etty Hillesum's testimony has become a treasure trove of reflections on spirituality for the modern women. The world of the masculine has marked out the way women may participate in the social, political, economic, and spiritual realms. There is still much work to do to explore the intuitions about the feminine in the mystical sphere. In the contemporary world, new proposals have emerged on how to constitute the identity of the humane. But many of these proposals still exclude the spiritual or the mystical, because they think these experiences prevent them from *being*. Approaching Hillesum's diaries provides an opportunity to defend the possibility that love can go beyond the human, and can allow us to be who we really are. In Etty Hillesum, three strong, authentic pillars are striking evidence for the modern human being's relationship to the divine: Identity, freedom, and full love.

Only when there is identity is there freedom, and if there is freedom, there is full love. Openness to life, reaffirmation of one's existence... these must not be an abstract alternative to the concrete world. Turning our gaze only to the external leads to the adoption of stereotyped identities of the human. Such a biased look towards the outside world gives rise to a chained

21 E.T., 519. *Het Werk*, 549; Thursday morning, 17 September 1942: En hiermee is misschien het meest volkomen uitgedrukt mijn levensgevoel: ik rust in mijzelve. En dat mijzelve, dat allerdiepste en allerrijkste in mij, waarin ik rust, dat noem ik "God".

freedom and an unsatisfactory love. But if we assume the battle for our inner liberation, with all its strength and meaning, we discover the vital wealth that allowed Etty Hillesum to take on the challenges of her daily world. Women today need to shape their own worlds and histories (herstories). Ultimately, Etty Hillesum embodied the voice of women of the 20th century and beyond, who search for and long to, experience a meaningful identity and an embodied affirmation of their womanhood. There is a longing in women today to hear the words that Max spoke to Etty Hillesum in their meeting on 12 March 1942: "I think you have turned into a real woman."[22]

About the Author

William Augusto Peña Esquivel (1982) is philosopher and theologian of the Pontifical Xavierian University in Bogotá, Colombia. He holds an Mg. in Philosophy and has taught Philosophy since 2010 in the areas of anthropology, aesthetics, and politics. He is an active member of the Seminary of Mystical Research and Humanism, part of the Faculty of Theology at the Pontifical Xavierian University.

22 E.T., 278. *Het Werk*, 289; Thursday evening, 12 March 1942 Ik geloof dat je nu een èchte vrouw geworden bent.

A Powerless God

Etty Hillesum and Dietrich Bonhoeffer

Maria Luísa Ribeiro Ferreira

Abstract

Etty Hillesum and Dietrich Bonhoeffer lived in what Hannah Arendt called "Dark Times." Their lives and work show us that in the worst places and situations light is possible and hope can be maintained. Besides emphasizing how they practised an ethics of care, this paper gives a particular importance to their concept of God – a powerless God who needs man's help.

Keywords: Dietrich Bonhoeffer, "Dark Times", ethics of care, powerless God, helping of God, Church and State, beauty, Hannah Arendt

1 Living in "Dark Times"

> [...] even in the darkest of times we have the right to expect some illumination, and that such illumination may come less from theories and concepts than from the uncertain, flickering, and often weak light that some men and women, in their lives and works, will kindle under almost all circumstances and shed over the time span that was given them on earth.
>
> – *Hannah Arendt*[1]

There is a deep contrast between our times and those when Etty Hillesum and Dietrich Bonhoeffer lived. We cannot classify our epoch as peaceful, yet the Western world is not directly engaged in the terrible events that

1 Hannah Arendt, *Men in Dark Times* (New York: Harcourt, Brace & Company, [1968] 1993), IX.

Smelik, Klaas A.D. (ed.), *The Lasting Significance of Etty Hillesum's Writings: Proceedings of the Third International Etty Hillesum Conference at Middelburg, September 2018.*
Taylor & Francis Group 2019
DOI: 10.5117/9789463722025_FERREIRA

can occur on our planet – most of them right now coming to us only via TV news or in newspapers. Hillesum and Bonhoeffer directly suffered the consequences of what Hannah Arendt called "Dark Times" – a painful period when the majority of the values conquered after centuries were neglected and contradicted and where people were not able to plan for the future. But Etty Hillesum and Dietrich Bonhoeffer succeeded in surpassing their destiny, showing us that in the bleakest places and situations, light was possible and hope could be maintained.

Both were victims of Nazism but the testimonies of their lives in dark times are quite different. Etty Hillesum's diaries and letters were not intended to be published. Their register was informal, revealing someone who was compelled to share her feelings and experiences with no presumption of making history or writing literature, philosophy, or theology. She died at the age of twenty-nine.

Dietrich Bonhoeffer was a renowned German theologian who resisted the Nazi dictatorship and became a founding member of the *Confessing Church*.[2] His texts were published and widely appreciated by European and American scholars. He was arrested by the Gestapo and imprisoned in Tegel where he stayed for more than one year. His letters from prison[3] show us how someone deprived of his civil rights can maintain integrity and persist as part of a social whole. Transferred to a concentration camp, he was condemned to death and hanged at the age of thirty-nine.

With Etty Hillesum's correspondence and diaries, we are acquainted with her intimate states, her doubts, her problems and fears. Her diaries began on 9 March 1941 and ended in October 1942, when she was deported from Camp Westerbork to Auschwitz-Birkenau. In her diaries and letters, she testified to the Jews' difficult condition under the Nazi Occupation in Holland: food scarcity, Jews banished from their jobs and daily occupations, not allowed to take public transport or go to cultural events, teachers and students expelled from their schools and universities. Even walking on the streets was controlled.

2 The Confessing Church was a dissident movement within the Evangelical Church which stressed the need of being attentive to the signs of history. According to this movement, there was no accord possible between Christianity and Nazism. Following the Lutheran tradition, Bonhoeffer pleaded for the autonomy of Church and State, although he admitted that the Church had the right to intervene when the State committed abuses.

3 Dietrich Bonhoeffer, *Widerstand und Ergebung: Briefe und Aufzeichnungen aus der Haft* (Munich: Christian Kaiser Verlag, 1970). We follow the English edition *Letters and Papers from Prison* (New York: Simon & Schuster, 1997).

> We are not allowed to walk along the Promenade any longer, and every miserable little clump of two or three trees has been pronounced a wood with a board nailed up: *No Admittance to Jews.*[4]

Although she does not complain, we can feel her anguish, her fear, her revolt. Some episodes, with an attitude of apparent neutrality, denounce the dramatic stages of Jewish persecution. Etty Hillesum described this collapsing world, where she tried to live "full of good heart and goodwill"[5] without losing touch with reality. In many passages of her writings, she comments on the arrests, the concentration camps, the terror of being in an occupied country. She assumed the role of witness to the darkness, but at the same time as someone whose life would prove that God was still present and that believing in Him could be a consolation.

Bonhoeffer condemned racial discrimination. In Germany after 1933, Jews were banished from public jobs. Non-Aryans were considered infra-humans and were deprived of civil rights. All social or political activities were forbidden. Bonhoeffer, the theologian from Berlin, criticized this politics in his article "Die Kirche vor der Judenfrage." There, he denounced the attitude of indifference, and even its opposite where Protestant churches considered the Jews as a sort of strange body in German society. Silence was the most common attitude in the Protestant churches and, sometimes, there was even collaboration. Parishes were the only entities that could prove baptisms before 1876 and so it was up to the clergy to sign certificates attesting to the purity of race. The separation of Church and State was made impossible when the demand was imposed on members of the clergy to grant certifications that could mean the difference between life and death.

2 Two strong characters; two different paths; the same goal

Etty Hillesum and Dietrich Bonhoeffer shared the same historical context – one in Holland, a member of a persecuted minority; the other in Germany, conspiring against the Nazis. Their familial, cultural, and religious origins were quite different. Hillesum described her family life as a madhouse, a mixture of barbarism and culture, where dialogue was impossible. She did not get along

4 E.T., 295. *Het Werk*, 308; Sunday morning, 22 March 1942: We mogen niet meer op de Wandelweg wandelen en ieder ongelukkig groepje van 2 en 3 bomen is tot bos verklaard en daar is dan een bordje opgeprikt: voor Joden verboden.

5 E.T., 50. *Het Werk*, 56; Tuesday, 25 March 1941: vol goede moed en goede wil.

with her mother, whose caprices and instability she loathed. She was aware of her father's weaknesses. She loved her brothers but recognized their psychological failures. Although she was Jewish, she received no religious education.

Bonhoeffer belonged to the German bourgeoisie, with connections to the aristocracy. Religion was part of his natural ambiance. Resistance to Nazism demanded great courage, separating him from his family and relations, and putting his life at risk. He suffered from being excluded and misunderstood in his religious community. The radicalism of his options threatened his reputation as a Christian. Nevertheless, he was strong-minded and chose to obey God, which put him in the difficult position of disobeying those who allegedly represented Him on earth. His comfort came from his family, who valued his choices and gave him indefectible support. The visits his parents paid to him at Tegel prison, his fiancée's letters, the sharing and prayers with his most intimate friends and familiars, gave him consolation. Those closest to him supported him and prevented him from being tempted to please the majority.

In spite of the differences that shaped their personalities and options, Hillesum and Bonhoeffer had many features in common. Both were non-conformists and fought against what they classified as intolerable. Both were resilient and thanked God for their endurance. When striving against adversity, they were confident – Etty Hillesum placed herself in God's arms and was therefore trusting and calm. Both were optimistic and enjoyed life. Notwithstanding all the horrors they witnessed and the experiences they went through, they proved that in the midst of utmost suffering it is possible to have a confident attitude and to be happy.

For each of them, religion did not follow canonical norms. By birth and culture, Etty Hillesum was a Jew but she was familiar with the New Testament, which she often read and enjoyed, believing it set forth the Christian morality of love and care. She looked for God in her intimate. Yet she accepted her Jewish status remembering the persecutions Jews had suffered. She interpreted the Inquisition and the pogroms as a sort of antechamber to the Nazis' persecution. But, for her, what mattered was how the Jews could bear the suffering and fit it into their lives. When compelled to use a yellow star, she began a new stage in her diary, where the pride of being Jewish was openly on display, "Something inside me has suddenly changed."[6]

Etty Hillesum and Dietrich Bonhoeffer were deeply conscious of being part of a whole, sharing the destiny and sufferings of their brothers and sisters.

6 E.T., 354. *Het Werk*, 372; Wednesday morning, 29 April 1942: [...] merk ik opeens, dat het vanbinnen zó in me gegroeid is.

They were demanding persons, passionately devoted to high ideals. The battles they fought took place in the Nazi terror, of which they were victims.

Love was present in Etty Hillesum's and Dietrich Bonhoeffer's lives. Hillesum felt she had "a strong erotic streak and a great need for caresses and tenderness."[7] She wrote openly about her physical enjoyments and assumed the mantle of her sensuality asking, "Why should it be just one man and just one bed?"[8] Bonhoeffer considered love as the sole fruitful relationship in humanity. He cherished earthly love, writing,

> God wants us to love him eternally with our whole hearts – not in such a way as to injure or weaken our earthly love, but to provide a kind of *cantus firmus* to which the other melodies of life provide the counterpoint. One of these contrapuntal themes [...] is earthly affection.[9]

Their courage was patent in the constant solidarity demonstrated towards other human beings. Hillesum refused opportunities to hide from the Germans; Bonhoeffer declined the American exile where he would have been safe. He could have accepted a position as Theology teacher in New York, but chose to share a common danger with his compatriots. Etty Hillesum and Dietrich Bonhoeffer accepted with hope the inevitability of their death. Hillesum's last letter that she dropped from the train out of Camp Westerbork is a hymn to life in the midst of death. In his testament Bonhoeffer wrote,

> In the event of my death [...] I write those lines in the grateful consciousness of having lived a rich and full life, in the assurance of forgiveness and in prayer for all those named here.[10]

3 Two main representatives of the "Ethics of Care"

Among contemporary ethical theses, the "Ethics of Care" plays a predominant role, favouring personal relationship and emotions and giving justice a secondary place. From the beginning of Etty Hillesum's diaries, we can see how the ethics of care were central in her life. She was concerned with

7 E.T., 123. *Het Werk*, 130; Monday morning, 6 October 1941: Maar ik ben wel sterk erotisch aangelegd en heb veel behoefte aan liefkozingen en tederheid.

8 E.T., 304. *Het Werk*, 316; Friday evening, 27 March 1942: [...] waarom zou dat juist een man en een bed moeten zijn?

9 Bonhoeffer, *Letters and Papers from Prison*, 303.

10 *Ibidem*, 112.

her family, with her deeply disturbed mother as well as with her gifted but mentally ill brothers. Her attention and her concern were also obvious in her relation with Julius Spier, the psychotherapist who became her lover and on whose illness and death she reported in detail. She cared for her many friends who appreciated her as a confidante. She cared for the Jewish people in general and was both shocked and moved by the dramatic situation of the Dutch Jews. Love and compassion were the main feelings we detect in her diaries.

> I have two great feelings deep inside: love, an inexplicable love, which perhaps cannot be analysed because it is so primitive, for creatures and for God or for what I call God; and compassion, a boundless compassion that can sometimes cause tears to spring to my eyes.[11]

Etty Hillesum showed solidarity with the Jews' tragic fate. On 15 July 1942, she began working as a staff member of the Jewish Council at Camp Westerbork. Her task was to "help" the floating population of deportees in imminent danger of being conveyed to death camps. She was a sort of social worker who tried to solve multiple problems with extremely limited resources. Her connection with the Jewish Council gave her a somewhat flexible status, guaranteeing some exits and delaying her own deportation. She was very much committed to her work.

Bonhoeffer took it upon himself to defend the Jews, the conscientious objectors, and all those who could not speak freely. He considered the Nazis' anti-Semitic laws an abuse of power and accused them of being theologically perverse. He challenged all members of the ecclesial community to fight against this status quo. He was one of the founders of the *Bekennende Kirche* [Confessing Church], a movement for renewal inside the *Evangelische Kirche* [Evangelical Church]. This movement represented a core of resistance to national socialism. Insisting on being attentive to the signs of the times, Bonhoeffer argued that sagacity and perspicacity were virtues that Christians should acquire. For him, the words preached in the pulpit should have their echo in the institutions of daily life. Therefore, he was implacable with the survival strategies of most Germans. Following the Lutheran tradition, he insisted upon the independence of Church and

11 E.T., 161. *Het Werk*, 170; Sunday morning, 30 November 1941: het zijn de 2 grote grondgevoelens in me: liefde, een onverklaarbare, misschien niet nader te analyseren, omdat het een oergevoel is, liefde voor de creatuur en tot God, wat ik dan God noem en medelijden, een grenzeloos medelijden, waardoor soms plotseling de tranen uit m'n hoofd kunnen storten.

State. Yet he maintained that the Church had the duty of intervening when State laws were abusive.

In those dark times, Etty Hillesum was a luminous presence, personifying the possible comfort given by the spoken word and the embrace. She called herself "the thinking heart of the barracks."[12] As persecution intensified, she questioned her own strength, as well as her capacity for helping those who suffered. She had an acute awareness of just how little her resistance could accomplish, and she could foresee that, if deported, she would not live long.

> Have I really made such progress that I can say with complete honesty, I hope they will send me to a labour camp so that I can do something for the sixteen-year-old girls who will also be going? And to reassure the distracted parents who are kept behind, saying: "Don't worry, I'll look after your children"?[13]

Taking care of other people prevented her from losing hope:

> [...] surrender does not mean giving up the ghost, fading away with grief; but offering what little assistance I can wherever it has pleased God to place me.[14]

From 18 November 1943 on, Bonhoeffer wrote to his friend Eberhard Bethge, to confide his anguish and share his fears. He complained of his painful solitude and lamented the cruelty of being deprived of visitors. In his letters, we become acquainted of his moods and sufferings. He experienced twelve days of complete seclusion and was treated like a criminal. Bonhoeffer related his worries and alarm to Bethge. He wrote about his psychological and physical suffering, his nights without sleep, his fear of dying without having finished his *Ethics*. He trusted Bethge with his testament and even chose the texts and hymns for his funeral service. Yet he maintained

12 E.T., 515. *Het Werk*, 545, Tuesday morning, 15 September 1942: Het denkende hart van de barak.

13 E.T., 483. *Het Werk*, 510; Thursday morning, 9 July 1942: Ben ik werkelijk voor mezelf al zover, dat het eerlijk is als ik zeg: ik hoop, dat ik meekom naar het arbeidskamp om iets te kunnen zijn voor de 16-jarige meisjes, die ook meegaan? Om van te voren tegen ouders, die achterblijven, te kunnen zeggen: wees maar niet ongerust, ik zal op jullie kinderen passen.

14 E.T., 478. *Het Werk*, 504; Tuesday morning, 7 July 1942: En voor mij houdt die overgave niet in een resignatie, een afsterven, maar dáár, waar God me toevallig plaatst, nog te steunen wat ik kan en niet alleen maar vervuld te zijn van eigen verdriet en gemis.

some optimism, accepting his prisoner's status with resignation and hope. Although he experienced indignation and sadness, he valued his capacity for facing facts with a new look, and his ability to consider the positive aspects of his painful experience. He did not accept prison as something natural but admitted it could be instructive, stressing the virtues of total renunciation of material things. He was moved and touched by the letters, the food packets and the small gifts he received, but did not lose his capacity for indignation over his unjust situation. He never accepted arbitrariness; he rose against it and denounced injustice.

In Camp Westerbork, Etty Hillesum faced horror. She tried to be hardy without being hard. She tried to keep her capacity for love and compassion. She wished to describe the camp's drama so that, later on, she would be able to be at peace with herself and with the whole of humanity. Her letter of 24 August 1943 was illegally edited and published a short time after being written. In it, we are made aware of the dramatic departures on the trains, of the evil visited on sick people, the elderly, the babies. We can see the mothers' anguish trying to hide their children, offering them to strangers, blackmailing, and using all possible stratagems to save them.

Against the hellish backdrop of mud and illness Etty Hillesum posed kindness and the beauty of life, emphasizing its intrinsic and everlasting value as well as her own regenerative capacity. She had no illusions about her destiny and appreciated the rare moments of happiness. Through her inward freedom she was able to rise above the meanness and cruelty of daily life in Camp Westerbork. She constantly wrote to her friends, exposing the tragic situation of the detained.

> There are moments, it's true, when I feel things can't go on. But they do go on. You gradually learn that as well [...]. The misery here is really indescribable. People live in those big barracks like so many rats in a sewer. There are many dying children.[15]

In June 1942, the condition of Jewish prisoners got worse and life in the camp became more and more difficult. But Hillesum sustained an inner happiness in spite of all these circumstances.

15 E.T., 615. *Het Werk*, 655-656; Letter 46, To Johanna and Klaas Smelik and others, Westerbork, Saturday, 3 July 1943: Er zijn wel eens momenten, waarop je denkt, dat het toch eigenlijk niet verder kan. Maar het gaat altijd verder, dat weet je langzamerhand ook wel [...]. De ellende, die hier heerst, is werkelijk onbeschrijfelijk. In de grote barakken leeft men als ratten in een riool. Men ziet vele wegstervende kinderen.

> Yes God, I am faithful to You, through thick and thin, I shall not succumb, and I still believe in the deeper meaning of life. I know that I must go on living and that there are such great certainties in me [...] and you must think it incredible, but I find life so beautiful and feel so happy. Isn't that strange? I wouldn't dare say to anybody, not in so many words.[16]

She was always trying to transcend suffering to seek the presence of God inside herself. She developed a spirituality of her own, seeing God where He appeared to be utterly absent.

Like Etty Hillesum, Dietrich Bonhoeffer discovered God in the vicissitudes of his daily life. He was intolerant when faced with what he considered a perversion of Christian values. He wanted to draw strict borders between Christianity and nationalism, to make a demarcation line that would definitely prevent them approaching each other. He denied that there could be a link between the two. Even when situated on secular ground, he wanted to demonstrate that it was impossible for two opposite values like patriotism (which he honoured) and Nazism (which he violently opposed) to approach one another.

4 A powerless God

Etty Hillesum had strong feelings of transcendence. Among the eleven exercise books that constitute her diaries, and in her letters, God scarcely appears. Only gradually does He becomes a companion, a constant presence and a partner in her intimate dialogues.

Of Bonhoeffer we cannot say he discovered God – he was educated in the Christian faith, studied theology and became a Protestant Minister. But prison gave him a new opportunity to re-examine his point of view and to check his criteria. The silence and isolation of his cell were unexpectedly favourable to his thought processes and there he consolidated theological issues and reformulated biblical concepts in accordance with a world that "was coming out of age."[17] In the quiet of his cell, he built the most significant thesis of his new theology: Our world had become free and we were living

16 E.T., 497. *Het Werk*, 526; 20 July 1942, Monday evening: Ja, mijn God, ik ben je heel erg trouw, door dik en dun en ik zal niet ten onder gaan en ik geloof nog steeds in de diepere zin van dit leven en ik wéét hoe ik verder moet leven en er zijn zulke grote zekerheden in me, en [...] en, je zult het onbegrijpelijk vinden, maar ik vind het leven zo mooi en voel me zo gelukkig. Is dat niet wonderlijk? Ik zou het ook aan niemand met zoveel woorden durven zeggen.

17 This idea of a world coming out of age and needing a new language to speak about God is recurrent in his *Letters and Papers from Prison*. See his letter of 8 June 1944, 324-329.

in an era without religion and without God: "Before God and with God we live without God."[18]

Yet both Etty Hillesum and Dietrich Bonhoeffer believed in God – a different God, devoid of power, weak, fragile, and silent.

4.1 Etty Hillesum's God

When reading Hillesum's diaries and letters, our first impression is of someone unstable and lonely. But step by step, she walks into the depths of her inner being and her thirst for transcendence increases. Like Teresa d'Avila, who finds God in the kitchen among the saucepans, Etty Hillesum can pray anywhere – at home, in the mud of the camp, on the rug in her bathroom, in the middle of a crowd. She considers the force of praying as "a dark protective wall"[19] and sometimes refers to prayer as a closed cell. When everything seemed to be falling apart, she showed an absolute faith in God's presence, "a faith of God that has grown so quickly inside me that it frightened me at first but has now become inseparable of me."[20] When she perceived that things would not change with the regime, noticing that people around her disappeared to concentration camps, she became aware that her God was different and needed to be helped. She wrote, "And if God does not help me to go on I shall have to help God",[21] and "one thing is becoming increasingly clear to me: that You cannot help us, that we must help You to help ourselves."[22]

She thought that Creation was as yet unaccomplished and that people should collaborate with God to achieve it. She wrote that our duty is to complete and fulfil God's work: "I shall merely try to help God as best as I can, and if I succeed in doing that, then I shall be of use to others as well."[23] Her God was deprived of power, He was a fragile God that we must help. God depends on our care, "if we just care enough, God is in safe hands with

18 Bonhoeffer, *Letters and Papers from Prison*, Letter to Bethge, 16 July 1944, 360.

19 E.T., 364. *Het Werk*, 380; Monday, 18 May 1942: [...] een donkere beschuttende muur.

20 E.T., 481. *Het Werk*, 508; Tuesday morning, 7 July 1942: [...] er is een godsvertrouwen in me, dat me eerst nog haast beangstigde door zijn snelle groei, maar dat steeds meer bij me gaat horen.

21 E.T., 484. *Het Werk*, 512; Saturday morning, 11 July 1942: En als God mij niet verder helpt, dan zal ik God wel helpen.

22 E.T., 488. *Het Werk*, 516; Sunday morning, 12 July 1942: Maar dit éne wordt me steeds duidelijker: dat jij ons niet kunt helpen, maar dat wij jou moeten helpen.

23 E.T., 485. *Het Werk*, 512; Saturday morning, 11 July 1942: [...] ik zal er altijd van uit gaan God zo veel mogelijk te helpen en als me dat lukt, welnu, dan ben ik er voor anderen ook.

us, despite everything"[24]. Therefore, we must collaborate with God in our everyday life, and not expect Him to solve our problems.

> Yes, my Lord, there doesn't seem to be much You Yourself can do about our circumstances, about our lives. Neither do I hold You responsible, although You may later hold us responsible. I become more aware almost with each heartbeat that You cannot help us, but we must help You and defend Your dwelling place inside us to the last.[25]

Hers is not a transcendent God. She finds His presence in nature as well as in the deepness of her inner self.

> I imagine that there are people who pray with their eyes turned heavenward. They seek God outside themselves. And there are those who bow their head and bury it in their hands. I think that these seek God inside.[26]

Her growing spirituality is almost mystical and she is capable of living her daily life united in a permanent dialogue with God. She found Him in her most trivial work, "A hint of eternity steals throughout my smallest daily activities and perceptions."[27]

Sometimes, she felt an urgent desire to kneel:

> This afternoon I suddenly found myself kneeling on the brown coconut matting in the bathroom, my head hidden in my dressing gown, which was slung over the broken cane chair. Kneeling doesn't really come easily to me, I feel a sort of embarrassment. Why? Probably because of the critical, rational, atheistic bit that is part of me as well. And yet every so often I

24 E.T., 657. *Het Werk*, 701; Letter 68, To Maria Tuinzing; Westerbork, Thursday, 2 September 1943.: En als wij er maar zorg voor dragen, dat ondanks alles, toch God bij ons in veilige handen is.

25 E.T., 488-489 [revised]. *Het Werk*, 517; Sunday morning, 12 July 1942: Ja, mijn God, aan de omstandigheden schijn jij niet al te veel te kunnen doen, ze horen nu eenmaal ook bij dit leven. Ik roep je er ook niet voor ter verantwoording, jij mag daar later ons voor ter verantwoording roepen. En haast met iedere hartslag wordt het me duidelijker: dat jij ons niet kunt helpen, maar dat wij jou moeten helpen en dat we de woning in ons, waar jij huist, tot het laatste toe moeten verdedigen.

26 E.T., 92. *Het Werk*, 97; Tuesday evening, 26 August 1941: Ik stel me voor, dat er mensen zijn, die bidden met hun ogen naar de hemel geheven. Die zoeken God buiten zich. Er zijn ook mensen, die het hoofd diep buigen en in de handen verbergen, ik denk, dat die God binnen in zich zoeken..

27 E.T., 466. *Het Werk*, 491; Saturday morning, 4 July 1942: [...] tot in m'n kleinste dagelijkse handelingen en gewaarwordingen sluipt een vleugje eeuwigheid.

> have a great urge to kneel down with my face in my hands and in this way to find some peace and to listen to that hidden source within me.[28]

Although she did not identify with any particular religion, she was conscious of being part of a spiritual stream: "I feel that I am one of many heirs to a great spiritual heritage."[29] According to her last diaries from July to September 1942, we know that she prayed to God at the beginning and at the end of each day. In letter 60, she thanked God for all the gifts He had given her and felt a responsibility to share them with others, "You have me made so rich, oh God, please allow me to share out with full hands."[30] Completely conscious of her own destiny, as well as that of the other Jews in Camp Westerbork, she kept proclaiming her faith in God, in the world's beauty, and in the meaning of life, "And yet I find life beautiful and meaningful. From minute to minute."[31]

Beauty gave her courage. When she condemned the inhumane conditions of life in Camp Westerbork, she always contrasted them to the natural beauty of the world that persisted in spite of human perversity:

> I am with the hungry, with the ill-treated and the dying, every day, but I am also with the jasmine and with that piece of sky beyond my window; there is room for everything in a single life. For belief in God and for a miserable end.[32]

Etty Hillesum placed God in each human's heart. For her, He is the friend who constantly appeals, to whom one can speak and who tries to help, both

28 E.T., 103. *Het Werk*, 109; Wednesday morning, 24 September 1941: Vanmiddag vond ik mezelf plotseling geknield op de bruine cocosmat in de badkamer, m'n hoofd verborgen in m'n badjas, die op die kapotte rieten stoel slingerde. Ik kan helemaal niet goed knielen, er is een soort gêne in me. Waarvoor? Waarschijnlijk voor het critische, rationele, atheïstische stuk, dat er ook in me zit. En toch is er af en toe een grote drang in me neer te knielen, met de handen voor m'n gezicht en op die manier een vrede te vinden en te luisteren naar een verborgen bron in me.

29 E.T., 521. *Het Werk*, 551; Friday morning, 18 September 1942: Ik voel me een van de vele erfgenamen van een grote geestelijke erfenis.

30 E.T., 640. *Het Werk*, 682; Letter 60, To Henny Tideman, Westerbork, Wednesday, 18 August 1943: Je hebt me zo rijk gemaakt, mijn God, laat me ook met volle handen uit mogen delen.

31 E.T., 456. *Het Werk*, 481; Monday morning, 29 June 1942: En toch vind ik dit leven schoon en zinrijk. Van minuut tot minuut.

32 E.T., 460. *Het Werk*, 485; Thursday, 2 July 1942: [...] ik ben bij de hongerenden, bij de mishandelden en bij de stervenden, iedere dag, maar ik ben ook bij de jasmijn en bij dat stuk hemel achter mijn venster, er is voor alles plaats in één leven. Voor een geloven aan God en voor een ellendige ondergang.

oneself and the other. She thought humans could help Him when touched by the beauty of His Creation. She was happy when offering Him her joy at experiencing His creatures,

> [...] oh God. You can see I look after You. I bring You not only my tears and my forebodings on this stormy, gray Sunday morning. I even bring you scented jasmine. And I shall bring you all the flowers I shall meet on my way, and truly there are many of those. I shall try to make You at home always. Even if I should be locked up in a narrow cell and a cloud should drift past my small barred window, then I shall bring you that cloud, oh God, while there is still the strength in me to do so.[33]

Hillesum's God needs people in order to act. He needs the works of humans as a complement to his own action:

> [o]ne thing is becoming increasingly clear to me: that You cannot help us, that we must help You to help ourselves. And that is all we can manage these days.[34]

Etty Hillesum was always trying to overcome the constant menaces she faced. Her deepest will was to find a place of silence and meditation. She tried to be in touch with God, even when her time was occupied with urgent tasks, such as writing reports, answering demands, settling the rucksacks of those who were getting ready to depart in trains. Reading her beloved Rilke was enough to comfort her in the most dramatic moments. And contemplating a flower was always something admirable to her, even when it was found in a place full of mud. She grew stronger in those scarce moments when she could enjoy the beauty of things, using them as an incentive to stay alive. So, on 23 July 1942, when walking home after a hard day's work, Etty Hillesum still had the spirit to buy a bunch of roses, a gratuitous gesture

33 E.T., 489. *Het Werk*, 517; Sunday 12 July 1942: [...] mijn God. Je ziet, ik zorg goed voor je. Ik breng je niet alleen mijn tranen en bange vermoedens, ik breng je op deze stormachtige, grauwe Zondagochtend zelfs geurende jasmijn. En ik zal je alle bloemen brengen, die ik op mijn wegen tegenkom, mijn God, en werkelijk, dat zijn er heel vele. Je zult het heus zo goed mogelijk bij me hebben. En om nu maar eens een willekeurig voorbeeld te noemen: wanneer ik opgesloten zou zitten in een enge cel en er zou een wolk langs het kleine tralievenster drijven, dan zou ik je die wolk komen brengen, mijn God, als ik daarvoor tenminste nog de kracht zou hebben.

34 E.T., 488. *Het Werk*, 516; Sunday morning, 12 July 1942: Maar dit éne wordt me steeds duidelijker: dat jij ons niet kunt helpen, maar dat wij jou moeten helpen en door dat laatste helpen wij onszelf. En dit is het enige, wat we in deze tijd kunnen redden.

that gave her courage. In that one small purchase, she subscribed to John Keats's statement that "A thing of beauty is a joy forever."[35]

4.2 Bonhoeffer's God

Bonhoeffer lived under Nazi rule, suffering its threat and resisting it. But his purpose went beyond that particular context. He aimed at future times, a new age without God but where, nevertheless, God's word would command. It is on behalf of the divine word that he wanted to reform the Church, to rethink theology, and to re-establish ethics. Being in prison gave him a new opportunity to revise his views and to check his judgements. His letter of 5 May 1944, written from Tegel prison, is especially significant in understanding his intentions. Reading it, we realize how important he considered foreseeing God's language in a new way. His design was to reformulate the Christian message, liberating it from being metaphysically outward, and acknowledging that the divine word should be placed at the service of people. He identified being a Christian with being human and living in a world emancipated from God. He felt this would put an end to a false idea of the divine, leading to an unconditional search that went on while engaged in everyday life. For Bonhoeffer, in a world that has come of age, religion loses its importance. He thought we found God in our world, in the centre of life, in human failures. When we speak of God, he insisted, we must use the language of the people, which is different from the one used by the cultured middle class. He also proposed a renewal of the liturgy.

The fallen man thinks he is the author of good and evil, that he has become God, is against God, and is constantly struggling with himself and with others. Bonhoeffer wanted to get out of this conflicted situation by means of just action. He felt strongly that in order to be capable of acting, we must learn to hear and be attentive to the present. Christians should be clear-minded, docile to God's word, acting instead of judging. His view was that the fairness of human action does not depend on judgements, nor on those who judge: "Not everyone that saith unto me, Lord, Lord, shall enter into the kingdom of heaven; but he that doeth the will of my Father which is in heaven" (Matthew 7:21).

To Bonhoeffer, the word of God loses all meaning when it stops being disruptive, when it is inserted in a cultural packaging that obscures its clarity. It is in God's name that free responsibility and civil courage are exalted as virtues. Germans got used to obeying and considered obedience an essential value. Against this attitude of submission, Bonhoeffer wrote that we must learn

35 John Keats, *Endymion* (1818).

to cherish the occasion where a truly free and responsible action is needed. Obedience to God implies courage, especially when it leads to disobeying our masters or when it demands an alteration of the establishment. If Bonhoeffer remained faithful to the Evangelical Church, of which he was part, he would have been compelled to side with its conciliatory attitudes. If he acted in accordance with the dominant group, he would have been obliged to accept the Nazis' theories. When he refused to do any of this, opting to be faithful to God and to God's principles, he was accused of civil disobedience and imprisoned.

Bonhoeffer's example goes beyond time and circumstance, making him a model for all situations where we cannot keep silent. It is true that we live in a secular context, where State and Church are healthily separated. But this condition should not prevent the Church from openly disagreeing with a situation it considers morally unbearable. The Church and its members have a triple mission of keeping vigilance, denouncing, and acting. Bonhoeffer did this, sacrificing himself. He loved music and we can compare his life to an attempt to compose a symphony with different tempos rising above the *obbligato* – the *cantus firmus* – of God's love.

Both Etty Hillesum and Dietrich Bonhoeffer were capable of feeling joy and hope in the midst of deep anguish and pain. Even when Hillesum realized that the deportees of Camp Westerbork were going to die and that both she and her family would be deported and killed, hope never left her and she still had the strength to make plans for the future. She did not feel herself a prisoner in German clutches, she felt safe in God's company,

> No matter whether I am sitting at this beloved old desk now or in a bare room in the Jewish district, or perhaps in a labour camp under SS guards – I shall always feel safe in God's arms.[36]

In his last letter to his fiancée, on 19 December 1944, Bonhoeffer wrote,

> You must not think that I am unhappy. What is happiness and unhappiness? It depends so little on the circumstances; it depends really only on what happens inside a person. I am grateful every day that I have you, and that makes me happy.[37]

36 E.T., 487. *Het Werk*, 514; Saturday morning, 11 July 1942: [...] of dat nu hier aan dit verschrikkelijk dierbare en vertrouwde bureau is, of over een maand in een kale kamer in de Jodenbuurt of misschien in een arbeidskamp onder S.S.-bewaking, in Gods armen zal ik me geloof ik altijd voelen.

37 Bonhoeffer, *Letters and Papers from Prison*, 303; 419.

Of both we can say they were inviolable fortresses, engaged in their tasks of helping God – a powerless God – to Whom they offered their lives and support.

About the Author

Maria Luísa Ribeiro Ferreira (1944) is Full Professor of Modern Philosophy at Universidade de Lisboa. She has taught Modern Philosophy, Didactics of Philosophy, Women's Studies, and several Seminars on Spinoza and Hume. She is chief coordinator of several projects. Her last publication is *Marginalidade e Alternativa: Vinte e Seis Filósofas para o Século XXI* (Lisbon: Colibri, 2016). In addition, the author has published twenty eight books and many articles in the areas of teaching philosophy, gender philosophy, and modern philosophy (mainly on Spinoza). She is a researcher at the Centro de Filosofia of Universidade de Lisboa, Deputy Director of Sociedade Científica of Universidade Católica Portuguesa, member of GT Benedictus de Spinoza, Universidade Estadual do Ceará, Brasil, and of the Seminário Spinoza, Spain, of the Association des Amis de Spinoza, France, and of Accion Integrada Hispaña-Portugal, Leibniz. She also belongs to the Boarding Direction of Sociedade de Ética Ambiental.

New Light on Etty Hillesum's Actions in Camp Westerbork

Bettine Siertsema

Abstract

Ies Spetter was one of Etty Hillesum's colleagues on the Jewish Council in Camp Westerbork. Like Hillesum, he was opposed to the ways in which the Amsterdam Jewish Council responded to the Nazis' demands. Recently, a testimony by Spetter from the autumn of 1945 surfaced. It refers very briefly to his cooperation with Etty Hillesum in smuggling children out of Camp Westerbork. Spetter managed to survive, and his postwar activities show that to a great extent he and Hillesum shared the same views on life and humanity. This testimony may well mandate a shift in how we interpret what has until now been viewed as Hillesum's placid acceptance of her fate.

Keywords: Ies Spetter, resistance, Westerbork Camp, Etty Hillesum's refusal to seek hiding, humanism

In the reception of Etty Hillesum's work, her refusal to go into hiding is a recurring theme. For many, that choice is difficult to digest. In Jewish circles, especially, it has been met with a lack of understanding, sometimes bordering on indignation. This is understandable because Hillesum's deliberate choice to share the fate of her people, as she put it, could be considered an implicit denunciation of the many others who chose to go into hiding. And sometimes the denunciation was not only implicit; Etty Hillesum said as much to Klaas Smelik Senior, the friend who did everything he could to convince her to go into hiding,

> It's the same with those Jews who go into hiding. They may say they're doing it because they don't want to work for the G., but it's not nearly

Smelik, Klaas A.D. (ed.), *The Lasting Significance of Etty Hillesum's Writings: Proceedings of the Third International Etty Hillesum Conference at Middelburg, September 2018.*
Taylor & Francis Group 2019
DOI: 10.5117/9789463722025_SIERTSEMA

as heroic and revolutionary as that. All they are doing is using a high-sounding excuse to dodge the fate they ought to be sharing with the rest.[1]

Hillesum's refusal to go into hiding

Hillesum decided not to hide, and she also pressed others, like her friend Leonie Snatager, to report for Camp Westerbork instead of fleeing to a hiding place.[2] Even without being aware of it, her attitude towards hiding affected the lives of those near her. The Mennonite pastor of Makkum, San van Drooge, who had been a student of Louis Hillesum, related that he, together with the resistance group C6, had devised a plan to smuggle the Hillesum family out of Amsterdam with the help of a reliable ferryman, so that they could go into hiding at his presbytery. Father Hillesum knew his daughter's thoughts on the matter, however, and realized that if he were to move into hiding without her, her life would be in danger. Thus, he refused to accept the pastor's offer.[3]

Scholars like Klaas Smelik Jr. and Lotte Bergen have reflected on Hillesum's choice and have tried to counter the negative views on her choice expressed by some of her readers.[4] Tzvetan Todorov, on the other hand, remains openly critical of Hillesum in his *Facing the Extreme* (1996) and in other essays.[5]

1 E.T., 523. *Het Werk*, 553-554; Sunday evening, 20 September 1942: [...] het is precies hetzelfde als met de Joden die onderduiken: ze zeggen soms, dat ze dat doen omdat ze niet voor de D. willen werken. Maar zo heroïsch en revolutionair ligt de zaak niet bij hun. Eigenlijk onttrekken ze zich, met een schoonklinkend excuus aan een lot, dat ze gemeenschappelijk met anderen hadden moeten dragen.

2 Cf. Alexandra Nagel, "Vriendschap en therapie: Verstrengelde relaties tussen Julius Spier, Leonie Snatager en Etty Hillesum," in: Klaas A.D. Smelik *et al.* (eds.), *Etty Hillesum en het pad naar zelfverwerkelijking* [Etty Hillesum Studies, 9] (Antwerpen/Apeldoorn: Garant, 2017), 207.

3 Cf. the website "Ministers who helped Jews": www.hdc.vu.nl/nl/Images/Predikanten_die_joden_hielpen_IV_tcm215-460512.pdf.

4 Klaas A.D. Smelik, "De keuze van Etty Hillesum om niet onder te duiken," in: Ria van den Brandt & Klaas A.D. Smelik (eds.), *Etty Hillesum in context* [Etty Hillesum Studies, 2] (Assen: Van Gorcum, 2007), 59-73. Lotte Bergen, "Handelingsvrijheid binnen nazi-begrenzing: Etty Hillesum en haar invulling van het 'Massenschicksal'" in: Klaas A.D. Smelik *et al.* (eds.), *Etty Hillesum weer thuis in Middelburg* [Etty Hillesum Studies, 7] (Antwerpen/Apeldoorn: Garant, 2015), 51-83.

5 Jurjen Wiersma and Gerrit Van Oord have discussed Todorov's view on Hillesum. For the sake of brevity, I refer to their articles: Jurjen Wiersma, "Tzvetan Todorov over Etty Hillesums verzet: Opstandig, ethisch maar niet politiek?" in: Klaas A.D. Smelik *et al.* (eds.), *Etty Hillesum en het pad naar zelfverwerkelijking* [Etty Hillesum Studies 9] (Antwerpen/Apeldoorn: Garant, 2017), 127-140. Gerrit Van Oord, "Oprecht bewonderd en streng beoordeeld: Tzvetan Todorovs beeld van Etty Hillesum in de Italiaanse vertaling van zijn werk en enkele reacties daarop," in: Klaas A.D. Smelik *et al.* (eds.), *Etty Hillesum en het pad naar zelfverwerkelijking* [Etty Hillesum Studies 9] (Antwerpen/Apeldoorn: Garant, 2017), 141-156.

Etty Hillesum herself used a concrete argument against going into hiding, namely that if she hid, someone else would be deported instead of her:

> Many accuse me of indifference and passivity when I refuse to go into hiding; they say I have given up. They say: everyone who can must try to stay out of their clutches, it is our bounden duty to try. But that argument is specious. For while everyone tries to save himself, vast numbers are nevertheless disappearing.[6]

From a purely logical point of view, this is not necessarily a valid argument, since Hillesum was already aware that "They are out to destroy us completely."[7] In Camp Westerbork, it was undoubtedly true that a prescribed number of Jews had to be loaded onto each deportation train. So, if anyone escaped, another person would simply fill his or her place on the train. But before Camp Westerbork, hiding or flight did *not* mean that someone else would be arrested instead of you. We find Hillesum's actual reason further on in the same diary fragment:

> And it is sheer arrogance, to think oneself too good to share the fate of the masses.[8]

Another much quoted diary passage offers an explanation too:

> And my acceptance is not indifference or helplessness. I feel deep moral indignation at a regime that treats human beings in such a way.[9]

6 E.T., 487. *Het Werk*, 514; Saturday morning, 11 July 1942: Velen verwijten mij onverschilligheid en passiviteit en zeggen, dat ik me zomaar overgeef. En zeggen: ieder, die uit hun klauwen kan blijven, moet dat proberen en is dat verplicht. En ik moet iets dóen voor mezelf. Dit is een sommetje, dat niet op gaat. Iederéén is op het ogenblik n.l. bezig iets voor zichzelf te doen om er onder uit te komen en er moet immers toch een aantal, een zeer groot aantal zelfs gaan? Note that the original Dutch uses a more arithmetic-like phrase for "specious." Also the last phrase is less unequivocal in the original: "disappearing" could encompass those people who went into hiding, thus disappearing from public life, but it is clear Hillesum is talking about the vast numbers of deportees.

7 E.T., 461, *Het Werk*, 486; Friday evening, 3 July 1942: het gaat om onze ondergang en onze vernietiging,

8 E.T., 487. *Het Werk*, 515; Saturday morning, 11 July 1942: En het is een zeldzame zelfoverschatting, om zichzelf te waardevol te vinden om een "Massenschicksal" samen mee te ondergaan.

9 E.T., 487. *Het Werk*, 515; Saturday morning, 11 July 1942: En mijn aanvaarden is geen resignatie of willoosheid. Er is nog altijd plaats voor de elementaire zedelijke verontwaardiging over een regiem, dat zó met mensen omspringt.

And though we have repeated statements about Hillesum not wanting to nurture hatred, and descriptions of her desire to counteract hatred in herself, it remains unclear in what way she acted upon the "deep moral indignation" that she felt.

Ies Spetter, Hillesum's Jewish Council colleague in Westerbork

Recently, a text has surfaced that reveals something of Hillesum's actions to relieve her indignation. It is a text by Ies Spetter, written in the autumn of 1945 after his return from Auschwitz and the terrible death marches. It is kept in the archive of the NIOD, the Dutch Institute for War, Holocaust and Genocide Studies, and had gone unnoticed all these years until it was published in 2018.[10]

Spetter's name occurs once in Hillesum's letters. In Amsterdam, in February 1943, Hillesum's friend Jopie Vleeschhouwer asks in passing about this man. The relevant sentence reads,

> Do let me know some more news about Ies Spetter. Everyone here says that he is getting divorced, and I'd be interested if that's true.[11]

Who was Spetter, and why did Jopie Vleeschhouwer think that Etty Hillesum had more to say about him?

Ies Spetter was born in 1921 in a left-wing, liberal Jewish family. He studied psychology in Amsterdam and married Suze Turksma. One day, when he saw how children from the Jewish orphanage were thrown into a truck, he decided to join the resistance. He became involved with the Westerweel group, which smuggled people to Spain.

Spetter was offered a position on the Jewish Council at the end of March 1942. Although he objected to doing the handiwork of the Nazis in any form, he decided to accept the job because it would enable him to continue his illegal work. After a few months of "fictional" work, he was called – together with a few dozen others – to prepare for "a heavy task, namely that of the administration of Jews to be employed in Germany." It was the first time that deportation abroad had been mentioned. At the time, there

10 Ies Spetter, "Buna," in: Bettine Siertsema, *Eerste Nederlandse getuigenissen van de Holocaust 1945-1946* (Laren: Verbum, 2018), 395-453.

11 E.T., 665; *Het Werk*, 708; Letter 77, Jopie Vleeschhouwer to Etty Hillesum, Westerbork, Friday, 26 February 1943.

was still a possibility that it really was for labour since the people called were between 16 and 45 years old, excluding the sick and pregnant women toward the end of their term. Initially, Spetter refused to do this job, but at the insistence of the leader of his resistance group, he consented and left for Camp Westerbork at the end of July 1942. At that point he still had the possibility of traveling back and forth to Amsterdam, the same possibility Hillesum had. Spetter had a faked personal identification card as an extra security measure.

Together with four others, presumably including Etty Hillesum, he founded a social department, "Fully intent on helping as much as possible without lifting a finger for the SD's administration machine."[12] The social department collected things in the camp from people who had still something to share, for those who had arrived completely empty-handed.

Back in Amsterdam, Spetter was temporarily assigned to the *Voorlichtingsdienst* [Information Service]. In that position, he could caution people who were concerned about their relatives in Camp Westerbork, not to join them there. This was contrary to what many of his colleagues in the Jewish Council did when asked about Westerbork. His wife, meanwhile, was able to find safe addresses for about one hundred children.

Back in Camp Westerbork, Spetter was a bewildered witness to the terrible chaos wrought by the mass transport that arrived on the night of 2 to 3 October 1942. His description was similar to Etty Hillesum's view of Westerbork in tone and vision – though Hillesum herself was in Amsterdam on that date, and did not describe that exact event.

> Who will describe the suffering of all these mothers, children who have been picked up on their own, pregnant women and men who have been beaten up, psychologically broken, desperately clinging to what's left of their possessions, cold and hungry, dully bearing their fate, but actually unaware of the terrible end awaiting them.[13]

In a few lines of poetry, Spetter next described the deportees' state of mind, a mood that Hillesum also sketched, but of which she seemed more judgmental than Spetter:

12 Spetter, "Buna", 403. In Dutch: [...] vervuld van het idee zoveel mogelijk te helpen zonder één vinger voor de SD-administratiemachine uit te steken [...]. SD = Sicherheitsdienst [Secret Service].

13 *Ibidem*, 406. In Dutch: Wie beschrijft het leed van al deze moeders, alleen opgepikte kinderen, zwangere vrouwen en afgebeulde mannen, psychisch gebroken, zich wanhopig klemmend aan hun restje bezittingen, verkleumd en hongerig hun noodlot dof dragend, maar eigenlijk onbewust van het vreselijke einde dat hen wachtte.

> Thus they want us to be, battered, beaten,
> the spirit broken and cracked the heart,
> A gang of wanderers without land or God,
> too tired too dull to bear their fate.[14]

Compare this to Etty Hillesum:

> The human suffering that we have seen during the last six months, and still see daily, is more than anyone can be expected to comprehend in half a year. No wonder we hear on all sides every day, in every pitch of voice: "We don't want to think, we don't want to feel, we want to forget as soon as possible." It seems to me that this is a very great danger.[15]

After the poem – and an added line space – Spetter continued with a sentence of particular importance to this article:

> Together with a friend, Mr. Hillesum, I managed to smuggle some children out of the camp. My wife went to pick them up and delivered them elsewhere.[16]

This line sheds new light on Etty Hillesum's activities in Camp Westerbork. One may easily miss it, because Spetter addresses her as "Mr." Etty Hillesum herself wanted to be addressed this way, as shown in her request to Christine van Nooten whom she advised to send parcels for the family, "[...] preferably registered. It's safest to address them to me: Mr. E. Hillesum, Assistant Jewish Council, Westerbork Camp (etc.)."[17] In Dutch, "Meester," abbreviated as "Mr.," is an academic title used for persons who graduated in Law. Mr. Hillesum was, quite simply, her surname and academic title.

14 *Ibidem*. In Dutch: Zoo willen zij ons hebben, gebeukt, geslagen,
de geest gebroken en het hart kapot,
Een bende zwervers zonder land of God,
te moe te dof hun lot te dragen.

15 E.T., 586; *Het Werk*, 624; Letter 24, To two sisters in The Hague, Amsterdam, late December 1942: Wat zich daar het laatste half jaar voor onze ogen aan menselijk leed heft afgespeeld en zich dagelijks nog afspeelt, is meer dan één enkeling in een half jaar zou kunnen verwerken. Men hoort het dan ook dagelijks om zich heen in alle toonaarden: 'We willen niet denken, we willen niet voelen, we willen zo gauw mogelijk vergeten.' En het lijkt me toe dat dit een groot gevaar is.

16 Ies Spetter, "Buna", 406.

17 E.T., 605, *Het Werk,* 645; Letter 41, To Christine van Nooten, Westerbork, Monday, 21 June 1943: Liefst aangetekend. Aan mijn adres het veiligste: Mr. E. Hillesum, employé Joodse Raad, Kamp Westerbork [...].

In the margin of the typescript of Spetter's text in the NIOD archive, a handwritten note was scribbled: "by ambulance to Groningen," apparently indicating the method by which this smuggling had been accomplished. How we would have loved to know more of this affair! How many children did it concern, and of what ages? Were there other methods to get them out of the camp apart from the ambulance? How were the children selected, were they on their own in the camp, or did their parents make urgent requests? But Spetter did not say another word about it.

It is possible the smuggling was arranged with the help of the resistance group around camp inmate Werner Stertzenbach. Hillesum mentions him as an acquaintance in letter 21, and the explanatory note on page 756 states that Stertzenbach's group helped people escape from the camp and found "underground" addresses for them.[18] Werner Stertzenbach himself kept silent on the hospital route in his testimony in the spring of 1945.[19] And in his letters from Camp Westerbork in the years 1941-1943, he did not mention that he helped people go into hiding – for obvious reasons.[20] In Niemeijer and Mulder's *Verzet in Groningen*, a book about the resistance in the province of Groningen, there is only one mention of a young child who arrived in the academic hospital as part of a group of sick and underfed children. That particular child was smuggled out of the hospital. All the other children in the group were collected by the SD after recovery – no doubt to be sent to their deaths.[21] In his book on resistance in and escapes from Camp Westerbork, Guido Abuys mentions several other cases of escape from the camp, but doesn't touch specifically on escapes via the academic hospital in Groningen, though he concedes that it was quite possible such a route existed.[22] The NIOD archive has a file with more than one hundred names of inmates of Camp Westerbork who were temporarily nursed in the academic hospital.[23] Since Ies Spetter mentions neither date nor name, the notes in the margin do not help us in trying to pinpoint the exact occasion of the smuggling, nor do they help us to know if such an escape was a regular occurrence. Because Spetter's testimony

18 E.T., 577 and 756. The English edition has his name wrongfully spelled as Sterzenbach. *Het Werk*, 613, 787.

19 NIOD archive file 250i no. 513.

20 Werner Stertzenbach, *Rood en jood* (Hooghalen: Herinneringscentrum Kamp Westerbork, 2005).

21 Jan A. Niemeijer & Ad A.J. Mulder, *Verzet in Groningen* (Groningen: Wolters-Noordhof/ Forsten, 1986).

22 Guido Abuys & Dick Mulder (eds.), *Een gat in het prikkeldraad: Kamp Westerbork, ontsnappingen en verzet* (Hooghalen: Herinneringscentrum Westerbork, 2003), and an e-mail from Guido Abuys d.d. 9 November 2018.

23 NIOD archive file 250i, numbers 451 and 459.

is from the post-war period, clearly he was not inhibited by considerations of caution. People writing during the war, like Etty Hillesum and Werner Stertzenbach, would have exercised an abundance of caution so as not to endanger others involved in their efforts to rescue children. Without this one post-war sentence, we would never have known about the rescue at all.

Ies Spetter after Camp Westerbork

When *Lagersperre* was proclaimed for employees of the Jewish Council, signifying a revocation of their exemptions, the reason given was that they allegedly had not performed their duties well enough to continue being given privileges. Spetter immediately fled the camp with the help of his forged identity card. He continued his work in Amsterdam. At one point, however, the situation grew too dangerous and he tried to flee to England with his wife and another couple. Their daughter went into hiding with friends of theirs.

Both couples were, however, arrested at the Spanish border. In his written text in the NIOD archive, Spetter is quite brief about the torture he subsequently underwent, saying simply the interrogations grew "more barbaric by the day."[24] Next, his wife was maltreated in his presence to get him to talk. In 1992, Spetter gave an interview in which he was more explicit, "It was a terrible time. Being beaten senseless by three, four men who jump on you together, once for more than a week against the wall as if you were being crucified, tossing around in your own excrements, no water."[25]

He and his wife got separated. She died from a disease after an attempt to escape, but Spetter did not know anything of that. He ended up in Auschwitz-Monowitz, his spirit unbroken. In the 1992 interview he related that even there he was involved in resistance activities:

> We even had a resistance group in Auschwitz, a group of people who were from the resistance. We tried to smuggle weapons made of small parts that some were able to smuggle from the warehouses. The people in that group knew for sure that they would never go into the gas chamber, in that case we would do something. I had a razor blade. They would not get me. Or you would attack a German.[26]

24 Ies Spetter, "Buna", 409: De verhoren [...] werden met de dag van barbaarsere aard.

25 Max Arian, "Overleven: Ies Spetter en het verzet in Auschwitz", *De Groene Amsterdammer*, 6 May 1992, 11.

26 *Ibidem.*

In addition to this (intended) "armed" resistance, Spetter talked of a form of spiritual resistance. "There were also people who tried to keep up a human life together, even if you were starving."[27] He conducted, for example, old-fashioned, courteous conversations with a Russian comrade who spoke French.

During the horrible death march after Auschwitz was evacuated by the Germans as the Red Army advanced, and by sheer luck, Spetter was reunited with Sally de Jong, the friend with whom he had tried to escape to England. As a doctor, De Jong was in slightly better condition than Spetter himself, as doctors often had a slightly privileged position in the camps. They pulled each other through, and even tried to help a boy by placing him between their bodies to share their warmth. When doctors were required for work in the concentration camp Sangerhausen, a sub-camp of Buchenwald, Spetter urged his friend to step forward because he thought it would grant him some chance of survival. The wry outcome was that Spetter survived, if only barely, and his friend did not.

Sally de Jong was the reason that Spetter's testimony remained intact and surfaced so many years later. Sally was the twin brother of Loe de Jong, the national historiographer of the Second World War in the Netherlands who worked at the National Institute of War Documentation (RIOD, now NIOD). Spetter's text, titled "Buna" and dedicated "To my brother S. de J.," was one of the sources for Boudewijn Smits's biography of Loe de Jong, published in 2014.[28]

After the war, Spetter was a witness at the Nuremberg trials, which started on 20 November 1945. However, he did not testify in the International Tribunal trial, but in Case 6 of Court 6, The United States of America v. Carl Krauch *et al.*, also known as the I.G. Farben Case. His testimony took place on 17 November 1947.[29] That same year, he emigrated to the United States, where he settled in the New York area. Known as Matthew Ies Spetter after his move to New York, he obtained a doctorate in social psychology. His study *The Jews of the Netherlands: A social psychology of the patterns of acculturation and transculturation of a national community during periods of cultural catastrophe* is a classic in the field. Spetter wrote many more books as well, such as *Man, the Reluctant Brother*; *The Courage to Stand Alone*; *To Deny the Night*: *Reflections on Life and Essence*; *Passing through Darkness;*

27 *Ibidem.*

28 Boudewijn Smits, *Loe de Jong 1914-2005: Historicus met een missie* (Amsterdam: Boom, 2014).

29 I am grateful to Dr. Sofia Stolk of the T.M.C. Asser Instituut who helped me find the transcripts of this trial: www.profit-over-life.org/rolls.php?roll=5&pageID=685&expand=no.

and *In Search of Man*. He founded the Riverdale Mental Health Association, worked as a family therapist, and was a teacher of peace education. He was also an activist in the Civil Rights Movement. In the 1980s he received the Dutch Resistance Commemoration Cross. Matthew Ies Spetter died in 2012.

Kindred spirits

There seems to be a remarkable harmony between Etty Hillesum's mindset and Ies Spetter's thoughts, as seen in the following quotes from his 1967 book, *Man, the Reluctant Brother*,

> There is before us the choice, as always, to be loyal to what is human.[30]

> Perhaps, instead of dwelling on those forces threatening mankind we need at least as much preoccupation with those things that hold life together, and conserve it.[31]

> Our most precious capacity therefore is the capacity to choose, and to break the shackles of crippling fear. Sometimes [we need] valuing a person more than he does himself, acting upon the inherent substance of his character even if he does not. Men thus can help each other reach a richer state of mind in which their mode of *being* will be what matters most.[32]

> To live does not mean just to snatch a bit of happiness here and a bit of pleasure or money there. It means to have our reach extended so that the ideal of life becomes a possibility. Life is, above all, possibility.[33]

In these words it seems as if we hear Etty Hillesum's voice. Clearly, there is a greater correspondence between Spetter and Hillesum than just their positions on the Jewish Council and their joint effort to smuggle children from Camp Westerbork.

It is quite clear that a rescue action such as getting children out of Westerbork by ambulances fits perfectly with Ies Spetter's attitude not to cooperate with the occupier, and matches the pattern of his earlier

30 Matthew Ies Spetter, *Man the Reluctant Brother* (New York: Fieldston Press, 1967), 5.

31 *Ibidem*, 61.

32 *Ibidem*, 72.

33 *Ibidem*, 289.

and later resistance work; he aimed at getting as many people as possible into hiding. We know Etty Hillesum, on the other hand, only as giving "legal" aid to the Jews in Camp Westerbork as part of her job. And whereas Spetter lived to recount the story of the smuggling of children in post-war testimony and documents, Hillesum left no record because she would have endangered many if she had brought the event to light in her letters during the war. I have written in a previous article that Hillesum's high-minded thoughts about primarily fighting the evil in herself may have taken a different direction when faced with the reality of Camp Westerbork.[34] The one inconspicuous sentence in the testimony of Ies Spetter that mentions "Mr. Hillesum," shows that this assessment may well have been correct, at least in this one instance. It may be that Hillesum's acceptance of her fate, for which her friends and some of her later readers reproached her, did not lead to passivity at all. Instead, she may have committed herself to actively helping children escape from the very same fate that she so readily accepted.

The later career and books of Spetter, her comrade in these efforts, show how much his resistance had its roots in a humanistic idealism. This is an outlook that he had in common with Etty Hillesum – at least in part – and which even the torture and humiliations of the Nazis could not extinguish. A look at the titles of Spetter's books and his contribution to peace studies and civil rights makes us wonder what Hillesum could have accomplished after the war, had she not been killed in Auschwitz-Birkenau.

About the Author

Bettine Siertsema (1955) is Assistant Professor of History at the Vrije Universiteit Amsterdam. Her early research addresses religious and ethical aspects of Dutch autobiographical literature on the Nazi concentration camps (*Uit de diepten*, Vught: Skandalon, 2007). Recent publications on Holocaust literature include *Eerste Nederlandse getuigenissen van de Holocaust, 1945-1946* (Hilversum: Verbum, 2018) and *"The kind of spirit that people still kept": VHA testimonies of Amsterdam's Diamond Jews* (Holocaust Studies, September 2018). Her latest book is a history of Amsterdam's "Diamond Jews" during the Second World War (Hilversum: Verbum, forthcoming).

34 Bettine Siertsema, "'Wij mogen die haat niet aankweken in ons': Etty Hillesums visie op de nazi's," in: Klaas A.D. Smelik *et al.* (eds.), *Etty Hillesum 1914-2014* [Etty Hillesum Studies, 6] (Antwerpen/Apeldoorn: Garant, 2014), 49-58, especially pp. 57-58.

"My Beloved Desk, the Best Place on this Earth"

Etty Hillesum Says Goodbye to Her Familiar Surroundings[1]

Klaas A.D. Smelik

Abstract

Etty Hillesum showed a special attachment to the desk in her room in Han Wegerif's house. It was her favourite place to be. Also other parts of her room were very dear and had a special meaning for her; for instance, the tree behind her window or the jasmine behind the house. Nevertheless, she had no grief to leave her room, her desk or the house where she had lived since 1939, because "in every place on earth, we *are* 'at home' when we carry everything within us." In this contribution, Hillesum's remarks on the various parts of Wegerif's house are analyzed as well as the special meaning they had for her.

Keywords: house of Han Wegerif, Etty Hillesum's room, Etty Hillesum's desk, book case of Julius Spier, attachments, being at home.

Kde domov můj – "Where is my home?" The beginning of the Czech national anthem is an appropriate opening for this contribution about the longing of a Jewish woman for her home: the familiar desk where she would write her diaries, but which she had to say goodbye to when she went to work in the Westerbork transit camp. That woman is Etty Hillesum.

Hillesum's birth house on the Molenwater in Middelburg carries a plaque with an inscription that offers a partial answer to the question "Where is my home?". It is a quotation from her diary:

1 Thanks to R.W.M. van Uum, who translated this contribution into English.

Smelik, Klaas A.D. (ed.), *The Lasting Significance of Etty Hillesum's Writings: Proceedings of the Third International Etty Hillesum Conference at Middelburg, September 2018*.
Taylor & Francis Group 2019
DOI: 10.5117/9789463722025_SMELIK

> In every place on earth, we *are* 'at home,' when we carry everything within us.[2]

It is no surprise that Etty Hillesum could feel at home anywhere. As a child, she did not have much opportunity to be rooted in one place. With clock-like regularity, father Hillesum changed from one appointment as a teacher of classic languages, to another: Middelburg, Hilversum, Tiel, Winschoten, and finally, Deventer. Etty was ten years old when she moved to the city of Geert Groote where her father finally found a working environment that suited him.

As well, during her days as a student in Amsterdam, Etty Hillesum continuously changed address.[3] In March 1937, she finally came to lodge with the widower Han Wegerif, who offered her a room in his maisonette on No. 6 Gabriël Metsustraat in Amsterdam. The intention was that she would be his housekeeper. A further dimension was added to this when the two started a love affair – despite the large age difference: "Pa Han" was born in 1879, Etty in 1914.

As opposed to her paternal home in Deventer, where chaos reigned, No. 6 Gabriël Metsustraat offered Etty Hillesum a real home, a place where she loved to be and where she could blossom. This was the place where she wrote the diaries that have given her a posthumous worldwide renown.

Let us have a look at these diaries and explore the maisonette on No. 6 Gabriël Metsustraat to see the way Etty Hillesum experienced this house and how she depicted it in the years 1941 and 1942. Today, these premises have been fully reconstructed and nothing remains of the original design. There is only a shield next to the front door to remind us that Etty Hillesum wrote her diaries here in 1941 and 1942.

Her room

On the second floor of the house, Etty Hillesum had her room which was, according to her friend Johanna Smelik (in the diaries: Jopie), a long, narrow room; in Dutch: "een pijpenla". There was a divan bed, a desk table, a small chair, and a little white table. Bookshelves were attached to the wall, as well as several photographs [see Figure 4], including a portrait of the young

2 E.T., 524 [revised]. *Het Werk*, 555; Sunday, 20 September 1942: Op iedere plek van deze aarde is men 'thuis', wanneer men alles in zich draagt.

3 Cf. Klaas A.D. Smelik, "A Short Biography of Etty Hillesum (1914-1943)," in: Klaas A.D. Smelik, Gerrit Van Oord & Jurjen Wiersma (eds.), *Reading Etty Hillesum in Context: Writings, Life, and Influences of a Visionary Author* (Amsterdam: Amsterdam University Press, 2018), 23-30, especially p. 25.

Stalin.[4] At the end of September 1941, a pear-wood bookcase with the library of Julius Spier arrived and was put in place, leaving her barely any space to move.

In her diary, Etty Hillesum herself refers to her room as small,[5] but nevertheless it meant a lot to her. On Sunday morning, 5 April 1942, she writes, "I have been living in this room for three years now, and am grateful for every day I am left to live and to work."[6]

The familiar desk

The central place in the small room was given to Hillesum's "trusty desk".[7] This was her favourite place and we see her depicted at this desk in a photograph taken in 1939 [see Figure 5]. The right hand is under her chin, the left hand on an unfolded book; she is staring out the window. No heavy leather desk chair, but a modest little chair with a rattan seat. A table cloth covers the desk, on top of which are some folders and, on the right-hand side, a stack of books. She calls it an untidy desk,[8] and she

4 Cf. Gerrit Van Oord's blog: https://zichtopitalie.wordpress.com/2010/12/03/etty-hillesum-en-de-jonge-stalin/.

5 Cf. E.T., 320: Last night at 10.30 when I came back to my small room [revised] = *Het Werk*, 334; Friday morning, 3 April 1942: Toen ik gisterenavond om half 11 m'n kleine kamer binnenkwam [...].
E.T., 386: Well, how was it last night in my small bedroom? = *Het Werk*, 404; Saturday morning, 30 May 1942: Ja, hoe was dat gisterenavond in mijn kleine slaapkamer?
E.T., 523: We were standing at the window of my small room. = *Het Werk*, 553: Sunday evening, 20 September 1942: We stonden voor het raam van mijn kleine kamer.

6 E.T. 325-326. *Het Werk*, 340; Sunday 5 April 1942: Al drie jaar leef ik in deze kamer, ik ben dankbaar voor iedere dag, dat ik er leef en werk.

7 Cf. E.T., 355: I am writing this at my trusty desk [...] = *Het Werk*, 372; Wednesday evening, 29 April 1942: Ik schrijf dit nu aan m'n vertrouwde bureau [...]; E.T., 359: Deserting this beloved desk, the most dependable refuge I know [...] = *Het Werk*, 377; Thursday evening, 30 April 1942: Ik had te kiezen tussen dit lieve bureau, mijn vertrouwdste plek die ik ken [...], and E.T., 487: at this terribly beloved and trusty desk [revised] = *Het Werk*, 514; Saturday morning, 11 July 1942: aan dit verschrikkelijk dierbare en vertrouwde bureau.

8 Cf. E.T., 379: I have been sitting here now for about five minutes, physically exhausted and not particularly inspired, staring across this untidy, precious desk = *Het Werk*, 397; Tuesday evening, 26 May 1942: Ik zit hier zo 5 minuten, lichamelijk oververmoeid en niet al te bezield, een beetje over dit slordige, lieve bureau te staren.
E.T., 383-384: I shall always prefer an untidy desk of my own, covered with books and papers, to even the most ideal and harmonious marriage bed. = *Het Werk*, 402; Friday evening, 29 May 1942: [...] een slordig bureau vol boeken en papieren, dat van mij alleen is, zal ik altijd weer verkiezen boven het ideaalste en harmonischte huwelijksbed.

Figure 4 Portrait of Etty Hillesum in her room next to pictures of favourite authors, ca 1937

Collection Jewish Historical Museum, Amsterdam

E.T., 400: Good morning, untidy desk! = *Het Werk*, 420; Wednesday morning, 10 June 1942: Goeiemorgen, m'n slordige bureau; E.T., 603: [...] sitting at a shaky table in the noisy little parlour,

Figure 5 Etty Hillesum sitting at her desk, ca 1939

Collection Jewish Historical Museum, Amsterdam

or working at my beloved, untidy desk. = *Het Werk*, 642-643: Letter 38, To Maria Tuinzing, Westerbork, undated, mid-June 1943: [...] ik zit op het ogenblik aan een rommelig klein tafeltje in een rumoerige kleine zaal, en zit tegelijkertijd ook aan m'n lieve slordige bureau.

regularly expresses the intention to tidy it up.[9] Sometimes, she even carries out her intention.[10]

The desk is cluttered. One Sunday morning, 21 June 1942, she sums up all the things she sees lying or standing on it:

> Goodness me, my desk looks just like the world on the first day of creation. Chaos and confusion. As well as exotic Japanese lilies, geraniums, faded tea roses, pine cones that are now holy relics, a Moroccan girl with a look that remains animal yet serene at the same time, there are also St Augustine and the Bible and Russian grammars and dictionaries and Rilke and countless little scribbling blocks with God alone knows what weighty notes, and pencils, a bottle of ersatz lemonade, typing paper and carbons and Rilke's collected works, and Jung. And this is only what just happens to be lying about, there are also the permanent inhabitants of the desk, leaning against the wall. And miraculously, there is still room for me and for this exercise book.[11]

See also E.T., 384: untidy workplace = *Het Werk*, 402; Friday evening, 29 May 1942: [...] m'n rommelige werkplaats [...], and E.T., 353: Such a mess has piled up on my desk. = *Het Werk*, 370; Wednesday morning, 29 April 1942: Er ligt te veel rommel op m'n bureau.

9 Cf. E.T., 521: I shall now tidy my desk. I must keep good order even in external things, precisely in external things, or else it will all get too much for me. If I put something down somewhere, a minute later I don't know where it's got to, and then it takes so much time to find it again, and that time could be devoted to better things. I shall do my best and tidy up my desk now. = *Het Werk*, 552; Friday morning, 18 September 1942: Ik zal m'n bureau gaan opruimen. Ik moet orde blijven houden ook in de uiterlijke dingen, juist in de uiterlijke dingen, anders gaan ze me over het hoofd groeien. Als ik ergens iets neerleg, weet ik een minuut later niet meer, waar het gebleven is en dan kost het alles zoveel tijd om het terug te vinden en in die tijd zou men iets beters kunnen doen. Ik zal m'n best doen en ga m'n bureau opruimen. Cf. also E.T., 323: It is now half past nine, I have to put some order into the dreadful jumble on this desk [...] = *Het Werk*, 337; Saturday morning, 4 april 1942: Het is al half 10, ik moet eens wat orde brengen in de beestenbende op dit bureau [...]. On Tuesday afternoon, 7 July 1942, she no longer speaks of tidying up, but of liquidating, see E.T., 479: And I had better get used to the fact that I shan't be about much longer, and prepare for my leave-taking in all sorts of little ways so as to be sure I am not hit too hard by the finale when it comes: liquidating letters and papers and other old junk in my desk. [revised] = *Het Werk*, 506; dinsdagmiddag 7 juli 1942: En aan het weggaan van hier zal ik me ook beter kunnen gewennen, wanneer ik met verschillende kleine daden me dat afscheid steeds beter realiseer, zodat het me "letzten Endes" niet tòch nog als een veel te zware slag treft: het liquideren van brieven en papieren en veel rommel in m'n bureau.

10 Cf. E.T., 233: Dreamed away Friday morning, tidied my desk and gratefully absorbed all my impressions. = *Het Werk*, 244; Monday morning, 19 January 1942: Vrijdagochtend verdroomd en bureau opgeruimd en de vele indrukken dankbaar verwerkt. See also E.T., 484: I have already cleared out one of the drawers in my desk. = *Het Werk*, 512; Sunday morning, 11 July 1942: Ik heb al één la van m'n bureau uitgeruimd.

11 E.T., 436-437 [revised]. *Het Werk*, 460; Sunday morning, 21 June 1942: Allemachtig dat bureau. Het lijkt wel de wereld op de eerste scheppingsdag. Zó een chaos en zoveel doorelkaar.

What she does not mention are the folders she bought in September 1941, at the Amsterdam stationary store, Gebroeders Winter, so that she could organize her scattered papers.[12] She had five folders, on which she had written the subject in Russian – because "I don't want everyone to know what I'm doing."[13]

For the things that no longer fitted on the desk, Etty Hillesum had a small, white, round table in her room, on top of which were lying, apart from art books, a few blooming tree branches.

> On the little round white table, there is a large bunch of twigs, some with catkins and others whose names I don't know, in a brown earthenware pot, and when I look at the twigs, they are just like a forest into which you can walk very far and deep. The twigs bend over the *Gothic Cathedrals,* over the *Impressionists,* over Goya and Vincent the Sunseeker.[14]

Flowers, books, her diary notebooks and folders – in this room she could feel at home for the first time in her life – despite the problems that were advancing towards her.

> I've noticed this again as well: no matter how tired and weary and out of sorts I am, when I sit down at my desk for a while, at my untidy workplace, the white face of the wall rising straight in front of me, the room behind me, and beyond that the whole world, I feel so nice and peaceful again, so completely 'at home.'[15]

Behalve exotische Japanse lelies, geraniums, overleden theerozen, denneappeltjes, die tot heilige reliquieën geworden zijn, een Marokkaans meisje met een blik, die nog steeds dierlijk en sereen is tegelijkertijd, zwerven daar nog rond de Heilige Augustinus en de Bijbel en een aantal russische grammaticas en woordenboeken en Rilke en ontelbare kleine blocnootjes met god weet wat voor gewichtige aantekeningen en potloden en een fles surrogaatlimonade en schrijfmachinepapier en carbonpapier en Rilke, verzameld en wel en Jung. En dit is dan nog alleen maar wat er zo toevallig rondzwerft, er staan dan nog de vaste stamgasten van dit bureau tegen de muur geleund. En het mooiste is, dat er dan ook nog een plaatsje is voor míj en dit schrift.

12 E.T., 113. *Het Werk*, 120; Monday evening, 29 September 1941.

13 E.T., 109. *Het Werk*, 115; Monday morning, 29 September 1941: niet iedereen hoeft te weten wat ik doe.

14 E.T., 325. *Het Werk*, 340; Sunday morning, 5 April 1942: Op het witte ronde tafeltje staat een grote bos takken, er zijn katjes bij en nog andere, waarvan ik de naam niet weet, ze staan in een bruine aarden pot en als ik in die takken kijk is het net een bos, waar men heel ver en diep in zou kunnen gaan. De takken buigen zich over de 'Gothische Kathedralen', over de 'Impressionisten', over Goya en de Zonzoeker Vincent.

15 E.T., 384. *Het Werk*, 402; Friday evening, 29 May 1942: Ik merk nu weer dit ook: hóe geradbraakt en vermoeid en uit elkaar gevallen ook, wanneer ik een poosje aan dit bureau zit, m'n rommelige

Thus, it is clear that Etty Hillesum, in her small room with her desk at the centre, had created a home of her own, where she felt very much at ease. Moreover, her desk was a workplace, albeit untidy,[16] where she could work on her inner development. In this way, there arose an interplay between the desk as a place to work on the one hand, and her head as "the workshop, in which all worldly things must be thought through until they become clear",[17] on the other. It is no surprise that she felt the temptation to disregard the outside world and withdraw to her desk. She wondered, however, if she was allowed to cherish this desire:

> At certain fixed times – though less and less often now – I have a tremendous need to cut myself off; to be quite alone for a time. On Sunday, I found it very difficult to leave my desk and go over to your place. Was that very selfish and antisocial of me?[18]

Later, she feels differently in this respect:

> It is sometimes hard to take in and comprehend, oh God, what those created in Your likeness do to each other in these disjointed days. But I no longer shut myself away from that all in my room, oh God; I try to look things straight in the face and do not want to run away from them. I try to understand even the worst crimes, and I try and try again to discover the small, naked human being amid the monstrous wreckage caused by man's senseless deeds. I don't sit here in my peaceful flower-filled room, wallowing poets and thinkers, and praising God. That would be too simple, and in any case, I believe that I am not as unworldly as my friends so kindly say.[19]

werkplaats, de witte wand van de muur loodrecht voor me opstijgend, de kamer in m'n rug en daarachter de hele wereld, dan ga ik me weer zo rustig en zo prettig voelen, zo helemaal "thuis".

16 E.T., 384. *Het Werk*, 402; Friday evening, 29 May 1942: een rommelige werkplaats.

17 E.T., 87. *Het Werk*, 92; Friday morning, 15 August 1941: de werkplaats, waarin alle dingen van deze wereld tot klaarheid gedacht moeten worden.

18 E.T., 336. *Het Werk*, 351; Wednesday morning, 22 April 1942 – a reply to a lost postcard written by Henny Tideman: Op gezette tijden – maar met steeds grotere tussenpozen, komt dat bij me terug: een verschrikkelijk sterke behoefte me af te zonderen en tijdenlang helemaal alleen te zijn. Zondag kostte het me al zo een grote moeite m'n bureau in de steek te laten en naar jullie te komen. Is dat erg egocentrisch en asociaal?

19 E.T., 384 [revised]. *Het Werk*, 402; Friday evening 29 May 1942: Het is soms nauwelijks te verwerken en te bevatten, God, wat jouw evenbeelden op deze aarde elkaar alles aandoen in deze losgebroken tijden. Maar dáárvoor sluit ik me niet op in m'n kamer, God, ik blijf alles onder ogen zien en wil voor niets weglopen en van de ergste misdaden tracht ik iets te begrijpen en te doorgronden en ik tracht altijd weer de naakte, kleine mens op te sporen, die dikwijls niet terug te vinden is midden in de monstrueuze ruïnes van zijn zinneloze daden. Ik zit hier niet in een

In her diaries, her desk grows to be the symbol of a peaceful existence among the great thinkers whose works she was reading. This is her reaction to the daily reality of threat and persecution. Etty Hillesum, however, grows more and more aware that a time is approaching in which she can no longer sit at her desk reading and writing, but in which she will be exposed to unprecedented ordeals in a prison camp. For this reason, she practises saying goodbye to her beloved desk and accepting the new phase in her life:

> And I had better get used to the fact that I shan't be here much longer, and prepare for my leave-taking in all sorts of little deeds so as to be sure that finally I will not be hit too hard when it comes to liquidate letters and papers and much old junk in my desk.[20]

She has faith in the fact that, though far removed from her "dearly beloved and trusty desk",[21] she would be able to continue following her chosen road. Faith in herself and faith in God:

> I am writing this at my trusty desk, surrounded by books, chestnut twigs, and celandine plus the pencil sketch of S.'s head diagonally across from me on the wall. I may be writing this in great comfort, but there is something inside me, tough and indestructible, that tells me I shall be able to bear different circumstances, too. —[22]

> [...] I don't feel in anybody's clutches; I feel safe in God's arms, to put it in a beautiful manner, and no matter whether I am sitting at this dearly beloved and trusty desk now, or in a month's time in a bare room in the

rustige kamer met bloemen zwelgend in Dichters en Denkers God te prijzen, dat zou heus geen kunst zijn en ik geloof ook niet, dat ik zo "weltfremd" ben, als m'n goede vrienden vertederd zeggen.

20 E.T., 479 [revised]. *Het Werk*, 506; Tuesday afternoon, 7 July 1942. En aan het weggaan van hier zal ik me ook beter kunnen gewennen, wanneer ik met verschillende kleine daden me dat afscheid steeds beter realiseer, zodat het me "letzten Endes" niet tòch nog als een veel te zware slag treft: het liquideren van brieven en papieren en veel rommel in m'n bureau.

21 E.T., 487. *Het Werk*, 514; Saturday morning 11 July 1942: verschrikkelijk dierbare en vertrouwde bureau.

22 E.T., 355. *Het Werk*, 372; Wednesday evening, 29 April 1942: Ik schrijf dit nu aan m'n vertrouwde bureau, boeken, kastanjetakken en geel speenkruid, de getekende kop van S. schuin tegenover me aan de wand, ik kan het nu misschien gemakkelijk schrijven, maar toch is er iets in me, iets heel hards en onverwoestbaars, dat weet, dat het ook andere omstandigheden zal kunnen dragen.—

> Jewish district, or perhaps in a labor camp under SS guards – I believe that I shall always feel safe in God's arms.[23]

On Tuesday, 22 September 1942, after her return to Amsterdam from her first contact with the reality of Camp Westerbork, she looks back at the days when she could sit down quietly to read and write, and thinks of the experiences she has subsequently gained in the camp. To her astonishment, she concludes that for her there is no essential distinction between the "protected, peaceful room"[24] in Amsterdam and life in "a flashpoint of human suffering"[25] inside the camp. For her, the connecting link turns out to be her love for human life. Because of this, she feels "one great, meaningful whole."[26] What she has trained herself to do at her desk, namely learning to read her interior, she feels she can apply in the camp in order to be able to read others. In this way, she expresses her yearning to touch with her fingertips "the contours of these times",[27]

> I once wrote in one of my diaries, 'I would like to run my fingertips along the contours of these times.' I was sitting at my desk with no idea what to make of life. That was because I had not yet arrived at the life in myself. I have reached it while I was still sitting at this desk. And then I was suddenly flung into a flashpoint of human suffering, at one of the many frontlines all over Europe. And there, I experienced this: in the faces of people, in thousands of gestures, in small changes of expression, life stories, I was suddenly able to read our age – and much more than our age alone. Because I could read in myself, I realized that I could read in others too. And it really was as if I was able to feel the contours of these times with my fingertips [...]. Surrounded by my writers and poets and the flowers on my desk, I loved life so much. And there among the barracks, full of hunted and persecuted people, I found confirmation of my love of life. Life in those drafty barracks was no other than life in this protected, peaceful room. Not for one moment was I cut

23 E.T., 487 [revised]. *Het Werk*, 514; Saturday morning, 11 July 1942: [...] ik voel me in niemands klauwen, ik voel me alleen maar in God's armen, om het nu eens beeldschoon te zeggen en of dat nu hier aan dit verschrikkelijk dierbare en vertrouwde bureau is, of over een maand in een kale kamer in de Jodenbuurt of misschien in een arbeidskamp onder S.S.-bewaking, in Gods armen zal ik me geloof ik altijd voelen.

24 E.T., 527. *Het Werk*, 557; Tuesday, 22 September 1942: beschutte, rustige kamer.

25 E.T., 526. *Het Werk*, 557; Tuesday, 22 September 1942: in een brandpunt van menselijk lijden.

26 E.T., 527. *Het Werk*, 558; Tuesday, 22 September 1942: één grote, zinrijke continuïteit.

27 E.T., 526. *Het Werk*, 557; Tuesday, 22 September 1942: de contouren van deze tijd.

> off from the life I was said to have left behind. There was simply one great, meaningful whole.[28]

Therefore, saying goodbye to her familiar desk turns out not to be an ordeal; on the contrary, she considers it a challenge to put her insights into practice in new circumstances. In this situation, she sees God's hand. After all, in this manner, she is given the chance to carry her God with her to the frontline of human suffering:

> Still, I am grateful to You for driving me from my peaceful desk into the midst of the cares and sufferings of this age. It wouldn't do, would it, to live an idyllic life with You in a sheltered study? Now I have to carry You intact with me and to remain faithful to You through everything, as I have always promised to You.[29]

Once she has been locked up in Camp Westerbork forever, however, Etty Hillesum's longing for her desk in Amsterdam remains unchanged. In a letter to her housemate Maria Tuinzing, dated 2 September 1943, she writes from the transit camp:

> And please will you give my love to my dear desk, the best place on earth?[30]

28 E.T., 526-527 [revised]. *Het Werk*, 557-558; Tuesday, 22 September 1942: Ik heb eens vroeger in één van m'n dagboeken geschreven: ik zou met m'n vingertoppen willen aftasten de contouren van deze tijd. Ik zat toen aan m'n bureau en wist niet goed hóe bij het leven te komen. Dat was, omdat ik nog niet bij het leven in mijzelf gekomen was. Het leven in mij heb ik weten te bereiken, terwijl ik nog achter dit bureau zat. En toen werd ik plotseling geslingerd in een brandpunt van menselijk lijden, aan één van de vele kleine fronten, die over heel Europa zijn. En daar beleefde ik plotseling dit: uit de gezichten van de mensen, uit duizenden van gebaren, kleine uitingen, levensgeschiedenissen, begon ik deze tijd – en veel meer dan deze tijd alleen – bijeen te lezen. Doordat ik in mezelf had leren lezen, bemerkte ik, dat ik ook in anderen kon lezen. Het is me daar werkelijk geweest, alsof ik met gevoelige vingertoppen getast heb langs de contouren van deze tijd en van het leven. [...] Tussen m'n schrijvers en dichters en bloemen aan dit bureau heb ik het leven zo lief gehad. En daar tussen de barakken, vol opgejaagde en vervolgde mensen, heb ik de bevestiging gevonden van mijn liefde voor dit leven. Het leven in die tochtig barakken stond in geen enkele tegenstelling tot het leven in deze beschutte, rustige kamer. Ik ben geen moment afgesneden geweest van een leven, dat zogenaamd voorbij was, er was één grote, zinrijke continuïteit.

29 E.T., 499 [revised]. *Het Werk*, 528; Wednesday morning, 22 July 1942. Toch ben ik er dankbaar voor, dat je [= God] me niet aan dit rustige bureau hebt laten zitten, maar me midden in het lijden en in de zorgen van deze tijd hebt gesteld. Het zou geen kunst zijn om een idylle met jou te hebben in een beschutte studeerkamer, maar nu gaat het erom, dat ik je onbeschadigd met me meedraag en dat ik je door alles heen trouw blijf, zoals ik je altijd beloofd heb.

30 E.T., 658. *Het Werk*, 701; Letter 68, to Maria Tuinzing, Westerbork, Thursday, 2 September 1943. En groet je m'n lieve bureau, de beste plek op deze aarde?

Five days later, she will have to leave Camp Westerbork for Auschwitz, never to return to her best place on this earth.

The Moroccan girl

The photographs on the wall of Hillesum's room were of a great variety. A picture that was especially dear to her was a poster with the portrait of a Moroccan girl[31] [see Figure 6]. This picture meant so much to her that it was kept after the war when her room was emptied. It is now placed in the Jewish Historical Museum in Amsterdam. The girl in Moroccan attire with heavy earrings and embellished headdress, was described by Etty Hillesum as staring into the distance "with her dark glance, serene and sensual."[32] Attempts to discover the identity of the photographer of this portrait have unfortunately been fruitless.

31 Cf. E.T., 175: The statue of the Moroccan girl stares out into the grey morning with a serious dark look that is carnal and serene at the same time. [revised] = *Het Werk*, 184; Friday morning, 12 December 1941: Het zwarte Marokkaanse meisje staart naar buiten in de grauwe ochtend, met die ernstige, donkere blik, die dierlijk is en sereen tegelijkertijd.
E.T., 212: It is now 8.30. A gas fire, yellow and red tulips, an unexpected piece of chocolate from Aunt Hes, the three fir cones from Laren Heath, which still float in the neighbourhood of the Moroccan girl, and Pushkin. [revised] = *Het Werk*, 221/2; Wednesday evening, 31 December 1941: Het is nu half 9, een gashaard, gele en rode tulpen, en opeens zomaar een drosteflik van tante Hes en de drie denneappels van de Larense hei, die daar nog steeds te zwerven liggen in de buurt van het Marokkaanse meisje en Poesjkin.
E.T., 295: My solemn, black Moroccan girl looks out at the flower garden again, [...] with her dark glance, serene and sensual. [revised] = *Het Werk*, 307; Sunday evening, 22 March 1942: Mijn ernstige, zwarte Marokkaanse kijkt weer in een bloementuin, of liever, ze kijkt er weer overheen als steeds met haar donkere blik, die sereen is en dierlijk tegelijkertijd.
E.T., 325: On my desk were small narcissi that lit up my jet-black Moroccan like radiant stars. = *Het Werk*, 340; Sunday morning, 5 April 1942: Op m'n bureau stonden kleine witte narcissen, die als stralende sterren mijn pikzwarte Marokkaanse beschenen.
E.T., 341/2: I should like to write about yellow daffodils, little yellow daisy flowers, and the southern face of my Moroccan girl looking down on me from above [revised] = *Het Werk*, 357; Friday morning, 24 April 1942: ik zou kunnen opschrijven: gele narcissen, kleine gele dotterbloemen en het zuidelijke gezicht van mijn Marokkaanse meisje, dat er boven uitkijkt [...].
E.T., 436: And my black Moroccan girl is hiding behind a pink cloud of tiny, wispy flowers [...] = *Het Werk*, 459; Sunday morning, 21 June 1942: En mijn Marokkaanse zwarte meisje gaat schuil achter een rose wolk van allemaal hele kleine ijle bloemetjes [...].
E.T., 436: [...] a Moroccan girl with a look that is animal yet serene at the same time [...] = *Het Werk*, 460; Sunday morning, 21 June 1942: [...] een Marokkaans meisje met een blik, die nog steeds dierlijk en sereen is tegelijkertijd [...].
32 E.T., 295. *Het Werk*, 307; Sunday evening, 22 March 1942: met haar donkere blik, die sereen is en dierlijk tegelijkertijd.

Figure 6 The Moroccan girl

Collection Jewish Historical Museum, Amsterdam

The window

Inside her small room, the window plays an important part. Etty Hillesum loved to look outside, at what was then called the Skating Club grounds

(Dutch: het IJsclubterrein),[33] and at the Rijksmuseum in the distance.[34] Especially at night and early in the morning:

> How I love you, my solitary nights! I lie stretched out on my back in my narrow bed, completely abandoned to the night [...] the curtain is open, the night is a grey expanse at the window, the Skating Club grounds are a broad, white snowy steppe.[35]

33 Cf. E.T., 246: [...] the curtain is open, the night is a grey expanse at the window, the Skating Club grounds are a broad, white snowy steppe. = *Het Werk*, 255; Friday morning, 20 February 1942: [...] het gordijn is open, de nacht staat grijs en wijd aan het raam, het IJsclubterrein is een wijde witte sneeuwsteppe.
E.T., 318: The morning lay ready-made outside my window. The green grass of the Skating Club and the Rijksmuseum seemed wide awake. = *Het Werk*, 332; Thursday morning, 2 April 1942: De ochtend lag daar zo kant en klaar achter m'n venster in de vroegte. Het groene gras van het IJsclubterrein en het Rijksmuseum, dat al klaar wakker leek.
E.T., 321: When I looked out of my window this morning at 6.30, the Rijksmuseum was still half asleep and the Skating Club dozing away [...] = *Het Werk*, 335; Saturday morning, 4 April 1942: Toen ik vanochtend om ½ 7 door m'n venster keek, lag het Rijksmuseum nog in een halfslaap verzonken, de IJsclub doezelde ook [...].
E.T., 352: That is just how the trees took flight along the Skating Club grounds at five o'clock this morning. = *Het Werk*, 369; Wednesday morning, 29 April 1942: Zo vluchtten de bomen langs het IJsclubterrein, vanochtend om 5 uur.

34 E.T., 296: The Rijksmuseum, too, was there outside the window, so invitingly fresh and new in its contours and at the same time so old and familiar. = *Het Werk*, 308; Sunday morning, 22 March 1942: Het Rijksmuseum stond daar ook achter de ramen, zo uitdagend fris en nieuw in z'n contouren en – tegelijk zoo oud-vertrouwd.
E.T., 297: and further away still the Rijksmuseum. = *Het Werk*, 309; Sunday morning, 22 March 1942: [...] en achter de ramen de zwarte takken tegen de lichte lucht en nog verder het Rijksmuseum.
E.T., 318: The morning lay ready-made outside my window. The green grass of the Skating Club and the Rijksmuseum seemed wide awake. = *Het Werk*, 332; Thursday morning, 2 April 1942: De ochtend lag daar zo kant en klaar achter m'n venster in de vroegte. Het groene gras van het IJsclubterrein en het Rijksmuseum, dat al klaar wakker leek.
E.T., 320: The Rijksmuseum with its towers looked like a turreted city far away [revised]. = *Het Werk*, 334; Friday morning, 3 April 1942: Het Rijksmuseum met z'n paar torens leek als een stàd van torens in de verte.
E.T., 321: When I looked out of my window this morning at 6.30, the Rijksmuseum was still half asleep and the Skating Club dozing away [...] = *Het Werk*, 335; Saturday morning, 4 April 1942: Toen ik vanochtend om ½ 7 door m'n venster keek, lag het Rijksmuseum nog in een halfslaap verzonken, de IJsclub doezelde ook [...].
E.T., 352: The sky was opal, and the outlines of the Rijksmuseum merged purple and yellow in the sky. = *Het Werk*, 369; Wednesday morning, 29 April 1942: De lucht was opaal en de contouren van het Rijksmuseum vervloeiden paars en geel in de lucht.
E.T., 415: The Rijksmuseum in the distance looked like a caliph's palace [...]. = *Het Werk*, 436; Monday morning, 15 June 1942: Het Rijksmuseum in de verte leek een khaliefenpaleis [...].

35 E.T., 246. *Het Werk*, 255; Friday morning, 20 February 1942: Ik heb je zo lief, m'n eenzame nachten. Men ligt maar neergestrekt op de rug in het smalle bed, vol overgave aan de nacht [...],

Despite the blackout regulation, she does not close the curtains in her room. She wants to look outside from her bed at night and early in the morning.[36] She looks out over the area of the Skating Club grounds, covered in snow during winter, but it is the view of the Rijksmuseum that particularly inspires her to remarkable metaphors:

> The Rijksmuseum with its towers looked like a turreted city far away.[37]

> The Rijksmuseum in the distance looked like a caliph's palace [...].[38]

Directly in front of her window are several trees, through which – when it is still dark – she can see the stars. The combination of the dark silhouettes of the trees and the shining stars between them, fascinates her.

She builds a special tie to one tree in particular, "the one tree which is mine alone."[39] For her, this tree is an important place of tranquillity in the contrast between her busy social life and her strong desire for peace and quiet:

> Sometimes my day is crammed full of people and talk, and yet I have the feeling of living in utter peace and quiet. And the tree outside my window, in the evenings, is a greater adventure than all those people put together.[40]

She even confesses to Spier that she speaks out loud to the tree:

> I said that I had been deep in conversation with my tree and that I had already gone to bed. Did I ever talk to my tree out loud? "Yes, indeed," I

het gordijn is open, de nacht staat grijs en wijd aan het raam, het IJsclubterrein is een wijde witte sneeuwsteppe.

36 Cf. E.T., 320: Last night at 10.30 when I came back to my little room, where the curtains at the one large window are always left open [...] = *Het Werk*, 334; Friday morning, 3 April 1942: Toen ik gisterenavond om half 11 m'n kleine kamer binnenkwam, waar het gordijn voor het éne grote raam altijd helemaal weggeschoven is [...]. See also E.T., 345: the gleaming uncurtained window = *Het Werk*, 361; Saturday afternoon, 25 April 1942: het glanzende gordijnloze venster.

37 E.T., 320 [revised]. *Het Werk*, 334; Friday morning, 3 April 1942: Het Rijksmuseum met z'n paar torens leek als een stàd van torens in de verte.

38 E.T., 415. *Het Werk*, 436; Monday morning, 15 June 1942: Het Rijksmuseum in de verte leek een khaliefenpaleis [...].

39 E.T., 459. *Het Werk*, 484; Thursday morning, 2 July 1942: die ene boom, die van mij privé is.

40 E.T., 305 [revised]. *Het Werk*, 318; Saturday morning, 28 March 1942: Soms is m'n dag boordevol mensen en gesprekken en heb ik toch het gevoel van in een volledige stilte en rust te leven. En die boom voor m'n venster 's avonds is dan een groter avontuur, dan alle mensen bij elkaar.

> said, "one day that tree will write my biography, it knows me better than anyone else does, a crazy girl in pyjamas."[41]

The contrast between the dark tree, bare in winter, and the shining stars is an inspiration for her to reach the following parallel:

> This morning, a few stars hung like glistening fruits in the bare black branches of the tree outside my window.[42]

One day, however, the branches of the tree are chopped off. Etty Hillesum reconsiders her comparison of the previous day. There are no more branches from which the stars can hang as shiny fruit:

> The night before, the stars had still hung like glistening fruit in the black branches, and now they climbed, unsure of themselves, up the bare, ravaged trunk.[43]

The pruning hits her hard, but Hillesum recovers miraculously quickly and comes to the following reaction, typical for her:

> For a moment, when the branches were being cut, I almost became sentimental. And for that moment I was deeply sad. Then I suddenly knew: I shall love the new landscape, too, in its own way.[44]

41 E.T., 454. *Het Werk*, 479; Sunday morning, 28 June 1942: En ik zei, dat ik al in hevig gesprek met m'n boom was geweest en al in m'n bed had gelegen. Of ik dan wel eens hardop tegen die boom praatte. Ja, waarachtig, zei ik, die boom schrijft later een biographie over mij, die kent me het beste van iedereen, ein verrücktes Mädchen im Pyama.

42 E.T., 194. *Het Werk*, 203; Saturday morning, 20 December 1941: Vanochtend hingen er een paar sterren als glanzende vruchten in de zwarte naakte takken van de boom voor mijn venster. Cf. also E.T., 215-216: Sometimes when I have woken up, the grey dawn has been no more than a piece of paper stuck to the outside of my window and the black branches of my tree nothing but scribbled pencil marks on that grimy piece of paper. = *Het Werk*, 225; Monday morning, 5 January 1942: Enige keren bij het wakker worden was de grauwe ochtend niets anders dan een stuk papier, geplakt tegen de achterkant van m'n raam en de zwarte takken van mijn boom waren slordige potloodstreepjes op dat groezelige papier.

43 E.T., 306 [revised]. *Het Werk*, 319; Saturday morning, 28 March 1942: Nog een nacht te voren hadden de sterren als glanzende vruchten in de zwarte takken gehangen en een nacht later klommen ze, nog onzeker, langs de kale, beroofde stam.

44 E.T., 306 [revised]. *Het Werk*, 319; Saturday morning, 28 March 1942: Ik dreigde één ogenblik sentimenteel te worden, toen de takken gekapt werden. En één ogenblik was ik heel zwaar treurig. En toen wist ik meteen weer: het nieuwe landschap, dat er ontstaat, zal ik weer op zijn manier liefhebben.

The solution for her is to choose a new metaphor. To cope with the loss she has suffered, she now speaks of the tree's "austere ascetic body."[45] And even more beautifully:

> [...] that one bare trunk outside my window. That looked like a gnarled carbine in a fairy tale from the East.[46]

The metaphor of the oriental carbine does not last long; she returns to the metaphor of the "austere ascetic body", that fitted so well with her spiritual quest to rid herself of everything that seemed to be redundant. Now, her private tree becomes, once again, a beacon in her life, a life undergoing fierce changes.

Yet even the tree that "will write my biography", does not escape the rupture in her life that takes place in the summer of 1942. Her experiences during her two stays in Camp Westerbork, and the death of her mentor and friend, Julius Spier, on 15 September 1942, change everything for Hillesum. The tree is no longer the same; it has now become part of the past:

> The tree is still there, the tree that could write my biography. But it is no longer the same tree; or is it I who am no longer the same?[47]

Spier's bookcase

On Monday morning, 29 September 1941, a shipment is delivered to Gabriël Metsustraat 6. It consists of 31 bundles wrapped in grey paper, two large jute bags, and a bookcase. Together, these items form the library of Julius Spier which now finds a home in Hillesum's small, narrow room.[48] After setting

45 E.T., 320 [revised]. *Het Werk*, 334; Friday morning, 3 April 1942: magere asketenlijf. See also E.T., 386: their naked, tough, ascetic limbs = *Het Werk*, 404; Saturday morning, 30 May 1942: hun naakte, harde asketenlichamen, and E.T., 318: my two gaunt ascetics = *Het Werk*, 332; Thursday morning, 2 April 1942: mijn twee magere asketen.

46 E.T., 352 [revised]. *Het Werk*, 369; Wednesday morning, 29 April 1942: [...] die éne kale stam voor mijn venster. Die was als een gekromde karabijn uit een oosters sprookje.

47 E.T., 515 [revised]. *Het Werk*, 544; Tuesday morning, 15 September 1942: Daar staat die boom weer, die boom, die mijn biographie zou kunnen schrijven. Het is toch niet meer dezelfde boom of komt het, omdat ik niet meer dezelfde ben?

48 E.T., 111-112 [revised]: Any moment now those "1100 books" will be arriving. I shall surely get drunk on words. [...] This morning's feeble drivel was suddenly cut short – thirty-one parcels in grey paper, a sort of bizarre Santa Claus, together with two large jute sacks and a case that turned out to be two cases. At first I felt dismayed, then wound up. *Het Werk*, 118; Monday morning, 29 September 1941: Straks komen de "1100 boeken", ik zal er wel dronken van worden. [...] Dat

up the bookcase, there is only one metre left between it and Hillesum's bed,[49] just enough space for her to kneel when she wants to pray.[50]

Her feelings about this acquisition are mixed. On the one hand, the cupboard is full of books she would like to read. On the other hand, being suddenly invaded by such a large treasure trove overwhelms her:

> Didn't even think it nice at first. A library someone else has been building up all his life suddenly dumped in your house. You'd do much better putting together a library, book by painful book, yourself.[51]

She expresses her contradictory feelings with the help of a special metaphor, one which she will henceforth use for Spier's bookcase: "a threatening temple in my little room"[52] or more extensively: "S.'s pearwood bookcase, that threatening book temple."[53] A temple, both holy and threatening – this is Hillesum's perspective on Spier's bookcase.

The great danger posed to Etty Hillesum by the 1100 books is her urge to drown herself in them. Books are her life, and she is tempted now to only read the books from Spier.[54] She intends to limit her hunger for books in the same way as she limits her craving for chocolate; the link between the two stands out:

flauwe gewauwel van vanochtend werd plotseling onderbroken vanochtend – 31 pakken in grauw papier, een grotesk Sinterklaasfeest en 2 grote jute-zakken en een kast, die twee kasten bleek te zijn. Eerst wanhopig, later opwindend.

49 E.T., 515 [revised]: And there is his bookcase, one meter from my bed. *Het Werk*, 544; Tuesday morning, 15 September 1942: En zijn boekenkast staat er, op een meter afstand van mijn bed.

50 E.T., 320: Between S.'s bookcase, wide and deep, still a mysterious temple of wisdom, and my small monk's bed, there is just enough room for me to kneel down. *Het Werk*, 334; Goede-Vrijdagochtend 3 April 1942: Tussen S. z'n boekenkast, die daar, groot en diep, nog altijd staat als een geheimzinnige tempel vol wijsheid, en mijn smalle monnikenbed, is nog nèt zoveel ruimte, dat men er soms kan neerknielen.

51 E.T., 112. *Het Werk*, 118-119; Monday morning, 29 September 1941: Niet eens leuk eerst. Een bibliotheek, die iemand een heel leven lang verzameld heeft, met één smak in je huis gegooid te krijgen. Je kunt veel beter boek voor boek zelf bloedig bij elkaar sparen.

52 E.T., 114. *Het Werk*, 120; Monday morning, 29 September 1941: een dreigende tempel in mijn kleine kamertje.

53 E.T., 120 [revised]. *Het Werk*, 127; Sunday morning, 5 October 1941: de perenhouten kast van S., die dreigende boekentempel. Cf. also E.T., 122 [revised]: that pearwood book temple. *Het Werk*, 129; Sunday morning, 5 October 1941: boekentempel van perenhout; E.T., 246: S.'s large bookcase still stands like a threatening, mysterious temple. *Het Werk*, 255; Friday morning, 20 February 1942: S.' grote boekenkast als een dreigende, geheimzinnige tempel, and E.T., 320: S.'s bookcase, wide and deep, still a mysterious temple of wisdom. *Het Werk*, 334; Goede-Vrijdagochtend 3 April 1942: S. z'n boekenkast, die daar, groot en diep, nog altijd staat als een geheimzinnige tempel vol wijsheid.

54 Cf. E.T., 130: Last night I told S. that all those books are really bad for me, some of them, anyway. That they make me lazy and passive, and I want to do nothing but read. *Het Werk*, 138; Monday

Figure 7 The sun lounge

Collection Uitgeverij Balans, Amsterdam

> This evening I require several things of you, my girl: you mustn't eat any more chocolates, you must leave those thousand books alone and you must go to bed on time. All acts of self-control.[55]

As it turns out, Pa Han's brother, Reverend W.J. Wegerif, has good pastoral insight. He notices Hillesum's dilemma as she goes about filling Spier's case with books. He realizes that for a bookworm like Hillesum, an abundance of books such as has arrived at her doorstep is too much of a good thing, though this seems paradoxical:

> This afternoon when I was standing in front of the overloaded bookcase with a few books in my arms and the Rev. Wegerif was on the point of leaving, he said to me, half ironically but with an undercurrent of seriousness, "May you have the strength to bear all that and to cope with it."[56]

morning, 20 October 1941: Gisterenavond zei ik tegen S. dat àl die boeken zo gevaarlijk voor me waren, soms tenminste. Dat ik er zo lui en passief van werd en alleen nog maar wou lezen.

55 E.T., 115. *Het Werk*, 122; Thursday evening, 2 October 1941: Vanavond eis ik enige daden van je: je mag geen chocolaadjes meer eten, je moet de 1000 boeken met rust laten en je moet bijtijds naar bed. Allemaal daden van zelfbeheersing.

56 E.T., 122. *Het Werk*, 129; Sunday morning, 5 October 1941: Toen ik vanmiddag voor de overladen boekenkast stond met enige boeken in m'n armen en Ds. Wegerif wegging, zei hij tegen me, half

The sun lounge

Although Etty Hillesum had only a tiny room in Han Wegerif's house, she could make use of the rest of the maisonette. Her room was a place where she could retire in peace, rather than a place of continuous stay.

The sun lounge was a favourite room of hers, one floor down from her room [see Figure 7]. Here, she could read in the company of Pa Han and enjoy the sun,[57]

ironisch, maar met een ondergrond van ernst: Ik wens U sterkte om dat alles te dragen en te verwerken.

57 Cf. E.T., 27: Something of this radiance passed into that nice fellow [= Kees de Groot], and it was a good afternoon in the sunny sun lounge, full of friendship and high spirits. [revised] = *Het Werk*, 28; Monday evening, 17 March 1941: En iets van mijn stralendheid ging op die aardige kerel [= Kees de Groot] over en het was een goeie middag in de zon in de serre, vol vriendschap en opgewektheid.
E.T., 27: Next Marjo rolled into our sunny sun lounge fresh from her concert platform and asked for a glass of water – a bit of a break and a friendly face. = *Het Werk*, 28/29; Monday evening, 17 March 1941: En vervolgens Marjo, die kersvers van het podium onze zonnige serre kwam binnenrollen en vroeg om een glas water, wat rust en een vriendelijk gezicht.
E.T., 111: Still, right now, sunning myself this Monday morning in the sun lounge, wearing my Japanese dressing gown, it feels as if everything is too much for me and I find myself unable to get down to work. = *Het Werk*, 117; Monday morning, 29 September 1941: Toch is me op dit moment, op deze Maandagochtend in de serre in de zon, in m'n Japanse ochtendjas alles me te veel en kan ik m'n werk niet aan.
E.T., 322: [...] while I stayed behind on my sunny sun lounge with *Symbols of Transformation* and another volume of Rilke's letters. [revised] = *Het Werk*, 336; Saturday morning, 4 April 1942 [...] en ik ben met 'Wandlungen und Symbole' en een andere band Rilke-brieven achtergebleven in m'n zonnige serre.
E.T., 344: 4 o'clock in the sun lounge, which is bathed in sunlight. = *Het Werk*, 360; Wednesday morning, 22 April 1942: 4 uur, in de serre, die uitbundig vol zon staat.
E.T., 355 [revised]: A few months ago, I was in two minds as to how I would choose, when it came to it, between this sunny sun lounge, my untroubled studies, and Han's faithful eyes on the one hand, and a concentration or some other camp where I could share my troubles with S. = *Het Werk*, 372; Wednesday evening, 29 April 1942: Voor enige maanden voerde ik nog in m'n phantasie een strijd, hoe ik zou moeten kiezen, wanneer dat acuut werd, tussen deze zonnige serre, ongestoorde studie en Hans trouwe ogen of een concentratie- of ander kamp en zorgen, gedeeld met S.
E.T., 359: A few months ago I asked myself if I wanted to follow him into exile or wherever. And my imagination then enacted a host of heart-rending scenes. Deserting this beloved desk, the most dependable refuge I know, this sunny sun lounge and Han's level-headed, ever-present succor – if I may put it like that – for an uprooted life in God knows what unfriendly spot on this earth, cut off from the past and from the future. That's what I thought. Et cetera. [revised] = *Het Werk*, 377; Thursday evening, 30 April 1942: Enige maanden geleden heb ik mezelf afgevraagd of ik hem zou willen volgen in een verbanning of waar ook heen. En in mijn phantasie hebben zich toen vele hartverscheurende tafrelen afgespeeld. Ik had te kiezen tussen dit lieve bureau, mijn vertrouwdste plek die ik ken, deze zonnige serre en Hans evenwichtige, altijd aanwezige beschermendheid – om het zo maar eens uit te drukken – en tussen een ontworteld leven op

especially when the window was left open[58] – and provided that the sun was shining, of course. In winter time, however, the sun lounge was cold, something she complains about in her diary.[59] But she also mentions the gas heater that warmed the room and made it a pleasant place, where she loved to read while Pa Han was sitting behind his newspaper, smoking his cigar or his pipe.

> Last night, I was sitting by the stove reading Rilke's letters, and Han was sitting reading his newspaper smoking a pipe. And suddenly I said, with heartfelt emotion, "Hello, my dear old friend." And he from behind his paper, "Hello, old girl." And then another long silence while we went on reading. And that was something else that's good![60]

And in the summertime too, with the windows left open, the sun lounge could be a place where the temptation to lead a conventional married life instead of her unbound existence as a free spirit could ambush Etty Hillesum:

God weet wat voor onvriendelijke plek van deze aarde, afgesneden van een verleden en van een toekomst, zo dacht ik enz.
E.T., 458: Sun in the sun lounge and a light breeze through the white jasmine. [revised] = *Het Werk*, 483; Wednesday afternoon, 1 July 1942: Zon in deze serre en een lichte wind door de witte jasmijn.
58 Cf. E.T., 433: And now the sun lounge windows are wide open and the summer night is right here in the middle of the room. = *Het Werk*, 456; Saturday evening, 20 June 1942: En nu staan de ramen van de serre wagenwijd open en de zomeravond staat midden in de kamer.
E.T., 433/4: Tonight we sat by the open sun lounge windows, in peace and friendship, with a newspaper, a pipe, a book and a cup of chocolate, as if we'd been married for twenty-five years. = *Het Werk*, 457; Saturday evening, 20 June 1942: We zaten vanavond voor de geopende serrevensters in vrede en vriendschap, met een krant, een pijp, een boek en een kopje chocola, als waren we 25 jaar getrouwd.
59 Cf. E.T., 158: And Pa Han tending his little plants with endless patience in the cold sun lounge. I am just sitting here on the Chinese rush matting, staring fixedly into the none too flourishing fire with wide open eyes. = *Het Werk*, 167; Saturday morning, 29 November 1941: En Pa Han, die in de koude serre met z'n eindeloze geduld bij z'n plantjes doende is. Ik zit daar maar in het Chineese gras en staar met wijd open, strakke ogen in de niet erg tierige haard.
E.T., 230: [...] there was a tremendous clash in the cold sun lounge for all that. = *Het Werk*, 239; Wednesday morning, 14 January 1942: Maar in die koude serre botste het toch even geweldig.
E.T., 230: And then that bitterly cold sun lounge and Han with his photomania had to get in the way of it all [...] = *Het Werk*, 240; Wednesday evening, 14 January 1942: En toen kwam die verdomde koude serre en Han met z'n fotomaniakkerij er tussen.
60 E.T., 321. *Het Werk*, 335; Friday morning, 3 April 1942: Gisterenavond zat ik aan de haard en las de Rilke-brieven en Han zat over z'n krant met een pijp. En plotseling zei ik, uit het diepst van m'n gevoel: Dag, lief kereltje. En hij van achter z'n krant: Dag, meid! En toen weer heel lang zwijgen en lezen. Ook dàt is goed!

> Tonight, we sat by the open sun lounge windows, in peace and friendship, with a newspaper, a pipe, a book and a cup of chocolate, as if we'd been married for twenty-five years.[61]

No matter how cosy, a married life did not appeal to Etty Hillesum, even though she did not want to miss out on one altogether. One question was on her mind: would she, when the time came, give up this sheltered life with Pa Han and the warm sun lounge to follow her new friend Julius Spier into the concentration camp? She expected that Spier, being a German Jew, would get a summons before herself, a Dutch citizen.

> A few months ago, I was in two minds as to how I would choose, when it came to it, between this sunny sun lounge, my untroubled studies, and Han's faithful eyes on the one hand, and a concentration or some other camp where I could share my troubles with S.[62]

In the end, Etty Hillesum changed the warm sun lounge for a barracks in Camp Westerbork, while Julius Spier died in Amsterdam, just a day before the Gestapo came to arrest him at his home. In the end, life turns out differently from what one imagines...

The bathroom

On the same floor as the living room and the sun lounge was a common bathroom, which Etty Hillesum used extensively – not only to wash herself, but also for reading and writing in her diary.[63] More than once, she occupied

61 E.T., 433-434. *Het Werk*, 457; Saturday evening, 20 June 1942: We zaten vanavond voor de geopende serrevensters in vrede en vriendschap, met een krant, een pijp, een boek en een kopje chocola, als waren we 25 jaar getrouwd.

62 E.T., 355 [revised]. *Het Werk*, 372; Wednesday evening, 29 April 1942: Voor enige maanden voerde ik nog in m'n phantasie een strijd, hoe ik zou moeten kiezen, wanneer dat acuut werd, tussen deze zonnige serre, ongestoorde studie en Hans trouwe ogen of een concentratie- of ander kamp en zorgen, gedeeld met S. See also E.T., 359 = *Het Werk*, 377 (quoted above in note 57).

63 For reading in the bathroom, cf. E.T., 410: But then you should not sit in the bathroom reading until one o'clock in the morning when you can barely keep your eyes open with fatigue. [revised] = *Het Werk*, 431; Saturday morning, 13 June 1942: Dan moet je ook maar niet in de badkamer tot 1 uur 's nachts zitten lezen, terwijl je je ogen al bijna niet meer open kunt houden van de slaap. E.T., 411: Last night in my bathroom novel I read the following passage about a priest: [...] = *Het Werk*, 432; Saturday morning, 13 June 1942: Gisterenavond in mijn badkamerroman las ik het volgende over een priester: [...].

the bathroom for half an hour,[64] for purposes for which she could just as well have used her own room. There was a reason behind this, as the bathroom was a special place for her. She writes on Tuesday morning, 7 October 1941,

> Something invariably happens in the early morning in that small bathroom with the brown coconut matting.[65]

In the bathroom specifically, she attains some clarifying insights. For instance, when a passage by her favourite author Rainer Maria Rilke comes

E.T., 412: [...] and, putting on a deeply tragic mask and in impressive silence, I left his room and came and sat down in the bathroom to read a novel. And he came in, looking a bit helpless and stroking my hair and not quite knowing what to do, finding me sitting there in the middle of the night with a bowed head and tears behind my glasses, reading a novel in the bathroom. = *Het Werk*, 433; Saturday morning, 13 June 1942: [...] met een diep-tragisch masker en indrukwekkend zwijgend verlaat ik dan zijn kamer en ga in de badkamer een roman zitten lezen. En hij komt en is wat hulpeloos en streelt me en weet niet goed wat hij met me beginnen moet, nu ik daar zo midden in de nacht met een gebogen hoofd en tranen achter m'n brilleglazen in de badkamer een roman zit te lezen.
For writing in her diary in the bathroom, cf. E.T., 7: Sunday evening in the bathroom [revised] = *Het Werk*, 7; Sunday evening, 9 March 1941: Zondagavond in de badkamer.
E.T., 163: Tuesday morning, 9.30, in the bathroom. = *Het Werk*, 172; Tuesday morning, 2 December 1941: Dinsdagmorgen half 10, in de badkamer.
E.T., 164: Wednesday morning, eight o'clock, in the bathroom. = *Het Werk*, 173; Wednesday morning, 3 December 1941: Woensdagochtend, 8 uur in de badkamer.
E.T., 373: Last night in the bathroom at half past twelve, having first brought myself to a state of calm by writing on these blue lines, I suddenly sank down beside the bathroom chair, crying my heart out. = *Het Werk*, 391; Sunday morning, 24 May 1942: Gisterenavond om half 1, in de badkamer, nadat ik me eerst op deze blauwe lijntjes tot kalmte geschreven had, viel ik opeens zo hartverscheurend huilende neer bij de stoel van de badkamer.
E.T., 392: At midnight, in the bathroom. [revised] = *Het Werk*, 411; Thursday evening, 4 June 1942: 's avonds om 12 uur, in de badkamer.
E.T., 393: Friday morning, 8.30 in the bathroom. = *Het Werk*, 413; Friday morning, 5 June 1942: Vrijdagmorgen, half 9 in de badkamer.
E.T., 395: 5 June '42. Friday, midnight, in the bathroom. = *Het Werk*, 414; Friday evening, 5 June 1942: 5 Juni '42. Vrijdagavond, 12 uur, in de badkamer.
E.T., 395: Saturday morning, 8 o'clock, in the bathroom. = *Het Werk*, 415; Saturday morning, 6 June 1942: Zaterdagochtend, 8 uur, in de badkamer.
E.T., 541: Saturday morning, 6.30, in the bathroom. = *Het Werk*, 574; Saturday morning, 3 October 1942: Zaterdagochtend, half 7, in de badkamer.

64 Cf. E.T., 468: And so is every occasion you can wash yourself with scented soap in a bathroom all to yourself for half an hour. [revised] = *Het Werk*, 490; Saturday morning, 4 July 1942: En iedere keer dat je je nog met geurige zeep wast in een badkamer, die voor dat halve uur helemaal van jou alleen is.

65 E.T., 124. *Het Werk*, 131; Tuesday morning, 7 October 1941: (in dat smalle badkamertje met de bruine cocosmat speelt zich op de vroege morgen altijd heel wat af).

to life for her while she is reading in the bathroom, she states, "I still have those crucial experiences in the bathroom."[66] In this respect, her friend and therapist Julius Spier wittily remarked, "You're not likely to get a good wash if you're having to dream up all those ideas."[67]

Etty Hillesum picks up another activity in the bathroom: she teaches herself to pray on her knees on the rough brown coconut matting that lines the floor there. Kneeling while praying is a new experience for Etty Hillesum; this gesture has not come down to her from her Jewish background, as she remarks herself in a passage written shortly after Spier's death:

> I think that I can bear everything life and these times have in store for me. And when the turmoil becomes too great and I am completely at my wits' end, then I still have my folded hands and bended knee. A posture that is not handed down from generation to generation with us Jews. I have had to learn it the hard way. It is my most precious inheritance from the man whose name I have almost forgotten but whose best part has become a constituent of my own life.[68]

Although she also knelt down to pray in other locations, for instance in her room near the small white table[69] or at the window,[70] the bathroom continued to be her favourite place. The intimacy of this space, where she could have complete privacy and not be disturbed, gave her the opportunity to overcome the embarrassment she initially felt about this religious gesture:

66 E.T., 269. *Het Werk*, 280; Tuesday evening, 3 March 1942: M'n beslissendste momenten beleef ik nog steeds in de badkamer.

67 E.T., 396. *Het Werk*, 415; Saturday morning, 6 June 1942: 'Sie werden sich wohl nicht sehr gut waschen, wenn Sie sich alle solche Sachen ausdenken müssen.'

68 E.T., 547. *Het Werk*, 580; Saturday evening, 10 October 1942: Ik geloof, ik kan alles van dit leven en van deze tijd dragen en verwerken. En wanneer de onstuimigheid te groot is, en wanneer ik er helemaal niet meer uit weet te komen, dan blijven me altijd nog twee gevouwen handen en een gebogen knie. Het is een gebaar, dat ons Joden niet van geslacht op geslacht is overgeleverd. Ik heb het moeizaam moeten leren. Het is mijn kostbaarste erfdeel van de man, wiens naam ik al bijna vergeten heb, maar wiens beste deel ik verder leef.

69 E.T., 256: All at once I was down on my knees beside the little white table. = *Het Werk*, 266; Friday morning, 27 February 1942: Opeens lag ik geknield bij het witte tafeltje.

70 E.T., 225: It was a difficult road to take, finding my way back to this intimate gesture towards God in the evening by the window, and to say, "Thank you, oh Lord." = *Het Werk*, 235; Sunday evening, 11 January 1942: Het was een moeizame weg om terug te vinden dit intieme gebaar tot God, 's avonds aan het venster en te zeggen: Heb dank, o Heer.

> This afternoon I suddenly found myself kneeling on the brown coconut matting in the bathroom, my head hidden in my dressing gown, which was slung over the broken cane chair. Kneeling doesn't really come easily to me, I feel a sort of embarrassment. Why? Probably because of the critical, rational, atheistic bit that is part of me as well. And yet every so often I have a great urge to kneel down with my face in my hands and in this way to find some peace and to listen to that hidden source within me.[71]

Initially, kneeling while praying was certainly not the natural gesture for her as it was for her Roman Catholic contemporaries. On the contrary, she was ashamed to kneel for prayer. For her, it was "my most intimate gesture, more intimate even than being with a man."[72] She did not even dare write about it in her diary – it was that intimate:

> Something I have been wanting to write down for days, perhaps for weeks, but which a sort of shyness – or perhaps false shame? – has prevented me from putting into words. A desire to kneel down sometimes pulses through my body, or rather it is as if my body had been meant and made for the act of kneeling. Sometimes, in moments of deep gratitude, kneeling down becomes an overwhelming urge, head deeply bowed, hands before my face. It has become a gesture embedded in my body, needing to be expressed from time to time. And I remember: 'The girl who could not kneel,' and the rough coconut matting in the bathroom. When I write these things down, I still feel a little ashamed, as if I were writing about the most intimate of intimate matters. Much more bashful than if I had to write about my love life. But is there indeed anything as intimate as man's relationship to God?[73]

71 E.T., 103. *Het Werk*, 109; Wednesday afternoon, 24 September 1941: Vanmiddag vond ik mezelf plotseling geknield op de bruine cocosmat in de badkamer, m'n hoofd verborgen in m'n badjas, die op die kapotte rieten stoel slingerde. Ik kan helemaal niet goed knielen, er is een soort gêne in me. Waarvoor? Waarschijnlijk voor het critische, rationele, atheïstische stuk, dat er ook in me zit. En toch is er af en toe een grote drang in me neer te knielen, met de handen voor m'n gezicht en op die manier een vrede te vinden en te luisteren naar een verborgen bron in me.

72 E.T., 547. *Het Werk*, 580; Saturday evening, 10 October 1942: m'n intiemste gebaar, intiemer dan die ik heb in het samenzijn met een man. Cf. also E.T., 148: Such things are often more intimate even than sex = *Het Werk*, 156; Saturday morning, 22 November 1941: Maar deze dingen zijn haast nog intiemer, dan de sexuele, and E.T., 181: Some time ago I said to myself, "I am a kneeler in training." I was still embarrassed by this act, as intimate as gestures of love that cannot be put into words either, except by a poet. = *Het Werk*, 190; Sunday morning, 14 December 1941: Een tijd geleden zei ik tegen mezelf: ik oefen me in het knielen. Ik geneerde me nog te veel voor dat gebaar, dat even intiem is als de gebaren der liefde, waarover men ook niet spreken kan, als men geen dichter is.

73 E.T., 320. *Het Werk*, 334; Friday, 3 April 1942: Iets, wat ik al dagen lang, of weken lang, wil opschrijven, maar dat ik uit een soort schuchterheid – of nog steeds valse schaamte? – niet

Once the act of kneeling in prayer becomes a familiar gesture to her, it resides inside her body like an automatic force bearing upon her;[74] she wants to write a short novel[75] about "the girl who could not kneel,"

> Still a lot of false shame to get rid of. And there is God. The girl who could not kneel but learned to do so on the rough coconut matting in an untidy bathroom. [...] The story of the girl who gradually learned to kneel is something I would love to write in the fullest possible way. —[76]

She considers the metamorphosis that she has undergone so important, so characteristic a part of the road she has taken that she wants to share it

formuleren kan: door mijn hele lichaam gaat soms een natuurlijke beweging van te willen knielen, nee, het is nog anders: het is of het knielgebaar gemodelleerd is door m'n hele lichaam heen, ik voel het soms door m'n hele lichaam heen. Soms, in momenten van grote dankbaarheid, is het me een onweerstaanbare behoefte neer te knielen, het hoofd diep gebogen, de handen voor het gezicht. Het is een gebaar geworden, dat ìn m'n lichaam zit en dat gebaar wil soms verwezenlijkt zijn. En ik herinner me: "Het meisje, dat niet knielen kon" en de ruwe cocosmat in de badkamer. En bij het schrijven van deze dingen tòch het gevoel van een zekere gêne, of men over het intiemste van het intiemste schrijft. Veel meer schuchterheid en schaamte, dan wanneer ik over m'n liefdesleven zou schrijven. Is er ook wel iets zo intiem als 's mensen verhouding tot God?

74 Cf. E.T., 212: But now I sometimes actually drop to my knees beside my bed, even on a cold winter night. = *Het Werk*, 221; Wednesday evening, 31 December 1941: En nu moet ik soms opeens zomaar knielen, zelfs op een winternacht in de kou voor m'n bed.

E.T., 216: But last night, driven by a unexpected welling up of inner plenitude, I had to kneel down again suddenly in the middle of the room = *Het Werk*, 225; Monday morning, 5 January 1942: Maar gisterenavond moest ik opeens weer, door een plotseling opkomende innerlijke overvloed gedreven, weer knielen midden in de kamer.

E.T., 296: That is when I suddenly have the urge to kneel down in some quiet corner = *Het Werk*, 308; Sunday evening, 22 March 1942: Ik heb dan opeens de behoefte, ergens in een rustige hoek neer te knielen.

E.T., 301: And nowadays I get a bit of a rest as well: sometimes between two deep breaths and sometimes by kneeling for five minutes, anywhere I may find myself in the house. = *Het Werk*, 313; Friday morning, 27 March 1942 En men rust nu ook uit: soms tussen twee diepe ademteugen in en soms door 5 minuten te knielen, ergens op een toevallige plek in dit huis.

E.T., 320: It has become a gesture embedded in my body, needing to be expressed from time to time. = *Het Werk*, 334; Friday morning, 3 April 1942: Het is een gebaar geworden, dat ìn m'n lichaam zit en dat gebaar wil soms verwezenlijkt zijn.

75 Cf. E.T., 145: It is odd that while I have been so full of creative impulses, busy covering sheets of paper with a novel – The girl who could not kneel, or something like that [...] = *Het Werk*, 153; Friday, 21 November [1941]: Interessant is het, dat terwijl ik de laatste tijd vol scheppingsdrang zit en schrijven zou willen, een novelle: Het meisje, dat niet knielen kon of zo iets [...].

76 E.T., 148. *Het Werk*, 156; Saturday morning, 22 November 1941: Maar nog valse schaamte om ervoor uit te komen. En dan God. "Het meisje dat niet knielen kon en het toch leerde op de ruwe cocosmat in een slordige badkamer." [...] Dit proces in mij, van het meisje dat leerde knielen, zou ik willen uitbeelden in al z'n nuanceringen.— See also E.T., 320 and 547 (= *Het Werk*, 334 and 580).

with her readers in a short novel, which ultimately, she never writes. The full title, "The girl who could not kneel but learned to do so on the rough coconut matting in an untidy bathroom",[77] demonstrates that the bathroom in the Wegerif house has played an essential role in her process, so important to her, that she was able to develop a unique form of religiosity, detached from any tradition.[78]

The flowers in her room

Etty Hillesum liked to surround herself with flowers. On her desk, on the white table, everywhere, flowers compensated for the dark times of war and persecution. Many people did not understand her, "How can you even think about flowers now?". But still she goes out, with blisters on her feet from walking (Jews were no longer allowed to make use of public transport), in the pouring rain, in search of a flower stand to buy a big bunch of roses. She says, "There they are. They are just as real as all the misery I witness each day."[79] She refuses to allow her joy for the beauty of life and flowers to be hampered by the war.

The jasmine

On 1 July 1942, Etty Hillesum discovers a jasmine shrub, which can be seen through a window at the back of the maisonette. She remarks with surprise:

77 Dutch: Het meisje dat niet knielen kon en het toch leerde op de ruwe cocosmat in een slordige badkamer.

78 See also Pierre Bühler, "Het lichamelijke gebed bij Etty Hillesum", in: Klaas A.D. Smelik *et al.* (ed.), *Etty Hillesum weer thuis in Middelburg* (Etty Hillesum Studies, 7), Antwerpen-Apeldoorn: Garant, 2015, 85-91.

79 E.T., 499-500 [revised]: My red and yellow roses are now fully open. While I sat there working in that hell, they quietly went on blossoming. Many say, "How can you still think of flowers!" Last night, walking that long way home through the rain with the blister on my foot, I still made a short detour to seek out a flower stall, and went home with a large bunch of roses. And there they are. They are just as real as all the misery I witness each day. There is room for many things in one life. *Het Werk*, 529; Thursday evening, 23 July 1942: M'n rode en gele rozen zijn helemaal opengegaan. Terwijl ik daar in die hel zat, hebben zij daar maar stilletjes verder staan bloeien. Velen zeggen: hoe kun je nu nog aan bloemen denken. Toen ik gisterenavond dat grote eind door de regen gelopen had met die blaar onder aan m'n voet, ben ik toch op het eind nog een straatje omgelopen om een bloemenkar te zoeken en ik kwam met een grote bos rozen thuis. En daar staan ze. Ze zijn net zo werkelijk als al de ellende, die ik op een dag meemaak. Er is voor veel dingen plaats in één leven.

> Oh, yes, the jasmine. My God, how is it possible, it stands there squeezed between the neighbours' bare wall and the garage, overlooking the flat, dark, muddy garage roof. It is so radiant, so virginal, so unrestrained and so tender among all that greyness and that muddy darkness, an exuberant young bride lost in a back street. I can't understand this jasmine. But there is no need to. It is enough simply to believe in miracles in the twentieth century. And this is a miracle. And I believe in God, even though the lice will be eating me up in Poland before long. That jasmine, words fail me when it comes to that jasmine. It has been there a long time, but only now are words beginning to fail me about it.[80]

From that moment on, she writes about the jasmine on several occasions.[81] For her, the blooming jasmine represents the light side of existence, in juxtaposition to the dark horrors of her time. In her life, she wants to take both sides into account; they constitute a unity which is, at first sight, incomprehensible:

> Living and dying, sorrow and joy, the blisters on my feet and the jasmine behind the house, the persecution, the countless senseless horrors – it is all as one in me, and I accept it all as one mighty whole and begin to grasp it better if only for myself; without being able to explain to anyone else how it all hangs together.[82]

But the jasmine stops blooming. On Sunday morning, 12 July 1942, she writes:

> The jasmine behind my house has been completely ruined by the rains and storms of the last few days; its white blossoms are floating about in muddy

80 E.T., 459. *Het Werk*, 484; Wednesday morning, 1 July 1942: O ja, die jasmijn. Hoe is het toch mogelijk mijn God, hij staat daar ingeklemd tussen de verveloze muur van de achterburen en de garage. Hij kijkt heen over het platte donkere modderige dak van de garage. Tussen dat grauw en dat modderige donker is hij zó stralend, zo ongerept, zo uitbundig en zo teer, een overmoedige jonge bruid, verdwaald in een achterbuurt. Ik begrijp niets van die jasmijn. Dat hoef je ook niet te begrijpen. Men kan nog best in deze 20ste eeuw in Wonderen geloven. Dit is een wonder. En ik geloof in God, ook als de luizen me binnenkort hebben opgevreten in Polen. Die jasmijn, ik ben sprakeloos over die jasmijn. Hij staat er al heel lang, maar nu pas begin ik sprakeloos over hem te worden.

81 Cf. e.g. *Het Werk*, 485; Thursday morning, 2 July 1942: die niet tot bedaren te brengende, overmoedige en tedere jasmijn.

82 E.T., 461-462 [revised]. Cf. *Het Werk*, 487; Friday morning, 3 July 1942: Het leven en het sterven, het lijden en de vreugde, de blaren aan de kapotgelopen voeten en de jasmijn achter mijn tuin, de vervolgingen, de ontelbare zinneloze wreedheden, alles en alles, het is in me als één krachtig geheel en ik aanvaard alles als één geheel en begin steeds beter te begrijpen, zo maar voor mezelf, zonder dat ik het nog aan iemand zou kunnen uitleggen, hoe het alles in elkaar zit.

> black pools on the low garage roof. But somewhere inside me, the jasmine continues to blossom undisturbed, just as profusely and delicately as ever it did. And it spreads its scent round the house in which You dwell, oh God. You can see, I look after You, I bring You not only my tears and my forebodings on this stormy, grey Sunday morning, I even bring you scented jasmine.[83]

The jasmine shrub behind her house has been destroyed by rain and storm. Nothing remains of its beauty, "its white blossoms are floating about in muddy black pools on the low garage roof".[84] It is not strange that Hillesum considers the destroyed jasmine a symbol of the fate of the people to whom she belongs, their "Massenschicksal". She notes occasionally that their blossoming lives have also been destroyed and they have been scattered in "camps all over the world".[85] Even though Etty Hillesum is aware that she and her people are doomed to die,[86] the symbolic jasmine within keeps blooming and she offers to her God, not just tears, but also fragrant jasmine. Her vision of life and death form a unity and there is no consequential contrast between the two.

Goodbye forever

On 5 June 1943, Etty Hillesum descends, for the last time, the steep staircase that leads from the maisonette to the front door of the house. In 1942, as part of her job with the Jewish Council, she had been in Camp Westerbork on several occasions, after which she always returned to Amsterdam. But this time, she pulls the door of the small house on Gabriël Metsustraat behind her for the very last time. One month later, on 5 July 1943, her appointment

83 E.T., 489. *Het Werk*, 517; Sunday morning, 12 July 1942: De jasmijn achter mijn huis is nu helemaal verwoest door de regens en stormen der laatste dagen, haar witte bloesems drijven verstrooid in de modderige zwarte plassen op het lage dak der garage. Maar ergens in mij bloeit die jasmijn ongestoord verder, net zo uitbundig en teder, als ze altijd gebloeid heeft. En ze verspreidt haar geuren rond de woning, waar jij huist, mijn God. Je ziet, ik zorg goed voor je. Ik breng je niet alleen mijn tranen en bange vermoedens, ik breng je op deze stormachtige, grauwe Zondagochtend zelfs geurende jasmijn.

84 *Ibidem*.

85 Cf. E.T., 486. *Het Werk*, 624; Letter No. 23, to two sisters in The Hague, Amsterdam, late December 1942: kampementen, waar ter wereld ook.

86 Cf. e.g. E.T., 461: I must admit a new insight into my life and find a place for it: what is at stake is our impending destruction and annihilation, we can have no more illusions about that. They are out to destroy us completely [...] = *Het Werk*, 487; Friday evening, 3 July 1942: Men moet een nieuwe zekerheid in zijn leven een onderdak geven, men moet er even een plaats voor vinden: het gaat om onze ondergang en onze vernietiging, daarover hoeft men zich geen enkele illusie meer te maken. Men is op onze algehele vernietiging uit [...].

with the Jewish Council is revoked, and she becomes a prisoner without privileges in Camp Westerbork.

Etty Hillesum had anticipated the day would come when her familiar desk would be out of reach. For this reason, before her departure, she handed over her stack of exercise books to her housemate Maria Tuinzing. She asked her friend to pass them along to the writer Klaas Smelik, with the request that he publish them in case she did not return.[87] With this act, she entrusted the words that she had written in the maisonette at Gabriël Metsustraat 6 to her friends Maria Tuinzing and to my father, Klaas Smelik Senior, with the hope that they would convince future generations that a better world is possible once we extinguish the hatred in our hearts. In this way, she wanted to do something for posterity as she herself noted:

> I wish I could live for a long time so that one day I may know how to explain it all, and if I am not granted that wish, well, then somebody else will do it, carry on from where my life has been cut short. And that is why I must try to live a good and faithful life to my last breath: so that those who come after me do not have to start all over again, need not face the same difficulties. Isn't that doing something for future generations?[88]

About the Author

Klaas A.D. Smelik (1950) studied Theology, Semitic Languages, Archaeology, and Ancient History in Utrecht, Amsterdam, and Leiden. He successfully defended his PhD in Amsterdam in 1977. He taught Old Testament and Hebrew in Utrecht, Amsterdam, and Brussels, Ancient History in Amsterdam and The Hague, Jewish History at KU Leuven, and Hebrew and Jewish Studies at Ghent University. Until recently, he was the director of the Etty Hillesum Research Centre (EHOC), first in Ghent, later in Middelburg. Smelik edited the Dutch, English, French, and Italian unabridged editions of Etty Hillesum's writings and is editor-in-chief of the Etty Hillesum Studies. He has published or edited around 60 books and 300 articles on the Hebrew Bible, Ancient Hebrew inscriptions, Ancient History, Jewish Studies, Anti-Semitism, and Etty Hillesum.

87 Cf. E.T., xv.

88 E.T., 462 [revised]. *Het Werk*, 487; Friday evening, 3 July 1942: Ik zou lang willen leven, om het later alles tòch nog eens te kunnen uitleggen en als me dat niet vergund is, welnu, dan zal een ander het doen en dan zal een ander mijn leven verder leven, daar waar het mijne is afgebroken en daarom moet ik het zo goed en zo volledig en zo overtuigd mogelijk leven tot de laatste ademtocht, zodat diegene, die na mij komt niet helemaal opnieuw hoeft te beginnen en het niet meer zo moeilijk heeft. Is dat ook niet iets doen voor het nageslacht?

Etty Hillesum's Humanism

Ethical, Philosophical and Theological Comments

Jurjen Wiersma

Abstract

An excellent moral status is a leverage for the *humanum*. It elevates human beings to increased humanity and inspired Etty Hillesum to oppose hatred, anger, and barbarism. First and foremost, she wanted to be faithful to God, but also to all living co-creatures, to her own best moments, and to her creative talent. She displayed a specific Jewish identity in committing herself to JHWH's humanism, Biblical humanism.

Keywords: humanism, *humanum*, Biblical humanism, Jewish identity of Etty Hillesum, Emmanuel Levinas, Primo Levi, Being-in-Creation

Etty Hillesum was a militant advocate for the *humanum*, a collective name for human, humankind, or humanity. As such, she opposed hatred, anger, and barbarity. She considered that even the German enemy should not be treated wrongfully:

> Nazi barbarism evokes the same kind of barbarism in ourselves, one that would involve the same methods if we could do as we wanted right here and now. We have to reject that barbarism within us, we must not fan the hatred within us, because if we do, the world will not be able to pull itself one inch out of the mire [...]. But you can be very militant and act in a principled way without being crammed full with hatred.[1]

1 E.T., 21. *Het Werk* 22; Saturday, 15 March 1941: Resumerende, wil ik dus eigenlijk dit zeggen: het nazi-barbarisme roept in ons eenzelfde barbarisme wakker, dat met dezelfde methoden zou werken, wanneer we mochten doen wat we wilden vandaag aan den dag. Dit barbarisme van ons moeten wij innerlijk afwijzen, wij mogen die haat niet aankweken in ons, omdat de wereld

Smelik, Klaas A.D. (ed.), *The Lasting Significance of Etty Hillesum's Writings: Proceedings of the Third International Etty Hillesum Conference at Middelburg, September 2018.*
Taylor & Francis Group 2019
DOI: 10.5117/9789463722025_WIERSMA

Humanism had three prominent spokesmen in the 20th century: Martin Heidegger (1889-1976), Jean-Paul Sartre (1905-1980), and Emmanuel Mounier (1905-1950).[2]

Heidegger's foundation was *Seinsvergessenheit* and he brought the question of "Being" to the forefront as the creative force in the universe. On the wave of Being, humans can liberate themselves from the dictatorship of the anonymous "Man", the masses. Heidegger's humanism is a relentless mission from "Man" to "human" or from *homo barbarus* to *homo humanus*. All things considered, Heidegger formulated anti-humanism as totally different from the human; a complete makeover of the human person, not just a choice among choices. Being in its truest form is liberated from inhumanity and barbarity and emancipated to a full humanity.

Sartre's humanism, on the other hand, was based upon the absolute and principled freedom of the rational human, the thinking subject, summarized in his short dictum, "existence precedes essence". Human beings construct themselves and their existence by freely developing themselves through self-actualisation or self-realization. The only prerequisite is that they respond to the call not be to a product or fabrication of their environment and its alienation, but to be a creator. Take the adage of Sartre's life partner, Simone de Beauvoir: "One is not born, but rather becomes a woman." Hence, for Sartre humanism was a powerful yes to showcasing, manifesting, and projecting the self.

Mounier can be mentioned in one breath with Jacques Derrida, Michel Foucault, Paul Ricœur, and Denis de Rougemont. The goal of humanism for these men was "to create humans that are capable of emphatically showcasing themselves" (Mounier). The personal/personalism stands in the middle between individualism and communalism. As soon as the human person unfolds, the community flourishes in the sense that binds the *Gesellschaft* and germinates the *Gemeinschaft*. That will be in extremis, according to Denis de Rougemont (1906-1985), the Swiss champion for whom "Europe, a Federal Europe!" was a model for this idea.

Moral status as leverage for the humanum

Moral status is crucial in ethics. Conserving and allocating moral status is a core task of ethics, yet even as it increases in importance, it hardly

dan geen stap verder uit de modder komt. [...]. Maar men kan zeer strijdbaar en principieel zijn ook zonder volgepropt te zitten met haat [...].

2 Urs Thurnherr & Anton Hügli (eds.), *Lexikon: Existentialismus und Existenzphilosophie* (Darmstadt: Wissenschaftliche Buchgesellschaft, 2007), lemma "Humanismus", 131-132.

seems achievable anymore. With the threat to plant life and animals, more than ever bees and butterflies in the garden, trees along the highway, and ecosystems demand earnest consideration. Nevertheless, in this contribution, I highlight the importance of the moral status of humans, and dwell on what elevates humans to increased humanity and gives power to the *humanum*.

On the one hand, humans are a biological entity of the species *homo sapiens*. On the other hand, they are embodied spirits and in possession of the precious capability of reason. Both of these attributes are relevant in assigning the moral status of humans. Humans can react to sensations from the environment, make plans for the future, and think about the motives that inspire and activate them. There is a reverse side; humans are also subject to failure, defeat, suffering, and grief. As always, the idea of the I is decisive. Through this (f)actor, human beings become conscious of their own identity on a daily basis. Yesterday, you had certain experiences and tomorrow you will have others. Humans roll along with the rhythm of time, not passively but rationally, and in action. It is important that the I is an indicator for human dignity and freedom, an eminently crucial word to test the moral status of *humanum*.

It is not only the I that participates in the conservation and allocation of moral status. Moral status also resonates from the impact and support of the Other. Feminist philosophers and medical ethicists place particular importance upon the relational approach to moral status. Humans are social creatures that maintain relationships with others during their life history. An individual with a network of human relationships that stretches from dependence to care is reasonably assured of attaining moral status.

Take childbirth. At birth, the moral status changes completely; the infant enters the public space and his or her life begins. This expands to a junction of relationships, in which parents and significant others contribute to the budding life story of the little one. Their incentive is not "impartial consideration of reasons" but connectedness to the concrete "other".

Medical ethicists and feminist philosophers quite rightly highlight that morals are connected to specific interpersonal relationships, compassion, concern, and empathy, rather than to general, universal rules about respect and the common good.[3]

3 Govert den Hartogh, Frans Jacobs & Theo van Willigenburg, *Wijsgerige ethiek: Hoofdvragen, discussies en inzichten* (Budel: Damon, 2013), 53-62, 295-299.

Primo Levi and the buried human being

Regrettably, relationships between human beings frequently occur without compassion and concern, as the Italian chemist Primo Levi recounts in his work on the Second World War. In Auschwitz, where he arrived in the spring of 1944, a brother bellowed at him in the infirmary in broken German: "Du Jude kaputt. Du schnell Krematorium fertig." Levi got lucky. The camp leadership valued him, a highly educated chemist, for his useful labour. In his story, he recalls appearing before SS officer Pannwitz for some sort of exam. He stood to wait in the workplace of the officer, a tall, thin, blond man with eyes, nose, and hair as all Germans were supposed to have.

Pannwitz was seated behind an impressive desk. Levi, *Häftling* 174517, stood in the room that looked like a real office; it was orderly, neat, and clean. If Levi touched anything, he would leave behind a dirty mark. When Pannwitz finished writing, he lifted his head and looked at Levi. After that day, Levi frequently contemplated the SS officer and tried to imagine how he, as a human being, functioned internally and how he passed his time. He yearned to meet him again as a free man, not out of revenge, but out of a personal need to understand him better.

Because the gaze between them was not between two people, but rather was more like a glance through the glass pane of an aquarium exchanged between two creatures occupying different worlds, Levi noted that he could expose the great insanity of the Third Reich. Everything the Nazis thought and stated about German superiority became at that moment an instant reality. The brain behind the blue eyes and the well-cared-for hands affirmed: "That nonentity in front of me apparently belongs to the sort that must be exterminated. In the present case, we need to first determine whether it has a capacity for something useful." Meanwhile, Levi's head rattles with impressions like pips in a hollow gourd and he notes: "Blue eyes and blond hair is bad. No communication possible. I specialized in minerals. I specialized in organic connections. I specialized in...."

The interrogation commences. "Wo sind Sie geboren?" Levi begins his narrative, responding that he obtained the title of doctor in organic chemistry in Turin in 1941, *summa cum laude*, however he finds that unbelievable with his filthy, damaged hands and dressed in his muddy clothes for forced labour. Fortunately, the examination turns out well. Levi feels himself growing. The tension flows out of him. He peers dazed at the white hand entrusting to white paper incomprehensible characters concerning his destiny. The Kapo (from the Italian word *capo*, "boss", "chief", "head", in the KZ – in fact, an assistant of the SS) is quickly informed and relays the news.

Doktor Pannwitz informed the Labour Office that three *Häftlinge* had been chosen for the laboratory. Levi, *Häftling* 174517, is one of them. The other two are a Belgian and a Romanian. The Kapo surveys the threesome with a hateful grimace. Is it possible, three "Franzosen" will work in the laboratory paradise? Many comrades congratulate the *Häftlinge* without jealousy on this opportunity. *Häftling* 174517 is promoted to specialist, with the right to a new shirt and new underpants. He must be shaven each Wednesday. Nobody can claim that he doesn't understand the Germans.

In his introduction to *The Witnesses*, Levi notes that he consciously wanted to write about the concentration camps; they have to be viewed by every human being "as a sinister alarm signal". He strongly felt the necessity to tell his story so that others could participate in it. For him, it was "an inner liberation", a satisfaction of his need to testify. The result of his writing was extensive; he was able once again to achieve for himself a feeling of human dignity.

In his description of various comrades who shared the fate of Auschwitz, he notes with striking clarity the following, "The characters in this book are not people," and immediately he adds that their humanity "is buried, or they have buried it themselves, due to what has been done to them or what they have done to others." He can still recall stupid SS men, Kapos, politicians, criminals, prominent people and ordinary ones, and the slave masses of the *Häftlinge*, all ranks of the insane hierarchy that the Germans had imposed. Levi says that, although everyone was different, they were all "one and the same inner emptiness".[4]

These sentences of Levi are factual. He experienced humans and humanity buried in Auschwitz, covered and hidden. There was nothing to do about it; it was the great tragedy of the war. Etty Hillesum deals differently with this in Camp Westerbork; she goes against it. Reality for humans must be different. With inner emptiness and without *humanum*, there is no life, or certainly, life is not liveable anywhere. She accepts this as a fact. She wants to make the best out of imprisonment.

4 Cf. Primo Levi, *If This is a Man* & *The Truce*, translated by Stuart Woolf (London: Abacus, 2013), 9, 54, 118-120, 154-157.

Etty Hillesum and her Jewish identity

With regard to the words "moral status" one can observe that Etty Hillesum acted on three levels:

1 She buried her inner "I".
2 She paid attention to the nakedness of the countenance of the Other – the other "I".
3 She described her relationship with God, her theological anthropology.

Ad 1. Sometimes, Etty Hillesum had psychosomatic symptoms. During those times, she turned to her therapist, the psycho-chirologist Julius Spier (1887-1942), a Jew who left Germany in 1939 and started a practice in Amsterdam. He helped her work on herself in order to establish order in her interior chaos, her buried interior. She entrusted her thoughts and feelings to the first pages of her diary. That resulted in healing, noticeable in the following remark:

> The 'spiritual blockage' is beginning to get less 'blocked'.[5]

She continued to write, fearing that otherwise she would become captive to a demonic restlessness, become obstructed and burdened again, and the healing process would languish. In addition, she needed to come to terms with her parents, their lack of civility and their chaotic household. She realized, writes Denise de Costa, "how disorganized the family in which she had grown up was, and she considered it her duty to bring order and harmony to the chaos she had internalized."[6] Regarding her "becoming obstructed", she concluded that one must first improve one's inner life in order to improve the external world. According to her, the war had taught us only one lesson: "That we must look into ourselves and nowhere else."[7] She noted that she was doing well in the first few months of 1942 and that she felt broad and expansive internally. Hillesum felt a new energy rising up in herself and with that she hoped to help other people along the journey to healing.

5 E.T., 22. *Het Werk*, 23; Saturday, 15 March 1941: De "verstopfte Seele" begint al minder "verstopft" te worden. See also E.T., 74. *Het Werk*, 77; Tuesday, 5 August 1941.

6 Denise de Costa, *Anne Frank & Etty Hillesum: Spiritualiteit, schrijverschap, seksualiteit* (Amsterdam: Balans 1996), 184. E.T.: *Anne Frank and Etty Hillesum: Inscribing Spirituality and Sexuality*, translated by Mischa F.C. Hoyinck & Robert E. Chesal (New Brunswick, NJ: Rutgers University Press, 1998), 147.

7 E.T., 245. *Het Werk*, 254; Thursday, 19 February 1942: En dat lijkt me de enige les van deze oorlog, dat we geleerd hebben, dat we het alléén in onszelf moeten zoeken en nergens anders.

> One should always be ready to meet one's fellow man constructively, and the more constructive one is, the better.[8]

Ad 2. Once she was spiritually unblocked in her interior world, Etty Hillesum could move forward and prepare to meet the Other eye to eye in the external world. She could move ahead with "forming the fellow man." She is self-formed and, in exchange, she wants to form her fellow (wo)man. She is convinced that people create their own destiny (their *Schicksal*) from the inside. The situations and circumstances in which they fare are given; a human is a man, a woman, a father, mother, young, old, prisoner or prison guard, "it doesn't make that much of a difference, one is surrounded by the same walls."
In modern jargon one could say that economic, legal, political, and social behaviours are regulated and structured by man-made institutions (associations, unions, parties, etc.). These groupings surround us with the same walls as Hillesum noticed. She posits enthusiastically:

> How rash to assert that man shapes his own destiny. All he can do is determine his inner responses. You cannot know another's inner life from his circumstances. To know that you must know his dreams, his relationships, his moods, his disappointments, his sickness and his death.[9]

Hillesum does not doubt that "we truly shape our fate from within."[10] She gives an example:

> Very early on Wednesday morning a large group of us were crowded into a classroom of the Gestapo, and at that moment the circumstances of all our lives were the same. All of us occupied the same space, the men behind the desk no less than those about to be questioned. What distinguished each one of us was only our inner attitudes.[11]

8 E.T., 254. *Het Werk*, 263; Sunday evening, 22 February 1942: Het moet zo worden, dat men steeds paraat is om vormend de medemens tegemoet te treden en hoe gevormder men zelf wordt, des te meer zal dat lukken..

9 E.T., 258. *Het Werk*, 268; Friday morning, 27 February 1942: Men kent iemands leven niet, als men de uiterlijke feiten kent. De uiterlijke feiten, ach, ze verschillen niet zo erg in ieders leven. Om iemands leven te kennen moet men z'n dromen kennen, z'n stemmingen, weten, wat voor verhouding er bestaat tussen hem en z'n vrouw en z'n dood en z'n teleurstellingen en z'n ziekten.

10 E.T., 254. *Het Werk*, 264; Wednesday, 25 February 1942: Eigenlijk schept een mens toch z'n lot van binnen uit.

11 E.T., 258. *Het Werk*, 268; Friday morning, 27 February 1942: We stonden daar met een grote groep in dat lokaal bij de Gestapo Woensdagochtend in alle vroegte en de feiten van alle levens

She noticed a young Gestapo man with a sullen expression, pacing up and down and making no attempt to hide his irritation. He kept looking for pretexts to shout at the helpless Jews. When it was Hillesum's turn to stand in front of his desk, he bawled at her, "What the hell's so funny?" His face was saying, "I'll deal with you later," which was presumably meant to scare her, but the manoeuvre was too transparent.

> And that was the real import of this morning: not that a disgruntled young Gestapo boy yelled at me, but that I felt no indignation, rather a real compassion, and would have liked to ask, "Did you have a very unhappy childhood, has your girlfriend let you down?" Yet, he looked harassed and driven, sullen and weak. I should have liked to start treating him there and then, for I know that these young men are merely pitiful as long as they cannot do harm, but that they become mortally dangerous and must be eradicated when they are turned loose on humanity. Yet only the system that uses such people is criminal, not these fellows.[12]

The reason that Hillesum grants priority to the Other is that the system is no good and the times are unfathomable. Thus, her attempt to come to life and to gauge suffering is essential. There was a moment when she interpreted the tenor of the times from human faces, from a thousand gestures, or small changes of expression and life stories. She had learned to perceive herself and then noticed that she could also perceive others. She wanted to know the century, "this century of ours," inside and out.

She recalled the two weeks in August 1942 that she had spent in transit camp Westerbork. Suddenly, she got an idea of what she could make of life. That was because she was suddenly flung into one of many flashpoints of human suffering. In the faces of people, in thousands of gestures, small

waren dezelfde op dat ogenblik: we waren allemaal in dezelfde ruimte, de mannen achter de lessenaar even goed als de ondervraagden. Wat ieders leven bepaalde, was hoe men er innerlijk tegenover stond.

12 E.T., 259 [revised]. *Het Werk*, 269-270; Friday morning, 27 February 1942: En dàt was het historische in deze ochtend: niet, dat ik door een ongelukkige Gestapo-jongen werd aangeschreeuwd. Ik had misschien verontwaardigd of bang moeten zijn, maar het belangrijke van die ochtend lijkt me daarin te liggen, dat ik een oprecht medelijden met die jongen had, dat ik hem het liefst gevraagd had: heb je zo een ongelukkige jeugd gehad of heeft je meisje je bedrogen? Hij zag er gekweld en opgejaagd – overigens ook heel onaangenaam en slap – uit. Ik had het liefst direct met een psychologische behandeling begonnen. Me er zeer sterk van bewust zijnde, dat deze jongens beklagenswaardig zijn, zolang ze geen kwaad kunnen, maar levensgevaarlijk en uitgeroeid moetende worden, als ze op de mensheid loskomen. Maar misdadig is alleen het systeem, dat deze kerels gebruikt.—

changes of expression, life stories, she was able suddenly to read her age – and also to fathom much more than just her age:

> And then it happened: I was suddenly able to read our age and feel the contours of these times with my fingertips [...]. How is it that this stretch of heathland surrounded by barbed wire, through which so much human misery had flooded, nevertheless remains inscribed in my memory as something almost lovely?[13]

The manner in which Hillesum approached the Other, her fellow wo/man, can be described more precisely. Her approach is inherent to Jewish identity and stands on the horizon of Jewish thought, seen particularly in the work of Emmanuel Levinas (1906-1995). This Lithuanian-French thinker distanced himself from ontology or the nature of being. According to Levinas, ontology did not correctly represent the truthfulness of events and it bypassed the experience of the Other. Levinas created the allegory: The Other shows himself and looks at me. Even before he speaks one word, his face speaks to me. He exposes himself. His face and his eyes are completely exposed: *naked*. More than his own awkwardness, he exposes my narcissism and the monopoly that I have appropriated. Like a dominant tree, I deprived myself of air and light. His eyes scan me and compel me to take him into my home and world. He who was a stranger, becomes a guest and settles in with me.

Levinas' thinking about moral status is characterized by the belief that living creatures must conform to this moral status as if to a commandment. That is, they must reject every form of dominance and totalitarianism. In front of and looked at through the visage of the Other, everything becomes different. Hence, we return to Hillesum's bellowing Gestapo boy.

> He represents violence and tyranny, phenomena characterized by the fact that he (as a symbol of the Gestapo) did not observe those to whom he related. Indeed, the Nazis generally didn't even see faces, only a counterforce and wild freedom that needed to be restrained, or worse. Concern, compassion, and empathy are estranged from this attitude. Yet

13 E.T., 526. *Het Werk*, 557-558; Tuesday, 22 September 1942: Het is me daar werkelijk geweest, alsof ik met gevoelige vingertoppen getast heb langs de contouren van deze tijd en van het leven. Hoe komt het toch, dat dat met prikkeldraad omrasterde stukje heidegrond, waar zoveel mensenlot en -lijden áán- en dóórspoelde, als bijna liefelijk in m'n herinnering is achtergebleven?

these are exactly the sources of Etty Hillesum's resilience – "je suis celui qui se trouve des ressources pour répondre à l'appel."[14]

Ad 3. It appears that being open to the Other characterizes Hillesum's Jewish way of thinking. It embodies living a life with God. According to Levinas, this basic ethical attitude is of the essence in the Hebrew Bible. Levinas warned against the absolutist aspirations of philosophy that expounds ideas and thinks in terms of systems without being sensitive to, or even losing contact with, human reality. Levinas opposed exclusivism in philosophy, notably that of Heidegger and his existential philosophy. Levinas's route brings him from ontology to ethics, a journey from "l'Être" to "l'Autre", or to social justice.[15] He recalls the spirit of the Hebrew Bible visible in the lives of Moses and the prophets. They are concerned with the plight of the poor, the widow, the orphan, and the refugee; they are not interested in the immortality of the soul. That is more closely associated with the Greeks.

Levinas does not hesitate to say that *atheism* is liberation from the mythical powers of primitive and Greek gods. For Levinas, those gods were limited in their powers, as opposed to the Creator who grants men and women freedom to engage as creators themselves. The primitive and Greek gods don't speak to man and woman on a personal level with the explicit question: *Adam, where are you? Eve, where are you?*

But Etty Hillesum was conscious of God asking this question, issuing this calling (*Inanspruchnahme*); she felt an appeal, was called and proved herself to be prepared. Abraham Joshua Heschel (1907-1972), a Polish-born Jewish theologian, clarifies Levinas's above-mentioned position and makes a meaningful distinction. Heschel wrote that the Bible does not contain a *human/ anthropological theology* – God is not considered from a human viewpoint. Heschel's view was that the Bible contained a *divine/theological anthropology.*

> The Bible does not portray God from a human perspective, but humans from God's perspective; or expressed differently: the Bible provides us with a language in which we can seriously consider the awareness of being called to an assignment; with our feeling that something has to happen in us and in our world.[16]

14 Cf. Emmanuel Lévinas, *Éthique et Infini: Dialogues avec Philippe Nemo* (Paris: Fayard Biblio essais, 1982), 83.

15 Cf. Joëlle Hansel, "Autrement que Heidegger; Levinas et l'ontologie à la française," in: *Levinas de l'Être à l'Autre: Sous la coordination de Joëlle Hansel* (Paris: PUF, 2006), 37-53.

16 Tom de Bruin (ed.), *Adam waar ben je? De betekenis van het mensbeeld in de joodse traditie en in de psycho-therapie* (Hilversum: B. Folkertsma Stichting voor Talmudica, 1983), 111 [own translation].

Etty Hillesum felt the same. She reflected upon herself from God's perspective – her own theological anthropology. She felt that something had to happen within and outside her own being, in the world. She felt she could deal with whatever came up, and repeats her insight:

> My life is increasingly an inner one, and the outer setting matters less and less. Hardy as distinct from hard.[17]

Her circumstances, however, put her in a state of anxiety, due to changes in the fate of the Amsterdam Jews whose removal from the city had been stopped for the time being. The Nazis had begun to concentrate on eradicating the Rotterdam Jews. She prayed to God for her people about to be deported: "Help them, oh God, help the Rotterdam Jews."[18]

She is determined and knows what to do. Sounding combative and resilient, she writes, "Then I knew: I should take the field against hatred." She predicts for the coming years, "two torrents will be unleashed on the world: a torrent of loving-kindness and a torrent of hate."[19] Call it her binary worldview. It has two sides, two torrents: humanism equals good and hatred equals bad. But indiscriminate hatred, as she underscored earlier, is the worst thing there is. It is a sickness of the soul.

Although she almost never explicitly wrote about humanism, it is surely implicit in her diaries and letters. Hillesum wrote, for example, that by reducing hatred one shines forth and increases humanism, read: the *humanum.* In regard to this, she was also certainly referring to hatred in oneself. The terms that she used remind us of the Sermon on the Plain in the Gospel of Luke as follows: "Love your enemies, do good to those who hate you" (Luke 6:27). Hillesum, too, pleaded that we should love our enemies.

Klaas Smelik Jr., using the same example of the Gestapo boy, has indicated that Etty Hillesum transcended adversarial thought.[20] Smelik pauses at this somewhat violent episode. He notes that Hillesum refused to participate

17 E.T., 512. *Het Werk*, 542; Tuesday evening, 28 July 1942: Omdat het een leven is, dat in de innerlijke gebieden zich voltrekt en het decor doet er dan steeds minder toe. Gehard: goed te onderscheiden van verhard.—

18 E.T., 513. *Het Werk*, 543; Wednesday morning, 29 July 1942: Het schijnt, dat de transporten voorlopig in Amsterdam stopgezet zijn. Men begint nu in Rotterdam. Sta ze bij, mijn God, de Rotterdamse Joden, sta ze bij.

19 E.T., 526. *Het Werk*, 556-557; Sunday night, 20 September 1942: 'Na deze oorlog zal er, behalve een stroom van humanisme, ook een stroom van haat over de wereld gaan.'

20 Klaas A.D. Smelik, "Voorbij het vijanddenken: De visie van Etty Hillesum geplaatst in een Bijbels kader", in: Klaas A.D. Smelik, Ria van den Brandt & Meins G.S. Coetsier (eds.), *Etty Hillesum in perspectief* [Etty Hillesum Studies, 4] (Gent: Academia Press 2012), especially pp. 130-131.

in a scenario where the Gestapo tried to impress and scare the Jews. She rejected the simple division of roles into friend or enemy. She did not hate the Gestapo boy but had compassion for him: hatred did not lie in her nature. In general, she was forceful in her view that "[...] each of us must turn inward and destroy in himself all that he thinks he ought to destroy in others." For Hillesum, the task was to stop hating the so-called enemies.[21]

Throwing oneself into the breach for a humanum in distress

Let's return to the concept of humanism as outlined in *The Oxford Companion to Philosophy*.[22] Clearly, this concept has different connotations. In general, it denotes the tendency to study humans as such (*studia humanitatis*, an offspring of early Greek thought). Additionally, it expresses some of the attributes of human persons – e.g. their rationality and scientific abilities. In the wake of Darwin's conflict with a fundamentalist reading of the Bible, humanism acquired its modern association with atheism or agnosticism, and this happened centuries after the Renaissance had moved away from the premise of a personal God toward a placement of man at the centre of the universe. Humanism advocates a worldview that elevates dignity, freedom, and the value of the human personality. It boils down to eagerly helping people make use of their highest emotional and intellectual capacities, departing from the fundamental question, "How do we make more people more human?" and moving to ask, "How do we make a morally elevated, civilized human person?"[23] The word "moral" (from the Latin *mores*, behaviour, habit, morals; *èthos* in Greek) brings us again to ethics.

21 E.T., 18. *Het Werk*, 19; Saturday, 15 March 1941. Cf. E.T., 529. *Het Werk*, 560; Wednesday, 23 September 1942. She conveys her strong conviction to Klaas Smelik Senior, "that we shouldn't even be thinking of hating our so-called enemies. We are hurtful enough to one another as it is." She claims not to believe in what people call "bad guys."

22 Ted Honderich (ed.), *The Oxford Companion to Philosophy* (Oxford/New York: Oxford University Press, 1995), 375-376.

23 Cf. Bert Gasenbeek (ed.), *Vrijdenken & humanisme in Nederland: 40 plekken van herinnering* (Bussum: Thoth, 2016), 9, 25. The author distinguishes three central themes in humanism: 1. A critical and self-conscious reflection with regard to religious authority and dogmatic thought processes. 2. The moral and political effort for social justice, resistance to fascist and intolerant powers, opposition to military force and in favour of open dialogue. 3. A clear ideal for advancement, development, and education (*Bildung*) of the individual. Freethinkers on the stage in the book in question include Agricola, Pierre Bayle, Boniface, Coornhert, Domela Nieuwenhuis, Aletta Jacobs, Multatuli, Henriette Roland Holst, Benedictus de Spinoza, Joke Smit, and Belle van Zuylen. Etty Hillesum would also have fitted well among them.

But what then is ethics? Actually, various descriptions exist. I have three in mind: ethics is the teaching of the difference between good and evil; it concerns responsible action; and it is the contemplation of the actual reality of being human. Hillesum seemed familiar with these three considerations, but in essence, biblical humanism was her credo.

Etty Hillesum abhorred hate and was a convinced advocate for the *humanum*, for the communal, worldwide "We". To begin with, she wanted to stand on the front line alongside suffering humanity. Moreover, she wanted to travel "through all the world" to achieve this.[22]

> One day, I would love to travel through all the world, oh God; I feel drawn right across all frontiers and feel a bond with all Your warring creatures [...]. And I would like to proclaim that bond in a small, still voice but also compellingly and without pause. But first I must be present on every battlefront and at the centre of all human suffering. Then I will surely have the right to speak out?[24]

Conclusion

Philosophers have thought and continue to think about Being, existence and *In-der-Welt-Sein*.[25] Frequently, human beings find themselves wandering on paths that lead nowhere or on paths where human beings lose themselves. That is what Heidegger wrote in his collection of essays *Holzwege* [Woodways]. With this title, he was getting at the winding roads without destination in the woods of our existence. In his dissertation on Heidegger, Jacob van Sluis explains the core inspiration of Heidegger's essay volume:

> Wood is an old word for forest. In the woods are paths, mostly overgrown, that suddenly end in an impasse. They are called "Holzwege". Each path runs separately, but in the same woods. Frequently, it appears that they are all alike. However, appearances deceive. Lumberjacks and foresters know the paths. They know what it is *auf einem Holzwege zu sein*.[26]

24 E.T., 531. *Het Werk*, 563; Thursday, 24 September 1942. Later wil ik gaan reizen door de verschillende landen van jouw wereld, mijn God, ik voel die trek in me, die over alle grenzen gaat en die in al jouw verschillende en elkaar bevechtende schepselen over de gehele aarde toch iets gemeenschappelijks ontdekt. En over dit gemeenschappelijke zou ik willen spreken, met een heel klein en zacht stemmetje, maar ononderbroken en overtuigend.

25 Thurnherr & Hügli, *Lexikon*, lemma "In-der-Welt-Sein", 133-135.

26 Jacob van Sluis, *Heidegger: Denkwegen en dwaalwegen* [Thesis, Groningen University] (Best: Damon, 1997), 108.

It is tempting to approach Etty Hillesum's winding paths in the dark woods of the Second World War from a philosophical standpoint. Is it not more appropriate, however, to typify her life as Being-in-Creation?

In the first place she is grateful to know that she is placed before the countenance of God (*coram Deo*):

> How can I thank You, oh God, for all the good You keep showering upon me. For all the friendship, for the many fruitful thoughts, for that great all-embracing love I feel within me and that I am able to apply at every step. Sometimes I almost believe that it is too much, and then I cannot tell how I shall ever do justice to it. But it is just as if, thanks to that great love, everything one does bears fruit. Perhaps I shall yet be able to put it into words.[27]

And secondly, she commits herself to other creatures and to learning their needs:

> How great are the needs of Your creatures on this earth, oh God. I thank You for letting so many people come to me with their inner needs. They sit there, talking quietly and quite unsuspectingly, and suddenly their need erupts in all its nakedness. Then, there they are, bundles of human misery, desperate and unable to face life.[28]

Etty Hillesum considered herself to be one of the many heirs of a great spiritual heritage and vowed to be "its faithful guardian".[29] She strove to be faithful in the most comprehensive sense: faithful to herself, to God, faithful to her own best moments. Her "doing" would consist of "being". This

27 E.T., 521-522. *Het Werk*, 552; Sunday morning, 20 September 1942: Hoe moet ik je danken, mijn God, voor al het goede dat je me doet toevloeien, ononderbroken. Voor alle vriendschap, voor de vele vruchtbare gedachten, voor dat grote gevoel van liefde, dat er in me is en die ik op iedere stap kan omzetten, voor alles. Soms geloof ik haast, dat het te veel is, dan weet ik niet, hoe ik dat alles goed moet maken. Maar het is net of door die grote liefde alles wat je doet vruchtbaar wordt, misschien zal ik het nog eens kunnen uitdrukken.

28 E.T., 519. *Het Werk*, 549; Thursday morning, 17 September 1942: Wat is de innerlijke nood van jouw schepselen op deze aarde groot, mijn God. Ik dank je ervoor, dat je zoveel mensen met hun innerlijke noden naar mij toe laat komen. Ze zitten rustig en argeloos met me te praten en opeens breekt het dan naakt naar buiten, hun nood. En opeens zit daar dan een stukje mens dat wanhopig is en niet weet hoe te moeten leven. See also E.T., 531. *Het Werk*, 562; Thursday, 24 September 1942. Hillesum refers to all of suffering mankind's nocturnal distress and loneliness passing through her small heart.

29 E.T., 521. *Het Werk*, 551; Friday morning, 18 September 1942: de trouwe behoedster zijn.

sentence has the character of a short statement of faith, a statement of faith that was doable. She also wanted to be faithful to her creative talent, which she hoped would increase. Sometimes "an almost diabolic presumption" seized her; however, she understood why:

> I know how to free my creative powers more and more from the snares of material concerns, from the idea of hunger and cold and danger. These are imaginary phantoms not the reality. Reality is something one shoulders together with all the suffering [...]. And as one shoulders them, so one's resilience grows stronger.[30]

Hillesum's "Being-in-Creation" is apparent in the way she used her power in order to assist God. "I promise You to live as fully as I can wherever it should please You to put me."[31] Here she also displays the constancy of her Jewish identity. G'd is the Faithful One, the G'd of the Covenant with humans, G'd's humanism, Biblical humanism. In turn, Hillesum wants to be a faithful human being, a *chassid* throwing herself into the breach for the *humanum*.

The years in which she lived were irrefutably hard times, but Hillesum was certain that better days would come. She wrote on 20 July 1942:

> Oh God, times are too hard for frail people like myself. I know that a new and kinder day will come. I would so much like to live on, if only to express all the love I carry within me; carry into that new age all the humanity that survives in me, despite everything I grow through every day.[32]

30 E.T., 536-537. *Het Werk*, 568-569; Wednesday, 30 September 1942: Ik weet ook hoe het komt: àl m'n scheppende krachten – ik dank je mijn God, dat je er mij zovele gegeven hebt – zijn intact en ongerept bij me. Ik weet ze steeds weer te ontroven aan de klauwen van de dagelijkse zorgen en angsten, ik weet ze steeds minder de gevangenen te doen zijn van de materiële noden van de voorstelling van honger en kou en gevaren. Het is toch immers steeds de voorstelling en niet de realiteit. De realiteit is iets, wat men op zich moet nemen, al het lijden, dat er bij komt, al de moeilijkheden, men moet ze op zich nemen en dragen, al dragende vergroot de draagkracht.

31 E.T., 538. *Het Werk*, 570; Friday morning, 2 October 1942. Ik beloof je, ik zal leven volgens m'n beste scheppende krachten op iedere plek.

32 E.T., 497. *Het Werk*, 526; Monday evening, 20 July 1942: Mijn God, dit tijdperk is te hard voor broze mensen als ik ben. Ik weet ook, dat er hierna weer een ander tijdperk komen zal, dat humanistisch zijn zal. Ik wil zo graag blijven leven om al de menselijkheid, die ik in me bewaar, ondanks alles, wat ik dagelijks meemaak, over te dragen in dat nieuwe tijdperk. Dat is ook het enige, waardoor wij de nieuwe tijd kunnen voorbereiden, door haar nu al in ons voor te bereiden. [...] Ik wil zo graag blijven leven om de nieuwe tijd te helpen voorbereiden en om dat onverwoestbare in mij behouden over te dragen naar de nieuwe tijd, die zeker zal komen, ze

Her "Being in Creation" is a kind of *co-creatio* and anticipates liberating and salvific work. It is the central theme of modern feminist creation theology. God's transcendence does not stand alone, writes the German liberation theologian, Dorothee Sölle (1929-2003), nor is it akin to an otherworldly Creator. This transcendence, found in an ordinary life, takes place in the praxis of a human being who, as a co-creator, helps G'd's peace and justice blossom and grow in the world.[33]

About the Author

Jurjen Wiersma (1943) studied theology at the University of Amsterdam and at the Chicago Theological Seminary. Dr. theol., Amsterdam 1981. He is Professor emeritus of Ethics and Philosophy at the Protestant Theological Faculty in Brussels, Belgium, and Member of the International Bonhoeffer Society, Dutch Section. Recent publications include *Bevrijdingstheologie actueel* [Current liberation theology] (Antwerpen/Apeldoorn: Garant, 2016). He contributes regularly to the series *Etty Hillesum Studies*.

groeit immers al in mij, iedere dag, ik voel het toch? She wants to be superior in "loving-kindness", חֶסֶד / chèsed in Hebrew.

33 Dorothee Sölle, *Gott Denken: Einführung in die Theologie* (Stuttgart: Kreuz Verlag, 1990), 72. Cf. Jurjen Wiersma, "Chipping away the ice that surrounds the soul: Etty Hillesum and Dorothee Sölle", in: Klaas A.D. Smelik, Meins G.S. Coetsier & Jurjen Wiersma (eds.), *The Ethics and Religious Philosophy of Etty Hillesum: Proceedings of the Etty Hillesum Conference at Ghent University, January 2014* [Supplements to The Journal of Jewish Thought and Philosophy, 28] (Leiden/Boston, MA: Brill, 2017), 221-232.

Etty Hillesum's Struggle to See Clearly

A Story of Two Worlds

Patrick Woodhouse

Abstract

This contribution explores the question: how could it be possible to go on trying to see the Nazis as human beings created in the Image of God? It begins with Etty Hillesum gazing at the brutal faces of the guards loading the train destined for the death camps, and explores her reaction to what she sees and how her reaction is a statement of what she has become. The essay then traces how, in the midst of a world collapsing all around her, Etty Hillesum learns to inhabit another inner world which saves her, and which shares characteristics common to the contemplative traditions of all the great faiths. The contribution is a reminder that her story is a story not of one, but of two worlds.

Keywords: description of Nazism by Etty Hillesum, inner world of Etty Hillesum, contemplative practices, metaphors used by Etty Hillesum, silence, prayer, kneeling.

I want to begin with an excerpt from the letter Etty Hillesum wrote to her friends in Amsterdam just two weeks before she went on the train to Auschwitz in which she describes the faces of the guards who are loading the train.

> When I think of the faces of that squad of armed, green-uniformed guards – my God, those faces! I looked at them, each in turn, from behind the safety of a window, and I have never been so frightened of anything in my life. I sank to my knees with the words that preside over human life:

Smelik, Klaas A.D. (ed.), *The Lasting Significance of Etty Hillesum's Writings: Proceedings of the Third International Etty Hillesum Conference at Middelburg, September 2018.*
Taylor & Francis Group 2019
DOI: 10.5117/9789463722025_WOODHOUSE

> "And God made man after His likeness." That passage spent a difficult morning with me.[1]

Within the limits of this contribution, I want to reflect on these words, and more importantly, what lay behind them. And in the process, I hope that we can glimpse something of the inner "feel" of her experience.

This passage comes at the beginning of the long letter of 24 August 1943. It is her greatest contribution to the literature of the Holocaust. In this letter, she uses one of her greatest gifts, the ability to write, so fulfilling one part of her vocation, to *see* what was happening in all its unvarnished awfulness and to record it. From behind the safety of a window just across from the platform where the train was standing, she looks, she gazes, she seeks to *see.*

"I looked at them," she writes, ... these guards ... "each in turn." It is a particular kind of looking ...: slow, painstaking, deliberate, a looking in which she is searching, searching for something that is hidden, something that she believes must be there in a human face – or at least faint signs of it. Perhaps a trace of sensitivity, or of humanity, or simply *any* kind of human feeling. She is searching for glimpses of what in the Judaeo-Christian tradition is called "the image", or "likeness", of God. She searches for it, but she cannot see it.

What she sees, terrifies her. It is the Nazi "Final Solution" in operation. Old people, sick people, hungry people, children, infants, being bundled like so much disposable rubbish into cattle wagons to be taken to their death. But it is not the system of death that shocks her. It is the faces of those carrying it out in all their dehumanized brutality. Etty Hillesum always tended to see through a personal lens. In the period of her diaries, she was not interested in political systems which she saw as "growing too big for men and holding them in a satanic grip, the builders no less than the victims."[2] It was the individuals caught up in those systems that mattered. So she concentrates on the individuals carrying out the orders. "My God,

1 E.T., 644. *Het Werk*, 686; Letter 64, To Han Wegerif and others; Westerbork, Tuesday, 24 August 1943: Als ik denk aan die gezichten van het groengeüniformeerde, gewapende begeleidingspeloton, mijn God, die gezichten! Ik heb ze stuk voor stuk bekeken, verdekt opgesteld achter een venster, ik ben nog nooit van iets zo geschrokken als van deze gezichten. Ik ben in de knoei geraakt met het woord, dat het leidmotief van mijn leven is: En God schiep de mens naar Zijn Evenbeeld. Dat woord beleefde een moeilijke ochtend met mij.

2 E.T., 259. *Het Werk*, 269; Friday morning, 27 February 1942: Het angstaanjagende is, dat systemen boven mensen uitgroeien en mensen in een satanische greep houden, ontwerpers zowel als slachtoffers van dat systeem [...].

those faces," she writes, "[...] I have never been so terrified of anything in my life." It is a moment of real shock.

What I want to explore, is how this young woman reacts to this shock, and how her reaction defines who she has become.

But first, let us reflect for a moment on how you or I might have reacted in such a situation. It is very hard to imagine but in the face of such a sight, such a shock, I guess we might well have fled in terror, or perhaps we might have surrendered to this hatred with a responding hatred, maybe mouthing some expletive at these brutes, or at the system that has dehumanized them and of which they are merely the instruments. Flight or fight. It is the normal human reaction in the face of such shock and threat. Etty Hillesum reacts in neither of these ways.

What does she do? She sinks to her knees. She adopts the posture that has become her defining reference point. "I sank to my knees," she writes, "with the words that preside over human life, 'and God made man after His likeness'." In this moment of acute shock, her mind grasps at, and gives voice to, the creed that over the months, with extraordinary rapidity has taken shape within her and has *reshaped* her mind. Though in this particular moment it is undergoing its severest challenge… "that passage spent a difficult morning with me."

When I wrote my little book about her, I called it *Etty Hillesum: A Life Transformed*[3] because it seemed to me that more important than her life being "interrupted" was the fact that in the brief time that we know her through her diaries, her life fundamentally changed. It was about "transformation" much more than it was about "interruption". These words capture this transformation and define who she has become. *Someone whose consciousness was reshaped by a religious practice.*

There is no space to elaborate on this in great depth, but over the last few months I have reread every word of the diaries seeking to chart the development of her faith experience.

Now I like to think that I am familiar with the writings of Etty Hillesum, but to read her diary again with this single-minded focus was, I found, freshly astonishing, for – to put it simply – I realized in a way that I had not seen so clearly before that her story is a tale of two fundamentally contradictory worlds, with the old world of violence and terror with all its power to destroy, being radically subverted by the frighteningly rapid emergence (and it was frightening to her) of a new one. As the violence and terror increased, and the outer architecture and infrastructure of people's lives – both the physical

3 Patrick Woodhouse, *Etty Hillesum: A Life Transformed* (London, etc.: Bloomsbury, 2009).

infrastructure and the psychological infrastructure – at first gradually, and then rapidly disintegrated, with all the terrible suffering that this involved, she dealt with it by at first occasionally, and then increasingly habitually, resorting to another world, to another dimension, to another universe of meaning which became, to quote the Psalms, a "refuge" and "a hiding place" from the chaos and sufferings of the everyday realities of the world that was collapsing all around her.

In the midst of the chaos, it was a journey into a different kind of meaning, into a totally contrasting dimension, which she learned to inhabit, to dwell in, to remain in.

In the limited space available, what I want to do is point to just a few of the many milestones on that journey, and then touch on the nature of her experience as she describes it herself.

On Sunday morning, 8 June 1941, she writes about meditation for the first time, the practice of turning "one's innermost being into a vast empty plain, with none of that treacherous undergrowth to impede the view. So that something of 'God'" – and she puts this tricky questionable word in inverted commas – "can enter you [...]."[4]

The next day, she tells herself she will ask Spier about meditation – *how* to do it? – and wanting this experience for herself, she determines that she will ask him, "can I learn to do it too?"[5]

Six months later, in December, she asks him about words in prayer: "what exactly" she innocently inquires "do you *say*?"[6]

On a Tuesday evening in August 1941, she gives us an image of a well that gets blocked as a metaphor for the human heart that gets cut off from God, and she declares resolutely, "Then He must be dug out [...]."[7]

A few days later, under the influence of Jung, she writes for the first time about the practice of inner listening.[8] It becomes a constant deepening theme throughout her writing and central to her emerging spiritual practice. Later, she captures this in the evocative German word "*hineinhorchen*" through which she seeks to express the full dimensions of this practice of listening, or "hearkening". "Truly," she writes, "my life is one long hearkening unto myself and unto others, unto God. And if I say that I hearken, it is really God who hearkens inside me. The most essential and deepest in me

4 E.T., 57. *Het Werk*, 60; Sunday morning, 8 June 1941: Dat er dus iets van "God" in je komt.

5 E.T., 59. *Het Werk*, 62; Monday morning, 9 June 1941: Kan ik dat ook leren?

6 E.T., 181. *Het Werk*, 190; Sunday morning, 14 December 1941: Was beten Sie denn?

7 E.T., 91. *Het Werk*, 97; Tuesday evening, 26 August 1941: Dan moet hij weer opgegraven worden.

8 E.T., 94. *Het Werk*, 100; Friday morning, 5 September 1941.

hearkening unto the most essential and the deepest in the other. God to God."[9]

In late September, there is a key moment. For the first time, she describes being overwhelmed by the need to kneel.[10] "I suddenly found myself kneeling on the brown coconut matting in the bathroom," she writes, and she goes on to reflect on the embarrassment of this distinctly un-Jewish practice which flies in the face of the "rational atheistic" bit of her. But the pressing urgency of it cannot be ignored for she discovers this is far deeper than any rationality. As the terror increases, this kneeling down becomes regular, habitual, urgent; there are something like seventeen references to it.

And then on a Sunday morning in early October, she rehearses key elements of her evolving practice. At the top of her list are the fundamental ingredients of any contemplative life: silence, an undistracted focus, and stillness. "Do not speak," she writes, "do not listen to the outside world, [...] be perfectly still."[11]

In late November, she tells us how, in this journey into a different kind of meaning, this journey of learning to pray, key teachings of her Jewish tradition have their place. "I have recently been picking odd sentences from the Bible and endowing them with what for me is a new, meaningful and experiential significance. God created man in his own image, Love thy neighbour as thyself."[12] But with her, these phrases are not just doctrines to be believed with the mind, they are *matters of the heart*, they have "*experiential* significance". Later, there are increasing references to her reading from the Psalms.

And then, she recognizes that if these elements of a contemplative practice which seem to offer glimpses into this "other world" are to have any potency, they require the development of a "technique", a practice that you improve *with* practice, or to use the technical word for sharpening something, you "hone". "When grace," she writes on a Friday morning in December, "makes one of its rare entrances, it must be greeted with a

9 E.T., 519. *Het Werk*, 549; Thursday morning, 17 September 1942: Eigenlijk is mijn leven één voortdurend "hineinhorchen", in mijzelf, in anderen, in God. En als ik zeg: ìk "horch hinein", dan is het eigenlijk God in mij, die "hineinhorcht". Het wezenlijkste en diepste in mij dat luistert naar het wezenlijkste en diepste in de ander. God tot God.

10 E.T., 103. *Het Werk*, 109; Wednesday morning, 24 September 1941: [...] vond ik mezelf plotseling geknield op de bruine cocosmat in de badkamer [...].

11 E.T., 122. *Het Werk*, 129; Sunday morning, 5 October 1941: niet spreken, niet luisteren naar buiten, maar helemaal stil zijn [...].

12 E.T., 157. *Het Werk*, 165; Friday morning, 28 November 1941: Ik heb het de laatste tijd dat af en toe een enkele zin uit de Bijbel voor me oplicht in een duidelijke, nieuwe, inhoudsrijke en doorleefde betekenis. God schiep de mens naar z'n Evenbeeld – Heb Uw naasten lief als U zelve.

well-honed technique."[13] And the honing of her "technique" leads her ever deeper. On Monday, 29 December 1941 at the end of the first crucial year of her developing spirituality, she writes of becoming "more and more conscious" – today we might say "mindful" – and of "dwelling more deeply within", and so – very significantly – she writes, "I am becoming more and more divorced from the chaos [...]." This is a crucial phrase for it captures the essence of what her practice is doing. *It is mentally separating her from the worst horrors of the terror.* Her mind is bifurcating, dividing, separating. *Two* worlds are emerging.

And then crucially at the heart of this "dwelling more deeply within", she finds she enters not a great emptiness, but rather there is a meeting, a relationship, some kind of mysterious knowing of Another, a knowing that is profoundly nourishing. And here, the essentially Jewish character of her experience shines through. On a Saturday morning in May 1942, in one of the most beautiful evocations of what her practice means, she writes of how in the midst of the barbarity, of "the mounting human suffering [...] the persecution and oppression and despotism and the impotent fury and the terrible sadism", in the midst of all this mayhem and hell, she feels safe and calmed, as "in unguarded moments" she lies "against the naked breast of life with her arms around me so gentle and so protective [...]."[14] There are clear echoes here of Psalm 131 where the psalmist speaks of being "like a weaned child lying on its mother's breast, so my soul is quieted within me."[15]

But as well as being "protective", she realizes paradoxically that this Divine Other whom she has come to know as she "dwells within", is vulnerable, is in need of protection, has to be looked after, can so easily disappear. His/Her dwelling place must be guarded *within* – so much more important, she writes, than guarding silver forks and spoons or vacuum cleaners.[16]

I could have quoted dozens of others but these are just some of the milestones, just a very few of the huge number of references to an emerging, constantly being "honed" practice which opened the door into another world – which felt like what? Can we glimpse from what she writes, something of the nature of her experience, its resonance, its inner *feel*?

Again not enough space to explore it in detail, but let me identify just some elements.

13 E.T., 190. *Het Werk*, 199; Friday morning, 19 December 1941: De genade moet bij haar schaarse komsten een welvoorbereide techniek aantreffen.

14 E.T., 386. *Het Werk*, 405; Sunday morning: tegen de naakte borst van het leven en haar armen zijn zo zacht en zo beschuttend om me heen [...].

15 Psalm 131:3.

16 E.T., 488-489. *Het Werk*, 517; Sunday morning prayer, 12 July 1942.

First, it opens up within her a sense of huge spaciousness. The metaphor of spaciousness abounds. "That one should carry such an awe-inspiring space in oneself!" she exclaims on 29 December 1941.[17] Seven days later, on 5 January 1942, she writes that when the chaos and the darkness overwhelm, "as if your inner light switch has been turned off", the practice of kneeling down restores "the spacious dimensions [...]."[18] On 4 June 1942, she writes of clearing again a "wide undivided space" in herself.[19] Frequently, the metaphor of retreating to an inner room is used as a way of evoking this inner spaciousness. "Now I carry this quiet room inside me," she writes on 9 January, "and I can escape into it at any moment."[20] And the quiet "inner room" has extensive walls. When she fears the coming of the call-up card to Camp Westerbork, she imagines what she will take, but photographs of those she loves will not be necessary, for "I'll just take all the faces and familiar gestures I have collected and hang them up along the walls of my inner space so that they will always be with me."[21] And early on 21 June 1942, the diary entry begins with a paragraph on spaciousness in which she describes "an almost tangible feeling [...] as if there were all sorts of spaces and distances locked up inside me," and she ends by declaring "that spatial feeling within me is very strong."[22]

In his little book *Into the Silent Land*, which is probably the best contemporary book in English that there is on the practice of contemplation, the Augustinian Friar Martin Laird speaks of a sense of "spaciousness" as being a distinctive hallmark of authentic spirituality. As he struggles to put into words what is beyond words, Laird says that in the deepest moments of silent meditation, "something of the groundless ground of God washes onto the shores of perception and registers as spaciousness, luminous vastness, a sense of the unity of all things, a sense of everything manifesting vastness."[23]

This, it seems, is what Etty Hillesum also knew.

17 E.T., 204. *Het Werk*, 214; Monday morning, 29 December 1941: Dat men een dergelijke ontzagwekkende ruimte in zich heeft [...].

18 E.T., 216. *Het Werk*, 225; Monday morning, 5 January 1942: haar wijdheid [...].

19 E.T., 391. *Het Werk*, 410; Thursday morning, 4 June 1942: ongedeelde wijde ruimte [...].

20 E.T., 224. *Het Werk*, 233; Friday, 9 January 1942: Nu draag ik die "stille kamer" zogezegd steeds in me mee en ik kan me er ieder ogenblik in terugtrekken [...].

21 E.T., 486. *Het Werk*, 513; Saturday morning, 11 July 1942: [...] maar langs de uitgestrekte wanden van mijn innerlijke wezen hang ik de vele gezichten op en de gebaren, die ik verzameld heb en ze zullen altijd bij me zijn.

22 E.T., 435. *Het Werk* 458; Sunday morning, 21 June 1942: Een bijna tastbaar gevoel. [...] Dat ruimtegevoel in me is heel sterk.

23 Martin Laird, *Into the Silent Land: The Practice of Contemplation* (Darton: Longman & Todd, 2006), 68.

And then to further describe what is beyond description, she uses the metaphor of depth. The image of the well recurs more than once. We have already mentioned how she refers to "the well being blocked" and God having to be dug out from some kind of great depth. Perhaps, here it was her reading of the Gospel of John, where the image of the well is particularly important, that validated her experience. On 19 January 1942, she writes of listening "all day long to what is within me, and even when I am with others I am able to draw strength from the most deeply hidden sources in myself."[24] A few days later, she writes, "I want always to keep in touch with those depths from which the words well up [...]."[25]

Again, this chimes in with the experience of other contemplatives. In his collection of sermons entitled *The Shaking of the Foundations*, the great American theologian Paul Tillich, who was the first theologian in the 20th century to bridge the gulf between psychology and theology, *defined* God as depth. "The name of the infinite and inexhaustible depth and ground of all being," he wrote, "*is* God. That depth is what the word God means."[26]

Again, this, it seems, is what Etty Hillesum also knew.

The other key ingredients of any deep contemplative life are all there in her diary. On 13 April 1942, she writes about her constant "longing for silence"[27]; more and more even as she is in the midst of so many people, she finds she needs solitude; and through the whole diary, she is perfecting the art of inner listening. I have already referred to this remarkable word "*hineinhorchen*". And then one morning in February 1942, she reaches a key conclusion: echoing the experience of contemplatives in all traditions, she realizes that this dwelling within is both constant and *wordless*. "I stopped saying my prayers," she writes, "because I genuinely kept praying inside."[28]

And then, most importantly, this sense of inner spaciousness, of a great fathomless depth, of a huge silence, of a vast stillness, this sense of being known and embraced ... cries out to be named. Though she sometimes sees it as a "primitive" word, more and more as the diary develops she uses the word "God". "God" is the name for all this, for that "which is deepest and

24 E.T., 234. *Het Werk*, 244; Monday morning, 19 January 1942: ik luister de hele dag naar wat er binnen me is, ook wanneer ik tussen anderen ben, ik hoef me niet meer af te zonderen, put geregeld krachten uit de verborgenste en diepste bronnen in mezelf.

25 E.T., 237-238. *Het Werk*, 247; Friday afternoon, 23 January 1942: En met die diepte, waaruit die woorden opwellen, wil ik steeds voeling houden [...].

26 Paul Tillich, *The Shaking of the Foundations* (Harmondsworth: Penguin Books, 1949), 63.

27 E.T., 330. *Het Werk*, 345; Monday morning, 13 April 1942: Een verlangen naar de stilte.

28 E.T., 246. *Het Werk*, 255; Friday morning, 20 February 1942: Ik heb toen niet meer gebeden [...].

best *in* me." And she grows to love this God ... to seek out this God ... to adore this God ... to dwell in this Ground of Life which is so fertile in her.

The word "God" is not a literary device as some have suggested in the writing of Etty Hillesum. It is an ineffable experience of some kind of extraordinary inner vastness and adventure which is constantly being given shape through her experience and through her reading – of the Psalms, of the Gospels, of the "Jew Paul", of St Augustine, and perhaps particularly of the poetry and letters of Rainer Maria Rilke.

And so to return to where we began. It is this inner life, this vast inner fathomless world, that enabled this young woman to keep her eyes open and to see what was going on, and to see with compassion and pity. "The clearer are the things within," she writes, "the more clearly one can see others."[29] It is this seeing that makes Etty Hillesum a universal rather than a tribal person, for the spacious inner world out of which the seeing comes is borderless, embracing both friend and enemy. "The soul has no fatherland," she writes, "[...] or rather it has so great a fatherland that there are no frontiers left."[30] (Note the double meaning of "fatherland").

In conclusion, we can say that Etty Hillesum's story is a story of not one reality, but two.

Outwardly, there is chaos, violence, cruelty, suffering, meaninglessness. It is the darkest moment of the 20th century. She is a Jew caught up in the Holocaust. Her life is being swept away by a terrible history. But there is another reality, another world, that with courage and dedication and extraordinary, almost ruthless perseverance, she learns to inhabit, and the inhabiting of it saves her. It is an inner terrain of spaciousness, depth, silence, stillness, beauty, calm and adoration to which she constantly resorts, and which releases her to be what one camp inmate called her, "radiant".[31]

Of course, it was not like that all the time. There are very dark moments when "nothing makes any sense",[32] when the other world seems to have evaporated and there is only one terrible catalogue of suffering all around her. But to a remarkable degree, this young woman was able to retain her access to this second world and from it, look out, largely without fear, at the

29 E.T., 253. *Het Werk*, 263; Sunday evening, 22 February 1942: hoe klaarder de dingen worden bij jezelf, des te klaarder zie je ze bij anderen [...].

30 E.T., 270. *Het Werk*, 281; Tuesday evening, 3 March 1942: De ziel is toch vaderlandsloos of liever de ziel heeft één groot vaderland en daarin zijn geen grenzen.

31 E.T., 607. *Het Werk*, 647; Letter 42, To Han Wegerif and others, undated, after 26 June 1943: stralend.

32 E.T., 604. *Het Werk*, 644; Letter 40, To Christine van Nooten; Westerbork, Monday, 21 June 1943: alles onbegrijpelijk is.

horrors and depredations of the first. To a degree untouched by the chaos, *she could see clearly*, her vision unclouded by her own distress. Hence, her gazing through that window at those guards.

In the incipient chaos of our own times, when so many people are caught up in despair about the future, and feel violently pulled this way and that by the news and noise of a world that in many ways seems to be collapsing around us, her story of making a breakthrough into this extraordinary contemplative depth, is a gift and challenge to us all.

About the Author

Patrick Woodhouse (1947) is an Anglican priest and writer. He has published an exploration of the life and writings of Etty Hillesum entitled *Etty Hillesum: A Life Transformed* (Bloomsbury, 2009). He contributed to both volumes of essays from the First and the Second International Etty Hillesum Conferences in 2008 and 2014, published by Brill. More recently, he published *Life in the Psalms: Contemplative Meaning in Ancient Texts* (Bloomsbury, 2015). From 2000 to 2012, he was a Canon of Wells Cathedral in Somerset in the UK. He now lives in south Somerset.

Present Traces of a Past Existence

Through the Lens of Photography

Lucrezia Zanardi

Abstract

What happens to a space if it is inhabited by different people after many years? Does the presence of its previous inhabitants persist? And is the space something merely architectural or does it pervade the acts of the subjects themselves and affirm that this exact space is bound to the subjectivity of the former occupant? The photographic research that the author presents here is a playful chance to explore these open questions. Photography is the perfect medium to work through these problems as it is able to suggest and maintain a trace of a presence alongside a look from the past. Photography is also a highly psychological medium that allows one, just like a diary, to review and rework a vision.

Keywords: photography, creativity, writing, subjectivity of space, art, artists, past and present

Lately I have been going through life
as if there were a photographic plate
inside me
making a foolproof recording
of everything around me,
down to the smallest detail.
I am well aware of it;
everything is sharply outlined inside me.
Later, much later perhaps,
I shall develop and print it all.[1]

1 E.T., 483. *Het Werk*, 511; Friday morning 10 July 1942: De laatste dagen ga ik door het leven of er een photographische plaat in me zit, die alles om me heen feilloos, tot in de kleinste details

Smelik, Klaas A.D. (ed.), *The Lasting Significance of Etty Hillesum's Writings: Proceedings of the Third International Etty Hillesum Conference at Middelburg, September 2018.*
Taylor & Francis Group 2019
DOI: 10.5117/9789463722025_ZANARDI

I That painful longing that could never be satisfied, the pining for something I thought unattainable, which I called "my creative urge"[2]

There are books that reflect our image perfectly, and others that shape us while accompanying our growth. The impact of Etty Hillesum's diaries has entered the lives of many people, and has been felt as a watershed moment for growth and for drawing new meaning.[3] If I were to seek the roots of the photographic project I have been carrying out since April 2017, I too, would trace it back to her exercise books; to the tangle of questions and the continuous balancing and redefinition of the young Dutch woman.

I organized a trip from Middelburg to Westerbork, researching and tracking all the houses and spaces that may have influenced the perceptive construction of Etty Hillesum. I rang bells and sent postcards, to try to get in touch with the current residents. It was a sort of ethnographic research, working in particular on the visuals and trying to trace the fragment of an atmosphere, always bearing in mind Hillesum's expressive diaries and other writings.

The basis of my trip was to meet with others who had lived in the same spaces as Etty Hillesum and to work together with those residents, to get to know her or, if they already knew her, to speak about her.

I wondered what happens to a space if it is inhabited by different people after many years? Does the presence of its previous inhabitants persist? And is the space something merely architectural or does it pervade the acts of the subjects themselves and affirm that this exact space is bound to the subjectivity of the former occupant?

The photographic research that I present here is a playful chance to explore these open questions. Photography is the perfect medium to work through these problems as it is able to suggest and maintain a trace of a presence alongside a look from the past. Photography is also a highly psychological medium that allows one, just like a diary, to review and rework a vision.

Etty Hillesum's diaries contain a particular passage that resurfaces again and again for me and has guided me since my very first reading. In this passage, Hillesum faces in depth for the first time the problem of the creative

opneemt. Daarvan ben ik me bewust, alles gaat in mij "hinein" met kantige contouren. Later, veel later misschien, zal ik dat alles eens ontwikkelen en afdrukken.

2 E.T., 24. *Het Werk*, 25; Sunday morning 16 March 1941: Daarom altijd dat pijnlijke gevoel van verlangen, dat nooit te bevredigen was, die Heimweh naar iets, wat ik dacht dat onbereikbaar was en dat noemde ik dan scheppingsdrang.

3 Cf. E.T., 586. *Het Werk*, 624; Letter 23, To two sisters in The Hague, Amsterdam, end of December 1942: [...] een nieuwe zin [...].

act: the need to write and the impossibility of formulating everything with ease. She senses the urgency and importance of expressing herself in writing and analyzes her approach by recalling a previous period in her life in which she had less time to assimilate, and so swallowed everything in an urgent impulse mixed with fear of loss. She defined this impulse as her "creative urge". By March 1941, things were different for Hillesum. The intention or potential to act is now expressed as the need to elaborate words on a page, to let thought and spirit grow through the creative act of writing.

While reading the diaries, we are as delighted as she was by the beauty of words and by her discovery of their definition and redefinition, by her sinking into language and endeavoring to make it as close as possible to her own essence.

The slightly "sick and obsessive" creative urge of Hillesum's early days is appeased, and as a writer, she eventually finds the right rhythm and the right constancy to be herself inside and out. Etty Hillesum lives in her diaries and creates; the diary itself becomes the "creative process" put into words. Certainly, a diary is an emblematic way to find one's self. As well, it is as an exercise in inner analysis aimed at establishing a true relationship between one's psyche and the surrounding environment. But as well for Hillesum, it is an artistic process; her "need to act", her intention to become a writer one day. Writing the diary is Hillesum's initial conception of herself as an artist.[4] There are many passages in which Etty Hillesum tries to deal with her relationship to writing and her articulation of stories. We often see her confronting the great philosophers and thinkers, citing and copying Carl Gustav Jung, or Rainer Maria Rilke as, for example, when he observes and tries to analyze Cézanne's artistic process inside the studio:

> 27 June [1942]
>
> Some more about Cezanne's work, but doesn't it apply to every one of us in every field? –
> 'It also struck me very much yesterday how different they (C.'s paintings) are, without being mannered, without the least striving after originality,

4 E.T., 478: [...] my joy, the artist's joy in observing things and in shaping them mentally into an image of his own. [...] I approach things like an artist and expect that later, when I feel the need to tell everything, I shall have what talent it takes to do so. *Het Werk*, 505; Tuesday morning 7 July 1942: [...] mijn vreugde, de vreugde van de kunstenaar, om de dingen waar te nemen en in zijn geest om te vormen tot een eigen beeld. [...] De instelling van de kunstenaar heb ik en ik geloof, dat later, wanneer ik zal voelen, dat het noodzakelijk is, dat ik alles vertel, er ook genoeg talent zal zijn.

> certain of not losing themselves in every approach to thousandfold Nature, but rather of discovering, earnestly and conscientiously, the inexhaustibility within, the multiplicity without.'[5]

The confluence of artistic practices such as writing, painting, or composition, are a single idea known as the "creative process", an artistic approach that is neither a pose nor a chase after originality. It is a natural flow from the self to the work of art.

I still lack the courage to deal with the word "art", to define it and to figure out what emotions it provokes. So far, I know only that the stimulation gained from the output of art arises from an internal "need to act", to affirm one's presence through a process of making something tangible, be it a song or a photograph. The art object, however, fails to provide full satisfaction and always suggests new possibilities or emerging ways to attempt to create again.

I will try to find my personal approach through the stories about Cézanne too, but for once I will head straight to the French philosopher, Merleau-Ponty's views on Cézanne rather than to Rilke. Merleau-Ponty defined the artistic act as a phenomenon of global magnitude, capable of giving value to life itself.[6] He recognized the uncertainties he had about his own work, which he called the "difficulty of the first word", and made a parallel with Cézanne and his need to paint. The act of painting became for Cézanne the only real means for communicating. And for him, the greatest challenge always came from future work, the work that was still left to be done and his research toward that aim. Everything then lies in the "difficulty of the first word", in finding it and being able to continue on from there.[7]

There is a similar tangle in Etty Hillesum's struggle to find the most suitable form of expression to describe a moment, a place or a feeling. Reworked, copied, and quoted texts, together with their repetition on different days, are parts of her search, and even include the most sincere and natural appropriation of the works in which she is immersed. She encourages her own growth by engaging in a dialogue between the sources and her own thoughts, ideas, and inspirations.

5 E.T., 451. *Het Werk*, 476; Saturday morning, 27 June 1942: Auch fiel mir gestern sehr auf, wie manierlos verschieden sie (n.l. de schilderijen van C.) sind, wie sehr ohne Sorge um Originalität, sicher, in jeder Annäherung an die tausendartige Natur sich nicht zu verlieren, viel mehr an der Mannigfaltigkeit draußen die innere Unerschöpflichkeit ernst und gewissenhaft zu entdecken.

6 Cf. M. Merleau-Ponty, *L'Oeil et l'Esprit* (Paris: Gallimard, 1964).

7 Cf. M. Merleau-Ponty, *Le doute de Cézanne: Sens et non-sens* (Paris: Gallimard, 1996).

II I am still waiting for things to come out and find a form of their own accord. But first I myself must find the right pattern, my own pattern[8]

It can be said that Etty Hillesum found herself through words, and that the act of writing, after that first page of diary dated 8 March 1941, became something necessary, a sort of internal duty that led to an in-depth search for her inner self through the medium of words.

In "Le beau danger", the art critic Claude Bonnefoy tried in an interview with Michel Foucault, to define the approach to writing of the philosopher as author. The search for the self *between the tip of the pen and the white surface of the paper* is an attempt to let one's substance flow into those tiny traces and for one's life to be *nothing else than those scribbles, dead and talkative at the same time, laying there.*[9] In this way, writing becomes for Etty Hillesum the medium of expression, without taking away from her curiosity toward the other artistic languages such as music, which she enjoys through her brother Mischa, or the poetic and visual transformation of the written text itself that evokes *silence and makes it emphatic.* Words for Hillesum are as *a few delicate brush strokes – with attention to the smallest detail – and all around them space, not empty but inspired.*[10]

An individual existing in a visual and perceptual universe is quite naturally attracted by the photographic medium which can be easily be compared to expressing one's self in words. As happens in writing, photography is capable of extending thought to something external and tangible.[11] Photography, as well as being a trace of a presence and a glimpse of the past, is also a presence of the past in the present.[12] A photograph is not just a representation of an objective instant of what has been, it is the honest image of they who have experienced it. It is variable yet objective in its materiality, and at the same time it can speak to many people differently, changing its sense over time even in the eyes of the one who took it. A text, and in particular a hand-written text such as Etty Hillesum's diaries, is a subjective legacy as strong as a fixed glance

8 E.T., 78. *Het Werk*, 72; Friday morning, 4 July 1941: Ik wacht nog maar, tot alles vanzelf naar buiten komt en vorm vindt. Maar eerst moet ikzelf nog de vorm, mijn eigen vorm, vinden.

9 Cf. M. Foucault & C. Bonnefoy, *Le beau danger* (Paris: Éditions de l'EHESS, 2011).

10 Cf. E.T., 394. *Het Werk*, 413; Friday evening, 7 June 1942: Een paar tedere penseelstreken – maar wèlk een weergave van het kleinste detail – en daaromheen de grote ruimte maar niet een ruimte, die een leegte is, maar laten we zeggen een bezielde ruimte.

11 Cf. R. Barthes, *La chambre claire: Note sur la photographie* (Paris: Gallimard, 1980).

12 Cf. St Augustine, *Confessions*.

in an image. This is the case not only in the objectification of thoughts into words, but also in the manifestation of the subjective handwriting impressed on the paper.

A photographic image can also be perceived as a space of silence and observation, floating above tension, not structured around answers or definitions, but moving toward a continuous reworking of questions. Similarly, the image escaping from the flow of words on a page, or the even more fragmented reality of a word extrapolated from its context, is capable of other infinite possible openings. The image is able "to call knowledge into question, reviving it again".[13]

Photographing the present, the same places that had been inhabited by Etty Hillesum, was one possible way to explore her life. It was to be a re-elaboration of the relatively large amount of archival material that, nevertheless, is still not sufficient to capture the past in such a way as to help us understand it in the present day.[14]

The encounter with the current tenants of the many houses in which Etty Hillesum had lived was fundamental to this project. It was a way to understand that space can be interpreted as bearing an "aura"[15] capable of preserving the presence of past occupants and their tensions. It is a way to grasp that space is something that naturally influences people. There have been cases in which it has been possible to trace an atmospheric coincidence between the present and the past. Dialogue also creates a temporal coincidence and Hillesum thus takes shape again in the context in which her passage is already known and familiar, and we were able to talk about it.[16] In our dialogue on Etty Hillesum, we renewed her presence and created the conditions from which a photographic and atmospheric vision of her life could take place. Thanks to our exchange, together we created the "present of past things",[17] able to suggest a point of view that could be captured in an image.

13 Cf. U. Eco, M. Augé & G. Didi-Huberman, *La condition des images par Georges Didi-Huberman entretien avec Frédéric Lambert et François Niney: L'expérience des images* (Bry-sur-Marne: INA Editions, 2011).

14 The archive referring to its visual level.

15 Cf. W. Benjamin, *Charles Baudelaire: Ein Lyriker im Zeitalter des Hochkapitalismus* (Berlin: Suhrkamp Taschenbuch, 1974); ["aura":] "a strange weave of space and time: the unique appearance [apparition, semblance] of a distance, however near it may be. Words, too, can have an aura." [in reference to Kraus:] "The closer one looks at a word, the greater the distance from which it looks back."

16 Cf. Martin Buber, *Ich und Du*, 1923; *Das Dialogische Prinzip*, 1973.

17 Cf. St Augustine, *Confessions*.

III Just go downstairs and have a look at the clean kitchen, it's an impression, a photograph, of my mental state[18]

The perception of the environment underpins human imagination and culture, and perception is as important as the actual inhabited place in the construction of memory. Our environment, our home with its scents, colors, and temperature are the means by which we store and organize our particular universe, and the basis upon which we can perceive the external world and orient ourselves in it.[19] Objects are important and necessary for the individual, since they have the ability to incorporate meaning. Things wield great power in the perception of doing, feeling, and looking.[20] The camera becomes the means for investigating and playing with inhabited space. It establishes relationships and associations. It focuses the forms, and facilitates the need to enter the context more intimately. It strives to analyze the perceptual universe of another person, looking for the topical elements and experiencing them directly.

To approach the world according to coordinates in temporal space is a psychological need. So is the assumption of a point of view that is logically balanced with respect to nature. Sensory perception of material objects is an evident and recognizable base from which to start orienting oneself in the external world.[21]

When Etty Hillesum speaks of the external and the internal, of the balance between the parts, she describes a cosmology of objects. She locates where they sit on her desk, or what material the carpet of her bathroom is made of, or what color Spier's comb is. As well, she defines the coordinates in space in which her room lies, or the veranda, the many objects on her desk, the yellow roses. She explains Camp Westerbork with its rows of shacks, or the streets and bridges which divide her from Courbetstraat 27. In all of this, Hillesum has found her view of the world and its environs, and has created a certain palette capable of bringing hope and positivity even in the worst situations. She incorporates every spatial relation so deeply into herself that the exterior and interior merge for her and she is left with the

18 E.T., 43. *Het Werk*, 45; Monday morning, 24 March 1941: Ga naar beneden en aanschouw de schone keuken, dat is een afdruk, een fotografie van m'n zieletoestand.

19 Cf. Franco La Cecla, *Perdersi: L'uomo senza ambiente* (Rome & Bari: Laterza, 1988).

20 Cf. L. Leonini, *Gli oggetti come beni di consumo: L'identità smarrita. Il ruolo degli oggetti nella vita quotidiana* (Bologna: il Mulino, 1988), 97-111; D. Miller, *The Comfort of Things* (Cambridge: Polity, 2008).

21 Ernst Mach, *Erkenntnis und Irrtum: Skizzen zur Psychologie der Forschung* (Leipzig: Johann Ambrosia Barth, 1906).

conviction that "we *are* at home in every place on earth, if only we carry everything within us".[22]

It was important to me to look for how she gazed and for the perceptive sense that she displayed day after day in her diaries. She wrote in it hoping it would not only remain a "source of inspiration", but could help her discover her own person – Etty Hillesum. There are objective traces that we can still find in the present day. These are not theoretical, but are rather entirely palpable.

My photographic journey was about looking for someone who through and despite time, had been able to influence me. I wanted to understand the difference between what I had read in the diaries and had internalized about Etty Hillesum, and what springs from myself, from my act of writing both with words and with light. This does not in any way mean that I do pretend to be neutral. It is simply an attempt to bend my point of view towards the outlook that Etty Hillesum would have had on reality.

IV Your photograph is in Rilke's Stundenbuch, next to Jul's photograph[23]

Today the meaning of the photograph doesn't have the same value as it had in the past. With new media, from camera phones to satellite TV, a current event is already historicized within minutes after it has occurred. Until recently, individual memories, but also collective memories, first passed into a sedimentation process, and visual memory had to be constructed step by step.

In parallel motion with my photography trip was my journey to the Archive of the Jewish Historical Museum in Amsterdam. All the extant documents and photographs of Etty Hillesum are preserved there. The first material traces I encountered were the fragile papers and photographs that remained intact, preserved by those who had passed them from hand to hand until they finally found a home at the Museum. These documents have an incredible narrative force. They are anthropological traces, small clues and fragments of a much larger body of material that has been lost or is not yet archived.

22 E.T., 524. *Het Werk*, 555; Sunday night 20 September 1942: Op iedere plek van deze aarde is men "thuis", wanneer men alles in zich draagt.

23 E.T., 640. *Het Werk*, 683; Letter 60, To Henny Tideman, Westerbork, Wednesday, 18 August 1943: Je photo ligt in het 'Stundenbuch' van Rilke, naast de photo van Jul.

From the fragments, an image-historian can investigate, recognizing and tracing the dynamics of the shot taken, noticing gestures, shapes, and frames.[24] But what interested me most, was not only an analysis of the images detached from the presence of the gaze, but the active elaboration of the past that re-emerges and grows. This especially takes place if one is armed with the knowledge of the conditions that were current at the time. The photograph-as-object incorporates meaning and does not present itself as only a snap from the past. It is an object that is subject to gradual deterioration. The presence of, on the one hand, the materiality, and on the other, the fragility of the photos becomes more and more manifest with each passing year. The back of a photo is also an integral part, and a date or a description of place and people often appear there.

I tried to enter these images, to explore the limits of the shots and their materiality. In traveling around the Netherlands, it was interesting to see the changes in the spaces after so many years and also to note the choices that had been made over time in terms of furniture and decoration of houses and gardens. My investigation then shifted to documents: correspondence, and texts and analysis by Julius Spier, often typed by Etty Hillesum. I photographed them. The experience of transforming the documents into images was immersive. I was able to enter even the typography and to sense the sheet of paper as it had been in the moment when Etty Hillesum herself had put her pen to paper.

I do not think there is any substantial difference between my approach to the archive and the approach I took to the houses inhabited by the Hillesums. These inquiries complemented each other by way of a fragmented dialogue between the preserved objects and the spaces where they were once held. To study a photograph, an image-historian can use the present trace to search for a possible past, or the other way around, they can retrace the past to construct the present, shifting in this way also the presumed historical meaning. Rereading in this way takes place over time, and today's gaze can become the bearer of new tensions capable of suggesting a new perspective on the past, hence modifying it. Thus, this shifting is also a political act, giving a new way to let the past be in the present. The house as well as the document is a fragment of the past that reaches us and makes itself readable for what it is – a stratification and sedimentation of a deeper memory, returning to the present only if we are willing to reactivate it.

24 Cf. Eco *et al.*, *La condition des images par Georges Didi-Huberman.*

V And now that I don't want to own anything anymore and am free, now I suddenly own everything, now my inner riches are immeasurable[25]

My research is an on-going project, and it will never end nor take a final form. It is something that naturally has to remain open, as we are talking about somebody else, about a person and the traces left to us. What is of greatest interest to me, is the possibility of giving new tensions to specific places, and imbuing them with a profound significance. As the project moves forward, I will smooth out the words and dig further back in time, proceeding through structural and visual associations dictated sometimes by the testimony, and at other times by the parallelism and elaboration of the visuals.

Etty Hillesum shaped her thought through the act of writing. My search to understand Hillesum's creative impulse developed along lines that she too, had experienced; it became a patient quest for *the right pattern* so that *things* [could] *find a shape at their own accord*. By means of writing, she accomplished an act of resistance to hatred. Hers were not just thoughts recorded in a diary. Rather her thoughts helped her sculpt her own duty to become the *thinking heart of the barracks* of Camp Westerbork.[26]

Her call to action, understood as a commitment to self-expression, has played an important role in my search for identity and art. Without internalizing the "creative urge" described so clearly in the 3 March 1941 entry, I would not now find myself taking pictures, nor would I be able to engage in such an intimate research project. If I have been true to my understanding of Etty Hillesum, my work will also become a political act.

Thinking about the past as an intrinsic part of the present brings up profound feelings. It embodies the notion of a deeper dialogue between time and space, a dialogue that never truly reaches an end.

About the Author

Lucrezia Zanardi (1994) studied at the IUAV University of Venice, Italy, and at the University of Arts and Design of Karlsruhe, Germany. She is Master in

25 E.T., 25. *Het Werk*, 25; Sunday morning, 16 March 1941: En nu ik niets meer wil bezitten en vrij ben, nu bezit ik alles, nu is de innerlijke rijkdom onmetelijk.

26 E.T., 515. *Het Werk*, 545; Tuesday morning, 15 September 1942: Het denkende hart van de barak.

Photography and Photographic Studies at the University of Applied Sciences and Arts of Dortmund, Germany. She did an internship at District Kunst- und Kulturförderung GmbH (Berlin) and took part in several group projects and exhibitions in Italy, Germany, France, and the Netherlands. Her work *Present Traces of a Past Existence: A Photographic Research* was presented on occasion of the Third International Etty Hillesum Conference in Middelburg parallel to the exhibition at Sjakie's Gallery, from 1 to 30 September 2018. She is a scholarship holder of the *Studienstiftung des deutschen Volkes* and lives in Dortmund.

Etty Hillesum Bibliography

This bibliography consists of two parts:

- The first part contains a list of Etty Hillesum's works in Dutch and their translations into various languages. Her original handwritten diaries and letters (1941-1943) are kept in the archives of the Jewish Historical Museum (JHM) in Amsterdam. Scans of the diaries and letters can be retrieved on the website www.geheugenvannederland.nl.
- The second part is a list in alphabetical order of books and articles on Etty Hillesum.

Works by Etty Hillesum

In Dutch

Sorted by date of publication

Drie Brieven van den kunstschilder Johannes Baptiste van der Pluym (1843-1912). Met twee reproducties: Uitgegeven en van toelichting voorzien door Mevr. A.C.G. Botterman-v.d. Pluym, Apeldoorn 1917 Apeldoorn: Boekenfonds 'Die Raeckse', 1917 [Underground publication. Edited by David Koning & Petra Eldering. Haarlem: *De Vrije Katheder* & *De Patriot*, 1943].

"Een transport vertrekt... En een ooggetuige vertelt van lief en leed in en om Westerbork." *Het Parool* (5 February 1944): 6-8.

"Twee brieven uit Westerbork van Etty Hillesum." *Maatstaf: Maandblad voor Letteren* 7, no. 1 (1959): 3-41.

Twee brieven uit Westerbork. Edited by David Koning. The Hague: Bert Bakker / Daamen N.V., 1962.

"Twee brieven uit Westerbork." *BulkBoek*, no. 73. Utrecht: Knippenberg, 1978.

Het verstoorde leven: Dagboek van Etty Hillesum, 1941-1943. Edited by J.G. Gaarlandt. Haarlem: De Haan, 1981 [37nd revised edition, 2018].

Het denkende hart van de barak: Brieven van Etty Hillesum. Edited by J.G. Gaarlandt. Haarlem: De Haan, 1982 [12th revised edition, 2012].

In duizend zoete armen: Nieuwe dagboekaantekeningen van Etty Hillesum. Edited by J.G. Gaarlandt. Haarlem: De Haan, 1984. [Prepublication in *De Tijd* (27 November, 1981): 51-63].

Etty: De nagelaten geschriften van Etty Hillesum, 1941-1943. Edited by Klaas A.D. Smelik, Gideon Lodders & Rob Tempelaars. Amsterdam: Balans, 1986 [5th revised edition, 2008].

Dat onverwoestbare in mij. Amsterdam: Balans, 2011 [Revised edition: 2014].

Het Werk 1941-1943. Edited by Klaas A.D. Smelik, Gideon Lodders & Rob Tempelaars. Amsterdam: Balans, 2012.

Twee brieven uit Westerbork. Amsterdam: Balans, 2013.

Etty Hillesum: The Complete Works 1941-1943: Bilingual, Annotated and Unabridged. Edited by Klaas A.D. Smelik & Meins G.S. Coetsier, 2 volumes. Maastricht: Shaker Verlag, 2014.

In duizend zachte armen: Gedachten bij elke dag van het jaar. Amsterdam: Balans, 2016.

Translations

Sorted by language; reprints are not mentioned.

Czech

Přervaný živót. Edited by J.G. Gaarlandt. Translated by Jindra Hubková. Praha: Karmelitánské nakladatelství, 2005.

Myslící srdce: Dopisy z Let 1941-1943. Edited by J.G. Gaarlandt. Translated by Petra Schürová. Praha: Karmelitánské nakladatelství, 2007.

Danish

Et kraenket liv. Edited by J.G. Gaarlandt. Translated by Birthe Lundsgaard Sørensen. København: Lindhardt & Ringhof, 1983.

English

Etty: A Diary 1941-1943. Edited by J.G. Gaarlandt. Translated by Arnold J. Pomerans. London: Jonathan Cape, 1983.

An Interrupted Life: The Diaries of Etty Hillesum, 1941-1943. Edited by J.G. Gaarlandt. Translated by Arnold J. Pomerans. New York: Pantheon Books, 1983.

An Interrupted Life: The Diaries and Letters of Etty Hillesum, 1941-1943. Edited by J.G. Gaarlandt. Translated by Arnold J. Pomerans. New York: Pantheon Books, 1984.

Etty: A Diary 1941-1943. Edited by J.G. Gaarlandt. Translated by Arnold J. Pomerans. London: Granada, 1985.

An Interrupted Life: The Diaries and Letters of Etty Hillesum, 1941-1943. Edited by J.G. Gaarlandt. Translated by Arnold J. Pomerans. New York: Washington Square Press, 1985.

Letters from Westerbork. Edited by J.G. Gaarlandt. Translated by Arnold J. Pomerans. New York: Pantheon Books, 1986.

Letters from Westerbork. Edited by J.G. Gaarlandt. Translated by Arnold J. Pomerans. London: Jonathan Cape, 1987.

Letters from Westerbork. Edited by J.G. Gaarlandt. Translated by Arnold J. Pomerans. Glasgow: Collins, 1988.

Letters from Westerbork: Etty Hillesum. Edited by J.G. Gaarlandt. Translated by Arnold J. Pomerans. Glasgow: Grafton Books / Collins Publishing Group, 1988.

"Etty Hillesum: A Letter from Westerbork." In: *Different Voices: Women and the Holocaust*. Edited by Carol Rittner, 46-58. St. Paul, MN: Paragon Press, 1993.

An Interrupted Life: The Writings of Etty Hillesum, 1941-1943. Edited by J.G. Gaarlandt. Translated by Arnold J. Pomerans. Washington: United States Holocaust Memorial Museum, 1995.

Etty Hillesum: An Interrupted Life: The Diaries, 1941-1943, and Letters from Westerbork. Edited by J.G. Gaarlandt. Foreword by Eva Hoffman. Translated by Arnold J. Pomerans. New York: Henry Holt, 1996.

An Interrupted Life: The Diaries and Letters of Etty Hillesum, 1941-1943. Edited by J.G. Gaarlandt. Foreword by Eva Hoffman. Translated by Arnold J. Pomerans. London: Persephone Books, 1999.

Etty: The Letters and Diaries of Etty Hillesum, 1941-1943. Edited by Klaas A.D. Smelik. Translated by Arnold J. Pomerans. Ottawa, ON / Grand Rapids, MI: Novalis Saint Paul University / William B. Eerdmans Publishing, 2002.

Etty Hillesum: Essential Writings. Edited by Annemarie S. Kidder. Maryknoll, NY: Orbis Books, 2009.

Etty Hillesum: The Complete Works 1941-1943: Bilingual, Annotated and Unabridged. Edited by Klaas A.D. Smelik & Meins G.S. Coetsier, 2 volumes. Maastricht: Shaker Verlag 2014.

Finnish

Päiväkirja, 1941-1943. Edited by J.G. Gaarlandt. Translated by Anita Odé. Helsinki: Kustannusosakeyhtiö Otava, 1984.

French

Une vie bouleversée. Edited by J.G. Gaarlandt. Translated by Philippe Noble. Paris: Éditions du Seuil, 1985.

Lettres de Westerbork. Edited by J.G. Gaarlandt. Translated by Philippe Noble. Paris: Éditions du Seuil, 1988.

La fille qui ne savait pas s'agenouiller: Un choix de passages de son journal. Edited by Alain Burnand. Le Mont-sur-Lausanne: Ed. Ouverture, 1993.

Une vie bouleversée: Journal 1941-1943: Suivi de: Lettres de Westerbork. Edited by J.G. Gaarlandt. Translated by Philippe Noble. Paris: Éditions du Seuil, 1995.

Hillesum: Les écrits d'Etty Hillesum: Journaux et lettres 1941-1943. Edited by Klaas A.D. Smelik. Translated by Philippe Noble & Isabelle Rosselin. Paris: Éditions du Seuil, 2008.

Faire la paix avec soi: 365 Meditations quotidiennes. Paris: éditeur Points, collection Point vivre, 2014.

German

Das denkende Herz: Die Tagebücher von Etty Hillesum, 1941-1943. Edited by J.G. Gaarlandt. Translated by Maria Csollány. Reinbek bei Hamburg: Rowohlt Verlag, 1985.

Das denkende Herz: Die Tagebücher von Etty Hillesum, 1941-1943. Edited by J.G. Gaarlandt. Translated by Maria Csollány. Reinbek bei Hamburg: Rowohlt Taschenbuch Verlag, 1985.

Das denkende Herz der Baracke: Die Tagebücher von Etty Hillesum, 1941-1943. Edited by J.G. Gaarlandt. Translated by Maria Csollány. Freiburg: F.H. Kerle, 1983.

Das denkende Herz der Baracke. Edited by J.G. Gaarlandt. Translated by Maria Csollány. Hamburg: Rowohlt, 1988.

Das denkende Herz der Baracke: Die Tagebücher 1941-1943. Mit einer Einführung von Christian Feldmann. Translated by Maria Csollány. Freiburg: Herder, 2014.

Hebrew

Chayim Kerutim: Yomana shel Etty Hillesum 1941-1943. Edited by J.G. Gaarlandt. Translated by Shulamit Bamberger. Jerusalem: Keter Publishing House, 1985.

Hashamayim Shebetokhi: Yomana shel Etty Hillesum 1941-1943. Edited by J.G. Gaarlandt. Translated by Shulamit Bamberger. Jerusalem: Keter Publishing House, 2002.

Hungarian

A megzavart élet: Etty Hillesum Naploja, 1941-1943. Edited by J.G. Gaarlandt. Translated by Judit Gera. Budapest: Gondolat, 1994.

Italian

Diario 1941-1943. Edited by J.G. Gaarlandt. Translated by Chiara Passanti. Milano: Adelphi Edizioni, 1985.

Diario 1941-1943. Edited by J.G. Gaarlandt. Translated by Chiara Passanti. Milano: Mondolibri, 2003.

Lettere 1942-1943. Edited by J.G. Gaarlandt. Translated by Chiara Passanti. Milano: Adelphi Edizioni, 1990.

"Dal Diario e dalle Lettere: Con una nota di Giancarlo Gaeta." In: *Lo Straniero*, no. 21 (2002): 5-24.

"Etty Hillesum: Lettere inedite." Translated by Gerrit Van Oord. In *Con Etty Hillesum: Quaderno di informazione e ricerca*, no. 1 (2008): 9-18.

Diario: Edizione integrale 1941-1942. Edited by Klaas A.D. Smelik. Translated by Chiara Passanti & Tina Montone. Milano: Adelphi Edizioni, 2012.

Lettere: Edizione integrale 1941-1943. Edited by Klaas A.D. Smelik. Translated by Chiara Passanti, Tina Montone & Ada Vigliani. Milano: Adelphi Edizioni, 2013.

Il bene quotidiano: Brevario dagli scritti (1941-1942). Edited by Lorenzo Gobbi. Cinisello Balsamo: Edizioni San Paolo, 2014.

Japanese

Eros to Kami to Shuyojo. Edited by J.G. Gaarlandt. Translated by Okoso Toshiko. Tokyo: Asahi Shinbunsha, 1986.

Ikiru koto no imi wo motomete. Edited by J.G. Gaarlandt. Translated by Okoso Toshiko. Tokyo: Shobunsha, 1989.

Norwegian

Det tenkende hjerte: Dagbok 1941-1943. Edited by J.G. Gaarlandt. Forword by Johanna Schwarz. Translated by Tove Alkan. Oslo: Gyldendal Norsk Forlag, 1983.

Polish

Przerwane życie: Pamiętnik 1941-1943. Edited by J.G. Gaarlandt & Wieslawa Otto-Weiss. Translated by Iwona Piotrowska. Kraków: Wydawnictwo WAM, 2000.

Myślące serce: Listy. Edited by J.G. Gaarlandt. Translated by Iwona Piotrowska. Kraków: Wydawnictwo WAM, 2002.

Portuguese

Uma vida interrompida. Edited by J.G. Gaarlandt. Translated by Antonio C.G. Penna. Rio de Janeiro: Editora Record, 1984.

Diário 1941-1943. Edited by J.G. Gaarlandt. Preface by José Tolentino Mendonça. Translated by Maria Leonor Raven-Gomes. Lisboa: Assírio & Alvim, 2008.

Cartas 1941-1943. Edited by J.G. Gaarlandt. Translated by Patricia Couto & Ana Leonor Duarte. Lisboa: Assirio & Alvim, 2009.

Russian

Я никогда и нигде не умру: Дневник 1941-43 гг. [Ja nikogda i nigde ne umru: Dnevnik 1941-1943]. Edited by J.G. Gaarlandt. Translated by Very Menis. Char'kov/ Belgorod: Klub semejnogo dosuga, 2016.

Slovak

Prertrhnutý život:Denníky z rokov 1941-1943. Edited by J.G. Gaarlandt. Introduction by Alexander Tomský, J.G. Gaarlandt & Józef Augustyn SJ. Translated by Marta Blašková-Maňáková. Bratislava: Karmelitánske nakladateľstvo, 2012.

Slovenian

Pretrgano življenje: Dnevnik Etty Hillesum; Pisma iz Westerborka. Edited by J.G. Gaarlandt. Translated by Martina Soldo. Ljubljana: Modrijan, 2008.

Spanish

Una vida interrumpida. Edited by J.G. Gaarlandt. Translated by Javier Vergara. Buenos Aires: Javier Vergara Editor, 1985.

Cartas desde Westerbork. Edited by J.G. Gaarlandt. Translated by Matilde Almandoz. San Sebastián: La Primitiva Casa Baroja, 1989.

El corazón pensante de los barracones: Cartas. Edited by J.G. Gaarlandt. Translated by Natalia Fernández Díaz. Barcelona: Anthropos Editorial, 2001.

Diario de Etty Hillesum: Una vida conmocionada. Edited by J.G. Gaarlandt. Translated by Manuel Sánchez Romero & Asunsión Sainz Lerchundi. Barcelona: Anthropos Editorial, 2007.

Swedish

Det förstörda livet. Edited by J.G. Gaarlandt. Translated by Brita Dahlman. Stockholm: P.A. Norstedt & Söners förlag, 1983.

Dagböcker och brev: I urval. Translated by Brita Dahlman & Olov Hyllienmark. Stockholm: Bokförlaget Faethon, 2018.

Works on Etty Hillesum

Sorted by author

Accart, Xavier. "S'agenouiller: une conversion." *Prier* no. 315 (October 2009).

Adinolfi, Isabella. *Etty Hillesum: La fortezza inespugnabile*. Genova: Il nuovo melangolo, 2011.

—. "Le Lettere di Etty Hillesum: Una cronaca poetica di Westerbork." In: *Dopo la Shoah: Un nuovo inizio per il pensiero*. A cura di Isabella Adinolfi. Roma: Carocci editore, 2011, 303-327.

—. "De naam van God in het werk van Etty Hillesum: De stilte en het woord." In: *Etty Hillesum 1914-2014* (Etty Hillesum Studies, 6). Edited by Klaas A.D. Smelik *et al*. Antwerpen & Apeldoorn: Garant, 2014, 75-92.

Adrian, Luc. "La prière du Cœur d'Etty Hillesum." *Famille Chrétienne* no. 1764 (November 2011).

Alberti, Olympia. *L'amour dans l'âme: Le journal disparu d'Etty Hillesum*. Paris: Presse de la Renaissance, 2011 [novel].

—. *Une année avec Etty Hillesum: Un jour, une pensée*. Paris: Presses de la Renaissance, 2014.

Allewijn, Herrianne *et al*. "Een voorbeeld voor de eeuwigheid? Over de huidige waardering voor de dagboeken van Etty Hillesum." *Werkschrift voor Leerhuis & Liturgie* 4 (November 1984): 164-173.

—. *'In niemands handen': Over de mythevorming rond Etty Hillesum*. MA-thesis, University of Amsterdam, 1984.

Aluffi Pentini, Anna. "A woman's all-embracing search of 'The other': Etty Hillesum as the basis of a 'pedagogy of care and attention'." In: *Reading Etty Hillesum in Context: Writings, Life, and Influences of a Visionary Author*. Edited by Klaas A.D. Smelik, Gerrit Van Oord & Jurjen Wiersma. Amsterdam: Amsterdam University Press, 2018, 479-500.

Anderson, Nancy JP *The Undercurrent of Music in the Burgeoning Spirituality of Etty Hillesum*. MA Thesis, St. Catherine University, 2017.

Angeli, Silvia. *Etty Hillesum: Le pratiche di scrittura come trasformazione*. Roma: Edizioni universitarie romane, 2010.

Badaracchi, L. "'Ho spezzato il mio corpo come fosse pane': Etty Hillesum, martire dell'olocausto." *La Vita in Cristo e nella Chiesa* (1999): 3.

—. "Il Dio di Etty Hillesum." *Segno nel mondo* no. 7 (2000): 24.

Baggiani, Anna. "Lettere dall'abisso." *L'Indice dei libri del mese* (March 1990): 3.

Bakker, Aalt. "Etty Hillesum, inspiratiebron voor een rijk innerlijk leven." *Geloven onderweg* 132 (spring 2014): 12-15.

Bakker, Sybe. "'De innerlijke gebieden': Over het dagboek en de brieven van Etty Hillesum." In: *Vuurproeven over literatuur.* Barneveld: De Vuurbaak, 1992.

Barban, Alessandro & Antonio Carlo Dall'Acqua. *Etty Hillesum: Osare Dio: Bisogna osar dire che si crede osar pronunciare il nome di Dio.* Assisi: Cittadella Editrice, 2012.

Barry, J. "An Interrupted Life." Screenplay adapted from the diaries and letters of Etty Hillesum, 1985 [not published].

Barry, William A., SJ "Mysticism in Hell." In: *God's Passionate Desire and Our Response.* Notre Dame, IN: Ave Maria Press, 1993, 81-89.

Baum, Gregory. "The Witness of Etty Hillesum." *Ecumenist* 1 (1985): 24-28.

Beattie, Tina. "Etty Hillesum: A Thinking Heart in a Darkened World." In: *Spirituality and Society in the New Millennium.* Edited by Ursula King with Tina Beattie. Brighton, UK: Sussex Academic Press, 2001, 247-260.

Beck, Ulrich. *Der eigene Gott: Von der Friedensfähigkeit und dem Gewaltpotential der Religionen.* Frankfurt am Main: Suhrkamp, 2008.

—. *A God of one's own: Religion's capacity for peace and potential for violence.* Cambridge: Polity Press, 2010.

Bedient, Calvin. "Etty Hillesum: Outward from the Camps Themselves." In: *Martyrs.* Edited by Susan Bergman. San Francisco: Harper, 1996, 169-181.

—. "Etty Hillesum, Polen 1943." In: *Martelaren: Literaire levensverhalen over bekende gelovigen van nu.* Edited by Susan Bergman. Baarn: Ten Have, 1997, 217-232.

Bendien, Hans. "Zelfverwerkelijking." In: *Men zou een pleister op vele wonden willen zijn: Reacties op de dagboeken en brieven van Etty Hillesum.* Edited by J.G. Gaarlandt. Amsterdam: Balans, 1989, 160-185.

—. "Mythevorming rond de heiligheid van Etty Hillesum." *De Gids* 159 (1990): 170-181.

Benima, Tamarah, *et al. Etty Hillesum '43-'93: Teksten van lezingen gehouden in de herdenkingsweek november 1993 te Deventer.* Deventer: Praamsma, 1995.

—. "Moord valt niet te accepteren: Etty Hillesum (als gelukkig promiscuë jodin Maria)." *Werkschrift* 14, no. 1 (1994): 21-25.

Benschop-Plokker, Julie. "Etty Hillesums vermogen tot verplaatsing als weg van verzet en bevrijding." In: *Etty Hillesum en het pad naar zelfverwerkelijking* (Etty Hillesum Studies, 9). Edited by Klaas A.D. Smelik *et al.* Antwerpen-Apeldoorn: Garant, 2017, 13-23.

—. "De werkelijkheid van het verhaal of het verhaal van de werkelijkheid: Josl Rakover en Etty Hillesum wenden zich tot God." In: *Etty Hillesum en de contouren van haar tijd* (Etty Hillesum Studies, 10). Edited by Klaas A.D. Smelik, *et al.* Oud-Turnhout / 's-Hertogenbosch: Gompel & Svacina, 2018, 13-34.

Bercken, Wil van den. "Dostojevski als literair thema in het dagboek van Etty Hillesum." *Tijdschrift voor Slavische literatuur* 52 (maart-april 2009): 14-25.

—. "Etty Hillesum's Russian vocation and spiritual relationship to Dostoevsky." In: *Spirituality in the Writings of Etty Hillesum: Proceedings of the Etty Hillesum Conference at Ghent University, November 2008* (Supplements to The Journal of Jewish Thought and Philosophy, 11). Edited by Klaas A.D. Smelik, Ria van den Brandt & Meins G.S. Coetsier. Leiden / Boston, MA: Brill, 2010, 147-171.

—. "'Denn wenn ich selbst gerecht wäre…': Etty Hillesum en Fjodor Dostojevski." In: *Veel mooie woorden: Etty Hillesum en haar boekje Levenskunst.* Edited by Ria van den Brandt & Peter Nissen. Hilversum: Verloren, 2017, 195-204.

Beretta, Gemma. "Etty Hillesum: La forza disarmata dell'autorità." *ALFAzeta* no. 60 (1996): 48-53.

Bergen, Lotte. *Handelingsvrijheid binnen nazibegrenzing: "Een mens schept zijn eigen lot van binnen uit." Dagboeken en brieven van Etty Hillesum, 1941-1943 Amsterdam-Westerbork.* MA-thesis, Universiteit Leiden, 2015.

—. "Handelingsvrijheid binnen nazibegrenzing: Etty Hillesum en haar invulling van het 'Massenschicksal'." In: *Etty Hillesum weer thuis in Middelburg* (Etty Hillesum Studies, 7). Edited by Klaas A.D. Smelik *et al.* Antwerpen-Apeldoorn: Garant, 2015, 51-83.

—. "Etty Hillesum en Hélène Berr: Reflecties op het nazikwaad en de moed de eigen koers te varen." In: *Etty Hillesum in weerwil van het Joodse vraagstuk* (Etty Hillesum Studies, 8). Edited by Klaas A.D. Smelik *et al.* Antwerpen-Apeldoorn: Garant, 2016, 79-110.

—. "Etty Hillesum & Albert Konrad Gemmeker: Een dubbele analyse van het daderschap van de commandant van Westerbork." In: *Etty Hillesum en het pad naar zelfverwerkelijking* (Etty Hillesum Studies, 9). Edited by Klaas A.D. Smelik *et al.* Antwerpen-Apeldoorn: Garant, 2017, 69-88.

—. "Agency within Nazi constraints: Etty Hillesum and her interpretation of the Jewish fate." In: *Reading Etty Hillesum in Context.* Edited by Klaas A.D. Smelik, Gerrit Van Oord & Jurjen Wiersma. Amsterdam: Amsterdam University Press, 2018, 103-141.

—. "De esthetische gelaagdheid in Hillesums dagboekteksten en brieven." In: *Etty Hillesum en de contouren van haar tijd* (Etty Hillesum Studies, 10). Edited by Klaas A.D. Smelik *et al.* Oud-Turnhout / 's-Hertogenbosch: Gompel & Svacina, 2018, 35-51.

Berger, Karima. "Dieu dans un sac à dos." *Études* 414, no. 2 (2011): 236-238.

—. *Les attentives: Dialogues avec Etty Hillesum.* Paris: Albin Michel, 2014.

Bériault, Yves. *Etty Hillesum, Témoin de Dieu dans l'abîme du mal.* Montréal: Médiaspaul, 2010.

—. *Etty Hillesum: Testimone di Dio nell'abisso del male.* (Spiritualità del quotidiano, 93). Milano: Paoline, 2013.

—. "The invincible hope of Christian de Chergé and Etty Hillesum." In: *Reading Etty Hillesum in Context.* Edited by Klaas A.D. Smelik, Gerrit Van Oord & Jurjen Wiersma. Amsterdam: Amsterdam University Press, 2018, 361-369.

Berk, Tjeu van den. "'Das Erlebnis ist das einzig Wirkliche': Etty Hillesum en Carl Gustav Jung." In: *Veel mooie woorden: Etty Hillesum en haar boekje Levenskunst.* Edited by Ria van den Brandt & Peter Nissen. Hilversum: Verloren, 2017, 223-228.

Beus, Jos de. *Na de beeldenstorm: Een beschouwing over de werking van de toeschouwersdemocratie in Nederland: Voordracht in het kader van de Etty Hillesumlezing 2002.* Heerde: Langhout & De Vries, 2002.

Blom, Hans. "La persecuzione degli ebrei in Olanda: Una prospettiva internazionale." In: *L'esperienza dell'Altro: Studi su Etty Hillesum.* Edited by Gerrit Van Oord. Sant'Oreste: Apeiron Editori, 1990, 21-42.

Bloom, Harold (ed.). *A Scholarly Look at the Diary of Anne Frank.* Philadelphia: Chelsea House Publishers, 1999.

Boas, Henriëtte. "Etty Hillesum in niet-Joodse en Joodse ogen." In: *Neveh Ya'akov: Jubilee Volume Presented to Dr. Jaap Meijer on the Occasion of His Seventieth Birthday.* Edited by Lea Dasberg & Jonathan N. Cohen. Assen: Van Gorcum, 1982, 255-279.

—. "In joodse en niet-joodse spiegel: Het dagboek van Etty Hillesum 1941-1943." *Hakehilla* 27, no. 3 (1982).

—. "Twee tentoonstellingen in Amsterdam: Studia Rosenthaliana en Etty Hillesum." *Hakehilla* 32, no. 2 (1986): 18-20.

—. "Meer egocentrisme dan heiligheid." In: *Men zou een pleister op vele wonden willen zijn: Reacties op de dagboeken en brieven van Etty Hillesum.* Edited by J.G. Gaarlandt. Amsterdam: Balans, 1989, 44-47.

Boas, Jacob. *Boulevard des Miseres: The Story of Transit Camp Westerbork.* Hamden, CT: Archon Books, 1985.

—. *Boulevard des Misères: Het verhaal van doorgangskamp Westerbork.* Amsterdam: Nijgh & Van Ditmar, 1988.

Boddeke, Frans. *Zo betoverend mooi.* Aalsmeer: Dabar-Luyten, 1996.

—. *Die glimlach vergeet ik nooit: Het verschijnsel Etty Hillesum.* Nijmegen: Verbod Writers & Publishers, 2000.

Boella, Laura. *Le imperdonabili: Etty Hillesum, Cristina Campo, Ingeborg Bachmann, Marina Cvetaeva.* Mantova: Tre Lune Edizioni, 2000 [On Hillesum: 21-43]. Reprint: *Le imperdonabili. Milena Jesenská, Etty Hillesum, Marina Cvetaeva, Ingeborg Bachmann, Cristina Campo.* Milano: Mimesis, 2013.

Bonanate, Mariapia. *Io sono qui: Il mistero di una vita sospesa.* Milano: Mondadori, 2012.

Bonnet, Hervé. "Le journal d'Etty Hillesum: Un baume verse sur tant de plaies." In: *L'Express*. See http://blogs.lexpress.fr/les-8-plumes/2012/09/12/le-journal-d%E2%80%99etty-hillesum-un-baume-verse-sur-tant-plaies/ [retrieved 5 November 2013].

Boon, Els & Han Lettinck. "Etty Hillesums Winschoter jaren (1918-1924) en de mensen die haar omringden." In: *Etty Hillesum in Relatie* (Etty Hillesum Studies, 5). Edited by Klaas A.D. Smelik *et al.* Ghent: Academia Press, 2013, 175-204.

Boonen, Rony. "De terugkeer van Etty Hillesum naar haar geboortestad Middelburg." *Joods actueel,* no. 113 (September 2016): 116-121.

Boonstra, Nelleke. "Etty Hillesum en de oorlog." *Ouderlingenblad,* no. 1057 (March 2015): 27-30.

Bori, P.C. & E. Picollo. "Etty Hillesum: La forza di una vita vissuta intensamente." *ALFAzeta* no. 60 (1996): 54-59.

—. "Developing sensitivity: A qualitative study on the inner development of Etty Hillesum." *Journal of Humanistic Psychology* (2 July 2013).

Borgman, Erik P.N.M. "Lezen als vorm van hoopvol wachten: Over de dagboeken van Etty Hillesum." *Tijdschrift voor geestelijk leven* 64 (2008): 79-90.

—. "De onmogelijkheid namens anderen te getuigen – de onmogelijkheid om niet namens anderen te getuigen: Idiosyncratie als redding." In: *Etty Hillesum in discours* (Etty Hillesum Studies, 3). Edited by Ria van den Brandt & Klaas A.D. Smelik. Ghent: Academia Press, 2011, 49-59.

Bosma, Hielke. *Spirituele ontwikkeling vanuit een humanistisch perspectief.* Thesis, Humanistic University Utrecht, 1997.

—. "Berusting: Aanvaarding is geen resignatie." *Praktische Humanistiek: Themanummer Etty Hillesum* 9, no. 1 (1999): 31-35.

Boterman, Frits & Marianne Vogel. *Nederland en Duitsland in het Interbellum: Wisselwerkingen en contacten: Van politiek tot literatuur.* Hilversum: Verloren, 2003.

Bouthors, Jean-François. "Etty Hillesum, la juste folie de l'amour." *Croire* (March 2009). See www.croire.com/Definitions/Vie-chretienne/Etty-Hillesum/Etty-Hillesum-la-juste-folie-de-l-amour [retrieved 5 November 2013].

Bovo, Giuseppe & Nadia Neri. *Il dodicesimo quaderno: Gli 83 giorni di Etty Hillesum ad Auschwitz.* Molfetta: La meridiana, 2009.

Bowie, Fiona. "Modern Women Mystics: Etty Hillesum and Simone Weil." *New Blackfriars* 76, no. 892 (1995): 175-187.

Brandt, Ria van den. "'Ik heb hem gebracht de schriften van Meister Eckehardt': Het Eckhartbeeld van Etty Hillesum." *De Gids* 153, no. 3 (1990): 182-192.

—. "Middeleeuwse filosofie en moderne levenswijsheid: Thomas van Aquino, Meister Eckhart, Albertus Magnus en Etty Hillesum." In: *Ergo cogito IV: Het ideeënmuseum.* Edited by F. Geraedts & L. de Jong. Groningen: Historische Uitgeverij Groningen, 1996, 20-36.

—. "Etty Hillesum e Meister Eckhart." In: *Etty Hillesum, Diario 1941-1943: Un mondo 'altro' è possibile.* Edited by Maria Pia Mazziotti & Gerrit Van Oord. Sant'Oreste: Apeiron Editori, 2002, 40.

—. "'... comme dans mille éclats d'un miroir': Le 'bricolage' d'Etty Hillesum." In: *Reconstruction et bricolage dans la réflexion théologique contemporain.* Edited by François Nault & Marcel Viau. Special issue of *Religiologiques* 26, no. 1 (2003): 163-174.

—. "Etty Hillesum en haar 'katholieke vereerders': Pleidooi voor een meer kritische benadering van een bijzonder document." In: *Etty Hillesum in facetten* (Etty Hillesum Studies, 1). Edited by Ria van den Brandt & Klaas A.D. Smelik. Budel: Damon, 2003, 57-75.

—. "Aantekeningen bij de vriendschap van Etty Hillesum en Henny Tideman: Vriendschap op het tweede gezicht." *Tijdschrift voor Humanistiek: Perspectieven op vriendschap* 5, no. 20 (2004): 79-87.

—. *Denken met Etty Hillesum.* Zoetermeer: Meinema, 2006.

—. "Vriendschap op het tweede gezicht: Aantekeningen bij de vriendschap van Etty Hillesum en Henny Tideman." In: *Etty Hillesum in Context* (Etty Hillesum Studies, 2). Edited by Ria van den Brandt & Klaas A.D. Smelik. Assen: Van Gorcum, 2007, 4-15.

—. "Comme 'des perles en verre dans un petit sac plein de trous': La nécessité du bricolage dans les textes de femmes juives." In: *Bricoler la mémoire: La théologie et les arts face au déclin de la tradition.* Edited by Ria van den Brandt & Mariska Koopman-Thurlings. Paris: Les Éditions du Cerf, 2007, 119-131.

—. "'Innere Emigration' als wapen." *In de marge* 17, no. 3 (2008): 30-37.

—. "Spiritualiteit, een grillige weg – Etty Hillesum." *Speling: Tijdschrift voor bezinning* 60, no. 1 (2009): 42-46.

—. "Introduction." In: *Spirituality in the Writings of Etty Hillesum: Proceedings of the Etty Hillesum Conference at Ghent University, November 2008* (Supplements to The Journal of Jewish Thought and Philosophy, 11). Edited by Klaas A.D. Smelik, Ria van den Brandt & Meins G.S. Coetsier. Leiden / Boston, MA: Brill, 2010, 1-20.

—. "Etty Hillesum and Her "Catholic Worshippers": A Plea for a more critical approach to Etty Hillesum's writings." In: *Spirituality in the Writings of Etty Hillesum: Proceedings of the Etty Hillesum Conference at Ghent University, November 2008* (Supplements to The Journal of Jewish Thought and Philosophy, 11). Edited by Klaas A.D. Smelik, Ria van den Brandt & Meins G.S. Coetsier. Leiden / Boston, MA: Brill, 2010, 215-231.

—. *Etty Hillesum: Amicizia, ammirazione e mistica.* Sant'Oreste: Apeiron Editori, 2010.

—. "Sylvie Germain, Etty Hillesum et le mal." In: *Sylvie Germain: Les essays – une espace transgenénérique* (CRIN Cahiers de recherche des instituts néerlandais de langue et littérature française, 56). Edited by Mariska Koopman-Thurlings. Amsterdam: Rodopi, 2011: 107-112.

—. "Een toonaangevende stem: De boodschap van Etty Hillesum volgens Sylvie Germain." In: *Etty Hillesum in discours* (Etty Hillesum Studies, 3). Edited by Ria van den Brandt & Klaas A.D. Smelik. Ghent: Academia Press, 2011, 17-26.

—. "'Dit boekje was Etty in haar laatste maanden tot troost': Aanvullingen op de Eckhartreceptie van Etty Hillesum." In: *Etty Hillesum in discours* (Etty Hillesum Studies, 3). Edited by Ria van den Brandt & Klaas A.D. Smelik. Ghent: Academia Press, 2011, 93-113.

—. "'Werde der Du bist' in oorlogstijd – Etty Hillesum." *Speling: Tijdschrift voor bezinning* 63, no. 4 (2011): 39-44.

—. "Het groeiend vertrouwen van Etty Hillesum." *Herademing: Tijdschrift voor spiritualiteit en mystiek* 20, no. 76 (2012): 36-39.

—. "Een 'stukje van God in mij': De groeiende religiositeit van Etty Hillesum tijdens de Tweede Wereldoorlog." *Franciscaans leven: Tijdschrift voor verdieping en vernieuwing van de Franciscaanse beweging in Nederland en Vlaanderen* 95, no. 5 (2012): 200-205.

—. *Etty Hillesum: An Introduction to Her Thought.* Münster: LIT Verlag, 2014.

—. "De buik van Etty Hillesum." *Speling: Tijdschrift voor bezinning* 66, no. 1 (2014): 37-43.

—. "'Is dat alleen maar die maandelijkse buik?': De cyclische spiritualiteit van Etty Hillesum." In: *Etty Hillesum 1914-2014* (Etty Hillesum Studies, 6). Edited by Klaas A.D. Smelik *et al.* Antwerpen & Apeldoorn: Garant, 2014, 59-70.

—. *Vrouwen van woorden: Een kleine canon tegen groot leed.* Heeswijck: Berne Media, 2015.

—. "Lopend onderzoek: De citaten van Etty Hillesum in *Levenskunst.*" In: *Etty Hillesum weer thuis in Middelburg* (Etty Hillesum Studies, 7). Edited by Klaas A.D. Smelik *et al.* Antwerpen-Apeldoorn: Garant, 2015, 171-188.

—. *Steeds een ander uitzicht: Een inleiding in het denken en leven van Etty Hillesum.* Heeswijk: Berne Media, 2015.

—. "Newly discovered sources of Etty Hillesum." In: *The Ethics and Religious Philosophy of Etty Hillesum: Proceedings of the Etty Hillesum Conference at Ghent University, January 2014* (Supplements to The Journal of Jewish Thought and Philosophy, 28). Edited by Klaas A.D. Smelik, Meins G.S. Coetsier & Jurjen Wiersma. Leiden / Boston, MA: Brill, 2017, 299-313.

—. "Etty Hillesum en haar boekje *Levenskunst*: Een document voor onderzoek." In: *Veel mooie woorden: Etty Hillesum en haar boekje Levenskunst.* Edited by Ria van den Brandt & Peter Nissen. Hilversum: Verloren, 2017, 121-133.

—. "'… when you overcome the pain…': Etty Hillesum en Julia de Beausobre." In: *Veel mooie woorden: Etty Hillesum en haar boekje Levenskunst.* Edited by Ria van den Brandt & Peter Nissen. Hilversum: Verloren, 2017, 213-221.

—. "'… wie de andere wang toekeert…': Etty Hillesum en Eli Stanley Jones." In: *Veel mooie woorden: Etty Hillesum en haar boekje Levenskunst.* Edited by Ria van den Brandt & Peter Nissen. Hilversum: Verloren, 2017, 273-281.

—. "'… eine magnetische Kraft…': Etty Hillesum en Charles Alexander Eastman." In: *Veel mooie woorden: Etty Hillesum en haar boekje Levenskunst.* Edited by Ria van den Brandt & Peter Nissen. Hilversum: Verloren, 2017, 299-303.

—. "'Dit is een tijd om in toepassing te brengen: hebt Uwen vijanden lief': Enkele notities bij Hillesums vijandsliefde in *Levenskunst*." In: *Etty Hillesum en de contouren van haar tijd* (Etty Hillesum Studies, 10). Edited by Klaas A.D. Smelik *et al.* Oud-Turnhout / 's-Hertogenbosch: Gompel & Svacina, 2018, 53-67.

Brandt, Ria van den & Alexandra Nagel. "'Driemaal ja en duizend keer nee!' Julius Spier schrijft aan Etty Hillesum." In: *Etty Hillesum 1914-2014* (Etty Hillesum Studies, 6). Edited by Klaas A.D. Smelik *et al.* Antwerpen & Apeldoorn: Garant, 2014, 93-103.

—. "De citaten van Etty Hillesum en Henny Tideman in *Levenskunst*: Facsimile, transcriptie en notenapparaat." In: *Veel mooie woorden: Etty Hillesum en haar boekje Levenskunst.* Edited by Ria van den Brandt & Peter Nissen. Hilversum: Verloren, 2017, 11-117.

Brandt, Ria van den & Peter Nissen (eds.). *Veel mooie woorden: Etty Hillesum en haar boekje Levenskunst.* Hilversum: Verloren, 2017.

Brandt, Ria van den & Klaas A.D. Smelik. *"Wachten jullie op mij?" Etty Hillesum in beeld.* Amsterdam: Balans, 2003 [2nd revised edition, 2016].

—. *Etty Hillesum in facetten* (Etty Hillesum Studies, 1). Edited by Ria van den Brandt & Klaas A.D. Smelik. Budel: Damon, 2003.

—. *Etty Hillesum in Context* (Etty Hillesum Studies, 2). Edited by Ria van den Brandt & Klaas A.D. Smelik. Assen: Van Gorcum, 2007.

—. *Etty Hillesum in discours* (Etty Hillesum Studies, 3). Edited by Ria van den Brandt & Klaas A.D. Smelik. Ghent: Academia Press, 2011.

Brandt, Ria van den, Klaas A.D. Smelik & Meins G.S. Coetsier. *Spirituality in the Writings of Etty Hillesum, Proceedings of the Etty Hillesum Conference at Ghent University, November 2008.* (Supplements to The Journal of Jewish Thought and Philosophy, 11). Edited by Klaas A.D. Smelik, Ria van den Brandt & Meins G.S. Coetsier. Leiden / Boston, MA: Brill, 2010.

—. *Etty Hillesum in perspectief* (Etty Hillesum Studies, 4). Edited by Klaas A.D. Smelik, Ria van den Brandt & Meins G.S. Coetsier. Ghent: Academia Press, 2012.

Brederode, Désanne van. "Etty Hillesum probeerde voluit te leven: Interview met Désanne van Brederode." *Opzij* 26, no. 7/8 (July-August 1998): 80-81.

Breggia, Luciana. *Parole con Etty: Un itinerario verso il presente.* Torino: Claudiana, 2011.

Brenner, Rachel Feldhay. *Writing as Resistance: Four Women Confronting the Holocaust: Edith Stein, Simone Weil, Anne Frank, Etty Hillesum.* Pennsylvania: Pennsylvania State University Press, 1997.

—. "Etty Hillesum: Self-Search as a Writer in the Hell of Westerbork." In: *Women in the Holocaust: Responses, Insights and Perspective.* Edited by Marcia Sachs Littell. Merion Station: Merion Westfield Press International, 2001, 97-103.

—. *Resistencia ante el Holocausto: Edith Stein, Simone Weil, Anna Frank y Etty Hillesum.* Translated by Federico de Carlos Otto. Madrid: Narcea Ediciones, 2005.

—. "Etty Hillesum: A portrait of a Holocaust artist." In: *Spirituality in the Writings of Etty Hillesum: Proceedings of the Etty Hillesum Conference at Ghent University, November 2008* (Supplements to The Journal of Jewish Thought and Philosophy, 11). Edited by Klaas A.D. Smelik, Ria van den Brandt & Meins G.S. Coetsier. Leiden / Boston, MA: Brill, 2010, 235-251.

Brezzi, Francesca. "... e continuo a lodare la vita malgrado tutto." In: *Etty Hillesum, Diario 1941-1943: Un mondo 'altro' è possibile.* Edited by Maria Pia Mazziotti & Gerrit Van Oord. Sant'Oreste: Apeiron Editori, 2002, 9-11.

—. "Etty Hillesum: An 'atypical' mystic." In: *Spirituality in the Writings of Etty Hillesum: Proceedings of the Etty Hillesum Conference at Ghent University, November 2008* (Supplements to The Journal of Jewish Thought and Philosophy, 11). Edited by Klaas A.D. Smelik, Ria van den Brandt & Meins G.S. Coetsier. Leiden / Boston, MA: Brill, 2010, 173-190.

Bridonneau, Yves. *Etty Hillesum cahiers et lettres.* [privately printed].

—. *Etty Hillesum: la Shoah et Dieu.* Saint-Rémy-de-Provence: Édisud, 2014.

Broca, Alexis. "Etty Hillesum: Une intellectuelle libertaire dans les camps." *Le Magazine litéraire* (December 2008). See www.magazine-litteraire.com/actualite/etty-hillesum-intellectuelle-libertaire-camps-01-12-2008-34748 [retrieved 5 November 2013].

Broers, Arjan. *Dwarsliggers in naam van God: Mystici van Hadewijch tot Hillesum.* Baarn / Tielt: Ten Have / Lannoo, 2002.

—. "Van iedereen of niemand zijn: Over het Etty Hillesum Centrum in Deventer." In: *Etty Hillesum in facetten* (Etty Hillesum Studies, 1). Edited by Ria van den Brandt & Klaas A.D. Smelik. Budel: Damon, 2003, 153-164.

Brouns-Wewerinke, Door. *Liefhebben in vrijheid: Het volkomen leven van Etty Hillesum.* Thesis, Tilburg University, 1985.

—. "'Doorgloeid zijn van een warm besef': Etty Hillesum en Kees Schuurman." In: *Veel mooie woorden: Etty Hillesum en haar boekje Levenskunst.* Edited by Ria van den Brandt & Peter Nissen. Hilversum: Verloren, 2017, 229-236.

—. "'Je tiefer es ins Innere geht...': Etty Hillesum en Friedrich Rittelmeyers Johannesevangelie." In: *Veel mooie woorden: Etty Hillesum en haar boekje Levenskunst.* Edited by Ria van den Brandt & Peter Nissen. Hilversum: Verloren, 2017, 245-253.

—. "'Zijt niet bezorgd om Uw leven...': Etty Hillesum, Matteüs en 'de jood Paulus'." In: *Veel mooie woorden: Etty Hillesum en haar boekje Levenskunst.* Edited by Ria van den Brandt & Peter Nissen. Hilversum: Verloren, 2017, 255-267.

Bühler, Pierre. "Het lichamelijke gebed bij Etty Hillesum." In: *Etty Hillesum weer thuis in Middelburg* (Etty Hillesum Studies, 7). Edited by Klaas A.D. Smelik *et al.* Antwerpen-Apeldoorn: Garant, 2015, 85-91.

Burnier, Andreas. "Al het grote is er desondanks." In: *Men zou een pleister op vele wonden willen zijn: Reacties op de dagboeken en brieven van Etty Hillesum.* Edited by J.G. Gaarlandt. Amsterdam: Balans, 1989, 186-191.

Burrell, David B. "Assessing Statements of Faith: Augustine and Etty Hillesum." Chapter 16. In: *Faith and Freedom: An Interfaith Perspective*: *Challenges in Contemporary Theology.* Malden, MA: Blackwell, 2004.

Cales, M.E. *Dagboeken van Etty Hillesum: Bestaat er een verband tussen het razendsnelle ontwikkelingsproces van Etty Hillesum en het ritme van haar schrijven?* Thesis, Paris: Sorbonne University, 1997.

Camarero Santamaría, D. *La chica que no sabía arrodillarse: Etty Hillesum, 1914-1943.* Burgos: Editorial Monte Carmelo, 2002.

Capó, Carme. "Etty Hillesum: Ayudar a Dios en Auschwitz." *Cristianismo Protestante* no. 36 (2005): 11-12.

Capovilla, Nandino & Betta Tusset. *Nei sandali degli ultimi: In Terra Santa con Etty Hillesum.* Presentazione di Tonio dell'Olio. Milano: Paoline Editoriale Libri, 2005.

Cartner, John. *Dialogising life: Etty Hillesum, carnival and the holocaust.* PhD thesis, Murdoch University, 2016.

—. "The carnivalesque in the writings and spirituality of Etty Hillesum." In: *The Ethics and Religious Philosophy of Etty Hillesum: Proceedings of the Etty Hillesum Conference at Ghent University, January 2014* (Supplements to The Journal of Jewish Thought and Philosophy, 28). Edited by Klaas A.D. Smelik, Meins G.S. Coetsier & Jurjen Wiersma. Leiden / Boston, MA: Brill, 2017, 119-143.

Cassells, Cyrus. "Life Indestructible." *Kenyon Review,* New Series 13, no. 4 (1991): 32-39.

Cazeaux, Brigitte. "Etty Hillesum ou l'amour de la vie." *Les cahiers du college* no. 39 (2009): 2-5.

Cereja, Federico. "La deportazione degli ebrei italiani: Alcune linee di lettura." In: *L'esperienza dell'Altro: Studi Su Etty Hillesum.* Edited by Gerrit Van Oord. Sant'Oreste: Apeiron Editori, 1990, 43-52.

Chalier, Catherine. "Une vie bouleversée: Journal 1941-1943 par Etty Hillesum." *Esprit* (August-September 1985): 122ff.

—. "Etty Hillesum: Rejoindre la vie que je portais en moi." In: *Le désir de conversion.* Paris: Editions du Seuil, 2011, 229ff.

Cherifi, Corinne. "Lettres de Westerbork, d'Etty Hillesum." *Artelio* (28 February 2005); see http://nerial.free.fr/artelio/artelio/print_337.html [retrieved 5 November 2013].

Clement, Marja. "'Hineinhorchen' en schrijven: De taal van Etty Hillesum." In: *Etty Hillesum weer thuis in Middelburg* (Etty Hillesum Studies, 7). Edited by Klaas A.D. Smelik *et al.* Antwerpen-Apeldoorn: Garant, 2015, 15-36.

—. "*Hineinhorchen* and writing: The language use of Etty Hillesum." In: *Reading Etty Hillesum in Context: Writings, Life, and Influences of a Visionary Author.* Edited by Klaas A.D. Smelik, Gerrit Van Oord & Jurjen Wiersma. Amsterdam: Amsterdam University Press, 2018, 51-77.

—. "Het meisje dat niet knielen kon: Etty Hillesum en de beweging naar binnen." In: *Etty Hillesum en de contouren van haar tijd* (Etty Hillesum Studies, 10). Edited by Klaas A.D. Smelik *et al.* Oud-Turnhout / 's-Hertogenbosch: Gompel & Svacina, 2018, 69-100.

Clement, Marja, Klaas A.D. Smelik, Meins G.S. Coetsier, Janny van der Molen, Gerrit Van Oord & Jurjen Wiersma (eds.). *Etty Hillesum weer thuis in Middelburg* (Etty Hillesum Studies, 7). Antwerpen-Apeldoorn: Garant, 2015.

Clerc, Jeanne-Marie. "Pour une sagesse concentrationnaire: Le journal d'Etty Hillesum." In: *Le registre sapiential: Le livre de sagesse ou les visages de Protée.* Edited by Sylvie Freyermuth. Bern: Peter Lang, 2007, 243-252.

—. *Etty Hillesum écrivain: Écrire avant Auschwitz.* Paris: L'Harmattan, 2012.

Coccia, Maria. *Etty Hillesum: L'amore oltre la giustizia.* Prefazione di Angela Ales Bello. Roma: Edizioni Universitarie Romane, 2014.

Coelho, Alexandra Lucas. "Etty vai ajudar Deus." *Ípsilon* (02/05/2008): 8-11.

Coetsier, Meins G.S. "God?... Licht in het duister: Twee denkers in barre tijden: De Duitse filosoof Eric Voegelin en de Nederlands-Joodse schrijfster Etty Hillesum." In: *Etty Hillesum in Context* (Etty Hillesum Studies, 2). Edited by Ria van den Brandt & Klaas A.D. Smelik. Assen: Van Gorcum, 2007, 16-35.

—. "Johanna Smelik: Friendship." Interview with Johanna Smelik. Film, *EHOC Archives*, June 2007.

—. "'Heaven in Hell': A Voegelinian Exploration of the Life and Writings of Etty Hillesum." *Annual Meeting of the American Political Science Association (APSA).* Chicago, 2007: 1-7.

—. *Etty Hillesum and the Flow of Presence: A Voegelinian Analysis.* Eric Voegelin Institute Series in Political Philosophy. Studies in Religion and Politics. Columbia, MO: University of Missouri Press, 2008.

—. "Etty Hillesum and the Light of Faith: A Voegelinian Analysis." *Modern Age: A Quarterly Review* 50, no. 3 (2008): 198-206.

—. "'God, the Creative Ground of Existence' in Voegelin, Etty Hillesum and Martin Buber: A Response to Richard Dawkins." In: *The God Delusion. Annual Meeting of the American Political Science Association* (*APSA*). Boston, 2008: 1-20.

—. "Etty Hillesum and the Experience of Reason: Voegelin, Buber & Levinas." In: *Visiting Speaker Series, Department of Philosophy*, Seminar Room of the Moore Institute, Galway University. Galway, 2008: 1-22.

—. "A Heaven-Gram for World Politics: Hillesum, Heschel and Rilke Rescuing God in Exile." In: *Annual Meeting of the American Political Science Association* (*APSA*). Toronto, 2009: 1-16.

—. "Strijd om God: Om het behoud van de menselijke waardigheid." *Tijdschrift voor theologie* 49, no. 4 (2009): 373-390.

—. "'*You-Consciousness*' – Towards Political Theory: Etty Hillesum's Experience and Symbolization of the Divine Presence." In: *Spirituality in the Writings of Etty Hillesum: Proceedings of the Etty Hillesum Conference at Ghent University, November 2008* (Supplements to The Journal of Jewish Thought and Philosophy, 11). Edited by Klaas A.D. Smelik, Ria van den Brandt & Meins G.S. Coetsier. Leiden / Boston, MA: Brill, 2010, 103-124.

—. "Etty Hillesum als hedendaagse spirituele figuur voor Joden en Christenen." In: *Wil er iemand mijn Messias zijn? Nieuwe verlossers en hedendaagse spirituele meesters.* Edited by Didier Pollefeyt & Ellen de Boeck. Leuven: Acco, 2010, 145-178.

—. *Etty Hillesum and the Spiritual Search: An Analysis of the Diaries and Letters 1941-1943. In the light of Martin Buber, Emmanuel Levinas and Dietrich Bonhoeffer.* PhD Thesis, Ghent University, 2012.

—. "Etty Hillesum and the Integral Spirituality of Dialogue: Explorations with Martin Buber." *Studies in Spirituality* 22 (2012): 243-274.

—. "'Humanity's Secret Code': Bonhoeffer and Hillesum and the New Science of Political Theology." *XI. International Bonhoeffer Congress*, Sigtuna, Sweden, 2012: 1-9.

—. "Dialogisch leven in tijden van 'Godsverduistering': Martin Buber en Etty Hillesum." In: *Etty Hillesum in Perspectief* (Etty Hillesum Studies, 4). Edited by Klaas A.D. Smelik, Ria van den Brandt & Meins G.S. Coetsier. Ghent: Academia Press, 2012, 33-47.

—. "'Nous sommes tous responsables': Etty Hillesum en Emmanuel Levinas." In: *Etty Hillesum in Relatie* (Etty Hillesum Studies, 5). Edited by Klaas A.D. Smelik *et al.* Ghent: Academia Press, 2013, 97-120.

—. "'Humanity's Secret Code': Bonhoeffer and Hillesum and the New Science of Political Theology." In: *Dem Rad in die Speichen fallen / A Spoke in the Wheel: Das politische in der theologie Dietrich Bonhoeffers / The Political in the Theology of Dietrich Bonhoeffer.* Edited by Kirsten Busch Nielsen, Ralf Karolus Wüstenberg, Jens Zimmermann. Gütersloh: Gütersloher Verlagshaus, 2013, 203-219.

—. "Time, Memory, and Restless Hearts: Notes on Augustine in Voegelin and Hillesum," In: *Monument and Memory: 4th Nordic Conference in Philosophy of Religion, Stockholm School of Theology,* Sweden, 2013: 1-12.

—. *The Existential Philosophy of Etty Hillesum: An Analysis of her Diaries and Letters* (Supplements to the Journal of Jewish Thought and Philosophy, 22). Leiden / Boston, MA: Brill, 2014.

—. "'Incipit exire, qui incipit amare': Augustinus en Etty Hillesum." In: *Etty Hillesum 1914-2014* (Etty Hillesum Studies, 6). Edited by Klaas A.D. Smelik *et al.* Antwerpen & Apeldoorn: Garant, 2014, 119-139.

—. "Esthetische spiegels: Etty Hillesum en Rainer Maria Rilke." In: *Etty Hillesum weer thuis in Middelburg* (Etty Hillesum Studies, 7). Edited by Klaas A.D. Smelik *et al.* Antwerpen-Apeldoorn: Garant, 2015, 107-134.

—. "Etty Hillesum's ethical consciousness and the history of Jewish philosophy." In: *The Ethics and Religious Philosophy of Etty Hillesum: Proceedings of the Etty Hillesum Conference at Ghent University, January 2014* (Supplements to The Journal of Jewish Thought and Philosophy, 28). Edited by Klaas A.D. Smelik, Meins G.S. Coetsier & Jurjen Wiersma. Leiden / Boston, MA: Brill, 2017, 23-48.

—. "Vrijheidsberoving als menselijke grenssituatie: Etty Hillesum en Viktor Frankl over de zin van het bestaan." In: *Etty Hillesum en het pad naar zelfverwerkelijking* (Etty Hillesum Studies, 9). Edited by Klaas A.D. Smelik *et al.* Antwerpen-Apeldoorn: Garant, 2017, 25-68.

—. "'Aesthetic mirrors': Etty Hillesum and Rainer Maria Rilke." In: *Reading Etty Hillesum in Context: Writings, Life, and Influences of a Visionary Author.* Edited by Klaas A.D. Smelik, Gerrit Van Oord & Jurjen Wiersma. Amsterdam: Amsterdam University Press, 2018, 183-225.

Coetsier, Meins G.S., Klaas A.D. Smelik & Ria van den Brandt (eds.). *Spirituality in the Writings of Etty Hillesum: Proceedings of the Etty Hillesum Conference at Ghent University, November 2008* (Supplements to the Journal of Jewish Thought and Philosophy, 11). Leiden / Boston, MA: Brill, 2010.

—. *Etty Hillesum in Perspectief* (Etty Hillesum Studies, 4). Ghent: Academia Press, 2012.

Coetsier, Meins G.S., Klaas A.D. Smelik, Gerrit Van Oord, Denise de Costa, Janny van der Molen & Jurjen Wiersma (eds.). *Etty Hillesum in Relatie* (Etty Hillesum Studies, 5). Ghent: Academia Press, 2013.

—. *Etty Hillesum 1914-2014* (Etty Hillesum Studies, 6). Antwerpen & Apeldoorn: Garant, 2014.

Coetsier, Meins G.S., Klaas A.D. Smelik, Marja Clement, Janny van der Molen, Gerrit Van Oord & Jurjen Wiersma (eds.). *Etty Hillesum weer thuis in Middelburg* (Etty Hillesum Studies, 7). Antwerpen-Apeldoorn: Garant, 2015, 37-49.

Coffey, Kath. "The Voice of Etty Hillesum." *Midstream* 34, no. 3 (1988): 24-25.

Cohen, Monique Lise. *Etty Hillesum: Une lecture juive.* Paris: Orizons, 2013.

Comer, Sylvia. "Etty Hillesum: The Girl Who Learned to Pray and the Spiritual Exercises." *Review for Religious* 49 (1990): 865-873.

Commers, Ronald. "Loving-kindness, hatred, and moral indignation: Etty Hillesum and Vladimir Jankélévitch, *Ordo amoris*." In: *Reading Etty Hillesum in Context: Writings, Life, and Influences of a Visionary Author.* Edited by Klaas A.D. Smelik, Gerrit Van Oord & Jurjen Wiersma. Amsterdam: Amsterdam University Press, 2018, 459-477.

Comte-Sponville, André. "Etty Hillesum: J'aurais aimé être son amant." *Clés* 69 (February-March 2011).

Cornuz, Michel. *Le ciel est en toi: Introduction à la mystique chrétienne.* Genève: Labor et Fides, 2003: 35-41.

Costa, Denise de. "Ceci n'est pas une cigarette: Een detaillistische lezing van Etty Hillesum." *Lover: Literatuuroverzicht voor de vrouwenbeweging* 18, no. 3 (1991): 140-145.

—. "Nageslacht: Over Etty Hillesum." *Lust & Gratie* (Winter 1993): 81-84.

—. "Etty Hillesum: Beeldhouwster van de ziel." In: *Een beeld van een vrouw.* Edited by Rosi Braidotti. Kampen: Kok Agora, 1993, 109-127.

—. "Hoe 'vrouwelijk' waren Anne Frank en Etty Hillesum? Interview met Denise de Costa." *Opzij* 21, no. 1 (January 1993): 82-83.

—. "Fifty years after the War: Anne Frank and Etty Hillesum Revisited." In: *(W) Righting the Nineties: Papers presented at the ERASMUS-conference: Ghent, May 1994.* Edited by Nicole Rowan. English Department, Ghent University, 1995, 11-16.

—. *Anne Frank en Etty Hillesum: Spiritualiteit, schrijverschap, seksualiteit.* Amsterdam: Balans, 1996.

—. *Anne Frank and Etty Hillesum: Inscribing Spirituality and Sexuality.* Translated by Mischa F.C. Hoyinck & Robert E. Chesal. New Brunswick, NJ: Rutgers University Press, 1998.

—. "Anne Frank and Etty Hillesum: Diarists." In: *Anne Frank: Reflections on Her Life and Legacy.* Edited by Hyman A. Enzer & Sandra Solotaroff-Enzer. Urbana & Chicago, IL: University of Illinois Press, 2000, 214-222.

—. "Etty Hillesum: Dagboekschrijven als innerlijke weg." *Speling: Tijdschrift voor bezinning* 53, no. 2 (June 2001): 65-68.

—. "Fel oranje en vuurrood: Hoe een Nederlands proefschrift over Etty Hillesum gekleurd werd door de Franse filosofie." In: *Etty Hillesum in facetten* (Etty Hillesum Studies, 1). Edited by Ria van den Brandt & Klaas A.D. Smelik. Budel: Damon, 2003, 77-91.

—. *Met pen en penseel: Levenskunst van Anne Frank, Etty Hillesum en Charlotte Salomon.* Etty Hillesum lecture. Deventer: Thieme, 2003.

—. "Etty Hillesum: 'Ecriture feminine'?" In: *Spirituality in the Writings of Etty Hillesum: Proceedings of the Etty Hillesum Conference at Ghent University, November 2008* (Supplements to The Journal of Jewish Thought and Philosophy, 11). Edited by Klaas A.D. Smelik, Ria van den Brandt & Meins G.S. Coetsier. Leiden / Boston, MA: Brill, 2010, 269-278.

—. "Un arancione vivace e un rosso scuro. Come una tesi di dottorato olandese su Etty Hillesum fu colorata dalla filosofia francese." In: *Etty Hillesum: Studi sulla vita e l'opera.* Edited by Gerrit Van Oord. Sant'Oreste: Apeiron Editori, 2013, 24-34.

—. "De ene eeuw is het massamoord en de volgende een economische crisis: De betekenis van Etty Hillesum voor onze tijd." *Spiegelbeeld* 21, no. 4 (april 2014): 66-69.

—. "De nieuwe tijd, die zeker komen zal: De actualiteitswaarde van Etty Hillesum." In: *Etty Hillesum 1914-2014* (Etty Hillesum Studies, 6). Edited by Klaas A.D. Smelik *et al.* Antwerpen & Apeldoorn: Garant, 2014, 15-26.

—. "Bright orange and crimson: How a Dutch dissertation on Etty Hillesum was coloured by French philosophy." In: *Reading Etty Hillesum in Context: Writings, Life, and Influences of a Visionary Author.* Edited by Klaas A.D. Smelik, Gerrit Van Oord & Jurjen Wiersma. Amsterdam: Amsterdam University Press, 2018, 431-444.

Costa, Denise de & Ton Jorna. *Van aandacht en adem tot ziel en zin: Honderd woorden uit het levensbeschouwend idioom van Etty Hillesum.* Utrecht: Kwadraat, 1999.

Costa, Denise de, Ton Jorna & Marijn ten Holt. *De moed hebben tot zichzelf: Etty Hillesum als inspiratiebron bij levensvragen.* Utrecht: Kwadraat, 1999.

Costa, Denise de, Klaas A.D. Smelik, Gerrit Van Oord, Meins G.S. Coetsier, Janny van der Molen & Jurjen Wiersma (eds.). *Etty Hillesum in Relatie* (Etty Hillesum Studies, 5). Ghent: Academia Press, 2013.

—. *Etty Hillesum 1914-2014* (Etty Hillesum Studies, 6). Antwerpen & Apeldoorn: Garant, 2014.

Costa, João Bernard da. "Etty, a rapariga que aprendeu a ajoelhar-se (I)" *Público* 2 (25 May 2008): 9.

—. "Etty, a rapariga que aprendeu a ajoelhar-se (II)" *Público* 2 (1 June 2008): 11.

Cottrau, A. "Etty Hillesum." *Una città per il dialogo* 70 (2002): 11-32.

Cousin, Roger. "Etty Hillesum." *Mémoires de guerre* (26 August 2012); see www.memoiresdeguerre.com/article-hillesum-etty-109427157.html [retrieved 5 November 2013].

Couto, Patricia. "Witnesses and victims of massacre: The literary testimony of Samuel Usque and Etty Hillesum." In: *Spirituality in the Writings of Etty Hillesum: Proceedings of the Etty Hillesum Conference at Ghent University, November 2008* (Supplements to The Journal of Jewish Thought and Philosophy, 11). Edited by Klaas A.D. Smelik, Ria van den Brandt & Meins G.S. Coetsier. Leiden / Boston, MA: Brill, 2010, 335-350.

—. "Saint, cyber phenomenon, thinker, or poet: Etty Hillesum in Portugal." In: *Reading Etty Hillesum in Context: Writings, Life, and Influences of a Visionary Author.* Edited by Klaas A.D. Smelik, Gerrit Van Oord & Jurjen Wiersma. Amsterdam: Amsterdam University Press, 2018, 419-430.

Daenen, Lies (ed.). *Etty Hillesum: Volledig Leven* (SPES cahier). Leuven & Ghent: SPES-forum & Yunus Publishing, 2015.

Dalsace, Rabbin Yeshaya. "Etty Hillesum dialogue intime avec Dieu." *Massorti* (November 2011). See www.massorti.com/Etty-Hillesum-dialogue-intime-avec [retrieved 5 November 2013].

Dam, Paul van. *Bijvoorbeeld Etty Hillesum.* Hilversum: Gooi en Sticht, 1983.

Dekker, Jeanine & Peter Sijnke. "Etty Hillesum: Monument van geestelijk verzet." In: *Het leven in Middelburg, no. 3: Middelburgers van naam en faam.* Edited by Jeanine Dekker. Middelburg: Optima & Zeeuws Archief, 2016, 74-75.

Delaye, Alain. *Sagesses concordantes: Quatre maîtres pour notre temps: Etty Hillesum, Vimala Thakar, Prajnânpad, Krishnamurti.* Paris: Accarias, 2003.

—. Etty Hillesum: Mystique sans frontières. Nantes: Editions Almathée, 2014.

Delforge, Jacques. "Faire front à la violence: Lecture et analyse de trois témoignages." A.I.E.M.P.R. (17 July 2008). See www.aiempr.org/articles/pdf/aiempr34.pdf [retrieved 5 November 2013].

Delville, J.P. *et al.*, *Mystiques et politiques: Une lecture de Bernard de Clairvaux, Claire d'Assise, Julienne de Cornillon, Edith Stein, Etty Hillesum et des sept Pères trappistes de Tibhirine* (Trajectoires, 15). Bruxelles: Lumen Vitae, 2005.

Deriu, Marco. "Etty Hillesum: La forza di una vita vissuta intensamente." *ALFAzeta* no. 60 (1996): 54-59.

—. "L'altro nell'io: Etty Hillesum ed il conflitto dell'essere: Intervista a Frediano Sessi." *ALFAzeta* no. 60 (1996): 32-37.

—. "La resistenza esistenziale di Etty Hillesum." *ALFAzeta* no. 60 (1996): 8-15.

Des Pres, Terrence. "Eros, God and Auschwitz." In: *Men zou een pleister op vele wonden willen zijn: Reacties op de dagboeken en brieven van Etty Hillesum.* Edited by G.J. Gaarlandt. Amsterdam: Balans, 1989, 68-73.

Devoto, Andrea. "Prospettività e assertività nel messaggio di Etty Hillesum." In: *L'esperienza dell'Altro: Studi su Etty Hillesum.* Edited by Gerrit Van Oord. Sant'Oreste: Apeiron Editori, 1990, 129-136.

Dijk, Annette van. "Verlangen en mystieke ervaring: Enkele gedachten over de relatie tussen mystiek, literatuur en de geschriften van Etty Hillesum." *Praktische Humanistiek: Themanummer Etty Hillesum* 9, no. 1 (1999): 36-46.

—. "'... de zich onnaspeurlijk wijzigende tijdgeest...': Etty Hillesum en Simon Vestdijk." In: *Veel mooie woorden: Etty Hillesum en haar boekje Levenskunst.* Edited by Ria van den Brandt & Peter Nissen. Hilversum: Verloren, 2017, 181-183.

—. "'Honestum petimus usque': Etty Hillesum en Albert Verwey." In: *Veel mooie woorden: Etty Hillesum en haar boekje Levenskunst.* Edited by Ria van den Brandt & Peter Nissen. Hilversum: Verloren, 2017, 185-190.

—. "'Wie grote kracht voelt is zacht': Etty Hillesum en Frederik van Eeden." In: *Veel mooie woorden: Etty Hillesum en haar boekje Levenskunst.* Edited by Ria van den Brandt & Peter Nissen. Hilversum: Verloren, 2017, 191-193.

—. "'Selig sind die Sanftmütigen…': Etty Hillesum en Giovanni Papini." In: *Veel mooie woorden: Etty Hillesum en haar boekje Levenskunst.* Edited by Ria van den Brandt & Peter Nissen. Hilversum: Verloren, 2017, 269-272.

Dijkstra, Carl. "Ex captivitate salus: Etty Hillesum en Carl Schmitt: een ongemakkelijke vergelijking." In: *Etty Hillesum en het pad naar zelfverwerkelijking* (Etty Hillesum Studies, 9). Edited by Klaas A.D. Smelik *et al.* Antwerpen-Apeldoorn: Garant, 2017, 89-125.

—. "Het gebeuren en de gebeurtenis: Een Hegeliaans perspectief op Etty Hillesum en Adèle d'Osmond." In: *Etty Hillesum en de contouren van haar tijd* (Etty Hillesum Studies, 10). Edited by Klaas A.D. Smelik *et al.* Oud-Turnhout / 's-Hertogenbosch: Gompel & Svacina, 2018, 101-136.

Di Porto, Bruno. "Etty Hillesum: La ragazza che prese Dio per mano." *Il Tempo e l'idea: Una finestra ebraica sul mondo. Quindicinale di attualità e cultura* 8 (2000): 59-65.

Dittrich, Kathinka. *Berlijn – Amsterdam 1920-1940: Wisselwerkingen.* Amsterdam: Querido, 1982.

Dobner, Cristiana. *Etty Hillesum: Pagine mistiche.* Milan: Ancora, 2007.

—. *Il Volto: Principio di interiorià: Edith Stein, Etty Hillesum.* Genova: Marietti, 2012.

Dongen, Marian van. "Tegenstelling in eenheid: Erotiek en mystiek in het werk van Etty Hillesum." *Lust & Gratie* 22 (Summer 1989): 8-23.

Downey, Michael. "A Balm for all Wounds: The Spiritual Legacy of Etty Hillesum." *Spirituality Today* 40 (Spring 1988): 18-35.

—. "Penning Patterns of Transformation: Etty Hillesum and Thomas Merton." *Merton Annual: Studies in Culture, Spirituality and Social Concerns* 4 (1991): 77-95.

Dreifuss, Gustav. "Individuation under Extreme Conditions: Men Zou Een Pleister op Vele Wonden Willen Zyn (We Should Be Willing to Act as a Balm for All Wounds); An Interrupted Life – The Diaries of Etty Hillesum 1941-1943." *The San Francisco Jung Institute Library Journal* 10, no. 4 (1992): 59-64.

Dresden, Sem. "Etty Hillesum: Identiteit als opgave en oplossing." *De Gids* 153, no. 3 (1990): 159-169.

Dreyer, Pascal. *Etty Hillesum: Une voix bouleversante.* Parijs, Desclée de Brouwer, 1997.

—. *Etty Hillesum: Una testimonianza del Novecento.* Roma: Edizioni Lavoro, 2000.

—. "C'est à nous d'aider Dieu." *La vie* no. 2920 (August 2001).

Driehuis, Jelka. *Holocaust-literatuur in Nederlands: Een studie naar de representatie van Westerbork in werk van Etty Hillesum, Philip Mechanicus, en Jacques Presser.* Thesis, University of Amsterdam, 1993.

Ducrocq, Anne. *Petite anthologie spirituelle pour réenchanter le quotidien.* Paris: Editions Albin Michel, 2011.

—. "Etty Hillesum, une vie bouleversante." See www.cles.com/enquetes/article/etty-hillesum-une-vie-bouleversante [retrieved 5 November 2013].

Dutter, Cécilia. *Etty Hillesum: Une voix dans la nuit.* Paris: Lafont, 2010.

—. "Habiter sa vie d'une paisible densité humaine." *La Vie* no. 3522 (February 2013).

—. *Un cœur universel: Regards croisés sur Etty Hillesum.* En collaboration avec Delphine Horvilleur, Alain Delaye, Ghaleb Bencheich, Jacques Arènes et Emmanuel Jaffelin. Paris: Editions Salvator, 2013.

Duval, Armand. *Etty Hillesum: Quand souffle l'Esprit: Essai.* Paris: François-Xavier de Guibert, 2010.

Eggehorn, Ylva. *Att ta ansvar för Gud: Om hängivenhet som motstånd.* Stockholm: Cordia, 2004.

Verantwoordelijk voor God: Denken en doen van Etty Hillesum en Dietrich Bonhoeffer. Kampen: Ten Have, 2005.

Eisenberg, J. "Connaissez-Vous Etty?" *Information Juive* (1999): 1-16.

Epicoco, Luigi Maria. *Il Dio "Salvato": Etty Hillesum tra storia e profezia.* Rome: Nova Itinera, 2006.

—. *Etty Hillesum: Introduzione ad una donna.* Todi: Tau editrice, 2013.

Ergas, Yasmine. "Growing up Banished: A Reading of Anne Frank and Etty Hillesum." In: *Behind the Lines: Gender and the Two World Wars.* Edited by M. Randolph Higonnet. New Haven, CT: Yale University Press, 1987, 84-95.

—. "Growing up Banished: A Reading of Anne Frank and Etty Hillesum." In: *A Scholarly Look at The Diary of Anne Frank.* Edited by H. Bloom. Philadelphia: Chelsea House Publishers, 1999.

Essunger, Maria. "The phantom of God in the (auto-)biographical writings of Hélène Cixous and Etty Hillesum." In: *The Ethics and Religious Philosophy of Etty Hillesum: Proceedings of the Etty Hillesum Conference at Ghent University, January 2014* (Supplements to The Journal of Jewish Thought and Philosophy, 28). Edited by Klaas A.D. Smelik, Meins G.S. Coetsier & Jurjen Wiersma. Leiden / Boston, MA: Brill, 2017, 205-220.

Ester, Hans. "De spiritualiteit van Etty Hillesum als wapen tegen het kwaad van de Nazi-terreur." *Sophie* 5, no. 1 (2015): 45-49.

—. "'Verschrikkelijker dan het godsgericht...': Etty Hillesum en Walter Schubart." In: *Veel mooie woorden: Etty Hillesum en haar boekje Levenskunst.* Edited by Ria van den Brandt & Peter Nissen. Hilversum: Verloren, 2017, 205-212.

—. "'Jede Gewalt in der Welt wirkt fort...': Etty Hillesum en Walther Rathenau." In: *Veel mooie woorden: Etty Hillesum en haar boekje Levenskunst.* Edited by Ria van den Brandt & Peter Nissen. Hilversum: Verloren, 2017, 237-244.

Etty, Elsbeth. *De pagina monologen: Waarden en normen in de media: Voordracht in het kader van de Etty Hillesumlezing 2001.* Heerde: Langhout & De Vries, 2001.

—. *Etty Hillesum: Introduzione ad una donna.* Todi, Tau Editrice, 2013.

Evans, Mary. "Gender and the Literature of the Holocaust: The Diary of Etty Hillesum." *Women: A Cultural Review* 2, no. 12 (2001): 325-335.

—. "Etty Hillesum: Gender, the modern and the literature of the holocaust." In: *Reading Etty Hillesum in Context: Writings, Life, and Influences of a Visionary Author.* Edited by Klaas A.D. Smelik, Gerrit Van Oord & Jurjen Wiersma. Amsterdam: Amsterdam University Press, 2018, 371-377.

Falque, Odile. "Mystique du quotidien avec Etty Hillesum." *Revue Adolescence* 26, no. 1 (2008): 23-39.

Fasani, Laura. *Guardare, nominare e giudicare le cose del mondo: Lo sguardo lucido di Etty Hillesum e Simone Weil.* Thesis, Università Ca' Foscari, Venezia, 2014/2015.

—. "Twee vrouwen in opstand: Simone Weil en Etty Hillesum." In: *Etty Hillesum en de contouren van haar tijd* (Etty Hillesum Studies, 10). Edited by Klaas A.D. Smelik *et al.* Oud-Turnhout / 's-Hertogenbosch: Gompel & Svacina, 2018, 137-151.

Fenoulhet, Jane. "Intimate Emancipation: Mystical Experience in the Work of Carry van Bruggen and Etty Hillesum." *Forum for Modern Language Studies* 42, no. 3 (2006): 214-225.

Fens, Kees. "Naar een woestijn van medemensen." In: *Men zou een pleister op vele wonden willen zijn: Reacties op de dagboeken en brieven van Etty Hillesum.* Edited by J.G. Gaarlandt. Amsterdam: Balans, 1989, 6-10.

Ferrière, Pierre. "Etty Hillesum, chemin de pauvreté." *Fois et Cultures* no. 4 (December 2008).

Ferrière, Pierre & Isabelle Meeûs-Michiels. *Prier 15 jours avec Etty Hillesum.* Bruyères-le-Châtel (Essonne): Nouvelle Cité, 2005.

—. *Meditiamo 15 giorni con Etty Hillesum.* Milano: Paoline, 2006.

—. *Doch, es gibt eine andere Wirklichkeit: Meditieren mit Etty Hillesum.* Oberpframmern: Verlag Neue Stadt, 2014.

Filippa, Marcella. "Etty, o la ricerca del silenzio e della semplicità." In: *Etty Hillesum: Una testimone del Novecento.* Edited by Pascal Dreyer. Rome: Edizioni Lavoro, 2000, 163-177.

—. "Ripensare Etty Hillesum." *L'indice del mese* 22, no. 2 (2002).

—. "Un mondo 'altro' è possibile: Roma celebra Etty Hillesum." *Via Po* (2002).

Fimiani, Antonella. *Donna della parola: Etty Hillesum e la scrittura che dà origine al mondo.* (Apeiron Saggi, 14). Sant'Oreste: Apeiron, 2017.

Flinders, Carol. *Enduring Lives: Portraits of Women and Faith in Action.* New York: Jeremy P. Tarcher/Penguin, 2006. [reprint: Maryknoll, NY: Orbis Books, 2013].

Fournier, Pierre-André. "Etty Hillesum, héroïne de la condition humaine." *Progrès Echo* (20 November 2011). See http://mondieuetmontout.com/Mgr.-Pierre-Andre-Fournier-2011-Etty-Hillesum-heroine-de-la-condition-humaine-Salon-du-livre.html [retrieved 5 November 2013].

Frank, Evelyne. *Avec Etty Hillesum: Dans la quête du bonheur, un chemin inattendu: Une lecture d'Une vie bouleversée et des Lettres de Westerbork.* Genève: Labor et Fides, 2002.

—. *Con Etty Hillesum alla ricerca della felicità un cammino inatteso: Una lettura del Diario e delle Lettere da Westerbork.* Milano: Gribaudi, 2005.

—. "Trouw zijn aan zichzelf, in de geschriften van Etty Hillesum zoals vertaald in het Frans." In: *Etty Hillesum in discours* (Etty Hillesum Studies, 3). Edited by Ria van den Brandt & Klaas A.D. Smelik. Ghent: Academia Press, 2011, 35-47.

Fromaget, Michel. *Un joyau dans la nuit: Introduction à la vie spirituelle d'Etty Hillesum.* Paris: Desclée de Brouwer, 2014

Funk, Viola. *La chose que je n'ose pas nommer: (Un)articulated lived experience in the journals of Marie Bashkirtseff and Etty Hillesum.* Thesis, Vancouver: Simon Fraser University, 1997.

Gaarlandt, Jan Geurt. "Introduction." In: Etty Hillesum. *An Interrupted Life: The Diaries of Etty Hillesum, 1941-1943.* New York: Pantheon Books, 1984, vii-xiv.

—. "Introduction." In: Etty Hillesum. *Letters from Westerbork.* New York: Random House, 1986, xi-xviii.

—. (ed). *Men zou een pleister op vele wonden willen zijn: Reacties op de dagboeken en brieven van Etty Hillesum.* Amsterdam: Balans, 1989.

—. "Men zou een pleister op vele wonden willen zijn." In: *Men zou een pleister op vele wonden willen zijn: Reacties op de dagboeken en brieven van Etty Hillesum.* Edited by J.G. Gaarlandt. Amsterdam: Balans, 1989, ix-xi.

—. "Context, dilemmas, and misunderstandings during the composition and publication of *An Interrupted Life: Etty Hillesum's Diary, 1941-1943.*" In: *Spirituality in the Writings of Etty Hillesum: Proceedings of the Etty Hillesum Conference at Ghent University, November 2008* (Supplements to The Journal of Jewish Thought and Philosophy, 11). Edited by Klaas A.D. Smelik, Ria van den Brandt & Meins G.S. Coetsier. Leiden / Boston, MA: Brill, 2010, 365-375.

Gaeta, Giancarlo. "La gratuità come categorie dell'agire politico." *Linea ombra* no. 74 (1992): 6-10.

—. "Costruire il futuro a partire da se stessi: Un vero senso della storia: La lezione di umanità di Etty Hillesum." *ALFAzeta* no. 60 (1996): 44-47.

—. "Woolf, Weil, Hillesum: La libertà di pensare le cose come sono." *Lo Straniero* 1, no. 1 (1997).

—. "Scrittura diaristica e trascendenza in Etty Hillesum." *Intersezioni* 19, no. 3 (1999): 379-388.

—. "Etty Hillesum: Destino di massa e coscienza storica." In: *Religione per il nostro tempo.* Edited by Giancarlo Gaeta. Roma: Edizioni E/O, 2000, 53-66.

—. "Genesi di una trasformazione interiore." *Lo Straniero* 4, no. 21 (2002): 5-9.

—. *Il privilegio di giudicare: Scritti su Etty Hillesum.* Sant'Oreste: Apeiron Editori, 2016.

—. "De vorm van het ik en het scheppend verlangen." In: *Etty Hillesum en het pad naar zelfverwerkelijking* (Etty Hillesum Studies, 9). Edited by Klaas A.D. Smelik *et al.* Antwerpen-Apeldoorn: Garant, 2017, 173-181.

Gagné, Laurie Brands. *The Uses of Darkness: Women's Underworld Journeys, Ancient and Modern.* Notre Dame, IN.: University of Notre Dame Press, 2000.

Gaillardetz, Richard R. "Etty Hillesum, Suffering and Sexuality: Reflections on Passionate Living." *Spirituality* 6 (May-June, 2000): 148-152.

—. "Sexual Vulnerability and a Spirituality of Suffering: Explorations in the Writing of Etty Hillesum." *Pacifica* 22, no. 1 (February 2009): 75-89.

Galen Last, Dick van & Rolf Wolfswinkel. *Anne Frank and After: Dutch Holocaust Literature in Historical Perspective.* Amsterdam: Amsterdam University Press, 1996.

Galotti, Agnese. "Etty Hillesum [Profili]." *Individuazione* 4, no. 22 (1997): 4.

Gastão, Ana Marques. "A mulher que desejava proteger e ajudar Deus." *Diário de Notícias* (28/04/2008): 50.

Gendron, Sylvie. *La joie dans le Journal d'Etty Hillesum.* Thesis, Université de Montréal, 1993.

Gentili, Antonio. *"Sarò io ad aiutare Dio": Il cammino spirituale di Etty Hillesum.* Milano: Ancora, 2014.

Gentiloni, Filippo. "Parole che resistono." *L'indice dei libri del mese* 6 (June 1986): 7.

—. "Le parole di Etty Hillesum per riscrivere il futuro quando salvare il corpo è troppo poco", *Il Manifesto*, 9/11/90.

Germain, Sylvie. *Etty Hillesum: Chemins d'éternité.* Paris: Pygmalion / Gérard Watelet, 1999.

—. *Etty Hillesum: Una coscienza ispirata.* Rome: Edizioni Lavoro, 2001.

—. *Etty Hillesum: Een spirituele biografie.* Amsterdam: Balans, 2001.

—. *Etty Hillesum: Una vida.* Santander: Editorial Sal Terrae, 2004.

—. "Kroniek van de eeuwigheid." In: *Etty Hillesum in discours* (Etty Hillesum Studies, 3). Edited by Ria van den Brandt & Klaas A.D. Smelik. Ghent: Academia Press, 2011, 27-35.

Geurts, Jan. *"Ongeremd in het menselijke" (dagboek 21 maart 1942): De verandering bij Etty Hillesum, aan de hand van één der Westerbork-brieven.* Thesis, Tilburg University, 1990.

Goetze, Maria C. *Etty Hillesums Rilke-Lektüre.* Thesis, Utrecht University, 2006.

Giebner, Beate. "Lichaam, ziel en geest: Bezield leven." *Praktische Humanistiek: Themanummer Etty Hillesum* 9, no. 1 (1999): 13-17.

Giles, Mary E. "Reflections on Suffering in a Mystical-Feminist Key." *Journal of Spiritual Formation* 15 (1994): 137-146.

Ginapri, Laura. *Paesaggio di un anima: Etty Hillesum: Uno sguardo diverso sulla Shoa.* Thesis, Università Ca' Foscari, Venezia 2000.

—. "Una donna coraggiosa." In: *Etty Hillesum, Diario 1941-1943: Un mondo "altro" è possibile.* Edited by Maria Pia Mazziotti & Gerrit Van Oord. Sant'Oreste: Apeiron, 2002, 28-29.

Gindre, Caroline. "Conversation imaginaire avec Etty Hillesum." *Hommes et faites* (June 2006). See www.hommes-et-faits.com/Dial/spip.php?article58 [retrieved 5 November 2013]. The first version of this text was published in revue *Conscience de,* no. 12 (March 1989).

Giuntella, V.E. "Gli scritti di Etty Hillesum come fonte storica." In: *L'esperienza dell'Altro: Studi su Etty Hillesum.* Edited by Gerrit Van Oord. Sant'Oreste: Apeiron Editori, 1990, 59-57.

Goetze, Maria. "'Erst muss man Gott irgendwo finden...': Etty Hillesum en Rainer Maria Rilke." In: *Veel mooie woorden: Etty Hillesum en haar boekje Levenskunst.* Edited by Ria van den Brandt & Peter Nissen. Hilversum: Verloren, 2017, 169-179.

Goldstein-Glaser, Yvonne. *Reacties op de werken van Etty Hillesum in binnen- en buitenland, april 1981-juli 1992.* Amsterdam: Etty Hillesum Stichting, 1993 [privately printed].

Gomel, Sara. *Il racconto di sé come apertura etica: Un'analisi filosofica del diario di Etty Hillesum.* Thesis, Sapienza Università di Roma, 2018.

González Faus, José Ignacio. *Etty Hillesum: Una vida que interpela.* Santander: Sal Terrae, 2008.

Granstedt, Ingmar. *Portrait d'Etty Hillesum.* Paris: Desclée de Brouwer, 2001.

—. *Ritratto di Etty Hillesum.* Milano: Paoline, 2003.

—. "Etty Hillesum: Une parole de Dieu dans la Shoah." *Théophilyon* 8, no. 2 (2003).

—. *De cendres et d'amour: Portrait d'Etty Hillesum: Amsterdam, Westerbork, Auschwitz.* Paris: Lethielleux, 2011.

Greif, Gideon. *Ein abgeschittenes Leben. Das Tagebuch von Etty Hillesum 1941-1943*: In: Walter Schmitz (ed.). *Erinnerte Shoah: Die Literatur der Überlebenden.* Dresden: Thelem, 2003.

—. "Jüdische Schicksale während der Shoah – basierend auf Tagebüchern: Der Fall von Hillesum und Perechodnik." *Psychosozial* 28, no. 100 (2005): 85-92.

Grimmelikhuizen, Frits. "Een mens kan hier niet gedijen." *Het Deventer Dagblad* (4 December 1999).

—. "Etty Hillesum." In: *De pagina Monologen*. Heerde: Langhout & De Vries, 2001, 31-46.

—. "Hass ist eine Krankheit der Seele." *Wir Frauen* 22, no. 4 (Winter 2003): 26.

—. "De TAO van Etty Hillesum." *Prana* no. 141 (2004): 32-36.

—. "The road of Etty Hillesum to nothingness." In: *Spirituality in the Writings of Etty Hillesum: Proceedings of the Etty Hillesum Conference at Ghent University, November 2008* (Supplements to The Journal of Jewish Thought and Philosophy, 11). Edited by Klaas A.D. Smelik, Ria van den Brandt & Meins G.S. Coetsier. Leiden / Boston, MA: Brill, 2010, 429-445.

—. *Alleen met heel je hart aanwezig zijn: De invloed van Rainer Maria Rilke op het kunstenaarschap van Etty Hillesum*. Deventer: Frits Grimmelikhuizen, 2011 [privately printed].

—. *Etty Hillesum leest Rainer Maria Rilke: De invloed van Rainer Maria Rilke op het kunstenaarschap van Etty Hillesum*. Deventer: Uitgeverij Oorsprong, 2016[4].

Groot, Anouta de. "Aandacht voor identiteit, spiritualiteit en verbondenheid: Centrale thema's in de Amerikaanse literatuur over Etty Hillesum." In: *Etty Hillesum in facetten* (Etty Hillesum Studies, 1). Edited by Ria van den Brandt & Klaas A.D. Smelik. Budel: Damon, 2003, 129-151.

Gruyter, Rentsje de. "Er duiken steeds nieuwe puzzelstukjes op: Directeur van Etty Hillesum Onderzoekscentrum." *JHMmagazine* 23, no. 1 (2014): 18-19.

Guasco, Maurilio. "Etty Hillesum: La religione della libertà." In: Luigi Gambino (ed.). *Stato Autorità Libertà: Studi in onore di Mario d'Addio*, Roma: Aracne, 2006, 325-337.

Gubar, Susan. "Falling for Etty Hillesum." *Common Knowledge* 12, no. 2 (2006): 279-302.

Guerreiro, António, "Etty: O espaço interior do mundo." *Expresso* (13 June 2008): 43.

Gur-Klein, Thalia. "From separation to communitas: Etty Hillesum, a Jewish perspective." In: *Reading Etty Hillesum in Context: Writings, Life, and Influences of a Visionary Author*. Edited by Klaas A.D. Smelik, Gerrit Van Oord & Jurjen Wiersma. Amsterdam: Amsterdam University Press, 2018, 333-359.

Hahn, Karel J. "Richtsnoer voor menselijkheid." In: *Men zou een pleister op vele wonden willen zijn: Reacties op de dagboeken en brieven van Etty Hillesum*. Edited by J.G. Gaarlandt. Amsterdam: Balans, 1989, 54-67.

—. "Etty Hillesum: Purificazione ai limiti dell'esistenza." In: *L'esperienza dell'Altro: Studi su Etty Hillesum*. Edited by Gerrit Van Oord. Sant'Oreste: Apeiron Editori, 1990, 59-75.

Halperin, Irving. "Etty Hillesum: A Story of Spiritual Growth." In: *Reflections of the Holocaust in Art and Literature*. Edited by Randolph L. Braham. New York: Boulder, 1990, 1-16.

Hannafey, Francis T. "Ethics as Transformative Love: The Moral World of Etty Hillesum." *Horizons* 28, no.1 (2001): 68-80.

Haumonté, Odile. *Je veux consoler Dieu: Etty Hillesum*. Saint-Céneré: Pierre Téqui Éditeur, 2014.

Heldring, J.L. "De heilige van het Museumplein." In: *Men zou een pleister op vele wonden willen zijn: Reacties op de dagboeken en brieven van Etty Hillesum*. Edited by J.G. Gaarlandt. Amsterdam: Balans, 1989, 22-24.

—. "Een tweede Carry van Bruggen?" In: *Men zou een pleister op vele wonden willen zijn: Reacties op de dagboeken en brieven van Etty Hillesum*. Edited by J.G. Gaarlandt. Amsterdam: Balans, 1989, 48-50.

Herlédan, Marie-Laure Jeanne & Joseph Thomas Gilles Herlédan. *Esther Hillesum: Entre fleurs et poésie: la trace du nom*. Assérac: Des sources et des livres, 2010.

Herzberg, Abel J. *Kroniek der Jodenvervolging*. Amsterdam: Van Loghum Slaterus, 1950.

—. "Esther Hillesum: In memoriam." *Werkschrift* 14, no. 1 (1994): 17-20.

Hick, John, Ninian Smart & David B. Burrell. *Hermeneutics, Religious Pluralism, and Truth: Lectures*. Winston-Salem, NC: Wake Forest University, 1989.

Hicks, Joshua A. & Laura A. King. "Meaning in Life as a Subjective Judgment and a Lived Experience." *Social and Personality Psychology Compass* 3, no. 4 (July 2009): 638-653.

Hinrichs, Jan Paul, "Franse paters vallen voor Etty Hillesum: Etty Hillesum in Frankrijk." In: *De Parelduiker* 17, no. 3 (2012): 46-48.

Hirt, Jean-Michel. "Résistance de la psyché." In: *Études, revue de culture contemporaine* 414, no. 2 (2011): 238-240.

—. *La dignité humaine: Sous le regard d'Etty Hillesum et de Sigmund Freud*. Paris: Desclée de Brouwer, 2012.

Hogenstijn, Clemens. *De akker van de geest bewerken: Geschiedenis van het voortgezet onderwijs te Deventer: Van Kapittelschool tot Etty Hillesum Lyceum*. Deventer: Arko Uitgeverij, 2005.

Holligan, Carrie Lynn. *An Interrupted Writer: Etty Hillesum and the Power of Expressive Journaling*. Thesis, State University of New York at New Paltz, 2005.

Hoogewoud, F.J. "A photograph of the Deventer Gymnasium on 29 November 1940 as a protest." *Studia Rosenthaliana*, 33, no. 1 (1999): 77-79.

—. "'Ware vreugde is iets ernstigs': Dr. Louis Hillesums gedwongen afscheid van het stedelijk gymnasium in Deventer, 29 november 1940." In: *Etty Hillesum in weerwil van het Joodse vraagstuk* (Etty Hillesum Studies, 8). Edited by Klaas A.D. Smelik *et al.* Antwerpen-Apeldoorn: Garant, 2016, 11-40.

Hulsebos, Anne-Marleen. *Een monument van levenskunst: Over de onthullende Westerbork-brieven van Etty Hillesum (1914-1943) in een verhulde oorlogsuitgave*. Thesis, University of Amsterdam, 2002.

Hulst, J.W. van. *Treinen naar de hel: Amsterdam-Westerbork-Auschwitz: Een aantal beschouwingen die verband houden met het dagboek en de brieven van Etty Hillesum.* Amsterdam: Buijten & Schipperheijn, 1983.

Iacopini, Beatrice & Sabrina Moser. *Uno sguardo nuovo: Il problema del male in Etty Hillesum e Simone Weil.* Cinisello Balsamo (MI): Edizioni San Paolo, 2009.

Jackson, Timothy P. "'Heroism on an Empty Stomach': Weil and Hillesum on Love and Happiness Amid the Holocaust." *Journal of Religious Ethics* 40 (March 2012): 72-98.

Jager, Karen de. "Hillesum typisch Joodse denker." *Joods nu* 1, no. 1 (2014): 11-13.

Joldersma, Hermina. "Mosaic Stones for the Holocaust: Etty Hillesum: 'Letters from Westerbork' and Jona Oberski: 'Childhood'." *Canadian Journal of Netherlandic Studies: The Journal of the Association for the Advancement of Netherlandic Studies = Revue canadienne d'études néerlandaises: La revue de l'Association canadienne pour l'avancement des études néerlandaises* 10, no. 2 (1989): 27-30.

Jollien, Alexandre. "Baume pour occlusion de l'âme." *Le Nouvelliste* (4 June 2005): 6.

Jorna, Ton. "Etty Hillesum als inspiratiebron bij het (leren) omgaan met zinvragen: De waarde van de overwegingen bij en de resultaten van het onderzoek naar de dagboeken en brieven van Etty Hillesum." *Praktische Humanistiek: Themanummer Etty Hillesum* 9, no. 1 (1999): 5-12.

—. *"En mijn verrukte ogen lezen maar": Aard en betekenis van het fenomeen inspiratiebron op basis van de nagelaten geschriften van Etty Hillesum.* Heerde: Langhout & de Vries, 2000.

—. "'M'n intiemste gebaar': Van meditatie tot gebed in de dagboeken van Etty Hillesum." *Herademing* 8, no. 2 (2000): 33-38.

—. "'De grote gevoelens en verbondenheden in hun afgerond geheel': Over mensenliefde en religiositeit in het werk van Etty Hillesum." In: *Humanisme en religie: Controverses, bruggen, perspectieven.* Edited by J. Duyndam, M. Poorthuis & Th. de Wit. Delft: Eburon, 2005, 215-228.

Jorna, Ton & Denise de Costa. *Van aandacht en adem tot ziel en zin: Honderd woorden uit het levensbeschouwend idioom van Etty Hillesum.* Utrecht: Kwadraat, 1999.

Jorna, Ton, Denise de Costa & Marijn ten Holt. *De moed hebben tot zichzelf: Etty Hillesum als inspiratiebron bij levensvragen.* Utrecht: Kwadraat, 1999.

Jorna, Ton & Julika Marijn (eds.). *Altijd Etty: Etty Hillesum, blijvende inspiratiebron voor een rijk innerlijk leven.* Utrecht: Ten Have, 2014.

Jorna, Ton, Manja Pach & Klaas A.D. Smelik. "Huiswerk voor de eigen werkplaats: De actualiteit van Etty Hillesum." *Rondom het Woord* 42, no. 2 (2000): 5-13.

Juliet, Charles, Dominique Sterckx & Claude Vigée. *Etty Hillesum: Histoire de la fille qui ne savait pas s'agenouiller.* Introduction by Liliane Hillesum. Orbey: Arfuyen, 2007.

Kamel, Rose. "Interrupted lives, inner resources: The diaries of Hannah Senesh and Etty Hillesum." *Women's Studies Quarterly* 17, no. 3-4 (1989): 45-58.

Keller, Hildegard Elisabeth. *Der Ozean im Fingerhut: Hildegard von Bingen, Mechthid von Magdeburg, Hadewijch und Etty Hillesum im Gespräch. Mit Beiträgen von Daniel Hell und Jeffrey F. Hamburger* (Trilogie des Zeitlosen 3). Zürich: Hochschulverlag AG an der ETH Zürich, 2011.

Kessler, Valerie Denise. *The Diaries and Letters of Etty Hillesum: Writing Journeys and the Creativity of Spirituality.* Thesis, Lexington, KY: University of Kentucky, 1996.

Kidder, Annemarie S. "Introduction." In: *Etty Hillesum: Essential Writings.* Maryknoll, NY: Orbis Bks., 2009, 7-24.

King, Peter. "Etty Hillesum: 'At One with All Existence'." In: *Dark Night Spirituality: Thomas Merton, Dietrich Bonhoeffer, Etty Hillesum: Contemplation and the New Paradigm.* London: SPCK, 1995, 35-45.

Kleef-Hillesum, Suse van. "Een oorlogsdocument dat bevrijdt van angst." In: *Men zou een pleister op vele wonden willen zijn: Reacties op de dagboeken en brieven van Etty Hillesum.* Edited by J.G. Gaarlandt. Amsterdam: Balans, 1989, 19-21.

—. "Haarscherpe beelden van een onbeschrijflijke werkelijkheid." In: *Men zou een pleister op vele wonden willen zijn: Reacties op de dagboeken en brieven van Etty Hillesum.* Edited by J.G. Gaarlandt. Amsterdam: Balans, 1989, 51-53.

Klooster, Leonie. *Etty Hillesum en de relatie tussen het Goede, het Schone en het Goddelijke: Een studie naar de ontwikkeling van Hillesums wereldbeschouwing aan de hand van de Weltanschauungslehre van Wilhelm Dilthey.* Thesis, Leiden University, 2011.

Koot, Corrie. *Maak 'gewoon' tot iets bijzonders.* Den Haag: Mirananda, 1987.

Kornblatt, Joyce. "Refuge in the Storm: A Meditation on Etty Hillesum." *Parabola* 33, no.4 (2008): 86-92.

Krabbendam, Hans. "Amerika in de schaduw: Etty Hillesum als bemiddelaar tussen de koude oorlog-perspectieven op de holocaust." In: *Etty Hillesum in weerwil van het Joodse vraagstuk* (Etty Hillesum Studies, 8). Edited by Klaas A.D. Smelik *et al.* Antwerpen-Apeldoorn: Garant, 2016, 159-170.

—. "America in the shade: Etty Hillesum as mediator between the cold war perspectives on the holocaust." In: *Reading Etty Hillesum in Context: Writings, Life, and Influences of a Visionary Author.* Edited by Klaas A.D. Smelik, Gerrit Van Oord & Jurjen Wiersma. Amsterdam: Amsterdam University Press, 2018, 379-393.

Kristel, Conny. *Geschiedschrijving als opdracht: Abel Herzberg, Jacques Presser en Lou de Jong over de Jodenvervolging.* Amsterdam: Meulenhoff, 1998.

Kroke, Roman. *L'araignée et sa toile, regards sur le cœur pensant d'Etty Hillesum, juive néerlandaise (1914-1943).* Wavre: Mediel, 2012.

—. *The Spider and its Web: Insights into the Thinking Heart of the Dutch Jew Etty Hillesum (1914-1943).* Wavre: Mediel, 2012.

—. *Die Spinne und ihr Netz: Einblicke in das denkende Herz der holländischen Jüdin Etty Hillesum (1914-1943)*. Wavre: Mediel, 2012.

Kroon, Ben & Corine Spoor. "Ze was iemand die alles gaf en alles nam, dat hoorde bij haar warmte." In: *Men zou een pleister op vele wonden willen zijn: Reacties op de dagboeken en brieven van Etty Hillesum*. Edited by J.G. Gaarlandt. Amsterdam: Balans, 1989, 25-40.

Labarile, Francesco. *Narrare la shoah oggi: Il contributo di Etty Hillesum*. Campobasso, 2016.

Laberge, Hélène. "Etty Hillesum." *Encyclopédie de l'Agora* (1 April 2012). See http://agora.qc.ca/Dossiers/Etty_Hillesum [retrieved 5 November 2013].

Lagerweij, Anneke. *Een vrije vogel vogelvrij: Etty Hillesum: Spiritualiteit in dialoog?* Thesis, Catholic Theological Academy Amsterdam (KTHA), 1986.

Lagrou, Els. *Etty Hillesum, 1914-1943: Een historisch-biografische studie*. MA Thesis, KU Leuven, 1986.

Landrot, Marine. "Les écrits d'Etty Hillesum, Journaux et lettres 1941-1943." *Télérama*, no. 3073 (December 2008). See www.telerama.fr/livres/les-ecrits-d-etty-hillesum-journaux-et-lettres-1941-1943,36468.php [retrieved 5 November 2013].

Lathouwers, Ton. "'De Waarheid: Dat is de sprong!': Etty Hillesum, 'De moed hebben tot zichzelf' en de Russische literatuur uit de periode van de zogenaamde 'Dooi' (1953-1975)." *Praktische Humanistiek. Themanummer Etty Hillesum* 9, no. 1 (1999): 18-30.

Lebeau, Paul. *Etty Hillesum: Un itinéraire spirituel: Amsterdam 1941-Auschwitz 1943*. Namur / Bruxelles: Éditions Fidélité / Éditions Racine, 1998.

—. *Etty Hillesum: Een spirituele zoektocht: Amsterdam 1941-Auschwitz 1943*. Tielt / Baarn: Lannoo / Ten Have, 1999.

—. *Etty Hillesum: Un itinerario spirituale: Amsterdam 1941-Auschwitz 1943*. Milano: Paoline editoriale, 2000.

—. *Etty Hillesum: Un itinerario espiritual: Amsterdam 1941-Auschwitz 1943*. Santander: Sal Terrae, 2000.

—. "Un itinéraire spirituel européen: Etty Hillesum (Amsterdam 1941-Auschwitz 1943)." *Nouvelle revue théologique* 121, no. 3 (1999): 397-416.

—. "Il Diario di Etty Hillesum." *Civiltà Cattolica* (5-19 August 2000): 235-248.

—. "The reception of Etty Hillesum's writing in French language." In: *Spirituality in the Writings of Etty Hillesum: Proceedings of the Etty Hillesum Conference at Ghent University, November 2008* (Supplements to The Journal of Jewish Thought and Philosophy, 11). Edited by Klaas A.D. Smelik, Ria van den Brandt & Meins G.S. Coetsier. Leiden / Boston, MA: Brill, 2010, 191-213.

—. "Sur les traces d'Etty Hillesum." [Lebeaux, Yves & Monique Durand]. *La maison de Tobie* 89 (2011): 1-6.

Leersum, Marijke van. *'Ziezo zusje, nu wordt er gewerkt of ik mep je dood !': The idiolect of Etty Hillesum in English and Swedish translation.* MA Thesis, Utrecht University, 2018.

Leibovici, Solange. "De Belle Juive." *De Groene Amsterdammer* 124, no. 3 (2000): 20-21.

Léna, Marguerite. "La trace d'une rencontre, Edith Stein et Etty Hillesum." *Études* 401, no. 7/8 (2004): 51-63.

Leroux, Georges. "Aimer «malgré tout»." *Le devoir* (September 2009). See www.ledevoir.com/culture/livres/266599/philosophie-aimer-malgre-tout [retrieved 5 November 2013].

Lettinck, Han & Els Boon. "Etty Hillesums Winschoter jaren (1918-1924) en de mensen die haar omringden." In: *Etty Hillesum in Relatie* (Etty Hillesum Studies, 5). Edited by Klaas A.D. Smelik *et al.* Ghent: Academia Press, 2013, 175-204.

Lewin, Lisette. "Er lijkt een cultus te ontstaan rond Etty Hillesum met griezelige kanten." *De Groene Amsterdammer* (8 June 8 1984).

Liebert, Elizabeth. "The Thinking Heart: Development Dynamics in Etty Hillesum's Diaries." *Pastoral Psychology* 43 (1995): 393-409.

Liempt, Ad van. "Dagboeken op de drempel van de ondergang." In: *Etty Hillesum in Relatie* (Etty Hillesum Studies, 5). Edited by Klaas A.D. Smelik *et al.* Ghent: Academia Press, 2013, 5-15.

Limentani, Giacoma. "Diario 1941-1943." *La Rassegna Mensile di Israel* 102, no. 1 (1986): 262-266.

—. "Il linguaggio del corpo." In: *L'esperienza dell'Altro: Studi su Etty Hillesum.* Edited by Gerrit Van Oord. Sant'Oreste: Apeiron Editori, 1990, 137-144.

—. "De taal van het lichaam." In: *Etty Hillesum en de contouren van haar tijd* (Etty Hillesum Studies, 10). Edited by Klaas A.D. Smelik *et al.* Oud-Turnhout / 's-Hertogenbosch: Gompel & Svacina, 2018, 157-165.

Lincoln, Ulrich. "The courage to write: Biography and religion in Etty Hillesum and Søren Kierkegaard." In: *The Ethics and Religious Philosophy of Etty Hillesum: Proceedings of the Etty Hillesum Conference at Ghent University, January 2014* (Supplements to The Journal of Jewish Thought and Philosophy, 28). Edited by Klaas A.D. Smelik, Meins G.S. Coetsier & Jurjen Wiersma. Leiden / Boston, MA: Brill, 2017, 158-169.

Linden, Saskia van der. "De wetenschap gaat toch altijd door: De docenten en medestudenten Russisch van Etty Hillesum." *Kolokol'cik* 16 (August 1997): 21-24.

Lindwer, Willy. *Kamp van hoop en wanhoop: Getuigen van Westerbork 1939-1945.* Amsterdam: Uitgeverij Balans, 1990.

Llontop, Rosamaría. *Eros, philia e agápe nella vita e negli scritti di Etty Hillesum.* Thesis, Rome: Pontificia Università Lateranense, 2007.

Lobet, B. "Etty Hillesum ou le cœur pensant." *Le Monde des Livres* (1999): 29.

Lucchetti Bingemer, Maria Clara. "The journal of Etty Hillesum from eros to agape." In: *The Ethics and Religious Philosophy of Etty Hillesum: Proceedings of the Etty Hillesum Conference at Ghent University, January 2014* (Supplements to The Journal of Jewish Thought and Philosophy, 28). Edited by Klaas A.D. Smelik, Meins G.S. Coetsier & Jurjen Wiersma. Leiden / Boston, MA: Brill, 2017, 68-89.

Maanen, Willem G. van. *Etty: Toneelstuk over Etty Hillesum.* Baarn: De Prom, 1988.

Maas, Frans. *Spiritualiteit als inzicht: Mystieke teksten en theologische reflecties.* Zoetermeer: Meinema, 1999.

—. *Spirituality as Insight: Mystical Texts and Theological Reflection.* Louvain, Belgium: Peeters, 2004.

—. "In me is heaven: An exploration of Etty Hillesum." *Mount Carmel* 54, no. 1 (2006): 28-34.

Makkonen, Anna. "Holocaust Chronicle, Spiritual Autobiography, Portrait of an Artist, Novel in the Making: Reading the Abridged Diary of Etty Hillesum." *Biography (Honolulu)* 22, no. 2 (1999): 237-261.

Manara, Fulvio Cesare. "Pagine mistiche di Etty Hillesum?" *Con Etty Hillesum: Quaderni di informazione e di ricerca*, no. 1 (2009): 28-36.

—. "Philosophy as a way of life in the works of Etty Hillesum." In: *Spirituality in the Writings of Etty Hillesum: Proceedings of the Etty Hillesum Conference at Ghent University, November 2008* (Supplements to The Journal of Jewish Thought and Philosophy, 11). Edited by Klaas A.D. Smelik, Ria van den Brandt & Meins G.S. Coetsier. Leiden / Boston, MA: Brill, 2010, 379-398.

—. "Oltre la ragione, un'altra filosofia: Etty Hillesum e la vita filosofica." In: *Etty Hillesum: Studi sulla vita e l'opera.* Edited by Gerrit Van Oord. Sant'Oreste: Apeiron Editori, 2013, 35-57.

—. "Dimensions of mystical experience in the thinking and behavior of Etty Hillesum." In: *The Ethics and Religious Philosophy of Etty Hillesum: Proceedings of the Etty Hillesum Conference at Ghent University, January 2014* (Supplements to The Journal of Jewish Thought and Philosophy, 28). Edited by Klaas A.D. Smelik, Meins G.S. Coetsier & Jurjen Wiersma. Leiden / Boston, MA: Brill, 2017, 49-67.

Manara, Fulvio Cesare & Gerrit Van Oord. "Presentazione." *Con Etty Hillesum: Quaderni di informazione e di ricerca* no. 1 (2009): 5-7.

Marchelli, Silvia. "Né vittima né aguzzino: Riflesssioni su Etty Hillesum nel mezzo di una guerra." *ALFAzeta* no. 60 (1996): 66-67.

Marcolivio, Pia. *Forme del destino: Etty Hillesum.* Bari: Palomar, 2005.

Mardones, José María. "Etty Hillesum: El corazon pensante del Barracon." *Vida Nueva* 2295 (2001).

—. "Etty Hillesum: El corazon pensante de los barracones." *Revista Anthropos* 203 (2004): 167-174.

Mariani, M. "Contro il sonno della ragione." *Il foglio de il paese delle donne* 15, no. 5-6 (2002): 15.

Marijn, Julika & Ton Jorna (eds.). *Altijd Etty: Etty Hillesum, blijvende inspiratiebron voor een rijk innerlijk leven*. Utrecht: Ten Have 2014.

Martins, Guilherme de Oliveira. "Etty, um comboio para Auschwitz." *Jornal de Letras* 987 (30/07/2008): 35.

Marujo, António, "Bonhoeffer e Etty: Testemunhas da Páscoa em tempos de sombra." *Viragem* 58 (January/April 2008): 2-3.

—. "Etty, Rilke e Eckhart: Viagens pela mão dos místicos." *Ípsilon* (19 June 2009): 22-25.

Marxer, François. "Etty Hillesum ou Rilke aux enfers." *Christus* 197 (January 2003): 117-125.

Maynadier, Martial. *Ecoute au-dedans: Journal d'Etty Hillesum, Premier Cahier.* Gravigny: Editions Le Parc [s.d.].

—. *Ecoute au profondeur tes sources intérieures: Journal d'Etty Hillesum, Deuxième Cahier.* Gravigny: Editions Le Parc, 2015.

—. *Le courage d'être-soi: Journal d'Etty Hillesum*, Troisième Cahier. Gravigny: Editions Le Parc [s.d.].

Mazziotti, Maria Pia & Gerrit Van Oord (eds.). *Etty Hillesum, Diario 1941-1943: Un mondo 'altro' è possibile.* Sant'Oreste: Apeiron Editori, 2002.

Mazziotti, Maria Pia & Simona Lattarulo. *La vita segreta delle parole: Alba de Céspedes, Etty Hillesum, Edith Stein, Simone Weil, Maria Zambrano.* Sant'Oreste: Apeiron editori, 2007.

McCarthy, Patricia. *The Girl Who Learned How to Kneel.* Strathfield, NSW: St. Pauls Publications, 2013.

—. *La jeune fille qui apprit à se mettre à genoux: Histoire d'Etty Hillesum.* Nouan-Le-Fuzelier: Editions des Béatitudes, 2014.

McDonough, William C. "Etty Hillesum's Learning to Live and Preparing to Die: *Complacentia Boni* as the Beginning of Acquired and Infused Virtue." *Journal of the Society of Christian Ethics* 25, no. 2 (2005): 179-202.

—. "Etty Hillesum as moral-theological guide: From fear to love's givenness and at-riskness." In: *The Ethics and Religious Philosophy of Etty Hillesum: Proceedings of the Etty Hillesum Conference at Ghent University, January 2014* (Supplements to The Journal of Jewish Thought and Philosophy, 28). Edited by Klaas A.D. Smelik, Meins G.S. Coetsier & Jurjen Wiersma. Leiden / Boston, MA: Brill, 2017, 90-118.

Meeüs-Michiels, Isabelle. "Avec Etty Hillesum: Sept clés pour simplifier sa vie intérieure." *Famille Chrétienne* no. 1737 (April 2011).

Meijer, Jaap. *Als Maggied vergeten: Doctor Levie Hillesum 1880-1943: De vader van Etty.* Heemstede: s.n., 1992 [privately printed].

—. *De Odyssee van een joods docent: Dr Levie Hillesum 1911-1924*. Heemstede: s.n., 1992 [privately printed].

—. "Als maggied vergeten: Doctor Levie Hillesum 1880-1943, de vader van Etty." In: *Etty Hillesum in Relatie* (Etty Hillesum Studies, 5). Edited by Klaas A.D. Smelik *et al.* Ghent: Academia Press, 2013, 135-150.

—. "De Odyssee van een joods docent: Dr. Levie Hillesum 1911-1924." In: *Etty Hillesum in Relatie* (Etty Hillesum Studies, 5). Edited by Klaas A.D. Smelik *et al.* Ghent: Academia Press, 2013, 151-174.

Melançon, Louise. "Etty Hillesum." *L'autre parole* 106 (June 2005). See www.lautreparole.org/articles/632 [retrieved 5 November 2013].

Melandri, V. *Fede e obbligo morale negli scritti di Etty Hillesum*. Thesis, *Università degli Studi di Bologna*, 2000.

Mendonça, José Tolentino. "A rapariga de Amesterdão." *Viragem* 58 (January/April 2008): 10-11.

Mennicken, Peter. "Gespräche mit Gott, der uns nicht helfen kann: Etty Hillesum: Tagebücher." In: *Herzstücke: Texte die das Leben ändern*. Edited by Georg Langenhorst & Christoph Gellner. Düsseldorf: Patmos, 2008.

Mercier, Jean & Isabelle Francq. "Etty Hillesum: Ses inédits retrouvés." *La vie* no. 3298 (November 2008).

Merlatti, Gabriella. *Etty Hillesum: Un cuore pensante*. Milano, Ancora, 1998.

Metz, Tineke. "Een zoektocht naar Etty Hillesum." Metz Audiovisuals, 2001 [Documentary].

Michman, Joseph & Hartog Beem. *Pinkas: Geschiedenis van de joodse gemeenschap in Nederland*. Ede: Kluwer, 1985.

Miconi, Emanuela. *Etty Hillesum: La forma perfetta*. Prefazione di Roberto Celada Ballanti. Trento: Il Margine, 2015.

Millot, Catherine. *La vie parfaite: Jeanne Guyon, Simone Weil, Etty Hillesum*. Paris: Gallimard, 2006.

Minardi, Marco, "L'Occupazione tedesca e la resistenza in Olanda." *ALFAzeta* no. 60 (1996): 16-19.

Minco, Marga. "Het verstoorde leven: Dagboek van Etty Hillesum 1941-1943." *Studia Rosenthaliana* 16, no. 2 (1982): 96-98.

—. "De kroniekschrijfster van onze lotgevallen." In: *Men zou een pleister op vele wonden willen zijn: Reacties op de dagboeken en brieven van Etty Hillesum*. Edited by J.G. Gaarlandt. Amsterdam: Balans, 1989, 1-5.

Molen, Janny van der. *Goed en Kwaad: Een studie naar de vraag in hoeverre dagboekschrijfster Etty Hillesum (1914-1943) in haar denken over goed en kwaad geïnspireerd en beïnvloed is door literatuur van psychiater Carl Gustav Jung (1875-1961)*. Thesis, University of Amsterdam, 2001.

—. "'Ik word alweer naar Jung getrokken': Goed en kwaad in het werk van Etty Hillesum en Carl Gustav Jung." In: *Etty Hillesum in Context* (Etty Hillesum Studies, 2). Edited by Ria van den Brandt & Klaas A.D. Smelik. Assen: Van Gorcum, 2007, 36-49.

—. "Besprekingen van en gedachten bij Tjeu van den Berk 'In de ban van Jung'." In: *Etty Hillesum weer thuis in Middelburg* (Etty Hillesum Studies, 7). Edited by Klaas A.D. Smelik *et al.* Antwerpen-Apeldoorn: Garant, 2015, 199-209.

—. "'I keep being drawn towards Jung': Good and evil in the work of Etty Hillesum and Carl Gustav Jung." In: *Reading Etty Hillesum in Context: Writings, Life, and Influences of a Visionary Author.* Edited by Klaas A.D. Smelik, Gerrit Van Oord & Jurjen Wiersma. Amsterdam: Amsterdam University Press, 2018, 227-243.

Molen, Janny van der & Klaas A.D. Smelik. *Ik zou lang willen leven: Het verhaal van Etty Hillesum.* Amsterdam: Balans, 2014.

Molen, Janny van der, Klaas A.D. Smelik, Gerrit Van Oord, Meins G.S. Coetsier, Denise de Costa & Jurjen Wiersma (eds). *Etty Hillesum in Relatie* (Etty Hillesum Studies, 5). Ghent: Academia Press, 2013.

—. *Etty Hillesum 1914-2014* (Etty Hillesum Studies, 6). Antwerpen & Apeldoorn: Garant, 2014.

Molen, Janny van der, Klaas A.D. Smelik, Marja Clement, Meins G.S. Coetsier, Gerrit Van Oord & Jurjen Wiersma, *Etty Hillesum weer thuis in Middelburg* (Etty Hillesum Studies, 7). Antwerpen-Apeldoorn: Garant, 2015.

Molder, Maria Filomena. "O coração pensante e a faculdade de julgar." *Intervalo*, no. 2 (May 2006): 22-48.

—. "Why is Etty Hillesum a great thinker?" In: *Spirituality in the Writings of Etty Hillesum: Proceedings of the Etty Hillesum Conference at Ghent University, November 2008* (Supplements to The Journal of Jewish Thought and Philosophy, 11). Edited by Klaas A.D. Smelik, Ria van den Brandt & Meins G.S. Coetsier. Leiden / Boston, MA: Brill, 2010, 399-418.

Montone, Tina. "Qualcosa su Westerbork: L'inferno concentrazionario di Etty Hillesum." *Intersezioni* 30, no. 2 (2010): 205-228.

Moormann, Christina. "Mystiek, psychotherapie en Etty Hillesum." *Prana*, 149 (June/July 2005): 44-52.

Mounic, Anne. "A propos d'Etty Hillesum." *Temporel* (September 2007).

Mucznik, Esther. "Esculpindo uma estátua interior." *Viragem* 58 (January/April 2008): 12-17.

Mulder, Hans. *Kunst in crisis en bezetting: Een onderzoek naar de houding van Nederlandse kunstenaars in de periode 1930-1945.* Antwerpen / Utrecht: Het Spectrum, 1978.

Nagel, Alexandra. "Julius Spier zocht en vond houvast in de Bijbel: Etty Hillesum volgde hem." In: *Etty Hillesum in discours* (Etty Hillesum Studies, 3). Edited by Ria van den Brandt & Klaas A.D. Smelik. Ghent: Academia Press, 2011, 77-91.

—. "Protocollen en vellen boterhampapier: Inventarisatie van een verzameling handanalysen uit de school van Julius Spier." In: *Etty Hillesum in perspectief* (Etty Hillesum Studies, 4). Edited by Klaas A.D. Smelik, Ria van den Brandt & Meins G.S. Coetsier. Ghent: Academia Press, 2012, 61-75.

—. "Uitgever Julius Spier en Iris-Verlag." *De Boekenwereld* 28, no. 4 (2012): 237-251.

—. "Een drieluik van Hes Hijmans." In: *Etty Hillesum in Relatie* (Etty Hillesum Studies, 5). Edited by Klaas A.D. Smelik *et al.* Ghent: Academia Press, 2013, 205-217.

—. "Figureerde Etty Hillesum als schoolmeisje in de Avonturen van Pieterjoris?" *Lessen* 8, no. 2 (2013): 34-37.

—. "Spier cercò conforto nella Bibbia ed Etty Hillesum lo seguì." In: *Etty Hillesum: Studi sulla vita e l'opera*. Edited by Gerrit Van Oord. Sant'Oreste, 2013, 58-73.

—. "Herta Levi, de onzichtbare figuur in de dagboeken van Etty Hillesum." *Tijdschrift voor Biografie* 3, no. 3 (2014): 27-38.

—. "'Met 26 jaar opnieuw beginnen ... is niet mogelyk': Een portret van Jan Bool, Etty Hillesums studiegenoot." In: *Etty Hillesum 1914-2014* (Etty Hillesum Studies, 6). Edited by Klaas A.D. Smelik *et al.* Antwerpen & Apeldoorn: Garant, 2014, 151-165.

—. "Herta Levi, de onzichtbare figuur in de dagboeken van Etty Hillesum." In: *Etty Hillesum weer thuis in Middelburg* (Etty Hillesum Studies, 7). Edited by Klaas A.D. Smelik *et al.* Antwerpen-Apeldoorn: Garant, 2015, 93-106.

—. "De Hillesum-stamboom." In: *Etty Hillesum weer thuis in Middelburg* (Etty Hillesum Studies, 7). Edited by Klaas A.D. Smelik *et al.* Antwerpen-Apeldoorn: Garant, 2015, 189-197.

—. "Leonie Snatager en het Joodse vraagstuk." In: *Etty Hillesum in weerwil van het Joodse vraagstuk* (Etty Hillesum Studies, 8). Edited by Klaas A.D. Smelik *et al.* Antwerpen-Apeldoorn: Garant, 2016, 51-69.

—. "Loekie, de onverwoestbare zwerfster op de hoge dansbenen." In: *Etty Hillesum in weerwil van het Joodse vraagstuk* (Etty Hillesum Studies, 8). Edited by Klaas A.D. Smelik *et al.* Antwerpen-Apeldoorn: Garant, 2016, 171-175.

—. "Vriendschap en therapie: Verstrengelde relaties tussen Julius Spier, Leonie Snatager en Etty Hillesum." In: *Etty Hillesum en het pad naar zelfverwerkelijking* (Etty Hillesum Studies, 9). Edited by Klaas A.D. Smelik *et al.* Antwerpen-Apeldoorn: Garant, 2017, 183-209.

—. "Wanneer schreven Henny Tideman en Etty Hillesum in *Levenskunst*?: Een reconstructie." In: *Veel mooie woorden: Etty Hillesum en haar boekje Levenskunst.* Edited by Ria van den Brandt & Peter Nissen. Hilversum: Verloren, 2017, 147-158.

—. "Henny Tideman en de wijsheden van Julius Spier en anderen." In: *Veel mooie woorden: Etty Hillesum en haar boekje Levenskunst.* Edited by Ria van den Brandt & Peter Nissen. Hilversum: Verloren, 2017, 159-167.

—. "Etty Hillesum, a devoted student of Julius Spier." In: *Reading Etty Hillesum in Context: Writings, Life, and Influences of a Visionary Author.* Edited by Klaas A.D. Smelik, Gerrit Van Oord & Jurjen Wiersma. Amsterdam: Amsterdam University Press, 2018, 273-284.

—. "Etty Hillesum en de Joods-Amsterdamse toneelwereld." In: *Etty Hillesum en de contouren van haar tijd* (Etty Hillesum Studies, 10). Edited by Klaas A.D. Smelik *et al.* Oud-Turnhout / 's-Hertogenbosch: Gompel & Svacina, 2018, 167-190.

Nagel, Alexandra & Ria van den Brandt. "'Three times yes and a thousand fold no!': Julius Spier writes to Etty Hillesum." In: *Reading Etty Hillesum in Context: Writings, Life, and Influences of a Visionary Author.* Edited by Klaas A.D. Smelik, Gerrit Van Oord & Jurjen Wiersma. Amsterdam: Amsterdam University Press, 2018, 303-312.

Nagel, Alexandra & Denise de Costa. "'Bij jou voor anker gaan': Vijftien brieven van Etty Hillesum aan Julius Spier." In: *Etty Hillesum 1914-2014* (Etty Hillesum Studies, 6). Edited by Klaas A.D. Smelik *et al.* Antwerpen & Apeldoorn: Garant, 2014, 105-117.

—. "'With you, I have my anchorage': Fifteen letters from Etty Hillesum to Julius Spier." In: *Reading Etty Hillesum in Context: Writings, Life, and Influences of a Visionary Author.* Edited by Klaas A.D. Smelik, Gerrit Van Oord & Jurjen Wiersma. Amsterdam: Amsterdam University Press, 2018, 285-301.

Navarro Sánchez, Rosana E. *De las razonas humanas de la mística a las raíces místicas de lo humano: desde la experienca espiritual de Etty Hillesum.* PhD Thesis, Pontificia Universida Javeriana Bogotá Colombia, 2015.

Nave, Jean-Pierre. "Mais qu'a donc à nous dire Etty Hillesum?" *La Croix* (20 April 2013). See www.amisdettyhillesum.fr/docs/Etty%20Article%20de%20JPN.jpg [retrieved 5 November 2013].

Neiman, Alven M. "Self Examination, Philosophical Education and Spirituality." *Journal of Philosophy of Education* 34, no. 4 (2000): 571-590.

Neri, Nadia. "Vrouwelijke identiteit en opoffering." In: *Men zou een pleister op vele wonden willen zijn: Reacties op de dagboeken en brieven van Etty Hillesum.* Edited by J.G. Gaarlandt. Amsterdam: Balans, 1989, 146-155.

—. "Etty Hillesum: Identità femminile e sacrificio." In: *L'esperienza dell'Altro: Studi su Etty Hillesum.* Edited by Gerrit Van Oord. Sant'Oreste: Apeiron Editori, 1990, 145-154.

—. "Etty Hillesum: Paradigma vivente di femminilità integrale." *ALFAzeta* no. 60 (1996): 38-42.

—. *Un'estrema compassione: Etty Hillesum testimone e vittima del Lager.* Milano: Mondadori, 1999.

—. "Etty Hillesum: Un'estrema compassione, la risposta esemplare di una vittima di fronte al male estremo." In: *Si può sempre dire un sì o un no: I Giusti contro i Genocidi degli Armeni e degli Ebrei.* Milano: Cleup, 2001.

—. "La scrittura in Etty Hillesum tra ricerca artistica ed ansia di memoria." In: *Oltre la persecuzione.* Edited by Roberta Ascarelli. Roma: Carocci, 2004.

—. "Etty Hillesum's psychological and spiritual path: Towards an ethics of responsibility." In: *Spirituality in the Writings of Etty Hillesum: Proceedings of the Etty Hillesum Conference at Ghent University, November 2008* (Supplements to The Journal of Jewish Thought and Philosophy, 11). Edited by Klaas A.D. Smelik, Ria van den Brandt & Meins G.S. Coetsier. Leiden / Boston, MA: Brill, 2010, 419-427.

Newell, John Philip. *A New Harmony: The Spirit, the Earth and the Human Soul.* San Francisco: Jossey-Bass, 2011.

Nissen, Peter. "'O – Meester, dat ik niet zo begerig zij': Etty Hillesum en Franciscus van Assisi." In: *Veel mooie woorden: Etty Hillesum en haar boekje Levenskunst.* Edited by Ria van den Brandt & Peter Nissen. Hilversum: Verloren, 2017, 283-287.

—. "'... onverdeeld van hart en innerlijk eenvoudig...': Etty Hillesum en Thomas a Kempis." In: *Veel mooie woorden: Etty Hillesum en haar boekje Levenskunst.* Edited by Ria van den Brandt & Peter Nissen. Hilversum: Verloren, 2017, 289-292.

—. "'De heilige lichtzinnigheid...': Etty Hillesum en Ebba Pauli." In: *Veel mooie woorden: Etty Hillesum en haar boekje Levenskunst.* Edited by Ria van den Brandt & Peter Nissen. Hilversum: Verloren, 2017, 293-298.

Nitzan, Tal. "I remember Etty Hillesum." *Bridges: A Jewish Feminist Journal* 12, no. 2 (2007): 65-66.

Noble, Philippe. "Het dubbel filter: De dagboeken en de brieven van Etty Hillesum in Franse vertaling." In: *Etty Hillesum in facetten* (Etty Hillesum Studies, 1). Edited by Ria van den Brandt & Klaas A.D. Smelik. Budel: Damon, 2003, 93-109.

—. "Le texte d'Etty Hillesum, de l'original à la traduction française: Un cheminement singulier." *Revue française de linguistique appliquée* 8 (2/2003): 19-31.

Noccelli, Maria Giovanna. "Etty Hillesum: Vedetta della verità." *Prospettiva Persona* no. 24 (1998).

—. "A te, cuore pensante del lager." *Lettere* 0 (April 1998).

—. "Il cuore moltiplicato del mondo: Etty Hillesum – Edith Stein." *Poietica* no. 11 (March 1999).

—. *Oltre la ragione: Risonanze filosofiche dal pensiero e dall'itinerario esistenziale di Etty Hillesum.* Sant'Oreste: Apeiron Editori, 2004.

—. *Se amare è chiedere troppo: Leggendo Etty Hillesum.* Roma: Edizioni Pro Sanctitate, 2004.

Nocita, Maria Gabriella. "Sentire la vita: Etty Hillesum si fa parola." In: *La comunicazione umanante: Ermeneusi di un mistero.* Edited by G. Scaramuzzo. Roma: Aracne, 2009.

—. "Feeling Life: Etty Hillesum *Becomes* Word." In: *Spirituality in the Writings of Etty Hillesum: Proceedings of the Etty Hillesum Conference at Ghent University, November 2008* (Supplements to The Journal of Jewish Thought and Philosophy, 11). Edited by Klaas A.D. Smelik, Ria van den Brandt & Meins G.S. Coetsier. Leiden / Boston, MA: Brill, 2010, 279-295.

—. *Etty Hillesum: Dalle tenebre della Shoah una paideia per umanarsi: Spunti ermeneutici dalla filosofia dell'Educazione di Edda Ducci.* Thesis, Rome: Libera Università Maria SS. Assunta, 2012.

—. "Etty Hillesum: quale Dio? Un modello del Dio personale di Ulrich Beck?" In: *Etty Hillesum: Studi sulla vita e l'opera.* Edited by Gerrit Van Oord. Sant'Oreste: Apeiron Editori, 2013, 74-93.

—. "Etty Hillesum en Primo Levi tussen de verdronkenen en de geleerden: Ervaringen van innerlijke vrijheid." In: *Etty Hillesum weer thuis in Middelburg* (Etty Hillesum Studies, 7). Edited by Klaas A.D. Smelik *et al.* Antwerpen-Apeldoorn: Garant, 2015, 139-158.

—. "Etty Hillesum and Primo Levi among the *drowned* and *saved*: Experiences of inner freedom." In: *The Ethics and Religious Philosophy of Etty Hillesum: Proceedings of the Etty Hillesum Conference at Ghent University, January 2014* (Supplements to The Journal of Jewish Thought and Philosophy, 28). Edited by Klaas A.D. Smelik, Meins G.S. Coetsier & Jurjen Wiersma. Leiden / Boston, MA: Brill, 2017, 170-191.

O'Connor, Elizabeth. "The Thinking Heart." *Sojourners* 14 (October 1985): 40-42.

Okken, Riet. *De kracht van de bestemming.* Deventer: Ankh-Hermes, 1988.

Oord, Gerrit Van. *L'esperienza dell'Altro: Studi su Etty Hillesum.* Edited by Gerrit Van Oord. Sant'Oreste: Apeiron Editori, 1990.

—. "Etty Hillesum: O perché l'odio non aiuta il mondo." *ALFAzeta*, no. 60 (1996): 60-85.

—. "Note biografiche su Etty Hillesum." In: *Etty Hillesum, Diario 1941-1943: Un mondo 'altro' è possibile.* Edited by Maria Pia Mazziotti & Gerrit Van Oord. Sant'Oreste: Apeiron Editori, 2002, 45-52.

—. "Het dagboek van Etty Hillesum in Italië." *Filter: Tijdschrift over vertalen* 9, no. 3 (2002): 49-55.

—. "Italiaans enthousiasme: Het dagboek van Etty Hillesum in Italië." In: *Etty Hillesum in facetten* (Etty Hillesum Studies, 1). Edited by Ria van den Brandt & Klaas A.D. Smelik. Budel: Damon, 2003, 111-127.

—. "Etty Hillesum en Edith Stein: Over een ontmoeting die nooit heeft plaats gehad." In: *Etty Hillesum in Context* (Etty Hillesum Studies, 2). Edited by Ria van den Brandt & Klaas A.D. Smelik. Assen: Van Gorcum, 2007, 50-58.

—. "Etty Hillesum ed Edith Stein: La storia di un incontro mai avvenuto." *Con Etty Hillesum: Quaderno di informazione e ricerca* no. 1 (2008): 46-57.

—. "Two Voices from Westerbork: Etty Hillesum and Philip Mechanicus on the Transport from Camp Westerbork on 24 August 1943." In: *Spirituality in the Writings of Etty Hillesum: Proceedings of the Etty Hillesum Conference at Ghent University, November 2008* (Supplements to The Journal of Jewish Thought and Philosophy, 11). Edited by Klaas A.D. Smelik, Ria van den Brandt & Meins G.S. Coetsier. Leiden / Boston, MA, Brill, 2010, 313-334.

—. "Het vertrek: Een reconstructie van de onverwachte deportatie van de familie Hillesum uit kamp Westerbork op 7 september 1943." In: *Etty Hillesum in discours* (Etty Hillesum Studies, 3). Edited by Ria van den Brandt & Klaas A.D. Smelik. Ghent: Academia Press, 2011, 115-130.

—. "Omnia salva: Brieven van Louis Hillesum en anderen aan Christine van Nooten." In: *Etty Hillesum in Perspectief* (Etty Hillesum Studies, 4). Edited by Klaas A.D. Smelik, Ria van den Brandt & Meins G.S. Coetsier. Ghent: Academia Press, 2012, 77-128.

—. "Historie en legende rondom het gezin van Louis en Riva Hillesum: Een beschouwing over *Mischa's spel en de ondergang van de familie Hillesum*." In: *Etty Hillesum in Perspectief* (Etty Hillesum Studies, 4). Edited by Klaas A.D. Smelik, Ria van den Brandt & Meins G.S. Coetsier. Ghent: Academia Press, 2012, 139-152.

—. "Rectificatie." In: *Etty Hillesum in Perspectief* (Etty Hillesum Studies, 4). Edited by Klaas A.D. Smelik, Ria van den Brandt & Meins G.S. Coetsier. Ghent: Academia Press, 2012, 153-156.

—. "Eerherstel of terugkeer? Jaap Meijers visie op Levie / Louis Hillesum." In: *Etty Hillesum in Relatie* (Etty Hillesum Studies, 5). Edited by Klaas A.D. Smelik *et al.* Ghent: Academia Press, 2013, 121-134.

—. "Introduzione." In: *Etty Hillesum: Studi sulla vita e l'opera.* Edited by Gerrit Van Oord. Sant'Oreste: Apeiron Editori, 2013, 8-18.

—. (ed.) *Etty Hillesum: Studi sulla vita e l'opera.* Sant'Oreste: Apeiron Editori, 2013.

—. "Amor Fati. Abel Herzberg intervistato da Wim Ramaker." In: *Etty Hillesum: Studi sulla vita e l'opera.* Edited by Gerrit Van Oord. Sant'Oreste: Apeiron Editori, 2013, 19-23.

—. "La partenza. L'inaspettata deportazione della famiglia Hillesum dal campo di Westerbork: Una ricostruzione." In: *Etty Hillesum: Studi sulla vita e l'opera.* Edited by Gerrit Van Oord. Sant'Oreste: Apeiron Editori, 2013, 149-167.

—. "Een Venetiaanse werkplaats: Het Hillesum-onderzoek van Isabella Adinolfi." In: *Etty Hillesum 1914-2014* (Etty Hillesum Studies, 6). Edited by Klaas A.D. Smelik *et al.* Antwerpen & Apeldoorn: Garant, 2014, 71-74.

—. "Elementen voor de vorming van een nieuwe mens: Maria Gabriella Nocita interpreteert Etty Hillesum en Primo Levi." In: *Etty Hillesum weer thuis in Middelburg* (Etty Hillesum Studies, 7). Edited by Klaas A.D. Smelik *et al.* Antwerpen-Apeldoorn: Garant, 2015, 135-138.

—. "Andermans veren: Hoe Etty Hillesum leentjebuur speelde bij Albert Verwey en Simon Vestdijk." In: *Etty Hillesum in weerwil van het Joodse vraagstuk* (Etty Hillesum Studies, 8). Edited by Klaas A.D. Smelik *et al.* Antwerpen-Apeldoorn: Garant, 2016, 139-158.

—. "Oprecht bewonderd en streng beoordeeld: Tzvetan Todorovs beeld van Etty Hillesum." In: *Etty Hillesum en het pad naar zelfverwerkelijking* (Etty Hillesum Studies, 9). Edited by Klaas A.D. Smelik *et al.* Antwerpen-Apeldoorn: Garant, 2017, 141-156.

—. "De dingen zeggen zoals ze zijn: Giancarlo Gaeta's visie op Etty Hillesum." In: *Etty Hillesum en het pad naar zelfverwerkelijking* (Etty Hillesum Studies, 9). Edited by Klaas A.D. Smelik *et al.* Antwerpen-Apeldoorn: Garant, 2017, 167-172.

—. "The departure: A reconstruction of the unexpected deportation of the Hillesum family from Camp Westerbork on Tuesday, 7 September 1943." In: *Reading Etty Hillesum in Context: Writings, Life, and Influences of a Visionary Author.* Edited by Klaas A.D. Smelik, Gerrit Van Oord & Jurjen Wiersma. Amsterdam: Amsterdam University Press, 2018, 157-180.

—. "Vertalen en vertellen: Giacoma Limentani." In: *Etty Hillesum en de contouren van haar tijd* (Etty Hillesum Studies, 10). Edited by Klaas A.D. Smelik *et al.* Oud-Turnhout / 's-Hertogenbosch: Gompel & Svacina, 2018, 153-155.

—. "Louis Hillesum, een 'stijf deftig' docent." In: *Etty Hillesum en de contouren van haar tijd* (Etty Hillesum Studies, 10). Edited by Klaas A.D. Smelik *et al.* Oud-Turnhout / 's-Hertogenbosch: Gompel & Svacina, 2018, 191-198.

Oord, Gerrit Van, Klaas A.D. Smelik, Meins G.S. Coetsier, Denise de Costa, Janny van der Molen & Jurjen Wiersma (eds.). *Etty Hillesum in Relatie* (Etty Hillesum Studies, 5). Ghent: Academia Press, 2013.

—. *Etty Hillesum 1914-2014* (Etty Hillesum Studies, 6). Antwerpen & Apeldoorn: Garant, 2014.

Oord, Gerrit Van, Klaas A.D. Smelik, Marja Clement, Meins G.S. Coetsier, Janny van der Molen & Jurjen Wiersma, *Etty Hillesum weer thuis in Middelburg* (Etty Hillesum Studies, 7). Antwerpen-Apeldoorn: Garant, 2015.

Oosterwijk, Corrie. *Etty Hillesum: Receptieonderzoek 1959-1989*. Thesis, Leiden University, 1990.

Overeem, Emmy van. "Esther." In: *Men zou een pleister op vele wonden willen zijn: Reacties op de dagboeken en brieven van Etty Hillesum*. Edited by J.G. Gaarlandt. Amsterdam: Balans, 1989, 16-18.

Pach, Manja. "Brief aan Etty Hillesum, maart 2006." *Agenda / Nieuwsbrief van het Etty Hillesum Centrum* (May/August 2006).

—. "Een dierbaar woord uit het werk van Etty Hillesum." *Praktische Humanistiek: Themanummer Etty Hillesum* 9, no. 1 (1999): 47-51.

Pach, Manja, Ton Jorna & Klaas A.D. Smelik. "Huiswerk voor de eigen werkplaats: De actualiteit van Etty Hillesum." *Rondom het Woord* 42, no. 2 (2000): 5-13.

Paillet, Paule. "Une jeune femme au péril de la mort." *Informations sociales* 145 (2008): 29-30.

Pantanella, Giorgio. *Etty Hillesum: La ragazza che ospitò Dio.* Villa Verucchio: Pazzini Stampatore Editore, 2012.

Parc Locmaria, Marie-Hélène du. *«Tant souffrir et tant aimer» selon Etty Hillesum.* Paris: Salvator, 2011.

—. "Etty Hillesum ou la joie dans la souffrance." See www.paroles.ch/entre-vous-soit-dit/395-hilleseum-parc-locmaria [retrieved 5 November 2013].

Parker, Judith. *The spirituality of Etty Hillesum: Its sources and legacy.* Thesis, Lampeter: University of Wales, 2007.

Passanti, Chiara. "Bij het vertalen van 'Het verstoorde leven'." In: *Men zou een pleister op vele wonden willen zijn: Reacties op de dagboeken en brieven van Etty Hillesum.* Edited by J.G. Gaarlandt. Amsterdam: Balans, 1989, 156-159.

—. "Tradurre Etty Hillesum." In: *L'esperienza dell'Altro: Studi su Etty Hillesum.* Edited by Gerrit Van Oord. Sant'Oreste: Apeiron Editori, 1990, 89-92.

Patterson, David. *Along the Edge of Annihilation: The Collapse and Recovery of Life in the Holocaust Diary.* Seattle: University of Washington Press, 1999.

—. "Through the Eyes of Those Who Were There." *Holocaust and Genocide Studies* 18, no. 2 (2004): 274-90.

Pellegrino, Vincenza. "Etty Hillesum: La capacità di riposare su se stessi: Intervista a Chiara Passanti." *ALFAzeta*, no. 60 (1996): 68-71.

Perrini, Marta. "Parallellen tussen Etty Hillesum en Sophie Scholl." In: *Etty Hillesum in perspectief* (Etty Hillesum Studies, 4). Edited by Klaas A.D. Smelik, Ria van den Brandt & Meins G.S. Coetsier. Ghent: Academia Press, 2012, 15-32.

—. "Etty Hillesum e Sophie Scholl: Itinerari paralleli." In: *La Rosa bianca: La sfida della responsabilità.* Edited by Marta Perrini. Milano: IPOC Press, 2013, 90-107.

—. "Etty Hillesum and Sophie Scholl: Sisters in fate." In: *The Ethics and Religious Philosophy of Etty Hillesum: Proceedings of the Etty Hillesum Conference at Ghent University, January 2014* (Supplements to The Journal of Jewish Thought and Philosophy, 28). Edited by Klaas A.D. Smelik, Meins G.S. Coetsier & Jurjen Wiersma. Leiden / Boston, MA: Brill, 2017, 192-204.

Petraglio, Renzo. "Un sigillo di amore contre il caos." *ALFAzeta,* no. 60 (1996): 76-81.

Petrignani, Sandra. "La scelta di Etty." *Panorama* (7 October 1990): 23.

Pevenage, Debbie. *'Het harmonisch rollen uit Gods hand lukte niet zo erg': Worsteling en evenwicht in de dagboeken van Etty Hillesum.* MA Thesis, Ghent University, 2007.
—. "'There was little of that harmonious rolling out of God's hand': Struggle and balance in the diaries of Etty Hillesum." In: *Spirituality in the Writings of Etty Hillesum: Proceedings of the Etty Hillesum Conference at Ghent University, November 2008* (Supplements to The Journal of Jewish Thought and Philosophy, 11). Edited by Klaas A.D. Smelik, Ria van den Brandt & Meins G.S. Coetsier. Leiden / Boston, MA: Brill, 2010, 253-268.
Philippe, Jacques. *La liberté intérieure.* Burtin: Éditions des beatitudes, 2002.
—. *Interior freedom.* New York: Scepter publishers, 2007.
—. "Etty Hillesum, maintenir la flamme." *Feu et Lumière* 226 (March 2004).
Piechowski, Michael M. "Etty Hillesum: The Thinking Heart of the Barracks." *Advanced Development* 4 (1992): 105-18.
—. "Is Inner Transformation a Creative Process?" *Creativity Research Journal. Special Issue: Creativity in the Moral Domain* 6, no. 1-2 (1993): 89-98.
Pisi, Guido. "I campi di concentramento nazisti e lo sterminio delle minoranze." *ALFAzeta,* no. 60 (1996): 20-27.
Pissinger, Stéphanie. *'... bis eines Tags es keinen Sinn mehr haben wird zu sagen: Morgen': Literarische Verarbeitung von KZ-Erfahrungen 1933-1994.* Thesis, Freiburg: Albert-Ludwigs-Universität, 2011.
Pita, Nélio, "Entre a vida e a morte: O universo interior de Etty Hillesum." *Viragem* 58 (January/April 2008): 18-21.
Pivot, Bernard. "Comme une soeur perdue et retrouvée." *Le journal du dimanche* (27 November 2010). See www.lejdd.fr/Chroniques/Bernard-Pivot/La-chronique-de-Bernard-Pivot-dans-le-JDD-236544 [retrieved 9 November 2013].
Pleshoyano, Alexandra. *L'expérience de la nuit chez Etty Hillesum à la lumière de Saint Jean de la Croix: Une herméneutique de la démaîtrise.* Thesis, Université de Sherbrooke, 2002.
—. "Croissance spirituelle et transformation des rapports femme-homme chez Etty Hillesum." In: *Femme-Homme: Considérations sur l'expérience de la rencontre: Lectures théologiques, spirituelles et littéraires.* Edited by P. Snyder & M. Pelletier. Sherbrooke: Ed. GGC, 2003, 121-141.
—. "Etty Hillesum: Désirs sexuels et désir spirituel." *Sciences Pastorales, Femmes et expériences spirituelles* 22, no. 2 (2003): 33-46.
—. "Etty Hillesum: For God and with God." *The Way* 44, no. 1 (2005): 7-20.
—. "L'autobiographie et le journal intime comme contemplation rétrospective de Dieu: À propos de Etty Hillesum et d'Ignace de Loyola." In: *Variations sur dieu: Langages, silences, pratiques.* Edited by François Coppens. Brussels: Facultés Universitaires Saint Louis, 2005, 281-305.

—. "Etty Hillesum: A Theological Hermeneutic in the Midst of Evil." *Oxford Journals, Humanities, Literature and Theology* 19 (September 2005): 221-237.

—. "Etty Hillesum: 'Ce sera à moi d'aider Dieu'." In: *Un Dieu qui agit?* Edited by Robert Mager. Montreal: Fides, 2006, 165-180.

—. "L'autoportrait spirituel d'Etty Hillesum." *La faute à Rousseau* 5 (2006): 28-29.

—. "Etty Hillesum: De l'écoute à la parole." *Cahiers de spiritualité ignatienne: Aujourd'hui dire Dieu*, Publication du Centre de Spiritualité Manrèse no. 116 (2006): 97-104.

—. *Etty Hillesum, l'amour comme 'seule solution': Une herméneutique théologique au cœur du mal.* Münster: LIT Verlag, 2007.

—. "L'espace 'inspiré' dans les écrits d'Etty Hillesum: Une spiritualité sans structure confessionnelle." *Cahiers de spiritualité du séminaire saint Charles* (2007).

—. "Bricolage et herméneutique au cœur du mal: À la mémoire d'Etty Hillesum." In: *Bricoler la mémoire: La théologie et les arts face au déclin de la tradition.* Edited by M. Koopman-Thurlings & Ria van den Brandt. Paris: Cerf, 2007, 133-149.

—. "L'héritage spirituel d'Etty Hillesum: 'Je me sens comme une des nombreuses héritières d'un grand legs spirituel'." *Studies in Religion / Sciences Religieuses* 37/1 (2008): 63-79.

—. "Etty Hillesum." In: *Et Dieu dans tout ça!* Edited by Louis Lesage. Montreal: Fides, 2008, 25-37.

—. *J'avais encore mille choses à te demander: L'univers intérieur d'Etty Hillesum.* Montreal / Paris: Novalis / Bayard, 2009.

—. "Etty Hillesum: Love Calls for Spiritual Discernment." *Religious Studies and Theology* (2009): 241-268.

—. "Etty Hillesum et Leonard Cohen: Deux Juifs errant vers une spiritualité sans 'églises'." In: *Études du religieux contemporains.* Edited by Patrick Snyder & Martine Pelletier. Montreal: Fides, 2010.

—. "Etty Hillesum: Prier dans la nuit." *L'aventure intérieure* (2010): 12-15.

—. "Etty Hillesum and Julius Spier: A 'Spierituality' on the fringe of religious borders." In: *Spirituality in the Writings of Etty Hillesum: Proceedings of the Etty Hillesum Conference at Ghent University, November 2008* (Supplements to The Journal of Jewish Thought and Philosophy, 11). Edited by Klaas A.D. Smelik, Ria van den Brandt & Meins G.S. Coetsier. Leiden/Boston, MA: Brill 2010, 43-75.

—. "Die Liebe als 'einzige Lösung': Das spirituelle Erbe der Etty Hillesum." In: *LIEBE – mehr als Gefühl: Philosophie – Theologie – Einzelwissenschaften.* Edited by Werner Schüßler & Marc Röbel. Paderborn: Schöningh, 2015, 249-271.

Pomi, Massimo. "Lavorando a noi stessi: L'educazione spirituale secondo Etty Hillesum." *Orientamenti Pedagogici* 61, no. 2 (2014): 297-321.

Popp, Friederike. *Bedrängt und unendlich geborgen: Begegnungen mit Etty Hillesum.* Münsterschwarzach: Vier-Türme-Verlag, 2014.

Porto, Bruno Di. "Etty Hillesum: La ragazza che prese Dio per mano." *Il Tempo e l'Idea: Una finestra ebraica sul mondo: Quindicinale di attualià e cultura,* no. 8-10 (2000): 59-65.

Pot, Mieke. *Doorkruist land: De contemplatieve weg.* ['s-Gravenhage:] Uitgeverij Lente, 2014.

Pres, Terrence Des. "Eros, God and Auschwitz." In: *Men zou een pleister op vele wonden willen zijn: Reacties op de dagboeken en brieven van Etty Hillesum.* Edited by J.G. Gaarlandt. Amsterdam: Balans, 1989, 68-73.

Presser, Jacques. *De nacht der Girondijnen.* Amsterdam: Meulenhoff, 1957 [novel].

—. *Ondergang: De vervolging en de verdelging van het Nederlandse Jodendom 1940-1945.* 's Gravenhage: Staatsuitgeverij, 1965.

—. *Ashes in the Wind: The Destruction of Dutch Jewry.* Transl. from Dutch by Arnold J. Pomerans. Detroit: Wayne State University Press, 1968.

Purcell, Brendan. "Foundations for a judgement of the Holocaust: Etty Hillesum's standard of humanity." In: *Spirituality in the Writings of Etty Hillesum: Proceedings of the Etty Hillesum Conference at Ghent University, November 2008* (Supplements to The Journal of Jewish Thought and Philosophy, 11). Edited by Klaas A.D. Smelik, Ria van den Brandt & Meins G.S. Coetsier. Leiden / Boston, MA: Brill, 2010, 125-146.

—. *From Big Bang to Big Mystery: Human Origins in the Light of Creation and Evolution.* Dublin: Veritas, 2011.

Putman, E. *Worden wie je bent: Etty Hillesum en het lot.* Thesis, Nijmegen University, 1986.

Putte, Josée van de. *Etty Hillesum.* Thesis, Titus Brandsma Institute, Nijmegen, 2017.

Puyo, Jean. "Etty Hillesum vit l'enfer de ses frères juifs." *La Vie* 2451 (August 1992). See www.lavie.fr/archives/1992/08/20/etty-hillesum-vit-l-enfer-de-ses-freres-juifs,1278203.php [retrieved 5 November 2013].

Quinzio, Sergio. "Attacamento alla vita e pietà." In: *L'esperienza dell'Altro: Studi su Etty Hillesum.* Edited by Gerrit Van Oord. Sant'Oreste: Apeiron Editori, 1990, 155-160.

Ramaker, Wim. "Amor Fati: Wim Ramaker in gesprek met Abel Herzberg." In: *Men zou een pleister op vele wonden willen zijn: Reacties op de dagboeken en brieven van Etty Hillesum.* Edited by J.G. Gaarlandt. Amsterdam: Balans, 1989, 11-15.

Rastello, Luca. "Etty Hillesum: Diario 1941-1943." *L'indice del mese* no. 1 (January 1986).

Rasy, Elisabetta. "Etty Hillesum: La luce del Lager." *Io Donna* (2002): 43-44.

Regenhardt, J.W. "De Weg Naar Westerbork." In: *Men zou een pleister op vele wonden willen zijn: Reacties op de dagboeken en brieven van Etty Hillesum.* Edited by J.G. Gaarlandt. Amsterdam: Balans, 1989, 192-209.

—. *Mischa's spel en de ondergang van familie Hillesum*. Amsterdam: Balans, 2012.

Reitsma, Anneke. "'Ik bloei van binnen met de dood tot bloem': Naar aanleiding van dagboek en brieven van Etty Hillesum." *BZZLLETIN* 107 (June 1983): 3-16 & 22.

—. "Ik bloei van binnen met de dood tot bloem: Naar aanleiding van dagboek en brieven van Etty Hillesum." In: *Men zou een pleister op vele wonden willen zijn: Reacties op de dagboeken en brieven van Etty Hillesum*. Edited by J.G. Gaarlandt. Amsterdam: Balans, 1989, 99-132.

—. "'Men moet zichzelf het vaderland zijn': Over Etty Hillesum en de innerlijke noodzaak van haar schrijverschap." *Parodos* 31 (April 1992): 29-37.

Remy, Gérard. "Etty Hillesum et saint Augustin: L'influence d'un maitre spirituel?" *Recherches de science religieuse* 95, no. 2 (2007): 253-280.

Reve, Karel van het. "Het korte leven van Etty Hillesum." In: *Men zou een pleister op vele wonden willen zijn: Reacties op de dagboeken en brieven van Etty Hillesum*. Edited by J.G. Gaarlandt. Amsterdam: Balans, 1989, 41-43.

Ribeiro Ferreira, Maria Luísa. "Spinoza and Etty Hillesum: Two different views of God." In: *The Ethics and Religious Philosophy of Etty Hillesum: Proceedings of the Etty Hillesum Conference at Ghent University, January 2014* (Supplements to The Journal of Jewish Thought and Philosophy, 28). Edited by Klaas A.D. Smelik, Meins G.S. Coetsier & Jurjen Wiersma. Leiden / Boston, MA: Brill, 2017, 147-157.

Rijper, Erna. *'Ernst maken met de dingen van het lichaam': Een onderzoek naar lichamelijkheid in het leven van Etty Hillesum aan de hand van de woordbeschrijvingen 'mond,' 'vermoeidheid,' 'menstruatie,' 'schaamte'*. Thesis, Humanistic University Utrecht, 2002.

Rogers, Gary P. *New life in attentiveness to our dying: A view of spiritual direction in the light of an analysis of an interrupted life, the dairies of Etty Hillesum and H.U. von Balthasar's A theological anthropology*. Thesis, General Theological Seminary, 1985.

Ruedin, Luc. "Une guerre à l'envers: Etty Hillesum." *Choisir, Revue Culturelle* 610 (October 2010): 13-16.

—. "Etty Hillesum: Un témoin pour notre temps." *Christus* 228 (October 2010).

Russo, Fabio. "Rainer Maria Rilke, Etty Hillesum, Giorgio Voghera: L'altro e la morte nell'esistenza compresso." In: *L'esperienza dell'Altro: Studi su Etty Hillesum*. Edited by Gerrit Van Oord. Sant'Oreste: Apeiron Editori, 1990, 93-108.

Salvo, Laura De. "Etty Hillesum: Un cuore pensante: Sentire ed esserci." *Annali di scienza della cultura e della religione* (2001): 289-311.

Saut, Charlotte Arnoux. *Le journal de la souche de bouleau*. Laboissière: Éditions Isoréa, 2011.

Sauto, Martine de. "Etty Hillesum, un long dialogue avec Dieu." *La Croix* (November 2008).

Scarsato, Fabio. *Francesco d'Assisi e Etty Hillesum*. Padova: Edizioni Messaggero Padova, 2013.

Scholtens, Wim. "Søren Kierkegaard en Etty Hillesum: Een vergelijking." In: *Men zou een pleister op vele wonden willen zijn: Reacties op de dagboeken en brieven van Etty Hillesum*. Edited by J.G. Gaarlandt. Amsterdam: Balans, 1989, 74-88.

Schrijvers, Piet. "Een filosoof in bezettingstijd: Over Seneca's brieven en het dagboek van Etty Hillesum." In: *De mens als toeschouwer: Essays over Romeinse literatuur en Westeuropese tradities*. Amsterdam: Ambo, 1986, 190-208.

—. "De dagboeken van Etty Hillesum en de brieven van Seneca." In: *Men zou een pleister op vele wonden willen zijn: Reacties op de dagboeken en brieven van Etty Hillesum*. Edited by J.G. Gaarlandt. Amsterdam: Balans, 1989, 89-98.

—. "I diari di Etty Hillesum e le lettere di Seneca." In: *L'esperienza dell'Altro: Studi su Etty Hillesum*. Edited by Gerrit Van Oord. Sant'Oreste: Apeiron Editori, 1990, 109-120.

—. "Etty Hillesum in joodse contexten." In: *Etty Hillesum in facetten* (Etty Hillesum Studies, 1). Edited by Ria van den Brandt & Klaas A.D. Smelik. Budel: Damon, 2003, 37-56.

—. "I contesti ebraici di Etty Hillesum." In: *Etty Hillesum: Studi sulla vita e l'opera*. Edited by Gerrit Van Oord. Sant'Oreste: Apeiron Editori, 2013, 94-106.

—. "Etty Hillesum in Jewish contexts." In: *Reading Etty Hillesum in Context: Writings, Life, and Influences of a Visionary Author*. Edited by Klaas A.D. Smelik, Gerrit Van Oord & Jurjen Wiersma. Amsterdam: Amsterdam University Press, 2018, 315-331.

—. "De dagboeken van Etty Hillesum en de brieven van Seneca." In: *Etty Hillesum en de contouren van haar tijd* (Etty Hillesum Studies, 10). Edited by Klaas A.D. Smelik *et al.* Oud-Turnhout / 's-Hertogenbosch: Gompel & Svacina, 2018, 201-210.

Semeraro, MichaelDavide. *Etty Hillesum: Dio matura: Un viaggio in quaranta tappe*. Foreword by Christiana Dobner & André Louf. Molfetta: Edizioni La Meridiana, 2005, 2013^3.

—. *Etty Hillesum: Umanità radicato in Dio*. Milano: Paoline Editoriale Libri, 2013.

—. *En Carême avec Etty Hillesum*. Translated by Soeur Ginevra Maria. Paris: Editions Salvator, 2016.

Semino, Gabriele. "Un ritratto di Etty Hillesum a cent'anni dalla nascita." *La Civiltà Cattolica* no. 3926 (18 January 2014): 142-156.

Sessi, Frediano. "L'altro nell'io: Etty Hillesum ed il conflitto dell'essere." *ALFAzeta* no. 60 (1996): 32-37.

Shirley, I.S. *Five Holocaust Diaries* (*Anne Frank, Moshe Flinker, Eva Heyman, Etty Hillesum, Dawid Sierakowiak*). Thesis, Union Institute and University, 2004.

Siertsema, Bettine. *Uit de diepten: Nederlandse egodocumenten over de nazi concentratiekampen*. Vught: Skandalon, 2007.

—. "Etty Hillesum (1914-1943) and Abel Herzberg (1893-1989): Two Dutch chroniclers of the Shoah." In: *Spirituality in the Writings of Etty Hillesum: Proceedings of the Etty Hillesum Conference at Ghent University, November 2008* (Supplements to The Journal of Jewish Thought and Philosophy, 11). Edited by Klaas A.D. Smelik, Ria van den Brandt & Meins G.S. Coetsier. Leiden/Boston, MA: Brill, 2010, 297-312.

—. "Niet haten: Etty Hillesums visie op de nazi's." In: *Etty Hillesum 1914-2014* (Etty Hillesum Studies, 6). Edited by Klaas A.D. Smelik *et al.* Antwerpen & Apeldoorn: Garant, 2014, 49-58.

—. "Etty Hillesum's views on the Nazis and their henchmen." In: *The Ethics and Religious Philosophy of Etty Hillesum: Proceedings of the Etty Hillesum Conference at Ghent University, January 2014* (Supplements to The Journal of Jewish Thought and Philosophy, 28). Edited by Klaas A.D. Smelik, Meins G.S. Coetsier & Jurjen Wiersma. Leiden / Boston, MA: Brill, 2017, 270-281.

—. "De spiritualiteit van A.J.C. van Seters (1885-1968), de samensteller van *Levenskunst.*" In: *Veel mooie woorden: Etty Hillesum en haar boekje Levenskunst.* Edited by Ria van den Brandt & Peter Nissen. Hilversum: Verloren, 2017, 135-145.

—. "Ies Spetter, collega van Etty Hillesum in kamp Westerbork." In: *Etty Hillesum en de contouren van haar tijd* (Etty Hillesum Studies, 10). Edited by Klaas A.D. Smelik *et al.* Oud-Turnhout / 's-Hertogenbosch: Gompel & Svacina, 2018, 211-224.

Sievers, Joseph. "'Aiutare Dio': Riflessioni su vita e pensiero di Etty Hillesum." *Nuova Umanità* 17, no. 3-4 (1995): 113-127.

—. "'To Help God': Reflections on the Life and Thought of Etty Hillesum," *SIDIC* 28, no. 3 (1995): 9-16.

—. "Aider Dieu: Réflexion sur la vie et la pensée d'Etty Hillesum." *Service international de Documentation judéo-chrétienne* 28, no. 3 (1995): 9-17.

Silverstone, Jennifer. "An Interrupted Life: The Diaries and Letters of Etty Hillesum 1941-43 by Etty Hillesum." *British Journal of Psychotherapy* 18, part 2 (2001): 291-295.

Smelik, Johanna F. "Het 'zusje' van Etty Hillesum: Interview by Anke Manschot." *Opzij* 21, no. 7 (July/August 1993): 118-121.

Smelik, Klaas A.D. "Het godsbeeld bij Etty Hillesum." *Rondom het Woord* 26, no. 2 (1984): 82-88.

—. "Reacties op Etty Hillesum." *Rondom het Woord* 27, no. 4 (1985): 65-70.

—. "Etty Hillesum veertig jaar na de Bevrijding." *OJEC periodiek*, no. 2 (April 1985): 3-4.

—. "Etty Hillesum." In: *Bewogen grensgangers: 52 overwegingen.* Edited by A. Bakker. Hilversum: Gooi & Sticht, 1987, 34-36.

—. "Reacties op Etty Hillesum." In: *Men zou een pleister op vele wonden willen zijn: Reacties op de dagboeken en brieven van Etty Hillesum.* Edited by J.G. Gaarlandt. Amsterdam: Balans, 1989, 210-219, 228-230.

—. "Etty Hillesum." In: *The Blackwell Companion to Jewish Literature: From the Eighteenth Century to the Present*. Edited by G. Abramson. Oxford: Blackwell, 1989, 335-336.

—. "Le edizioni dell'opera di Etty Hillesum." In: *L'esperienza dell'Altro: Studi su Etty Hillesum*. Edited by Gerrit Van Oord. Sant'Oreste: Apeiron Editori, 1990, 121-125.

—. "L'immagine di Dio in Etty Hillesum." In: *L'esperienza dell'Altro: Studi su Etty Hillesum*. Edited by Gerrit Van Oord. Sant'Oreste: Apeiron Editori, 1990, 161-168.

—. "Geen heilige maar een begenadigd schrijfster." *Werkschrift* 14, no. 1 (1994): 26-32.

—. "Una testimone in anticipo sui tempi." *ALFAzeta* no. 60 (1996): 28-31.

—. "Schipper, Klaas Abe." In: *Bibliografisch Lexicon voor de geschiedenis van het Nederlandse protestantisme*, deel 4. Edited by J. van den Berg *et al.* Kampen: Kok, 1998, 387.

—. "Invalshoeken in het onderzoek naar de nagelaten werken van Etty Hillesum." *Praktische Humanistiek: Themanummer Etty Hillesum* 9, no. 1 (1999): 52-58.

—. "Gedenken is doen: Van een bundel cahiers tot een wereldwijde publicatie." In: *Etty Hillesum in facetten* (Etty Hillesum Studies, 1). Edited by Ria van den Brandt & Klaas A.D. Smelik. Budel: Damon, 2003, 21-36.

—. "Hillesum: Heilige of martelares?" *Tertio* 4, no. 198 (2003): 8-9.

—. "Nieuwe publicaties over Etty Hillesum in haar zestigste sterfjaar." *De Stem van het Boek* 14, no. 4 (2003): 1-5.

—. "Volledig leven tot de laatste ademtocht: Etty Hillesum, heilige of martelares?" *VolZin* 3, no. 2 (2004): 28-32.

—. "De keuze van Etty Hillesum om niet onder te duiken." In: *Etty Hillesum in Context* (Etty Hillesum Studies, 2). Edited by Ria van den Brandt & Klaas A.D. Smelik. Assen: Van Gorcum, 2007, 59-73.

—. "Hillesum, Esther (Etty)." In: *Joden in Nederland in de twintigste eeuw: Een biografisch woordenboek*. Edited by Rena Fuks-Mansfeld. Utrecht: Spectrum, 2007, 137-138.

—. "Wat is het EHOC? Het Etty Hillesum Onderzoekscentrum (EHOC) in Gent opgericht." In: *Etty Hillesum in Context* (Etty Hillesum Studies, 2). Edited by Ria van den Brandt & Klaas A.D. Smelik. Assen: Van Gorcum, 2007, 116-118.

—. "Etty Hillesum congres in Gent – Durf denken." *Joods Actueel* no. 23 (December 2008): 45.

—. "A short biography of Etty Hillesum (1914-1943)." In: *Spirituality in the Writings of Etty Hillesum: Proceedings of the Etty Hillesum Conference at Ghent University, November 2008* (Supplements to The Journal of Jewish Thought and Philosophy, 11). Edited by Klaas A.D. Smelik, Ria van den Brandt & Meins G.S. Coetsier. Leiden / Boston, MA: Brill, 2010, 21-28.

—. "Etty Hillesum and her God." In: *Spirituality in the Writings of Etty Hillesum: Proceedings of the Etty Hillesum Conference at Ghent University, November 2008*

(Supplements to The Journal of Jewish Thought and Philosophy, 11). Edited by Klaas A.D. Smelik, Ria van den Brandt & Meins G.S. Coetsier. Leiden / Boston, MA: Brill, 2010, 75-102.

—. "Een merkwaardige vondst: Nieuwe teksten van Etty Hillesum uit een vuilnisbak." In: *Etty Hillesum in discours* (Etty Hillesum Studies, 3). Edited by Ria van den Brandt & Klaas A.D. Smelik. Ghent: Academia Press, 2011, 5-10.

—. "Is Etty Hillesum een martelaar?" In: *Etty Hillesum in discours* (Etty Hillesum Studies, 3). Edited by Ria van den Brandt & Klaas A.D. Smelik. Ghent: Academia Press, 2011, 69-75.

—. "Romantiek aan de IJssel: De eerste ontmoeting tussen Etty Hillesum en Klaas Smelik senior." In: *Etty Hillesum in Perspectief* (Etty Hillesum Studies, 4). Edited by Klaas A.D. Smelik, Ria van den Brandt & Meins G.S. Coetsier. Ghent: Academia Press, 2012, 49-60.

—. "Voorbij het vijanddenken: De visie van Etty Hillesum geplaatst in een Bijbels kader." In: *Etty Hillesum in Perspectief* (Etty Hillesum Studies, 4). Edited by Klaas A.D. Smelik, Ria van den Brandt & Meins G.S. Coetsier. Ghent: Academia Press, 2012, 129-137.

—. "Preface." In: Roman Kroke, *The Spider and its Web: Insights into the Thinking Heart of the Dutch Jew Etty Hillesum (1914-1943)*. Wavre: Mediel, 2012, 1-2.

—. "Etty Hillesum 1914-1943." In: Roman Kroke, *The Spider and its Web: Insights into the Thinking Heart of the Dutch Jew Etty Hillesum (1914-1943)*. Wavre: Mediel, 2012, 5-7.

—. "Vorwort." In: Roman Kroke, *Die Spinne und ihr Netz: Einblicke in das denkende Herz der holländischen Jüdin Etty Hillesum (1914-1943)*. Wavre: Mediel, 2012, 1-2.

—. "Etty Hillesum 1914-1943." In: Roman Kroke, *Die Spinne und ihr Netz: Einblicke in das denkende Herz der holländischen Jüdin Etty Hillesum (1914-1943)*. Wavre: Mediel, 2012, 5-7.

—. "Préface." In: Roman Kroke, *L'araignée et sa toile: Regards sur le cœur pensant d'Etty Hillesum (1914-1943), Juive néerlandaise*. Wavre: Mediel, 2012, 1-2.

—. "Etty Hillesum 1914-1943', In: Roman Kroke, *L'araignée et sa toile: Regards sur le cœur pensant d'Etty Hillesum (1914-1943), Juive néerlandaise*. Wavre: Mediel, 2012, 5-7.

—. "Biografia di Etty Hillesum." In: Etty Hillesum, *Diario 1941-1943: Edizione Integrale*. Rome: Adelphi, 2012, 17-26.

—. "De houding van Etty Hillesum tegenover de vervolging van haar volk." In: *Etty Hillesum in Relatie* (Etty Hillesum Studies deel, 5). Edited by Klaas A.D. Smelik *et al.* Ghent: Acacemia Press, 2013, 17-42.

—. "La scelta di Etty Hillesum." In: *Etty Hillesum: Studi sulla vita e l'opera*. Edited by Gerrit Van Oord. Sant'Oreste: Apeiron Editori, 2013, 107-120.

—. "Oltre l'immagine del nemico." In: *Etty Hillesum: Studi sulla vita e l'opera*. Edited by Gerrit Van Oord. Sant'Oreste: Apeiron Editori, 2013, 121-127.

—. "Knielen op de ruwe kokosmat." *VolZin* 13, no. 4 (2014): 42-44.

—. *Il concetto di Dio in Etty Hillesum*. Sant'Oreste: Apeiron, 2014.

—. ""Ik geloof eigenlijk helemaal niet in wat men noemt 'slechte mensen'": Etty Hillesums visie op het kwaad in de mens." In: *Etty Hillesum 1914-2014* (Etty Hillesum Studies, 6). Edited by Klaas A.D. Smelik *et al.* Antwerpen & Apeldoorn: Garant, 2014, 27-47.

—. "Hillesum: La libertà di Etty 'Credo in Dio e negli uomini': L'attualità del suo messagio giovedi alle Cede." *Corriera della Sera* (9 December 2014): 17.

—. *Odio e inimicizia in Etty Hillesum*. Sant'Oreste: Apeiron, 2015.

—. "Ulrich Becks visie op Etty Hillesum." In: *Etty Hillesum weer thuis in Middelburg* (Etty Hillesum Studies, 7). Edited by Klaas A.D. Smelik *et al.* Antwerpen-Apeldoorn: Garant, 2015, 159-169.

—. "Het Etty Hillesum Onderzoekscentrum opent in Middelburg zijn deuren." *Zeeuws Tijdschrift* 65, no. 3-4 (2015): 48-49.

—. "'Mystiek moet rusten op een kristalheldere eerlijkheid': Etty Hillesum over God en mens." In: *Etty Hillesum: Volledig Leven* (SPES cahier), edited by Lies Daenen. Leuven & Ghent: SPES-forum & Yunus Publishing, 2015, 63-75.

—. "'Dat merkwaardige bemiddelingslichaam': Etty Hillesum en de Joodsche Raad." In: *Etty Hillesum in weerwil van het Joodse vraagstuk* (Etty Hillesum Studies, 8). Edited by Klaas A.D. Smelik *et al.* Antwerpen-Apeldoorn: Garant, 2016, 51-69.

—. "Perspectives of research on Etty Hillesum's writings." In: *The Ethics and Religious Philosophy of Etty Hillesum: Proceedings of the Etty Hillesum Conference at Ghent University, January 2014* (Supplements to The Journal of Jewish Thought and Philosophy, 28). Edited by Klaas A.D. Smelik, Meins G.S. Coetsier & Jurjen Wiersma. Leiden / Boston, MA: Brill, 2017, 11-19.

—. "Etty Hillesum's reaction to the persecution of her people." In: *The Ethics and Religious Philosophy of Etty Hillesum: Proceedings of the Etty Hillesum Conference at Ghent University, January 2014* (Supplements to The Journal of Jewish Thought and Philosophy, 28). Edited by Klaas A.D. Smelik, Meins G.S. Coetsier & Jurjen Wiersma. Leiden / Boston, MA: Brill, 2017, 235-269.

—. "Esther in tweevoud: Een vergelijking tussen de Bijbelse koningin Esther en de schrijfster Esther Hillesum." In: *Etty Hillesum en het pad naar zelfverwerkelijking* (Etty Hillesum Studies, 9). Edited by Klaas A.D. Smelik *et al.* Antwerpen-Apeldoorn: Garant, 2017, 157-165.

—. "Etty Hillesum." In: *Middelburg en de Mediene: Joods leven in Zeeland door de eeuwen heen*. Edited by Klaas A.D. Smelik & Arjan van Dixhoorn. Antwerpen & Apeldoorn: Garant, 2017, 193-206.

—. "A short biography of Etty Hillesum (1914-1943)." In: *Reading Etty Hillesum in Context: Writings, Life, and Influences of a Visionary Author*. Edited by Klaas A.D.

Smelik, Gerrit Van Oord & Jurjen Wiersma. Amsterdam: Amsterdam University Press, 2018, 23-30.

—. "To remember is to act: From a bundle of notebooks to a worldwide publication." In: *Reading Etty Hillesum in Context: Writings, Life, and Influences of a Visionary Author.* Edited by Klaas A.D. Smelik, Gerrit Van Oord & Jurjen Wiersma. Amsterdam: Amsterdam University Press, 2018, 33-49.

—. "Etty Hillesum's choice not to go into hiding." In: *Reading Etty Hillesum in Context: Writings, Life, and Influences of a Visionary Author.* Edited by Klaas A.D. Smelik, Gerrit Van Oord & Jurjen Wiersma. Amsterdam: Amsterdam University Press, 2018, 81-101.

—. "Romance down by the River IJssel: The first meeting between Etty Hillesum and Klaas Smelik Senior." In: *Reading Etty Hillesum in Context: Writings, Life, and Influences of a Visionary Author.* Edited by Klaas A.D. Smelik, Gerrit Van Oord & Jurjen Wiersma. Amsterdam: Amsterdam University Press, 2018, 259-271.

—. "Ulrich Beck and Etty Hillesum." In: *Reading Etty Hillesum in Context: Writings, Life, and Influences of a Visionary Author.* Edited by Klaas A.D. Smelik, Gerrit Van Oord & Jurjen Wiersma. Amsterdam: Amsterdam University Press, 2018, 445-457.

—. "Gabriël Metsustraat 6, Amsterdam." In: *Joodse huizen 4: Verhalen over vooroorlogse bewoners.* Edited by Frits Rijksbaron, Esther Shaya & Gert Jan de Vries. s.l.: Gibbon Uitgeefagentschap, 2018, 27-34.

—. "'M'n lieve bureau, de beste plek op aarde': Etty Hillesum neemt afscheid van haar vertrouwde omgeving." In: *Etty Hillesum en de contouren van haar tijd* (Etty Hillesum Studies, 10). Edited by Klaas A.D. Smelik *et al.* Oud-Turnhout / 's-Hertogenbosch: Gompel & Svacina, 2018, 225-248.

—. "Onuitwisbare levenskunst van Etty Hillesum." *AdRem* 29, no. 6 (2018): 12-13.

—. "Het zondagochtendgebed van Etty Hillesum." *NTT Journal for Theology and the Study of Religion* 73, no. 1 (2019): 33-41.

—. *Flarden van gesprekken: Etty Hillesum discussieert met vrienden over God, lot, lijden en haat*, Oud-Turnhout / 's-Hertogenbosch: Gompel&Scavina, 2019.

Smelik, Klaas A.D. & Ria van den Brandt. *"Wachten jullie op mij?" Etty Hillesum in beeld.* Amsterdam: Balans, 2003.

—. *Etty Hillesum in facetten* (Etty Hillesum Studies, 1). Edited by Ria van den Brandt & Klaas A.D. Smelik. Budel: Damon, 2003.

—. *Etty Hillesum in Context* (Etty Hillesum Studies, 2). Edited by Ria van den Brandt & Klaas A.D. Smelik. Assen: Van Gorcum, 2007.

—. *Etty Hillesum in discours* (Etty Hillesum Studies, 3). Edited by Ria van den Brandt & Klaas A.D. Smelik. Ghent: Academia Press, 2011.

Smelik, Klaas A.D., Ria van den Brandt & Meins G.S. Coetsier (eds.). *Spirituality in the Writings of Etty Hillesum: Proceedings of the Etty Hillesum Conference at Ghent University, November 2008* (Supplements to The Journal of Jewish Thought and Philosophy, 11). Leiden/Boston, MA: Brill, 2010.

—. *Etty Hillesum in Perspectief* (Etty Hillesum Studies, 4). Ghent: Academia Press, 2012.

Smelik, Klaas A.D. & Janny van der Molen. *Ik zou lang willen leven: Het verhaal van Etty Hillesum*. Amsterdam: Balans, 2014.

Smelik, Klaas A.D., Gerrit Van Oord, Meins G.S. Coetsier, Denise de Costa, Janny van der Molen & Jurjen Wiersma (eds.). *Etty Hillesum in Relatie* (Etty Hillesum Studies, 5). Ghent: Academia Press, 2013.

—. *Etty Hillesum 1914-2014* (Etty Hillesum Studies, 6). Antwerpen & Apeldoorn: Garant, 2014.

Smelik, Klaas A.D., Marja Clement, Meins G.S. Coetsier, Janny van der Molen, Gerrit Van Oord & Jurjen Wiersma (eds.). *Etty Hillesum weer thuis in Middelburg* (Etty Hillesum Studies, 7). Antwerpen-Apeldoorn: Garant, 2015.

Smelik, Klaas A.D., Marja Clement, Meins G.S. Coetsier, Gerrit Van Oord, Jurjen Wiersma (eds.). *Etty Hillesum in weerwil van het Joodse vraagstuk* (Etty Hillesum Studies, 8). Antwerpen-Apeldoorn: Garant, 2016.

Smelik, Klaas A.D., Meins G.S. Coetsier & Jurjen Wiersma (eds.). *The Ethics and Religious Philosophy of Etty Hillesum: Proceedings of the Etty Hillesum conference at Ghent University, January 2014*. (Supplements to the Journal of Jewish Thought and Philosophy, 28). Leiden / Boston, MA: Brill, 2017.

Smelik, Klaas A.D. *et al.* (eds.). *Etty Hillesum en het pad naar zelfverwerkelijking* (Etty Hillesum Studies, 9). Antwerpen-Apeldoorn: Garant, 2017.

Smelik, Klaas A.D. *et al.* (eds.). *Etty Hillesum en de contouren van haar tijd* (Etty Hillesum Studies, 10). Oud-Turnhout / 's-Hertogenbosch: Gompel & Svacina, 2018.

Smelik, Klaas A.D., Gerrit Van Oord & Jurjen Wiersma (eds.). *Reading Etty Hillesum in Context: Writings, Life, and Influences of a Visionary Author*. Amsterdam: Amsterdam University Press, 2018.

Smelik, Klaas A.D., Manja Pach & Ton Jorna. "Huiswerk voor de eigen werkplaats: De actualiteit van Etty Hillesum." *Rondom het Woord* 42, no. 2 (2000): 5-13.

Snyders, Jos. *Etty Hillesum: Ik heb zo lief: De menselijke en gelovige groei van Etty Hillesum: Geloofsgetuigen*. Averbode / Den Bosch: Altiora / KBS, 1993.

—. *De spiritualiteit van Etty Hillesum*. Mechelen: Secretariaat van de religieuzen, 1993.

Spaltro, Kathleen. "'A Symbol Perfected in Death': Etty Hillesum as Moral Exemplar." *Advanced Development Journal* 3, no. 3 (1991): 61-74.

Spoor, Corine. "Het succes van Etty Hillesum." *De Tijd* (7 May 1982): 34-37.

Steeg, Maria ter. *De verlokking van de liefde: Eenzaamheid en erotiek bij mystieke vrouwen*. Aalsmeer: Dabar / Luyten, 1994.

—. "De verlokking van de liefde: De geestelijke ontwikkeling van Etty Hillesum." *Streven* 61 (April 1994): 291-303.

Stein, Leon. "An Interrupted Life: The Diaries of Etty Hillesum, 1941-1943." In: *Holocaust Literature*. Edited by John K. Roth. Pasadena, CA: Salem Press, 2008, 259-263.

Stelling, Marleen. "'Jij lieve, grote, goede': Etty Hillesum bereidt zich voor op haar afscheid van Julius Spier." In: *Etty Hillesum in weerwil van het Joodse vraagstuk* (Etty Hillesum Studies, 8). Edited by Klaas A.D. Smelik *et al.* Antwerpen-Apeldoorn: Garant, 2016, 111-119.

Stouten, Johanna. *Dagboeken van Etty Hillesum 1941-1942: Bestaat er een verband tussen het razendsnelle ontwikkelingsproces van Etty Hillesum en het ritme van haar schrijven?* Thesis, Université Paris IV, Sorbonne, 1996-1997.

Stewart, Dolores. "Etty Hillesum-Cín Lae 1943." *Comhar* 64, no. 5 (2004): 11.

Strien, Ans van. "Ik zag publicatie als familieplicht." *NCRV-gids* no. 18 (2014): 54.

Swart, Loet. "Ik bloei van binnen met de dood tot bloem." In: *Men zou een pleister op vele wonden willen zijn: Reacties op de dagboeken en brieven van Etty Hillesum.* Edited by J.G. Gaarlandt. Amsterdam: Balans, 1989, 133-145.

—. "Etty Hillesum e la tradizione mistica." In: *L'esperienza dell'Altro: Studi su Etty Hillesum.* Edited by Gerrit Van Oord. Sant'Oreste: Apeiron Editori, 1990, 169-184.

—. "Een verzamelplaats voor het lijden van de mensheid." In: *Tot op de bodem van het niets: Mystiek in een tijd van oorlog en crisis: 1920-1970.* Edited by Hein Blommestijn. Kampen / Averbode: Kok / Altiora, 1991, 26-41.

Swart, Loet & Hein Blommestijn. *Teksten en thema's uit de mystiek 5: Etty Hillesum.* Nijmegen: Titus Brandsma Instituut, 1983.

Taylor, Dennis. "Examined Lives." *Boston College Magazine* 52 (Winter 1993): 32-40.

—. "The Need for a Religious Literary Criticism." *Religion and the Arts* 1 (1996): 124-150.

Terzi, Maria Grazia, Stefana Terzi & Silvia Treves (eds.). *Il pensiero di un'estrema compassione: Atti degli incontri di Torino su Etty Hillesum XII maggio 2000.* Torino: Associazione Culturale Nautilus, 2000.

Thompson, Margie. "Stones of Norwich, Ashes of Auschwitz: Julian of Norwich and Etty Hillesum Finding Wisdom by Praying Life Experience." In: *Not Etched in Stone: Essays on Ritual Memory, Soul, and Society.* Edited by Marie A. Conn & Therese McGuire. Lanham, MD: University Press of America, 2007, 43-60.

Thooft, Lisette. "Etty Hillesum als voorloopster van de Nieuwe Spiritualiteit: 'Beluisteren, wat er opstijgt uit je zelf'." In: *Etty Hillesum in discours* (Etty Hillesum Studies, 3). Edited by Ria van den Brandt & Klaas A.D. Smelik. Ghent: Academia Press, 2011, 61-68.

Thurston, Ann. "Hope in Hell: The Diaries and Letters of Etty Hillesum." *Doctrine and Life.* 54, no. 3 (2004): 5-20.

Todorov, Tzvetan. *Di fronte all'estrema: Quale etica per il secolo dei gulag e dei campi di sterminio?* Milano: Garzanti, 1992.

—. *Face à l'extreme.* Paris: Seuil, 1994.

—. *Facing the Extreme: Moral Life in the Concentration Camps.* New York: Henry Holt, 1996.

Tol, Gé & Manja Pach. *Het Etty Hillesum Centrum en Manja Pach.* Deventer: Etty Hillesum Centrum, 1999.

Tomè, Simona. *Etty Hillesum testimone di Dio nell'inferno nazista.* Thesis, Università degli studi di Padova, 2000.

Tommasi, Wanda. *Simone Weil: Esperienza religiosa, esperienza femminile.* Napoli: Liguori, 1997.

—. *Etty Hillesum: L'intelligenza del cuore.* Padova: Edizioni Messaggero, 2002.

—. "Etty Hillesum Mistica?" In: *Etty Hillesum, Diario 1941-1943: Un mondo 'altro' è possibile.* Edited by Maria Pia Mazziotti & Gerrit Van Oord. Sant'Oreste: Apeiron Editori, 2002, 41-43.

—. "Il silenzio interiore in Etty Hillesum e in Simone Weil." In: *La vita segrete delle parole.* Sant'Oreste: Apeiron Editori, 2007, 28.

Tommasi, Wanda & C. Ballester Meseguer. *Etty Hillesum: La inteligencia del corazón.* Madrid: Narcea, 2003.

Vacante, Franca Maria. "Lettere prima del Lager." *L'Osservatore romano* (17 April 17 1991): 7.

Van Den Drissche, "Thibault: Entre éthique et mystique: Quand Edith Stein et Etty Hillesum se rencontrent." *Revue d'éthique et de théologie morale* 247 (2007): 65-91.

Vandewalle, Ellen. "De invloed van André Suarès' Dostojewski in de dagboeken van Etty Hillesum." In: *Etty Hillesum in Context* (Etty Hillesum Studies, 2). Edited by Ria van den Brandt & Klaas A.D. Smelik. Assen: Van Gorcum, 2007, 74-94.

—. "L'influenza del Dostoevskij di André Suarès sui diari di Etty Hillesum." In: *Etty Hillesum: Studi sulla vita e l'opera.* Edited by Gerrit Van Oord. Sant'Oreste: Apeiron Editori, 2013, 128-148.

Vertone, V. "Memorie di un'ottimista che fu condannata a morte." *Corriere della Sera* (22 January 1986): 13.

Villela-Petit, Maria. "Résister au Mal: Simone Weil et Etty Hillesum." *Cahiers Simone Weil* 18 (1995): 343-356.

—. "Etty Hillesum ou l'itinéraire spirituel d'une jeune femme au milieu d'un désastre historique." *Transversalités, revue de l'Institut catholique de Paris* 117 (January-March 2011): 103.

Villeneuve, Camille de. *Etty Hillesum: La paix dans l'enfer.* Paris: Points Sagesses, 2013.

Vissel, Achsa. "De nagedachtenis van een verstoord leven." *Nieuw Israelietisch Weekblad* 149, no. 17 (2013-2014): 26-27.

Vrielink, Herman & Dick van der Molen. *Louis Hillesum: Een portret.* Deventer: Etty Hillesum Centrum, 2006.

Vrijland-Postma, F. Joke. "Tide – mijn tante Henny: Persoonlijke herinneringen aan Henny Tideman." In: *Etty Hillesum en het pad naar zelfverwerkelijking* (Etty Hillesum Studies, 9). Edited by Klaas A.D. Smelik *et al.* Antwerpen-Apeldoorn: Garant, 2017, 211-219.

Wallner, Josef. "'Aber irgendwo in mir blüht der Jasmin': Lesungen im Musiktheater Linz brachten die Tagebücher der Jüdin Etty Hillesum ins Gespräch." *Kirchen-Zeitung, Diözese Linz* no. 11 (17 March 2016): 6-7

Walters, Kerry. *The art of dying and living.* Maryknoll, NY: Orbis Books, 2011.

Walton, Heither. "Sex in the War: An Aesthetics of Resistance in the Diaries of Etty Hillesum." *Theology & Sexuality: The Journal of the Institute for the Study of Christianity & Sexuality* 12, no. 1 (2005): 51-61.

Walvis, Jaap. "Etty Hillesum hield een dagboek bij om later een roman te schrijven: In gesprek met Swiep van Wermeskerken." *Het Oog in 't Zeil* 1, no. 4 (1984): 2-6.

Walvis, Jaap & Almar Tjepkema. "Het verstoorde leven." NOS, 1984 [Documentary].

Weinstein, Bernard. "Etty Hillesum's An Interrupted Life: Searching for the Human." In: *The Netherlands and Nazi Genocide: Papers of the 21st Annual Scholars' Conference.* Edited by G. Jan Colijn & Marcia S. Littell. Lewiston, NY: Edwin Mellen Press, 1992, 155-166.

Wel, Anna van der. "Eenzaamheid en één-zijn: Het werk van Etty Hillesum bekeken vanuit een spiritueel-psychologisch perspectief." *InZicht* 10, no. 1 (February 2008): 28-31.

Whitehead, Anne. "A Still, Small Voice: Letter-Writing, Testimony and the Project of Address in Etty Hillesum's Letters from Westerbork." *Cultural Values* 5, no. 1 (2001): 79-96.

Wiersma, Jurjen. "Etty Hillesum en Dietrich Bonhoeffer: Er zijn met en er zijn voor anderen." In: *Etty Hillesum in perspectief* (Etty Hillesum Studies, 4). Edited by Klaas A.D. Smelik, Ria van den Brandt & Meins G.S. Coetsier. Ghent: Academia Press, 2012, 5-14.

—. "Het ijs van de ziel klieven: Over Etty Hillesum en Dorothee Sölle." In: *Etty Hillesum in Relatie* (Etty Hillesum Studies, 5). Edited by Klaas A.D. Smelik *et al.* Ghent: Academia Press, 2013, 85-96.

—. "'... merken, dat het leven werkelijk eenvoudig is': Etty Hillesum en Walter Rathenau." In: Etty Hillesum 1914-2014 (Etty Hillesum Studies, 6). Edited by Klaas A.D. Smelik *et al.* Antwerpen & Apeldoorn: Garant, 2014, 141-149.

—. "'Men zou de kroniek moeten schrijven van Westerbork.'" In: *Etty Hillesum weer thuis in Middelburg* (Etty Hillesum Studies, 7). Edited by Klaas A.D. Smelik *et al.* Antwerpen-Apeldoorn: Garant, 2015, 37-49.

—. "Studente Hillesum en professor Bonger: De democratie zal overwinnen." In: *Etty Hillesum in weerwil van het Joodse vraagstuk* (Etty Hillesum Studies, 8). Edited by Klaas A.D. Smelik *et al.* Antwerpen-Apeldoorn: Garant, 2016, 41-49

—. "Chipping away the ice that surrounds the soul: Etty Hillesum and Dorothee Sölle." In: *The Ethics and Religious Philosophy of Etty Hillesum: Proceedings of the Etty Hillesum Conference at Ghent University, January 2014* (Supplements to The Journal of Jewish Thought and Philosophy, 28). Edited by Klaas A.D. Smelik, Meins G.S. Coetsier & Jurjen Wiersma. Leiden / Boston, MA: Brill, 2017, 221-232.

—. "Tzvetan Todorov over Etty Hillesums verzet: Opstanding, ethisch maar niet politiek?" In: *Etty Hillesum en het pad naar zelfverwerkelijking* (Etty Hillesum Studies, 9). Edited by Klaas A.D. Smelik *et al.* Antwerpen-Apeldoorn: Garant, 2017, 127-140.

—. "One ought to write a chronicle of Westerbork." In: *Reading Etty Hillesum in Context: Writings, Life, and Influences of a Visionary Author.* Edited by Klaas A.D. Smelik, Gerrit Van Oord & Jurjen Wiersma. Amsterdam: Amsterdam University Press, 2018, 143-156.

—. "'To realize that life is truly simple': Etty Hillesum and Walther Rathenau." In: *Reading Etty Hillesum in Context: Writings, Life, and Influences of a Visionary Author.* Edited by Klaas A.D. Smelik, Gerrit Van Oord & Jurjen Wiersma. Amsterdam: Amsterdam University Press, 2018, 245-255.

—. "Etty Hillesums humanisme: Ethische, filosofische en theologische overwegingen." In: *Etty Hillesum en de contouren van haar tijd* (Etty Hillesum Studies, 10). Edited by Klaas A.D. Smelik *et al.* Oud-Turnhout / 's-Hertogenbosch: Gompel & Svacina, 2018, 249-261.

Wiersma, Jurjen, Klaas A.D. Smelik, Gerrit Van Oord, Meins G.S. Coetsier, Denise de Costa, Janny van der Molen & Jurjen Wiersma (eds.). *Etty Hillesum in relatie* (Etty Hillesum Studies, 5). Ghent: Academia Press, 2013.

—. *Etty Hillesum 1914-2014* (Etty Hillesum Studies, 6). Antwerpen & Apeldoorn: Garant, 2014.

Wiersma, Jurjen, Klaas A.D. Smelik, Marja Clement, Meins G.S. Coetsier, Janny van der Molen & Gerrit Van Oord, *Etty Hillesum weer thuis in Middelburg* (Etty Hillesum Studies, 7). Antwerpen-Apeldoorn: Garant, 2015, 37-49.

Wind, Peter de. "Gelatenheid volgens Meister Eckhart en Etty Hillesum." In: *Etty Hillesum in weerwil van het Joodse vraagstuk* (Etty Hillesum Studies, 8). Edited by Klaas A.D. Smelik *et al.* Antwerpen-Apeldoorn: Garant, 2016, 121-138.

Wolfswinkel, Rolf & Dick van Last Galen. *Anne Frank and After: Dutch Holocaust Literature in Historical Perspective.* Amsterdam: Amsterdam University Press, 1996.

Woodcock, John. "The Therapeutic Journals of Joanna Field and Etty Hillesum." *A/B: Auto/Biography Studies* 5, no. 1 (1989): 15-25.

Woodhouse, Patrick. *Etty Hillesum: A Life Transformed.* London & New York: Continuum, 2009.

—. *Credo in Dio e negli uomini: Storia di Etty Hillesum.* Torino: Lindau, 2010.

—. "The roots of the chaos and the process of change in Etty Hillesum." In: *Spirituality in the Writings of Etty Hillesum: Proceedings of the Etty Hillesum Conference at Ghent University, November 2008* (Supplements to The Journal of Jewish Thought and Philosophy, 11). Edited by Klaas A.D. Smelik, Ria van den Brandt & Meins G.S. Coetsier. Leiden/Boston, MA: Brill, 2010, 31-42.

—. *Etty Hillesum: uma vida transformada.* Prior Velho: Paulinas, 2011.

—. "The influence of the work of Rainer Maria Rilke on the mind and heart of Etty Hillesum." In: *The Ethics and Religious Philosophy of Etty Hillesum: Proceedings of the Etty Hillesum Conference at Ghent University, January 2014* (Supplements to The Journal of Jewish Thought and Philosophy, 28). Edited by Klaas A.D. Smelik, Meins G.S. Coetsier & Jurjen Wiersma. Leiden / Boston, MA: Brill, 2017, 285-298.

Woolfson, Tony. "Dear God, There Is So Much To Do: Etty, The Letters and Diaries of Etty Hillesum." *Jung Journal: Culture and Psyche* 2, no. 2 (2008): 89-101.

Wunderlich, Hannah. "Und damit muss ich nun versuchen, fertig zu werden... Eine psychologische Studie zu Etty Hillesums Bewältigung der nationalsozialistischen Verfolgung." In: *Etty Hillesum in Relatie* (Etty Hillesum Studies, 5). Edited by Klaas A.D. Smelik *et al.* Ghent: Academia Press, 2013, 43-84.

Yankova-Brust, Genka. *Die Opfer schreiben: Tagebücher aus der Holocaustzeit.* Studienarbeit, Philipps-Universität Marburg, 2009.

Yokohata, Yukiko. "Het beeld van Etty Hillesum in Japan." In: *Etty Hillesum in Context* (Etty Hillesum Studies, 2). Edited by Ria van den Brandt & Klaas A.D. Smelik. Assen: Van Gorcum, 2007, 95-115.

—. "La popolarità di Etty Hillesum in Giappone." In: *Etty Hillesum: Studi sulla vita e l'opera.* Edited by Gerrit Van Oord. Sant'Oreste: Apeiron Editori, 2013, 168-183.

—. "Perceptions of Etty Hillesum in Japan." In: *Reading Etty Hillesum in Context: Writings, Life, and Influences of a Visionary Author.* Edited by Klaas A.D. Smelik, Gerrit Van Oord & Jurjen Wiersma. Amsterdam: Amsterdam University Press, 2018, 395-417.

Ypma, Sytze. *Voorbij het verstoorde leven: Een zelfpsychologisch lezing van het zelfbeeld en godsbeeld van de ik-persoon uit 'Etty: De nagelaten geschriften van Etty Hillesum, 1941-1943.'* Thesis, Groningen University, 1990.

Zamboni, Chiara. "Etty Hillesum: Quel che resta della vita." *Via Dogana* no. 48 (2000): 11-12.

—. "L'efficacia di saper dire quel che accade." In: *Etty Hillesum, Diario 1941-1943: Un mondo 'altro' è possibile*. Edited by Maria Pia Mazziotti & Gerrit Van Oord. Sant'Oreste: Apeiron Editori, 2002, 41-43.

Zee, Nanda van der. *De Trein*. Soesterberg: Uitgeverij Aspekt, 2003.

Ziegler, Sandra. *Gedächtnis und Identität der KZ-Erfahrung: Niederländische und deutsche Augenzeugenberichten des Holocaust.* Würzburg: Köningshausen & Neumann, 2006, 215-275.

Index of Names and Subjects

Index of Citations

For Product Safety Concerns and Information please contact our EU representative GPSR@taylorandfrancis.com
Taylor & Francis Verlag GmbH, Kaufingerstraße 24, 80331 München, Germany

www.ingramcontent.com/pod-product-compliance
Lightning Source LLC
Chambersburg PA
CBHW071932130726
47908CB00015B/122

* 9 7 8 1 0 4 1 1 8 8 3 4 6 *